Fernando De Lucia

(signature: Fernando De Lucia)

OPERA BIOGRAPHY SERIES, NO.3

Series Editors
Andrew Farkas
William R. Moran

Fernando De Lucia

Son of Naples

1860 – 1925

Michael E. Henstock

Amadeus Press
Reinhard G. Pauly, General Editor
Portland, Oregon

First published in 1990 by
Gerald Duckworth & Co. Ltd.
The Old Piano Factory
43 Gloucester Crescent, London NW1 7DY

First published in North America in 1990 by
Amadeus Press (an imprint of Timber Press, Inc.)
9999 S.W. Wilshire
Portland, Oregon 97225, U.S.A.

ISBN 0–931340–30–6

Library of Congress Cataloging-in-Publication-Data
Henstock, Michael E.
    Fernando De Lucia : son of Naples, 1860–1925 / Michael E.
Henstock.
        p.   cm. — (Opera biography series : no. 3)
    Discography: p.
    Includes bibliographical references (p.)
    ISBN 0–931340–30–6
    1. De Lucia, Fernando, 1860–1925.   2. Singers—Italy—Biography.
I. Title.   II. Series.
ML420.D43H4   1990
782.1′092—dc20
[B]   90–33660
                                                                              CIP
                                                                              MN

Typeset by
Michael E. Henstock
Printed in Great Britain by
Redwood Press Ltd, Melksham

Contents

For all who love Naples,
and for
Desmond Shawe-Taylor,
whose writings first aroused my interest
in
Fernando De Lucia

Preface

The question has been asked: Why does Fernando De Lucia now merit a first biography, more than sixty years after his death?

The reasons are several. Foremost is the recognition that his records preserve more of the vocal style and mannerisms of a century or more ago than do those of any other singer. For this reason, virtually every modern book or essay on vocal style, especially in relation to the gramophone, makes extensive reference, along with Battistini, Patti, and Plançon, to De Lucia.

Battistini and De Lucia together left some 520 records. No other contemporary Italian singers of comparable ability have bequeathed us so much. They have been described as their generation's 'ambassadors to posterity',[1] preserving characteristics of style and technique which were soon to disappear. They exemplify an age when the singer was the *raison d'être* of the opera and not just one element of it; when the 'band' was the loyal, self-effacing follower of the voice, and never its rival; when the task of the conductor was to keep the orchestra in time with the singers, who were not mere servants of the composer but active collaborators, valued for their skill in embellishing the music, and when operatic effect did not depend on thrilling high notes and on voices with sufficient volume to penetrate orchestras which grew ever larger as the nineteenth century neared its close. Without the records, those features would have vanished beyond recall. Because both men recorded copiously and continued to do so into the 1920s they are often thought of as idiosyncratic singers of this century; as such, they might be dubbed 'glorious eccentrics'. In fact, they represent an earlier artistic generation. They may well be even more significant now, as historical figures, than they were in their heyday for, though each enjoyed an immense vogue, what they then represented was already beginning to pass out of fashion.

Of the two, Fernando De Lucia was by far the more prolific recording artist. He was not a perfect singer but his records, when played at speeds which correctly reflect their often extensive transposition, show the heights of the artistry that made him the dominant Italian tenor of the 1890s.[2] Across the technical imperfections of three-quarters of a century

---

[1] Will Crutchfield, 'Twin Glories', *Opera News*, Dec. 19 1987 and Feb. 27 1988.

[2] The speeds have an importance that cannot be emphasised too strongly. See Chapter 18, pp. 336-7 and the Discography, pp. 438ff.

ago, through more than 400 records, he continues to stimulate
discussion, not to say controversy. One critic summarises his charm and
uniqueness in a single sentence: 'There is not, and in recorded vocal
history, never has been, anyone quite like him: no one else who could
caress a word, a note, in so beguiling and personal a way, spin the tone
so delicately, twist a phrase so fancifully, and achieve so remarkable a
variety of timbres, here subtly blended, there suddenly contrasted.'[3] He
demonstrates clearly the contribution of the Italian school to the *legato*
style and to the cultivation of virtuosity in florid work.[4] He exemplifies a
technique based on the *messa di voce*, the swelling of tone from *piano* to
forte and back again entirely at the singer's bidding, at any speed and at
any dynamic, an instrument of his will. His records combine agility with
flexibility and vocal charm in a way that has never since been equalled,
offering us some of the most beautiful purely vocal effects on record. His
exquisite vocalisation, limpid coloratura, and vividly imaginative
approach stamp him as the most individualistic of singers, one who
fascinates with the variety of his interpretations. When, in an apparently
effortless way, he adds an ornament and a note blossoms with a
spontaneity which is beyond the reach of other singers he reminds us of
the literal meaning of the term *'fioritura'*. He is one of the few singers
who can offer us an utterly individual pleasure which is almost
independent of the composition. His effects of chiaroscuro are legendary.
Of his 1918 recordings of Rossini's *Il Barbiere di Siviglia* one critic has
written: 'There has been no one to equal him in this music since this
recording was made. With it we come as close as we shall ever come to
pulling back the curtain on nineteenth-century *bel canto* style in its
fullest flower.'[5] Another writes that he 'might well be called the last
singer of the rococo age'.[6] Yet others describe him as 'the technician of
technicians, the most refined vocal magician' or as 'one whose art we
may review as an echo of a world that has ceased to exist'.[7] His records
have been termed 'unlike anything else in the annals of recording, and
worthy of the closest study both for their historical interest and for their
fascinating spontaneity and originality'.[8]

But the records, however enthralling they are as exhibitions of vocal
technique, assume even greater significance in the context of nineteenth-
century performance practice. Some scholars entertain no doubt that
their eccentricities, their textual and musical alterations, and their
transpositions mirror his stage performances. Others maintain that such
liberties would have been possible only in the recording studio. To this

---

3 Andrew Porter, *Gramophone*, April 1971, p. 1683.

4 J.B. Steane, *The Grand Tradition*, p. 149.

5 John Ardoin, *Opera Quarterly*, Vol. 4, No. 1, Spring 1986, p. 51.

6 Desmond Shawe-Taylor, *Opera*, Vol. 6, No. 7, July 1955, p. 433.

7 Max de Schauensee, *Opera News*, Mar. 19 1960, pp. 10-12.

8 Desmond Shawe-Taylor, 'A Vanished Style', Notes to Rubini RS 305: *Fernando De Lucia. The
G&T/Gramophone Company Recordings, 1902-1909* (released 1980).

writer it has always seemed desirable to determine, from the contemporary reviews of critics who heard him in person rather than those who have judged him from records, whether De Lucia's stage performances showed the freedom and capriciousness which characterise his records. That they did, and that the critics berated him for them, suggests that he was not wholly typical of even his own generation. I have drawn at length on such contemporary accounts, allowing the critics to speak to us in their own words, and, because unfavourable reviews are frequently more informative than are eulogies, I have been at pains to quote every traceable adverse notice which tells us something specific.

Another compelling stimulus for this biography is the link that detailed reviews of De Lucia's performances enable us to make with the singing of the great tenor triumvirate of the last thirty years of the nineteenth century: Gayarre, Masini, and Stagno. Through them, the singing of Rubini and Mario is brought to the fringe of our imagination. That is not to argue that De Lucia compares with or rivals these latter great figures, but to remark upon him as our closest and most convincing parallel.

Yet to think of him solely as the virtuoso and supreme technician in the graces of the *bel canto* period is to overlook his dominance among Italian tenors of the 1890s. It was a position that made him the preferred interpreter of the composers of the *verismo* epoch, when he was in his prime: Giordano, Mascagni, and Puccini courted him to create rôles in their new operas, whose arias he invested with a fluency, an easy elegance, and a command of nuance which were denied to less well-equipped singers, and in which his remarkable dramatic talents were allowed full play. He was prominent in the establishment of such operas in the repertory and he remains as a link with that school, whose music he recorded all too rarely.

Finally, De Lucia was quintessentially Neapolitan. Apart from brief periods in his youth he always lived in his native city. He had the warm, passionate, even violent nature of the South. His life opens for us a window on to the vigorous musical world of Naples at a time which, as its school of native operatic composers flickered on the edge of extinction, coincided with the finest flowering of the genre now known as the Neapolitan song.

Nottingham, October 1989   M.E.H.

Plates
(between pages 234 and 235)

1. Portrait, c. 1890.
2. As a pupil of the Conservatorio di San Pietro a Maiella, Naples.
3. Portrait in clean-shaven days.
4-5. The young concert artist.
6-7. As Faust in his operatic début, 1885.
8. A Falk portrait, c. 1893.
9. The man-about-town, c. 1893.
10. Falk portrait, c. 1893.
11. The dandy, c. 1886.
12. As Turiddu, c. 1891-2.
13. De Lucia and Calvé as Turiddu and Santuzza, London, c. 1892.
14. A fiercely-dramatic Turiddu.
15-20. As Canio in *Pagliacci*, with Mario Ancona (Tonio) and Nellie Melba (Nedda), London, 1893.
21. De Lucia with Mario Ancona and Luigi Mancinelli, London, 1893.
22. *En famille* at Cava de' Tirreni, c. 1894.
23. Portrait dedicated to Carlo Clausetti, 1893.
24. Sketch from the period of his New York début, December 1893.
25. Cartoon from *Punch* showing De Lucia as Fritz and Calvé as Suzel at Covent Garden, 1892.
26. Cartoon from *Punch* showing De Lucia, Mascagni, and Calvé at Covent Garden, 1893.
27. The father: De Lucia with Armando and Nadir, 1898.
28. Portrait from the period of the La Scala première of *La Bohème*, March 1897.
29. *Iris* at La Scala, January 1899.
30. Portrait inscribed to Elvira Giommi.
31. Cartoon from *Papiol*, 1902.
32. Cartoon from *Rastignac*, 1905.
33. Portrait, c. 1905.
34. Elvira Giommi.
35. Portrait, c. 1905.
36. Portrait, c. 1900.
37. Portrait, dated 1908 but probably of earlier date.

Acknowledgements

The writer, now that his work is concluded, is not inclined to dwell on the difficulties under which he laboured in the preparation of the present volume.

So wrote a nineteenth-century author, and such are my sentiments. I will not, however, deny myself the pleasure of thanking those who have made the current work possible.

Fernando De Lucia attracted no biographer during his lifetime. There are no contemporary memoirs of him and any diaries that he may have kept have disappeared without trace. Relatively few of his letters survive in accessible collections. Most of the memorabilia still in his possession at his death have since been dispersed. Thus, the present work necessarily draws on material from many sources, both printed and oral. Without the kindnesses of numerous people, some of whom have become fast friends, it could never have been written. To them I owe a debt which, if it cannot adequately be repaid, is a pleasure to acknowledge.

Some correspondents have died since work began on this book. Others have changed their affiliation. In what follows, the terms 'the late' and 'formerly of' have been eschewed in favour of the form that would have been appropriate at the time when they provided their help.

Members of the De Lucia or De Giorgio families who have been generous with their time and recollections are, first and foremost, his children Amalia, Fernando, Giuseppina, and Rosa, whom I also thank for their kind permission to quote their father's correspondence. Other family members include Atelio Amato, Mario Ciampi, Fernando Cirenei-De Giorgio, Felice Forino, Raffaele and Olimpia Forino, Amedeo Tosini, and Fabio Trabucchi.

For other personal reminiscences of De Lucia and his family I gratefully acknowledge the help of Enzo Aita, Tom Burke, Luigi de Lillo, Luigi Caggiula, Carmine Giordano, Giuseppina Giordano, Franz Gleijeses, Giovanni Martinelli, Rodolfo Mele, Maria Németh, Angelo Notariello, Angeles Ottein, Edward E. Petrillo, Mikhail Popov, Riccardo Ricciardi, Vincenza Senatore, and Georges Thill.

Extracts from Queen Victoria's diaries are reproduced by gracious permission of Her Majesty the Queen.

I am much indebted to Sheila de Bellaigue, Elizabeth H. Cuthbert, Julia Gandy, and Robert Mackworth-Young, of the Royal Archives, Windsor Castle, for their unstinted help.

Roberto Esposito, the Benedikt and Salmon collection, James Camner, the Stuart-Liff collection, the La Cañada Memorial Library, and the Stanford Archive of Recorded Sound have generously given me unrestricted access to their holdings of published and unpublished autographs and other documents, books, photographs, and records, and permission to quote or reproduce them.

For the writings of Emilio De Gogorza on De Lucia, and for permission to publish them, I am indebted to Stephen B. Fassett. The verses of Giovanni Capurro are reproduced by kind permission of Edizioni Bideri, s.p.a., and of Capurro's heirs. For his patient researching of family papers, and for communicating the reminiscences of his father, Mario Ancona, I thank Giacomo R. Ancona. The writings of Saverio Procida are reproduced by permission of Roberto Procida.

The chronology of De Lucia's performances owes a great debt to Charles A. Jahant, for cast lists, first names of many minor singers, and numerous pieces of information gleaned in a lifetime spent researching often obscure publications; to Thomas G. Kaufman, who allowed me free access to his well-ordered files; to Francesco Canessa, who made available data on performances at the Teatro San Carlo, Naples; to Carlo Marinelli, who provided many cast lists; and to Lorna Principe Gillespie, who spent much time checking performance notices. The efforts of George S. Shepherd enabled me to make contact with the Forino family in Scotland and in Italy. Gilbert H. Boggs, G.W. Fury, Juan Carlos Mazondo, Rudi B. Sazunic, and R.A. Martin (British Council, Montevideo) each supplied reviews, dates, and critiques of De Lucia's performances, as did D. Miguel Angel Robles, Virginia Benvenuty, and Miranda Buttimore, all of the British Institute, Seville. For his good offices in gaining me access to the Ufficio Registri Successioni of Naples I thank Malcolm Holding, Consul General of Great Britain, Naples.

It would be impossible to overstate the value and importance of the collections of the Emeroteca Vincenzo Tucci, Naples, where I have spent untold hours, and of the friendship and cooperation of Salvatore Maffei and his colleagues there. To them I express my warmest thanks.

Documentation of De Lucia's recording activities for the Gramophone Company and for the Società Italiana di Fonotipia was achieved with the kind cooperation of Keith Hardwick, Alan Kelly, and, especially, of Ruth Edge and her colleagues Jenny Keen and Suzanne Lewis, EMI Archives. Access to the files of Phonotype Record was possible through the good offices of Fernando, Raffaele, Roberto, and Vincenzo Esposito, Naples.

Mario Rosario Pepe and Sergio Pepe, of Naples, provided information regarding the former De Lucia villas at Cava de' Tirreni. Sergio Pepe also guided me through Neapolitan officialdom (which at times seemed impenetrable), obtained many legal documents, and arranged for me to have direct access to the official records of the Comune di Napoli. Only researchers who have worked in Naples can know how greatly I am in his debt.

Grateful thanks are due to Antonio Cappiello, Vincenzo De Marco, Ciro Fabbricini, and Mario Marasco of the Ufficio di Stato Civile, Naples. Without their help, documentation of many of the prominent characters in this book would have been impossible. Similarly, particular mention must be made of Arrigo Benedetti, Rome, and of Lucio Parisi, Naples, for considerable practical assistance and for their tenacity in solving seemingly intractable bureaucratic problems.

The extensive library of G. Michael Aspinall, Rome, provided details and sheet music of many elusive songs. Malcolm Stacey and the staff of the Business Library, Nottinghamshire County Libraries, have been patient and efficient in supplying answers to numerous arcane queries. Very rarely have they had to admit defeat.

The following librarians and archivists have gone to great pains on my behalf:

Vittorio di Donato, Archivio di Stato, Caserta; Mrs. Paul Rhymer, Chicago Historical Society; Vittorio Mezzomonaco, Istituti Artistici e Culturali della Città di Forlì; Francesca Franchi, Covent Garden Archives, London; Francesco Cozzolino and Ciro Di Martino, Archivio di Stato, Naples; Giovanni Marcello, Biblioteca Nazionale, Naples; Ernesto Giangrasso, Biblioteca Lucchesi-Palli, Naples; Francesco Bossarelli, Marta De Concilis, Michele Pilla, Bianca Spinazzola, and Andrea Vampore, Conservatorio di Musica di San Pietro a Maiella, Naples; Mary Ellis Peltz, Metropolitan Opera, New York; Cesarina Vighy, Biblioteca di Storia Moderna e Contemporanea, Rome; Pasquale Natella, Biblioteca Provinciale, Salerno; and Franco Ramella, Ordine Mauriziano, Turin.

Other museums and libraries which have contributed material are: Biblioteca Nazionale, Bari; Biblioteca Comunale dell'Archiginnasio, Bologna; Boston Public Library; National Széchényi Library, Budapest; Biblioteca Nacional, Buenos Aires; Biblioteca Comunale, Cava de' Tirreni; Nordica Memorial Association, Inc., Farmington; Biblioteca Nazionale Centrale, Florence; Biblioteca Nacional and Biblioteca Teatro S. Carlos, Lisbon; Municipio di Livorno; British Library, Gabrielle Enthoven Theatre Collection (formerly at the Victoria and Albert Museum, now at the Theatre Museum), Guildhall Library, and London Library, London; Biblioteca Nazionale and Biblioteca Livia Simoni, Teatro alla Scala, Milan; Royal Archives, Monaco; Biblioteca Nacional, Montevideo; Biblioteca di Storia Patria, Naples; Marcella Sembrich Memorial Association, Inc., New York City; New York Public Library; Biblioteca Nazionale, Palermo; Philadelphia Public Library; Biblioteca Comunale, Piacenza; Biblioteca Nazionale Centrale, Rome; Museo Puccini, Torre del Lago; Library of Congress, Washington, D.C.

To Luciana Pestalozza, of Casa Ricordi, Milan, I express my grateful thanks for access to the business and confidential files of Giulio Ricordi, and for permission to quote from them. Teresita Beretta and Fausto Broussard have given me much of their time. Above all, the days and weeks spent in the Archivio Storico of G. Ricordi & C. were made greatly more productive through the unfailingly helpful and informed interest of Carlo Clausetti, to whom I owe much.

For their painstaking analysis of the medical history of De Lucia I thank Peter Sprackling and Harold Wayne. The latter also kindly made for me transfers of many records which I had not previously heard.

It is a pleasure to thank Jean-Paul Getty, through whose philanthropy the surviving matrices were preserved, for the fact that so many of De Lucia's Phonotype records are now widely available.

For the many hours which he devoted to the pitching of the Phonotype and Fonotipia recordings I am greatly indebted to my colleague John Morehen. Paul Steinson kindly made freely available to me the results of his detailed studies of Phonotype speeds. Richard Bebb, Eliot Levin, Vivian Liff, Jerrold Northrop Moore, William R. Moran, and Desmond Shawe-Taylor have all devoted much time and effort to resolving the complexities of speed and pitch presented by the records made by De Lucia for The Gramophone Company.

Other assistance has come from: Luigi Abbro, Giacomo R. Ancona, Dorothy Anderson, Carlo Annunziata, Domenico Apicella, Giovanni Artieri, Marcella Barzetti, Luciano Villevieille-Bideri, Ester Bolaffi, Renato Caccamo, Luigi Caccavale, James Camner, Valerio Canonico, Mosco Carner, Arthur Carter, Rodolfo Celletti, Gianni Cesarini, Marcello Conati, Ivor Davies, Mario De Luca, Ettore De Mura, Fernando Dentoni-Litta, Domenico de' Paoli, Max de Schauensee, Juan Dzazópulos, Domenico Farina, Andrew Farkas, Dennis Foreman, John Freestone, Antonio Gagliardi, Eugenio Gara, Georges Girard, Amedeo Gleijeses, S.C. Greaves, Robert Gregory, Giorgio Gualerzi, John Gualiani, P.G. Hurst, Gianni Infusino, Cyril Jacob, Edward Lack, Peter Lack, Philip L. Miller, Paul Morby, Mario Morini, Raffaele Moscatiello, Otto Müller, Carlo Pandolfini, Graham Peel, William F. Porter, Simonetta Puccini, Leo Riemens, Harold Rosenthal, John Rosselli, Aldo Stefanile, Khushroo Suntook, Julie Thornhill, Carmelo Tito, Ruffo Titta, and Henry Wisneski, as well as all those who contributed to the discography.

To my friends and academic colleagues G.W. Connell, Walter Grauberg, N. Horton-Smith, P. Jolivet, Ron Keightley, Martine Lafon, Cynthia Marsh, Brian Tate, Fern Utton, and Christine Whitbourn goes my gratitude for linguistic assistance in French, German, Hungarian, Portuguese, Russian, and Spanish.

Grateful acknowledgement is made to the University of Nottingham for the provision of research facilities.

Thanks are due to Pat Andrew and Joy Armstrong for secretarial assistance; to Michael Brown, MJB Data Systems Ltd; to Alan Odell, Cripps Computing Centre, University of Nottingham; and to Joanne Osman, Microsoft Ltd, for help in preparing the manuscript for publication. Particularly appreciated was the patience of Deborah Blake and Ray Davies, Gerald Duckworth & Co. Ltd., who guided me through the intricacies of book production.

The work has profited greatly from many fruitful and enjoyable discussions with Cora Alter, Euan Gibby, Eliot Levin, Jerrold Northrop Moore, George Stuart, and Michael Wyler.

A particular tribute is due to three friends who, despite their many onerous commitments, have never failed to respond to my requests for help: publication may be almost as great a relief to them as it is to me. Without the enthusiam of Vivian Liff this book would have been very much the poorer. Whether devoting his time to the details of the dust-jacket, drawing my attention to references in arcane publications, or searching his library on my behalf, little escaped his notice and nothing was ever too much trouble for him. William R. Moran has sustained my sense of proportion: his penetrating, but always kindly, constructive and well-informed criticism has spared me 'many a blunder ... and foolish notion'. Desmond Shawe-Taylor, whose writings first aroused my interest in De Lucia, kindly read various drafts of the manuscript. His knowledge, experience, and limitless capacity for taking pains have produced innumerable improvements.

To Francesca Terry my gratitude is immense: for helping me to acquire a working knowledge of Italian; for transcribing many tapes of conversations; for assistance in deciphering pages of crabbed and faded calligraphy, and for clarifying numerous points of Neapolitan life and custom. Above all, I thank her for her continuing guidance and support over many years.

No incidents, scenes or quotations stem from the imagination; all are based on documentation or on the testimony of those with credible claims to personal knowledge of the matter under discussion. In the few cases where, in the absence of the facts, I have resorted to supposition, this is made plain in the text. Every possible care has been taken to verify the facts as presently known. However, further material will undoubtedly come to light which may present a new aspect to the conclusions that I have drawn. In thanking the above for their help I must, therefore, absolve them from any errors in my interpretation of the material that they have so freely given.

Finally, and quite inadequately, I thank my wife Ann and daughter Luisa for their indulgence during the many years for which this work has absorbed almost all of my free time.

Glossary of Terms

The reviews of De Lucia's performances employ certain Italian musical terms. Some are too well-known to require explanation. Others, however, are archaic, obsolete, or at least uncommon. Yet others persist but with an altered meaning. Few permit of concise translation. Accordingly, for brevity and to preserve the flavour of the original, I have retained the Italian terms in the text and included definitions here.

corona: The *fermata* or pause (pl. *corone*).

falsetto: This term is used with some frequency in critiques of De Lucia. In the nineteenth century it described the entire head register, or *voce mista,* between chest voice and what we now term *falsetto.* It did not then have its modern meaning, i.e. the register used by the male alto, or counter-tenor. No De Lucia record known to the writer shows *falsetto* in its modern sense.[1]

filata: Literally 'a spun note'. In practice, a note held while the sound is diminished (pl. *filate*).

fioritura: Literally 'flowering'. The term applied to the type of decoration or flourish, often extemporised, designed to show the quality and agility of the voice. It was especially common in eighteenth-century operatic arias (pl. *fioriture*).

gruppetto: The Italian term for a turn, i.e. the four-note ornament employing the note above, the note itself, the note below, and the note itself once again (pl. *gruppetti*).

legato: A smooth, flowing line.

mezza voce: Half-voice, i.e. with half the available power.

morendo: Literally 'dying'. A note diminished to a thread of sound.

picchiettato: 'Knocked', 'knocking', i.e. (in the playing of bowed instruments) detaching the notes (or *picchettato*).

portamento: The carrying of the voice from note to note, each blending into the other, without gaps or change of quality, both ascending and descending.

puntatura: Alterations of the *tessitura* (q.v.) or of the extreme notes of the vocal line to accommodate a voice of different range but with the original accompaniment. There is no clear line between a change for

---

[1] See Conrad L. Osborne, 'The Evolution of the Tenor Voice from Handel to the Present', *Musical Newsletter,* Vol. III, July 1973, pp. 3-8, 17-20.

reasons of range and one made for artistic effect (pl. *puntature*).[2]

sfumatura: Literally 'to evaporate, disappear, vanish, or come to nothing'. Musical meanings include shading, gradation of colours, or nuance (pl. *sfumature*). (See also *smorzatura*.)

smorzatura: Literally to extinguish, shade or attenuate; hence, in some senses it can be synonymous with *filata, morendo*, or *sfumatura* (q.v.). In musical contexts it most often signifies a fading away to nothing (pl. *smorzature*) (also *smorzando, smorzi*).

spianato: Smoothed, thus *canto spianato* signifies even, sustained singing, or so-called Plain Style.

striscio: Smoothing, or gliding.

tessitura: Literally 'texture'. Distinct from the actual range, which is determined by the compass of the voice, the *tessitura* is the general position or lie of the vocal lines. Parts containing excessive numbers of high or low notes - none of which need be inaccessible - are said to have high or low *tessitura*, and to place a corresponding strain on the voice.

---

2 Crutchfield, 'Vocal Ornamentation in Verdi: the Phonographic Evidence', *19th Century Music*, Vol. 7, No. 1, Summer 1983, p. 12, and private communication, June 1988.

Conventions

A foolish consistency is the hobgoblin of little minds, adored by little statesmen
and philosophers and divines.   Ralph Waldo Emerson[1]

Conversations: Conversations are reproduced only when they may be
documented from credible contemporary written or oral evidence.

Dates: Dates in the text are given in the form October 11th 1860. Months
are abbreviated in footnotes.

Language: The writer has not adopted strict uniformity in the matter of
language other than to give opera titles in the language in which the
works were sung and to favour the style used in references such as
Kobbé's Complete Opera Book, namely (for example) *La Forza del Destino*
rather than *La forza del destino.* Place names and geographical features
generally take their Anglicised forms, such as Florence, Leghorn, Milan,
Naples, Seville, and Vienna. For its conciseness as well as for its common
usage, 'River Plate' has been preferred to the local name, 'Rio de la Plata'
('River of Silver'). Titles of songs and arias are given in roman, within
quotation marks; other foreign phrases are italicised, as are opera titles.

Levels of emphasis: Many letters quoted contain double underlinings. No
attempt has been made to discriminate between different levels of
emphasis. Except in those few cases where an underlined phrase is given
in the original language all underlinings appear as italics. Some
correspondents, notably Giulio Ricordi, frequently employ ellipses in the
form of a series of five dots, and this has been preserved in the current
work. Words omitted by the present writer are indicated by the
customary three dots.

Names: Generally, forenames are given on the first appearance in this
work of the person concerned. Forenames are subsequently omitted
except in cases of possible ambiguity, eg. Fabbri or Rossi.

Reference to records: Reference to De Lucia's records is made by
Discography Number, enclosed in square brackets. Since he recorded
many items more than once, and since not all have been heard,

---
[1] *Essays: First Series. History* (1841).

comments relate specifically to the recordings so identified but not necessarily to his other versions of the same piece. In mentioning individual notes the presumed downward transposition has been taken into account.

Sources: Reference is made by the following abbreviations:

A	G.R. Ancona.
BLP	Biblioteca Lucchesi-Palli, Naples.
BLS	Biblioteca Livia Simoni, Teatro alla Scala, Milan.
BS	Benedikt-Salmon Collection.
CGA	Covent Garden Archives.
DL	De Lucia family.
E	Enthoven Collection, Victoria and Albert Museum, London.
EMI	EMI Archives.
G	Georges Girard.
H	P.G. Hurst.
LCML	La Cañada Memorial Library, La Cañada, California.
MP	Museo Puccini, Torre del Lago Puccini.
PC	Private collection.
R	G. Ricordi & C.
RE	Roberto Esposito.
SLC	Stuart-Liff Collection.
SPM	Conservatorio di Musica di San Pietro a Maiella, Naples.
TM	Theatre Museum, London.
TPN	Tribunale Penale di Napoli.

As down the stage again,
With Spanish hat and plumes, and gait inimitable,
Back from the fading lessons of the past, I'd call,
  I'd tell and own,
How much from thee! the revelation of the singing voice
  from thee!
(So firm - so liquid-soft - again that tremulous,
  manly timbre!
The perfect singing voice - deepest of all to me the
  lesson - trial and test of all:)
How through those strains distill'd - how the rapt ears,
  the soul of me, absorbing
Fernando's heart, Manrico's passionate call, Ernani's,
  sweet Gennaro's . . .
From these, for these, with these, a hurried line,
  dead tenor,
A wafted autumn leaf, dropt in the closing grave, the
  shovel'd earth,
To memory of thee.

Walt Whitman, *Leaves of Grass* [1]

It is a sign of genius if an artist has been able to create a
world which by the force of his imagination and gifts he
compels us to recognise as peculiarly his own. This is not
necessarily synonymous with greatness, but it argues a high
degree of individuality - one of the most precious of creative
gifts.

Mosco Carner, *Puccini*

---

[1] Published Nov. 1884 as a tribute to the tenor Pasquale Brignoli.

1

Son of Naples

Naples - The pure, translucent sky, the carefree sun and fecund earth!
Hector Berlioz, *Mémoires de Berlioz*

Of the the cities of Europe, none has deeper flaws than Naples. Yet few can have exerted so compelling an attraction for authors and artists, bewitched by the splendour of its setting:

> There is something in the soft and limpid loveliness of the Bay of Naples that may well appeal to our Northern races with the intensity of a passion. . . . It is a beauty which the hand of man cannot destroy. The midland sea is as blue, the curves of the bay are as sweeping, as in the days when lovers of Nature heard there the voices and songs of their Gods. . . . the harbour, which lies like a great opal reflecting colours and sunshine as glowing as those of the East, and yet far softer. There is something Homeric in the setting of this cluster of sea-washed towns, extending in a wide half-circle from Posillipo to Sorrento. . . . purple Vesuvius, whose ravelled cloud extends across the heavens.[1]

Thus was described a city that for centuries had suffered the dominion of oppressors, of Spaniards, Austrians, and French, before, on September 6th 1860, the last Bourbon King, Francesco II, left his capital by sea. The following day Giuseppe Garibaldi, summoned from Salerno, entered the city without bloodshed. On October 21st 1860 the Kingdom of Naples was annexed to Italy by plebiscite.

In that year of liberation the 38-year-old Giuseppe De Lucia[2] and his 29-year-old wife Rosa, *née* Barbella, were living with their children at 45, Strada Capuana, an old street in the populous Vicaria quarter of Naples. At 10 pm on October 11th 1860 their responsibilities increased once more, when a second son was born to the couple; in the Cathedral, next day, he was baptised with the family names Ferdinando Salvatore.[3]

The precise nature of Giuseppe's occupation is not clear. Some official documents describe him as a trader or shopkeeper, others as a musician or music teacher. The latter description is supported by family tradition and by the presence of two music masters at the registration of

---

[1] Augustine Fitzgerald and Sybil Fitzgerald, *Naples*, p. 2.

[2] Giuseppe signs with the lower case *de* as, initially, did Ferdinando. Later, both employed the upper case *De* which, for consistency, is used throughout this work.

[3] Though some sources give 1861 De Lucia's birth certificate clearly states 1860.

Ferdinando's birth. Giuseppe is variously credited with proficiency in the
clarinet,[4] the guitar, and the double-bass.[5]

Ferdinando De Lucia was an Italian of the South, with the natural
warmth, the spontaneous passion, and the latent intensity of the people
of that region. But, specifically, he was born a Neapolitan. He was
always to remain a son of Naples. To understand the nature of the man
that he was to become we must explore his background and examine in
some detail the city and the times which moulded him.

The final years of Bourbon rule have been held to be the last great
days of Neapolitan society, when the diplomatic corps, distinguished
foreign visitors, and wealthy residents joined the aristocracy in functions
then considered to be the most brilliant in Europe.[6] The sumptuous balls
of the Accademia Reale; the San Carlo opera house; the receptions and
soirées at the villas of the Riviera di Chiaia, in their secluded, palm-
fringed gardens; the entertainments in private theatres: these were the
diversions of the aristocracy or of the merely well-to-do as they divided
their time between their homes and the concerts, plays, and operas at
the many theatres of the city - six or more different opera seasons each
year was not unusual - or at gatherings of musical societies. In spring
and summer, attended by armies of servants, they would occupy the long
days and balmy evenings at the races or in excursions and picnics
all'aperto at Capri and Ischia.

Apart from the departure of the diplomats, the sweeping away of the
Bourbons in 1860 saw little change in the agreeable social order of the
comfortably-off. The promenade on the Riviera di Chiaia still presented a
spectacle perhaps unique in Europe, as stately carriages, bearing
fashionable women and famous *coquettes*, filed slowly around the bay in
the diffuse light of a sunset that threw purple and gold on to the hill of
Posillipo. Public social life continued to be centred on the San Carlo and
on the Caffè d'Europa, where, amid the gilt, crystal, and glass, the
theatre's habitués could sup after the performance in the company of the
wits of the day, the *dilettanti* of the arts, and the *jeunesse dorée*. Lighter
refreshment was still to be had at Benvenuto's in Via Chiaia, where the
finest water ices in Naples were made. For the sweet of tooth, Luigi
Caflisch, in Via Toledo, continued, as he had for nearly forty years, to
provide exquisite pastries.

To those with shorter pockets but hearty appetites the *pizzerie* offered
a cheap, filling repast. Macaroni, though, was an unattainable luxury for
the very poor, whose single meal of the day would be a bowl of vegetable
soup and a lump of coarse bread. Such, or less, was the fare of those
whom the Spaniards had termed the *lazzaroni*, the lowest class, with the

---

4 Arturo Lancellotti, *Le Voci d'Oro*, p. 186.
5 De Lucia family.
6 Peter Gunn, *Naples: A Palimpsest*, p. 195.

humblest occupations and no fixed abode or way of life, whose numbers dwindled after independence to such an extent that Mathilde Marchesi, during a visit in 1871, looked in vain for one.[7] By the 1890s the term was almost confined to boatmen and fishermen, some of the most industrious of Neapolitans.

In this old-world city, its narrow, tortuous thoroughfares climbing hills by steps and ramps in every direction, it seemed that the tall houses were held up only by the arches which spanned the streets. Below, every kind of itinerant trader touted for custom. The *acquaiolo*, water tub on his back and string of lemons on his arm, mingled with the flower seller, the fruit merchant, the tinker, and the charcoal vendor - all the endless variety of commerce, money and goods changing hands in baskets let down on cords from balconies. In the alleys and among the fish-booths of Santa Lucia the cries of the vendors were deafening. Fresh milk was provided by the herds of cows and goats which were driven daily from the countryside, adding to the noise, congestion, and insanitariness.

Yet there was much that was stylish about Naples. The old Via Mezzo-cannone had been replaced by the long, broad Via Toledo as the virtual town centre. In the seventeenth and eighteenth centuries the Toledo had held the palaces of many noble families. By the nineteenth, however, it was the main business artery and reputedly the noisiest street in Europe. The cracking of whips and rumble of wheels over the uneven roads were ear-splitting. Alexandre Dumas is said to have described it as a promenade for the noble, a bazaar for the merchant, and a dwelling place for the *lazzaroni*. But even the Toledo could fall almost silent on one day a year, when on Maundy Thursday the shops stayed open late and carriages were banned from the street, thronged with people making the promenade called *Lo Struscio*, from the rustling of the silk dresses which the women allowed to drag in the dust.[8] The Largo Santa Trinità Maggiore, flanked by the immense stone wall of the former Sanseverino palace, and under the windows of the mansion of Prince Pignatelli, had a calm dignity.[9] Even the poorest quarters, Porto and Pendino, had their narrow mediaeval streets, with noble houses rising six floors and more, their balconies almost closing out the sky. Tranquil above the busy town centre lay the winding, still incomplete, Corso Vittorio Emanuele, skirting the hill of St. Elmo and offering unequalled views of the Bay.

To a greater extent than most Italian cities, Naples remained a loose association of so-called *quartieri*: almost a separate and self-contained village, each quarter had its own web of relationships in a great extended family and was characterised by the class, dress, and psychology of its

---

[7] Mathilde Marchesi, *Marchesi and Music*, p. 138.

[8] In 1870 it was renamed Via Roma, so remaining for a more than a century. Now, it is again named after the Spanish Viceroy Don Pedro de Toledo.

[9] Now Piazza del Gesù Nuovo; the church of that name occupies part of the site of the former Sanseverino palace.

inhabitants. In the poorer quarters, life revolved about the *basso*, the small shop with a door like a coach-house, with neither window nor chimney to carry away the smoke of its charcoal stove. The *basso* was devoted more to the business of the occupant than to his comfort and needs. Its door stood open by day while the tenant exercised his trade within. The furnishings were few: on the wall a picture of the Madonna, with an oil lamp continuously burning before it; the stove; the huge family bed, often scarcely able to contain the large families. In summer the men would sleep outside - and little wonder when the alternative was the shuttered darkness shared with a dozen others. Indeed, life could be said to be centred in the streets, where the women dressed their hair and bathed their children, and where many local people took their meals at the street cookshops, with their pots of oil simmering on a wood fire. From the single door of the *basso* refuse was thrown out as convenient, to await human or animal scavengers or the daily visit of the dustcart.[10]

The Vicaria, where De Lucia was born, had been described by Charles Dickens in 1844 as 'the dirtiest quarter of dirty Naples'. Though it was not without its imposing palaces and its middle class it also had its *lazzaroni*.[11] When they did not sleep in the open air they dwelt in cellars and caves or in the so-called *fondaci*, *'O fúnneco* in dialect. In these high, windowless blind alleys, formerly warehouses, each floor of fifteen or more rooms was home to the destitute, who slept on the boards amid the odours of rotting offal, where mothers guarded their children at night against the voracious rats, and where the well adjoined the cesspit in the courtyard.[12] Called by Axel Munthe 'the most ghastly human habitations on the face of the earth', these vile rookeries were home to thousands in the capital of the former Kingdom of the Two Sicilies.[13]

These, then, were the violent contrasts of De Lucia's Neapolitan youth. Little is known of his childhood. He evidently spent periods at his mother's birthplace, San Vitaliano, near Nola, north of Naples, where the family probably resided at some stage; of his two brothers and eight sisters, Federico (1851) and Maria (1865) were born there.[14] But they always returned to Naples and to the Vicaria, where two of the children died in infancy. In the early 1870s they lived at 52, Strada Fontana Capuana and subsequently at other addresses in the area of Porta Capuana. In 1873-4, Ferdinando attended the Day School for Boys in Via Monte di Misericordia, in the Pendino quarter, where he occupied himself profitably and behaved as well as any other young Neapolitan.[15]

---

10 Eustace Neville-Rolfe and Holcombe Ingleby, *Naples in the Eighties*, p. 37ff.
11 Charles Dickens, *Pictures from Italy*.
12 Lacy Collison-Morley, *Naples through the Centuries*, p. 177ff.
13 Axel Munthe, *Letters from a Mourning City*, p. 76.
14 (SPM) Medical certificates for Ferdinando, dated 1874 and 1876, were issued at S. Vitaliano.
15 (SPM) Director's report, Feb. 16 1875.

Rumour has it that he at one time intended to train as a house-painter. However, at the age of fifteen - when he is said to have sung, as an alto, Mercadante's *Miserere*[16] - he was admitted for a trial period as a day pupil at the Royal College of Music, of Naples, to study the double-bass.[17] His elder brother Federico, for many years a violinist at the Teatro San Carlo, had entered the same school some twelve years earlier.

Centuries before, Naples had boasted four conservatories, founded to provide home and education for orphans of the city; by degrees, that education had become centred on music. From them had come composers of the stature of Bellini, Cimarosa, Mercadante, Paisiello, Pergolesi, and Porpora. Changing economic and artistic conditions, however, had obliged one institution after another to close and, in 1807, the schools were consolidated as the Collegio Reale di Musica. The following year, more ample premises were found in the buildings of a former convent, and the name correspondingly changed to the Reale Collegio di San Sebastiano. In 1826 it moved again, into a former monastery in Via San Pietro a Maiella, whence it takes its present name.[18]

This institution, inheritor of the traditions that had made eighteenth-century Naples the centre of the musical world, was one of the most distinguished colleges of music in Italy, enjoying a reputation such that eminent composers vied for the post of Director. Donizetti, who taught composition there, had been passed over for the position in favour of Mercadante; the latter had grown up in Naples, where he had attended San Sebastiano, and he was for this reason preferred by King Ferdinando II.[19] After presiding over the college for three decades, Mercadante was succeeded by another of the college's graduates, Lauro Rossi (1812-1885), a former pupil of Niccolò Zingarelli and of the male mezzo-soprano Girolamo Crescentini, and the composer of almost thirty operas. The professoriate, appointed exclusively by competitive examination, included Beniamino Carelli (father of Augusto, Bice, and Emma, and author of several books on singing), Beniamino Cesi, Vincenzo Lombardi, and Paolo Serrao, established composers and performers in their own right. Longest-serving of all was Francesco Florimo (1800-1888), who had been a fellow student of Bellini at San Sebastiano; in 1826 he had become librarian and archivist of the college, a position that he held until his death. In addition to writing, the teaching of singing, and the glorification of his friend Bellini, his life was spent collecting for the Library, housed in its elegant, high-ceilinged rooms each named after a composer. Already well endowed, it was

---

16 *Gil Blas*, May 10 1905.

17 (SPM) Application dated November 4 1875. There is no evidence for the statement that he studied the bassoon and the flute.

18 Guido Pannain, *Il R. Conservatorio di Musica 'San Pietro a Maiella' di Napoli*, p. 17ff. The development of the Conservatories is discussed at length in Michael Robinson, *Naples and Neapolitan Opera*, p. 13ff.

19 Herbert Weinstock, *Donizetti*, p. 136.

greatly enriched by his shrewd purchases of books, letters, pictures, manuscripts, and other items which made it one of the most interesting musical archives in Italy.[20] His autograph books contain respectful or affectionate words from many of his eminent musical contemporaries. When Wagner came to Naples in 1880, it was to meet its archivist that he visited San Pietro a Maiella. By then, still writing books and music, Florimo seemed almost as permanent as the college itself.

Passing from the narrow, cobbled street, under the archway with its unobtrusive nameboard, the young De Lucia entered the first of two cloistered courtyards, with their palm trees and the statues of composers, dominated by a powerful, brooding figure of Beethoven. The air was filled with music, of piano and organ, of singers' scales, all the everyday activity of a place that would be the centre of his life for most of the next ten years.

Initially, he attended the external school, which was *gratis* and which served to groom suitable candidates for the fee-paying boarding school. At the age of 17, however, he entered the competition for two scholarships offered for the study of the double-bass.[21] After some characteristic Neapolitan procrastination, in July 1879 the Council awarded him a place; in accepting it, Giuseppe De Lucia undertook to keep him at the college until the prescribed age - the double-bass involved studies of five years - and to pay for any damage to the furniture, instruments, and other equipment. As a concession to his modest income Giuseppe was permitted to pay the entry fee of 120 lire in two instalments.[22]

In addition to music, students at San Pietro a Maiella received a sound general education: they learned arithmetic, calligraphy, geography, national history, and the Italian language, with opportunities to study Latin, declamation, mythology, and Italian poetry and literature. The working day, although shorter than in Bellini's time, was still a long one. From 6.30 am until the students retired at 10 pm, only meals, the two half-hour periods of recreation, and the daily walk relieved the succession of lessons and religious activities, both in college and in city churches, and the continual traffic between practice rooms, college theatres, and library. The older students led a less regimented life; among other privileges they enjoyed regular visits to the operas at the former Royal theatres - the San Carlo and the Fondo (now the Mercadante) - where they could hear the greatest singers of the day.

These were fine times for the young Ferdinando, dashing in his uniform of black gloves, black cloak with gold buttons, and with the lyre emblem glittering on his cap.[23] The school of double-bass was directed by

---

20 Weinstock, *Vincenzo Bellini*, p. 15ff.
21 (SPM) Undated application.
22 (SPM) Agreement dated Nov. 12 1879. The sum was then about £5.
23 Edoardo Boutet, *Sua Eccellenza San Carlino*, p. 173ff. Boutet was a theatrical critic and teacher of

Gaetano Negri, under whose tuition he made steady - if not spectacular - progress, learning to execute all kinds of variations and ornaments on the instrument. For his playing in the orchestra which accompanied Francesco (Checco) Marconi in some trifle of Mario Costa, De Lucia was later to be termed 'first among tenors, last among double-bass players'.[24] He retained a lasting affection for Negri, who taught for fifty years at the college, sending him tickets for his performances, keeping his photograph in his studio, and always describing him as his true Maestro. Forty years later, the tenor Angelo Notariello found 'FDL' carved on the back of the smallest college double-bass instrument. None the less, Ferdinando was not to remain an instrumentalist for long. At the age of 19, his performance of a song written by one of his classmates was heard by the professor of advanced vocal studies, the former operatic baritone Alfonso Guercia (1831-1890). Guercia, struck by the facility and beauty of the voice, persuaded him to study under his guidance.[25] No precise date can be given for this change but it is known that Ferdinando was successful in the competition on May 18th 1880 for free places in the school of singing. So enthusiastically did he work, and so rapid was his progress that, after only a few months, he took first place in a student vocal competition, performing the romanza 'Ah! se sapessi!'[26] This first triumph was crowned by the traditional chairing of the winning student on the shoulders of his fellows beneath the vaults of the old cloister, while the professors looked on and applauded.[27]

The few surviving documents for the scholastic years 1880-2 do not identify De Lucia's first vocal teacher. All that is certain is that his was one of six free places in singing and that Guercia took some part in his training until at least 1884. Other sources state that Emanuele De Roxas also taught him.[28] An oral tradition suggests that he may have taken private lessons with Guglielmo Vergine.[29] Connections with Beniamino Carelli were most probably during the well-known *Tornate* (gatherings) at Carelli's house, where musical gossip alternated with discussion of advanced vocal technique.[30] Lombardi, however, was to have a profound effect on De Lucia's career.

Florimo soon noticed the young singer's worth. In his small but elegant rooms, crowded with souvenirs of a lifetime among composers and artists, he would invite the select few for coffee and liqueurs. In this

dramatic literature; he wrote for several Neapolitan newspapers and magazines, often under the pen-name 'Caramba'.

24 Oreste Giordano, article 'Mario Costa', in an unidentified Italian newspaper, Aug. 1919, referring to an event of c. 1885.

25 *Mattino*, Feb. 22 1925.

26 *Phonodart*, Year 1, No. 1, Mar.-Apr. 1931; this was published in Naples by the Esposito family, proprietors of the Phonotype recording company.

27 Boutet, op. cit.

28 *Occhialetto*, Dec. 10 1887.

29 Angelo Notariello (a De Lucia pupil). Vergine later taught Enrico Caruso.

30 Augusto Carelli, *Emma Carelli*, p. 14.

cordial atmosphere the student would hear his host recount the background to some item in his personal museum of musical history. That conviviality constituted his diploma. It was said that when the glass of wine became two or more, and affability became an exchange of confidences, it was a sign of Florimo's conviction - in which he was rarely mistaken - that the student would become a famous maestro or singer. Ferdinando De Lucia belonged to this group. But Florimo was not alone in his confidence; the knowledge that De Lucia was to participate in a concert was sufficient to fill the college theatre. In that dimly-lit room, hung with the portraits assiduously collected by the old archivist, the appreciative crowd might include such contemporaries as Francesco Cilea, Umberto Giordano, and Niccolò Van Westerhout who, time and again, would cross the tenor's path in the years ahead.[31]

Conservatory pupils had once been exempt from conscription, but De Lucia's studies were now to be interrupted. Scarcely a week after his 20th birthday he was declared fit for military service and called upon to cast off the cloak and don uniform. In the hope of continuing his studies he applied to a local regiment for admission as a Musician, a position of privilege and with better rates of pay than in the ranks, but requiring him to serve for eight years. The Regiment pointed out that entry for three years as an ordinary soldier would permit him, after initial training, to take service in music - although, under current economic conditions, it could not pay him any monthly supplement.[32]

The Director hastened to reply:

Naples, November 23rd 1880

The Commandant of the 16th Infantry Regiment (Savona)

Finding Your Excellency's note I beg to inform you that De Lucia, as talented a double-bass player as [he is] a singer (tenor voice), in order not to interrupt his musical studies, aims to enter the Regiment under your worthy command as a soldier to be, at an appropriate time, assigned to service in music, contracting only for the normal three years. These reasonable aspirations of De Lucia are intended to allow him to come to the College in his free time to pursue his studies.

I take the present opportunity to recommend to Your Excellency the young De Lucia, who has brought honour on the College, and who promises rather a bright musical career.[33]

This plea was denied.[34] Thus, in the bleakness of winter, the young conscript found himself as a private soldier in the 8th Infantry Regiment, garrisoned at Caserta, where his formal musical responsibilities soon became clear: he was to beat the bass drum in the regimental band. He

---

31 Boutet, op. cit.
32 (SPM) Letter from Admissions Office to the Director of San Pietro a Maiella, Nov. 21 1880.
33 (SPM) Draft reply, unsigned.
34 (SPM) Correspondence dated Dec. 21 1880.

seems to have born the indignity with cheerfulness and despite his small stature - only 1.64 m (5 ft. 6 in.) and slight of build[35] - he cut a fine figure in uniform. Further, since his singing made him popular with the officers, invitations to perform at their parties provided both a welcome change from parade-ground discipline and an opportunity to charm the daughters of the senior ranks. Among so many officers few noticed Private De Lucia until he started to sing. Then, the ladies gathered around the piano, each finding an excuse to sing a 'romanza' with him.

Once, he was invited to sing at the Military Circle in Caserta, in a concert in honour of a visit by Minister Pasquale Mancini, who was accompanied by the young Carmelo Errico, poet of Tosti's 'Ideale'.[36] At the end of the concert the rain was torrential. With the concern of a singer for his throat, and aware that a cold could impair his voice for weeks, De Lucia borrowed a woman's shawl, to cover his head and throat, and sheltered under a borrowed umbrella. Returning in uniform to the barracks he heard behind him the sound of steps and the jingle of officer's spurs. There came a shout to stop. Knowing that the officer would inevitably order him to discard his meagre protection from the elements, he ignored the call. Then came the second cry: 'Soldier of the Pope - Halt!' A swift assessment of the implications for his throat or for his military career could produce only one answer: he ran for the protection of the barracks where, intercepted and charged, he was at least sheltered from the rain.

Next day, he was called before the Colonel; on the stairs outside his office he was resourceful enough to sing a snatch of 'La donna è mobile', to jog the memory. The tactic was successful, and he was leniently treated by a Colonel who agreed that his throat was too precious to be put at risk. 'But,' he said, 'it is as well that you sang outside a moment ago!'[37]

He served only two years before returning to the Conservatory.[38] His debt paid to his country, it was a carefree time, with pleasant memories. A trip to a country inn at San Giovanello saw a good-natured shooting match before dinner; while the ladies massacred small chalk puppets Boutet watched the young tenor continue to miss larger and larger targets, testimony - as Ferdinando would later admit - to never having fired a shot in anger. Not until the fruit course did he redeem his reputation as he sang sentimental romanzas, to applause and many toasts. He sang again during the tram journey home, and the ticket-collector did not have the courage to interrupt to demand the fare.[39]

---

35 Military records.

36 Francesco dell'Erba, *Giornale d'Italia*, Feb. 24 1925.

37 De Lucia's military service has been described by several authors, including Boutet, op. cit., Lancellotti, op. cit., and Dell'Erba, 'Il debutto di un divo', *Napoli. Un Quarto di Secolo*, pp.169-175. This particular episode was also a favourite anecdote of De Lucia himself, who related it to his family.

38 The last date in his military record is Dec. 4 1882.

39 Boutet, op. cit.

At about this time Ferdinando accompanied a fellow student, Alfredo De Giorgio, to Salerno to give a concert and to sing in churches. There he stayed for a month with Alfredo's family.[40] His parents, Cav. Eduardo De Giorgio, who held the important post of Chief Civil Engineer for the province of Salerno, and his wife Penelope[41] had moved there from Naples in the mid-1870s. The house in which they and their ten children lived reflected the high social and financial status that a qualified engineer would then have enjoyed. Without doubt, Eduardo was a prominent and prosperous local figure.

Alfredo, a bass who later taught music in Rome, was to remain Ferdinando's lifelong friend.[42] He was not the only De Giorgio with artistic inclinations. His younger sisters, Flora and Pia, showed promise as pianist and singer, respectively. A brother, Rodolfo, was a painter. Their parents moved in musical circles; the conductor Carlo Scalisi[43] and his wife, the singer Fanny Rubini-Scalisi, were frequent visitors to the house, and it is possible that Ferdinando met them there. Achemenide De Giorgio, probably Eduardo's brother, wrote musical criticisms notable, it must be said, more for pedantry and flowery prose than for penetrating insight.

Of De Lucia's engagements in Salerno no details can now be found.[44] During his stay, however, he met Alfredo's eldest sister, the 19-year-old Itala, to whom he was attracted. Although she would accompany her mother to concerts in which her sisters were participating, Itala had no marked musical leanings. Neither, to judge from surviving photographs (dating from much later), was she any great beauty. Temperamentally, she and Ferdinando were to prove ill-suited. Nevertheless, the youthful fascination was strong. It is possible that the impecunious singer, who was later described as 'stingy',[45] was beguiled by the solid comforts of the De Giorgio home, a marked contrast to his own modest background.[46] For her part, Itala was not indifferent to her brother's handsome friend,

---

40 De Roberto, Scardaccione, and Majolo, *De Giorgio contro De Lucia, Memoria a Stampa*, Tribunale Civile di Napoli, 1ª Sezione, 1895, pp. 7-8. In this legal document, the source of much of our knowledge of De Lucia's domestic life, Itala - whose recollections, though, are sometimes unreliable - states that they met in 1882. Probably, the stay in Salerno came after his military service, i.e. after December 1882.

41 In some documents named Filomena, *née* Siciliano.

42 Alfredo (1861-1926) later became an enthusiastic and accomplished photographer. His earliest extant photographs date from around 1897; surviving record books carefully document his work from 1908 onwards, when he numbered among his subjects musical celebrities such as Battistini, Cotogni, De Lucia, Marconi, Mascagni, Ruffo, and Tosti, as well as his own pupils. Though few of his portraits have survived, his depictions of contemporary Rome were displayed in an exhibition there in 1985. See: Biblioteca di Storia Moderna e Contemporanea, *Memoria fotografica (1908-1923)*.

43 Sometimes Scalise.

44 Boutet, op. cit., implies that his concert début preceded his military service, but there is no other evidence for this.

45 Nicola Daspuro, 'Memorie Postume', ch. XXII, suggests that it was De Lucia's ability to drive a hard bargain which caused the publisher and impresario Edoardo Sonzogno to consider him the 'most miserly of tenors'.

46 Twenty years later, and very wealthy, he was described by the recording engineer Fred Gaisberg as 'generous'.

who was already showing promise as a concert artist.

After about a year of further study, with Guercia,[47] the tenor began to accept engagements in the fashionable drawing-rooms, the *salotti*, of Naples. Much had changed since the departure of the Bourbons but, although many of the great town houses had fallen into the hands of *parvenus* who had split them up into tenements, social gatherings in the others were still as grand and formal as when the Neapolitan nobility adorned its own court.[48] Their spacious salons, where wealthy Neapolitans attended private concerts of *musica da camera*, were in plain contrast to the dirty and ill-kept streets only a marble staircase away. In the 1880s, to wander through the maze of streets and squares of old Naples, from the Cathedral to the Royal Palace, or from Porta Capuana to the Conservatory, was to marvel at the imposing buildings, the fine patrician palaces of the fifteenth and sixteenth century with their towering iron-bound gates and their carved stone porticoes, flanked by ornate lamps, and at the numbers of the maids and footmen who attended the gleaming carriages.

De Lucia's first verifiable engagement was in Naples, on September 23rd 1883, in a concert in memory of Bellini. It was held at the home of Michele Ruta, co-director of the Conservatory. In the presence of Florimo, visibly moved by the occasion, the assembly crowded the principal salon and listened attentively from under the arches of the doors of adjacent rooms as the programme unfolded. The tenor Spanò sang Arturo's romanza from *I Puritani*. De Lucia and Anna Ruta sang the duet from *La Straniera*; later, they were joined by the veteran Luigi Colonnese and by a Signor De Giorgio (almost certainly Alfredo) in the quartet from *I Puritani*.[49] A correspondent wrote:

> De Lucia (tenor) has a beautiful voice. He sings with sentiment [and] has all the qualities [needed] to become a distinguished artist; but he offends by exaggerated effects and frequently, to obtain a 'Bravo' from the ignorant, he somewhat overdoes things.[50]

A scattering of other concerts followed before a more important engagement, at the Società Filarmonica of Naples, on January 25th 1884. Founded in 1867 by a group that included Luigi Filiasi, a musician with strong links with the Conservatory, the Filarmonica occupied lavishly decorated rooms in the Palazzo Cassano. It was a fashionable gathering-place where success was sure to lead to other prestigious and lucrative engagements in the city.

After the youthful maestro Camillo De Nardis had conducted two brief

47 *Piccolo*, Jan. 31 1884.
48 Mattia Limoncelli, *La musica nei salotti napoletani tra l'800 e il 900*.
49 *Piccolo*, Sept. 24 1883. The unspecified quartet was presumably the (offstage) 'Preghiera' from Act I, 'La luna, il sole, le stelle'.
50 *Gazzetta Musicale di Milano*, Sept. 30 1883.

orchestral items De Lucia, in wing collar and borrowed tailcoat, took the
stage for his first song, the barcarolle 'L'Alba', by Rotoli. A correspondent
wrote of

> ... a young man from our Conservatory, Sig. Ferdinando De Lucia, who is truly
> a rare tenor, because he has a most beautiful voice and sings very well and with
> spirit. He took an excellent B from the chest and he reinforces the voice and
> shades it as, perhaps, few tenors from our greatest theatre can do.[51]

He also sang Gounod's 'Medje', then much in vogue, and, to great
applause, was obliged to repeat it.

Meanwhile, at the Teatro San Carlo, the impresario and principal
conductor, Carlo Scalisi, was in trouble with the subscribers and the city
council. The season had opened with a performance of *La Gioconda* given
by singers who were clearly not of the first rank. In noting that the San
Carlo was 'sometimes a temple of art, more often a meeting-place for
good society' the newspaper *Piccolo* remarked that Scalisi had better
ensure more of the former if his contract was to be renewed. A
performance of *Lucrezia Borgia* was not well received, principally
through the inadequacies of the tenor Giovanni Battista De Negri. The
indisposition of Leopoldo Signoretti and the declaration by the theatre
Commission that Frapolli, the only other available tenor, was
unacceptable, led to suggestions that De Lucia should take over the
part.[52] In the event, Signoretti recovered and the idea had no further
currency.

Concert engagements continued to arrive for the young tenor, still
officially a pupil of the Conservatory. That of March 1st 1884 involved
his fellow student, Niccolò Van Westerhout, who conducted a concert at
the Circolo del Commercio. In response to the insistent acclaim for his
performance of three of the conductor's own songs De Lucia gave 'L'Alba'
and 'Ideale' as encores.[53] Another request for his services came from the
soprano and singing teacher Maria Migliaccio, to appear at the Collegio
dei Nobili, in Vico Nilo, on April 22nd. In his most ambitious programme
to date he gave, with his hostess, a Rossini duet and, joined by the
baritone Marini, the trio from *Lucrezia Borgia*. Tosti's 'Aprile' followed
and, as an encore, 'L'Alba'.[54] While the congratulations showered upon
the jubilant tenor many a society hostess noted his name in her
engagement book. As he made his way home to the Conservatory on that
Spring evening the dim, narrow streets with their pools of gaslight must

---

[51] *Piccolo*, Jan. 29 1884.

[52] *Gazzetta Musicale di Milano*, Feb. 3 and 17 1884. The authorities seemed ready to overlook the general
requirement that a singer at the San Carlo should already be an *artista di cartello*, i.e. have had success in a
major theatre. Shortly afterwards, by Deliberation of May 20 1884, the City Council abolished this
prerequisite.

[53] *Piccolo*, Mar. 3 1884. The source implies that 'Ideale' is by Rotoli, but it is probably that by Tosti.

[54] *Pungolo*, Apr. 23/24 1884. Though the reference gives the composer as Tosti the song 'L'Alba' is almost
certainly that by Rotoli.

have seemed bright with promise; the long years of existing on a pittance were surely over, and soon the fashionable would compete to engage him for their soirées.

True recognition, however, still lay some way ahead and he had a more immediate problem. It seems that he had been summoned to sing at the house of Prince Pignatelli, a notable local patron of the arts. Such social circles required something more than borrowed tails, and he lacked the means to buy his own coat. At the suggestion of a friend, he went to see Luigi Caggiula, a tailor with premises in Piazza San Ferdinando, where he explained his difficulty. Caggiula, a shrewd businessman and enthusiastic opera-goer, doubtless saw the eventual benefit of allowing him to pay by instalments. At any rate, De Lucia got his tailcoat, only the first of many purchases from the firm of Caggiula in a personal and business relationship with Luigi, his son Antonio, and his grandson - also Luigi - that lasted for more than forty years.[55]

Two days after his heady success in Vico Nilo the young man asked the Director's permission to be away from Naples for fifteen days on account of 'most urgent family business'.[56] The family involvement, if indeed there was one, is unknown, but business there certainly was, on or around May 7th, in the distant town of Ortona a Mare, east of Pescara on the Adriatic coast. There, he sang in De Nardis's new oratorio, *I Turchi in Ortona*. If the journey - some 200 km as the crow flies but much further in the horse-drawn carriages and hot, slow, crowded trains that wound their tortuous way around the Apennines - was tiring, it was also an adventure, and the engagement doubtless provided a useful fee well away from Naples. But he underestimated the vigilance of the Neapolitan press and, possibly to his embarrassment, the event was reported.[57] However, if the news reached his teachers their complaints are not recorded in his Conservatory file. On May 18th 1884, 'the pupil De Lucia ... in a warm, baritonal voice that reminds us of Negrini' closed a vocal concert at San Pietro a Maiella with 'Il mio tesoro', from *Don Giovanni*.[58] On the same day, he also sang in a concert at the church of San Domenico Maggiore.

His name and his interpretation of Tosti songs were by now well-known in Naples. But he could look forward to very little more activity and profit before the suffocating heat and miasma of summer would drive away everyone free to leave the city. Soon, concert activity would wither as, in the rite of *villeggiatura* (country holiday), wealthy Neapolitans streamed to villas and hotels at Posillipo and Marechiaro to

---

55 Luigi Caggiula, grandson, in conversation with the writer, April 1968. Piazza San Ferdinando is now named Piazza Trieste e Trento; in 1988 the firm of Caggiula is located in Via dei Mille.

56 (SPM) Request dated Apr. 24 1884.

57 *Piccolo*, May 8 1884.

58 *Roma*, May 19 1884. The tenor Negrini (real name Carlo Villa) (1826-1865) was renowned for the masterly expressiveness of his singing and for his great dramatic powers.

the west, and to Torre del Greco and Castellammare-di-Stabia to the
south.

This last, an airy and delightful spa a mere 25 km from Naples,
provided the singer with an engagement in the sultriest days of August.
Castellammare, though somewhat faded from its days of greatest glory
as the most elegant of the local resorts, was still a popular watering
place for the people of Naples and Salerno. Among the visitors that
summer was Minister Grimaldi, in whose honour the local choral society
gave a concert in the Royal Villa Quisisana. De Lucia sang 'L'Alba' well
enough to be invited to the Minister's suite to repeat it.[59]

On August 24th he was back in Naples, at the Gran Sala Tarsia. Of
this period, Boutet wrote:

> I have never forgotten 'Primavera' by Ciccillo Tosti, sung by De Lucia:
>
> > *'Non odi tu nell'aere'*
>
> In his inflections on the last notes, spring blossomed and sang joyously in the
> soul.[60]

Nothing in the surrounding city suggested spring. The summer of
1884 was exceptionally hot in many parts of Europe. As early as June,
ominous reports had been received of the quarantine of some French
ports against cholera. By mid-July the newspapers carried entire
columns about the spread of the disease throughout Italy; a month later
it was at the very gates of Naples.

On the breezy cape of Posillipo the heat was bearable. But in the
reeking lanes - the *vicoli* - of the fishermen's quarter at Santa Lucia the
foetid air hung heavily. In the *bassi* and *fondaci*, even more crowded
than usual, the rats grew bolder, attracted by the overpowering and
pervasive stench of putrefying refuse. The *acquaiolo*, his one tumbler
constantly in use as he moved about the narrow streets, squeezing the
juice from fresh lemons into the cool water, could scarcely satisfy the
demand. When, on August 19th, a carter named Giovanni Velvito was
admitted to hospital and his condition diagnosed, the great cholera
epidemic of 1884 had reached almost half a million people living under
conditions where the disease was uncontrollable.

Initially the outbreak was confined to a few areas. However, on the
last Saturday in August, there was an outbreak of merrymaking among
the poor, whose weekly hopes and expectations in the lottery had for
once been rewarded with a win. All night and the next day they feasted
on a surfeit of overripe fruit. Within a week, the number of cholera cases

---

[59] *Piccolo*, Aug. 22 1884.

[60] Boutet certainly refers to Pagliara's 'Aprile', set by Tosti; the opening words are actually *'Non senti tu
nell'aria'*.

had reached five hundred.[61]

Along the streets rumbled the convoys of carts and omnibuses as they carried the corpses to the immense pits in the cholera cemetery. As the epidemic reached a climax the afflicted dropped in the streets, as though struck by lightning. While the song festival of Piedigrotta was banned and the theatres were closed, the churches and chapels of Naples remained open day and night, thronged with people and ablaze with the light of votive candles in a frenzy of prayer for salvation. At the Farmacia of San Gennaro (the patron saint of Naples) a brisk trade ensued in Don Bartolo's famous anti-cholerical mixture, a family recipe that reputedly had saved the population during the epidemic of 1834. At its height the cholera killed almost five hundred every day.[62] Munthe saw eighty-three bodies arrive at the cemetery in one hour.[63] Over the whole city hung a pall of smoke as the victims' clothing was burned.

Gradually, though, the pestilence relaxed its grip. The great fires that had burned all night in the squares were allowed to die, and the smell of sulphur faded from the atmosphere. Shopkeepers took down their shutters and the traffic restarted. By mid-October, the cholera cemetery had closed its gates, the theatres had reopened, and life was returning to normal. However, the epidemic, the seventh in the city since 1836, was to have a permanent effect on Naples:

'Bisogna sventrare Napoli.'[64]

Thus, in a famous phrase, spoke Mayor Depretis in belated official recognition of the foul conditions in parts of the old city. Earlier outbreaks had been met with a wholly Neapolitan fatalism. Now, though, began the work of *sventramento* (disembowelment), the clearing away of whole quarters to admit light and air into the ancient town. Much of the four oldest regions - the Mercato, Pendino, Porto, and Vicaria quarters - disappeared. Within a year, the pure water of Serino ran from jets in the streets. The picturesque squalor that had endeared Santa Lucia to the traveller gave way to a region of fashionable hotels. But with the clearance (*risanamento*) departed much of what, for better and for worse, had made Naples unique, for with the wretched slums fell the fine palaces with which they had been cheek by jowl. Before the epidemic the city had still had a mediaeval character, in which her Angevin, Aragonese, and Spanish history could clearly be read. After it, the broad stretches of the Corso Umberto I and the Via del Duomo would drive through the Porto, and the oyster stalls and the barrows of the vendors of sulphur-water from the fountain at Santa Lucia would be replaced by

---

61 Neville-Rolfe and Ingleby, op. cit., p. 263.
62 *Piccolo*, Oct. 5/6 1884.
63 Munthe, *The Story of San Michele*, p. 157ff.
64 'Naples needs to be disembowelled.'

the arid reaches of Via Partenope. It would, however, be years before the changes were more than superficial and any improvement would be noted in the malodorous conditions behind the imposing new façades. The indefatigable Neapolitan writer, journalist, and social reformer Matilde Serao makes the flesh creep as she describes the utter destitution which, even twenty years later, characterised the mean streets and alleys which still remained after the reconstruction money had gone in grander and more visible improvements.[65] Even now, the observant may find evidence of the splendour and the misery that was old Naples.

Even while so much was changing for the better, many yearned for what had vanished. The song 'Napule ca se ne va!' of 1920 had its roots in the headlines of the late eighties, when the face of Naples was changing daily.[66] No longer would the *posteggiatori*, those bands of minstrels and popular singers who were one of the most pleasing and characteristic aspects of the old city, the very essence of the Naples of that era, roam its harbour restaurants, streets, and taverns. The Santa Lucia of Cottrau's song had gone for ever.[67] Its memory, though, has maintained on Neapolitan sentiment a grip that has never faltered; thirty years after its destruction, E.A. Mario (Giovanni Gaeta), in 'Santa Lucia luntana', expressed all the longing of the emigrant who saw it slowly disappear into the wake of the steamer as it headed westwards. *Lo sventramento* itself has passed into folklore and is immortalised in a song of that name.

No purer voice, no more perceptive picture of the essence of old Naples, may be found than in the rich personality and writings of its greatest dialect poet, Salvatore di Giacomo (1860-1934), whose work - set by Costa, Di Capua, Tosti, and a dozen others - exercised a dominant influence during the greatest flowering of the genre now known as the Neapolitan song. Through half a century of journalism, in numerous newspapers, pamphlets, and magazines, and under many pen-names, he portrayed the joy and suffering of his city. Some of his work makes gruesome reading but, perhaps in reaction to the horrors he saw about him, he also produced verses of incomparable, perfumed delicacy. The moon, the streets, the sea, the fishermen, love - these were his materials. To him, more than to any other poet, we owe our images of air redolent of citrus groves, or of the stench of *'O fúnneco verde*.

---

65 Matilde Serao, *Il ventre di Napoli*, 2nd ed., 1906. The first edition, 1884, describes Naples before the *risanamento*. Serao wrote under several pseudonyms, notably *'Gibus'* and *'Chiquita'*.

66 'Naples that is vanishing' (E. Murolo - E. Tagliaferri).

67 Written (1848) in Italian not Neapolitan. See: Ettore De Mura, *Enciclopedia della Canzone Napoletana*, Vol. I, pp. 47-8.

2

Influences and Ill Winds

It was a school [of singing] that exercised a singer till he had a technique that
made him feel lord of creation and then allowed him the freedom to exploit his
good or bad taste to the full.   J.B. Steane, *The Grand Tradition*

De Lucia was now studying with Vincenzo Lombardi, a singing teacher,
talented piano accompanist, and conductor of dash and taste.[1] With his
brothers Carlo and Eduardo, Vincenzino, as he was affectionately called,
was well-known in the musical world of Naples, not least through the
concerts and operas given by pupils and guests at his home, in Via
Egiziaca. His sister Annunziata, who seems to have inspired these
events, also sang in them, along with dilettanti such as Prince Federico
Pignatelli. Lombardi had a great influence on De Lucia and it may well
have been his advice that formed the basis of the tenor's lifelong
dedication to the study of singing.

Lombardi was also known as a point of contact between young singers
and theatrical agents such as Carlo D'Ormeville, a powerful figure in the
operatic world of Italy and South America, where he had strong links
with the impresario Angelo Ferrari. D'Ormeville was also a poet,
librettist of operas such as Marchetti's *Ruy Blas*, proprietor and Director
of the magazine *Gazzetta dei Teatri*, and former impresario of the Teatro
San Carlo, Naples. Ten years later he recalled:

> On one of those splendid December nights which, under the sky of Naples, are
> more springlike than our May, Maestro Vincenzo Lombardi said to me:
> 'Carlo, I want you to hear my pupil. He is a boy who promises something,
> and I believe that he will make a decent career, if well guided and helped.' . . .
> To his remark I therefore replied immediately:
> 'Vincenzino, I am at your disposal. When would suit you?'
> 'Would midday tomorrow suit?'
> 'Tomorrow midday would be excellent.'
> The following day I went to Lombardi's house. The young man was there,
> and he sang various pieces, among which I well remember the 'Epilogue' from
> *Mefistofele*, and he made such an impression on me that I said to him:
> 'My dear boy, in a few years you will earn two thousand lire a performance.'

---

[1] (1856-1914). The few registers extant from this period do not place De Lucia in Lombardi's Conservatory
classes; probably, his concert earnings allowed him to take private lessons. Ferdinando also appears to have
assisted in the training of newcomers to the Lombardi school.

' - Uh!. . . . . *cavaliè*, what are you saying?', he replied. 'God grant that it should be two hundred.'[2]

In December 1884, the opera to be given at Casa Lombardi was Boito's *Mefistofele*. These showcases of the Lombardi school were more than mere concert performances for fashionable audiences. They attracted agents, correspondents of the theatrical press of Milan, the best of the local critics, and the representatives of the operatic publishers, ever in search of promising singers. One such representative was Nicola Daspuro, newly-appointed agent for Southern Italy of Casa Editrice Sonzogno, the Milan publishing house then locked in grim conflict with Casa Ricordi and with its long-established dominance of the Italian operatic repertory. But Sonzogno's star was rising. He was on the brink of enlarging his sphere of influence. De Lucia's timely contact with Daspuro would lead to an close and immensely advantageous association with Sonzogno and with the operas of a new school.[3]

Since 1861, when he inherited his father's publishing business, Edoardo Sonzogno (1836-1920) had made a considerable fortune from popular editions of literature. In 1866, he founded the daily newspaper *Secolo*, which soon achieved the widest circulation of any in Italy. In 1874, he enlarged his editorial activities to music publishing. His artistic director was Amintore Galli, a composer, musicologist, and Professor of Counterpoint and Musical Aesthetics in the Conservatory of Milan. Galli was also musical critic for *Secolo* and Editor of *Teatro Illustrato*, another Sonzogno publication. A year later, Sonzogno became an impresario, assuming the concession of a theatre in Milan, where he presented operettas. Inspired by an genuine passion for the theatre he became the third force, to Ricordi and Lucca, in Italian music publishing. He acquired the Italian rights to almost the entire contemporary French lyric output, including the works of Adam, Auber, Berlioz, Gounod, Massenet, and Thomas. His masterstroke was the capture, in 1879, of the Italian rights to *Carmen*.[4] Later, his championship of the operas of the *verismo* school, of which he became virtual monopolist, gave him the initiative against Giulio Ricordi, who - while uniquely powerful in his ownership of Italian operas - had not yet purchased the firm of Lucca and so secured the Italian rights to the works of Meyerbeer and Wagner.

Sonzogno was a cultured man who, in his youth, had written successful plays. The impressive literary, musical, and political gatherings at the Milan home of this *bon vivant* were renowned for distinguished company and generous hospitality. The attractive women who accompanied him, and with whom he enjoyed being seen, were

2 *Gazzetta dei Teatri*, Apr. 11 1895.
3 Daspuro's 'Memorie Postume' (1936) remain, unedited and unpublished, in the Biblioteca Lucchesi-Palli, Naples.
4 Vittorio Frajese, *Dal Costanzi all'Opera*, Vol. I, p. 94.

almost an appendage, a decorative element in his urbane personality; to them he represented an *amante putativo* and protector.[5] He was known as a formidable but not insensitive businessman, who was disturbed by the fact that operatic seasons were so often the sole artistic province of one or other of the two major publishing houses. As he sought, with generous financial offers and with the famous *Concorso Sonzogno*, to attract young Italian composers to his colours it was with the avowed aims of enlarging his own sphere of influence and of creating a modern national operatic repertory.

As the power of the old-fashioned impresarios waned so did the publishing houses come to assume dictatorial influence over the terms of performance, fees, scenery, and costumes, the choice of singers, and every other aspect of opera production in Italy and beyond.[6] In the latter part of the nineteenth century they were the real controllers of Italian music. Singers who had offended the publishers could find themselves excluded from their operas, even in remote parts of the globe. It paid, therefore, to be on good terms with local representatives such as Daspuro. They, in turn, took care to cultivate the friendship of singers whose goodwill might well be needed at short notice.

Some biographers have been unduly dismissive of Daspuro (1853-1941), depicting him as an opportunist, entrepreneur, part-time impresario, and man-about-town.[7] In fact, someone who had to tread the narrow line between his employer's interests and those of the theatre management, to soothe ruffled tempers and to flatter the egos of singers, required singular qualities: a practised dissimulation, an extensive circle of contacts, and some fleetness of foot. His indefatigable efforts for Sonzogno involved him in arranging entire seasons - often exceedingly brilliant - designed to display the properties of the house. He was also a journalist for *Secolo* and a poet of some talent. His literary works include the *libretti* for Giordano's setting of Di Giacomo's *Mala Vita* - a victim of prevailing social prejudices against works depicting low life - and a substantial contribution to Mascagni's *L'Amico Fritz*. Notwithstanding these several gainful activities, he was usually short of money.

As fear of the cholera receded, Daspuro, overjoyed at being able to spend his days and evenings among the impresarios, authors, and artists with whom he felt so much at ease, embarked with a will on his new duties. In retreats such as the Caffè d'Europa, the Gran Caffè - once fashionable but now slightly seedy[8] - or the old Birreria Strasburgo, haunt of poets and musicians, of Salvatore di Giacomo and Mario Costa,

---

5 Daspuro, 'Memorie', ch. XII.

6 See, for example, John Rosselli, *The Opera Industry*, p. 173ff or George Marek, *Puccini*, p. 64ff.

7 See, for example, T.R. Ybarra, *Caruso*, p. 15ff.

8 In 1885 the Gran Caffè closed down. In 1890 it was refurbished by Mariano Vacca, proprietor of the Caffè d'Europa, who reopened it under its present name, the Birreria Caffè Gambrinus. Until 1938 it was the preferred meeting place of Neapolitan intelligentsia.

of Roberto Bracco[9] and Ferdinando Russo, he made his contacts. To the sound of the most famous *posteggiatori*, amid the chatter, the shouted orders for refreshment, and all the noise of Naples at its most voluble, the business of Casa Sonzogno was conducted. The salon of his spacious rooms in Via Chiaia, furnished with a grand piano and a set of vocal scores of the Sonzogno operas, became a rendezvous for resident and visiting artists, for all the lyric life of Naples. When his success in selling *Carmen* to the management of the San Carlo brought the promise of a visit from Signor Edoardo himself, his reputation was assured. To Lombardi it seemed politic to call on him personally, with the invitation to hear *Mefistofele*. Daspuro, eager to recruit, accepted with alacrity; already, the newspapers had written of the young tenor at rehearsal, of

> ... De Lucia, to whom a prodigious voice, with a phenomenal C from the chest, and skilful singing of exquisite art, promise a most successful future.[10]

Half an hour before the performance of *Mefistofele*, on December 20th 1884, the salon of Casa Lombardi was crammed and the air was warm with the fragrance of candle smoke, as still more people sought to find a patch of floor even in the farthermost corners. All of high society was there. The applause, as Lombardi took his place at his Kaps piano, was for a favourite son; the hush for the first notes was of high expectation.

Daspuro's attention was taken by De Lucia, whom he described as singing with

> ... a most charming voice ... perfect enunciation ... great sentiment and fire.

The critic of *Pungolo* was more fulsome:

> Of the tenor De Lucia one has said everything when one calls it the dawn of a powerful artist, certain to increase the ranks - ever thinner - of the famous singers. He is one of those born to *empoigner* [thrill] the stalls and to enrich an impresario. He has a simply phenomenal voice ... [11]

In the second performance, note was taken of the 'sumptuous richness' of the voice.[12] Daspuro, enthusiastic, invited him to sing for Sonzogno when he came to Naples two weeks later. Together, they judged the voice a trifle constricted but, none the less, of good range, bright timbre and warm accent, with a vivid delivery. Sonzogno approved, and ordered that he be given scores of *Carmen*, *Mignon*, and *Lakmé* to study.

De Lucia was now well known in Naples, both professionally and socially. Concert activity increased and so did the interest in his progress

---

9 Sometime music critic of the *Corriere di Napoli*, under the *nom de plume* 'Baby'.
10 *Pungolo*, Dec. 19/20 1884.
11 Ibid., Dec. 21/22 1884.
12 *Piccolo*, Dec. 24/25 1884.

shown by friends such as the singing teacher Adriano Galanti and his daughter, Amalia, who was a singer. She and her own daughter, Elvira, had lived with Adriano since moving to Naples from Rome in 1882.[13] The entire household eagerly followed the young tenor's career. For the child, Ferdinando's visits to her grandfather always meant dolls and toys for her.[14] For De Lucia, it was the start of a friendship with Elvira that would last until his death. Meanwhile, however, it was the De Giorgio family which principally concerned him, more especially Itala, to whom - not without the misgivings of his family - he became betrothed.

Further afield, in February 1885 he and two Conservatory piano students, Vincenzo Galassi and Oreste Lambiase, secured a concert engagement in Palermo. De Lucia's performance of arias from *L'Africana* and *La Favorita* brought the first of many comparisons, for his enchanting and ingratiating *mezza voce*, with the three great tenors Julián Gayarre (1844-1890), Angelo Masini (1844-1926), and Roberto Stagno (1836-1897). In the high notes,

> . . . to which he brings the self-possession and assurance of the veteran artist . . .

he was also likened to Ernest Nicolini (1834-1898).[15]

Three days later, the young artists had a success at the Filarmonica Bellini, Palermo. De Lucia, who sang more encores than programme items, concluded the evening with 'Salve! dimora' from *Faust*:

> . . . the audience . . . broke into an absolute *urrà* when Sig. De Lucia, wishing to exhibit the vocal means that he can command, gave them a clear, full and ringing *do di petto* [C from the chest], such as to satisfy the farthest reaches of the vast room.[16]

The concert over, the audience began reluctantly to disperse; some lingered to congratulate De Lucia who, still fresh, gave an impromptu recital. He might have sung for much longer had someone not reminded the enraptured listeners that it was after midnight.[17]

Well satisfied, the trio returned to Naples, where the affairs of the San Carlo opera house had assumed their customary prominence in the local press. For many years that theatre had suffered recurrent crises, as competing candidates for the concession haggled with the city council over the programme, the subsidy, and their freedom to make 'private arrangements', such as the mounting of operas for aspiring composers

---

13 The surname is often misspelled 'Galante'. Amalia's sister was probably the Adelina Galante (*sic*) who appeared with an Italian operetta company at the Teatro Fiorentini, Naples, in June 1884.

14 Elvira Giommi (Rome, 1871 - Naples, 1952). Amalia's husband, Antigono Giommi, a shadowy figure, appears to have died before the family left Rome.

15 *Nuova Gazzetta di Palermo*, Feb. 8 1885.

16 Ibid., Feb. 11 1885. From the wording of the source it is possible that a *Stornello* sung by De Lucia was his own composition.

17 Ibid.

who were willing to pay for their production. The subsidy, though usually cash, sometimes took the form of the concession to operate the gambling in the theatre. Negotiations often turned on whether the programme offered local singers or new works, especially by Neapolitan composers. Such so-called bell-tower loyalty (*campanilismo*) existed all over Italy, but was especially well developed in Naples.

For some years the San Carlo concession had been held by Carlo Scalisi, latterly assisted by Pasqualino Galeota, Director of a local theatrical journal, *Occhialetto*. In the spring of 1884, Scalisi, with some ambitious pledges regarding both roster and artists, had applied for renewal of his concession. Municipal procrastination had delayed confirmation of his tenure until July, by which time most singers of repute were already engaged elsewhere. However, Scalisi was a man of energy; having paid his caution money (which, in fact, came from Galeota's wife) to the Mayor, he soon assembled a company which included Masini and the celebrated Virginia Ferni-Germano, mainstay of the previous San Carlo season. Hardly, though, had he announced his roster when the cholera epidemic had closed the theatres, with little likelihood that there could be a lyric season. Under these conditions he agreed - and was probably glad enough to do so - to release some of his singers, fearful of a commitment in the disease-ridden city, to take up hastily-arranged engagements elsewhere.[18]

But he had been too precipitate. By October, the theatres were already reopening. While Naples began to regain its animated, careless aspect and to anticipate the opera season, the remaining operatic artists were being assured by the theatrical press that rumours of the continued closure of the San Carlo were unfounded. Clearly, however depleted the ranks of his singers, and no matter how reluctant they were to come to Naples, the wretched Scalisi would have to honour his contract with the city. A few changes of programme might be permissible but there could be no repudiation of the contract.[19]

The season started as scheduled, with *La Forza del Destino*, but delays soon arose with *Carmen*, the second production, when Sonzogno, as was his right, dismissed the Don José - the Neapolitan Francesco Percuoco - and summoned Alfonso Garulli from Venice. The management, obliged to continue with *Forza* for a full month, fell behind with its obligations to the subscribers and to the City Council; even Ferni-Germano could not placate them when, eventually, *Carmen* appeared. All through February, while Scalisi struggled with recalcitrant singers as they tried to avoid the terms of their contracts, the press deprecated both Don José and the numerous repetitions of the 'makeshift' production. Percuoco huffily left the company and defected to

18 *Teatro Illustrato*, Sept. 1884.
19 *Gazzetta dei Teatri*, Dec. 4 1884.

the Teatro Fondo, compounding a shortage of tenors. Some evenings the San Carlo remained in darkness as tired artists demanded rest. Finally, the Council presented Scalisi with an ultimatum: reopen the theatre or be deemed to be in default and lose the deposit.[20]

Ruin was imminent. Casting about for a solution, Galeota suggested that an easy opera to mount would be *Faust*, with Ferni-Germano as Margherita; the title rôle might be sung by young De Lucia, already known to many of the subscribers who, although never exposed to débutants at the San Carlo, would surely accept him. There was, though, a problem: the soprano declared that never, even at the cost of tearing up her contract, would she agree to sing with someone who had never even set foot on a stage. Many prominent Neapolitans had tried to persuade her, and all had failed.

What was needed was a conciliator and it was Daspuro who saved the situation. According to him, it was at 8 am that Scalisi and Galeota burst into his rooms, shouting that only he, a great friend of Ferni-Germano, could rescue them. The matter could not wait: they had a carriage below to take him to the Hôtel Royal. As they pushed him into his clothes he pondered on Sonzogno's reactions if the season failed and *Carmen* were not given. There, perhaps, lay his best argument with Ferni.[21]

Ferni-Germano, still in bed, was at first adamant; then she listened in silence as Daspuro used all his southern charm to explain that De Lucia was well-liked by the influential; that she ran no personal risk, since her own success was assured by the Jewel Song; and that her popularity in Naples would increase through her concern for the career of a local singer. The final, cogent argument was that her own continued appearance as Carmen - and, perhaps, her entire future relationship with a disappointed Sonzogno - depended on the success of the season. She began to weaken:

'Oh . . . . . Very well, if you are so convinced,' exclaimed Ferni-Germano, 'if it will please you and you think that Signor Edoardo will be happy . . . . . I will do as you wish: let us say that you have convinced me and I will sing . . . . . with a *boy*.'

Thanking her profusely, Daspuro went out to the salon to announce the good news to Scalisi and Galeota, who embraced him in relief.[22]

In the 1880s, the opera in Naples was still as much a social as a musical attraction. In the theatrical hierarchy, the San Carlo, as the

---

20 *Piccolo, Pungolo, Caporal Terribile, Occhialetto* (all of Naples), *Gazzetta dei Teatri, Gazzetta Musicale di Milano* (both Milan) Apr. 1884 - Mar. 1885.

21 Daspuro, 'Memorie', ch. XXII.

22 Daspuro's memoirs incorrectly place this in mid-January 1886 and state that only four days elapsed between his intercession with Ferni and the actual première. In fact, the Milan weekly *Gazzetta dei Teatri* had, as early as Feb. 12, mentioned a possible *Faust* with Ferni. Piano auditions, with De Lucia, were reported locally on Feb. 21, a full two weeks before the first performance. Hence, although the choice of tenor was obviously left somewhat late, the decision to stage the opera was not quite the hasty affair that Daspuro suggests.

leading theatre, attracted the most aristocratic audiences who came to
opera seria during the carnival, or winter season. Audiences then became
less exclusive as one descended the scale of seasons and theatres, and
from *opera seria* to *opera buffa*. Many people went to the San Carlo night
after night, as the upper-class Englishman might go to his club, and for
similar reasons.[23] The aristocracy, preferring to meet at the opera rather
than at home, seldom missed a performance. This practice encouraged a
certain ennui towards the performance itself, and has been given as one
reason why there was a particular need for the singers at the San Carlo
to devise whatever variations and embellishments they could to hold the
attention of audiences.[24] Draughts was regarded as an excellent game to
play whilst sipping chocolate and waiting for the end of the recitative
and the beginning of the aria. In 1770, Burney had written that 'not one
of the present voices is sufficiently powerful for such a theatre when so
crowded and so noisy'.[25] Though by 1885 the worst excesses of those days
were over, the opera remained a place for seeing and for being seen. A
box continued to be a rendezvous for chatter, refreshment, and gambling
during the performance; for entertaining friends during the intervals;
and for all the activities which had caused Chorley to describe Italian
opera-houses as 'virtually so many social music-halls'.

Performance standards were judged by the famous *patiti* (factions),
each group of enthusiasts posturing as sole legitimate guardian of what
were usually termed the sacred, solemn - Naples took itself very
seriously - artistic traditions of the San Carlo. Operatic Naples was
virtually ruled by the pronouncements of their leaders, Cav. Alfredo
Monaco, Prince Adolfo di Castagneto, Marchese Cocozza, and Barone
Savelli, on new works and new singers. Like every great theatre of the
day the San Carlo had its *claque* - its captain's name was Ambrosino -
paid by singers or management to draw the public's attention to
meritorious points. However, the *patiti* were not *claques* in the normal
sense, and there is no evidence that avarice played any part in their
activities in the theatre. Patronage and power were their objectives.
Deference and complimentary tickets, not money, were the keys to their
approbation. Above all, they were jealous of their right to make their own
judgement. Fierce rivalries existed between the audiences of the San
Carlo, the Teatro alla Scala, Milan, and, to a lesser extent, the Costanzi,
of Rome. The Neapolitan *patiti* accepted musical advice from no one,
least of all from the Milanese. Emma Calvé described the San Carlo as
having

>   ... the most amusing public it has ever been my privilege to encounter. A group
>   of *dilettanti*, gentlemen of taste and leisure assisted regularly at every

---

23 Rosselli, op. cit., p. 39ff.
24 Robinson, op. cit., pp. 9 and 102.
25 Charles Burney, *The Present State of Music in France and Italy*, p. 340.

performance, criticising the actors and actresses, praising and blaming in loud tones, punctuating the performance with exclamations and ejaculations, to the vast amusement of the rest of the audience.[26]

Few singers found them so diverting. The pronouncements of these groups, termed by Salvatore Mormone, music critic of the Naples newspaper *Roma*, the *'sicofanti'* (sycophants), were often couched in the pompous language of the law, with themselves cast as Supreme Court. Artists ignored them at their peril. 'In our greatest theatre', wrote Mormone, 'there is one who *organises* successes.'[27] Such factions were not unique to Naples or to the San Carlo. Indeed, in other theatres, the various cabals, not content with hurling insults, would throw fruit at each other. The Neapolitan audience was, though, especially feared for its unpredictability. Successes were seldom unanimous or, in theatrical parlance, 'unopposed'. What appealed to one faction was *ipso facto* almost certain to antagonise another. The *patiti* were dominated by individuals, people with particular preferences for this or that artist. The currents between them were constantly in a state of flux and the unfortunate singers could unwittingly find themselves in the middle.[28] It was advisable to ensure that the most influential subscribers, those connoisseurs whose views carried some weight, were consulted and their cooperation secured. Some of them would require convincing that the quality of the voice might compensate for its modest volume. Thus, invitations were issued to hear De Lucia sing his 'romanza' at the piano; Ferni-Germano condescended to join him in the duet; everyone left well-satisfied.[29] Protocol had been observed. Rehearsals could commence.

The tenor, overwhelmed by his good fortune and by the impresario's confidence, was happy to sing *gratis*. Though failure in such a major theatre could ruin his career, in many a lesser house he would, by the custom of the day, have been obliged to pay for a trial. But Scalisi's brow was troubled again when Ferni-Germano was indisposed. Possibly, her intention was only to remind him that she, the famous *diva*, was the real attraction, but while she held court in her suite to a stream of admirers the performance was postponed, finally being set for March 9th.

The immense, gaslit auditorium of the San Carlo was crammed with spectators. Not a box, not a seat, not even a small space in the gallery remained empty. Manifestly, the début of a local singer made the audience well-disposed. But for many this was a serious musical occasion. A concert singer who had not served the customary operatic apprenticeship in small theatres, such as the Fondo and Bellini, had to be evaluated very critically.

---

26 Emma Calvé, *My life*, p. 55.
27 *Roma*, Feb. 16 1891.
28 See also Pierre V.R. Key and Bruno Zirato, *Enrico Caruso*, pp. 148-50.
29 *Occhialetto*, Feb. 21 1885.

While family and friends waited anxiously in their seats Scalisi went to De Lucia's dressing-room to encourage him. The débutant's confident words:

'Cavaliè, voglio fà cose' e pazze'[30]

belied the apprehension of an artist who, even in full career, suffered from nerves. On the stage he appeared pale and even confused. A burst of applause before he had sung a note identified his friends.

As sceptical as any were the gentlemen of the press whose doyen, the respected Michele Uda, is worth quoting at length as illustrating how the Neapolitan musical public thought of itself:

Signor De Lucia - the impresarios are writing this name in their memoranda books - has gambled his artistic future on a single card, and has won.

To make his début at the San Carlo!

Even yesterday the association of these two ideas would have been thought nonsensical. To pass from the concert-room to one of the major stages of the world; to renounce the easy triumphs of the romanza and of the duet sung and applauded in family gatherings, to widen the sphere of impressions and ventures, a recruit in a field where only veterans fight, and frequently die; to take his first step where others stride in the full maturity of their talent and in the awareness and security of their powers ... to succeed in having himself baptised by a public which administers the sacrament of confirmation, but more frequently the last rites: yesterday all this was called rashness, presumptuousness, and even shamelessness, and some laughed up their sleeves; today it is courage, it is valour, and it is applauded.

The first impression of the public was one of surprise. That voice had such caressing sweetness of expression, the phrasing was so clean [and] the intonation so secure! The annoying chatter had stopped in the vast auditorium: from the boxes and from the stalls, all the opera-glasses were pointed; all eyes turned towards the stage where a tenor finally revealed himself, born suddenly to us in the house ... where, truly, we had had no expectations ...

Meanwhile, De Lucia was still applauded ... but his voice, which speaks of love with such tenderness, did not find virile accents of rage in the duel trio, nor of sadness during Margherita's agony. Also, the *mezza voce alla Stagno* hardly - and not always - penetrated the noisy orchestra to pause at the front row of the stalls. Was it weariness, was it the exquisite delicacy of the vocal organ, made for the softness of an idyll, but breaking in the emotion of the drama?

After only one hearing, speaking of a very young artist, who must have exhausted a great part of his energy in the venture, the reply would be risky.

There was great affection in that triumph ... We wait, then, contenting ourselves with a splendid promise. To have made a début at the San Carlo, and to be acclaimed there by a public which does not waste its enthusiasm, is already a start to De Lucia's career that no singer ever had, and one that old and young, great and small artists envy him.[31]

It was, wrote *Roma*,

... a *little Faust* ..... if we measure the height of Signor De Lucia, who played

---

30 Dell'Erba, *Giornale d'Italia*, Feb. 24 1925: *'Cavaliere*, I want to do great things!'
31 *Pungolo*, Mar. 10/11 1885.

him, a *Faust alla napoletana*, since tenor, baritone and bass were all Neapolitan. There was a family atmosphere in the calls ... De Lucia reached the ears of his audience *with a thread of voice*.[32]

The critic of *Occhialetto* warned that

... De Lucia should not allow himself to be dazed by facile adulation ... We can say this to him: first, he must consolidate the placing of the high register, still lacking in support from the head, for which [reason] it is not resonating; second, he must take care that the voice is not entirely supported in the throat: this will make it easier when singing *voce mista* ... he cannot find the note of impetuosity when he needs it ... and one cannot hear his voice in the ensembles; it almost always remains hidden when the orchestra does not play softly.

But this is not to discourage: the voice is an organ that can be strengthened ... but it can also be lost when the necessary rules are not followed to support the fatigue of a score. ...

De Lucia, besides, has expression and taste; he signifies sentiment delightfully. But it appears that he feels little because he communicates little, or because, not yet having the 'theatrical mask', he shows little.[33]

In an otherwise enthusiastic despatch to Milan, Daspuro, too, included a warning:

De Lucia should not be too enraptured by this true success. He is very young ... and he must understand that if he wants to make his fortune he must sing a light repertory until his voice becomes more extensive and more secure, [and] until he finds means of consolidating his high notes with greater facility than at present.[34]

Another writer good-naturedly chided the tenor's friends for their excessive enthusiasm, but continued:

[He is] destined for a brilliant career. And thus it will be if De Lucia ... will school his voice to acquire the power and volume that it does not yet possess ... It would be a pity if so pleasant and *simpatica* a voice, extensive, equalised between the registers, responsive in the most difficult modulations, ringing in the high notes and sweet in the mixed voice, had to remain of such limited volume and not gain that power in the high register and that security of placing that it lacks today.[35]

Daspuro telegraphed Sonzogno:

That *tenorino* De Lucia, whom you know, made his début with Ferni tonight, having a most gratifying success. He has the stuff of a good artist of the future.

---

32 *Roma*, Mar. 10 1885. Baritone and bass were, respectively, Giuseppe Del Puente and Francesco Vecchioni (sometimes Vecchione).
33 *Occhialetto*, Mar. 14 1885.
34 *Teatro Illustrato*, Apr. 1885.
35 *Piccolo*, Mar. 10/11 1885.

Sonzogno telegraphed his reply:

As soon as he is free, engage De Lucia for me, and send him to me at Bologna.

It would be months, however, before the start of an association that was to make him, virtually, the Sonzogno 'House Tenor' and in which Daspuro, for some time, at least, was his agent. It is not clear whether, as some sources claim, his formal studies were complete.[36] At any rate, the advice of several critics to continue them seems to have been ignored, if in the euphoria it had even been noticed. Like many students who had already commenced a career he does not appear to have graduated formally from the Conservatory. He was, doubtless, happy in his status as *artista di cartello*. There were more performances of *Faust* to be sung for the equally content Scalisi who, it is to be hoped, paid him for them; more performances of *Mefistofele*, in a vain attempt to accommodate the crowds that flocked to Lombardi's door; and both Rossini's and Pergolesi's *Stabat Mater* in Passion Week.[37] Maestro Angelo Siani dedicated his *stornello* 'Il bacio' to him.[38] The indisposition of the tenor Giovanni Sani brought an engagement to appear with Ferni-Germano and Giuseppe Del Puente at the Sala Vega of the Hôtel Royal in a charity concert for the cholera victims. It was, perhaps, even welcomed as an opportunity to substitute the bright new attraction from the San Carlo. He was introduced by a witty speech of the patron, the Prince of Cassano, before

. . . we had the great aria of Vasco from *L'Africana*, sung by De Lucia with a sweetness of voice, a warmth of accent and an effectiveness of expression that made one think of Gayarre. He then sighed with even greater tenderness Tosti's 'Aprile' . . . The concert closed with Rossini's duet 'Mira la bianca luna'. . . . The two voices [De Lucia and Ferni-Germano] blended in a delightful reverie.[39]

Then there was an opportunity of hearing the great Angelo Masini, 'the angelic tenor' as he was termed. All musical Naples had eagerly anticipated his performances in *Gli Ugonotti* (April 14th) and *Rigoletto* (April 27th), and by the time that he arrived the excitement had reached fever pitch. That the tenor travelled with an entourage of agent, barber, cook, journalist, lawyer, physician, secretary, under-secretary, treasurer and valet, a group spitefully described by Mapleson as doubling as a useful *claque*, made a great impression.[40] For weeks, no trifle went unreported as they virtually monopolised the theatrical columns of the

36 *Gazzetta Musicale di Milano*, Mar. 1 1885.
37 *Occhialetto*, Mar. 28 1885. The Pergolesi work is scored for female voices only; however, De Lucia later recorded its 'Vidit suum' [Nos. 206/7].
38 *Roma*, May 28 1885.
39 *Pungolo*, Mar. 17/18 1885.
40 J.H. Mapleson, *The Mapleson Memoirs 1848 - 1888*, Vol. II, pp. 148-9. By the standards of the day the entourage was not in fact unusually large.

newspapers with their doings.

For the paramount influence that Masini exerted on the style of De Lucia this dominant figure must be examined in some detail.[41]

Masini was a man of very few words. Clara Kellogg, who rehearsed with him for an entire season, could not recall the sound of his speaking voice.[42] Bellincioni described him as combining a crude artistic soul with a sweet and pliant voice, whose flexibility rivalled that of the most accomplished sopranos. Strong and masculine in appearance, always dishevelled, he carried on to the stage the strange fascination, on colleagues and public alike, of an undisciplined personality, reluctant to espouse any tradition or style. In performance he was difficult to follow:

> ... the poor conductor swore like a Turk ... when, becoming animated in the great passionate phrases, he forgot time and beat, but aroused a shout of enthusiasm from the delirious crowd![43]

Giulio Gatti-Casazza described his qualities thus:

> [He had] handsomeness, elegance and distinction of appearance, a voice of gold that was both insinuating and penetrating, a marvellous facility of song, and an accent, diction and warmth that were truly rare. His one flaw was his lack of exactness - a habit of varying the text, a continuing abuse. He seemed to require the employment of his variations at every moment. Some were really in good taste; others were not. But undoubtedly he was a great virtuoso and captivated his public. One should have heard him sing the Serenade of the first act of 'The Barber'. It was an enchanting thing. ... whatever gifts the soprano revealed in the second act, it was extremely difficult for her to efface the effect of Masini's Almaviva in the first act.[44]

The impression that Masini made on even the great Chaliapin may be judged from a conversation between the Russian bass and his son, Boris, who asked him: 'And tell me, Papa, was Masini a good singer?' Chaliapin looked at his son and said: 'Masini was not a singer. I, your father, am a singer, but Masini was an angel of God.'[45]

Two distinctive vocal features characterised Masini: a *mezza voce* of incomparable sweetness, and a lofty technical virtuosity that, in the opinion of many, made him the legitimate heir to Rubini.[46] An absolute facility of vocalisation enabled him to achieve the sparkling *fioriture* that typified his performances. Daspuro wrote of him, in *Rigoletto*, during that Naples season:

> Masini is a truly great artist ... with a *divine, fascinating mezza voce*. In *mezza voce*, he performs trills, [feats of] agility, *picchiettati*, like a light soprano, like

41 Readers who prefer not to digress from De Lucia may pass to page 34.

42 Clara Louise Kellogg, *Memoirs of an American Prima Donna*, p. 341.

43 Gemma Bellincioni, *Io e il palcoscenico*, pp. 87-8.

44 Giulio Gatti-Casazza, *Memories of the Opera*, pp. 38-9.

45 Konstantin Korovin, *Chaliapin: encounters and life together*, quoted in Borovsky, *Chaliapin*, p. 297.

46 Giovanni Battista Rubini (1795-1854).

Patti, and without using *falsetti* or any other device. He feels that he excels in
this type of singing, and perhaps he shades a little too much, and perhaps he
executes too many trills; perhaps, for whatever reason, he has lost something of
his *full voice* in the high register. In full voice, in fact, if he reaches *B natural*,
he has to reach it and to leave it immediately - he cannot hold it.

Another point that the purists might note is that he changes the *tempi* to his
own liking and follows his own taste entirely, paying no attention to the
composer's writing. Therefore, the effects attained in each piece are new,
original, they surprise and, because they are well contrived, they delight.[47]

This notice is significant in the context of the history of the *tenore di
grazia*, then often termed *tenore paradisiaco*. The tenor, as known today,
using the chest register to sing high C and above, has existed only since
about 1830 and the heyday of Gilbert-Louis Duprez. Before then, tenor
voices lay low by modern standards - most of Handel's writing for this
voice has an upward limit of only an A natural - and were dominated by
the head register.[48] The disappearance of the *castrati* had presented the
problem of voices to sing the romantic parts which they had hitherto
assumed. Bellini's answer to the challenge lay in the great tenor
Giovanni Battista Rubini, who had extraordinary agility and an
exceptional range above the stave, achieved by use of a head register
(then termed *falsetto*) which he had strengthened almost to the power of
a full voice. If we may believe contemporary accounts, Rubini had some
superb full-voice high notes, such as a B flat of exceptional ring and
brightness. Above this, however, he entered the so-called *falsetto*
register, seldom giving a B natural, and never a C, from the chest.[49] He
was, effectively, the founder of the school of the romantic tenor, the
tenore paradisiaco, of sweet, bright timbre. Subsequently, the works of
Verdi and Meyerbeer required an alternative, i.e. the *tenore di forza*, still
of clear colouring but of more metallic and biting timbre, and of explosive
top notes. Finally came the *tenore di mezzo carattere*, who was part
tenore paradisiaco, part *tenore di forza*. In the last quarter of the
nineteenth century Tamagno was the dominant *tenore di forza*, Gayarre
di mezzo carattere, and Masini *di grazia*.[50]

Masini derived in direct line from Rubini, of whom he had the
inherently clear vocal colouring and, albeit to a less remarkable extent,
the same agility and mastery in *falsetto*. Like Rubini, he never disposed
of chest notes which were exceptional for power or ring. There are
occasional references to a C but, as seen above, B flat was judged the
practical limit of his chest register in 1885. However, in the judgement of
Clara Kellogg, Masini, around 1880, surpassed any other tenor in that
combination of voice production and breath control which permitted him

47 N. Daspuro, *Teatro Illustrato*, June 1885.
48 Conrad L. Osborne, loc. cit.
49 See Glossary of Terms, xviii.
50 Rodolfo Celletti, 'La voce di Angelo Masini', *Atti del convegno su Angelo Masini*, Forlì, Comune di Forlì,
1976, pp. 47-8.

to sing phrases that seemed interminable:

> I have never heard a length of breath like his. No phrase ever troubled him; he
> had the necessary wind for anything. In *L'Africaine* there is a passage in the big
> tenor solo needing very careful breathing. Masini did simply what he liked with
> it, swelling it out roundly and generously when it seemed as if his breath must
> be exhausted. When the breath of other tenors gave out, Masini only just began
> to draw on his.[51]

In this lay the secret of the virtuosity that made him, probably, the
greatest male vocal acrobat since Rubini.

Daspuro asserted that Masini's high register had been atrophied
through the excessive use of the *mezza voce*, a feature for which he was
renowned and which Francesco Tamagno, who much admired him,
described to Edmondo De Amicis:

> A nightingale . . . . . a violin! . . . you can have no idea of the sweetness, of the
> angelic softness of that voice. Never in my life have I heard anyone who so
> deeply enters the heart and wrenches tears as he does, with that voice of
> paradise, that seems to come not from the mouth but from the air.[52]

If Masini was inferior to Rubini in the high register, he was probably
superior to him in two respects. First, though Rubini's singing was a
fascinating alternation of *forte* and *piano*, he could not always span long
phrases in *mezza voce*. Masini, on the other hand, used it to sing entire
arias. Second, Rubini was a great elegiac interpreter of Bellini and
Donizetti. So also was Masini but with moments, in addition, of blazing
dramatic fire, consistent with the more robust style of Verdi. Monaldi,
writing that Masini was characterised by 'warm and vigorous' outbursts
and impulses, remembered him as a great Radames and Don Alvaro.
Today, these rôles are not associated with the *tenore di grazia*, who is
thought of as a light tenor, of slender and almost white voice. But the
real light tenors, then, were little more than comprimarios, while the
tenore di grazia often had the vocal stamina to sing operas of the *spinto*
type, albeit with a volume and phrasing that distinguished him from the
dramatic tenor. Thus, Masini's repertoire included *Gli Ugonotti*, *Aida*,
La Forza del Destino, and *L'Africana*. His Raoul - which he sang,
without apparent effort, for many years - was particularly celebrated. In
this part, during his Spanish seasons of 1881-2, critics described his
splendid timbre, great interpretative originality, strong emotional
capacity in *canto spianato*, grace and agility in vocalised passages, and
enchantment in *mezza voce*. However, he did not escape criticism for his
aspirations toward the dramatic genre without having the vocal capacity,

---

[51] Kellogg, loc. cit.

[52] Edmondo De Amicis, *Nuovi ritratti letterari ed artistici*, quoted in *Ad Angelo Masini, 27 Novembre
1924*, Edito a cura del Municipio di Forlì, 1924, p. 16.

and for being an exhibitionist who wanted to give a very personal relief to everything he performed, 'including commas and full stops'.[53]

The critic Vincenzo Valle wrote:

> More than a strong voice he has that of a tenor - so far as intensity goes - of *mezzo carattere*, but of the sweetest temper. In some phrases his voice can equal the power of his musical and dramatic sentiment, gifts that have no counterpart in any other tenor known today. ... From the lips of Gayarre, for example, pours serene song, exquisite melody; from that of Masini the tumult of passion, of the most powerful emotion and animation.[54]

Masini took the view (in which he was probably correct) that the public attended his performances to hear him sing; it followed that the *tempi* used should be those which showed his voice to its best advantage and he personally instructed the conductor in this matter.[55] Like Patti, he attended as few rehearsals as possible. Nevertheless, for all the deification (*divinismo*) of which he was the object, he remained among the singers favoured by Verdi who, in correspondence with Ricordi and others, considered the possibility that he should create Fenton. Verdi felt that no one would sing it better than Masini, but he feared an outburst when the tenor discovered that Falstaff, Alice, Quickly, and Ford all had more important parts. He also thought that the well-known *divinismo* of Maurel, in the title part, would provide sufficient temperament for one production.[56]

That Masini's fame is less secure than Rubini's arises from the latter's indissoluble links with Bellini and his place in a substantial literature of the history of opera in London and Paris. Memories of Masini are, instead, predominantly chronicled in Barcelona, Madrid, and St. Petersburg, cities somewhat removed from the cultural mainstream. But he was Rubini's equivalent in a different historical period; and if Rubini is still thought of as the greatest lyric tenor who has ever lived it is clear that Masini was hardly less exceptional.

In the end, concluded Daspuro,

> ... weighing his merits and defects, and those of other tenors, the unanimous judgement is that Masini is the best tenor among those living, and his artistic structure is of the best balanced and most agreeable.[57]

At the age of more than 60, and after a career of almost forty years, he retained an absolute mastery of his instrument. When Masini visited the premises of the Gramophone Company in Milan in 1903 the Company's

---

53 José Subira, *Historia y Anecdotario del Teatro Real*, pp. 319-20 and p. 328.

54 *Musica Popolare*, Anno I, No. 7, May 18 1882.

55 Mapleson, op. cit., Vol. I, pp. 220-3, gives an entertaining account of Masini's dealings with Sir Michael Costa in this regard.

56 See Giorgio Gualerzi, 'Appunti per la carriera di Angelo Masini', *Atti del convegno su Angelo Masini*, Forlì, Comune di Forlì, 1976, pp. 40-1.

57 *Teatro Illustrato*, No. 54, June 1885.

representative there, Alfred Michaëlis, could write to Head Office in London:

> The two greatest names in the modern history of Italian lyric art are Tamagno and Masini. Masini has been, and still is, a kind of ideal Caruso. A contemporary of Tamagno, these two stars have arisen and are shining contemporaneously, and their triumphs were and are parallel: the two being perfect contrasts.[58]

Even in his final operatic appearances, in 1905, Masini's agility and modulations were described by Titta Ruffo as 'insuperable'. Effectively, he was the last of the great ornamentist tenors.[59] With his retirement from the stage there ended not only the career of a great singer but also an historic cycle. The history of recording holds many a missed opportunity, and the failure to capture the voice and technique of Masini, who lived until 1926, is arguably the most regrettable loss of all.

Some evidence, though, survives of his style. The ornaments that he introduced served to demonstrate his own skills, but have become established in the tenor repertoire. To his capricious improvisations are attributed variations and cadenzas still in use in *Il Barbiere*, *L'Elisir d'Amore*, and *Rigoletto*, where he was said to have had seven different ways of ending 'La donna è mobile', including a solution of the problems presented by the high B. Of his performance in Naples we read:

> The voice of Masini is not of the colossi . . . but sufficient for any theatre. In compensation, though, it has a timbre that lends itself to every effect. If [he] wishes to convey fury, the voice supports it perfectly, and if he wants to move [us] he modulates it in such a way as to reach the heart and draw tears from us. . . . it is equalized from *piano* to a clarion tone and back. It is not one of those voices that is feeble in the low and strong in the high notes, or weak in the centre and strong both high and low. . . . all the notes are proportioned one to another as on a Stradivarius or an Erard of the very first quality. He sang 'La donna è mobile' five times and always in a different way, most of all in the so-called *puntature*, which he varies every evening, and in all the encores.[60] He has a breath control which seems impossible for human lungs, and a method of singing all his own, adapted to his chosen manner of rendering the thought. To obtain a dramatic effect I have heard him unfold a note moderately and force it to the point of hoarseness: I have trembled, thinking that he would never be able to utter a sound afterwards: my fears were groundless, and the surprise was bewildering. Immediately after the forced note Masini has come out on a C and has shaded it with an ease and facility that any celebrated soprano might envy. They call him *divo*. I leave the divinities to the sky; and, remaining on earth, I believe that Masini is a true celebrity.[61]

---

58 (EMI) A. Michaëlis - W.B. Owen, Apr. 6 1903, commenced: 'This morning at 11 o'clock Masini is coming here.' Negotiations evidently foundered because of the fees demanded by Masini, who claimed that he had, in Russia, been offered 50,000 roubles (£5,000) to record. In 1902, Tamagno had negotiated the then astonishing sum of £200 per disc as soon as recorded and a royalty of £0.20 for each record leaving the factory. In Nov. 1902 Caruso commanded £40 per record, and De Lucia received a similar sum from Oct. 1904 onwards.

59 Celletti, *L'Enciclopedia dello Spettacolo*, Vol. VII.

60 See Glossary, pp. xviii-xix. If *puntature* were a necessity, Masini clearly made them into a virtue.

61 *Gazzetta dei Teatri*, May 14 1885.

In Naples that season Masini also gave 'Questa o quella' three times, a generosity of spirit that did not spare him an uproar when, as was often done in the nineteenth century, he coolly omitted the second act aria. This was characteristic of a man who would sometimes - especially in Russia, where audiences idolised him for almost thirty consecutive seasons - allow a substitute to sing acts which, he considered, lacked interesting music for the tenor.

All this the young De Lucia certainly absorbed. He, too, had the ability to sing a passage several times in as many different ways, and he would often be compared with Masini whose influence probably stretched even into the recording studio. Thirty years on, De Lucia's recordings of 'Questa o quella' [Nos. 119 and 218] almost certainly owed their audacious embellishments to those heard on the lips of *il tenore angelico*, and the same is true of 'La donna è mobile' [Nos. 3 and 106]; here, he transforms the opening lines but with rhythmic nuances of such subtlety and refinement that the overall shape of the phrases is unchanged. A favourite ornament, the rising two-note embellishment, or slide, is heard before '*e di pensiero*'. Later in the recording [No. 3] come departures, especially the *filata*, which change the rhythm, for instance on the word '*accento*'. Such mannerisms have the Masini stamp.[62] De Lucia's breath control and the facility with which he passes from *pianissimo* to the most glittering *fortissimo* recall the older tenor's method; the languor observable in his recordings is after the fashion of Masini; and references to the latter's 'blazing dramatic fire' resemble reviews of De Lucia's Canio and Don José. De Lucia, too, drew criticism for undertaking rôles which were too heavy, and for being an exhibitionist; and, like Masini's, his highest notes - which were probably never well-developed - faded away well before the end of his career.

For the moment, however, the younger tenor was more concerned with the concert bookings that fame had brought. It was the season of the races, when the Chiaia by day was thronged with open carriages carrying the fashionable to the course, and by night with broughams taking them to elaborate entertainments in the great houses. At one such, in the home of Lady Eliza Otway, an accomplished singer and harpist whose Wednesday soirées were then a feature of Neapolitan social and musical life, there was an gathering of more than a hundred. Fortified by the oysters, soups, pâtés, stuffed turkey, lamb cutlets, and sorbets with which the evening had commenced, it was then entertained, first, with an instrumental concert, in which their hostess participated on the harp. The vocal programme included the baritone Giuseppe Kaschmann,[63] who sang duets with his wife Emma, and De Lucia, who was warmly applauded as he sang 'Ideale' and, with Eliza Otway,

---

62 Emilio De Gogorza. See pp. 185-6.

63 Kaschmann, 1850 (or 1852)-1925 is one of the earliest singers on record.

shimmering with diamonds, the duet from *Un Ballo in Maschera*. In a softly-lit salon, its crystal chandeliers as far removed from the oil lamps of the Vicaria as the sumptuous supper awaiting him was from the *pizza* of the Pendino, he gallantly - and diplomatically - accorded to his hostess the lion's share of the ovation.[64]

Then there were concerts in support of former fellow students; at the Sala del Quartetto and the Hôtel Riviera, for the violinists Metauretta Torricelli and Maria Smitti; an entire evening of music by Niccolò Van Westerhout, performed by De Lucia, Kaschmann, Beniamino Cesi, and others; at the Sala Vega, in honour of the Queen; and at private houses. In a concert by the violinist Carlo Lombardi, the tenor's more solemn repertoire of arias from *L'Africana* and *Mefistofele* was leavened by a spirited rendering, with Giuseppe Rapp, of 'I Mulatieri', to send the audience home in high good humour.

All added something to his reputation and to his experience as he prepared his new rôles for Bologna. Domestic responsibilities also claimed his time; a move from Naples was now imminent, for on September 17th 1885, in the Town Hall of Salerno, the civil marriage to Itala was celebrated.[65] On the certificate the singer was described as *possidente* (man of means), a reflection of his increasing substance; he signed himself Fernando, not Ferdinando, an affectation that would long preoccupy some Neapolitan critics. The religious ceremony would have to be delayed until after Bologna: Sonzogno could not be kept waiting.

As De Lucia boarded the train for the journey north his career as a local prodigy fell behind him. Ahead lay audiences who would not judge him as a *concittadino* (fellow citizen). Not for another four years would he reappear at the San Carlo, and he would by then be a seasoned artist.

---

[64] *Occhialetto*, Apr. 11 1885.

[65] Subsequently, De Lucia's address was 30, Via Flavio Gioia, Salerno; this seems to have been, at that time, the home of the De Giorgio family which, by 1888, had moved to Via Indipendenza, Salerno.

3

Santa Lucia luntana

Any tenor standing upon the threshold of success is a magnet.
Pierre V.R. Key and Bruno Zirato, *Enrico Caruso*

After the massive stone palaces of his native city, Bologna, with its high brick wall pierced by twelve gates, its characteristic brick buildings, its colonnades against the summer sun and winter rain, and its clean and well-paved streets, was almost a foreign land. However, there was no time for sightseeing: the expense of travelling from Salerno - notwithstanding the concessions that the Italian railways then allowed lyric artists - meant that the *quartale*, that quarter of an artist's salary available on arrival, had to be claimed without delay.

The current season was a minor one. De Lucia's name was among those of its 'First Tenors' on the posters around the theatre. However, Bologna had once been the centre of the Italian lyric world, and its principal theatre, the Teatro Comunale, was one of the largest in Italy. In 1885, it was managed by Giovanni Bolelli, a man who shared Verdi's opinion that success was measured by the thermometer of the takings.[1] Nothing raised his enthusiasm more readily than a full cashbox, and the poor houses of the season had, so far, given him little pleasure.

Since 1881 the musical director of the Comunale and head of the Liceo Musicale di Bologna had been the composer and conductor Luigi Mancinelli.[2] He had assembled a company of which a major attraction was undoubtedly the handsome soprano Gemma Bellincioni (1864-1950). Scarcely 21 years old but already a veteran of tours with singers as eminent as Enrico Tamberlick and Julián Gayarre, she had only recently turned from the *coloratura* of Lucia and Rosina to the rôles which would make her the great singing-actress of later years.

The season started on October 3rd, when Goldmark's *La Regina di Saba* generated only lukewarm enthusiasm. De Lucia was to make his début on October 27th[3] in *La Traviata*, with Bellincioni and Senatore

---

1 Bellincioni, op. cit., p. 70.

2 Luigi Mancinelli (1848-1921), whose compositions included operas and sacred pieces, later had long seasons at Madrid, London, and New York, where his work at the Metropolitan was caught by the cylinder recording machine of Lionel Mapleson. His brother, Marino Mancinelli (1842-1894), was also a conductor.

3 Not October 17th, as given by Trezzini, *Due Secoli di Vita Musicale*.

Sparapani. As the day approached so did the tempo of the till quicken, as Bellincioni and Verdi together ensured the first financial success of the season, and Bolelli's face began to brighten.

The performance was successful artistically as well as financially, with generally favourable critical opinion. Bundles of Bologna papers were soon on their way to the Milan theatrical journals, publications usually run by agents for the benefit of their clients; such journals had their own correspondents (who sometimes worked for more than one such periodical) but would reprint notices sent to them by their clients or, on payment, by other artists. Generally, they printed what it paid them - sometimes in the most literal sense - to print. That they were widely used is clear from the fact that it was considered newsworthy that Masini did not send such despatches.[4]

Predictably, audiences were fascinated by Bellincioni's '...truly powerful interpretation of the drama', but of De Lucia one critic wrote:

...he is presented under most happy auspices. His beautiful, tuneful and ringing voice, the agreeable sonority of his high notes, and his facility of expression are fully demonstrated in the congenial part of Alfredo. Here is a truly talented and praiseworthy artist, sure to have a brilliant career.[5]

Elsewhere we read of:

...an Alfredo [with] a certain grace in modulating a rather weak voice, but he is an artist who will please even more when he has somewhat corrected his method of singing, [which is] harsh and uneven at times, and [when he] makes his study of the character a little more accurate.[6]

The voice of Ricordi, in the *Gazzetta Musicale di Milano*,[7] commented:

...the voice easily encompasses a wide range of notes; the middle [ones] have a slight baritonal tendency; the high are beautiful, ringing and of the genuinely touching tenor timbre. ...De Lucia is also a capital actor, with sentiment ...that betrays his southern ardour.[8]

The old-established Milan theatrical paper *Trovatore* remarked:

...Possessed of a rather slender voice, of caressing timbre, obedient to the subtlest shadings, he sings with excellent schooling ...Full of goodwill, an intelligent musician, he is dedicated to singing through a true love of art ...[9]

---

4 *Gazzetta dei Teatri* and *Mondo Artistico* were only two of these publications. They carried almost identical groups of Bologna reviews, doubtless sent by De Lucia.

5 *Gazzetta dei Teatri*, Nov. 5 1885.

6 *Mondo Artistico*, Nov. 1 1885.

7 This old-established paper was published by Ricordi and, though not exclusively so, was strongly linked with his operas. It would often give detailed coverage of a minor Ricordi season whilst ignoring a more important Sonzogno season in the same city. The Sonzogno paper *Teatro Illustrato* operated similarly. Both, however, offered serious musical criticism and are important sources.

8 *Gazzetta Musicale di Milano*, Nov. 8 1885.

9 *Trovatore*, Nov. 5 1885.

The daily press was somewhat more critical. One critic described the tenor as possessing a 'beautiful *vocina* [little voice] of a light tenor [quality]'.[10] Another wrote:

> The tenor De Lucia ... is young and, inevitably, has some slight faults that time and study will certainly eradicate. His voice, of *baritonal* timbre, is inherently most agreeable and inspiring and, without being overpowering, is sufficiently robust and extensive. [He] sings with much art and can execute delicate and very refined inflections and *smorzature*. He sings with expression, although he sometimes abuses it a little.
>
> ... he was much applauded, [especially] at the dramatic phrase '... *pagata io l'ho*', but in ... '*O ciel, che feci*' he could not find the necessary interpretation. ... In the third act ... he achieved true dramatic passion at the phrases '*No, non morrai, non dirmelo*'.[11]

Others described him as being 'a very correct singer',[12] with '... a most tender *mezza voce*. ... The accent is almost always good and sometimes excellent. Altogether, he has the soul of an artist.'[13]

News of his success soon travelled, for the telegraph brought an extension of his engagement for Florence; he was to sing at the Teatro Pagliano, which was under the same management as the Teatro Pergola for which he was already booked. In Bologna, Bolelli asked him to sing *Linda di Chamounix* as replacement for the indisposed Brasi; he declined, in view of his involvement with rehearsals of *Dinorah*. In the latter, he was to appear with Ernestina Bendazzi-Secchi (1864-1931), later the wife of the tenor Alfonso Garulli (1866-1915). At Bologna, she was in the charge of her formidable mother, Luigia, herself a former singer.[14] Operatic Bologna had by now become divided into two camps, the *bellincioniani* and the *bendazziani*. Bolelli, fearing that Puccini's *Le Villi*, in which the young - and inexperienced - Ernestina was to sing, might be scanty fare for an entire evening, had proposed adding an act of *La Traviata*. Signora Bendazzi felt slighted by this proposal and a furious row ensued:

> 'When Titina sings, there is no need for other names on the bill to draw the public. She is already famous enough!'

shouted the outraged mother at the myopic, imperturbable Bolelli.[15] De Lucia might easily have found himself in the middle of a theatrical vendetta. Fortunately, the dust settled in time for the *prima* of *Dinorah*. In what has been termed 'certainly the most lunatical [*sic*] opera ever

---

10 *Resto del Carlino*, quoted in *Gazzetta dei Teatri*, Nov. 12 1885.

11 *Patria*, quoted in *Gazzetta dei Teatri*, Nov. 12 1885.

12 *Stella d'Italia*, quoted in *Gazzetta dei Teatri*, Nov. 12 1885.

13 *Piccolo Faust*, quoted in *Gazzetta dei Teatri*, Nov. 12 1885.

14 Luigia Bendazzi (1833-1901) created the part of Maria in the first version of *Simon Boccanegra*.

15 Bellincioni, op. cit., pp. 70-1.

composed'[16] he pleased as '. . . the strange and unrewarding character of Correntino'. He was frequently interrupted by cries of *'Bravo!'* and was termed

> . . . a capital Correntino, whether because he was able to give to the part that comic flavour that belongs to it, or whether through his musical and unexaggerated performance.[17]

Significantly, *Trovatore* noted that it was clear that the applause resulted from sincere admiration on the part of the public, and not from other motives.[18] It was observed that he had evidently profited from the advice of Pietro Neri-Baraldi (1828-1902), formerly a notable Correntino.

As the season drew to a close it was the time of benefit performances, those occasions when the other artists contributed their services and the managements escaped paying full fees to anyone. The theatre was illuminated as for gala occasions, while poems and flowers rained on to the stage and an animated, festive, and demonstrative crowd bestowed medals, laurel wreaths, and elaborate gifts on the artists. For Bendazzi-Secchi, the programme included Acts I and II of *Dinorah* and the Jewel Song and love duet from *Faust*; after the Shadow Song the stage resembled one large garden.[19] For Bellincioni, the final performance of *La Traviata* was followed by the rondo from *Lucia di Lammermoor*. Such a substantial *pourboire* did not come the way of De Lucia, as he prepared to leave for Salerno and the religious marriage ceremony; however, twenty performances had not been unprofitable, and the benefit nights would certainly come. Now, it was less than three weeks to the opening of the season at Florence, a milestone in his career. Naples had been fortuitous, and Bologna a second-rank season. Florence was his first appearance, won by reputation, as a regular member of the company in a theatre of the first order.

The stages of Florence no doubt lacked the *cachet* of Milan or Rome. However, more than a dozen theatres gave drama and music and the citizens were accustomed to the very best in operatic singing. In the autumn of 1885, patrons of the Teatro Nuovo had heard *Maria di Rohan*, with the baritone Mattia Battistini (1856-1928), while at the Pagliano the renowned tenor Francesco Marconi (1853-1916) had appeared in works as diverse as *Aida* and *La Favorita*. The Florentines were an urbane and discriminating audience. De Lucia's engagement was with Alessandro Barilati, confidant of Sonzogno and impresario of the two principal theatres, the small, intimate Pergola, frequented by the fashionable, and the much larger, popular, Pagliano. In both the manager spared no expense to ensure the quality of his performances.

---

16 H. Sutherland Edwards, *The Lyrical Drama*, Vol. I, p. 285.

17 *Mondo Artistico*, Dec. 2 1885.

18 *Trovatore*, Dec. 3 1885.

19 Ibid., Dec. 10 1885.

The Pergola season opened on December 26th, with *Mignon*, in which De Lucia was joined by Lison Frandin and by Maria Paolicci-Mugnone, mezzo-soprano and wife of Leopoldo Mugnone, who was principal conductor at the Pergola. 'Popo' Mugnone (1858-1941), a Neapolitan and former pupil at San Pietro a Maiella, was composer of several operas and many songs. He was a mild man until he mounted the conductor's podium. Then, he was transformed as his fiery and excitable Southern temperament asserted itself; all of his youthful vitality and nervous energy were concentrated in the rapid glances with which his lively and lucid eyes commanded the orchestra, his mobile features expressing the mood of the music as he threw his entire being into reaching his desired effects. He could be a hard, even brutal taskmaster to his orchestras, who none the less revered him.[20] He followed his instincts; his performances were sometimes criticised for being too exuberantly coloured, but they always bore the impression of his strong personality. 'This man is all fire, like the lands that saw his birth' wrote the tenor Giuseppe Borgatti.[21] One writer likened him to 'an urn of phosphorus'.[22]

In the operatic world of that era Mugnone was a colourful character, a noted wit, and the subject of many anecdotes. He was intensely superstitious; any unwelcome incident on Friday 17th was certain to produce fulminations from him on the *jettatura*, the Evil Eye.[23] Such convictions characterise the Neapolitans, many of whom believe firmly in the gift of fascination implanted in people whose malevolent influence may be exerted on any object on which their gaze may light. The laziest citizen will cross the street and even walk in the sun to avoid a known *jettature*, a person who supposedly can fascinate humans or animals, even becoming a specialist, such as a 'fascinator of horses'.[24] Charms may ward off their worst influences; alternatively, certain hand movements are thought efficacious.[25] There is a copious literature on the *jettatura*. Neapolitan newspapers devoted entire pages to solemn discussion of the subject. In the lyric world, Mugnone's preoccupation with it was shared not only by Neapolitans, such as De Lucia and Caruso, but by many others. For Bellincioni, who had the world première of *Cavalleria Rusticana* deferred by four days rather than sing on the scheduled Tuesday May 13th 1890, the 17th was evidently preferable.[26] Calvé, Blanche Marchesi, Patti, Puccini, and Jean de Reszke were only a

---

20 *Stampa Artistica*, Dec. 18 1913.

21 Giuseppe Borgatti, *La Mia Vita d'Artista*, pp. 54-5.

22 *Pungolo*, Mar. 16 1905.

23 For many superstitious Italians the 13th, 17th, and Friday are dreaded in equal measure. Several of Puccini's biographers incorrectly state that the Palermo première of *La Bohème*, which Mugnone conducted (not without incident), was on Friday Apr. 13th. In fact it took place on Friday Apr. 24th 1896.

24 Neville-Rolfe and Ingleby, op. cit., p. 146ff. The *jettatura* (or *iettatura*) of Neapolitan dialect becomes *jettatora* in Italian; the words appear in the literature of many languages.

25 Such gestures are still commonly seen in Southern Italy.

26 Pietro Mascagni - Lina Mascagni, May 6 1890, quoted in Edoardo Pompei, *Pietro Mascagni*, p. 80.

few of the others who were quite ready to believe the widespread rumour that Offenbach had the Evil Eye.

In 1885, Mugnone had strong links with Sonzogno, for whom he edited opera scores and conducted on especially important occasions; later he was to forge equally firm ones with Ricordi, when he prepared and conducted the world première of works as important as *Tosca*.

On the first night of the season, December 26th 1885, the society of Florence crowded into the Pergola to hear *Mignon*. The occasion was perhaps judged more important than the music, for the distinguished audience gave unstinted applause to a performance which some critics found lacking. The principal artists were called repeatedly to the footlights. De Lucia was praised for good schooling, distinguished style, elegant phrasing, and for a voice which was thought to be perfectly adapted to the opportunities offered by the part of Wilhelm Meister for the display of graces and *sfumature*.[27] One enthusiastic critic wrote:

> The major success belonged to the tenor De Lucia. It was an absolute triumph. He had to repeat the two *romanzas* 'Non lacrimar' ['Addio, Mignon'] and 'Ah qual guardo strano' ['Ah! non credevi tu'] from the 3rd act and also the 'andante' of the duet with Mignon, 'La tua bell'alma alfin'. These repeats took place amid enthusiasm [which is] unusual for the Pergola and [which] was justified because De Lucia sings *admirably*. He puts into his beautiful and very tender voice all the passion of his heart and communicates it to the public. His *legato* and shadings are masterly. Go and hear him . . . [28]

Another critic commented that from the phrases '*Con quella vesta bianca*' ('La tua bell'alma') he made a true poem, and only the dignity of the staid Pergola audience restrained it from requesting an encore in the manner beloved of the gallery at the Pagliano.[29]

Even as Barilati reconfirmed De Lucia for the whole of March there came evidence of the tenor's growing fame. Two new contracts were announced. The first was for South America during the European spring and summer; the second was for the winter season at the Teatro Real of Madrid, where Luigi Mancinelli was principal conductor.

When Itala, who had accompanied Fernando to Florence, fell ill her parents - from whom, for their initial travelling and subsistence expenses, the young couple had evidently accepted financial help - came from Salerno to care for her. It was soon clear that she was pregnant, and would be unable to accompany her husband to South America.

Meanwhile, there were unfamiliar works to be learned. The next rôle in De Lucia's calendar was that of Ernando, in Pinsuti's *Margherita*. Florence received the work enthusiastically, the third and fourth acts proceeding amid continual applause. The composer, who was well-known

27 *Mondo Artistico*, Jan. 6 1886.
28 *Vedetta*, quoted in *Gazzetta dei Teatri*, Jan. 14 1886.
29 *Trovatore*, Jan. 1 1886.

locally, had more than thirty curtain calls during the first two performances. Success was constant as later performances continued to fill to overflowing both the Pergola and the much larger Pagliano.

But this achievement, in a work that he never sang again, was minor alongside the success that his next part would eventually bring him. On February 11th 1886 he made his début as Don José. At its first performances there, Florence had given *Carmen* a cool reception. Now, in his impersonation of the distraught soldier, it witnessed De Lucia in what, for many, would be his most unforgettable rôle. Twenty-five years later the tenor wrote in the front of his score:

Here [is] my great career. Fernando De Lucia

However, it cannot yet have been more than the pale glimmer of that creation, for the press, except in noting his animation on the stage, gave few details.[30] He had not then developed that feeling for the part where intuition, natural ability, and profound feeling would appear as instinctive, savage impulses, terrifying in their spontaneity. There was, as yet, barely a hint of the violence that he would instil into the moment when, overcome by jealous rage, Don José would seize Carmen by the hair and hurl her to the ground with the cry: 'You are mine at last, accursed soul!' while the audience shuddered.[31] It was in Florence that the ferocity of his attack once so alarmed a Carmen that she backed off the stage and only the camaraderie of the curtain calls proved to the audience that the quarrel was not a real one.[32] He so lived the part that one soprano is even said to have reminded him, before the opera, that he was only acting, and to be careful not to hurt her.[33] But the character was to undergo years of refinement before its realism would make audiences in Boston and Chicago gasp in stunned horror. For now, Florence had to agree that, possibly because of a translation described as 'more Chinese than Italian', it had previously misjudged the opera. Large and enthusiastic audiences attended its many performances. Another milestone for its tenor was reached on February 27th, when *Carmen* and a performance of 'L'Alba' comprised his benefit, his first *serata d'onore*.

A little over a week after his last performance at Florence, a *Mignon* recast with the striking American Costanza Donita as protagonist, he was due to sail for South America. New repertoire had to be learned, ready for polishing during the voyage. On April 8th he was part of the Ciacchi-Rainieri Company on board the liner *Regina Margherita* as she slipped out of Genoa *en route* for the River Plate.

[30] *Nazione*, Feb. 16 1886.
[31] Lancellotti, op. cit., p. 185.
[32] De Lucia family.
[33] Franz and Amedeo Gleijeses, in conversation with the writer, Naples, 1968. Their information probably came from Bellincioni, who resided in Naples for many years.

For the unworldly tenor it was a great adventure, this chance to sing in the Eldorado of the lyric world, where fees greatly exceeded those paid in Europe. He would be away four, perhaps six months, returning to Salerno scarcely in time for the birth of the child in November. But he would not feel isolated; the young republics of South America were full of Italians, and southerners too, for these were the years of mass emigration as more than a million people a year fled to South America from the grim poverty of Calabria, Campania, Sicily, and other distressed areas of Europe. Indeed, the *Regina Margherita* carried 600 such emigrants, each hoping for prosperity in Argentina and Uruguay. Buenos Aires had a large and influential Italian community with its own newspapers and entertainments, bakers and pasta-makers, the whole comprising a frugal, hard-working section of society, largely independent of the Spanish-speaking hinterland. Visiting companies with the operas of their native land could be sure of a welcome which, although perhaps owing more to native exuberance than to refined taste, would send them away glowing with artistic success, patriotism, and financial rewards. Depressed the economy might be, with the first signs of the smouldering inflation that would flare up a few years later, but the troupes could still rely on enthusiastic audiences and their managers on rich returns. Every year, as the theatres of Italy and Spain closed their doors for the summer, ships laden with one ballet, dramatic, or lyric company after another left Genoa and Naples to give Society a chance to air its finery and to bring a whiff of the homeland to the immigrant population of Argentina, Brazil, Chile, and Uruguay.

Seventeen days from Genoa the troupe caught its first glimpse of Montevideo; next day, the ship anchored in the roads of Buenos Aires. Italian colony or no, there was at first sight little to remind De Lucia of home; the chessboard regularity of the wide streets was a far cry from the *vicoli,* and the flat-roofed houses held little in common with the brooding tenements of Naples. The houses presented an aspect of stucco and the occasional glimpse of Carrara marble. Ten years earlier, most main streets had been tolerably paved in granite, but time and traffic had played havoc with the planners' intentions; now, the only streets safe for wheeled traffic were those main thoroughfares with tramway lines, which carried both private carriages and public conveyances. Footpaths often towered above the morasses that served as roads. Only a dozen airy squares, where statues of generals and politicians rose among the trees and flower beds, provided the focus for the evening *paséo* and a glimpse of the imposing city in the making. In the shady courtyards of their mansions, cattle and grain magnates gave extravagant parties and paid well for the services of the principal artists from the opera houses.

The modest Ciacchi company was overshadowed by that shortly to follow them, a troupe assembled by Angelo Ferrari and including the

Sicilian tenor Roberto Stagno. Ferrari (1830-1897) occupied a prominent theatrical position in South America. From 1868 onwards he had brought out a succession of companies including artists such as Battistini, Ferni-Germano, Figner, Gargano, Gayarre, Marconi, Navarrini, Tamagno, and many others, to appear at the old Teatro Colón and, later, at the Teatro de la Opera.[34] In 1884, whilst also impresario of La Scala, Milan, he was decorated with the Ordine della Corona d'Italia for his work - which would eventually span almost thirty years - in making Rio de Janeiro and Buenos Aires two important centres for the spread of Italian opera abroad. It was the custom of this honest and serious man, latterly assisted by his wife Amelia, to arrive in Milan deep in the Italian winter to gather as many as a thousand recruits into four opera and ballet companies, with which he would depart by steamer early in April.

Ranged against Ferrari was his great rival, the Florentine Cesare Ciacchi (d. 1913), proprietor of the Teatro Politeama Argentino of Buenos Aires, an impressive pavilion which he and his associates had transformed from a circus into a lyric theatre. Ciacchi, too, had long theatrical experience; since 1871 he had managed companies in many of the principal houses of South America. Anything that he lacked in knowledge he made up in flair. In partnership with managers such as Ducci, Grau, and Rainieri he was a formidable competitor as, with promises of great rewards, he secured artists of the calibre of Sarah Bernhardt for his seasons in Argentina, Brazil, and Chile. So fierce was the rivalry between Ciacchi and Ferrari that they would sometimes stage the same opera at their respective theatres in the same city, often within days of one another. But, while they vied to engage the most celebrated artists, they sowed the seeds of disaster as singers' fees rose to levels which would eventually prove unsustainable.

The 1886 season was eagerly anticipated as the greatest operatic and dramatic year on record for Buenos Aires. The Tartini Opera Company, already at the Colón, was quickly eclipsed by the Ciacchi troupe. Interest in the opera became still more intense when, in mid-May, Ferrari arrived and he and Ciacchi strove to outdo one another. Boxes were at a premium at both theatres.

Proceedings opened at the Politeama with *Faust* on April 29th. In the newly refurbished theatre, glittering with Argentinian and English society - there was a large English colony - 'decked with diamonds enough to save an empire', De Lucia sang with 'grace and with a thread of voice such that he forced the public to perfect silence with their eyes and ears open'.[35] To some he seemed unnerved by the audience, since

> ...[he] certainly showed to little advantage, and he would have shown
> discretion beyond his years had he taken the sense of the house and not

---

34 The present Colón was not inaugurated until 1908.
35 *Trovatore*, May 28 1886.

annihilated, in a second attempt, the aria 'Salve! dimora'. But, like Caesar, he paid for his ambition. . . . [We] expect that [he] will improve on acquaintance, as he is still very young and probably correspondingly nervous.[36]

The critic 'Mefistófeles' noted:

He sang with good taste and perfectly in tune . . . We must, however, reproach [him] for the way that he raises the head and fixes his eyes on the ceiling whenever he wants to produce some tender effect. But he is young and very slightly inexpert. After the 'Salve! dimora', which he sang with *appuntature* and variations which, in homage to the composer, he ought to omit, he was applauded . . . [in the encore] the unfortunate C natural which . . . had come out well the first time, suffered a lamentable lapse. . . . The voice [is] of good timbre in spite of a tendency to be a little throaty and white, a defect noted above all in the *smorzando*.[37]

In his next rôle, that of Gennaro in *Lucrezia Borgia*, the same critic wrote of his 'white and throaty voice and his inelegant bearing' which afforded only mediocre success. Even so, he was perhaps the best of a poor cast, since 'Mefistófeles' added:

Let us have no more of the companions of Gennaro, by Heaven! How long must we wait for the poison to give us justice? [38]

However, Buenos Aires was preoccupied with the impending arrival of 'The Divine Sarah', with a reputed 100,000 francs worth of new dresses.[39] Ciacchi even went in person to greet her on arrival at Rio and, incidentally, to safeguard his investment by trying - unsuccessfully - to persuade her to start her season in the cities of the River Plate instead of in Brazil, with its risk of yellow fever.

Meanwhile, the foggy weather did not discourage a crowd from gathering at the harbour to welcome the Ferrari company to Buenos Aires; Stagno's lungs were not proof against it, though, and the début of the company in *Roberto il Diavolo* at the Colón was in all senses a muted affair. He had recovered by the time that the same work was given during the May Fêtes. Then, the Colón featured performances by both the opera companies. The festivities reached their height on May 25th, when the wealthy of the city filled the theatre. What should have been a dignified occasion was, however, marred when fire - started by a lighted cigar stub among old costumes in a store-room - threw the audience into great but temporary confusion.

Buenos Aires and Montevideo provided an opportunity for De Lucia to

---

36 *Standard*, May 1 1886 (Buenos Aires English language daily).

37 *Prensa*, Apr. 30 1886.

38 Ibid., May 12 1886.

39 In the so-called Latin Union of that time the Belgian, French and Swiss francs, Greek drachma, Italian lira, and Spanish peseta had identical value, at 25.2 to the pound Sterling.

observe and analyse Stagno, who was another major influence on him. In
Argentina the admiration for the Sicilian, the idol of local theatregoers,
was immense.[40] Women were fascinated by him, and he seldom
discouraged them. His gentlemanly and cultivated qualities had gained
him friends at all levels, including the President of Argentina himself.
His voice, according to Bellincioni,

> ...was of less beautiful timbre than that of his great rivals Gayarre and
> Masini, but they did not possess the vibrant power of his top notes, ringing like
> a silver bell, while he sustained them with breathing that was an absolute
> miracle, adding to these vocal qualities a refinement and an elegance which
> made him the most finished and aristocratic artist of the age.[41]

Bellincioni and Stagno had met on the voyage from Genoa and on
arrival were, as she charmingly expressed it, singing their love duets
with no need of a conductor. She was to remain his devoted companion
for the remaining eleven years of his life. Since she cannot be considered
a disinterested observer, Bellincioni's reservations have the stamp of
honest comment.

Her praise is amply corroborated elsewhere. All agreed that Stagno
could essay a greater range of parts than could any other tenor of that
period.[42] It could almost be said that his repertoire was limitless, and in
few operas, old or new, did he fail to find one of those characteristic, very
personal moments, in which he ravished the public. Aware of his powers,
legitimately proud of his aura, *el mago siciliano* (the Sicilian magician),
as he was known in Spain, could - like Rubini - permit himself the luxury
of easing his way through half his part and of exerting himself only in
the other half where, at will, he would bring the public to delirium in two
or three places.[43] One critic wrote:

> He ... so rarely condescends to use his voice that one might well wonder whence
> his reputation came. When ... he wishes to rise to the occasion, his marvellous
> tones, pure and clear as a bird's, carry everyone away in a fury of enthusiasm
> and his manoeuvres are forgotten.[44]

He espoused the maxim, attributed to Duprez, that the singer who wants
to make an effect in everything makes it in nothing. By such economies
he preserved his voice, almost untouched, to a late age. Masini
customarily referred to him as an 'extraordinary mosaic', a reference to
the structure of the voice of this Lamperti pupil. Unlike more fortunate

---

40 Real name Vincenzo Andreoli Stagno (1836-1897). He took the name Roberto following his first major
success, in the title rôle of *Roberto il Diavolo*.

41 Bellincioni, op. cit., p. 77. Some sources incorrectly refer to them as husband and wife.

42 Masini sang 107 rôles in his career, but Stagno was thought to be the more versatile.

43 Gino Monaldi, *Cantanti Celebri*, p. 149. Monaldi (1847-1932) was a historian, musicologist, music critic
for *Gazzetta d'Italia*, and sometime impresario. He was the author of several books on composers, operas, and
singers.

44 *Standard*, Aug. 6 1887.

singers he could not draw on a bountiful natural voice. Instead, by ceaseless work, he had come to terms with the disjointed, unequal organ, drawing, as necessary, from the chest and head registers whatever was lacking for the complete and precise formulation of his scale. Such a combination of sounds from different sources was certainly not simple to manage, and the public had been slow to accept it. In 1890 it was described as 'a voice of an artist, a *boîte-à-surprises*, and these surprises do not always please'.[45] But an extensive and sparkling upper register compensated for defects in the centre, while a prodigious flexibility and agility lent themselves to *sfumature* and to all kinds of virtuosity. Thus, he became renowned in works which were beyond most tenors; for decades his fame rested on operas of high *tessitura* - *I Puritani* and several of the Meyerbeer works, especially *Roberto il Diavolo* - or those lending themselves to embellishment, such as *La Sonnambula* or *Il Barbiere di Siviglia*:

> He possesses in the highest degree the art of attacking the high notes with freedom, without exertion, without artifice, and of fining them sweetly away in a *pianissimo*, spinning out the note at great length, always with the same purity, and also the art of swelling high notes, showing the [dynamic] range of the voice. [In *I Puritani*] the agility of the voice is phenomenal; his singing of *fioriture* . . . can rival a light soprano . . . [46]

In 1886, as Lindoro in *Il Barbiere*, he was considered

> . . . one of the, by now, few, if not the only tenor, who through a rare musical education can perform that type of music, so different from that which singers are accustomed and required to perform today. For the *fioriture*, the *gruppetti*, the delicacy which are the form and substance of the Rossinian comedy, voice does not suffice when not coupled with a perfect knowledge of the art of singing, such as Stagno possesses to a high degree.[47]

By then, Stagno was already fifty, but apparently still very much a vocal force. Four years later, his decline more evident, he would find the *verismo* operas increasingly congenial, vocally and temperamentally. Photographs show him as a vivid, dashing, and powerfully dramatic Turiddu; even then, however, he could not restrain his virtuoso nature, as in the cadenza and trill with which he ended the 'Brindisi'. His natural ability as an actor was supported by a command of languages and a strong literary and cultural background that had led him to study his characters in their historical context.[48] The care and artistic discrimination with which he chose his costumes might, in a lesser artist, have seemed mere pedantry, but were perfectly consistent with

---

45 *Occhialetto*, Dec. 29 1890, quoting *Gazzetta Teatrale* (of Naples).

46 *Gazzetta dei Teatri*, May 28 1885, quoting the Palermo paper *Nuovo Precursore* (undated).

47 *Piccolo*, quoted in *Gazzetta dei Teatri*, Apr. 22 1886.

48 G. Piccini, *Attori, Cantanti, Concertisti, Acrobati*, p. 129ff.

his cultured fastidiousness. His prowess with both pistol and sword lent realism to many of his rôles. He lived in the almost regal style expected of the great luminaries of the lyric stage.

When Stagno died, on April 26th 1897, many a nostalgic story was told of the great days of the Stagno-Tamagno rivalry in Buenos Aires, when all the girls were either 'Stagnites' or 'Tamagnites'.[49] The affection for him was clear from the obituaries carried in most of the newspapers.

From all accounts, De Lucia was much impressed by Stagno's magnetism: vocally, dramatically, and even socially we may detect traces of the older singer, whom Fernando would almost certainly have heard during his seasons at Naples in 1877-8 and 1881-2, and on other occasions elsewhere. Later, the young man was a frequent visitor to Mergellina, the fishing village a carriage-ride west of Naples, where Stagno, enchanted with the area, had established one of his three residences. There, this enthusiastic and discriminating collector had furnished his villa with antique furniture, bronzes, porcelain, silver, and paintings, and there Fernando had many opportunities to study his accomplishments. Like Stagno, he would in turn be termed a mosaic. In 1890, De Lucia was described as

> ... an artistic bee, who collects the honey from so many different flowers. ... Perhaps the artist from whom he drew most was Stagno. ... this year he is more exquisite in the *mezza voce*, [which] merges better with the other registers.[50]

Critics wrote of Stagno and De Lucia as a priceless statue and a likeness. Comparing the Venus de Milo with its copies, the

> ... first is ... Roberto Stagno, the only *Almaviva* today. The second is Fernando De Lucia, a copy in bronze of the original marble. ... Comparisons are odious, but necessary [here] because we speak of imitation. ... De Lucia has great qualities, and draws serious profit from his studiousness; more than criticising him for a tendency to imitate Stagno, we applaud him, since whoever wants to shape himself ought to have great models ... but without debasing himself.[51]

De Lucia, a master of the *mezza voce*, preserves on records the techniques of *diminuendo* and *crescendo* for which Stagno had been so celebrated a generation earlier. His acting, too, was touched by the influence of the Sicilian. In 1895, a South American critic exclaimed:

> We may say that De Lucia is Stagno's pupil: not that his voice is the same, but his school and his acting are identical. Stagno was about the most finished actor that ever appeared on the stage, and De Lucia is certainly worthy of being his successor.[52]

---

49 *Standard*, Apr. 28 1897.
50 *Roma*, Dec. 17 1890.
51 *Nación*, in *Gazzetta dei Teatri*, June 20 1889.
52 *Standard*, Sept. 17 1895.

While admiring crowds - including, it seems, most of the critics - flocked to hear Stagno at the Colón, the Ciacchi company continued, poorly attended and almost unreported, with a lavishly-costumed *L'Ebrea* (*La Juive*), in which De Lucia took the small part of Leopoldo, gaining applause for several of his pieces. His next part was that of Fernando, in *La Favorita*. The accolade was for Eva Tetrazzini,[53] the tenor drawing only faint praise for being

> ...not at all bad overall, and good in the aria 'Spirto gentil', sung without amending Donizetti, for which we should be thankful.[54]

But many theatre-goers preferred to save their entrance money for the eagerly-awaited Sarah Bernhardt; despite the unseasonable cold, the steamer *Apollo*, laden with her admirers, left for Montevideo to escort her to Buenos Aires where, in a grand gesture for a city packed to the limits, Ciacchi had taken for her the entire Globo hotel. Subscriptions for the Politeama changed hands for unheard-of sums. Theatrical fever raged, as four thousand crammed the theatre for her début.

De Lucia's final new rôle of the season was in *La Gioconda*, which also provided his benefit on July 14th in the last performance before the Ciacchi troupe departed for Montevideo.

The Uruguayan capital was usually the first point of call for the dozen or so steamship lines then plying between Europe and the River Plate. It had only half the population of Buenos Aires, yet the installation of modern comforts, such as the electric light, was making rapid headway. It was a city where fully one-third of the population was Italian: it was a prosperous city, avid for culture after a period when an attempted revolution had emptied it of its once-flourishing night life.

On July 17th 1886, Montevideo's Teatro Cibils was crowded, especially the *cazuela* - the women's gallery characteristic of Spanish theatres - to hear Lucignani and Tetrazzini in *L'Ebrea*. De Lucia had 'gallantly' agreed to sing the high-lying part of Leopoldo.[55] Not all of the interest was musical; the distinguished audience included many cabinet ministers and the President, General Santos, whose admiration for Tetrazzini did not stop with applause. He presented her with a bouquet worthy of an Empress. The company did not enjoy the limelight for long, however, since four days later the Ferrari opera company arrived to replace his ballet troupe at the Teatro Solis. Some of his artists took advantage of their leisure to appraise the opposition; Stagno shared a box with Amelia Ferrari to hear the Ciacchi company give *La Gioconda*, in which De Lucia contributed 'with his beautiful high notes to the

53 Eva (1862-1938), was the elder sister of Elvira and Luisa Tetrazzini (1871-1940).
54 *Prensa*, June 18 1886.
55 *Tribuna Popular*, July 19 1886.

excellence of the fourth act trio'.[56] Also present was the distinguished tenor Antonio Aramburo (1838-1912), a singer to whom the Neapolitan was likened when *La Favorita* was given on August 7th; the third act was singled out as a revelation of De Lucia's dramatic power.

The proceedings of August 17th 1886 were enlivened when an assassin fired a revolver at Santos, slightly wounding him as he entered the packed Cibils theatre for Tetrazzini's benefit performance. Although the offender was swiftly shot dead, within ten minutes the panic-stricken audience had fled and the theatre was deserted.

Nor were the worries of the Italian artists confined to terrorism. In April, cholera had reappeared in Italy; by August it was rampant and Brazil had closed its ports to ships from Naples, where the situation was so serious that Piedigrotta was again forbidden. Moreover, it was becoming clear that Buenos Aires and, particularly, the smaller Montevideo could not support the direct competition between the Ferrari and the Ciacchi-Rainieri companies - for Ciacchi, too, had three troupes operating - and, equally important, pay the salaries of artists such as Stagno and Bernhardt. All the impresarios lost money heavily. For Ferrari, especially, it was a disaster; one company was stricken by yellow fever in Rio, and some singers had not been paid for a month or more.[57] A truce was inevitable but it came too late to save the remnants of the current season, as the Ciacchi troupe resumed in Buenos Aires on September 4th and the Ferrari company three days later. The exhausted managers would fight many another theatrical war, but never with quite the same profligate independence.

---

[56] *Trovatore*, Sept. 3 1886.
[57] *Standard*, July 16 1886.

4

Galley Slave

... when great artists have to be dealt with, only keenly analytical observation
and comparison of them with artists who, however agreeable, are not great, can
enable a critic to distinguish between what everybody can do and what only a
very few can do, and get his valuations right accordingly.

G.B. Shaw, *London Music in 1888-89 as heard by Corno Di Bassetto*

As the *Regina Margherita*, bound for Genoa, steamed out of the River
Plate on October 1st 1886 it was the start of a working voyage for De
Lucia. Within days the season would start at the Teatro Real, Madrid,
and domestic matters would leave little time for learning new operas
once he reached Italy. The long season in Madrid - at the Real they
typically stretched to 120 performances of 20 or more operas - was his
greatest challenge to date. In the context of his entire career, De Lucia's
seasons there would be his equivalent of Verdi's years in the galleys;
they would hone his technique and his experience, and expand his
repertoire and reputation. From them he would emerge a finished artist,
and Madrid would be proud of the part that it had played in the
metamorphosis.[1]

Spain was the country where, perhaps more than anywhere else, the
operatic kingdom was ruled by the tenor, for whom there were
aficionados who would come to blows over their idol even more readily
than over politics. Naturally, it was the tenor who most attracted the
attention of the notorious *claque* of the Teatro Real. The *claque* has not
always had its modern, pejorative overtones. At that time, it still
retained vestiges of its legitimate function.[2] However, advantages or not,
many informed opera-goers considered it an intolerable nuisance, and
nowhere more so than in Madrid. Arrogant and unchallenged, it
connived with the impresario for the engagement of the most prestigious
and expensive singers, who were paid much better than in Italy. But the
extra cost was recovered nightly from the singers themselves; whilst his
men applauded, hushed or hissed in unison, the *chef de claque* would

---

[1] *Gazzetta dei Teatri*, Nov 15. 1894.

[2] There is a considerable literature on the *claque*. See, for example, Sutherland Edwards, *The Prima
Donna*, Vol. I, p. 137ff, or Hector Berlioz, *Evenings in the Orchestra*, p. 71ff. The *chef de claque* often received
a stipend and attended the final rehearsals.

present himself between acts at the dressing-room door, vehement in his denunciation of some other cabal which could be defeated only by the chink of coin.[3] The *claque* took its duties rather seriously. Tamberlick recounted that, on one occasion, he had had to beg the *claqueurs* to stop applauding and to let him go home when no one but they, led by his cwn barber, remained in the theatre.[4]

Few singers would admit to paying such people; Bellincioni, however, who sang frequently with the greatest tenors of her time and had ample opportunity to observe, recalled how even they, acknowledged masters of the lyric art and yet prey to their own vanities and uncertainties, were reduced at each première to frightened children, in the power of the parasites who trafficked in nerves:

> ... and all were so, Stagno ..... Gayarre ..... Masini ..... no one excluded,
> from the greatest to the smallest ..... [5]

As the Ciacchi company made its way to Italy, the *tamagnisti* of the Real were already ecstatically acclaiming their hero in *Guglielmo Tell*, *Poliuto*, and *Aida*, and the *gayarristi* were preparing to welcome theirs like the colossus that, in Madrid, he was. While Fernando lingered in Salerno, awaiting Itala's confinement, an exasperated management put *Mignon* into rehearsal with Giuseppe Oxilia in his place. When, eventually, De Lucia could delay no longer, it was to arrive in Madrid on the day of the première, November 2nd, have two very long rehearsals and, finally, to make his début.

On the whole the performance did not please, largely because Giuseppina Pasqua was not well cast as Mignon. By the time that Meister appeared on the stage the enthusiasm of the audience had all but evaporated, and any applause at all was no small honour.[6] The Madrid press echoed previous critics: it noted his limited range and power, but also the correctness of his schooling and the refined and tasteful manner with which he delivered his *filate* and *gruppetti*.[7] The correspondent 'Nelusko' wrote:

> ... in 'Addio, Mignon, fa core' he ingratiated himself at a stroke with the
> audience. ... In the last act his success increased further ... he had to repeat
> the very delicate phrases of the duet with Mignon, 'La tua bell'alma', which he
> finished with an exquisite softening on the D sharp.[8]

This modest success, though, was no reason for complacency. His next

3 Carelli, op. cit., p. 91.
4 *Occhialetto*, Nov. 7 1885.
5 Bellincioni, op. cit., p. 89.
6 *Gazzetta Musicale di Milano*, Nov. 28 1886.
7 *Epoca* and *Imparcial*, Nov. 3 1886.
8 *Gazzetta dei Teatri*, Nov. 11 1886.

rôle was Boito's Faust, a part in which both Masini and Gayarre had left recent memories among robust and fiercely partisan supporters. And the *gayarristi*, especially, could compare him closely with their hero, when that great man returned to the Real in *L'Africana* on November 6th.

Julián Gayarre was the last of the tenor triumvirate who so markedly influenced the development of Fernando De Lucia. In appearance he was unprepossessing: of barely medium height, with reddish hair and beard, and with small but lively eyes, he had an expression which, in its profound sadness, was almost hard. He seldom smiled. Latterly, he seemed to have been preoccupied with death.[9]

He was a *tenore di mezzo carattere*. Compared with Marconi, whose repertoire was similar, the voice of Gayarre was not of golden timbre but was lightly veiled and guttural, with a less unstudied attack on the high notes.[10] However, by virtue of its colouring, it appeared more masculine and sonorous, and its veil added a harmonious sweetness. In the flute-like passages, supported on the breath, it had a voluminous, velvety quality that only Stagno could emulate.[11] At its best it was a voice of marvellous tenderness, full of a strange fascination said by some to suggest the sounds of angels and to produce shivers of emotion beyond the capacity of other tenors, no matter how powerful. Gayarre was the singer with the *voce di paradiso*, the poet of the stage.[12]

To others, the voice was less pleasing. Hermann Klein described him as an exponent of the new quasi-nasal school of tenor singers, of which Tamagno was one of the leading exponents. To his ears (1877) Gayarre's production sounded strange and not wholly pleasant; it was an organ that could occasionally emit tones which earned the name of the 'Gayarre bleat'[13] or, as Shaw acidly termed it, 'goatbleat', being 'harsh, acute, piercing, [and] disquieting, probably as a result of forcing his voice to produce too much volume'.[14] Yet, when this was not in evidence, for Klein the tone had a superb tenor quality with a resonant power that grew stronger as it mounted easily to a high C capable of filling the largest auditorium. He was a highly artistic singer with a singular command of colour and nuance, thanks to breath control that enabled him to make a slow crescendo from the most delicate *mezza voce* to the loudest *fortissimo*.

In the succeeding decade Gayarre proved to be the most interesting of the operatic tenors heard in London. Italo Campanini and Giuseppe Fancelli had finer voices; of the French school, Nicolini and Victor Capoul were perhaps more attractive. But in certain operas Gayarre

9 Sebastián Julián Gayarre, Roncal, 1844 - Madrid, 1890. Although the name is often written Gayarré, an autograph survives where he writes: '*Je m'appelle Gayarre et non Gayarré*' (BLS).

10 Francesco Marconi (1853-1916) made almost thirty records in 1903-8.

11 Giovanni Borelli, 'Il necrologio', in *Angelo Masini: Il tenore angelico*, p. 56.

12 Bellincioni, op. cit., pp. 47-8 and 88.

13 Hermann Klein, *Thirty Years of Musical Life in London*, p. 100.

14 G.B. Shaw, *London Music in 1888-89 as heard by Corno Di Bassetto*, pp. 288 and 337.

stood by himself: in *La Favorita*, *Le Prophète*, and *La Gioconda*, in which he was the first Enzo. Thought by Wagner himself to be in the very front rank of Lohengrins, he was said to have been the first to vary the charm of the Bridal Chamber scene by the judicious use of a particularly lovely *mezza voce*. Above all, in *Lucrezia Borgia* he was positively unrivalled.[15] Of his Gennaro, Uda wrote:

> [He speaks] the word *'madre'* as no human voice ever spoke it. It bursts forth from the throat with an inexpressible power of swelling melody, but from its warm and impassioned vibrations you understand, you feel what was in the heart ...

Of his acting in the third act, the critic continued:

> The anguish for his dying friends, the rage against the terrible and monstrous woman who has caused their death, the profound desperation that takes possession of him on learning that that monster is his mother ... the voice of Gayarre says everything; and the face - that countenance that seemed to me, and was, impassive, with no reflection of the feelings so admirably spoken by the voice - radiates, contorts, suffers agonies with that of the character ... It was an enthusiastic triumph, not of the singer and not of the virtuoso. The God-given throat, the prodigious lungs, the marvellous art of the sweetest *smorzature* in the ringing fullness of the chest voice, all played their part, but the heart predominated.[16]

His Latin temperament was evident in the passionate force of his acting on his Covent Garden début in *La Favorita* (1876). In 'Spirto gentil' his vocal defects disappeared, leaving purity, steadiness and charm, together with a wonderfully sustained breadth of phrasing and a thrilling *ut de poitrine* at the close, when the whole audience, staid Victorian matrons and *habitués* of the old guard alike, burst into an outbreak of enthusiasm so spontaneous and unanimous as to leave no doubt of his triumphant success.[17] Monaldi, who otherwise thought him almost perfect in this part, remarked on the excessive pride that he took in his breath control, with which he made great play, sometimes to the detriment of the music. He recounts that a venerable peer, long a Covent Garden regular, 'through one of those idiosyncrasies not uncommon in the English' habitually timed the duration of every piece in the operas he heard. By his reckoning, 'Spirto gentil' should take an absolute maximum of 5 minutes 10 seconds; Gayarre, it seems, customarily took almost 7 minutes. On the night in question the noble lord sat in his stall, listening with religious attention as the Spaniard sang the aria. After precisely his maximum permitted period he could tolerate no more; watch in hand and oblivious to the protests of those eagerly awaiting the

15 Klein, *Thirty Years*, p. 101.
16 Michele Uda, *Arte e Artisti*, Vol. II, pp. 198-9.
17 Klein, *The Golden Age of Opera*, p. 58.

cadenza, he leapt to his feet and rushed from the theatre.[18]

The singing of Gayarre was celebrated for the *mezza voce*, a feature that was always eagerly anticipated, its voluptuous inflections the envy of others. In *I Puritani*, in which he had a great vogue, there were pleas from the critics that he should exercise it rather more in 'A te, o cara'.[19] The Turin critic Depanis contended that no one who had not heard him in that quartet, or in 'Spirto gentil', could form an idea of virtuosity, free of affectation.[20] His chest range, described as exceptional, is held to have ended at high C; he would, however, occasionally employ it, rather than the head voice which he normally used at that point, in the high C sharp of the *I Puritani* piece.[21]

There were claims that he was unable, physically or dramatically, to project the character that he was playing, or to assume the appropriate musical style; he was said to render Bellini, Donizetti, Meyerbeer, and Ponchielli all in the same way. To such critics, his best - and only - dramatic gesture was to throw his arms wide and then to place one hand on the chest.[22] Though few singers escape occasional disapprobation, it is difficult to reconcile the conflicting, even diametrically opposed views, of some of the critics. It is, however, well known that, after a long history of ill-health, Gayarre's performances, especially towards the mid-eighties, had become unequal; he had superb moments, and periods of tiredness. In the opinion of Klein, he was not a great tenor in the highest sense of the term, one who could fulfil the hopes entertained of him as Mario's successor. Nevertheless, he judged him a *primo tenore* of the first order, one who possessed vocal and histrionic attributes of a very distinguished kind and who was capable, to a large extent, of bridging over the interval between the final retirement of Mario and the coming of Jean de Reszke. On his death, in 1890, he was described as full of noble qualities.[23]

De Lucia evidently studied the more effective vocal devices of the Spaniard of whom, time and again, he reminded critics. The recollections came in the timbre, in the emotional effects of his voice on the listener, in certain similarities of style, and especially in the *mezza voce*. Seven years after Gayarre's death a Neapolitan critic compared him with De Lucia:

> But because the memory still lives of that *cantore paradisiaco* one can say that the legitimate heir to his enchantment is now our De Lucia, the only [one] who, in his clear, velvety, responsive, supple voice, in his sweetness, in the spell cast by his sentiment, can create an echo [of Gayarre], can recall him for us, through the softness of a melodious illusion, abounding with passion and tenderness.[24]

18 *Teatro Illustrato*, Aug. 1 1906.
19 *Gazzetta dei Teatri*, Mar. 24 1887.
20 Giuseppe Depanis, *I concerti popolari ed il Teatro Regio di Torino*, quoted in Eugenio Gara, *Cantarono alla Scala*, p. 126.
21 Gara, *Cantarono*, p. 122.
22 Leone Fortis, quoted in Gara, *Cantarono*, p. 124.
23 *Standard*, Jan. 5 1890.
24 *Fortunio*, Feb. 14 1897.

Of the works that Gayarre sang in Madrid that year, only *La Favorita* was to enter the repertoire of De Lucia, who would certainly have heard him as Fernando and as Vasco da Gama at Naples in 1883. But these and other seasons would allow the Neapolitan to judge him also in *Faust*, *Lucia di Lammermoor*, *I Pescatori di Perle*, and other operas, and it is in De Lucia's recordings of some of these that we may, perhaps, glimpse the great Spaniard. His singing (with Josefina Huguet) in the duet from *I Pescatori di Perle* [No. 37] is particularly suggestive. It does not seem fanciful to imagine that, in the use of the head voice, in the soft, high A, shimmering in its iridescent beauty, and in that indolence, that same wilfulness with *tempo* with which Gayarre so enraged the nobleman at Covent Garden, De Lucia evokes echoes of him in one of his favourite rôles.[25] The record displays the most subtle vocal colours as he 'builds a great arch to his fullest power and back, then finishes off the verse with a passionate accelerando and a floated high note of the purest quality'.[26] Others have commended his shaping of the piece:

> ... the flow of his singing is a feature that memory retains as one of his most remarkable characteristics. ... If one follows the score and De Lucia's breathing there is no very remarkable span, yet so smooth is the production, with such fine instrumental 'bowing' of the line, that one has the impression of completely unbroken melody. It all comes back to the exact and disciplined matching of technique and imaginativeness.[27]

Among Gayarre's supporters, opinion on the new tenor, in *Mefistofele*, was divided, with one side hissing some forced and flagging high notes and the other applauding his taste and delicacy.[28] But all were agreed upon his value to the now mollified management. Soon after, his artistic elation was mingled with pride in the news from Salerno that, on November 17th 1886, Itala had given birth to a son, who was named Armando.

The season now brought De Lucia into harness with Mattia Battistini; neither *Linda di Chamounix*, which was dominated by the celebrated baritone, nor the première of *Il Barbiere di Siviglia*, overshadowed by recollections of Masini, yielded him any great success. His later performances in *Il Barbiere* were better received, evidently for the modesty with which he presented himself;[29] 'modesty' was a word often used of him at that time, both in reviews and theatrical gossip columns,

---

25 This record (a copy of which, with 23 recordings by other notable artists, was deposited in two sealed boxes in the Paris Opéra on Dec. 24 1907) is apparently transposed by a semitone. De Lucia's record of 'Spirto gentil' [No. 159], which omits the recitative, lasts 4 min. 2 sec. (at 78.95 rpm, in B), 4 min. 14 sec. (at 75 rpm, in B flat, the most probable transposition), or 4 min. 27 sec. (at 71.43 rpm in A). Presumably, he did not feel it necessary to use two sides, as he later did for the *Faust* aria: 'Qual turbamento ... Salve! dimora' [Nos. 165/6].

26 Crutchfield (1988), p. 13.
27 Steane, op. cit., p. 33.
28 *Imparcial* and *Epoca*, Nov. 17 1886.
29 *Imparcial* and *Epoca*, Jan. 2 1887.

as if he realised that to gain acceptance in this stronghold of established tenors it was unwise to provoke comparisons.

After requests to hear De Lucia's delicately-sung Correntino, *Dinorah* was given on January 20th 1887, with Gargano, Battistini, and Guerrina Fabbri.[30] Given the nature of their respective parts, it was no surprise that the success of the evening was again Battistini's, especially in 'Sei vendicata assai'.[31] However, the tenor was felt to have portrayed the timid and ridiculous character perfectly. One critic wrote:

> It has been a long time since we heard ... Correntino performed with such perfection as last night. Sr. De Lucia ... sang with true *amore*, the gleaming middle notes [having] a most pleasing timbre.[32]

In increasingly bitter weather the illness of some of the artists caused rearrangement of works and still further reduced the takings of impresario Michelena who, like most operatic managements outside Italy, was losing large sums.[33] The opera was still drawing fashionable society, though, with the two Infantas present almost every evening. *Fra Diavolo* offered De Lucia an opportunity to repeat the 'Barcarolle', but he gained only lukewarm praise overall and unfavourable comparisons with Naudin[34] and Stagno.[35] In *La Traviata* he had, despite memories of Masini, probably his best success of the season, interpreting the part with great mastery.[36]

The season was now nearing its end, the time of benefits and other eccentric programmes. Mancinelli's *serata*, well-supported as befitted the popular conductor, featured Act I of his own *Isora di Provenza*, sung by Battistini, Beltramo, De Lucia, Kupfer-Berger, and Pasqua, and a chorus of pages made up of other principal artists, including De Vere, Fabbri, Garrido, Adele Gazul, and Pérez. The single performance of *L'Elisir d'Amore*, at popular prices, was for Baldelli's benefit.

De Lucia had succeeded well enough to be reconfirmed, under greatly-improved conditions, for next winter at the Real. Further, on the recommendation of Mancinelli, who was to be its principal conductor, he had secured an unexpected engagement in London. There, at the height of the London Season, Italian opera was to be given at Drury Lane Theatre, whose lessee was Augustus Harris.

In 1887, Italian opera in London had for some time been in the financial doldrums. At Covent Garden, Mapleson and Lago had each mounted seasons which, despite the novelty of some of their offerings

30 Reviews do not always distinguish between the contralto Guerrina Fabbri (1866-1946) and her less-celebrated sister, the mezzo-soprano Vittorina.
31 *Gazzetta dei Teatri*, Feb. 3 1887.
32 *Epoca*, Jan. 21 1887.
33 *Gazzetta dei Teatri*, Jan. 27 1887.
34 Emilio Naudin (1823-1890).
35 *Imparcial* and *Epoca*, Feb. 1 1887.
36 *Epoca*, Feb. 17 1887.

and the strength of their casts, had failed to draw the fashionable society essential for success. All at once, opera was revitalised by a new contender, in the person of Harris, the young and energetic son of a father, also Augustus, who had been stage manager for Gye, and a mother who ran a theatrical costumiers' business.[37] After a period as Mapleson's assistant stage manager, Augustus *fils* had in 1879 assumed the management of Drury Lane, where he proceeded to mount dramas and, especially, pantomimes of unprecedented lavishness.[38] His first experiences of operatic management were with the German troupe of Franke and Pollini and the annual visit to his theatre of the Carl Rosa Opera Company; thus inspired, 'Druriolanus' had conceived the idea of an experimental Italian season whereby, with prestigious artists and with the standards of presentation for which he was now renowned, he hoped to revive the institution then still known as the 'Royal Italian Opera'. In this enterprise he had secured the support of the Prince of Wales. Equally important had been the cooperation of Lady de Grey (later Marchioness of Ripon, and a great influence on operatic life in London until the Great War) and of Lady Charles Beresford; they, it seems, had left Harris in no doubt regarding their wish to see Jean de Reszke engaged for the season.

Klein recalls that it was over lunch at the Albion Restaurant, opposite Drury Lane Theatre, that Harris chose to break to him the news of his venture and to ask him to accompany him to Madrid to hear artists recommended by Mancinelli. Klein, unaware that the idea was already in Harris's mind, independently suggested that he consider the De Reszkes. Accordingly, their journey took them first to Paris, to secure the services of the brothers, and thence to Madrid.[39] There, they engaged Battistini, Kupfer-Berger, Guerrina Fabbri - known as the 'Tamagno of Contraltos' - and De Lucia, who was described in Harris's publicity as 'leading *primo tenore leggiero* of the Teatro Real' and who was given equal billing with Jean de Reszke.

London, that Jubilee summer, was in animated mood, the confident hub of the empire on which the sun never set. Always cosmopolitan, it was more than usually thronged with visitors from every land. They had come to honour the Queen-Empress who, after reigning for longer than most people could remember, symbolised the stability of everything that Englishmen considered to be the natural order of things.

Operatically, London enjoyed an *embarras de richesse*. Mapleson, on yielding Covent Garden to Lago, had taken Her Majesty's Theatre where,

---

37 Harold Rosenthal, *Two Centuries of Opera at Covent Garden*, p. 222.

38 W.J. McQueen Pope, *Theatre Royal Drury Lane*, p. 284ff.

39 The background to the venture is given at length in the two Klein works cited above. However, since he writes that the Real season (whose subscription closed on Mar. 30) was still in progress, Klein's statement that he and Harris set out at Easter (Apr. 10 was Easter Day) is incorrect. Their impending visit to Madrid hardly explains why De Lucia, whose last scheduled performance was on Mar. 9, was still there for Baldelli's benefit on Mar. 29, since his London engagement had been announced in the Milan press as early as Mar. 24.

on June 4th, he opened a season that featured Lilli Lehmann, Oxilia, and Trebelli. On July 1st he presented his trump card, *La Traviata*, with Adelina Patti, recruited at £600 per night plus other perquisites, such as travel from Craig-y-Nos by special train;[40] it was, though, her only appearance in that season. Lago opened at Covent Garden on May 24th, his roster including Albani, Antonio De Andrade,[41] Figner, Gayarre, Mei, and Scalchi.

On their visit to London, Fernando and Itala were accompanied by her brother, Alfredo De Giorgio, who had also been engaged by Harris.[42] They and the other Italians would not have lacked for company of their fellow-countrymen, of whom London had a thriving and hospitable community. Musicians of the stamp of Tosti and Denza frequented the small shop in Great Portland Street where Signor Pagani, who had once been in the service of Grisi and Mario, prepared excellent spaghetti. There, too, came Carlo Pellegrini, the Neapolitan nobleman who then served *Vanity Fair* as its caricaturist, 'Ape'.[43]

The Drury Lane season began on June 13th, with a spectacular performance of *Aida* in which, twelve years after his first appearance there, as a baritone, Jean de Reszke made his London début as a tenor. He was an immediate sensation in what was possibly the most successful tenor début since that of Mario. The furore that he caused continued as he went on to sing *Lohengrin* and *Gli Ugonotti*. In securing him for a fee of £100 per performance Harris had struck an excellent bargain.

On June 14th, De Lucia sang Alfredo, to the Germont of Del Puente and the Violetta of Lillian Nordica. She had initially been turned down by Harris; later, grudgingly, she was added to the roster as stand-by at £40 per performance, 'if needed'.[44] She then had some unexpected luck when Kupfer-Berger, whose *vibrato* was thought excessive, was replaced after three performances.[45]

The press was enthusiastic about the *mise-en-scène*, in the period of Louis XV. Opinions on De Lucia's performance were decidedly mixed. For every critic who would recognise that his light and flexible tenor was most pleasant when not being overstrained, another would agree with the dismissive verdict: 'Alfredo [was] Signor De Lucia, who, besides boasting the *tremolo*, sang out of tune'[46] or with:

This gentleman is a *tenorino leggiero*, whose voice has been carefully cultivated and who acts with intelligence. The audience, though limited in number, was

---

40 *Gazzetta dei Teatri*, July 7 1887. A two-bedroom house could then be purchased for £300.

41 Brother of the baritone Francisco De Andrade (1856 (not 1859)-1921), who made records for Lyrophone in 1906-7.

42 Alfredo sang in *Il Barbiere* (Fiorello), *Carmen* (Zuniga), *Faust* (Wagner), *Gli Ugonotti* (a monk), and *La Traviata* (D'Obigny). The company included both Francesco and Vittorio Navarrini.

43 Isidore De Lara, *Many Tales of Many Cities*, p. 62.

44 Ira Glackens, *Yankee Diva*, p. 137.

45 Glackens incorrectly implies that Kupfer-Berger sang no performances.

46 *Graphic*, June 18 1887.

not wanting in sympathy and the débutant was favourably received. His voice is
so limited in power that his repertory must be limited, but in certain light tenor
parts he is likely to be of service.[47]

There were, however, more mature judgements. To Klein he seemed

... too nervous to do himself justice. ... My belief is that Signor De Lucia will in
due time prove himself a very valuable artist.[48]

The *Daily Telegraph* (June 16th) commented:

Sig. De Lucia ... recommends himself ... by the possession of excellent and
serviceable qualities. He has a good appearance, a pleasant voice, a cultivated
style and obvious intelligence. These advantages were quite good enough to
secure a cordial reception for the débutant, whose future efforts should be
watched with an interest proportional to existing needs for a superior
representative of his class.

In his next work, *Don Giovanni*, where Maurel took the honours, his
Don Ottavio attained only respectable mediocrity,[49] though he had a
success in 'that sentimental and exemplary gentleman's popular air'.[50]
Nor did Almaviva revive his fortunes: while Sigrid Arnoldson had a
notable success as Rosina, 'Signor De Lucia, a more than indifferent
Almaviva, sang the "serenade" in a truly detestable manner'.[51] The *Daily
Telegraph* (June 21st) termed him a 'weak' Almaviva. Klein, in the
Sunday Times (June 26th) was more encouraging, writing that he

... was, perhaps, not up to the level of his associates, but he did tolerable justice
to the florid music of his part, which is saying something. In 'Ecco ridente' it
struck me that this pleasant youngster attempted too much; he exaggerated the
sentiment of the piece and his contrasts of tone colour were so frequent as to be
irritating. As usual he acted well, especially when embodying the tipsy Lindoro;
the legs, however, were too stiff at the knees.

He was scheduled to sing Don José but the rôle went, instead, to Paroli.
Overall, the Harris venture had been successful. His careful, lavish
productions made a rare impression on audiences accustomed to the dull
or slipshod efforts at other London theatres. Although the brief season
was almost over by the time that its virtues became clear to its intended
public, the £10,000 that Harris had lost turned out to be an investment

---

47 *Illustrated Sporting and Dramatic News*, June 18 1887.
48 *Sunday Times*, June 19 1887.
49 *Illustrated London News*, June 25 1887.
50 *Daily Telegraph*, June 20 1887. The air was presumably 'Il mio tesoro'.
51 *The Times*, June 22 1887. In *Chicchere e Chiacchiere*, pp. 61-2, Alfredo De Giorgio states that he sang
Figaro in a performance, which included one act of *Il Barbiere di Siviglia*, given for Queen Victoria at Windsor
Castle by Patti, De Lucia, Francesco Navarrini (Basilio), Ciampi (Bartolo) and Desvignes (Berta), conducted
by Luigi Mancinelli. The Royal Archives cannot, however, trace the event.

which paved the way into Covent Garden theatre itself.

The cool reception accorded De Lucia - and other continental singers making their London début that season - is attributable to what was termed *tremolo* to which, as the *Graphic* remarked, British audiences had a special aversion.[52] By contrast, as Blanche Marchesi has pointed out, Italian audiences

> ... simply hate *cold* voices that possess no sympathetic vibrations. ... The vibrations of the human voice form its sympathy. But the vibrations must be natural, deriving from the quality of the vocal cords. Vibrations can never be mistaken for *tremolo*. The first is a quality, the second is a fault - more than fault.
>
> When you hear the *tremolo* in a voice, you will know that it will steadily increase with time and that at the en⸂ ⸃he career of the artist will be stopped.[53]

De Lucia made his first recordings in 1902, some fifteen years after these first London notices, and he continued to record for a further twenty years. His records certainly show a voice with a pronounced, characteristic *vibrato*. But, provided always that they are played at the correct speed, they show no progressive deterioration of the kind that Marchesi describes as an inevitable consequence of the *tremolo*. The voice, which by 1902 had undoubtedly lost some of its upper range, remains, from the first records to the last, unmistakable. And there were other qualified observers who would specifically deny that De Lucia had a *tremolo*. The Welsh tenor Ben Davies, who made his Covent Garden début in the same season as did De Lucia, and who once sang with him a duet, arranged by Randegger on Tosti's *La Serenata*, wrote:

> What I remember of De Lucia is that he had not so much of the *tremolo* as a *vibrato*, which is different; his voice was of the 'white' order, which was suited (not that I ever admired that kind of production) to the *Pagliacci*, especially to the 'Vesti la giubba' ... I never heard the *tremolo* in the real good old singers ..... Reeves, de Reszke, Battistini, never had it even when old. Santley, in later years, had a slight touch of it.[54]

Elsewhere, Davies distinguishes between *vibrato* and *tremolo*:

> A true *vibrato* is on a steady note and is the result of intense expression - just as a violinist vibrates on his violin. A *tremolo* is on two notes.[55]

On the same subject, Zélie De Lussan wrote:

> The term *vibrato* is more often than not used erroneously, and the average

---

52 *Graphic*, July 30 1887.
53 *Gramophone*, Jan. 1936, pp. 349-50.
54 (H) Letter Ben Davies - P.G. Hurst, Jan. 24 1935.
55 *Gramophone*, Jan. 1936, p. 350.

person, when speaking of a singer with a *vibrato*, means nine times out of ten a voice with a *tremolo*; but since that evil tendency cannot be tolerated, the term *vibrato* has taken its place. *Vibrato* in Italian and French means *une voix vibrante*. No beautiful voice or instrument exists without it. ... All my contemporaries, and their name is legion, the de Reszkes, Caruso, Plançon, Alvarez, Calvé, Melba, Nordica, Eames, Ternina ... and the present artists Tauber, Melchior, McCormack, Ponselle, Leider, and so many more ... had and have *des voix vibrantes*, and could never have obtained their great reputations without *vibrante* voices.[56]

And Emma Nevada, too, draws the important distinction between the terms:

Every well-trained voice has *vibrato* in some degree. ... There is no comparison between *vibrato*, as I understand it, and *tremolo*, which is a serious fault caused by wrong breathing and production or ill-health.[57]

Nevertheless, as Emma Eames has pointed out, whereas the ideally beautiful sound in many other countries is based on that of the stringed instruments, with their strong timbre, to the English ear it is that which approaches as nearly as possible to the flute or wood-wind.[58] Throughout De Lucia's career in London the imputation of a *tremolo* would pursue him and would do more to obstruct his wholehearted acceptance there than any other factor. The modern judge should note that Giovanni Martinelli, who first heard him in the theatre in 1905, recalled that the records exaggerate the *vibrato*,[59] and that his views are supported by those of other contemporary professional singers (see p. 339).

After almost two years of more or less constant activity, De Lucia could now contemplate a summer with his wife and son. His own family was presently at Saviano, very close to San Vitaliano, and he persuaded them to come to live with him.[60] He devoted himself, probably with the help of his old mentors at Naples, to the serious business of strengthening the voice. But Naples was less than restful; the city's face was changing rapidly as the old quarters were demolished and ancient landmarks disappeared. By comparison, Salerno was a tranquil oasis, and the nearby mountains a cool refuge in the dog days of summer. All too soon, it was time to return to Madrid.

The Teatro Real season of 1887-8 had a strong tenor wing, including Stagno, Tamagno, and Marconi, who opened it in *Gli Ugonotti*. This time, De Lucia took care to arrive in good time, for he was to appear in the

---

56 Ibid., p. 349.
57 Ibid., p. 350.
58 Ibid., p. 349.
59 Private communication, April 1967.
60 The date of this is not clear. Itala (De Roberto, op. cit., p. 11) suggests that her husband's family came to share his house *in Naples* soon after the return from London. If so, the theatrical press, at least as late as March 1888, erred in continuing to give his address as Salerno. In the period November 1890 - May 1892 he resided at two known addresses in Naples, at Largo Mercatello (now Piazza Dante), and at Via Fuori Portamedina. Both are near the Conservatory.

second production, *La Traviata*, on October 5th. Immediately, note was taken of the increased power and range of his high register.[61]

Of his singing in *L'Ebrea* - an opera not much to Madrid's taste - the correspondent of the *Gazzetta dei Teatri* reflected the local press when he reported:

> [He] gave an unusual prominence to the part of Leopoldo [and was] deservedly applauded at the end of the difficult serenade, for his perfect diction, beautiful notes and singular taste. With fresh and powerful notes he contributed to the great march. He added filigree to the splendid duet with Rachel in the second act, in which he found hitherto unknown effects and, in the dramatic trio that follows, he distinguished himself with his ringing high notes.[62]

In reviewing *L'Elisir d'Amore* the press began, for the first time, to produce the glowing and eulogistic but, in truth, uncritical and uninformative reviews which characterise much of the Latin school of musical criticism. Improvements over the previous season were again noted as was his apparent realisation that his reputation no longer depended upon a willingness to sing encores.[63] For *Epoca*,

> De Lucia showed a voice and an artistic talent which ... gleamed in extraordinary fashion. He unfolded his part with exquisite delicacy ... and painted a miniature in the romanza 'Una furtiva lagrima' ... With last night's performance, the young tenor has made a mark for himself at the Teatro Real.

In congratulating him, though, the same critic reminded him that '*chi va piano va sano e più lontano*'.[64]

De Lucia's Nemorino is well represented on records. His list includes 'Quanto è bella' [No. 326], with its wholly characteristic turn on '*quanto è cara*'; 'Adina, credimi' [No. 327]; and 'Una furtiva lagrima' [No. 132], where his wistful effects are obtained through observance of dynamic markings, for example in the phrase '*che più cercando io vo?*', as well as from decoration such as the two-note slide on the descending second of '*cor*'. Less commonly recorded is the duet with Adina, 'Una parola ...Chiedi al rio' [Nos. 308/9], which displays a wide variety of vocal effects: the turn, the sudden diminuendo, and the fining away of the note to a silken thread. All of Nemorino's pleading is conveyed in '*Perchè! ...perchè!*' But the most attractive of the group is arguably the enchanting duet 'Obbligato, obbligato' [No. 42], where De Lucia and Ernesto Badini (Dulcamara), with perfect intonation, complete control of *filata*, and marvellous timing recreate the *opera buffa* style.

On November 4th 1887, in a concert given at the Real in memory of

---

61 *Gazzetta dei Teatri*, Oct. 20 1887.
62 Ibid., Nov. 10 1887.
63 Ibid.
64 *Epoca*, Nov. 2 1887 'He who goes slowly goes wisely and further'.

Mozart, he sang 'Il mio tesoro', with 'much taste and delicacy'.[65] By now, he was the *enfant gâté* of that theatre. The flower of society eagerly sought the company of the handsome and accomplished young tenor. On November 11th 1887 he was received in audience by Her Majesty Queen María Cristina and by the Infanta Donna Isabel, for whom the Real artists frequently sang at the Palace. They invited him to return to give a concert of extracts from *Carmen*, a work that the Queen, who had not attended public performances since the death of her husband, was eager to hear.[66]

From good to better. In *Il Barbiere di Siviglia* he had an unqualified success; the *sfumature* with which he decorated 'Ecco ridente' were thought to be in the most refined taste. After unanimous approval of the 'Serenata' (Se il mio nome) and of the duets with Figaro (Ramón Blanchart), four curtain calls concluded the act. He also ingratiated himself with the theatre management by agreeing to substitute at short notice for Signoretti in *La Gioconda* on December 1st, earning him reconfirmation for 1888-9 and revealing to the Madrilenos some previously unsuspected talents as a dramatic tenor.[67] De Lucia,

> ... thought by all to be a tenor of *mezzo carattere*, or even *leggiero*, last night convinced [us] at a stroke that he was more a dramatic tenor than many others of high artistic reputation.[68]

After *Mefistofele* his next hurdle was *La Favorita*, in which - despite inevitable comparisons with Gayarre, the 'Nightingale of Navarre' - he was well received. He had five calls with Pasqua after Act IV, where he showed

> ... delicacy, flexibility and sweetness in the romanza, and energetic and brilliant tones in the duet.[69]

His treatment of a more slender part, that of Danilowitz in Meyerbeer's *La Stella del Nord*, was commended for exquisite phrasing in the aria 'Così detta dei pasticcetti!' But the reviews were almost an irrelevance as, ever eager for novelty, opera-goers looked forward to the arrival of Patti from Paris, where she was reported to have spent two days trying on the clothes and the 60 costumes that would fill 44 trunks for her forthcoming tour of South America. This level of comment typified the view of the press which, after such eager anticipation of her arrival and the novelty of her début, was soon reduced to filling space with articles dwelling on - and exaggerating - her age and urging her to

---

65 *Imparcial*, Nov. 5 1887.
66 *Epoca*, Nov. 12 1887.
67 Ibid., Dec. 2 1887.
68 *Gazzetta dei Teatri*, Dec. 8 1887.
69 *Imparcial*, Dec. 30 1887.

retire. But Patti knew the value of the publicity that enabled her to command 12,500 pesetas a performance, when Marconi had been refused 5,000. At her début, on February 4th, the opera - most exceptionally - was front-page news. Descriptions of her inclusion of Arditi's 'Il bacio' in *Linda di Chamounix* occupied more press space than notices of her Linda. Moreover, the fact that they wrote only of her, ignoring De Lucia, Fabbri, and the rest of the cast, suggested that Donna Adelina was still the most newsworthy of singers; even a decade later, more objective critics than the vitriolic breed of Madrid were still finding much to delight them. And De Lucia, conscious of sharing the stage with a soprano who had sung with Giuglini and Mario, and with Alboni, Nilsson, and Titiens, an artist among the greatest of that or of any other age, may have found it hard to resent the omission.

Subsequently, De Lucia and Patti sang together in *Il Barbiere, La Traviata*, and *Rigoletto*. In the *Rigoletto* of February 21st the critics again stressed the decay of Patti's vocal powers; De Lucia, however, pleased greatly in the love duet, and he repeated 'La donna è mobile'.

In a private musical event he sang at Court for the Queen; shortly afterwards came the announcement of his decoration as Cavalier (Caballero) of the Order of Isabella Cattolica.[70]

The season was over and he found himself at leisure, albeit involuntary, when an engagement for the Politeama of Palermo did not materialise.[71] Soon after, his availability from May to August was announced, but no engagements have been traced.[72]

Instead, there was time to spend with his family and to revisit old haunts, an entire summer to renew acquaintances in the extraordinary musical world of Naples.

---

[70] The Court concert, which cannot be dated precisely, was reported in *Occhialetto*, Feb. 18 1888. The same source also stated that he had been honoured with the title of Commander. In fact, the decree elevating him to Caballero was not signed by Queen María Cristina until Mar. 12 1888, and not until Oct. 19 1891 was he made Commander (Comendador) of the same order.

[71] *Occhialetto*, Mar. 24 1888.

[72] *Mondo Artistico*, Mar. 29 1888.

5

Naples and her Songs

That was the time in which Naples dreamed as her great artists, her fanciful painters, sculptors and poets dreamed; and in so great a variety of expression one form prevailed ... : song. In those days they sang all over Naples: ... It was the time which, more than any other, was dominated by the aesthetic and melodious enchantment of Posillipo, where from every silver beach, traced by boats and wandering torches, from every terrace, from every merry and festive group of trippers, from every still and pensive pair of lovers rose in the air a voice, now like a cry of love, now like a murmur of voluptuous rapture in song ..... Times long ago, dreamed rather than lived.

Enrico De Leva, 'Ricordo di Mario Costa'[1]

From Naples, the coast sweeps westwards from Santa Lucia to Mergellina. Here, where the mountains meet the sea, is Piedigrotta, for centuries the site of a shrine to Venus; in the Christian era the fishermen rededicated it to the Madonna, whose church of S. Maria now stands nearby. This sanctuary is the heart of the most famous of all Neapolitan feasts, that of the Madonna of Piedigrotta, the Festival of Festivals, celebrated at this spot for more than five hundred years.

Setting aside the legends which depict Piedigrotta simply as a place of pagan revelry, the custom of celebrating the nativity of the Madonna each September 7th began around the middle of the fifteenth century. Sovereigns, princes, and ministers went to give thanks at the little shrine for blessings received during the year; their gilded carriages passed in procession, preceded by bands and detachments of soldiers and accompanied by fireworks and naval salvoes from ships in the bay, while the festivities were enjoyed by thousands, drawn by the occasion from every city in the kingdom. After the departure of the royal family on the night of the feast, the merrymakers would dance in the grotto, illuminated by torches, and would sing the songs currently in favour. Certain songs came to be associated with the event, and new ones were written for it, but not until 'Te voglio ben assaie' (1839) was the term 'Songs of Piedigrotta' first used. Many early collections of 'Neapolitan songs' are transcriptions of traditional melodies whose origins and composers are unknown. The new songs and those still popular from

---

[1] 'Ricordo di Mario Costa', *Roma della Domenica*, Oct. 3 1933 (a Naples weekly), quoted in Di Massa, *Il Café-chantant e la Canzone a Napoli*, p. 259.

earlier years banished boredom while convivial crowds, drinking copious quantities of wine, awaited the opening of the sanctuary.

Although the formal celebrations at Piedigrotta vanished with the departure of the Bourbons the songs continued to appear. There was, however, a marked preference for the older melodies, notably of Florimo and Cottrau, and the songs originating in the immediate post-Bourbon period are now almost unknown.

In 1876, on the initiative of a newspaper wholesaler, Luigi Capuozzo, the festival was revived. The lack of royal and military patronage was no obstacle to this resourceful entrepreneur; make-believe sovereigns and troops, recruited from the news-stands of all Naples, travelled on the wagons bearing the allegorical tableaux of that first Piedigrotta of modern times, to the accompaniment of songs describing the ancient folklore of the feast, or celebrating the subject of individual floats.

The true Piedigrotta of the songs may be traced from the birth of the *caffè-concerto* or *café-chantant*. Long before the birth of today's bar, the café was an important social element of everyday life. In Naples, it was an open-air microcosm of all but the poorest classes. Businessmen at any time of day; teachers at the end of the scholastic hour; professionals between visits; artists and writers; tourists from every land; the retired; students; the crowd that daily invaded Naples from the suburbs; aristocrats and *viveurs* in the evenings; officialdom and the *demi-monde* at the hour of aperitif or tea: all were to be found in the café. Attracted by the ambience, citizens of all categories were wont to linger over their coffee - said to be consumed in Naples in greater quantities than in any other city - for light conversation, assignations, business talk, and for a thousand other reasons, not excluding pure pleasure. Naples, like most great cities of the period, was rich in cafés and beerhouses; moreover, for much of the year its climate lent itself to the placing of tables on footpath or adjacent square. In the summer, life moved into the open where a water ice or glass of beer offered relief in the great heat.

The public that crammed these places of refreshment was an ideal audience for the songs, written in increasing numbers for the swelling ranks of singers, and the general enthusiasm for them induced some proprietors to arrange for the songs to be performed when their premises were at their most crowded, especially after the cares of the day. The audience, initially the habitués of the café, appreciated the entertainment, accepted the higher prices of the fare, and made donations when the artists came round with the plate.[2] The initiative had rapid and wide success; from the street and from the lowliest retreats of the labourers and artisans the songs passed to small stages in the more important places of public resort. The Caffè del Commercio is said to have led the way in demanding a modest entrance fee. Thus, the

---

2 Di Massa, *Il Café-chantant*, pp. 31-2.

outpouring of new songs spawned the *café-chantant*, whose proprietors turned to the *posteggiatori*, the performers best prepared to display them; they, wheeling their cylinder pianos from café to street to tavern, in turn disseminated the new compositions throughout the city.

During the spring and summer months, from San Giuseppe to San Martino, the immense, resonant sea-shell of Naples echoed to the sound of *'e ccanzone* in the open. From the Birreria Strasburgo in Via Foria and the Caffettuccio in Via Costantinopoli, hard by the Conservatorio San Pietro a Maiella, to the richly-ornamented establishments of the Galleria Umberto, which opened in 1890, and to numerous other places of refreshment, the *café-chantant* acquired dignity, consistency, and favour at every level of society. Gradually, it became customary to present groups of new compositions in the afternoons and evenings of September 7th, 8th, or 9th. From 1891, these events spread to the more important theatres of variety of the city - the Masaniello, the Eden, and the Rossini - always on the same three days. Still later, they were featured in normal theatrical performances in August and September.

In all this the leading music-publishing houses played a prominent rôle. Open-air song competitions had taken place as early as 1848 but they were not formalised until 1877, when Luigi Chiurazzi, poet, bookseller, and publisher of the newspaper *Spassatiempo*, organised a competition for the best setting of the poem 'Dimane po facimmo sto servizio', by Lucia Riughizzi, a pseudonym for Chiurazzi himself. The entries were to be judged by Lauro Rossi, Director of the Music Conservatory. The example set was enough to stimulate the commissioning of songs by newspapers and magazines such as *Don Marzio, Fortunio*, and *Occhialetto* throughout the eighties and nineties.

In 1880, the Neapolitan song took a decisive turn when Luigi Denza, already an established and prolific composer of songs ('romanzas'), set some verses written by the journalist Peppino Turco to celebrate the opening of the Vesuvius funicular railway.[3] 'Funiculì, funiculà', with its infectious melody and crackling rhythm, spread like wildfire to every continent, selling untold thousands of copies to the profit of Ricordi, who had been publishing popular songs in Naples since taking over the business of the Clausetti brothers, Pietro and Lorenzo, in 1864. It was the first great triumph of what was to become a hugely successful idiom, and marked the birth of the modern Neapolitan song.

If the musical impact of Denza had been great, of even greater influence on the verse, from 1882, was Salvatore di Giacomo, '... the most limpid voice of Naples ... a plant which was to bear the most delightful fruit, the most tender flowers, sweet perfumes and previously unheard beauties in our poetry and song.'[4] 'Nannì!', to music that the young

---

3 Starting in 1889 four funicular lines were also built in Naples.
4 De Mura, *Enciclopedia della Canzone Napoletana*, Vol. I, p. xx.

P. Mario Costa wrote (it is said) in the Caffè di Napoli, was the first of a long line of Di Giacomo successes for Piedigrotta. Costa was to set many more Di Giacomo poems: 'Oilì, oilà', sponsored by *Occhialetto* for the Piedigrotta of 1886, proved irresistible to a populace which braved the cholera to hear it sung both in the Caffè d'Europa and in the gardens of the Villa Comunale, the splendid public gardens which stretch beside the bay from Piazza Vittoria to Mergellina.[5] In his conservative suits, Panama hat at its characteristic angle, Di Giacomo was a familiar figure in this little world of the *fin-de-siècle*. And he was as well-known in the streets and taverns of Naples, the inspiration for much of his writing, as he was to the publishers and editors of the score of newspapers and magazines to which he at various times contributed. By common consent, as a Neapolitan dialect poet he stands supreme. It is ironic that the most widely-known work in his prodigious output is the poem which, set by Tosti, lives on in a song, 'Marechiare', that Di Giacomo came to loathe. He prophesied - correctly - that it would follow him to the grave.[6]

With Di Giacomo as an example, other poets turned to the new genre: the fertile and dynamic Ferdinando Russo (1866-1927); the elegant and witty Roberto Bracco (1858-1943); the introspective and poverty-stricken Giovanni Capurro (1859-1920), poet of ' 'O sole mio', much of whose best work saw the light of day only long after his death. The next generation brought the prolific and versatile Libero Bovio (1883-1942), a poet whose view of Naples hovered between dream and reality, and whose love of his native city shines in every stanza.

Amid the dialect compositions, Neapolitan composers such as Costa, De Leva (1867-1955), Denza, Leoncavallo (1857-1919), and Mugnone (1858-1941), wrote many beautiful romanzas. Verses by Neapolitan poets such as the creative Rocco Pagliara, who had worked with Florimo and, in 1888, succeeded him as Librarian at San Pietro a Maiella, provided composers such as Tosti (1846-1916) with verses for some of their happiest inspirations.[7] Pagliara was also an opera librettist, renowned art collector, music critic for the newspaper *Mattino* and, under the name Mario Perla, a composer. Overwhelmed in their day by the triumphant march of the *canzone in dialetto*, the singular delicacy and fragrance of songs such as Tosti's 'Aprile' and 'Malìa', and Denza's 'Torna', all to verses by Pagliara, have always appealed to discriminating audiences.

In 1892, the song competition advanced another step. Ferdinando Bideri (1851-1930), publisher of *napoletana* since 1818 and founder, in 1891, of the weekly literary-artistic-musical magazine *Tavola Rotonda*, lent the weight of his powerful organisation (which later absorbed such influential Neapolitan publishing houses as Gennarelli, Gill, Santa Lucia

---

[5] Franco Schlitzer, *Salvatore di Giacomo*, p. 685n.

[6] The background to the song is given in Chapter 20. The tune was played at his funeral.

[7] Denza (1846-1922) and Pagliara (1857-1914) were actually from nearby Castellammare, and Costa (1858-1933) from Taranto. All, however, are considered Neapolitan by training and adoption.

and Santojanni) to an annual competition. The first such *Piedigrotta La Tavola Rotonda* attracted an entry of 81, with the prize of 200 lire being taken by ' 'O pumpiere', by Pasquale Cinquegrana and Eduardo Di Capua. At the rehearsals for *mattinate*, given by *Tavola Rotonda* to unveil its new songs, singers of the reputation of De Lucia and Elvira Donnarumma would be accompanied by song composers as noted as Enrico Cannio and Enrico De Leva.[8]

Not to be outdone, Bideri's rivals, Neapolitan or otherwise, promoted their own competitions, mounted auditions, and each year produced handsome booklets of their new songs for Piedigrotta. Thus, to name but a few, arose Piedigrotta La Canzonetta, Piedigrotta Ricordi, and eventually Piedigrotta Polyphon, as the German pianoforte and musical instrument-maker, under the local guidance of Russo, established itself in the lucrative business of Neapolitan songs. This it did by the unprecedented means of paying monthly stipends of 125-250 lire to its authors, in return for one song per month. In so doing at a time (1910) when 5 lire a day could provide a living, it drew upon itself the charge of industrialising the song which had once belonged to Naples alone.

Nothing was too insignificant, or too serious, to provide inspiration for the poet; songs were written on subjects as diverse as the funicular railway or the subtleties of a cup of coffee, the *sventramento* or the state visit of the Emperor and Empress of Germany. Nor did authors and composers hesitate to dedicate their work to their mistresses, to singers, or to members of the Royal Family of Italy. So it is that the name of Donna Nina Arcoleo, wife of the lawyer and politician Giorgio Arcoleo and a woman described as the most beautiful in Naples, lives on through Di Capua's ' 'O sole mio'. Just as it did when it took first prize at the *Concorso La Tavola Rotonda* in 1898, every copy of this song published by the heirs of Bideri carries its dedication to Nina, the gracious spirit of a salon frequented by musicians, painters, politicians, and writers.

Not only the songs but also the associated ephemera bear testimony to the astonishing vitality of Naples in those years. The covers of the sheet music of the period are minor masterpieces of art. In their romanticised but always delicate, ingratiating, and evocative designs we might see a slim and lovely girl playing the mandolin beneath an orange tree, a luncheon party *all'aperto* on a dream-like terrace overlooking the sea at Posillipo, or a group of peasants dancing the *tarantella*, while the cone of Vesuvius smokes in the distance. And these striking covers were not fortuitous, for the substantial profits of the publishers could well support the services of artists such as Enrico Rossi and Pietro Scoppetta, highly accomplished and specialised craftsmen who could bestow a blend of line and colour perfectly suggestive of their theme, whether the lemon groves of Sorrento or the vitality of a flower girl.

---

8 Di Massa, *Il Café-chantant*, p. 170.

In this setting, the popularity of the songs was all-pervasive. As September approached, snatches of the new *canzonette* would be heard on the lips of carters and fishermen, as well as of *posteggiatori*. In Neapolitan folklore the cycle would culminate on a cloudless, starlit night. The sea, bright as polished crystal, would reflect the volcano, with its column of smoke, and the glitter of lights as tens of thousands enjoyed the festival until far into the morning hours. Coloured lanterns waved on poles, gleaming warmly on the copper pots of the vendors of snail soup or fried fish. Around great iron stoves the smell of roasting chestnuts and baking pizza scented the air. Garlands of paper flowers festooned the barrows of the lemonade and sulphur-water sellers, with their slabs of melting ice. As a further solace to the throat, parched by heat and dust, mountains of melons and figs tempted the *soldi* from the pockets of the merry-makers along the road to the grotto. A great noise, a booming roar, arose from the trumpets, wooden mallets, large shells, and *putipù*,[9] sounded by men and boys.

At midnight, the procession of floats began. Each would stop outside the grotto for its occupants to sing their new songs, while the crowds stamped and cheered. All night long the music continued until, before the stars faded from the sky, the prizes in the various competitions were awarded.

If, as is probable, De Lucia spent at least part of the spring and summer of 1888 in Naples, he would have found himself in the midst of the most fruitful period of the Neapolitan song. A walk to revisit his old teachers at the Conservatory would have been to the reverberation, in the narrow alleys, of ' 'A retirata', 'Luna nova', ' 'O Munasterio' and 'Scètate', last year's successes, sung and whistled by the street urchins, the *scugnizzi*.[10] Former fellow-students ready to congratulate him on his rapid progress certainly included Enrico De Leva, a student of only 21 but already with several successful songs to his credit. He had just completed his setting of Di Giacomo's 'Lacreme amare' and, perhaps in admiration but possibly with an eye to the advantages of a performance - in influential company, even - by a rising artist, he dedicated it to the tenor.[11] Such may also have been the case with other songs dedicated to De Lucia: Nunzio Cosentino's ' 'Ammore è tuosseco', published (1894) by the magazine *Fortunio*;[12] Daniele Napoletano's setting (1897) of Di Giacomo's 'Furtunata'; and 'Di Te!' (Antonio Fogazzaro - Pier Adolfo Tirindelli, 1902). 'Carulina' (Michelino Testa - Vincenzo De Crescenzo), 'Mandulinata', (Gustavo Di Giacomo - Carlo Donato), and 'Palummella'

---

[9] A drum with a perforated skin, though which a stick is worked up and down.

[10] A century later they remain among the most durable songs of the period. That all were by Mario Costa, the first three to verses by Di Giacomo, is evidence of the dominant position of these two men.

[11] De Leva's later compositions included the opera *La Camargo*.

[12] 'Ammore mio' by Cosentino's son, Alfonso, is to verses by a Giuseppe De Lucia, possibly the tenor's father.

(Teodoro Rovito - Giuseppe De Crescenzo) made their appearance at the Piedigrotta of 1900, and all were dedicated to De Lucia. 'Il Marinaro canta', by his son Nadir De Lucia, to words by Bianca Franci (1919), is the last traceable obeisance. No doubt there were others.

Such accolades came also from the famous. Tosti dedicated at least two songs - 'Per morire' (1893) and 'Solo!' (1900) - to De Lucia. Costa, another product of the Naples Conservatory, had rapidly established himself as not only the leading composer of Neapolitan songs but also as an accomplished singer, in his 'vocina, his tenor-mosquito'. Conspicuously successful, he was surrounded at every social function by an adoring audience of beautiful women. By 1897, when he dedicated his 'Donn'Antonio 'o cecato' to De Lucia, who was also at the height of his fame, his list of prize-winning songs was impressive and he had little to gain from sycophancy. Riccardo Barthélemy (b. 1869), another fellow Conservatory student and a popular pianist of the salons, was well-established by 1899, when he dedicated 'Triste ritorno' to De Lucia. Salvatore Gambardella (1871-1913), composer of the enduring ''O marenariello' (1893), had written dozens of successful songs when, in 1905, the words 'Al Divo De Lucia' appeared on the cover of his 'Nun me guardate cchiù', to words by Ferdinando Russo. Similarly, the unprepossessing Ernesto De Curtis (1875-1937), his small circular spectacle lenses misted by the smoke curling from the inevitable cigarette, had no need of further fame when, in 1904, De Lucia accepted the dedication of his 'Voce 'e notte', to words by the eloquent poet and brilliant humorist Edoardo Nicolardi.[13] Ernesto already had to his account one immortal success, 'Torna a Surriento', to verses by his brother, Giambattista De Curtis. A musician who was better known as a poet, Giambattista (1860-1926) was passionate in his love of Sorrento, whose enchanting beauty inspired him to live a great part of his life in its Hotel Tramontano. There, he painted frescos and canvasses and wrote his fresh and spontaneous verses and music; in songs such as 'Carmela' and ' 'A surrentina' it is eternally spring.[14]

De Lucia never forgot these friendships of his youth or his early associations with the songs of Naples. When, in another century, he made records, almost one quarter of them spoke of his origins. From a legacy of napoletana greater than that of any other operatic singer we know both the classics of the repertory and the more transient successes - the lilting 'Serenata a Surriento', the melancholy 'Luna, lù!', and the almost forgotten 'Lu cardillo', songs neglected by most or all of the operatic singers who recorded the better-known examples in such profusion. In the close-knit musical world of Naples he probably knew most, if not all, of their authors and composers and, since his earliest

---

13 Pen-name C.O. Lardini.
14 De Mura, Poeti Napoletani dal '600 ad oggi, p. 191.

recordings of their songs were made at a time when he might easily have met almost any of them during a morning walk in the Galleria, his interpretations may be fancied to have unequalled authenticity. To some, even his voice epitomised Naples, evoking 'the murmur of wavelets which lull at dead of night, under the moon on the beach of Posillipo'.[15]

The tenor may even have tried his own hand at composition; unfortunately, of 'Gerolomini terra d'amore', with 'Words and music by Fernando De Lucia', only the verses can now be found.[16] They extol a restaurant, 'Vincenzo a Mare', at Pozzuoli. There is no proof that the tenor wrote the piece, but it is known that he used to take the spa waters in the area, spending weekends at the home of his friend Raffaele Esposito.[17] It seems plausible that he wrote this crude advertisement as a favour to the restaurateur.

The enthusiasm, the naïve sincerity of another epoch is illustrated by an anecdote related by Emilio De Gogorza, who was once present at a gathering of Neapolitan musicians, centred around De Lucia, or 'Don Fernando', the title with which, even now, the Spanish heritage of Naples accords respect to an eminent citizen. The ageing but 'still flamboyant' tenor had just sung one of Denza's romanzas when the composer rushed up to him and, kissing him full on the lips, exclaimed *'Tu sei divino'*.[18]

At its best, the Neapolitan song is an inspired combination of the most delicate of dialect poetry with the music of composers classically trained by the best schools of Italy, notably by San Pietro a Maiella itself. Its words speak as directly now as they did then, and its melodies, a century old and more, are fresh and vibrant as if they had sprung only yesterday from the imagination of their authors. Their unity, the inseparability of text and melody, gives to such songs a singular character, style, and purity. Though echoing the popular tone they are often distinguished by a refinement which transcends the limits of popular song. As such, their summary dismissal by some critics seems unjust. The impenetrability of the vernacular apart, they seem almost to have been a victim of their own tunefulness and popularity. Their originality, however, testifies to the blissful inspiration of an unrecapturable - and simpler - time.

Describing an audition of Neapolitan songs at the Teatro Costanzi, Rome, in 1884, Matilde Serao, under the name 'Chiquita', wrote of 'Napulitanata', by Di Giacomo and Costa:

> Listen to those words and that music. They are so amorous and insinuating and tender, they have in them so much of the unforgettable poetry of Naples, that they make the eyes weep the burning tears of nostalgia.[19]

---

15 *Corriere di Napoli*, May 2 1895.

16 (BLP) Published by Tipi F. Feola. No other Fernando De Lucia is known.

17 Roberto Esposito. Gerolomini is an area of Pozzuoli.

18 Max de Schauensee, loc. cit.

19 Schlitzer, op. cit., p. 62.

6

Virtuoso

Whenever individuality is not mere eccentricity there is always interest in it -
there is always the chance of that interest becoming a charm.

H.F. Chorley, *Thirty Years' Musical Recollections*

As De Lucia set out once more for Madrid in the autumn of 1888 the
tempo of his career quickened again. The summer had held its tragedies
for, on August 4th, with Fernando away from Salerno, Itala had had a
daughter, christened Maria, who was stillborn.

The season of 1888-9 brought De Lucia true artistic recognition by
both management and public of the Teatro Real, for he was to open the
season there. Further, in his pocket was a contract with Ciacchi and
Rainieri for South America the following summer. For four months of
work he was to receive 150,000 lire.[1]

After some delay, while electric lighting was installed in the Real, on
November 10th he opened the season in *La Gioconda*, with Elena
Teodorini, Emma Leonardi, and Delfino Menotti. He was adjudged to
have '...returned to us even better than last year [having made] truly
great progress'.[2] Another critic wrote:

> De Lucia, in the opinion of many, engages in the fad of imitating Stagno in his
> postures and movements but he retains, and improves, his good school of
> singing [and] his humility (which is considerable).[3]

In an apparent criticism of the fees paid to operatic singers - albeit
that De Lucia was one of its own subscribers - *Occhialetto* noted acidly
that he had declined to repeat 'Cielo e mar', '...the artist not being in the
habit of wasting breath uselessly. He is right, now that tenors are paid a
cachet for a single breath.'[4]

He had to be persuaded to undertake his next rôle, that of Elvino in

---

1 Then about £6,000, or $29,000. We must, however, take published accounts of fees *cum grano salis*.
Figures were often manufactured, with the connivance of the impresario, to spread abroad an exaggerated
sense of a singer's value.

2 *Gazzetta Musicale di Milano*, Nov. 25 1888.

3 *Imparcial*, Nov. 11 1888.

4 *Occhialetto*, Nov. 24 1888.

La Sonnambula.[5] Though the press affected surprise, his reluctance is understandable given the virtual certainty that he would be overshadowed by Emma Nevada as Amina;[6] this Marchesi pupil, already very popular in Madrid, had made her London début in the part, in which she came to be particularly celebrated.[7] The reviews now reflected that fame, praising her attention to the smallest details and the expressiveness of her 'Ah, non credea mirarti'.[8]

But De Lucia, as Elvino, had his greatest success so far at the Real. Attacking the most difficult and taxing passages with assurance and skill, he was tender and sentimental in the duet 'Prendi, l'anel ti dono', where his vocal inflections were described as infinitely graceful and tender. In the second act finale his accents were 'heart-rending'.[9] Another critic marvelled:

> The part bristles with difficulties, and it is almost impossible to avoid them all. They are found in the first act duet ['Prendi, l'anel ti dono'] and in the aria ['Ah! perchè non posso odiarti'], where the tenor must phrase on very high notes, without orchestra to lean on or chorus to save him. De Lucia overcame the hurdles.[10]

Others remarked that he did much more than *donner la réplique* when he sang; he was a phenomenon who monopolised and absorbed the interest of the public. He embodied the part, drawing from it all its tender poetry and communicating it to the listeners in touching accents which won them over completely;[11] in the second act he rose to extraordinary heights as singer and artist.[12] He showed serenity and mastery in the most difficult and culminating phrases, and gained applause and shouts of 'Bravo', especially in the third act aria.[13]

His Elvino was thought by some to have been the most perfect since Mario.[14] Indeed, in tackling a part that had belonged to him, to Rubini, and to so many other great and important tenors, De Lucia had shown that he was no longer a *tenorino* but a singer who need have no fear in *il gran repertorio*.[15] Nevada is quoted as having, during rehearsals, described him as the best Elvino who had ever sung with her.[16]

The following day he wrote to Negri:

---

5 *Occurencias*, quoted in *Gazzetta dei Teatri*, Dec. 13 1888.

6 *Née* Emma Wixom, Nevada (1859-1940) took her stage name from her birthplace near Nevada City, California.

7 Blanche Marchesi, *Singer's Pilgrimage*, p. 39.

8 *Gazzetta dei Teatri*, Dec. 6 1888.

9 *Voz de la Patria*, quoted in *Gazzetta dei Teatri*, Dec. 13 1888.

10 *Pais*, quoted in *Gazzetta dei Teatri*, Dec. 13 1888.

11 *Epoca*, Nov. 26 1888.

12 *Imparcial*, Nov. 26 1888.

13 *Izquierda Dinastica*, quoted in *Gazzetta dei Teatri*, Dec. 13 1888.

14 *Estandarte*, quoted in *Gazzetta dei Teatri*, Dec. 13 1888.

15 *Correo*, quoted in *Gazzetta dei Teatri*, Dec. 13 1888.

16 *Epoca*, Nov. 26 1888.

Madrid, November 26th, 1888

My dear Maestro:

Last night I sang *La Sonnambula* for the first time, with the celebrated
Nevada, and I assure you that I had a colossal, unforgettable success. Nevada
herself, like the public and the press, judged me the ideal Elvino, unique in art
today. They praise me to the skies and tell me that I am a master of the Italian
school, and especially the Neapolitan. I have given you this information
knowing how much you wish me well. . . .

Commendatore Fernando De Lucia[17]

His records from *La Sonnambula*, especially the duets with Galvany
[Nos. 58 and 59] must be reckoned among those in which De Lucia is
incomparable, in the strict sense of that word. In their tenderness, their
freedom, their shaping, and their exquisite vocalisation and limpid tone
they perfectly suggest the sentimental character of Elvino. In 'Prendi,
l'anel ti dono' [No. 58] the swiftness and perfection of the turns on words
such as *'gentil'* is characteristic of this tenor; the way he lingers on *'un
Dio'* is inimitable: they are the hallmarks of masterly vocal control.

His next part was Almaviva, to the Rosina of Emma Nevada. The keen
public anticipation was reflected in the prices asked for tickets. Even
Queen Cristina, who generally enjoyed her music in the privacy of the
Palace, made a rare visit to the theatre for the occasion. Hence, the
disappointment was all the greater at the realisation that Nevada was
not really suited to the part. Only the inclusion of the 'romanza' from *La
Perla di Brasile* justified the usual rain of flowers at the Lesson Scene.
By contrast, the tenor was very well received, drawing favourable
comment on his exquisite style in 'Ecco ridente' which, to frantic
applause, he repeated. With equal facility he delivered the serenade 'Se
il mio nome', to which he added 'a cadenza of much taste and of
extraordinary effect'.[18] While Gargano replaced Nevada in later
performances De Lucia continued to win approval, especially in the
difficult passages of the duet with Figaro.

Even in so arduous a season, with many singers falling ill, there was
still time for social activities. There were benefit concerts for visiting
musicians, given at his home by the convivial, hospitable, and ever-
considerate Mancinelli; these splendid events were supported by the
conductor's colleagues from the Real and were attended by ambassadors

17 (SPM) It is not clear why he styles himself Commendatore (Commander); several contemporary Italian
newspapers used this title when he was first decorated with the Order of Isabella Cattolica, even stating that
the 'Honorary title of Commendatore was given to him by the Infanta'. Official Spanish records, however,
confirm that the grade was then only that of Cavalier (Caballero). At any rate, the tenor and the press were
using the title of 'Commendatore' for some years before the Queen of Spain formally invested him in that
grade (Comendador), in October 1891; so proud was he of the distinction that *'Il Commendatore'* later became
almost a nickname in Naples.

18 *Gazzetta dei Teatri*, Jan. 10 1889.

and by the élite of society. However, despite such evenings away from the stage, the strain on De Lucia may have started to show. Less than two weeks after the première of *Il Barbiere* came that of *Mignon*, where they noted his increased power and greater discipline;[19] he was scheduled then to sing Danilowitz in *La Stella del Nord* but, probably to afford him some rest before *L'Elisir d'Amore*, he was replaced by Enrico Giannini. De Lucia's voice was judged 'perfectly adapted to the *tessitura*' of the Donizetti work, but the honours were taken by the *buffo* Antonio Baldelli, and by Gargano, who interpolated into the finale of the opera a 'Bolero' by Bottesini.[20]

Barely a week after making his bow as the rustic Nemorino, on February 2nd he sang his second new part of the season, Idreno, in what was evidently a realistic production of *Semiramide*. There was a minor disturbance in the stalls when, at the appearance of the ghost of Nino, Emma Leonardi, apparently fearful of some *jettatura*, covered her face with her fan and two or three other women did the same.[21] De Lucia, though, was very much at ease, singing the difficult phrases of 'Là, dal Gange, a te primiero' with an aplomb that won him an encore and, in the third act, restoring the usually-omitted 'La speranza più soave'.[22]

> The honours of the evening were genuinely due to De Lucia, who swept the audience away in the difficult *cavatina* that preceded Assur's departure. He sang it in a masterly manner, with extraordinary vigour and breath control. ... He had to repeat the third act *cavatina*, and attained a new and tumultuous triumph in his singing of a very beautiful aria not previously heard in Madrid.[23]

Next came *Dinorah*, with Marie van Zandt, whose remarkable facility above the stave - including a reported trill on E *in alt* - took most of the attention.[24]

His final opera of the season, Petrella's *I Promessi Sposi*, reached the stage on March 21st. Adjectives applied to the work by the critics included 'arid', 'monotonous' and 'vulgar'. De Lucia, who sang the part of Renzo '*con amore*', won most of the applause, especially after his fourth act aria, but all the efforts of the artists could not save the opera.[25]

Early in April he again set sail for Buenos Aires. For the 1889 season at the Politeama, Ciacchi, with Abbey and Grau, had assembled a company which, in addition to Vittorio Arimondi, Ramón Blanchart, De Lucia, Guerrina Fabbri, Giulio Rossi, and Eva Tetrazzini, boasted the presence of Patti, for her second consecutive season under their management. She did not travel with the rest of the company, preferring

---

19 *Epoca*, Dec. 30 1888.
20 Ibid., Jan. 24 1889.
21 *Imparcial*, Feb. 3 1889.
22 *Gazzetta dei Teatri*, Feb. 21 1889.
23 *Imparcial*, Feb. 3 1889.
24 *Epoca*, Feb. 8 1889.'
25 *Epoca* and *Imparcial*, Mar. 22 1889.

to make her own way via Bordeaux.[26] Never one to overlook the value of
a good press agent, she became, inevitably, the centre of attention in
Buenos Aires. She was even the subject of an elaborate April Fool prank,
when many prominent people received invitations to attend a non-
existent *soirée* at her house.

Against Ciacchi were arrayed the forces of Ferrari, including
Battistini, De Negri, Eugenia Mantelli, Masini, Teodorini and Fanny
Toresella, marshalled at the Teatro de la Opera under the baton of
Marino Mancinelli. Ferrari had, however, been denied Tamagno, who
had refused his offer of 750,000 lire and had demanded one million. Each
management enjoyed a handsome subsidy, giving many a subscriber
pause to wonder why ticket prices should be so high. In fact, each had
spent heavily on his respective theatre. Ciacchi was the first to unveil his
improvements; the Politeama, redecorated and refurbished, with new
stage curtains and with its old-fashioned chairs replaced by comfortable
fauteuils, presented a cheerful aspect for the subscribers when the
season opened with *Aida* on April 7th.

In spite of the rain, mud, and cold - usually enough to keep many of
the opera-goers of Buenos Aires at home - rows of carriages lined the
streets outside as all society came to the rejuvenated Politeama to hear
Patti, as Violetta, on her début on April 9th. In a house that was 'without
o'erflowing, full', the audience greeted her as a favourite; the unrivalled
freshness and beauty of a voice which was still perfectly under control
again won her the affection of all.[27] She followed this success with less
tangible ones in *Lucia di Lammermoor* (with Nicolini), and *Dinorah*.

In a house crowded from top to bottom, De Lucia made his début on
May 2nd, in *La Gioconda*, with Eva Tetrazzini, Blanchart and both
Fabbris. A critic much given to vivid writing exclaimed:

> ... the splendid voice of [Guerrina] Fabbri was heard to great advantage [as La
> Cieca] in the first act, but her makeup [was] needlessly repulsive. The efforts of
> De Lucia were violently applauded, but his metallic voice and marionette style
> of acting will never appeal favourably to a British sense of art.[28]

But most of the reviews reflected the Latin taste which had produced a
hurricane of applause on his very appearance on the stage. The critic of
Censor, recalling the callow youth of three years ago, remarked on the
immense change in someone whose style of singing and phrasing now
recalled that of Stagno; one could not, he insisted, imagine 'Cielo e mar'
being sung with greater taste and delicacy:

> His ascendency started in the first act duet with Barnaba, which was repeated;
> his success was brilliant, and only after hearing him now can we understand

26 (LCML) Edwin Tribble, 'The Prima Donna as Goddess'.
27 *Standard*, Apr. 11 1889.
28 Ibid., May 4 1889.

and explain to ourselves all the praise of the Madrilenos. Today, De Lucia figures among the first tenors of the time and is worthy to stand beside Masini and Gayarre.[29]

Generally, he was thought deserving of the applause. The critics took care to distinguish between genuine enthusiasm and that of the noisy, intemperate, infuriating *claque* which several times incensed the true enthusiasts.

On May 7th, the Politeama was the setting for the second performance of *Il Barbiere di Siviglia*, in which De Lucia replaced De Bassini as Almaviva. The theatre was crammed, the feminine element resplendent in its finery. Although the audience's interest was principally in Patti, De Lucia also found favour for a captivating voice; he sang 'Ecco ridente' very well. Again came the comparisons:

> De Lucia, with his superior artistic gifts, has aroused the admiration of the public. They say that he imitates Stagno; if this were said of *La Gioconda*, it can be repeated, and with greater reason, now that he is shown to us in an opera of his *maestro*, the insuperable Lindoro of the lyric stage. In fact, imitation is not perhaps the term one needs to affirm the similarity of the school and method of an artist as talented as De Lucia and one as notable as Stagno, [a similarity] brought about also, perhaps, by the similarity of their quality and by the admiration that the master can inspire in his follower. In *Il Barbiere* De Lucia showed us clearly . . . the delicacy of a throat that allows him to vocalise with astonishing agility.[30]

Others, though, were ready to criticise this perceived mimicry of Stagno, *'l'unico Lindoro'*. Should not, it was murmured, singers of De Lucia's talents be prepared to place their own stamp on their work?[31]

One critic stressed the rare *mezza voce* and the elegance and good taste with which he carved the *cantabile* passages, qualities which were amply demonstrated throughout the opera.[32] His acting, though, was again criticised, some correspondents complaining of the constant smile which gave his features an inane appearance and which caused the audience, also, to smile at what was purely a stage expression.[33] Further, he was felt to lack balance, his acting passing with immoderate ease from excessive gentleness to excessive vigour.[34]

As always, Patti's music in the Lesson Scene was a focus of interest. On June 22nd she started with the *rondo* from *La Sonnambula*. The wild applause, which continued even as the orchestra gave the first notes of 'Home, sweet home', instantly changed to a silence that could almost be

---

29 *Censor*, quoted in *Gazzetta dei Teatri*, June 20 1889.

30 Ibid.

31 *Nazione Italiana*, quoted in *Gazzetta dei Teatri*, June 20 1889.

32 *Nacional*, quoted in *Gazzetta dei Teatri*, June 20 1889.

33 *Standard*, May 9 1889.

34 *Nazione Italiana*, quoted in *Gazzetta dei Teatri*, June 20 1889.

felt as Patti stepped forward. When the last note died away, in a perfect *diminuendo*, to a soft whisper distinctly heard at the farthest part of the house, a 'caramba' escaped the lips of many a stern Argentine.[35]

While the subscribers at the Colón waited for the Ferrari season to open, the Ciacchi company continued, in a sparsely-attended house, with *Don Giovanni*. Mozart, lamented the critic of the *Standard*, had ever lacked appreciation in Buenos Aires. De Lucia, as the anaemic Ottavio, was applauded for his two arias. One critic even claimed that 'Il mio tesoro' was the whole point of the evening; there was, though, no denying that the performance belonged to its Zerlina, Patti.[36]

Except for Masini, for whom a wealthy admirer had fitted out a house in the most luxurious Oriental style, the members of the Ferrari company had now settled into their respective hotels throughout the city, and operatic Buenos Aires was in a ferment of eager anticipation. Signora Ferrari profited substantially from the interest by selling her personal box. On May 16th 1889, society and the Diplomatic Corps heard Masini and Teodorini open the season in *Mefistofele* at the Teatro de la Opera - also renovated - whose acoustics the tenor had pronounced excellent. But not all the subscribers were gratified with the new electric lighting; this novelty, which made the fashionable ladies look pale as sheets, resulted in a theatre temperature at which the subscribers shivered. Moreover, the occupants of the *cazuela* complained that the alterations impaired the view of their admirers in both pit and boxes. Despite these discomforts, though, Ferrari had achieved the ascendancy.

Ciacchi swiftly announced a counter-attraction, a gala performance at the Politeama on May 24th in honour of President Tajes of Uruguay. There began another period of the competition that had so nearly ruined the same impresarios in 1886; by early July the Opera was reported as being half-empty every night, with tickets readily available at greatly-reduced prices at the theatre entrances. The cold of the theatre was held partly responsible; as were frost-bitten journeys in open, horse-drawn, tramcars after the performance, but Italian opera seemed, for the moment, to induce a certain apathy which responded only to a Patti.

Notwithstanding, less than a week after the Ferrari *Mefistofele*, Ciacchi mounted the same opera, with De Lucia and Eva Tetrazzini. In the tenor, the critics noted an ability to give the required colour and accentuation even to the less-important phrases; from the outset, it was clear that the rest of the part of Faust would not be sacrificed to 'Giunto sul passo estremo'. Elegantly costumed, impassioned, interpreting with *élan* phrases which passed almost unnoticed when sung by others, he had a complete triumph.[37]

---

35 Patti also gave 'Home, sweet home' after the *Linda di Chamounix* of June 1.

36 *Patria Italiana*, quoted in *Gazzetta dei Teatri*, July 4 1889.

37 *Censor*, quoted in *Gazzetta dei Teatri*, June 27 1889.

His next opera was *Romeo e Giulietta*, with Gounod's recent additions. From her first bars of music it was clear that Patti's presence would itself have assured a complete success. For the fair-haired Ciacchi, smilingly contemplating the vast theatre, thronged with society and with even the standing-room exhausted, it was a moment of satisfaction.

The opera pleased very much. In the view of the *Standard*, Patti excelled herself. Her irreproachable singing elicited thunderous applause and an encore of the waltz. Her acting was no less excellent, the timid girl and the loving woman being carefully delineated. But the divide between the Anglo-Saxon and the Latin critic was again evident:

> The opera would have been greatly improved had the *diva* been supported by a more able Romeo. It must not, though, be imagined that De Lucia was bad, far from it, he was in fact much better than usual, but the peculiarly metallic timbre of his voice and his jerky style of acting must always militate against his acquirement of a high position among operatic tenors.[38]

The 'Madrigal' ('Angiol regina'), sung by Patti and De Lucia in the first act, set the tone for the evening, with five calls and prolonged applause. The dramatic situation was well developed in their duets, where his acting evidently surpassed hers. In the balcony scene, which culminated in the lovers' first kiss, they created an idyllic atmosphere; the subsequent tenor aria, 'Angelico un sorriso', was sung with great gentleness in a moment which, in its tenderness and mysticism, recalled Stagno's Lohengrin.[39] De Lucia even succeeded in drawing the attention of the public during Patti's more brilliant moments. It was no small feat for a young man, noted one critic, who continued:

> De Lucia is of the school of Stagno, finding [his] effects in rapid changes of the voice and in very agile transitions from *mezza voce* to *falsetto*, and we must agree that he has equalled the master, singing with unparalleled grace and uncommon elegance of method.[40]

On July 2nd the ever-fresh *La Sonnambula* drew a capacity crowd to the Politeama, to hear Patti in one of her favourite parts and to be spellbound by her in the *rondo*. De Lucia was described as a capital Elvino, whose acting reminded the critic of Mario.[41]

Patti's engagement was now nearing its end; indeed, to fulfil her contract with Ciacchi and to depart in time for her English concert tour, she was obliged to sing on as many as three consecutive nights. Her benefit, a miscellaneous programme given on July 6th, was sold out days in advance and hundreds had to be turned away from the box-office. For the three thousand fortunates she sang 'The Last Rose of Summer', both

38 *Standard*, June 15 1889.
39 *Censor*, quoted in *Gazzetta dei Teatri*, Aug. 1 1889.
40 *Patria Italiana*, quoted in *Gazzetta dei Teatri*, Aug. 1 1889.
41 *Standard*, July 4 1889.

in Italian and in English, and 'Ombra leggiera'. In the subsequent interval, on a stage piled high with floral tributes, lackeys came and went with jewel cases which they opened to produce a kaleidoscopic effect of diamonds and other gems, all to the apparent surprise of Patti. She expressed her thanks by singing the Mad Scene from *Lucia*, after which, evidently quite overcome by her reception, she gave no fewer than three encores. The *Standard* doubted whether she ever did as much for any other audience.[42] For the Gala performance of July 9th, attended by the President of the Republic, *La Sonnambula* was repeated and again Patti overshadowed the other singers.

De Lucia's benefit performance was *Romeo e Giulietta* (July 11th). The audience braved a fog worthy of London to hear Patti sing like a nightingale and to see the tenor receive splendid garlands of flowers from her and from Elvira Colonnese, and several valuable presents. The exercise was repeated with *Semiramide*, to the nominal benefit of Guerrina Fabbri; rumour had it, though, that neither she nor De Lucia was any the richer as a result of these events. However, the contralto was the object of a little scene on stage, when Patti kissed her *con effusione* and insisted that she keep all the flowers. Well could Patti afford to be magnanimous as she prepared, amid mounting Argentine inflation, to return to England with £20,000 in bills of exchange. In her *addio* and final *Barbiere*, for which a frenzied public was glad to find tickets even at double their usual price, De Lucia saw Patti called 23 times before the curtain. Then came Ciacchi's turn; during the performance, handbills had been distributed informing the public that he had engaged Tamagno, Maurel, and De Lucia for 1890. From every side came cries of 'Viva Ciacchi!', and the roar, when De Lucia and Patti dragged him on to the stage, made the gas flames dance.

Even in her departure, Patti was no less of an attraction. As the Ciacchi company, bound for Montevideo, left the quayside the onlookers were impressed by a tender, entirely filled with her baggage, steaming towards the *Elbe* in the outer roads.

Ciacchi had taken the Teatro Cibils in Montevideo for a month and had sent many furnishings and decorations from Buenos Aires. His subscription of fifteen performances opened with Tetrazzini and De Lucia in *La Gioconda* on July 25th, a few hours after an infernal machine, intended to blow President Tajes to eternity, had been discovered in the theatre. Coincidentally, it was the same theatre, opera, and principal singers as that of the evening, three years earlier, when an attempt had been made on the life of President Santos.

Montevideo shared the surprise of Buenos Aires at the progress made

---

42 Ibid., July 9 1889. For a detailed account of the stage-managing of such presentations to prima donnas, and particularly for the part played in them by their husbands, see Sutherland Edwards, *The Prima Donna*, Vol. I, pp. 282-6.

by De Lucia in three years. He sang the romanza, 'Cielo e mar', with great delicacy and feeling, yet in the duet with Barnaba attained extraordinary brilliance and showed himself as a tenor of considerable power and range.[43] In the second performance he was in fine voice '...which he manages very cleverly, especially when merging into *falsetto*'.[44] Indisputably, critics wrote, he was a tenor of the first rank; in strengthening the voice he had also invested it with delicate *sfumature* and modulations, revealing himself as a true successor to the great masters of *bel canto*.[45]

Mefistofele, despite disparaging references to the dilapidated scenery and - in so small a theatre - to the limited room for the ballet, was also well received. De Lucia's benefit, *Romeo e Giulietta* on August 22nd, was given in the larger Teatro Nuevo Politeama, taken by Ciacchi for extra performances; some 2,500 people made the tenor the object of great enthusiasm and he received numerous bouquets and gifts. As the Ferrari troupe arrived, Ciacchi closed his season with *La Gioconda* and with the announcement that he had secured the Teatro Solis for 1890.

De Lucia's contract with Ciacchi for next season, with a *cachet* of 200,000 lire, represented a satisfactory increment after a season of solid endeavour. However, comparison with the million, plus 250,000 for two benefit performances, reportedly promised by Ferrari to Masini clearly showed that he had not yet reached the pinnacle of fame.[46]

He returned to Naples in mid-September, with the prospect of a winter at leisure.[47] Once again, he could be the real Neapolitan, the *verace napoletano*, as he was often affectionately described in the highest encomium that one Neapolitan can apply to another. He was now the man-about-town, quite the dandy. Excessively proud of his luxuriant moustache, he declined to shave it for any reason; instead, he would - when unavoidable - conceal it with stage makeup. A similar pride in his hair usually caused him to eschew the use of a wig on stage. Polished in appearance and animated in his mannerisms, he was a familiar sight about the streets and in the *salotti* of Naples. Impeccable in his dress, his studs and tie-pins glinting with jewels, he was a frequent visitor to the Sartoria Caggiula, to be fitted for the suits and coats of a seemingly limitless wardrobe. Always, much in the mould of Stagno, he carried one of the elegant walking-sticks with which one or other of his admirers had presented him.

Naples was a community which, *sventramento* or no, pursued its old ways. In a city where, at unification, ninety per cent of the population

---

[43] *Tribuna Popular*, July 26 1889.

[44] *Express* (a Montevideo daily), July 30 1889.

[45] *Razon*, quoted in *Gazzetta dei Teatri*, Oct. 3 1889.

[46] Klein, *The Reign of Patti*, pp. 246-7, states that, in 1888, Patti was paid £1,600 (40,000 lire) per night, a figure which, he claims, was still (1920) unsurpassed.

[47] In July 1889 *Occhialetto* had noted his reconfirmation for Buenos Aires for 1890 and, apparently for the information of interested managers, his availability for the coming winter.

had been illiterate, the letter-writers mentioned by Dickens still sat with
their century-old paraphernalia under tattered umbrellas beneath the
portico of the San Carlo. The *cantastoria*, or story-singer, still
entertained evening gatherings at the Mole.[48] The Neapolitans
themselves remained as fiery and excitable as ever, masters of a
vernacular which is one of the most expressive known, unintelligible to
foreigners and even to most other Italians.

A feature peculiar to Naples was - and is - the *camorra*. Originally, it
was a union of individuals, formed for mutual support and protection
against rapacious officials, especially of the more repressive Spanish or
Bourbon régimes. From these more-or-less high-minded beginnings it
had evolved into an organisation for the 'protection' of gambling,
prostitution, smuggling, and so forth. With great powers of terrorising
anyone who opposed it, it was the local equivalent of the better-known
Mafia. By grace and favour of the *camorra* alone were trade and
commerce, legitimate or otherwise, conducted. Everywhere, it collected
its tribute. Hardly a boatman, porter, shopkeeper, or carriage-driver
plied his trade without its permission. Every section of the docks, the
markets, and the prisons had its *camorrista*. At every street corner of the
poorer *quartieri* would be an arrogant bully, the *guappo*, in characteristic
broad-bottomed trousers, intimidating, cajoling, battening on the weak.[49]

Nowhere was it easier for the *camorra* to exploit the ignorant than in
their gambling, where it took its share of the winnings as of right. For
gambling is a Southern Italian passion, inextricably bound up with the
superstitions which flourish among ignorance and which pervade the
communities of the *vicoli*.[50] The overwhelming urge to obtain money
without toil makes the Neapolitan an obsessive gambler, for no citizen -
including, reputedly, De Lucia - could imagine playing a game without a
stake. Card games of fashionable French origin were enjoyed by the
aristocracy; noisier were the local games, such as 'Scopa', played by
workmen at midday, with the Neapolitan pack of forty cards. In a society
where a man's rank was judged by the position of his box at the opera
and by the number and splendour of his carriages, the racetrack
provided an opportunity to combine gambling with ostentation, notably
in the 'show drive' to and from the course. And if the society papers
chanced, on the morrow, to mention the first rate equipage and the
ladies' finery, the cup of joy overflowed.

But, for the spectacle of greatest credulity, one must turn to the *lotto*,
the public lottery. Every Saturday, in each of eight principal cities of
Italy, five numbers were drawn from a drum containing the numbers one

---

48 Gunn, op. cit., pp. 185-6.

49 Accounts of the *camorra* may be found in Gunn, op. cit., pp. 217-24, and Collison-Morley, op. cit.,
pp. 166-72. A Neapolitan - and more benevolent - view of the *guappo* is that of Giuseppe Marotta, *The Gold of
Naples*, ch. XI.

50 Clara Erskine Clement, *Naples*, pp. 232-5.

to ninety. The appeal of the *lotto* to the poorest classes lay in that its lowest stake was minute enough to be accessible to all. This, with its prospects of unimaginable wealth, presented a great temptation to steal the small sums required to buy a ticket. With good reason was it termed 'that terrible canker of Italian institutions'.[51]

No city surpassed Naples in its passion for the lottery. Serao wrote powerfully of 'a contagious illness of the spirit', and of how

> ...the Neapolitan population, every week, rebuilds its great dream of happiness, it lives for six days in growing, intrusive hope, which spreads, widens, [and] leaves the confines of reality: for six days the populace dreams its great dream, in which there is everything of which it is deprived, a house purified by cool and healthy air, a ray of sun, warm on the earth ... *macaroni* and meat every day, and a litre of wine ...[52]

Neapolitans rejected the mathematical certainty that one number is just as likely to be drawn as any other. Instead, they resorted to professional *cabalisti*, or diviners who, for a small fee, would supply winning numbers. Another strategy was to ask a monk - for monks are supposedly lucky - for three numbers. But superstition dictated that anyone might divine lucky numbers from circumstance. Each ticket office kept a printed book, the lottery dictionary, where a number was assigned to every conceivable happening and incident.[53] Most Neapolitans, however, knew the principal numbers by heart. For instance, a woman run over in the street by a cab was a clear omen for the onlooker. The woman corresponded to the number 22, cab (empty) to 42, cab with passengers to 78, street to 44, and accident to 17. From these, a Neapolitan witnessing such an event would play a so-called *ambo* of two numbers, or a *terno* of three, rewarding him, respectively, with prizes of three hundred or five thousand times his stake. A *quaterna*, of four numbers, would yield sixty thousand times his stake. If, in his haste to reach the lottery office to register his good fortune in finding such a powerful presage, he took cab no. 5786, this might itself suggest 57 and 86 as an *ambo*, or 5, 7, and 86 as a *terno*. Before 1888, when the old cemetery closed, it was customary for gamblers to count the corpses, in a presumed connection with winning numbers in the lottery. Dreams were considered very significant, as were natural disasters. Dickens suggested that, were the roof of the San Carlo to collapse, so many people would play the numbers attaching in the dictionary, or 'Universal Lottery Diviner', to the accident that the Government would soon close these numbers to avoid the risk of further losses on them.

---

[51] Neville-Rolfe, *Naples in the Nineties*, pp. 12-15.

[52] M. Serao, *Il ventre di Napoli*, 1st ed. See also Serao, *Il Paese di Cuccagna*.

[53] In 1884, the locally-published *Nuova Smorfia pel Giuoco di Lotto* was already in its 24th edition. A century on, the almost 600 pages of the 1985 edition still provide the numbers reputedly associated with events. Other publications record the winning numbers in every drawing of the lottery since September 1682.

A single example from the many stories of the lottery illustrates its hold on public imagination. Any event of importance has its numbers; inevitably, they are played by many who, by the laws of chance, sometimes win. In August 1884 the schools in three districts were closed through fear of cholera, and their numbers were played by the whole town. Prodigious sums were won and the resultant feasting had much to do with the subsequent turning of a minor outbreak into an epidemic.

The cheerful, lively, and humorous De Lucia was, in such matters, entirely Neapolitan. He was an enthusiastic card-player, particularly of baccarat, both at private soirées and at the Circolo Artistico. With close friends, 'Scopa' was a favourite afternoon pastime, for token stakes of 1 soldo.[54] To a friend known to be somewhat unhappy when losing even such small sums he would hand back the money, saying:

'I merely desired to win!'

In the years of his greatest fame and prosperity his coach would frequently take him to the races, to the lottery offices, and even, it is said, to nearby towns to play particular combinations of numbers when the omens were favourable. His preferred number was 90. Holidays at Monte Carlo would include evenings in the Casino - where, like every other player, he had his 'system' - and drives to Ventimiglia, the nearest Italian frontier town, to play the lottery. Since his own fortunes were variable to poor, his gullible and intensely superstitious nature made him easy prey for the tipsters, with their dubious and expensive advice.[55]

On a lighter note, he would impulsively make wagers that were not without their amusing side. When in Naples, he always had his shoes polished by Vincenzo, a bootblack of almost 80 years of age, who plied his trade under the arches of the San Carlo. In broad Neapolitan, De Lucia would tease him, saying:

'*Vicienzo*, life is finished for you, you are past it!'

Once, Vincenzo replied:

'You often say that, but we shall see. I will wager you the price of a girl that I can demonstrate that I am still a good man!'

The tenor accepted the wager. In nearby Via Nardones they found a *casa di tolleranza* where, in the singer's presence, Vincenzo made good his claim and De Lucia had to pay.[56]

---

54 About 5 centesimi, or one twentieth of a lira.

55 Conversations with the De Lucia family and with former friends and acquaintances of the tenor at Naples and Cava de' Tirreni.

56 Luigi de Lillo.

The extent and duration of any serious gaming remains uncertain. In Naples at large he has always been thought of as an inveterate gambler. According to Daspuro, he sometimes staked 12,000-15,000 lire in a week, and this 'ruinous vice' continued even when he had ceased to earn the sizeable fees of his prime years.[57] Even family opinion is divided. Some members insist that his losses were modest, and insufficient to prejudice his position. Others assert that gambling so obsessed him that, when he could not go in person, he would ask an aunt to place his bets; that he would send money to friends who would buy lottery tickets for him in other cities; that his losses were heavy; and that they were reflected in a much-reduced standard of living in his last years. But, as will be seen, there are other possible explanations. There were those of his close friends who believed that De Lucia - by common consent, a shrewd and intelligent man - used supposed gambling as a convenient ruse to conceal from Itala and, more especially, from her family, funds that he needed for his own purposes. By their very nature - irregular and largely untraceable - gaming losses would have been ideal for such a purpose.

In the autumn of 1889, however, he was not to remain idle for long enough to enjoy the distractions of Naples. Within a month he had, 'by mere chance', been found to be available and had been engaged by the impresario Marino Villani for three months and three operas, including *La Regina di Saba*, at the San Carlo, Naples; the first announcement of a fee of 45,000 lire, described as a 'coup' for the management, was later corrected to 75,000 lire, and viewed as 'no small sum'.[58] The contract also gave Villani the option of renewing the engagement the following season. On the posters, De Lucia's name appeared beside that of Gayarre, who was to have opened the season in *Gli Ugonotti*. However, the Spaniard, already stricken by his final illness, did not arrive, and negotiations with Masini to deputise came to nothing. Thus, the theatre opened on December 21st with *Aida*, which inaugurated the cycle of balls, receptions, and parties with which Neapolitan society diverted itself in winter. The social round continued despite an influenza epidemic which produced cartoons and leader columns in the newspapers and which brought to a halt much of the Chiaia and San Ferdinando quarters.

De Lucia, as he plunged into rehearsals, could not have enjoyed much of the abundant social life of the city, nor had time to read the many tributes to Gayarre, who had died in Madrid. But the whole pages devoted to the Spaniard, and the expressions of loss, were accompanied by eulogies on the return of De Lucia and by well-publicised indiscretions on the vocal wonders that he would soon display to the subscribers.

His first performance of the season, in *I Pescatori di Perle*, took place on January 15th 1890. No one present that evening in the San Carlo, its

---

[57] Daspuro, 'Memorie', ch. XXII.
[58] *Occhialetto*, Oct. 26 1889.

gas jets now replaced by electric lamps and its stalls and boxes occupied
by the handsome ladies of Turno C, could have imagined that the city
had more than 100,000 cases of influenza.[59] It was, as the chronicler
remarked, a sign of how Naples, when sufficiently distracted, laughed at
epidemics. The presence of the soprano Félia Litvinne showed that not
even other singers were deterred by the threat to their health, or - since
the ballet *Excelsior* was also to be given - by the prospect of staying in
the theatre until 1.30 am.[60]

There was great curiosity concerning the appearance of Emma Calvé
as Leila, not least among the roués, who would rather have seen her in
something 'more abbreviated than a costume suggestive of a Roman
toga'. Above all, however, both public and critics were eager to hear De
Lucia after an absence of almost five years, and to welcome him as soon
as he appeared.

And, at the end of the evening, it was agreed that the tenor, scarcely
recognisable as the singer of his début, had returned like a conqueror. At
his entrance he made, if not an excellent impression, at least a good one.
The slim, dapper figure, the self-possessed gestures, and the elegant
diction were quickly attractive to an audience already well-disposed
towards a fellow Neapolitan. None the less, the chatter that persisted
throughout the great friendship duet of the first act ('Del tempio al
limitar') was probably the usual social gossip rather than a lively
discussion of his artistic progress.[61] Not until 'Mi par d'udir ancora',
which he repeated, did he engage the full attention of the audience.
When he sang 'Della mia vita', an A natural, held to the limits of his
lungs, brought applause that gained him two encores.[62]

Uda wrote:

What an evening! There was a moment in which I feared that De Lucia would
leap out of his costume before the stalls which were applauding him so
enthusiastically. His entire person shook in nervous exultation, as his face was
transfigured by the radiance of the great ecstatic eyes. One hand, stretched out
convulsively to the hand of Signora Calvé, conveyed the indivisibility of the
triumph, while the other, raised from low to high, or turned with the slowness
of a magical invocation, spread the indescribable elatiɔn of joy aɹd thanks
throughout the crowded room.

In the glorious uproar, everyone must have thought of the *tenorino* whose
début we heard and encouraged ... in a *Faust* of indulgence. To me ... the
transformation ... seemed truly miraculous. The voice has been extended and
strengthened, has acquired timbre and colour and, while the exquisite art of the
singer remains, the cold virtuosity of the concert has already become sentiment
and, almost, passion. One could not believe one's own ears, hearing those warm,
baritonal tones contrasting with the ringing top notes and the tender sighs of

---

59 The subscription was of three *turni*; Turno A, the most fashionable, had the grand opening and most of
the important first performances. Turno C generally included the younger and less wealthy subscribers.

60 *Corriere di Napoli*, Jan. 16/17 1890.

61 In De Lucia's score this duet and 'Mi par d'udir' are marked 'Semitone down'. The annotations are
undated.

62 *Piccolo*, Jan. 16/17 1890.

the middle [range]. De Lucia has finesse and with it the attack, the warmth that penetrates, and the charm that invades. At times he is a little too studied, affected, and mannered, like a momentary reminder of school, the artistic personality still incomplete. One feels in the singing, as in the acting, the long, industrious study, the patient eclecticism. In De Lucia there is already much of himself but still much of two or three celebrated tenors whom, like us, he evidently admires. Above all, he shows the vocal delivery of Stagno, not only in passionate outbursts but also in the convulsive movements of bearing and gesture . . . the young tenor has too much talent and refined artistic intelligence not to have the right to what painters call his own cipher.[63]

Capitan Fracassa wrote:

De Lucia is a phenomenon through his authority and through his vocal art, where others are phenomena through the voice. Nevertheless, his voice has sweetness, [and] exquisite finish. . . . he has returned to Naples the complete artist, having robbed Gayarre, Masini, and Stagno of almost all the secrets of their art, cleverly managing the voice, always striving to obtain all the effects that he demands of his vocal organ.[64]

To others his success was the more laudable in that study, perseverance, and genius, together with energy and audacity, had overcome his lack of an exceptional throat. To their ears the *striscio* on the word 'gioir', was a most beautiful device, a little nuance that would by itself dub him a great artist.[65] Another critic wrote:

These four years of lucrative and glorious exile have done very well by our De Lucia. Spain has made him not only Fernando, not only Commendatore, but also an almost perfect singer. His voice, not voluminous but very agreeable, has gained much, especially in the centre. He has learned all the graces and the wiles of art to which are added, for a not very robust organ, *all* the effects.[66]

However, the same writer, while generally commending his acting and remarking that he also enunciated very well, criticised his habit of beating the ground with his foot to give force to phrases

. . . perhaps in conformity with the exhortation of Horace: *nunc est bibendum* etc.,[67] and of stretching the legs in emitting the high notes - almost a question of uncorking the bottle - so making obvious the effort that it cost him.

Roberto Bracco took a poetic, characteristically Neapolitan view:

. . . the exhausting delight of five hours left sweet and voluptuous memories . . . certain bacilli, unknown to Pasteur, in the souls of spectators who, in perfect health, without fear of contagion or infection, went to dream . . . . .

---

63 *Pungolo*, Jan. 16/17 1890.

64 Quoted in *Occhialetto*, Jan. 18 1890.

65 *Occhialetto*, Jan. 18 1890.

66 *Piccolo*, Jan. 16/17 1890.

67 'Now we must drink. Now the earth must be struck [i.e. in the dance] with free foot.' Horace, *Odes*, Book I, Ode 37.

...He - the tenor - is the sum of many things: a touching, fresh, most agreeable voice, incessant study, superior artistic intelligence ...and a fascinating *napoletanità* [Neapolitan nature], whereof the bewitching poetry of Mergellina and Posillipo vibrate in his heart and voice. ...And that sensual mellifluousness is the most singular aspect of the singing. ...Not infrequently it borders on affectation - a danger from which his intuition will save him - but he obtains effects, many effects, too many effects which, in defiance of criticism, inspire in the spectators, especially the female, shivers of sweet delight.[68]

That severe critic Baron Procida ('p.c. dario'), warned, however, that

...he indulges too much in embroidery of the throat, in that superhuman *tessitura*[69] which - as in all forms of art made of caresses and refinement - offers a danger of degeneration. His good taste saves him from that mawkishness which, fleeting or not, is harmful to art; but he could become infatuated with it ...The intonation is of a marvellous perfection, the evenness of his middle notes [is] a factor in the effective and coloured diction in the recitatives ...De Lucia remains one of the most delicate tenors ...he is a true singer: *rara avis* among the various purveyors of *B flat* and *C* from the chest.[70]

Perhaps the most effusive review - though still some way short of the uncritical comment of later seasons in Italy - was that of 'Argo':

We shall not analyse the intrinsic value of these two pearls [Calvé and De Lucia]. ...We come down to details: how would we remember the *divine mezza voce* of De Lucia, the embroidery of his phrasing, the accent, the passion, the impulses of the great artist ...Three times De Lucia created the magic *barcarolle* [Della mia vita] amid the wildest enthusiasm. ...

And the love duet? What *charme, what flirtation of poetry and music. 'O merveille de l'art! Rien avant toi, rien après toi!'* The exclamation is a little daring, but is for the *moments* in which he seemed to touch the summit of his art and, if it is not the summit, it is certainly a height from which De Lucia can glory in being Neapolitan, and Naples can admire him in such a splendid career.[71]

Though there were friendly warnings not to 'abuse his precious throat' by too many encores,[72] the press was unanimous in declaring it a spontaneous, enthusiastic, and well-deserved triumph for De Lucia, who was worthy of the fame that he had achieved. Typical was:

On Wednesday evening, entering the San Carlo after a year, the heart bled for the memory of a genius of song, whom art had mourned for several days! Ferdinando De Lucia, with the sweetness of his voice, has come to fill the artistic void left by that death. Gayarre is no more. De Lucia inherits his fascination, glory, and triumphs.

Le roi est mort, vive le roi![73]

---

68 *Corriere di Napoli*, Jan. 16/17 1890.
69 Certainly in reference to the *falsetto* (head voice).
70 *Fortunio*, Jan. 19 1890.
71 *Paese*, Jan. 17/18 1890.
72 *Corriere di Napoli*, Jan. 17/18 1890.
73 *Caporal Terribile*, Jan. 19 1890.

It was also a night of encores for Calvé, a dark beauty, full of abandon, who intrigued by her black, impassioned eyes and supreme voluptuousness as well as by her timbre and extraordinary top notes; she repeated her second act aria and, with De Lucia, the *stretta* of the love duet. Both had numerous calls to the proscenium.

In a fulsome exchange, Calvé sent De Lucia her photograph, evidently with a flattering dedication. The tenor's reply expressed similarly gracious - not to say effusive - sentiments:

Dearest Signorina,

Heartfelt thanks for your most beautiful picture and for the most kind dedication. In your modesty you have forgotten that in your fascinating voice, too, there are the rarest pearls, so much more beautiful and precious for the radiance and charm of the jewel-case which holds them.

If it is true, which does not seem to be so, that you have not been compelled to assume an *air bête* in posing, the picture is all the more appreciated, since you have chosen the moment when you are looking at your Nadir, sacrificing your personal *charme* to a kind thought.

. . . you are always most gracious and your intelligence shows itself in your face and in your bewitching eyes!

I am sure that you will have a fresh triumph in *Amleto* [*Hamlet*] and, for myself, I hope always to be your companion in art, as I am ever your sincere friend and enthusiastic admirer.

Greetings to your mother and an affectionate handshake for you.[74]

So began a long - too long, as it turned out - series of performances of *I Pescatori*. After half a dozen repetitions, to general approval, the *patiti* were restless and eager for novelty. By now, they had their favourite artists. In the stalls the francophile *'calvénisti'* predominated. Elsewhere the audience was solidly behind the tenor, their *concittadino*. Matters came to a head on February 8th; after a well-received first act the stalls asked for an encore of Calvé's aria. De Lucia's supporters, who sought primacy for their man, demanded a further repeat of 'Della mia vita'. There was immediate, noisy dissent. The tenor threw an anxious glance at the stalls; he seemed uncertain over whether he should give an encore. Then came a crescendo of *'Bis!'* and *'Basta!'*[75] It was a battle without projectiles. Some of the ladies retreated from their boxes; others made ready to leave the theatre. Some bewildered Germans vainly asked their neighbours for an explanation. Shouts, protests, and tumult reigned for a good half-hour and an Inspector of Police was called to the stalls; at this, the aggrieved subscribers retired to fulminate in the corridors behind the first row of boxes. To the annoyance of those who wished to know nothing of the *claque* or the counter-*claque*, the curtain was lowered while Villani

---

[74] (G) (No date or place) De Lucia concludes his letter by writing out four bars of the duet 'Non hai compreso' from *I Pescatori di Perle*. Calvé sang *Amleto* at Naples in the 1890-1 season.

[75] 'Encore!' and 'Enough!'

and the theatre commission reasoned with the subscribers. Finally, the performance restarted under a flag of truce. All next day, the dignitaries of the San Carlo discussed a *modus vivendi* and reached an agreement which, despite its quaint period flavour, was forged by feelings running at white heat. Parity of encores was agreed between Calvé and De Lucia, with the activities of the public *claque* of the management and the private one of each singer to be limited to cases of 'prearranged unanimity' of applause.[76] 'At Naples, as in all the theatres of Italy, the *claque* is intolerable' complained *Piccolo*.

As the number of performances increased so also did the boredom with *I Pescatori*. On February 20th, as Calvé took her leave, shouts of 'Absolutely no more *Pescatori!*' accompanied the applause, the calls, and the garlands and baskets of flowers. Undeterred, Villani - who had no other works ready - engaged another Leila, Fanny Toresella, and continued despite threats from the *patiti*, who clearly wanted no more pearls or fishermen. At the San Carlo they had built a fish-hatchery, muttered *Roma*.[77]

But they were performances which would be recalled for children and grandchildren. A lifetime later the musician, painter, poet, and sculptor Francesco Cangiullo, born within weeks of that première, wrote to the poet Alberto Canna:

Leghorn, Roses of May, 1967

... The name De Lucia is like a key on my keyboard. In that divine, irreplaceable voice was all Naples. There were my youth and my parents. In the *Pescatori di Perle* at the San Carlo there were the fishermen at the seashore and the fishermen at Santa Lucia. ... (DL)

While *I Pescatori* continued, Villani persuaded the City Council to permit him to substitute *La Gioconda* for *La Regina di Saba*, in which De Lucia and Litvinne had been scheduled to sing. Opposition from subscribers who wished to hear the Goldmark work, new for Naples, prevailed, and by February 16th the chorus was rehearsing it, together with *Carmen*. Within a week, however, and for no obvious reason, it had again been abandoned by the management, in favour of *L'Ebrea*, with Litvinne and Toresella. Preparations for *Carmen* were protracted, with so many rehearsals that, when the scenery was finally ready, the singers were too tired to perform on the day set for the first performance. The opera finally went on stage on March 8th.

De Lucia's conception of the part of Don José had developed in the four years since Florence. The *prova generale* of *Carmen* had caused the critic of *Occhialetto* to describe him as combining the sweetness of Giuglini

---

[76] *Roma*, Feb. 10 1890.
[77] Ibid., Feb. 28 1890.

with the power of Negrini. Now, the première achieved a success which sent the same writer breathless to his office to stop the presses for his immediate reactions. A week later, on March 15th, his mature views were scarcely less intemperate:

> The young Comm. Fernando De Lucia, now the sole heir to the few stars of the tenor clef, sent the spectators into raptures ... He is a conscientious artist because he gives the audience all he possesses, and to the detriment of his vocal organ. In all, De Lucia feels much, and this sentiment is transfused into the listener, imparting, like a magnetic current, an outburst of enthusiasm such as we rarely see ... Nothing is neglected by him, nothing, from the delightful *sfumature* and from the impassioned singing of the first act to the vehement shudder and enraged impulses of the last. There is nothing of artifice in his theatrical mask, in his movements, in his accents, which are different in every performance: something that clearly demonstrates what has been said: that De Lucia is a born artist. It is a Southern nature: the passion [and] the drama are inherent and appear spontaneously with great power.
>
> It is strange that artifice is retained in the voice; but he is such an artist that, in the most vibrant moments of the tragedy, he forgets vocal artfulness and is incarnated in the body, lost in the character.[78]

His 'superlative qualities as a dramatic artist' made as great an impact as did his singing, and not only on his audience, for his calls brought him forth pale and drained of all emotional force. In the tremendous scene of the last act, it was said next day, few stage actors could equal him. In happiness he was likened to Maieroni, in the moments of the highest tragedy to Salvini, and, in the devices of the great actor, to Rossi:[79]

> In the 3rd and 4th acts of *Carmen* you no longer find the singing artist, the restrained professor who, with refined skill, limits himself to an admirable interpretation of the piece. No, it is another De Lucia who ... transfuses all the ardour of passion, the frenzies of love, the spasms of jealousy, the furies of desperation. A shiver came over the listener ... [80]

For Procida, De Lucia was shown as an artist of the very first order, and his Act IV as a creation:

> The actor is unsurpassable in truth, in pain, in the jealous impulses of rage, in love; the swelling agonies in his singing are reflected in the movements of his face, transfigured in the tortures of love. It could not be more effective. There can be no greater artistic splendour. Everything remains inferior to that moment, and I forget the sweet singer of the Flower Song, the fiery curses of the third finale, the colourist - too much, perhaps, if one observes some slightly exaggerated colours in the first act - of the entire part, to remind myself of a more human José, more terribly real than I have [ever] witnessed in this terrible scene.[81]

---

78 *Occhialetto*, Mar. 15 1890.
79 Maieroni, Ernesto Rossi, and Tommaso Salvini were three notable actors of the period.
80 *Arlecchino*, quoted in *Occhialetto*, Mar. 22 1890.
81 *Fortunio*, Mar. 16 1890.

In some scenes of the last two acts he achieved extraordinary effects by speaking, instead of singing. The applause, wrote *Roma*, was not always justified. But other critics were carried away by their enthusiasm. Typical was the reference to

> ... sweet, tender notes, which are not lost in the air but meet their end in a sweet echo in the heart. In the unfolding of the drama he had marvellous outbursts, especially in the third and fourth acts. What desperation, what anguish in the last phrase: *'Io l'ho ammazzato'* to which, more than a cry of rebellious conscience, he gave the impression of a broken heart.
>
> In the third and fourth acts ... the enthusiasts for phrasing and *bel canto* must resign themselves. In the fourth, with a dagger being brandished and a woman slain, there is no place for musical notes. At best, there can be cries ... In the final scene José *spoke*: from the gallery to the stalls they hung upon the clash of those two personalities. [The voice] soared above the orchestra with a strange, unexpected effect, the natural voice of the man who threatens. And another, the whimpering of a woman in fear.[82]

De Lucia's contract allowed him to refuse to sing two nights in succession and, although he had waived that right for *I Pescatori*, he declined to do so in the more strenuous part of Don José.[83] On March 9th the San Carlo remained closed. Uda, who had not seen the première, attended the second performance. Seldom, he wrote, had he known the stalls so ecstatic:

> Fernando De Lucia was revealed as a dramatic tenor, *hors ligne*. Whoever, after hearing him in the love duet, in the third act finale, and in the wonderful scene of the fourth, said of him that he recalled Negrini, judged fairly. He has his warm, penetrating singing - a Frenchman would write *troublant* [disconcerting] - but in the dramatic expressions of the last act, he is incomparable. The interpretation is his: bold, very successful, the phrases more than sung and delivered. ... The gesture is restless, and the eyes glitter sombrely. In the presentiment of the blade about to be unsheathed, to stab, is the impression of awful reality and, after Carmen's death, physical prostration and moral annihilation. [84]

Significantly, Uda, who had been among the first to notice the influence of Stagno on the young Neapolitan, was also the first to note De Lucia's personal imprint. By the third performance of *Carmen* he could write:

> De Lucia, I have already said, gave to the character a stamp that is his; today, no one could repeat the criticisms made of him in *Pescatori*. Not the slightest trace remains [of the style] of the great artist [Stagno] whom he loves and emulates. In his passion he enters into the personage and is absorbed. Every phrase has his warmth and his expression; the eye and the gesture, even in the

---

82 *Cronaca Partenopea*, quoted in *Occhialetto*, Mar. 22 1890.

83 The terms of a singer's contract, stating the number of performances to be given each week, were often waived under pressure or in an emergency. Until the late nineteenth century, singers in Italy frequently sang five times a week. See Rosselli, op. cit., p. 127.

84 *Pungolo*, Mar. 11/12 1890.

smallest details of the by-play, annotate wonderfully. The perversion of a man infatuated with a smugglers' woman: you see it born, grow, burst forth ... The final scene, which every night transports the public to wild enthusiasm, is only the paroxysm of an illness of the senses, where reason is clouded and the moral man collapses.

I have said that this is new. ... it is also bold, but audacity was never accompanied by talent such as this.[85]

The tenor's growing reputation, with its associated authority and independence, did not, however, impair his sense of duty. His Nadir had been a pillar of the season. On March 16th, despite a fever, he was induced, apparently by a management that stood to lose the receipts of a full house, to attempt *Carmen*. After struggling through Act I in half voice it was announced that he would omit 'Il fior' and the song of the Dragoon of Alcala. Money would, if required, be refunded and the performance would not count towards the subscription. Half the gallery and part of the stalls emptied; the tenor was reduced almost to humming his music but gained sympathetic applause for the spoken parts of his rôle from those who had remained and from a highly-cynical press.[86]

Such select musical societies as the Casino dell'Unione were by now willing to rearrange their performances to secure De Lucia's services. The Casino still occupied what would have been the foyer at the San Carlo had not King Vittorio Emanuele - believing it to be his property - given that part of the theatre to it. It was the most lavish of all the Neapolitan musical societies in the entertainments offered to its members. Several times the society postponed its presentation of Beethoven's *Cristo all'Oliveto (Christus am Ölberge)* before, on March 24th, the tenor was finally fit to sing. In this well-reported appearance in sacred music De Lucia - the 'demi-God' as *Roma* termed him - joined Toresella, Terzi, and the San Carlo chorus, conducted by Lombardi. He gave to the part of Christ an interpretation which some found too human and theatrical.[87] To others, he was a Christ

... all tenderness, all ..... *freely expressed* divinity. (Thus the view of someone nearby, doubtless a purist.)[88]

In the usual end-of-season haste to give each *turno* its due, the San Carlo management asked De Lucia, whose formal engagement finished on March 31st, to give three extra performances of *Carmen*; after some negotiation he was persuaded to moderate his demand for 4,000 lire per appearance.[89]

85 Ibid., Mar. 14/15 1890.
86 *Roma*, Mar. 17 1890.
87 Ibid., Mar. 25 1890.
88 *Caporal Terribile*, Mar. 30 1890.
89 *Roma*, Apr. 5 1890.

And so, on April 10th 1890, ended his first full season at the San Carlo. It was a festive evening. There were flowers for Novelli, Toresella, and the dancer Cornalba. The curtain calls, the cheering and the applause seemed endless. But for De Lucia there was something more: the admiration of his own people. Down from the gallery rained the silk banners carrying his name and verses - traditional for the *addio* - in praise of the *concittadino* of the Neapolitans, and he received five enormous garlands from well-wishers. Already, with a cachet of 100,000 lire, he had been reconfirmed for next season, to sing Don José. The emotional occasion was not *Addio* but *Arrivederci*.

7

A Man of Substance

When a composition is ill-suited to the means of the vocalist, he may resort to changes or to transposition; but it is often wiser to abandon a work rather than spoil it and incur blame or impair the organ.   Manuel Garcia, *Hints on Singing*

Two weeks after his last performance in Naples, De Lucia again embarked at Genoa for Argentina. This year the *Duchessa di Genova* carried the Ciacchi-Ferrari Company, an involuntary amalgamation of the forces of those two old adversaries. In 1890, Argentina was racked by social and economic crises and opera had become too costly for competition at such a level, though minor companies continued to function. The operatic troupe, said to have been the most powerful ever to visit Buenos Aires, included Armand Castelmary, Elvira Colonnese, Emilio De Marchi, Adalgisa Gabbi,[1] Kaschmann, Leonardi, Maurel, Francesco Navarrini, Amelia Stahl, Tamagno, and Paolo Wulman.[2] Its principal conductor was Marino Mancinelli. The press hinted that the managers were looking to governments as well as subscribers to assist them with the costs of providing such entertainment.[3]

The amalgamation did not mean that the two impresarios were any better friends. In fact, they were still locked in bitter litigation over Verdi's *Otello*. As early as January 1890, Ferrari had sought to dispel the rumour that he and Ciacchi had formed a partnership. To the Editor of *Italia*, of Montevideo, Ferrari wrote:

It is not true that there is any partnership between me and Sig. Cesare Ciacchi. The truth is this. It was proposed to me, and I have accepted, that I complete my company for the Teatro de la Opera in Buenos Aires with artists engaged by Sig. Ciacchi, with the condition that, at the end of the season at this theatre, the same company would operate in the theatres of Sig. Ciacchi.

Not only does a partnership not exist, but there is not even a fusion of interests and business between me and Sig. Ciacchi. ... Our agreement does not prejudice the litigation between us ... and if Signor Ciacchi gives Verdi's *Otello* he will give it with my permission, according to the agreement with the Publisher [Ricordi].[4]

---

1 Adalgisa's sister, Leonilda, was less well-known.
2 Sometimes Wulmann.
3 *Italia*, May 13 1890.
4 Quoted in *Gazzetta dei Teatri*, Jan. 16 1890.

The mention of *Otello* referred to Ricordi's practice of limiting performance rights to a single management in a country, so depriving rivals of a vital part of the repertory. In practice, this made no difference in countries such as Argentina, where no treaty of artistic property existed and where illegally-copied scores attracted, at worst, only the stigma of a supposed lack of authenticity. As Stagno pointed out, no practical difference existed between legal and illegal scores.[5]

Passengers for Buenos Aires had always had to make the last part of their journey by tender, from their steamer anchored far out in the roads of the shallow River Plate. This year the water level was spectacularly low, the result of the worst storms in two decades. Natural calamities were mirrored in Argentina itself. Not only was immigration, a barometer of national prosperity, falling fast, but emigration was now taking money from the country. The ship bearing the singers was only one of the large vessels to turn for Europe bearing disappointed former settlers, many of whom had lost everything.

Notwithstanding the economic gloom, Ferrari had already invested more than $70,000 in the new Colón theatre, now taking shape. There was, however, outrage at the rumour that the Government was to give him $300,000 'to enable the wealthy folk of the city to enjoy their Italian opera without loss to him'.[6]

Despite her dislike of long journeys, Itala had decided to accompany Fernando to South America. Since her health was not good at the time, she was, apparently at her mother's suggestion, accompanied by her cousin, Adelina De Palma, daughter of Cav. Lodovico De Palma and of Eduardo De Giorgio's sister, Adelgonda. Adelina, who was four years older than Itala, had been orphaned at an early age and had been brought up by Eduardo and his wife, with whom she still lived.[7]

After a leisurely voyage by way of the Canaries the company reached Buenos Aires on May 16th 1890. On the 20th, Tamagno, Maurel, and Adalgisa Gabbi opened the season with *Otello*: ominously, several boxes remained empty.[8] The poor houses continued in later performances. For *L'Africana*, with Tamagno and Kaschmann, there were forty empty boxes, a state of affairs which many attributed to the 'scandalous' prices required to meet the artists' fees. The gloomy predictions of the press were quickly proved correct. Although the artists had agreed to be paid in gold at the official, rather than the free market rate, almost four-fifths of the receipts of the opening night went to Tamagno and Maurel alone. The possible loss for the season was calculated as $200,000.[9]

De Lucia made his début in *Mefistofele* on May 24th. The critics noted

---

5 (BLS) Letter Stagno - D'Ormeville, 1888.
6 *Standard*, May 31 1890.
7 De Roberto, op. cit., p. 12.
8 *Standard*, May 22 1890.
9 Ibid., May 23 1890.

his 'fresh and beautiful voice'. The public, remembering Masini, who had had a great vogue in this part, was at first unmoved:

And what a public! Cold, grudging of applause, stone-faced ... it allowed 'Dai campi, dai prati' to pass with not the slightest sign of approval. ... It was, however, seduced by the music of the Garden Scene quartet ... and called the artists twice.

In the Prison Duet, 'Lontano, lontano', ... Gabbi and De Lucia lent enchantment to the music ... [In Act IV] he delivered the phrase 'Forma ideal purissima della bellezza eterna' with the elegance and intensity of expression that Stagno gave to it and he and his partner sang the heavenly duet 'Cantiamo l'amore' with *brio*.

We reached the epilogue. The theatre silently awaited the romanza 'Giunto sul passo' to judge, authoritatively, the tenor who had presented himself for the first time on the stage of the Opera. ... The outcome surpassed our expectations without reservation. Penetrating the lofty philosophical spirit that surrounds the work ... using every one of his vocal faculties, realised through extensive study, De Lucia achieved a miracle. It is impossible to sing more sweetly or vocalise more softly.[10]

His success was also reported in Montevideo:

De Lucia was a little overawed, having to contend with the still-fresh memories of Masini ... [He] is not yet Masini, but seeing his rapid progress year by year it is to be hoped that it will not be long before he draws level with the great tenor. De Lucia is very young, very studious, finely intelligent, and adopts the maxim: *Prendo il buono, dove lo trovo*.[11] He has taken from the three great artists Gayarre, Masini, and Stagno all the beauty that he can, creating an individuality which, although preceded by those three, is still a novelty. His singing is full of the sweetness of sentiment and passion.

He has very powerful outbursts, where the voice has accents [that are] now vibrantly sonorous, now very sweet, passing from one to the other with a masterly security which reveals profound study.[12]

He was billed to sing in *La Gioconda* on May 26th but was evidently replaced by Emilio De Marchi. In De Lucia's next opera, *La Favorita*, it was said that he sang and acted Fernando excellently and that his singing of 'Spirto gentil' was as good as Gayarre's.[13] His method of attacking and ending the phrases received particular praise. 'His singing has the soul of a purist, highly and ideally expressive.'[14] At the first well-known notes of the air a menacing 'Ssst' imposed silence.

He does not possess the angelic voice of Giuglini, nor ... the breath, two measures long, which allowed Gayarre to do miracles, nor ... the power of Masini, in his famous spun notes. What, then, will he do?

The other three colossi sang it divinely, blissfully, reaching the height of

---

10 *Censor*, May 25 1890.
11 'I take the good, where I find it.'
12 *Italia*, May 27 1890. The same notice appeared in *Patria Italiana*.
13 *Standard*, June 1 1890.
14 *Nazione Italiana*, quoted in *Occhialetto*, July 19 1890.

perfection, De Lucia did not sing so much as 'sigh' the heavenly music, and the effect was marvellous.[15]

Nothing [could be] simpler and more artistically beautiful.

The sweet music, a celestial flash from a human brain, depicts Fernando's state of mind wonderfully and, with a fusion of tear and sigh, De Lucia delivers the anguished, sublime phrases.

What marvellous art, and what shrewd intuition.[16]

The same critic noted, though, two faults that he admonished the young tenor to cure. The first was his tendency to shut his eyes tightly each time he spun a note. Consequently, 'he sings three quarters of the part with closed eyes'. The other was 'an awkward motion of the right arm, held half-bent, which he swings, invariably, at every pace, always with the same monotonous movement'.

Rigoletto, two days later, and at only three days notice, marked his first appearance with Victor Maurel. The baritone's performance of the title rôle was generally agreed to be a masterpiece of singing and acting, unequalled on the stages of Buenos Aires. The part of the Duke demanded of De Lucia a complete change of mood and, from all accounts, he succeeded well in the transition from monk to libertine. He entranced in the gay, thoughtless measures of 'Questa o quella' and in the duet with Gilda. In 'La donna è mobile', which he sang three times, the notes came forth with the brilliance of a display of fireworks. On the third occasion he changed the cadenza, also to great effect.[17] In the high notes of '*e di pensier*' he displayed a *brio* which recalled Stagno in the same passage.[18] The effect on the audience, more especially on the female members, was prodigious; Tamagno, too, was seen to be among those applauding vigorously.[19]

On June 5th, when *Rigoletto* was to have been repeated, Maurel was ill. To forestall any rumour that he might not have received his fee Ferrari posted in the vestibule the baritone's receipt for $4,000, paid to him in gold a few hours earlier. Even so, the hissing, groaning, and stamping of feet amply justified the precaution. Eventually, a *pot-pourri* was staged by the other members of the cast and by Kaschmann who, at ten minutes notice and apparently with considerable success, gave Act I of *Rigoletto*.[20]

The liveliest event of the season was undoubtedly *Gli Ugonotti* on June 24th. A waiter in the *cazuela* set fire to his napkin on a coffee stove,

---

15 The numerous possible meanings of the Italian word 'sospirare' collectively convey a sigh of sorrow and longing.

16 *Gazzetta dei Teatri*, July 10 1890.

17 *Argentina*, quoted in *Gazzetta dei Teatri*, July 31 1890.

18 *Censor*, June 2 1890.

19 *Nazione Italiana*, quoted in *Gazzetta dei Teatri*, July 31 1890.

20 *Standard*, June 7 1890. There are conflicting accounts of this performance. *Censor* (June 6) reported that, after the audience had shown its disapproval of the proposed composite programme, Kaschmann sang the entire opera (*Rigoletto*) without rehearsal.

whereupon one of the fair occupants shrieked. In an immediate rush for the doors, many fainted and the remainder became hysterical. Tamagno, the hero of the hour, sang the National Hymn and order was restored. Wulman, the St. Bris, was finally found running for his life in the direction of the river. When brought back and induced to go on to the stage the storm of laughter made the theatre ring.

July 19th saw the company at Ciacchi's Teatro Politeama, where it was to give *Gli Ugonotti, Don Carlo, Faust, Otello*, and *La Gioconda*. However, the season of fifteen performances was poorly attended and reported. On July 26th the Union Civica, a body formed by leading citizens to oppose the excesses and corruption of the administration, took to the streets supported by units of the army. The fleet began to bombard the city. On July 31st the President resigned and Buenos Aires was *en fête* for three days. But it was no climate for opera. On August 11th the company embarked for Europe instead of continuing at the Solis in Montevideo, as originally scheduled by Ciacchi.[21] It was doubtless a subdued group of artists that made its way back to Italy.

To De Lucia, the early return was probably less disappointing than for some of the other artists. Itala was expecting another child. A lucrative San Carlo season lay ahead. Moreover, there were exciting new artistic possibilities. News had reached Buenos Aires of the sensational new opera, *Cavalleria Rusticana*, which had won the second *Concorso Sonzogno* for its young composer, Pietro Mascagni. Sung by Bellincioni and Stagno, and conducted by Mugnone, it had received frenzied popular acclaim - with no fewer than sixty curtain calls - at the Teatro Costanzi, Rome, on May 17th 1890. Impresarios and agents flocked to Rome to secure performing rights. Within a few months it had been given at Bologna, Florence, Genoa, Leghorn, Milan, Naples, Palermo, Trieste, Turin, and Venice.[22] Italy was in the first grip of *mascagnitis*.

In Naples there was an air of civic pride. On October 5th 1887, only five months after the start of demolition of the adjacent Via Santa Brigida, the foundation stone of the Galleria Umberto I had been laid in the city centre. Modelled on the building that, since 1867, had provided a focal point for the lyric activity of Milan, the Galleria of Naples set out to be more beautiful, costly, and luxurious than its precursor. It was now nearing completion, for its inauguration on November 9th 1890.[23] Astonishingly, in view of the running battle in the press in favour of electricity, this new building was at first lit by gas. It was less magnificent than might have been the case had it not needed to accommodate in its structure two churches and several private houses. But it was - and is - a most striking and effective building. Its central

---

21 *Italia*, May 13 1890.

22 Morini, *Pietro Mascagni*, Vol. II, p. 183.

23 Vittorio Paliotti, *Il Salone Margherita*, pp. 51-6 gives a detailed account of the design, decoration, and furnishing of the Galleria.

octagon, beneath a glass dome that rises almost sixty metres, forms an imposing setting for its richly impressive stucco and gilded decoration. In its Salone Margherita the personalities of the 'Belle Époque' of Naples finally had somewhere with the flavour of Paris - then much in vogue - in which to spend their evenings and to squander their inherited fortunes. So great was the interest in the Galleria that, for a month after its opening, the citizens meekly paid even to enter it.

In the shadow of the Galleria, the San Carlo had experienced its customary complications regarding the concession. Villani's tenure still had two years to run when, in April 1890, he announced his roster and programme - including Van Westerhout's new opera *Cimbellino*, based on Shakespeare's *Cymbeline* - for the coming winter.[24] However, he failed to pay the deposit to the municipality in time and was deemed to be in default. Rival bids were then submitted by Scalisi and by Pasquale Mario Musella, an experienced manager of seasons in Italy and South America. Eventually, Villani agreed - for a subsidy of 10,000 lire - to present *Cavalleria Rusticana*, with Bellincioni and Stagno; by June 1st, however, the press was linking the names of Calvé and De Lucia with the rôles. Villani also offered another novelty, *Spartaco*, by Pietro Platania, and was again awarded the concession.[25] A weighty influence in the decision was the public refusal of Sonzogno to allow Villani's rivals to give *Cavalleria Rusticana*.[26] The publisher had not forgotten that it was Villani who, at a critical moment in her career, had engaged Calvé, now Sonzogno's regular companion.[27] Where, though, wondered some, would chorus and orchestra find time to prepare so many new operas?

De Lucia, who was *tenore d'obbligo*[28] for the season, lost no time in judging *Cavalleria* for himself: on September 14th, he and Lombardi, having travelled especially from Naples, were in the audience at the Pergola, Florence, to hear the new work, sung by Fernando Valero and Emma Calvé.[29]

In that autumn of 1890 few in Naples were aware of the impact of the new musical genre. The 'romanza', its golden age as yet undisturbed by the brutal realism of *verismo*, was still to be heard in every fashionable drawing room of Naples. As society took up its winter activities the traditional Monday evening concerts resumed at Uda's house. The Carelli sisters and Annunziata Lombardi, Nina Arcoleo and the young Princess Rosa Pignatelli were 'at home' to De Leva and Costa, to Van Westerhout and Giordano, to De Nardis and De Lucia, and to other former scholars at San Pietro a Maiella. All were intimates of another

---

24 *Occhialetto*, Apr. 26 1890.

25 *Occhialetto* and *Corriere di Napoli*, Apr.-July 1890.

26 *Piccolo*, July 4/5 1890.

27 Daspuro, 'Memorie', ch. XXIX.

28 An opera or singer *d'obbligo* was one whose production or engagement was made a condition of awarding the concession.

29 *Occhialetto*, Sept. 13 1890.

favourite guest and habitué of the *salotti*, Carlo Clausetti. A cultivated and sensitive young lawyer and *dilettante* poet and composer, Clausetti had only two more years of such agreeable irresponsibility before, on the death of his father, Pietro, he would be called upon to direct the Naples branch of Ricordi and so assume a prominent place in local musical circles. But these new burdens did not stem his creative writing, nor restrain him from a host of musical activities, and the young artists remained his faithful friends.[30]

As preparations continued for the season at the San Carlo the weather in Naples became increasingly severe. There was even the novelty of snow as De Lucia went back and forth between home and the theatre. Otherwise, as a concerned parent and prudent singer, he stayed at home. To Marchese Filiasi he wrote:

> I earnestly beg you to excuse my lateness in thanking you for your courteous and most kind gift that, unfortunately, I shall not be able to preserve for ever (because I shall drink it) but of which I shall always preserve the memory. I wanted to come personally, as was my duty, but the recent bad weather and my child's illness forbade it. Instead, I write to do what I should *viva voce*, and I thank you indeed from the heart for your goodness towards me. Permit me to enclose my photograph, so that you may sometimes remember me.
>
> Please accept my distinguished respects and deference to the Signora Marchesa, while to you I extend a cordial handshake.[31]

Like most singers, De Lucia was preoccupied with his health and was conscious of the risk of illness or of vocal overwork. There can be few callings more completely dependent upon a single, specialised, physical faculty, and one which is so unpredictable and vulnerable to minor ailments. The fear of loss of voice and livelihood was never far from his mind, and his precautions were thorough. Though a simple eater, he nevertheless believed that food and wine of the finest quality were essential for vocal well-being. His vade-mecum was a collection of the remedies and prescriptions which he had found beneficial. On the day of a performance he spoke *sotto voce*, would mime or write his requests to his valet, Enrico, and would barely clear his throat to try out his voice. Bellincioni recalled how he would, minutes before going on stage, say:

> 'I don't feel well, I can't go on - I've lost my voice!'

On leaving his dressing room he would be swathed in wraps, a handkerchief in his mouth to protect throat and larynx from cold air. Enrico, with his master's cape, was always present in the wings during the performance. De Lucia never forgot the ice and snow of Russia, scarcely bearable for a Southerner. There, as he would later recount to

---

[30] Unpublished writings of Clausetti's grandson, Carlo C.

[31] (SPM) Dec. 9 1890.

his pupils, he saw nothing of the beauties of St. Petersburg, but only the railway station, the hotel, the theatre, the Imperial palace, and the inside of a closed carriage.[32] In such conditions he wore several coats and a bearskin. Concern for the voice overcame even his normal courtesy when, in the few paces between stage door and conveyance, he would scarcely speak to the admirers, mostly women, who would wait outside the theatre. During Spanish winters, to the displeasure of Itala, who did not care for the hotel cooking, he went out only for performances. Long summer holidays at Monte Carlo, always at Villa Lotus, were preceded by a week or two at a spa, usually Salsomaggiore, where he could take curative baths and where his voice could benefit from inhalations. During a prolonged period of diminished vocal powers he consulted many doctors; subsequently, he collected together in an exercise book the various cures that these eminent men had prescribed for him to recover his voice.

Despite the unusual severity of that Naples winter, he attended a nuptial mass at the church of S. Giuseppe a Chiaia, for the wedding of Cav. Arturo Catalano Gonzaga di Cirella. Accompanied by the three Lombardi brothers, at the harmonium, cello, and harp, he sang 'Ave Maria' (Bach-Gounod), giving to it an impassioned fervour which, the chronicler noted, was perhaps not to be found in the music. Instead of applause - then not allowed in such surroundings - he had to content himself with tears of emotion from his listeners. The Neapolitan baritone Colonnese sang Rossini's 'O salutaris hostia'.[33]

On December 15th *La Gioconda* had its *prova generale*, a full dress rehearsal to a house packed with spectators. Critics making their notes in preparation for the actual première; friends and relations of the singers; assorted sycophants, and acquaintances of the impresario crowded into the daytime gloom of the San Carlo, where the singers performed in a festive air and to uninhibited applause. They also heard the unusual sound of Vincenzo Lombardi, as he half-sang and half-spoke the part of the indisposed Novelli. Critical comment before the official first performance was forbidden but, as critics sought to inform without actually breaking this time-honoured rule, many a so-called 'indiscretion' saw the light.

On December 17th the opening of the season saw the theatre full to capacity. The press took care to report on the presence of the numerous princesses, duchesses, and lesser members of the aristocracy. What was unusual was the appearance of three local artists: Aurelia Cattaneo,[34] Lombardi, and De Lucia, now freely discussed as the first Neapolitan for years who could stand among the great tenors of the time.

---

32 Mikhail Popov, letter to the writer, June 1973.

33 *Pungolo*, Dec. 11/12 1890.

34 Sometimes Cataneo.

As in Buenos Aires, enthusiasm for electric lighting had not considered the need for additional heating. The theatre was cold, and many fashionably-dressed woman shivered in *robe décolletée*. However, the jewels displayed in the boxes flashed as never before. As the lights were dimmed, critics were still noting the details of the more spectacular gowns, including Emma Calvé's magnificent white and gold creation.

Act I was already in progress when the Princess of Naples, accompanied by Princess Victoria Schaumberg-Lippe, sister of Emperor Wilhelm, appeared in a box. Immediately, the audience rose to its feet and loyally applauded while the orchestra played the National Anthem.[35]

But such an interruption - taken for granted - scarcely touched the extraordinary atmosphere of that evening and of a Neapolitan festival. It was an ambience which imposed itself on all, like an electric impulse, at the appearance '...of *our* Gayarre, of our De Lucia, of our tenor',[36] an 'incomparable Genoan Prince'. The critics were in self-indulgent mood. Entire pages of local newspapers were filled with exuberant admiration for 'the King of the evening', for

> ...the colossal success of Fernando De Lucia who ...has truly astounded the public ...through the vocal power that he has acquired, and which he demonstrated with so many high notes, always full and ringing, among which were not a few B flats. But these B flats, delivered in quantity, do not impress us, always lovers of the *bel canto* of which De Lucia is master, and we admonish him, for [the sake of] the future, not to be estranged from it. One can always find someone to produce a B flat but one less easily finds someone who produces *voce mista* as does the young *divo*. De Lucia produced it delightfully at the end of his *romanza*, where he made an *acciaccatura* on the B flat that would alone justify his fame, his fee and the enthusiasm of the public.[37]

In characteristically poetic flight, Bracco wrote:

> The young tenor spoke to the audience with all the passion of Enzo, and with a voice which seemed to be of two, three, of ten De Lucias gathered together. To the well-known, ingratiating sweetness of the middle notes, to the touching *filature*, to the caressing *smorzi*, to the exuberance of an artistically expansive youth, he added last night an unexpected vocal power ... in the vocal clamour of the [second act] finale [he had] secure, ringing and triumphal notes.[38]

It was his unshakeable *authority*, decided *Napoli*, that had increased; he was now 'an absolute magician ...of power ...of sentiment ...of art ...of melody'.[39] And *Arlecchino* noted that, from the *tenore di grazia* of the aria and the duet, he became a fully dramatic tenor.[40]

---

35 *Piccolo*, Dec. 18/19 1890.
36 *Paese*, Dec. 18/19 1890.
37 *Occhialetto*, Dec. 20 1890.
38 *Corriere di Napoli*, Dec. 18/19 1890.
39 *Napoli*, quoted in *Occhialetto*, Dec. 29 1890.
40 *Arlecchino*, quoted in *Occhialetto*, Dec. 29 1890.

The most coldly-considered view was, perhaps, that of Uda:

> Today's *Gioconda* has, over the two that preceded it, the great advantage that
> Enzo is sung by De Lucia. . . . From the *Gioconda* of Sani and of Signoretti one
> would not suspect that, in Ponchielli's music, where the major dramatic effects
> lie in power, a tenor could gain for himself a climactic success but achieve it
> with opposite effects, in those very parts of the opera in which he could be at the
> greatest risk.
>
> With his voice, De Lucia has *created* a character: he has made a man of the
> tenor who, at the most critical time, at the moment of greatest passion, had the
> resoluteness to free himself from the arms of the soprano . . .
>
> I said the voice, because the *creation* of Fernando De Lucia is essentially and
> necessarily vocal. The character is revealed more clearly in the warm sweetness
> or in the exquisite sentiment of the singing than in the action of the melodrama.
> In the musical phrases he sketches, colours and animates. At the beginning of
> the romanza 'L'angel mio verrà dal cielo', into which the artist puts
> unspeakable expressions of impassioned *reverie*, and at the end in the cry that
> bursts from the heart: 'Tu sei morta, tu sei morta!' whose agonising inflections
> were heard in the imposing concerted finale of the third act, there stood out, in
> proper relief from the singing population that covered the stage, a tragic
> personality - Enzo - which previous *Giocondas* have ignored.
>
> This, for me, is the major worth of De Lucia's interpretation, and this [is] the
> praise that must be dearest to him. It is true that he has returned to us with
> greater strength of voice. But the critic, if he is cautious in his praise, should
> hardly notice it, nor the artist dwell on it. . . . With a power that is not [mere]
> resilience of the lungs, nor audacious subtleties of sound, De Lucia is a complete
> singer. His is an assiduous and progressive work towards perfection, from
> which emerges . . . a warm and refined painter.[41]

While *La Gioconda* enjoyed its long and successful series of
performances Naples was working itself into a frenzy of anticipation for
Cavalleria Rusticana. The expectation created by high ticket prices
increased when the *prova generale* took place in unusual secrecy. Only
the theatre commission, the press, and the pupils of San Pietro a Maiella
were permitted to witness Sonzogno's preparations as he supervised
every detail of the performance. Mascagni, though modestly concealed by
the shadow of the pit, maintained his reputation for being anything but a
compliant observer - at Rome the completely unknown composer had
changed two Alfios and three Lolas[42] - by requesting that Eugène
Dufriche should replace Salvatore Vinci, as Alfio. The work was finally
presented on January 14th 1891, when De Lucia - now with a light beard
- joined Calvé, Cucini, Dufriche, Patalano, and Lombardi before an
audience the like of which had not been seen at the San Carlo since the
first performance there of Verdi's *Otello*.

Cavalleria was preceded by the overture from *Der Freischütz*,
applauded with the courtesy of a handshake which accompanies the
departure of a respectable bore. As Lombardi lifted his baton for the

---

41 *Pungolo*, Dec. 20/21 1890.

42 Letter from Mascagni to the librettists Guido Menasci and Giovanni Targioni-Tozzetti, Rome, May 14
1890. See Ugo Bernardini Marzolla in *Pietro Mascagni: Contributi alla Conoscenza della Sua Opera nel 1o
Centenario della Nascita*, p. 73.

principal work there was an imposing silence in the great golden auditorium.

Initially, the transformation of Calvé from the pale and vapid Ofelia of Thomas's *Amleto*, which she had sung a few nights earlier, into the love-lorn Sicilian girl was what caught the attention of the audience. But, as the effects of passion, rage, and emotional outburst turned the agile nightingale into a dramatic soprano of great power, so did the enthusiasm of the audience for the music smoulder and burst into flame.

In *Corriere di Napoli*, Bracco thought it necessary to impress upon his readers that his chronicle - the ritual Italian recitation of the applause, the encores, and the curtain calls - was no more than the truth. After the prelude and 'Siciliana' - the latter encored - there were four calls for the tenor and the composer. Stifled applause for Alfio's aria was followed by satisfied acclaim for the Easter Hymn. An encore of 'Voi lo sapete' brought a call with Mascagni. The duet between Santuzza and Turiddu electrified the public ... and so the success continued until, at the end, there was pandemonium as the audience, on its feet applauding tirelessly, called the composer, the singers, and the conductor seven, eight, nine times to the footlights. As Turiddu,

> Fernando De Lucia ... sang without the preoccupations of a tenor-divinity, and his voice burst forth, caressed, compelled, [and] penetrated the heart. In the excess of effect, we again found a wholly human excess of vigour. Turiddu, powerful, arrogant, bold, no longer had anything in common with the tenor. And from the mouth of Turiddu - tormented by the thought of leaving his mother, perhaps for ever - with the enchanting notes of that already famous 'Addio' came the voice of a profoundly moved soul. In that agitation, hardly concealed by the feigned drunkenness, Ferdinando De Lucia asserted his superiority over every other possible Turiddu.[43]

As Uda remarked, the musical and dramatic effects of *Cavalleria Rusticana* were already well known; the curiosity of the critic lay in knowing whether the success was born in the mind or in the heart:

> Last night we all had this sad curiosity ... It left us when, in the principal scenes of the drama, the music gripped the critic by the throat, forcing him to abandon his reservations and to shout his emotions. Four times we shouted, honourably confessing our rout, a defeat that started with the 'Siciliana' and, through Santuzza's 'racconto', the duet with Turiddu, the 'Intermezzo' and the 'Addio', gathered pace in a crescendo of enthusiasm to the triumphal conclusion.
> ... The impression of these four pieces remains indelible. It endures for the music, it will remain for the performance. A Santuzza such as Calvé and a Turiddu such as De Lucia are difficult to find. The great dramatic actress was enthusiastically acclaimed in the exquisite singer that was Calvé. In particular, it was the wordless scene before the church and the outburst of weeping at the end that obliged them to repeat the duet with Turiddu. Eleonora Duse, the Santuzza of Verga, did neither more nor less. De Lucia vied with [Calvé] when the singing called for sensual grace or passion and, despite the unsympathetic

---

[43] *Corriere di Napoli*, Jan. 15/16 1891.

nature of the part, attained effects of the deepest sorrow in the 'Addio alla madre'.[44]

In *Fortunio*, Procida wrote of him:

His voice ... was reflected in bewitching sweetness in the impassioned 'Siciliana', which conquered our public through the curtain the other night, and in living colour, in magnificent vigour in the duet with Santuzza, where the phrase: *'Bada, Santuzza'*, in De Lucia's throat, gives off sparks of surging menace ... in the 'Addio alla madre' [he] employed all the exquisite sweetness of his throat to bring us to tears ... It was one of my finest artistic sensations.[45]

In the early hours of January 15th the musicians and critics, as was their custom after an important première, gathered at the Birreria Dreher. Their talk was of *Cavalleria* and of its performance. Lombardi thought it a work that transcended talent to attain genius.[46] Others dismissed it as derivative and meretricious, a mere musical sketch which had attained undeserved success. 'Was it true glory?' asked Mormone, in his first review.[47] But most agreed that it had had a breathtaking triumph with an audience that was oblivious to the disruptive effects of too many encores.

In the many later performances the critiques became more detailed. The 'Brindisi', in which De Lucia displayed his more experimental vocal graces, should not, suggested Bracco, reinforcing some views expressed at the première, be sung with too much seriousness, too great a desire to astonish the listener, too earnest a search for effect ..... or, sometimes, to substitute for the composer. There was a danger that an excessive attention to minor details could disturb the balance. Subsequently the tenor seemed to have heeded his critics. It was noted that he preserved his 'marvellous and fascinating artistic vitality', which pervaded the stage with his gestures and the surroundings with his voice, but he became less impetuous and emotional, and he portrayed the rustic Sicilian Don Giovanni with greater accuracy. After a dozen performances the exaggerations had disappeared. Musically, if not dramatically, he was thought to be perfect.[48] Only the austere Mormone continued to rail against an interpretation that the *sicofanti* found increasingly to their taste.

Something of the power of De Lucia's Turiddu is suggested by the several surviving photographs of him in the part. A hint of what the critics heard that evening may endure in his records of music from *Cavalleria Rusticana*, including three versions - the earliest dating from

---

44 *Pungolo*, Jan. 15/16 1891.
45 *Fortunio*, Jan. 15 1891.
46 *Caporal Terribile*, Jan. 18 1891.
47 *Roma*, Jan. 15 1891.
48 *Corriere di Napoli*, Jan. 18/19 and Feb. 24/25 1891.

1902 and the latest from 1920 - of the 'Siciliana' [Nos. 11, 123, 332]. They illustrate his way with music that is not usually embellished; the rapid, flickering, almost casual figurations that he inserts into the long, sensuous phrases have the indelible stamp of his times.

Mascagni and Sonzogno were understandably jubilant. The first three performances had been entirely sold out and only bad weather was able to keep the public away. *Cavalleria Rusticana*, in which De Lucia later alternated with Zerni, achieved more than thirty performances, for which the supply of tickets was exhausted within hours. Some boredom then obtruded and the intense rivalry of the previous year reappeared among the *patiti*, but even at the 24th performance the whisper that the composer was in the house brought forth a roar of 'Mascagni!' until he appeared on the stage.

Both publisher and composer were impressed with De Lucia, and quickly took steps to secure his future services; the morning after the première came the news that he had been chosen to create the part of Giorgio in *I Rantzau*, Mascagni's new opera.

On January 19th, at the Casino dell'Unione, Monaco and other *sicofanti* gave a banquet in honour of Mascagni and Sonzogno. As the champagne glasses were raised, the flowery speeches quoted the *'vino spumeggiante'* in *'bicchiere scintillante'*, the words and phrases which were on the lips of half of Naples. Mascagni, who - after much teasing in the press - had changed his pea-green trousers for more conservative attire, expressed his gratitude to Villani and Lombardi, proposing a toast to them and to all the interpreters of *Cavalleria Rusticana*. As he seated himself at the piano to play pieces from *I Rantzau*, the enthusiasm expressed general goodwill towards the new work which, Mascagni promised, Naples would be the first to hear after Rome.[49] After the première of *I Rantzau* - almost two years later and, as it turned out, at Florence - it was to be remarked that Naples was the city where the terms *'mascagnisti'* and *'antimascagnisti'* had real meaning, and where friends, family, and relatives daily argued bitterly over the Livornese maestro and his works. For two years, in some circles, thoughts of the *sventramento*, the misery, the workers' houses, or the administration of the city and the province were put aside in a city obsessed with Mascagni.[50]

While De Lucia continued with *Cavalleria Rusticana*, on January 25th 1891 Itala gave birth to a son. The child, though born dead, was named Nadir, in tribute to the tenor's first great success in his native city. Personal sorrow was following hard upon certain artistic difficulties. The latter were soon to come to an embarrassing climax.

But there was still time to sing in a fashionable concert in the old

---

49 *Piccolo*, Jan. 20/21 1891.
50 *Tribuna*, Nov. 28 1892.

Hôtel Nobile, now renamed Hôtel West End, taken for the afternoon of February 6th 1891 for the benefit of the orphans of Queen Margherita's refuge. As the patron, the Royal Prince, took his seat between Princess Rosina Pignatelli and Princess Torella Murat it was realised that Lombardi was still rehearsing at the San Carlo. Fortunately, the young composer Riccardo Barthélemy was there, to ingratiate himself by deputising at the piano.[51]

Even the ascetic Serao, apparently impressed by the lavish gowns - Cattaneo in black, Novelli in dark green silk and velvet, Calvé again showing her preference for white embroidered with gold, with the aristocratic audience an array of human flowers - and the worthiness of the cause, indulged in immoderate prose to describe the splendid occasion. The distinguished company heard Maurel in Tosti's 'Ninon' and, as an encore, the mandolinata 'Su andiam, la notte è bella', which was itself repeated; De Lucia in 'Scetate' and Tosti's 'Sera'; Calvé rivalling the flute for agility and trills in the couplets from *La Perle du Brésil*; these were some of the highlights of the concert, which was followed by a masked ball.[52]

The following day, De Lucia sang the Duke of Mantua to the Rigoletto of Victor Maurel, an event thought worthy of increased prices. The public's excitement was intense and its restlessness spread to the stage. The work was badly under-rehearsed. The inexperienced Carolina De Rossi-Trauner, summoned by telegram to sing Gilda at short notice, was clearly unable to project her voice in so large a theatre and dissolved into tears at the first cruel jeer from the stalls. During some stage business with Rigoletto, Giovanna fell, breaking her nose. A stagehand rushing to help her also fell, amid general hilarity. Gilda's grey felt hat fell off. A ducal armchair rocked on unsteady legs, and a bottle and Sparafucile's lantern overturned. By contrast, while all beneath it slithered and toppled, the curtain, its pulleys obstinately jammed, refused to descend at each finale. It was, as several critics remarked, a performance attended by the *jettatura*.[53]

All unintentional comedy aside, the performance was dominated by Maurel, a vocal and dramatic genius. For De Lucia, striking in an extravagantly rich costume, it was only a mediocre success. Certainly, he was applauded in his usual pieces, and the very inclusion of 'Parmi veder le lagrime' was unusual enough (at that date) to cause comment. The audience listened raptly to the 'delicate inflections that only De Lucia can produce.'[54] But the critics were generally severe. While Uda confined himself to writing that he had sung 'all his part delightfully, perhaps too

---

51 Barthélemy (b. 1869), a graduate of San Pietro a Maiella, wrote songs and *musica da camera*.
52 *Corriere di Napoli*, Feb. 7/8 and 9/10 1891.
53 *Occhialetto*, Feb. 7 1891.
54 *Piccolo*, Feb. 8/9 1891.

much so',[55] Bracco was more specific:

> [He] sang with fine and fascinating grace. He had to repeat the romanza
> 'Questa o quella' in which he produced marvellous refinements and, I would
> almost say, [showed] delightful and surpassingly *chic* vocal self-possession. In
> the second act ... the influence of the atmosphere impaired the effects that he
> would certainly have attained, especially in the 'adagio' of the duet. ... He had
> to repeat 'La donna è mobile'. And in this romanza he paraded all the
> tenderness, all the flirtatiousness, all the impassioned warmth of his singing.
> But when, in an excessive desire to please, affectation and intemperate
> 'virtuosity' damaged his excellent singing, the public felt a kind of scorn, giving
> vent to its nervousness. Though seemingly disrespectful, [it] could perhaps be a
> useful lesson to the young tenor ... [56]

Mormone complained that De Lucia was

> ... unable to cast off his habits as a tenor of *mezzo carattere*. ... 'La donna è
> mobile' is a *canzone* not an *adagio*: it is inappropriate to spin out the notes.[57]

Procida, too, commented on 'an excessive concern for effect, [and] the
delicate *smorzature* and frivolous *fioriture*, so beloved of the tenor but
inappropriate to the part'. A lighter approach, he suggested, was
required.[58]

The second performance was better received. Gilda was Cattaneo,
Rossi-Trauner having left Naples the morning after the première. De
Lucia's work, though still characterised by sweetness, grace, and
refinement in runs, in shading, and in fine-spun notes, was judged free of
the defects that had been criticised three nights earlier,[59] and he did not
permit himself the same licence in pauses.[60] Procida applauded him,
remarking that neither Verdi nor De Lucia needed affectation.[61] None
the less, the lesson was a sharp one, and it was soon to have quite
unforeseen results. For now Fernando became embroiled in theatre
politics, as manifested in the tortuous progress of *Cimbellino*. The opera
itself has long been forgotten. However, an examination of the
background to its first performance is revealing for the light that it sheds
on De Lucia's character. It shows him as indecisive and self-serving, torn
between friendship for its composer and the self-interest of refusing a
part which he knew was not for him.

Italian-born, of Dutch parentage, Niccolò Van Westerhout
(1862-1898) had studied at San Pietro a Maiella alongside De Lucia,
whose earliest concerts had included some of his songs. Even at that

---

55 *Pungolo*, Feb. 8/9 1891.
56 *Corriere di Napoli*, Feb. 8/9 1891.
57 *Roma*, Feb. 8 1891.
58 *Fortunio*, Feb. 12 1891.
59 *Corriere di Napoli*, Feb. 11/12 1891.
60 *Roma*, Feb. 11 1891.
61 *Fortunio*, Feb. 12 1891.

time, the studious composer, fastidious in his dress, his slim features and neatly turned-up moustache framed by the thin wire loops of small, oval-rimmed spectacles, was a well-known and popular figure in the *salotti*. He had remained in Naples, where he had a considerable following, devoting himself to teaching and composition; many of his songs were to words by local poets, such as Pagliara. The local press encouraged him assiduously. Casa Ricordi had published some of his romanzas, and the young composer had made pianoforte transcriptions of 'Serenata Francese', written by Giulio Ricordi under his pseudonym 'J. Burgmein'. Van Westerhout's first opera, *Cimbellino* (originally entitled *Imogene*), had impressed Ricordi sufficiently for him to take an option on the publication rights and to contemplate a production at La Scala in the season 1889-90. In the event, this did not materialise.

By this time, however, Naples thought of Van Westerhout as a local composer whose work the city council felt that it ought to foster and thereby gratify those critics who thought that, in return for its subsidy, the San Carlo should more actively promote new works. As early as January 1890 it had been agreed that *Cimbellino* would be given at the San Carlo the following year.[62] It had seemed entirely proper to make it an *opera d'obbligo* - a condition of awarding the concession to Villani.

It appears that De Lucia, whose triumphs at the San Carlo in 1889-90 had assured him of re-engagement for the following season, and Van Westerhout then read the score together at the singer's home. But the part of Leonato Postumo was for a dramatic tenor. After a brief audition De Lucia said to the composer: 'Adapt the part to my means and I will sing it.'[63]

If, at that time, Van Westerhout actually agreed to adapt the part the obligation does not seem to have weighed heavily with him. Possibly, he thought it merely a singer's whim, which would be forgotten during De Lucia's negotiations with Ricordi and Villani. For his part, the tenor may not have regarded the rôle as a definite commitment, especially so far in the future. There is adequate evidence that he often worked with composers on compositions that he may never have sung.[64]

The matter was, though, of political as well as artistic concern. In the struggles over the concession, one of Villani's arguments in support of his bid was his contract with Ricordi to present *Cimbellino*; this contract specified the artists, including - apparently at Van Westerhout's

---

[62] Ibid., Jan. 12 1890.

[63] S. Mormone, 'Cimbellino', *Roma*, Feb. 20 1891. This long and detailed article, which drew on a number of conversations with De Lucia and in which Mormone did not shrink from exposing his own errors, gives the best available insight into the tenor's reasons for his subsequent actions.

[64] For example, Achille Simonetti (Mar. 11 1897) sent him the music of his 'Madrigale', seeking advice on the key most suitable for tenor voice (R). In Feb. 1904 De Lucia invited an unidentified composer to lunch at the Grand Hôtel, Florence, in order to hear his work (BS). An undated letter from Leoncavallo to Mario Ancona strongly suggests that he wanted Ancona and De Lucia for the first performance of one of his operas, which is unidentified (A); in fact, De Lucia never created a Leoncavallo rôle at a world première.

insistence - De Lucia. There were those who - noting the lively interest shown in the opera in the cafés and the *salotti*, among journalists and men of letters alike - claimed that Villani's undertaking to mount it had been decisive in securing the concession.[65] In fact, as early as May 1890, Villani and Ricordi were already at odds over *Cimbellino*, the manager having found the publisher's demands 'excessive'. Ricordi countered by arguing that, to facilitate production of Van Westerhout's work, he had been 'generous' over *Lohengrin* and *La Gioconda*.[66]

Meanwhile, *Cavalleria Rusticana* had created a sensation at Rome. In the second round of negotiations for the concession Villani's promise to give that opera assumed primacy, principally to satisfy the curiosity of those with weighty influence at the San Carlo. The new contract eventually negotiated in the summer of 1890 did not oblige Villani to give *Cimbellino*, but left it to his discretion.

As the 1890-1 season drew nearer, De Lucia realised that he had, perhaps, been insufficiently emphatic a year earlier. He declared that the part was unsuited to his voice, and declined to sing it.

The news was received with dismay by Ricordi, who sent the tenor a telegram:

> With the greatest displeasure we learn [of] your refusal [of] *Cimbellino*. [In] arranging this work we had counted on your acceptance, the more so knowing the composer [to be] willing to make necessary changes at the point [that is] unsatisfactory to you. Such a refusal makes it impossible to give the opera [and] causes serious harm to a young composer. We beg you to re-examine the part with the composer, certain that you will agree to accept it.[67]

The tenor evidently agreed to reconsider since, next day, Ricordi again telegraphed:

> Very happy at the last telegram, I hope that new, diligent scrutiny can convince you [of the] possibility of acceptance. I trust that the Maestro will be able to make adequate arrangements for those points which need changing, such that you can assume the engagement with full confidence, this being an important point in our common interest. I thank you for new proof of friendship towards the composer.[68]

Fresh examination of the problems, however, failed to resolve them. Barely three weeks before the opening of the season, Villani announced that *Cimbellino* would not, after all, be given because De Lucia - 'God almighty' as Bracco termed him - had declared, by implication recently, that the part was unsuitable for his voice, and because no replacement

---

65 *Fortunio*, Nov. 16 1890.

66 Ibid., May 25 1890.

67 (R) Ricordi - De Lucia, Nov. 13 1890. 'Ricordi' *tout court* here denotes a communication (usually a telegram) not specifically identifiable as from Giulio or Tito Ricordi.

68 (R) Ricordi - De Lucia, Nov. 14 1890.

was available.[69] Others, however, pointed out that

> ... De Lucia has always said this, despite which he was included among the performers notified to the Council and to Ricordi. Thus, the situation is not unexpected.[70]

The tenor was actually under no obligation to Villani to sing the part; indeed, according to Mormone, he had declared, succinctly, shortly after his return from America, that he could not do so, judging it unsuitable.[71] Mormone applauded his reluctance to 'commit sacrilege in destroying a work of art'. Villani, he wrote, should look for another tenor.[72] The crisis at the San Carlo continued, as did the ecclesiastical parallels:

> Today there are two Popes, Leo XIII and Fernando De Lucia. Together they reply: 'Non possumus!'[73]

One evening, Mormone - who evidently enjoyed the singer's confidence - found himself, by chance, in a music shop in the company of Van Westerhout, De Lucia, and mutual friends. He sought to persuade the tenor to accept the part. There ensued a technical discussion between maestro and singer, one seated at the piano and the other softly singing the new music to prove that its *tessitura* was beyond his capabilities. In the ensembles he would have to remain silent - not an unusual operatic practice - especially in the final trio of the opera. Van Westerhout offered to lower the part for him, and suggested that he should rest at the points where the score required him to sing in unison with the others.

Mormone did not press the matter, since each had a legitimate point. De Lucia feared a fiasco for himself and for his friend Van Westerhout; the composer would not consider any solution not involving De Lucia, since he doubted that Villani would engage another artist of his calibre.

Later, De Lucia explained his objections further. As he accompanied Mormone to his home, he exclaimed:

> What do you want? Would you have me cause my own ruin, [while] damaging my voice to no one's benefit? [I accept that] it is a college companion, a brother in art, who asks my help. Well then, ... I solemnly undertake to sing the music of another Conservatory pupil, Daniele Napoletano, [music] which, with two other pieces, obtained an honourable mention in the Concorso Sonzogno, and which Uda, Bracco, and you tried in vain to have mounted last year. If *Cimbellino* succeeds it will be said that, with another tenor, it would have been a triumph, and if it fails everything will fall on to my shoulders![74]

69　*Corriere di Napoli*, Nov. 15/16 and 16/17 1890.

70　*Roma*, Nov. 14 1890.

71　Only one newspaper, *Piccolo*, Feb. 14/15 1891 actually specified that the *tessitura* was too high for his voice. Others said merely that it was unsuitable.

72　*Roma*, Nov. 15 1890.

73　Ibid., Nov. 16 1890. *Occhialetto*, too, favoured Papal comparisons.

74　Mormone, loc. cit.

Villani suggested the tenor Eugenio Galli, already engaged for *Ernani* and *Spartaco*, for the part of Postumo and, despite some doubts, the Commission exhorted Van Westerhout to accept him. The composer then found himself in a dilemma: to accept a less-than-ideal singer or to reject him and lose the rare opportunity of a production at the San Carlo. He agreed to accept Galli '*in principle, providing that the part is amenable to his means as a dramatic tenor*' (Mormone's italics).[75]

Galli duly came to Naples and studied for a month with Van Westerhout. Initial reports were encouraging; the composer was reported to be very happy with him, especially with his 'Tamagno-like high notes'.[76] Privately, however, the omens were less good. A letter from the composer to Villani, alluding to Galli, complained:

I have to confirm that his vocal means [are] powerful, but in no way compatible with singing that is all *sfumature*, to which he cannot lend himself.[77]

Behind the scenes, fresh representations had already been made to De Lucia, the favourite of the *sicofanti*. And, this time, he agreed to sing the part. On January 2nd 1891 he wrote to Ricordi, confirming this; it was doubtless a relieved publisher who, in expressing his thanks, reassured him:

Among all the equivocation regarding *Cimbellino*, we have never heard any reproach of you: we know how theatrical matters sometimes proceed. In any event, we are very pleased at the favourable outcome . . . [78]

It was announced, probably to save Galli's face, that he had laryngitis and that De Lucia, as 'the only healthy tenor, the only *distinguished tenor*', had agreed to assume the rôle and thus to rescue Van Westerhout from serious embarrassment. Mormone reported that the part was to be modified, including changes in the concerted pieces and the replacement of the original tenor aria by one written specially for De Lucia.[79]

The source of this intelligence on the changes is not clear. However, Van Westerhout responded immediately to the announcement with a letter that Mormone published without comment, in order to avoid embarrassment to the composer, who had written:

Naples, January 5th 1891

Dear Cav. Mormone,

I have read your otherwise well-disposed words regarding *Cimbellino*. It is true that the eminent tenor De Lucia, through my solicitude and that of mutual

75 Ibid.
76 *Roma*, Jan. 4 1891.
77 Mormone, loc. cit. The date of this letter was not given.
78 (R) Letter Ricordi - De Lucia, Jan. 3 or 5 1891.
79 *Roma*, Jan. 4 1891.

friends, has kindly agreed to assume the part of Leonato Postumo, thus giving
me a solemn proof of brotherhood. This was my first and most heartfelt wish,
being certain that no other artist could better interpret such a dramatic and
passionate part. It is not equally true that I have had to modify it profoundly,
since the means of the distinguished De Lucia permit him to surmount many
other difficulties. The truth is that, as with the other parts, I have revised the
part of Leonato according to my most recent inspirations. . . .
   I take this opportunity to thank my friend De Lucia publicly.[80]

This defiant and quite unexpected revelation set the scene for an
inevitable clash between a tenor who knew his limitations and who,
further, insisted on being seen to have his own way, and a composer who,
whatever changes he might privately have accepted, in public resolutely
maintained his artistic integrity.

Some time later, as Mormone was reproaching De Lucia for his
indecisiveness, the tenor retorted:

'What did you want me to do?'

He was committed to go on stage with *Cavalleria Rusticana*. He did
not want to make an enemy of anyone.

'If they were to hiss me, to speak ill of me in the press! I had a fear of refusing
any longer. I consented . . . . . '[81]

Hereafter the accounts, as recorded by Mormone, conflict. Van
Westerhout insisted that the agreement with De Lucia had involved
'suitable and opportune modifications' to the part, made during 'many
visits to the artist's house to study it'. The singer claimed that hardly
anything had been changed, nor had they reached the fourth act, where
there is a trio which requires an exceptional vocal range.[82]

Van Westerhout may have been sincere when promising, at the outset,
to adapt the part: if he was not, lip-service to the singer's concerns was a
cynical attempt to keep him without altering the opera. De Lucia, a
trained musician, certainly realised that rewriting would change the
nature of the part: unless he believed that his own importance now
demanded no less, he must have known that only minor changes were
likely and so felt under no moral obligation to someone who, he believed,
had not honoured his promise. Even Bracco, a staunch ally of Van
Westerhout, admitted that, despite the changes, the part of Postumo was
still not easy for De Lucia. What, above all, was lacking was an effective
intermediary between the stubborn composer and the volatile tenor.

---

80 Ibid., Jan. 5 1891.
81 Mormone, loc. cit.
82 Ibid.

Rehearsals eventually started at the beginning of February. Ricordi was far from pleased at the delay.[83] Moreover, the atmosphere at the San Carlo had changed, and to the detriment of *Cimbellino* and its composer. His understandable desire for a good *mise-en-scène*; the hurdles encountered but (apparently) overcome in the tenor part; the difficulty of the music; the character of the maestro himself, who, with cronies who cared for nothing except *Cimbellino*, was seen entering and leaving by the steps of the theatre instead of by the stage entrance; even the composer's name, with its supposed Germanic and Wagnerian overtones, and the flower that he customarily wore in his buttonhole: all this - trivial or serious - served to generate a hostile current which soon communicated itself to the performers.[84] The imagined obstacles - the only real one had, perhaps, been resolved when De Lucia changed his mind, and accepted the part - multiplied. *Cimbellino* and its composer had now become anathema to those with influence at the San Carlo. There were problems with the chorus. For the artists, some of whom felt demeaned in secondary parts, *Cimbellino* was clearly too difficult to be learned in the time available. Cattaneo was quoted as saying that it was even more demanding than *Tristan*: *Cimbellino* could be called the 'future of the future'.

By mid-February, it was obvious that those who feverishly awaited De Lucia in the new opera would now be disappointed. At the fourth rehearsal the difficulties were at last admitted to be insurmountable, and he finally renounced the part. When, shortly afterwards, he went to the principal critics, it was to state that all involved were alarmed. The artists felt that excessive work was necessary to mount it. The management was concerned over the number of rehearsals necessary for a work that might well be a failure.

Clearly, however, the difficulty of the music was not the whole story. With the season about half over, Villani still had outstanding commitments. Time was short. Neither *Spartaco* nor Giannetti's *L'Erebo* could be neglected for *Cimbellino*. *L'Erebo*, although outside the subscription, was the subject of a private contract between management and composer who, in a common enough practice, was evidently paying for its production. *Spartaco* was a delicate matter through the position of its composer - Platania was Director of San Pietro a Maiella - and of its status as a contractual opera with the Council but, above all, because its publisher owned the rights to *Cavalleria Rusticana* and *Carmen* and was therefore the real arbiter. Inexplicably, this was not foreseen by Van Westerhout and Ricordi as, from December 1890, they worked to present *Cimbellino*.[85]

---

83 (R) Letter Ricordi - Van Westerhout, Jan. 28 1891.

84 R. Bracco, 'La volontà di un tenore', *Corriere di Napoli*, Feb. 16/17 1891.

85 *Spartaco* (3 performances) had its première on Mar. 29; the single performance of *Erebo* took place on Apr. 9 1891.

Villani could not afford heroic gestures. *Cimbellino* was impossible without sacrificing *Spartaco* and, should this antagonise Sonzogno, there would be no *Carmen*, with a consequent loss of revenue; moreover, *Carmen* needed De Lucia, who would by then be occupied with *Cimbellino*.

De Lucia also wanted *Carmen*, to assure a successful end to the season. He had, however, accepted the part of Postumo, and he was probably resigned to singing it. He had made his promise in good faith, and there is no evidence of duplicity as, time and again, he reassured a puzzled and dubious Van Westerhout. It was the poor reception of *Rigoletto* that appeared to change his mind. Until then, trusting in his local popularity, De Lucia had always yielded to his artistic impulses. After *Rigoletto*, he took heed of his own position: he realised that he needed a success, and this was the death sentence for *Cimbellino*. He saw that his support among the *sicofanti* would not overcome their hostility towards Van Westerhout, and that the benevolence of the critics, most of whom had hitherto praised him for refusing an unsuitable part, would not save him from severe, albeit just, criticism if the opera failed. The dark forecasts of impresario, critics, and company reinforced his pessimism. *Cimbellino* seemed to offer only the prospect of leaving Naples, after two seasons of work, amid hisses. He was continually assailed by nervous doubts. In the charged atmosphere of the fourth rehearsal he could restrain himself no longer, and exclaimed: 'I will not sing *Cimbellino*.'[86]

When, on February 13th, he conveyed his decision to Uda and other critics he promised that he would explain his reasons in full, first to Van Westerhout and then in public. Uda still hoped that the tenor could be swayed and would again change his mind. He emphasised the grave responsibilities that, as a Neapolitan, he would assume by clouding the future of a Neapolitan maestro. That he was insufficiently persuasive is seen from the letters which followed:[87]

Naples, February 14th 1891

Dear Cav. Uda,

I am sure that you will wish to publish in *Pungolo* the enclosed letter from me to Van Westerhout, from which you will [be able] to assess, with your impartial judgement, the reasons.

To this letter I must today add the following declaration: Regarding my refusal to sing *Cimbellino*, isolated voices, which impugn my loyalty, seek to repudiate a *jury* of our most notable maestros, chosen in common with Van Westerhout, which will judge whether or not the part of Leonato Postumo in that opera is suited to my vocal means. I undertake to accept the verdict of the jury and abide by it.

---

86 Mormone, loc. cit.
87 *Pungolo*, Feb. 15/16 1891. Identical letters were addressed to other Neapolitan newspapers, including *Corriere di Napoli, Piccolo,* and *Roma*.

Pungolo then published the tenor's letter to Van Westerhout:

Naples, February 13th 1891

Carissimo Maestro Van Westerhout,

Through the affection that binds us I undertook the rehearsals of *Cimbellino*, notwithstanding that, even before commencing them, I had expressed to you my feelings on the impossibility of adapting it to my vocal means.

Today, then, after the rehearsals, I am entirely convinced that *Cimbellino*, for all that it is a work worthy of your highest genius, cannot be adapted and, despite all the goodwill between us, its *tessitura* and musical character make it unsuitable for my means.

You know my repertoire, and you know very well that it includes neither *Ugonotti* nor *Otello* nor *Africana;* and this [is] because I am conscious that, at least for now, it is not possible for me to interpret such operas.

Nor is my doubt the child of my own opinion; our distinguished conductors can testify to my goodwill, and have confirmed my doubts in your presence.

I would never permit you, on my account, to alter your work. In such a case, I would assume responsibility for a failure that, in any case, several notable critics are believed to have anticipated already, while *Cimbellino* would undergo modifications which would alter your beautiful opera.

From this moment, I promise you that, in other scores, better adapted to my means, I shall be most happy to lend you, with fraternal affection, my work.

Embracing you, Always your friend,
Fernando De Lucia

It was generally felt that this came, at best, tardily. Certainly, there had been misgivings about the work, not least on the part of Mormone himself.[88] For him, two facts were inexplicable: for two years, Niccolò Van Westerhout had not realised that his friend's gifts were unsuited to the part of Postumo and, perhaps at a time when De Lucia needed work, had persuaded Ricordi to insist that he be engaged to sing the part.[89] Moreover, De Lucia - described by Mormone as a very shrewd man, who knew both the pressures on Villani and the hostility of other factions - had allowed himself to become everyone's scapegoat. And the press berated him not for his decision - with few exceptions its wisdom was not questioned - but for his vacillation, when a resolute 'No!' would have given time for other solutions. One of those exceptions was Bracco who, still maintaining that the part had been modified to meet De Lucia's needs, accused him of being unwilling to disrupt his

... enormously remunerative and triumphantly successful career to help a friend, a companion, a Neapolitan ... [and] to keep his word. Ferdinando De Lucia ... who [was] born in Naples, and for whom the unstinted applause of his native city has led to many profitable triumphs in America, is a most excellent tenor, a most respected artist, but a bad friend and a very bad Neapolitan.[90]

---

88 *Roma*, Feb. 15 1891.

89 Both Mormone and Bracco make it clear that the opera had had a wide exposure at Naples, possibly as early as 1887-8, and long before there were definite plans to produce it there.

90 *Corriere di Napoli*, Feb. 16/17 1891.

For Bracco and for others De Lucia's worst crime was that he had not kept his word. The matter rumbled on acrimoniously. Letters in the newspapers debated the rôles accessible to a tenor of *mezzo carattere* and whether or not Van Westerhout was a Wagnerian.[91] Were not tenors really the third sex, who thought and loved only with the throat?[92] De Negri and Oxilia were in turn proposed for the part, but were quickly discarded. Marconi, latterly engaged to sing *Spartaco* at the San Carlo, read the score with Van Westerhout and agreed to undertake it. It would then be necessary to extend the season.[93] Villani demanded 20,000 lire for scenery and other expenses. Ricordi, it seems, was unwilling to provide funds and the matter was quietly dropped. Not until April 1892 did *Cimbellino* have its première, not at Milan or Naples but at the Teatro Argentina, Rome, with Benedetto Lucignani, the Radames and Eleazar of that season, as Postumo. Even then, Procida's review pilloried De Lucia in absentia; without naming him, he referred to 'precious tenors of half - or no - character'.[94]

With *Carmen* in rehearsal, De Lucia, on safe ground once more, had time to relax in a box at the San Carlo to hear Zerni sing Turiddu. His confidence in his own reception as Don José was amply justified. While the press found the general effect lacking in vitality, De Lucia and Giulia Novelli repeated their triumphs of the previous year. Procida noted that 'he put into the part a certain affectation that is by now the signature of De Lucia'.[95] Others found his acting more controlled and correct. His 'excessive vitality' found a 'natural and legitimate vent in that part, an effusion of intense life'. He had abandoned the *parlando* of the previous year.[96] He no longer yielded to certain perversions of taste.[97] He was:

> ... so impassioned, so tender, so terribly fascinated by a fatal passion, in other words a Don José so human that the public was obliged to ignore the defects of an otherwise imperfect performance to concentrate on the miracles of singing and acting of the ideal Don José.[98]

At the final *Carmen* he took ten curtain calls. For him, at least, it was a satisfactory end to a turbulent season.

---

[91] A long analysis of rôles sung by various tenors appeared in *Occhialetto*, Feb. 21 1891, one of the few papers to defend De Lucia. Bracco indulged in intemperate and fanciful speculation on the subject (*Corriere di Napoli*, Feb. 16/17 1891).

[92] Arturo Colautti, open letter in *Pungolo*, Feb. 25/26 and Feb. 26/27 1891.

[93] *Roma*, Feb. 23 1891.

[94] *Fortunio*, Apr. 15 1892. The autograph score of *Cimbellino* is in the library of the Conservatory of San Pietro a Maiella.

[95] *Fortunio*, Mar. 2 1891.

[96] *Occhialetto*, Mar. 7 1891.

[97] *Roma*, Mar. 1 1891.

[98] *Piccolo*, Mar. 1/2 1891.

8

Villas and Verismo

The wife of an artist has a mission different from that of wives of ordinary men. This is something you have never wanted to understand. Indeed, you sneer when the word 'art' is pronounced.   Giacomo Puccini[1]

From the San Carlo of Naples De Lucia went to the Teatro Costanzi of Rome. In 1888, Edoardo Sonzogno had obtained a three-year concession of that theatre as a platform for his operas in the capital of Italy. At a time of intense competition between the publishing houses the word 'war' was not simply a fiction of the press. It was a campaign waged with ruthlessness and enormous financial resources. Sonzogno, his operas blocked at La Scala by the hegemony of Ricordi, had eventually to make his own entry into Milan by building the Teatro Lirico Internazionale, which was inaugurated on September 22nd 1894 on the site of the old Teatro Canobbiana. Meanwhile, the Sonzogno season of 1888-9 at the Costanzi had included works over which Ricordi claimed absolute control. Long legal cases ensued as Ricordi sought damages, but the season, including some of the disputed works, went ahead with a prestigious roster of singers, among whom were Calvé, Cotogni, Ferni-Germano, Garulli, Kaschmann, Litvinne, Nevada, and Tamagno.[2] Subsequently, however, Sonzogno sought to establish his own lyric repertoire.

De Lucia made his début at the Costanzi in *I Pescatori di Perle*, with Calvé, on May 5th 1891. The reserved Roman public, determined not to be impressed by the fame that had preceded him, withheld the courtesy of a salute on his appearance. Soon, however, he created one for himself. His opening phrases

> ... were delivered with an absolutely surpassing vocal eloquence and dramatic effectiveness. Gradually, the public was transported by the strength and consistency of his voice ... the impassioned warmth of the phrasing ... the tenderness of diction, the facility, the ease of emission ... the fascination of the voice, of the expression, and of the gesture which are the true prerogatives of the first rank singer. Master of a beautiful voice, formidable in the middle notes

---

1 Giacomo Puccini, writing to his wife, Aug. 30 1915, Marek, op. cit., p. 92.

2 Frajese, op. cit., Vol. I, p. 94ff.

and equally powerful over the entire range of the scales he can, with art and delicate mastery, make it obedient and docile and with it he can design the softest and most subtle line.[3]

Eugenio Checchi, one of the most respected and influential Roman critics, wrote in *Fanfulla*, under his pen-name, 'Tom':

Fernando De Lucia ... intoned his first notes, secure, vigorous, limpid, into the air with unusual vibrancy, launched them like a man who wants to give battle, and to win it at once.

The victory was his, full and undisputed. The first sign was a murmur of surprise and approval; then, hard on the heels of those fleeting and brilliant notes, came full, unanimous, completely enthusiastic applause. Not only a victory, it was a true conquest of the public ...

[He] conquered and fascinated with the extraordinary power of some notes, with the tenderness of others, with passages [sung with] skill and with admirable *smorzature*, with accents and modulations which are always fitting. Rich in natural gifts, he can make them, so to speak, more polished or more resplendent with the most exacting of all arts, that which conceals art ... Sometimes, something that seems a spontaneous outburst of passion is the result of considered reflection and patient research, unfailing in effect.

For De Lucia, acting and singing are of equal importance and the one never obscures the other, nor *vice versa*: but they are alloyed together, blending to support one another in turn ... [4]

The presence of De Lucia and Calvé had given *I Pescatori di Perle* the character of a novelty. Of greater interest, though, was the revival of *Cavalleria Rusticana*. A year earlier, a sparse Costanzi audience had arrived blasé and had departed almost delirious after the first performance of the opera. Now, the rich and the influential crowded in, eager to compare Calvé and De Lucia with Bellincioni and Stagno.

The success started with the 'Siciliana', which De Lucia sang with

... secure voice and with very good taste. ... [In the] 'Brindisi', the reef for all Turiddus who are not called Stagno, he sang very well but ... the liveliness of gesture had no counterpart in the resilience, the vigour, the *portamenti* of the voice in those intrinsically vulgar phrases which, rather than sung, need to be hurled audaciously in the face of the audience.[5]

Despite general approval, it was asked why Calvé and De Lucia, in performing a new opera, had not given an original and personal interpretation. When physical, intellectual, and vocal gifts were different, was it not inevitable that the imitators would always fall short of the imitated? The Costanzi audience, expecting from these two artists a more idyllic, less *veristico* performance, had instead witnessed something more realistic than truth itself.[6]

---

3 *Popolo Romano*, May 6 1891.
4 *Fanfulla*, May 6/7 1891.
5 *Tribuna*, May 14 1891.
6 Ibid., May 14 1891.

On May 17th, the anniversary of its première, *Cavalleria Rusticana* was conducted by Mascagni. The performance of May 23rd was the *serata d'onore* of De Lucia and Calvé. The profusion of flowers gave the soprano the appearance of standing in a garden; the tenor was completely surrounded by wreaths. One was from Mascagni. It bore the words: '*Al mio Fritz*'. For there was exciting news of his next work.

Soon after the initial success of *Cavalleria Rusticana*, Mascagni had asked its poets, Menasci and Targioni-Tozzetti, for another libretto; they had suggested *Les deux frères*, by the Alsatian writers Emile Erckmann and Alexandre Chatrian. Mascagni found the play 'immensely pleasing', and by August 1890 he was working on Sonzogno's commission to write an opera on it, under the title *I Rantzau*.[7] But, even then, Sonzogno was seeking a more suitable subject for Mascagni's next exposure to the public, a solution to the problem caused by the success of *Cavalleria*, and one that could be ready for the Costanzi autumn season of 1891.[8]

The topic arose soon after the San Carlo production of *Cavalleria Rusticana*. On or around January 20th 1891, Mascagni, Sonzogno, and Daspuro were travelling by train from Naples to Cerignola, where the publisher was to be godfather to Mascagni's second son. All agreed on the difficulty of finding a libretto for an opera which would not be an anticlimax. Mascagni was irritated by hints that *Cavalleria* owed its success to its subject, and his reaction is significant:

. . . as if the same subject, set by others, would have been successful. It is for this reason, above all, that I want a simple libretto, where the action is tenuous, flimsy. I want to be judged for the music, for nothing but the music . . . [9]

One alternative was to choose an idyllic rather than a dramatic subject, and Sonzogno already had a likely candidate; he produced from his case a slim volume, *L'Ami Fritz*, also by Erckmann and Chatrian, which Mascagni immediately settled down to read. After an hour he was convinced. He agreed to defer *I Rantzau* and to compose an opera on this fresh subject, asking Daspuro to prepare the libretto.

According to Daspuro, it was in March 1891 that he started his work at Cerignola, where he spent eleven days in the composer's house.[10] Nearly fifty years later he wrote of that period and of the speed with which his verses were set by Mascagni, whom - despite the personal qualities which he later abominated to the point of obsession - Daspuro unfailingly regarded as an authentic and astonishing genius. He was now experiencing what Menasci had described as the white heat of

7 Letter Mascagni - Lina Mascagni, Aug. 6 1890.

8 *Guglielmo Ratcliff*, on which Mascagni had worked since his student days, was not produced until 1895.

9 Pompei, op. cit., p. 119ff reports this conversation and also (p. 432) the failure of Gastaldon's *Mala Pasqua*, another setting of Verga's Sicilian drama, on which *Cavalleria Rusticana* is based.

10 David Stivender, *Mascagni*, p. 275, states that Mascagni started work on *Fritz* on Feb. 4 1891. No source is cited.

Mascagni's creativity, when he and Targioni-Tozzetti had been unable to produce verses quickly enough for the composer.[11] Particularly impressive was his ability, when his melodic inspiration was in full flood, to write with hardly a pause or a correction.[12]

Mascagni, though, had greatly changed since achieving fame and wealth. Socially, his uncommon intelligence, sparkling wit, and animated and brilliant conversation at the café, the club, and the *scopone*[13] table made him gracious, even delightful, company. An excellent mimic, he had a wicked sense of humour and a talent for clever puns.[14] He fascinated and enchanted almost all those with whom his dealings lay outside business, and it was theirs - those to whom he owed nothing in a professional sense - whose company he preferred.[15] But his relationships had quickly deteriorated with those who had helped him in his success. Dismissive of the contribution of Giovanni Verga, on whose play the libretto of *Cavalleria* had been based but whose name does not even appear on the title page of the score, he refused, until so ordered by the courts, to pay him royalties.[16] He soon came to regard the performances of Bellincioni, Stagno, and Mugnone as subtracting some of the credit that belonged to his music. He forgot the glee with which, on May 6th 1890, he had written to his wife:

What luck, Lina, to have this colossus [Stagno]. Yesterday morning he sang the finale astoundingly ... and I expressed my sincere admiration.[17]

Within three years he was at daggers drawn with his first Santuzza and Turiddu.[18] While always conscious of Mugnone's eccentricities, his correspondence with him soon after the first success of *Cavalleria* was fulsome in its praise and thanks.[19] Yet, there was soon a disagreement over the conductor's work in reducing the score of *Cavalleria* for voice and piano.[20] When Mugnone was passed over for the première of *L'Amico Fritz* it was an action widely criticised as, at least, ungrateful.

It is easy to understand the frustration of Daspuro, whose position involved frequent and detailed dealings with someone whom Sonzogno was anxious not to upset. Daspuro was well situated to observe the composer both professionally and socially, and we might excuse his almost obsessive fixation with Mascagni's alleged arrogance, ingratitude,

---

11 Richard Specht, *Giacomo Puccini*, p. 79.
12 Daspuro, 'Memorie', ch. XXXIV.
13 A game which uses a pack of forty cards.
14 Klein, *Thirty Years*, p. 384.
15 Daspuro, 'Memorie', ch. XXXII.
16 Morini, *Mascagni*, Vol. I, p. 290, documents some of the litigation between Mascagni, Sonzogno, and Verga. Daspuro, 'Memorie', recalls the composer's colourful language on the subject.
17 Pompei, op. cit., p. 80.
18 Bernardini Marzolla, loc. cit., p. 107.
19 Letters Mascagni - Mugnone, of June 1890, appear in *Gazzetta dei Teatri*, Jan. 15 1891.
20 Letter Mascagni - Galli, July 25 1890, see Morini, *Mascagni*, Vol. I, pp. 293-4.

and psychotic jealousy of anyone with whom he had to share his fame. However, though he gave vent to his feelings more freely than did most others, Daspuro was not alone in finding him impossible.[21] The chronicle of Mascagni's stormy career provides many examples of more or less bitter open letters to the press and of public quarrels - occasionally leading to fisticuffs - with singers, conductors, and even with Sonzogno.[22]

Daspuro, who - by omission - implies that the libretto of *Fritz* was his alone, writes of the compromises that Mascagni obliged him to make, including the elimination of the chorus from the stage in the interest of making the opera cheap to mount and, therefore, the potential source of, in the composer's words, '*danari a cappellate*'.[23] Nevertheless, as he departed for Naples, Daspuro seems to have believed that he had left behind a composer who was content with what they had achieved together.[24] Subsequently - he alleges - Mascagni became resentful of the interest created by the libretto. In order to placate him, he offered to waive his own royalties and suggested that Sonzogno devise a pseudonym for the poet. If true, it was a futile gesture: not only was it already widely known that the libretto was by Daspuro, but the *nom-de-plume* (P. Suardon) was far from profound.

Half a century later, the composer - by then much mellowed - stated in 1942 or 1943 that Daspuro's verses had been unsatisfactory and that other help had had to be enlisted.[25] The second part, at least, of this statement is supported by Mascagni's correspondence with Amintore Galli, whence it emerges that contributions were made by Angelo Zanardini, by Menasci and Targioni-Tozzetti, and by Mascagni.[26] The librettists of *Cavalleria* evidently prepared the verses for Act III but when, at the railway station in Naples, Mascagni was robbed of the case containing it the composer himself wrote the poetry for the love duet.

Some qualification must therefore attach to the view that P. Suardon is a simple pseudonym for N. Daspuro, who was content to use his own name for the libretto of Giordano's *Mala Vita* (1892), recast in 1897 as *Il Voto*. Mascagni, in his old age, stated that Suardon was used because none of the authors subsequently involved wished to acknowledge an involvement.[27] It is more likely that none felt able to claim sole authorship and that the name finally chosen was a face-saving device which nodded in the direction of the principal part played by Daspuro in

---

[21] Daspuro's memoirs, which - he stresses - were not intended for publication, return repeatedly to Mascagni, and little that he writes is complimentary towards him as a person. He must have realised that, given Mascagni's fondness for litigation, they could never be published while the composer lived.

[22] *Mattino*, Mar. 15/16 1905 documents an incident of two days earlier, when Mascagni had assaulted the baritone Lequien during rehearsals of *Amica* at Monte Carlo.

[23] 'Money by the hatful'.

[24] Daspuro, 'Memorie', ch. XXXV.

[25] Salvatore De Carlo, *Mascagni Parla*, pp. 189-90.

[26] Mascagni - Galli, Aug. 24 and Sept. 7 1891 (Morini, *Mascagni*, Vol. I, p. 298).

[27] De Carlo, op. cit., p. 190.

arrangement of scenes and in partial versification. That Daspuro ignores the contribution of the others is either dissimulation or self-delusion. What is indisputable is that, late in April, he returned to Naples bearing his libretto and the news that the music was now substantially complete. On May 15th, Mascagni arrived there with the score of the opera, at that stage named *Suzel*, and the announcement that he was to resume work on *I Rantzau*. Within days he was in Rome, to read the work - now renamed *L'Amico Fritz* and still lacking one or two pieces - to a group comprising Daspuro, De Lucia, Mugnone, Sonzogno, and three or four journalists, gathered at the Costanzi.[28] Mascagni sketched his musical ideas and detailed many of the vocal effects. As he did so, De Lucia closed his eyes, concentrating like a man unwilling to waste time, taking notes for the future.[29]

For De Lucia, the summer of 1891 was free from strenuous travels and appearances. It saw, however, significant changes in his personal life. He was now truly a man of substance, and he and Itala were able to consider acquiring a country house.

Some ten kilometres from Salerno and forty from Naples is Cava de' Tirreni, the *Città della Cava*.[30] It was, and remains, an unremarkable southern Italian small town in a pleasant valley. In the 1890s the long, winding main street, so heavily arcaded that the very light seemed to be shut out, was a jumble of carriages and oxen, wedding parties and tinkers, residents and visitors. The unpaved road was a morass in winter and a source of the thickest dust in summer. Cava's few architectural features included a square, a cathedral, and, following the extension of the line from Naples to Salerno and southwards, a railway station.

The charm of Cava lies in its setting. Often called 'the little Switzerland of Italy', it is characterised by the hills and mountains which surround it, and by the thick chestnut woods on their heights. Its pyramid-like peaks, crowned by cross or monastery, slope one beyond the other, casting long shadows into the valleys. In the late nineteenth century it was a strange, striking, still unspoiled landscape. The peace of its sylvan surroundings, its beautiful panoramic views over the Gulf of Salerno, and its healthy summer climate, high above the stifling heat of the cities, had made Cava a popular place of *villeggiatura* for the nobility and the prosperous professional classes since the eighteenth century. When, in 1857, Ferdinando II inaugurated the railway extension from Nocera, still more visitors came to Cava.[31] From Naples, the journey itself now made a pleasant day excursion through plum and pear orchards and orange and lemon groves, whose fragrance overpowered even the smells of the passing steam engines. The opening of the Teatro

28 Mascagni was still improving *L'Amico Fritz* a year after its première.

29 Peppino Turco in *Capitan Fracassa*, quoted in *Gazzetta dei Teatri*, May 28, 1891.

30 Often spelled Cava dei Tirreni, see Valerio Canonico, *Noterelle Cavesi*, Vol. II, p. 52.

31 Domenico Apicella, *Sommario Storico-Illustrativo della Città della Cava*, p. 83.

Municipale in 1879 made Cava additionally attractive, and was an important cultural event for the summer colony.[32]

The *villeggiatura* was more than a simple holiday. It was based on comfortable private villas and on hotels which catered for visitors who returned each year for a stay of several months. Thus, the communities that it formed were, in their way, as formalised, stable, and rigid as those of the city in winter. Each resort had its habitués. At the Hôtel Tramontano of Sorrento, Neapolitan *villeggianti* would be joined by their counterparts in Roman society to form yacht parties which would cruise down the peninsula, pausing for luncheon at the inns and hotels of Amalfi. Others, turning their backs on the sea, preferred the mountains of Val d'Aosta or the healing waters of Salsomaggiore. Some fled the city as early as May and the stragglers might not return until November.

Cava de' Tirreni was a favourite resort of the wealthy of Salerno and Naples. One of the most picturesque of its outlying villages, accessible only by a track which wound its way between the olive trees of the mountainside, was Rotolo, which was then a place of few residents and remarkable chiefly for a dozen or so villas of the *villeggiatura*. Around 1886, Itala's father, Eduardo, had built there a substantial house, Villa Erminia, distinguished from the others by severe yet harmonious architecture, and by a size and quality that indicated his prosperity. All the furniture was designed especially for it. Here, in the company of friends from Salerno and Cava, the De Giorgio family spent its summers, and here Itala and Fernando often came to visit them.[33]

In May 1891 Itala purchased a neighbouring villa.[34] Although built on less grand a scale than the family house nearby, its situation was irresistible. From its commodious master bedroom and from the shady terraces of its hillside site spread a view of fields, woods, vineyards, and, between the mountains, of the Gulf of Salerno. It was a place of tranquillity, of cool air, and of the sound of rushing water and singing birds, a refuge from the cacophony of Naples. Over a period of years the De Lucias enlarged and improved it by adding a spacious salon and creating extra terraces. Luxuriously furnished, it was a comfortable and peaceful refuge for their family, and there, cared for by numerous servants, they spent their summers.

In addition to gardeners, chambermaids, and scullions, the household now included a valet, Enrico Onesti, who invariably accompanied De Lucia on his tours. When the singer travelled *en famille* the entourage might also include the coachman Pasquale Coppola, the chef Luciano,

32 Canonico, *Noterelle Cavesi*, Vol. I, pp. 73-81.

33 Ibid., Vol. III, p. 70.

34 The villa was always registered in Itala's name and, years later, she stated that she had bought it with her father's help. Since, on his death only six weeks after the purchase, Eduardo had considerable debts it seems more likely that De Lucia provided most or all of the purchase price. Indeed, the tenor wrote of having made her a gift of the property, which was probably registered in Itala's name for tax purposes. She, as will be seen, later had every reason to wish to depreciate her husband's contribution to the purchase.

and the maid Rosa. All four remained for many years in De Lucia's
employ. He treated them not as servants but as equals from a
background not unlike his own. Enrico, a small man, no taller than his
master, took his meals with the De Lucia family. Luciano, when he had
finished his work in the kitchen, would be bidden to join them. On the
chef's days off, Enrico - 'Errico' in the Neapolitan dialect in which he and
his master conversed - would deputise most ably in the kitchen. He was
much given to speaking for De Lucia, using the royal 'we'. When
conversing with the Director of the San Carlo, Enrico would say:
'Tomorrow we will come to rehearsal' and, on returning home after the
performance, it would be: 'Tonight we sang very well.' With De Lucia, to
whom he soon became indispensable, he travelled *au grand seigneur*; he
smoked only the best Havana cigars because, he said, he had to be a
reflection of his master's life.[35] He enjoyed the singer's complete
confidence: on performance days at the opera only Enrico could approach
him. To Itala, who had certainly been brought up amid servants who
knew their place, he quickly seemed to assume unwonted, even
insufferable, familiarity.[36]

In June 1891, apparently after a heart attack, Eduardo De Giorgio
died. It was soon clear that he was in debt, including 13,000 lire owed to
De Lucia, and that his widow, Penelope, had financial difficulties. These
were temporarily resolved when, in a reversal of fortunes for the two
families, De Lucia lent her almost 27,000 lire against the security of
Villa Erminia and other properties.[37]

The summer saw a slow crescendo of preparation for *L'Amico Fritz*. In
September, De Lucia went to Cerignola to study the work with Mascagni.
Calvé was to sing Suzel. The part of David, originally assigned to Victor
Maurel,[38] was eventually sung by Paul Lhérie, who was selected by
Mascagni himself.[39] Rodolfo Ferrari would conduct. The intense
expectation weighed heavily on the composer who, conscious of his
responsibilities, lived in continuous anxiety, unable to eat or to rest. No
longer the young maestro, he was the Maestro from whom much was
expected. Incapable of preserving the element of surprise, he allowed
groups of confidants - and his confidence was sometimes misplaced - to
hear the opera at the piano, incautiously nourishing ill-considered
discussion and judgement. Months before the first night, the work was
being subjected to detailed analysis by the critics.[40]

Five days before the première, with the Costanzi closed for rehearsals,
Mascagni arrived and heightened the interest still further by inviting

35 De Lucia family.
36 De Roberto, op. cit., p. 14.
37 *Atto privato* No. 217, Naples, May 1 1892, of Notar Gaetano Catalano.
38 *Occhialetto*, May 16 1891.
39 Letter Mascagni - Checchi, Cerignola, Sept. 11 1891, printed in *Fanfulla*, Nov. 1/2 1891.
40 *Gazzetta dei Teatri*, May 28 1891.

selected critics and musicians to a full-dress *antiprova*. In the general avidity for the smallest morsels of intelligence the press reported with increasing interest the most minute details of the scenery and properties, from Suzel's watering-can to the authentic Alsatian tablecloths.[41]

On October 31st 1891 the Costanzi was filled to overflowing; Roman society had been joined by an unusually large number of musicians, eager to learn of the development of the young composer. Bellincioni - strikingly dressed and bejewelled - and Stagno were joined by Hariclea Darclée, Maurel, and Tamagno. Lombardi and Villani were there to assess the prospects for Naples; the massed ranks of the press of Milan, Naples, and Venice were only part of what was thought to have been the largest gathering of musical critics, from many countries, to attend the première of an opera.[42]

Of the singers, perhaps only Calvé emerged with a clear triumph. She was variously described as a soprano of purest voice, with a refined and tender interpretation, an inspired artist of great good taste, and as 'absolutely divine', although somewhat overweighted by the final duet. Mascagni appears to have disagreed; it is reported that, when taking calls with Calvé after the second act, he turned to her and said: 'At the Quirino, chorus-girls paid one-and-a-half lire a night sing less out of tune than you do.' Not surprisingly, she retired to her dressing-room, and required much persuasion to appear for the last act.[43]

For the rest, not even De Lucia, an unquestioned celebrity and, since October 19th, officially Commander of the Order of Isabella Cattolica, was master of the situation. An indisposition that had kept him from the *antiprova* had persisted. The critic of *Perseveranza* attributed the coldness of the public, at least in part, to his inability to extract all the effects that were expected of him in such a beautiful rôle as that of the 'Romeo of the Vosges'.[44] Galli termed him '... intelligent, a Fritz of golden voice and of wholly graceful singing,'[45] but *Riforma* was harsher:

> De Lucia was not well but, vocally, he left nothing to be desired especially in the second and third acts, while in the first he displeased through certain affectations which were out of place. Oddly, he neither felt nor explained the character. He is, in fact, as an artist, a passionate one, and here passion is not everything.[46]

In his last comment, the critic was taking up an admonishment to De Lucia in *Tribuna* after the *prova generale*, to wit that the Alsatian Fritz Kobus can never, even during his strongest passions, become Turiddu.

41 *Fanfulla*, Oct. 29/30 1891.
42 *Florence Gazette*, Nov. 14 1891.
43 Morini, *Mascagni*, Vol. I, p. 229n.
44 Quoted ibid., Vol. I, p. 214.
45 *Secolo*, Nov. 2 1891.
46 Quoted by Morini, *Mascagni*, Vol. I, pp. 214-15.

By the end of the second act, which Checchi thought the most inspired, '... a silver thread of melody that could have been spun by the hands of Spring herself', the success of the evening was assured. After the first part of the 'Cherry Duet', the *clou* of the evening, there was insistent applause, three calls for composer and singers, and an encore. At the conclusion of the duet there were five more calls and another encore. By comparison, Checchi considered the third act to be less impressive, partly because of its lack of melodic invention and partly because of

> ... the uncertainty of the tenor De Lucia, still unwell. When he can make us appreciate the broad and impassioned phrases of ... 'O amore, o bella luce del core', which was, however, repeated; when those two worthy artists Emma Calvé and Fernando De Lucia can put into the final duet, one of the pearls of the opera, all the force of passion, where last night it was paralysed by the indecision of someone who was unsure of himself, the third act will rise again.[47]

Attilio Luzzatto, in *Tribuna*, detected no sign of De Lucia's indisposition in the first or second acts, where he could lay claim to a part of the triumph,

> ... for the warmth and the effectiveness with which he sang the great phrases

> > 'Tu sei bella, o stagion primaverile!
> > Rinovella fiori e amor il dolce aprile!'

> In the third act duet a little tiredness was observed and, with it, some of that exaggeration noticed at the *prova generale*.
> But fairness dictates that I say today that the defect or, better, the excess, is not entirely of the artist but is in good part inherent in the piece.[48]

The audience had demanded more than thirty curtain calls, with encores for seven pieces, and the honours had gone principally to the composer. To many it seemed a mere *succès d'estime*, and it was a poor house on the second evening. However, the lull was only temporary, and later repeats were to capacity audiences. The last two performances had to be cancelled when De Lucia left for Naples, on the death of his father. In bereavement he did not neglect the proprieties, writing to Checchi to express his thanks to the people and press of Rome for their support.[49]

Fernando had been close to his parents. With so many children, they had doubtless found it difficult to support his musical education, and he had sought to repay his debt as soon as it became possible. Even as a serving soldier, he is said to have given lessons in double-bass in order to help provide for his family, his father having gone blind.[50] He was

---

[47] *Fanfulla della Domenica*, Nov. 1/2 1891.
[48] *Tribuna*, Nov. 2 1891.
[49] *Fanfulla*, Nov. 22/23 1891.
[50] Dell'Erba, *Giornale d'Italia*, Feb. 24 1925.

particularly devoted to his mother; though he preferred her not to be present in the theatre when he performed, he would sing for her at home. Her photograph, framed with a lock of her hair, was always in his dressing-room as a talisman. As his success grew so also did the scale of his provision for parents and for nearer relatives. Now, they were dependent on him for more essential needs than the dowry that he provided for each sister.

The première of *L'Amico Fritz* at the Teatro Pergola of Florence had been scheduled for November 26th 1891, as the work began its progress around the opera houses of Europe. Once again, an important opening night found De Lucia far away, engaged with family matters. But the Florentines waited patiently and, on November 28th, they confirmed the success of Rome. The audience abandoned its usual reserve. All around the theatre could be heard, *sotto voce*, *'Bravo, bravo'* as he sang *'Un strano turbamento'*.

> It was a succession of notes tender as virgins' sighs, sonorous as thunderclaps. At the passing of the final note, sweet as paradise, of *'La vita è amor'*, there was a burst of applause which moved even the artist.[51]

With little respite, he travelled to Madrid where, after an acute attack of bronchitis, he reappeared at the Real, first in *La Sonnambula* and then in *Il Barbiere di Siviglia*. His success was immediate. Of his performance in the former, on December 30th, one critic wrote:

> There is surely no one today, in Italy or elsewhere, who can rival De Lucia in the music of Elvino.[52]

But he was soon involved in controversy. One of the most admired rôles of Gayarre in Madrid had been Nadir, in *I Pescatori di Perle*. It was, however, a part which held tragic associations. In the season of 1889-90, despite failing health, the Spaniard had had a great triumph in *Lohengrin* at the Real. As a favour to the impresario he had then agreed to sing one performance of *I Pescatori*, on December 8th 1889. In the duet with Zurga he seemed to be at the peak of his powers but, when he attacked the highest note of the romanza, the sound broke in his throat. Near to collapse, he left the stage but returned after medical attention, determined to conquer the same piece. And so he did, but the note which had previously failed him came out only with a supreme effort and it lacked its usual purity. Immediately after the performance he had left the theatre. He had contracted the *grippe* then sweeping Madrid. A pulmonary infection soon followed. At dawn, on January 2nd 1890, the 'King of the Tenors' breathed his last.

---

51 *Vedetta*, quoted in *Teatro Illustrato*, Dec. 1891.
52 *Epoca*, Dec. 31 1891.

Snow covered the streets and squares of Madrid. Notwithstanding the weather and their fear of the *grippe*, people lined the streets to see the coffin pass to the station for the journey to El Roncal, the singer's home. Thousands wept openly. In front of the Royal Coliseum the cortège halted while the orchestra of the Real played Chopin's Funeral March and a choir sang the chorus of friars which precedes 'Spirto gentil', the aria most closely linked with the singer. 'All saw with sorrowful emotion ...the coffin that bore away the silent fountain-head of that extraordinary voice.'[53]

On January 13th 1892 Gayarre was commemorated in a gala performance: De Lucia and Giuseppina Pasqua gave Act I of *La Favorita*; other artists gave acts of *I Puritani* and *L'Africana*. The Queen and the Infanta Isabella watched from the Royal Box as, on stage, wreaths were placed around the bust of the dead tenor.[54]

Now, De Lucia was asked to sing *I Pescatori di Perle*. Aware of the circumstances and apprehensive of public reaction, he asked to be excused. The management insisted. On February 7th 1892 the Queen was present for this controversial revival, but many critics stayed away as a mark of respect for Gayarre. From the gallery came the sounds of lively disapproval of the irreverence. The audience was otherwise cold and unresponsive. Before the performance, De Lucia was seized with trepidation. He recalled:

> I carry a little coat given to me, as a boy, by my mother. I was alone in my dressing room and, kissing it and murmuring a prayer, I quickly thrust it beneath my costume.
>
> My reception was icy enough to have scared anyone. When I reached the point in the romanza at which the voice of the divine Gayarre began to fail I saw the audience bow its head, and the ladies covered their faces with their hands. I felt my legs shaking. The performance ended without applause. Two days later I was received with enthusiastic and prolonged ovations.[55]

On completion of his season, with *Cavalleria Rusticana*, *L'Elisir d'Amore*, and *Faust*, De Lucia returned to Naples and to family matters. It was time to buy a residence in keeping with his status, and one which was adequate for two families. In April 1892 he purchased from Arturo Gonzaga di Cirella an impressive and prestigious property, nothing less than the entire third floor of the Palazzo Cirella, at No. 228, Via Roma, Naples. It comprised some forty rooms, including a ballroom and a billiard-room, arranged as three apartments, and it overlooked Piazza San Ferdinando, a stone's throw from the San Carlo.[56] For this, together

---

53 Subira, op. cit., pp. 412-17.

54 *Gazzetta dei Teatri*, Feb. 18 1892.

55 De Lucia himself often recounted this story. Dell'Erba, *Giornale d'Italia*, Feb. 24 1925, wrongly gives the opera as *L'Africana* and incorrectly states that he took over the rôle within a week of Gayarre's last performance. In fact, he was at Naples at that time and did not sing Nadir at the Real until two years later. Far from receiving no applause, he gave an encore of the romanza (*Imparcial*, Feb. 8 1892).

56 Originally describing a palace, '*palazzo*' is now commonly applied to any tenement or block of flats.

with its cellar, coach-house, and stables for three horses, he paid the then immense sum of 170,000 lire.[57] It became very much a family colony. His mother and sisters lived there. For many years, his brother Federico had some rooms there, and his mother-in-law and some of Itala's brothers lived upstairs in the same building.

De Lucia had expected to make his début at La Scala, Milan in the Quaresima (Lent) Season of 1892.[58] Instead, early in May, he found himself back in London where, in operatic terms, much had changed since his début there. Harris - 'Sir Druriolanus Operaticus', as *Punch* referred to him - was lessee of both Drury Lane and Covent Garden, now named the Royal Opera House. For 1892, Harris had announced his intention of giving a special German subscription during the traditional opera season. His other innovation, electric lighting which was dimmed during the German works, very much annoyed those society ladies whose main requirement of the opera was that they should be seen.[59]

The success of Lago's production of *Cavalleria Rusticana* the previous year had persuaded Harris that the Mascagni work should open the season on May 16th, paired with *Philémon et Baucis*. 'The event', wrote Klein, 'was in the nature of a revelation.' Santuzza was sung by Calvé, who made a strong, immediate and 'indescribable ... impression [with her] strangely poignant tones, ... the extraordinary charm of her expressive singing, the tragic power and intensity of her acting. ... We realized that we were in the presence of a new and towering genius.'[60] By contrast, De Lucia was generally compared unfavourably with Francisco Viñas,[61] the first London Turiddu, but was judged '... an accomplished and spirited actor, and when he forgets his *tremolo* an excellent singer'.[62] Elsewhere '... though the quality of the voice in some of the loud passages was not altogether pleasant, he gave a vivid rendering of the part'.[63] Another critic wrote:

> His voice is powerful and his intonation is satisfactory, but his persistent tremolo mitigated against his success ... [In the duet with Santuzza his] acting was powerful, but on most occasions he sang to his audience what should have been sung to personages on stage.[64]

Punch (May 28th), however, considered his singing and acting unsurpassable. For the *Sunday Times* (May 22nd), his careless, easy-going manner was well in keeping with the character.

---

57 Conservatoria Registri Immobiliari. The sum would then have purchased, perhaps, twenty-five small houses.
58 *Occhialetto*, May 30 1891.
59 Rosenthal, op. cit., pp. 246-7.
60 Klein, *The Golden Age*, pp. 155-6.
61 In Italian sources, Francesco Vignas. In his native Catalan his forename is Francesc.
62 *Musical Times*, June 1 1892.
63 *Magazine of Music*, June 1892.
64 (CGA) Unidentified cutting.

A week later came *L'Amico Fritz*. The house, 'typical and representative of musical and artistic London, with more than a *soupçon* of the fashionable element', was at first apathetic, but became animated during the second act. One reviewer wrote:

> To drink in the beauties of the 2nd act of *Amico Fritz* is quite sufficient enjoyment for one evening, save, perhaps, to the greedy music lover who stipulates for his full three hours of ceaseless bliss. ... The gem of the act, however, and of the opera also, is the celebrated 'Cherry Duet'. ... This is a genuine inspiration, and Madame Calvé and Signor De Lucia well merited the rapturous encore.[65]

The Cherry Duet was, indeed, the focus of critical attention. Described by some as graceful, original, full of tender feeling, and going far to compensate for the other shortcomings of the work, it proved irresistible to Shaw - no admirer of Harris - who condescendingly pronounced:

> *L'Amico Fritz* ... is an opera which will pass the evening pleasantly enough for you, but which you need not regret missing if you happen to have business elsewhere. The libretto is as delightfully free from blood and thunder as that of *La Sonnambula*: it is more an idyllic picture than a story. The cherry-tree duet ought really to be hung in the Royal Academy. ... when Madame Calvé climbed the ladder with an apron on, and threw down cherries to the tenor on the other side of the wall, I was transported as if on a magic carpet to Burlington House, where I remained in imagination until it suddenly occurred to me that I had paid a guinea instead of a shilling for my stall, when I came to myself in rather a melancholy frame of mind. ...
> The duet ... 'caught on' immensely; and there was a frantic encore a little later when Madame Calvé and Signor De Lucia finished a number with a sudden pianissimo on a sustained high note, the effect - a favourite one with Mascagni - being that of a ravishing caterwaul. ... As to the performance, it was more than good enough for the occasion. Signor De Lucia succeeds Valero and Lubert as artificial tenor in ordinary to the establishment. His thin strident *forte* is in tune and does not tremble beyond endurance; and his *mezza voce*, though monotonous and inexpressive, is pretty as prettiness goes in the artificial school. I cannot say that I like that school; but I must admit that its exponents have hitherto set a good example by minding their business and identifying themselves with their parts; and this, considering the lax discipline of the operatic stage at present, is a considerable merit.[66]

The novelty of the work afforded it seven performances, more than any work other than *Cavalleria Rusticana* which, in its double bill, achieved many repetitions both at Covent Garden and Drury Lane. If London critics had still to warm to De Lucia's voice and style, Harris had no doubts of the financial rewards of the operas of Sonzogno, for whom the Neapolitan was now considered almost 'House Tenor', and he reconfirmed him for 1893. So great was the *réclame* of *Cavalleria Rusticana* that Queen Victoria, for whom the Lago company had given it

---

65 (E) Unidentified cutting, dated May 28 1892.
66 Bernard Shaw, *Music in London 1890-94*, Vol. II, pp. 102-4.

at Windsor Castle the previous year, expressed a wish to hear it again. Calvé, De Lucia, and Tosti were duly commanded to perform there on July 2nd 1892.

Calvé wrote of that evening:

> ... the Queen entered, leaning on the shoulder of a young Maharaja of India. What an extraordinary picture they made; he, a slender youth, handsome, exotic, his turban surmounted by a flashing spray of diamonds, his canary-coloured tunic covered with precious stones; the Queen, in black, as usual, the severity of her widow's weeds hardly lightened by the little white tulle cap ... Yet it was the Queen who held every eye! She was impressive, dominating, a real presence ... [67]

The event took place without scenery or costumes, but at least part of the illusion was preserved when De Lucia sang the 'Siciliana' from behind a screen. In her diary the Queen wrote:

> July 2, 1892 Windsor Castle
>
> ... had a very great treat. Mlle Calvé, the new singer, whom Tosti & many others have told me so much about sang, also a Signor De Lucia, who has sung & acted a great deal with her. Tosti accompanied them. They sang first the lovely 'Cherry Tree' Duet from 'L'Amico Fritz'. We were at once enchanted with Calvé's rich, full, touching voice, & wonderful way of singing without any effort. She is very handsome. She asked whether she might *'faire quelques gestes'* in the Duo from 'Cavalleria', between Santuzza and Turiddu, which I readily granted. She acted as well as sang it in the most beautiful way imaginable, so touching, as to make one almost cry. Acting is Calvé's great forte passion ...

The two artists went through their scene with action, gestures, and sentiment, just as though they were on the stage. As was customary, the Queen presented them with mementoes of the occasion, Calvé receiving a bracelet and De Lucia a ring and tie-pin.[68]

The Covent Garden season ended on July 28th but De Lucia lingered in London for some while longer. It appears that he was not in Naples when, on August 24th 1892, Itala gave birth to a healthy son, but he returned in time to register the birth on the 28th. The child was baptised Nadir. He was to be the last child of the marriage. Soon afterwards, relations between husband and wife became intolerable, and Itala - not for the first time - moved into her mother's house.

The deterioration in their relationship was neither sudden nor recent. The De Lucia family had opposed the marriage, possibly on the grounds of the very different social extraction of the two families. Indeed, the difference in status between Chief Engineer De Giorgio and Signor - at best, Maestro - De Lucia was almost certainly a more potent influence

---

67 Calvé, *My Life*, pp. 87-8.
68 *Occhialetto*, Aug. 6 1892.

than the obvious initial differences in wealth, differences which had, in any case, by now been reversed. There were also very obvious temperamental differences. They seem to have had little in common.

Much of the available material concerning the marriage and its turbulent progress is drawn from a legal document supporting Itala's application for a personal separation from her husband, in 1895.[69] It summarises the outcome of two years of litigation, from 1893, involving several lawsuits between husband and wife. Since it was prepared by Itala's lawyers it doubtless shows Fernando in the worst possible light. Its dates are vague, and some of those that it supplies, or implies, are demonstrably wrong. However, since it was prepared for legal purposes and it reviews past lawsuits, it presumably claims nothing that had not, in essence, already been substantiated in court during those suits. It was not contested when, in 1909, it was produced in evidence in yet another suit.

De Lucia was said to have been a loving and affectionate husband in the early days of their marriage. However, this quickly changed - the lawyers continue - and he began to subject his wife to continual torment, on one pretext after another. Itala claimed that she had been only a passing affection for him. She maintained that during their stay in Florence, early in 1886, Fernando ill-treated and injured her on the pretext that she was not yet pregnant. Shortly afterwards this excuse disappeared, when her pregnancy with Armando was confirmed. Thus it was that, instead of accompanying her husband to South America that year, she remained at her parents' house. During this period, it is alleged, De Lucia contracted a liaison with an (unnamed) artist at the theatre in which he was singing in Buenos Aires; moreover, he is said to have suggested to Itala that their child, if female, should be named after his *paramour*.

Husband and wife made their first overseas journey together when they went to London in 1887. In England, his alleged ill-treatment took the form of 'unjustified jealousy', De Lucia forbidding his wife to come down to dinner in the hotel. Instead, she was obliged to remain in their room, and was denied the pleasures of sightseeing.

Matters did not improve when Fernando's family first came to live with the couple, probably in 1887. Instead of recognising the injustices, his parents and sisters are said to have assumed the right to rearrange the household for their own convenience, ignoring Itala's legal and moral rights. They are also alleged to have embarked on a course of 'systematic humiliation', making insinuations which De Lucia pretended to believe, to give scope to the savage side of his nature. She claims that he denied

---

[69] De Roberto, op. cit. The supporting documentation, including De Lucia's defence, has been destroyed with other pre-1900 court proceedings. This *'Memoria a Stampa'* has survived through its inclusion in a post-1900 lawsuit.

her money, forcing her to turn to her family. Over a comb, bought for a few pence, he is said to have launched at her a terrible insult: 'You are only the last servant of my household.'

These allegations cannot now be confirmed or refuted. The tensions of living with in-laws cannot be dismissed. Clearly, a thoughtless, even trivial, remark might be construed as an assault on Itala's authority in her household, or as a jibe at the *nouveau riche* De Lucia. We may also imagine the possible effect of unaccustomed luxury on his family, people of modest means, and Itala's resentment of their assuming rights in it in a reversal of the former status of the two families. Years later, De Lucia would have cause to rage at the proprietorial behaviour of Itala's family in his house.

For her part, Itala may have believed that it was her husband's actions which had led to the relative impoverishment of her family. For matters had taken a much more serious turn during the visit that the De Lucias made to South America in 1890, with Itala's cousin, Adelina De Palma, whom Fernando seduced and made pregnant. On their return to Italy, he revealed to Itala, who was also pregnant, this news which, though already known to others, had been concealed from her. From the liaison with Adelina a son, Enzo, was born in Milan. Itala's submission states that the shock of this revelation caused her own miscarriage.[70] Distraught, she went to live with her parents.

De Lucia is said to have attempted to take the infant Armando and to follow Adelina to Milan. However, the period held a further tragedy in the death of Eduardo De Giorgio. It is not clear whether his heart attack of June 1891 resulted from financial worries or, as stated by Itala's lawyers, from his horror at the humiliation and dishonour brought upon his daughter and family.[71] The advocates maintained that it was guilt and shame at the results of his behaviour that brought a contrite De Lucia to the De Giorgio house where, on the body of his father-in-law, he swore to mend his ways and to be a proper husband and father. Such was the gravity of the moment - and there may have been little alternative for the bereaved family - that his assurances were eventually accepted. In any event, Itala returned to her husband.

The only known, documented, source of information on this sorry chain of events is the legal submission, the '*Memoria a Stampa*' of 1895. It refers to letters, no longer to be found, from Adelina De Palma, asking De Lucia for money. Adelina remains a shadowy figure. If she went to Milan, her stay there was brief. She is known to have been resident in Rome in January 1892. In 1904 she resided in Ancona and, in 1910, in Palermo. Surviving records at Naples, Milan, and Rome indicate that she remained single, and provide no evidence that she ever married or had a

---

[70] Presumably the stillbirth of January 1891.
[71] De Roberto, op. cit., p. 13.

child.[72] She died at Naples, in 1933. It appears, though, that De Lucia, whether through conscience, compassion, demands, or duty, provided on a considerable scale for his wife's bereaved family. In 1909 he estimated that, over seventeen years, he had already contributed about half a million lire.[73]

Independent testimony irresistibly suggests that the principal cause of progressive alienation was jealousy. In his youth and early maturity De Lucia was a handsome, dashing, distinguished figure of a man, whose stage performances were of an intensity attainable only by someone of burning, exceptionally passionate temperament. Like many personable tenors he attracted women, who were infatuated with the romantic figure that he cut on the stage. On one occasion, what he had thought was a casual love affair in Madrid assumed serious proportions when a Spanish noblewoman, bent on leaving husband, family, and the honours of the Court, followed him to the station on his departure, and he delayed his journey home by a day to persuade the agitated woman not to take such an irrevocable step.[74] There can be no doubt that he made many such conquests in what Daspuro described as a 'terribly ruinous weakness'. When he entered a room 'it was like a cockerel entering a hen-coop: old or young, widows, married or single, any or all had to be his'.[75] At Naples and Rome, rumours of his philandering lie thick as autumn leaves. He was very close to Itala's sisters. Nothing suggests that his relationship with Flora involved anything more than shared musical interests: during the long summer evenings of the *villeggiatura* she often played the piano while he sang. But at Naples and, especially, at Cava de' Tirreni - then very prudish and much given to gossip - persistent murmurs still link him romantically with the other sister, Pia, described as 'a raven-haired beauty', with whom De Lucia was very taken. Within the De Giorgio family children's ears would be boxed for asking too many questions about 'Uncle Fernando and Aunt Pia'. Other rumours maintain that he had children by a celebrated - but unidentified - opera singer. In 1897, the newspapers in Montevideo clearly linked him with the soprano Elisa Petri (1869-1929).[76] He had close relationships with at least one of Alfredo De Giorgio's pupils - Alfredo and Fernando were accomplices in many a romantic escapade - and almost certainly with more than one of his own. Tom Burke knew him, even in his latter

---

72 The Servizi Demografici of Milan and Naples find no trace of Enzo De Palma. However, since war damage and the passage of almost a century have produced gaps in official records, the lack of evidence for the birth of a child to Adelina is now no proof that there was none. The allegations were not denied when they were cited in a 1909 lawsuit brought by Itala against Fernando.

73 The difficulties of interpreting such sums in modern terms are those of identifying a commodity which has retained a constant value. Such a sum, almost £20,000 at the then exchange rate, would amount to at least one million sterling in terms of 1988 purchasing power. By criteria such as property prices or labourer's wages it might easily be two million.

74 *Roma*, Mar. 2 1929.

75 Daspuro, 'Memorie', ch. XXII.

76 *Siglo*, Aug. 17 1897.

years, as a man who was still 'adored by women'.[77] Clearly, particularly
in his younger days, he was an habitual gallant for whom supposed
gambling losses would have provided a convenient explanation for the
disappearance of the considerable sums that he undoubtedly spent on his
obsession with women.

Itala's interests lay neither in music nor in her husband's life at the
theatre. Only rarely did she accompany him there, and she customarily
retired before he returned home. She showed little concern for his
success other than in the jewels which he would bring back from his
tournées and which, through fear of theft, she would carry with her in a
small black bag. These gifts, it was whispered, were to win her
indulgence for some peccadillo involving another woman. And, indeed,
the evidence suggests that, until such gifts came to an end, she connived
at his womanising. One report suggests that Itala was 'sweet-natured',[78]
but another, that she was 'never content, and very abrupt',[79] is supported
by the tenor's own reference to her 'venomous and cutting tongue, [and]
her arrogance and insolence'[80] He was particularly affected by the
disparaging manner in which she would say to him: 'You are an artist!'

Domestic harmony seems also to have suffered from the presence of
Enrico Onesti, whom Itala obviously thoroughly detested, perhaps for no
reason other than that he was her husband's confidant. He, too, she
claimed, tormented her with every kind of insult. The last straw came in
1892, when Fernando went to London accompanied only by Enrico. Itala
- who must actually have been in the final weeks of pregnancy - claimed
that he had refused to allow her to go with him because he wanted to
'continue to live the fast life' in London, and that he had left her only
fifteen lire 'for your vices!'

In his absence, Itala was subjected to slights from her husband's
mother and family who, she alleged, attempted to deprive her of her
clothes, jewels and even, on some occasions, of her child. Their ultimate
insult - which might easily have started as a joking reference to a
supposed resemblance - was to claim that the father of the infant Nadir
was the cook. This was the point at which she moved into her mother's
house.

But, for the moment, domestic matters were left behind as, in
September 1892, De Lucia departed for Vienna. Italian seasons there
had been the traditional gateway from Italy to the Germanic world. Now,
a company set out from Milan for the annual *Theater-und-Musik-
Ausstellung* where, at the Internationales Ausstellungs Theater in the
Prater, it was to display the work of the *Nuova Scuola Italiana*; in
practice, this comprised the properties of Sonzogno, who had taken the

---

77 In conversation with the writer, 1967.
78 Giuseppina Giordano, family friend, in conversation with the writer, Cava de' Tirreni, 1974.
79 Vincenza Senatore, Itala's dressmaker at Cava, in conversation with the writer, London, 1974.
80 (TPN) Letter Fernando De Lucia - Nestore Siciliano (Itala's uncle), Venice, Jan. 21 1908.

theatre for two weeks or so. The company was to give *Tilde* (Cilea), *Mala Vita* (Giordano), *Il Birichino* (Mugnone), *Pagliacci*, *L'Amico Fritz*, and *Cavalleria Rusticana*. No expense had been spared to show the works, and Italian art, to their best advantage; as well as De Lucia the roster included Bellincioni, Cotogni, Stagno, and Toresella.

Mascagni had travelled to Vienna in a blaze of publicity. During his stay in Venice, while the band in Piazza San Marco played selections from *Cavalleria Rusticana*, someone recognised him in a café and the resulting mêlée caused a great breakage of bottles and glasses.[81] In Vienna he was immediately the centre of attention; a crowd waiting outside the Hôtel Continental fell on him for his autograph as soon as he arrived with Sonzogno. Similar scenes ensued at the station as he greeted the arriving artists, and at the theatre.[82] Hundreds of letters and many bouquets, mostly from female admirers, arrived each day at the 'princely' suite in which, by courtesy of the hotel proprietor, he had installed himself and where he ingratiated himself daily with the many journalists who called upon him. Vienna was embarking on what was to be a long love affair with Mascagni. After the general rehearsal of *L'Amico Fritz* - at which he took the opportunity to make changes to the orchestration - Mascagni lunched with the artists, fellow composers, and journalists at Tommasoni's restaurant, where the toast was to Viennese hospitality.

The season opened on September 15th with *L'Amico Fritz*. The scenery was borrowed from an earlier Vienna production at the Hofoper, where, to quote Mascagni,

> ... they performed well enough, but not excellently, as did we, who had at our disposal, among others, De Lucia as the tenor. It was difficult to rival the artists that we had. [83]

The opera had a noisy success; at the first performance, Mascagni took seventeen calls, the audience on its feet shouting *'Viva Mascagni! Viva il grande Maestro!'*; at later ones he received gold laurel wreaths, their tricolour ribbons bearing legends such as *'Onore d'Italia'*, and *'Ritorna presto'*.[84] That the other works were received less rapturously was no disrespect to their composers, for Mascagni could do no wrong. Financial success was less marked, with so many expensive singers in so small a theatre. At the Teatro Nazionale, Rome, where the company repeated much of the Vienna programme, the house was crammed, despite increased prices.

---

81 Mascagni - Lina Mascagni, Sept. 11 1892, quoted in Pompei, op. cit., p. 137. De Carlo, op. cit., p. 109, incorrectly gives Vienna as the scene of this incident.

82 De Carlo, op. cit., pp. 108-10.

83 Mascagni, quoted in De Carlo, op. cit., p. 113. A letter from Menasci to Sonzogno, relating to the earlier performance and to the inadequacies of the tenor Müller, remarks: '... as to the singing, one must forget De Lucia!' (Bernardini Marzolla, loc. cit., p. 102).

84 *Neue Freie Presse*, Sept. 23 1892.

It is difficult, now, to imagine the scale of the operatic activity in those exuberant times, as chronicled in the dozens of periodicals devoted to it; to imagine the sheer traffic of artists who, by steamer, train, and, on at least one disastrous occasion, by mule over the Andes,[85] moved continually between hundreds of theatres in Moscow and Madrid, Milan and Buenos Aires, New York and Warsaw, or to comprehend the financial cornucopia associated with the new operas, and especially with those of Mascagni. Indeed, it was said that on a single day in 1891 over sixty theatres in Italy alone gave *Cavalleria Rusticana*;[86] 43 consecutive performances at one Berlin theatre were of this one opera, and a series of 15 took place in even so unlikely a spot as Constantinople. The appetite for Mascagni seemed insatiable.

85 The *Gazzetta Musicale di Milano*, Mar. 4 1888, quoting *Italia* of Montevideo, reported the vicissitudes of the Ciacchi-Rainieri lyric company on its journey from Valparaiso to Argentina.

86 De Carlo, op. cit., p. 194.

9

Cigno canor

In Naples, the singer is the most effective invitation to buy an opera ticket.
                                                        Michele Uda[1]

On the completion of *L'Amico Fritz*, Mascagni had again turned to *I Rantzau*; the première had been fixed for November 10th 1892. Casting was complete by July.[2] On his return from London, De Lucia went to Mascagni's house at Livorno to work with Battistini, Darclée, and the composer on the interpretation of the new opera.[3] Ferrari was to conduct.

Against his better judgement Sonzogno, who had favoured Milan, had been persuaded by Mascagni, 'with his foolish pretensions', to take the Teatro Pergola, Florence, for the première of his new opera.[4] The publisher again took a detailed personal interest in the preparations. For the dress rehearsal he had invited the directors of the principal opera houses of Berlin, Prague, and Vienna, and many Italian and foreign critics.

Florence had its first glimpse of the new opera on November 7th, at the concert of the Associazione della Stampa Toscana. A distinguished musical audience, which included most of the Pergola company, heard De Lucia sing the 'Romanza' from *I Rantzau* and the 'Siciliana' from *Cavalleria Rusticana*.[5]

In the days before the première, Mascagni and his entourage took to frequenting Cornelio's restaurant, almost in the shadow of Giotto's *campanile*. Every night, he and his friends - some from his student days - were to be found there until the small hours. It was a diverse group. Sonzogno's talk, even in such informal moments, was of serious matters. The baritone Edoardo Sottolana, an admirable mimic, was always likely to cause an uproar at his table with his imitations of some of the best-known people of theatrical Italy. But it was Mascagni who was the centre of attraction; 'thoroughly *bon garçon*', a flamboyant character who, at home, was said to wear a suit of flaming scarlet, he appeared in

---

1 *Pungolo*, May 5/6 1895.
2 *Occhialetto*, July 4 1892.
3 *Tavola Rotonda*, June 12 1892.
4 Bernardini Marzolla, loc. cit., pp. 106-7.
5 *Fortunio*, Nov. 11 1892.

the very best light so far as the press was concerned. When, after the dress rehearsal, he relaxed at the café with his wife, Lina, and his young son Domenico, nicknamed Mimì, they made an attractive picture.[6]

The composer was less affable in other circles. De Lucia, by now one of those colleagues whom Mascagni 'detested' - apparently because critics had suggested that the tenor had given vividness and life to his operas - was singled out for attention when the composer went to greet friends and musical critics at the railway station. To each new arrival Mascagni, holding up a walking stick with its handle in the form of a dog's head, delivered himself of a witticism: *'Di' un pò: ti piace questo De Lucia? Oh! volevo dire questo cane!'*[7]

The audience for the first night of *I Rantzau*, on November 10th 1892, was described as 'brilliant'.[8] All the ladies were presented with souvenir hand-painted fans, with roses attached. Among the singers present were Lelio Casini, Antonio Cotogni, Francesco Marconi, and Regina Pinkert. Italy's two best-known tragic actors, Ernesto Rossi and Tommaso Salvini, attended. All the most prominent impresarios were there. De Lucia, anxious that the Neapolitan press should be well represented, had offered stalls to Mormone, Pagliara, and Serao.[9]

The plot of *I Rantzau* is simple: it deals with the feud between the brothers Giacomo and Gianni Rantzau, who are divided by bitter hate, and the love between Giacomo's son, Giorgio, and Gianni's daughter, Luisa. In a family reconciliation, the lovers are united.

Within this flimsy dramatic framework, the Roumanian soprano Hariclea Darclée[10] produced 'an immediate, profound, impression, with her magnificent, ringing tone, intense and passionate',[11] her 'exceptional voice resounding with unique vigour in the Pergola'.[12] For D'Ormeville her voice was '... fresh, and of enviable facility ...; hers remains the most beautiful, secure, and agreeable soprano voice that I have heard for several years.'[13]

In his part of Giorgio Rantzau De Lucia was described as: 'Incomparable tenor, for sentiment and for the powerful beauty of the notes.'[14] At the second performance Galli wrote of him:

> De Lucia is always the *bel canto* tenor, for his refined subtleties, for the felicitous contrasts between vigorous sonority and delicate vocal *sfumature*. ... As an actor, also, he distinguishes himself, especially in the last act.[15]

---

6 *Magazine of Music*, Dec. 1892.

7 'Tell me then: do you like this De Lucia? Oh! I meant to say "this dog." ' Daspuro, 'Memorie', ch. XXII. *'Cane'* is a disparaging term for a bad singer.

8 *Magazine of Music*, Dec. 1892.

9 (BS) Letter De Lucia - Pagliara, Florence, Oct. 31 1892.

10 Darclée, whose birth year is variously given as 1860, 1863, or 1868, died in 1938.

11 *Perseveranza*, Nov. 11 1892.

12 *Secolo*, Nov. 13/14 1892.

13 *Gazzetta dei Teatri*, Nov. 17 1892.

14 *Secolo*, Nov. 11/12 1892.

15 Ibid., Nov. 13/14 1892.

D'Ormeville complained that the tenor part in *I Rantzau* relied too much on De Lucia's rare talents, yet did not adequately display them. Whereas, as Fritz,

> ... a single word sufficed to savour the sweetest sounds of a *mezza voce* which seemed to me a great treasure that only he can command and use ..., in this opera he has a 'romanza' ['Quando volevano ci dividessero'] in which he pours out all his genius, all his envied qualities as a singer, and this romanza will lose its effect the day it ceases to be interpreted with similar artistry, finesse and passion.[16]

The Milanese critic Nappi, writing of his *mezza voce* 'for which one might say that he has a special gift', observed that De Lucia was, for his taste, 'somewhat mannered'.[17] None the less, the audience obliged him to repeat his third act romanza, 'which he sang like a God'.[18]

For the Viennese critic Hanslick, the tenor piece 'Quando volevano ci dividessero' was interesting for some high notes which he thought of good effect.[19] Mascagni's tenor rôles are characterised by their high *tessitura*.[20] Although, unlike those of Bellini and Donizetti, they do not abound in very high notes, they often stay for relatively long periods above the stave as, for example, in the 'Siciliana' in *Cavalleria Rusticana* where, at a point at which he has hardly warmed up, the tenor must twice sing six successive A flats. To remain so long on a single high note is to produce a certain inelasticity of the vocal cords, to the potential detriment of the next phrase, and many a tenor has found it easier to transpose it a semitone, to E minor. In fact, during the piano rehearsals for the première Mascagni had had to transpose two pieces for Stagno. One was the duet with Santuzza, originally written a semitone higher in what Bellincioni herself described as a *'tessitura crudele'*; the other remains unidentified.[21] Even Marconi, who regularly sang *I Puritani* and *Lucrezia Borgia*, was daunted by the demands and by the *tessitura* of Mascagni's *Guglielmo Ratcliff* (1895).[22] And the problem would recur in later works.[23] The *Rantzau* piece noted by Hanslick rises on four occasions to A natural, two of them involving repeated notes, and lingers around the area of F - F sharp - G. Though neither it nor the passages

---

[16] *Gazzetta dei Teatri*, Nov. 17 1892.

[17] *Perseveranza*, Nov. 11 1892.

[18] *Tribuna*, Nov. 12 1892.

[19] Eduard Hanslick, *'Die Rantzau'*, in *Fünf Jahre Musik (1891-1895) (Der 'Modernen Oper' VII Teil)*, pp. 70-9. It is not clear which performance he was describing.

[20] See Gino Roncaglia, 'Pietro Mascagni: L'Operista' (pp. 27-8) and Giorgio Gualerzi, 'Cavalcata canora', (pp. 356-7), in *Pietro Mascagni nel 1⁰ Centenario della Nascita*, and Gara, 'Cantanti Mascagnani fra pregiudizio e verità', in Morini, *Mascagni*, Vol. I, pp. 205-6 and 249.

[21] Bellincioni, op. cit., p. 97.

[22] (BLS, CA 3614) Marconi - Angelo Eisner, Sept. 17 1901. 'Mascagni ... has asked me to sing *Ratcliff* but I cannot because of the very high *tessitura*. ... Mascagni, so dear as a man, so impossible as a maestro, would cut off his penis before cutting a note.'

[23] Gualerzi, 'Cavalcata canora', loc. cit.

containing the numerous A flats in the opera makes demands similar to those of the 'Siciliana', it has the general Mascagnian feature of requiring prolonged efforts from the tenor in his upper register. He moves above the stave in the first act finale, with several B flats and, in one passage of the Act IV duet with Luisa, remains above it for two entire bars, rising to B natural.

As Gianni Rantzau, Mattia Battistini undoubtedly took the honours, 'completely conquering the public ...[He was] shown as a supreme artist.'[24] His acting was no less impressive, and Rossi and Salvini were warm in their praise; even Mascagni would remember him with relish:

> How great he was in that opera. No one has been able to give the public the profound emotions that he could. Oh! Those beautiful performances of *Rantzau* at Florence, with Battistini and De Lucia.[25]

After the première, Mascagni, haggard with excitement, made his appearance at Cornelio's. Soon, however, he began to savour the occasion and the revelry continued until the early hours. The morning papers, though, were decidedly cool towards the opera. The work to which *L'Amico Fritz* was to have been a mere prelude was judged inferior to it, as *Fritz* had been thought inferior to *Cavalleria Rusticana*.

From Florence, *I Rantzau* was taken to Rome where Arturo Toscanini, then conductor at the Costanzi, was to direct it with the same three principal singers. When the news came of the success in Florence the Costanzi orchestra, without consulting its conductor, sent a telegram of congratulation to Mascagni. This the composer interpreted in his own fashion, and replied that he 'would be proud to conduct the famous orchestra of Rome in the *prima* of my opera'.

Toscanini's reaction was predictable. When the newspaper *Fanfulla* suggested that it had been his idea the affair rapidly developed into one of the public rows which characterised Mascagni's career, as the irate conductor used the columns of other papers to renounce the engagement:

> The *Fanfulla* of yesterday ... would have one believe that, of my own accord, I yielded to Mascagni the honour of directing *I Rantzau*.
> This is not true. Far from yielding it, I would have held the honour dearly and felt able, without difficulty, to meet the challenge fully, *even given the time limitations*; but Mascagni wanted to reserve for himself the honour of the first three performances . . . . . I invite him also to reserve the remainder.[26]

So it was that, on the opening night, November 26th 1892, the Costanzi had an air of tension. Mascagni was pale and his lower lip trembled slightly as he took his place on the rostrum.

24 *Corriere della Sera*, Nov. 11/12 1892.
25 Mascagni to his wife, Moscow, Mar. 7 1900, quoted in Pompei, op. cit., p. 288.
26 *Tribuna*, Nov. 18 1892.

Again, the reception was lukewarm. Again, De Lucia's third act aria was one of the few pieces to raise the artistic temperature. 'It is very beautiful and Fernando De Lucia made it so for us, with the treasure of his voice and art.' The love duet, 'notable for the charm of certain melodic hints, for the golden voice of Darclée and for the delightful emphases of De Lucia' was repeated, despite not a few cries of 'Enough!'[27]

Mascagni was judged an accomplished conductor, who had brought out many nuances missed at Florence. Here, there was greater unity and warmth, more care in vocal and instrumental detail, enviable security, and never an instant of affectation. 'Mascagni as a conductor - if nothing else - has real worth' was the cutting verdict of the critic of *Tribuna*. He went on to praise the singers:

> Darclée ... is a first-class Luisa. The dedication, the intelligence and the vocal and artistic treasures of her interpretation justly make her Mascagni's favourite. What shall I say of De Lucia? Can I say any less? Can one believe that Mascagni does not cherish him as an image of himself? Is he not perhaps one of the indispensable elements comprising the light that illuminates, [one] that gives life to his pictures? ... And Battistini, marvellous singer and actor. Where does he find the power that he gives to his voice, of a sweet, almost tenor-like, timbre in the more vigorous moments ... ?[28]

These were comments which would certainly fan any hostility in Mascagni towards De Lucia. But the composer's desire, expressed at the time of *L'Amico Fritz*, for a libretto that would not detract from the music had certainly been gratified. Many agreed with the *Florence Gazette* that, since it would be difficult to find a 'flatter, staler story or a more flaccid libretto', any success for the opera must lie elsewhere. Hanslick described it as 'a most unfortunate action, based on a single theme, developed in only one direction, without engaging episodes and with no secondary characters of any interest. ... It leaves us with the memory of successful and pleasing details despite its feeble overall structure.' He advised Mascagni to let his talent rest for at least two years.[29] In Germany, its failure to make money in the principal theatres discouraged the managements of the secondary houses. In Berlin, receipts diminished night by night until performances were suspended.[30]

For all that it was strongly pro-Ricordi and anti-Sonzogno, the verdict of *Gazzetta dei Teatri* is the one that posterity has endorsed:

> ... without the remarkable casts of Florence and Rome, the presence of Mascagni, the almost paternal affection of the Costanzi public for him, and the massed clients of the publisher, what remains of the opera's success?[31]

---

27 *Popolo Romano*, Nov. 27 1892.
28 *Tribuna*, Nov. 28 1892. Mascagni's own recordings of his works often ignore his markings of fifty years earlier.
29 Hanslick, op. cit.
30 Letter Sonzogno - Menasci, Oct. 6, 1893, quoted by Bernardini Marzolla, loc. cit., p. 106.
31 *Gazzetta dei Teatri*, Dec. 8, 1892.

Though *I Rantzau*, as a work, was severely and almost universally condemned, the detailed contemporary analysis is sometimes not convincing. Critics such as Hanslick charge, for example, that the duet for soprano and tenor in Act IV lapses into mannerism. Yet, to listen to its great sweeping phrases: '*Oh, dammi ascolto: Luisa non piangere, non vo' negli occhi lacrime*' is to be persuaded that *I Rantzau* is a work of passionate melody. It is one which may well have been unjustly neglected, not least by its creators, none of whom recorded a bar from it.

The final performance at Rome was on December 8th; De Lucia and Darclée went thence to a gas-lit Naples for the opening of the San Carlo season on December 17th. Marino Villani, who still held the concession, had made De Lucia the tenor mainstay of his season; indeed, he had reputedly refused another manager's offer of 55,000 lire to release him from his engagement.[32]

The season opened controversially, with *L'Amico Fritz*. It was an event which gave little pleasure to anyone. The more conservative could not accept an opening night without a ballet. Many subscribers and critics resented anything that delayed *Lohengrin*. Moreover, *Fritz* was not a novelty, having been given at the San Carlo, amid some chicanery, by Bellincioni and Stagno in December 1891. Though now deriving added interest from the presence of Mascagni on the rostrum it was actually a compromise choice, forced on Villani by his disagreement with members of the orchestra and a consequent need to minimise rehearsal time, a period of unproductive expense.

The première took place in even greater splendour than usual, in the presence of the Prince of Naples, heir to the throne of Italy. Darclée, who was evidently not in her best voice, drew attention chiefly for her costumes. Pagliara remarked on the harshness of the top notes, no longer sweet, but at least, another critic noted, they were not the flute-like tones with which Calvé was too often satisfied.[33]

De Lucia was eagerly awaited. There was much interest in hearing what he could do in an opera less dramatic than the well-remembered *Carmen* of two seasons ago. He knew the expectations, and the movement of the eyes and slight tremor of the hand betrayed it. But, as gradually he disciplined himself, he drew continual applause from the audience for 'the sweetest and most accurate singing, free and limpid'.[34] Typical descriptions were:

> . . . tenor of the wonderfully tinted voice, a Fritz of a charm and sprightliness which permit of no regrets for other interpretations.[35]

> . . . now, without doubt, the only tenor who can employ such treasures of voice

---

32 *Occhialetto*, Aug. 6 1892.

33 *Tavola Rotonda*, Dec. 25 1892.

34 *Fortunio*, Dec. 22 1892.

35 *Corriere di Napoli*, Dec. 18/19 1892.

and art. Colouring the naturally idyllic nature of the opera, he displays all his marvellous resources, [born] of assiduous study and of a throat full of sweetness.[36]

... his voice [is] melodious and vibrant, such that his notes seemed like discs of gold, launched to ring magically in the resonant air ... [37]

De Lucia is at the summit of Olympus, and is now a *divo*. I shall no longer dispute his deification. He was equal to his most subtle intention: his art has completed the miracle. He has a stupendous *mezza voce*. The passage to the high notes is easier. The low notes are not exaggerated. He is a secure and exquisite singer.[38]

Procida criticised a certain crudeness, some disjointedness, as he passed from dramatic intensity to exquisite tenderness, but was quick to note the improvement of later performances.[39] There were also warnings against 'ruthless enemies', who encouraged De Lucia - disposing, as he did, of a delightful *voce mista* - to disregard the cardinal rule never to weight the centre of the voice, making a baritonal trumpet of it, when to lighten it would permit him to develop the notes with which to sing a greater variety of rôles.[40] Procida's notice, too, hinted at potential vocal damage, as the tenor's voice moved rapidly between gentleness and passion:

... and I allude [in the Cherry Duet] to that *'Tutto tace'*, which De Lucia sang with the most consummate fascination of his voice, of his melodious and vigorous singing alternating with a *mezza voce* which is a marvel of vocal education. [He] surprised us through the robustness of his middle notes; there is a baritonal ductility [and] a quality of admirable resonance in his middle register, and if this studied strengthening were in time to succeed, without detriment to the high register, I would enthusiastically applaud the magnificent evenness of those resonant notes, so secure and effective.[41]

And the singer may have heeded the warning since in later performances he was reported to have enraptured the audience by lightening the voice, where previously he had forced it.[42]

When, almost thirty years later, De Lucia recorded the 'Cherry Duet' [Nos. 297/8], he was in fine voice. As a link with the première of *Fritz* the record - though lacking either the additional *cachet* that the presence of Calvé would naturally have lent to it, or yet the overall charm of Mafalda Favero and Tito Schipa in the same music - has singular interest. Moreover, it amply displays those enchanting touches that the reviews of his performances as Fritz lead us to expect. The contemplative inflection

---

36 *Tavola Rotonda*, Dec. 25 1892.
37 *Mattino*, Dec. 18/19 1892.
38 *Roma*, Dec. 18 1892.
39 *Fortunio*, Dec. 22 1892.
40 *Occhialetto*, Dec. 19 1892.
41 *Fortunio*, Dec. 22 1892.
42 *Occhialetto*, Jan. 3 1893.

on '*mature*'; the unwritten *gruppetto* on '*roseo*'; and the crispness of '*Una
primizia certo*', where the diction on the 1919 record shames many
singers who enjoy modern recording, are inimitable. The second part is
transposed downwards by a semitone relative to the first; how tenderly
he delivers '*Tutto tace*', observing Mascagni's '*pp*'. A decoration on '*mi
parla*' does not reappear in the reprise, a curious reversal of convention.
His singing of '*Tu sei bella, o stagion primaverile!*' is joyful. The record
ends in a dreamy pianissimo. It is a performance of imagination.

While the subscribers enjoyed Battistini in *Maria di Rohan*,
rehearsals of *Pagliacci* started. The work was new for Naples and it
assumed a special interest from the presence of its Neapolitan composer.
The première took place at the San Carlo on January 14th 1893, after a
brouhaha which at one time threatened the production. Following the
custom of many years, the *prova generale* was attended by certain groups
of people - journalists, students of the Conservatory, privileged
subscribers, the inmates of the Albergo dei Poveri, and the principal
sicofanti, some two hundred people in all. The conductor was Riccardo
Bonicioli.[43] He took his place among the tiny lights of the orchestra pit
where, baton in hand, he harangued the onlookers in a manner which
seemed strained. He - he told the assembly - took his duties seriously.
Despite the beauties of the music the success or failure depended on him.
He made it abundantly clear that he resented the onlookers, foisted on
him despite a contract that had assured him of an empty theatre for
rehearsals. Villani and Leoncavallo seemed particularly disturbed by
this speech, suspecting that his state of mind was ill-suited to the
occasion. The first scene was characterised by a prickliness and
excitability which were in marked contrast to Bonicioli's austere and
lofty appearance. To their evident displeasure, he admonished the
orchestra members and he sang with the soloists.[44] When the baritone
Buti had to repeat a phrase Bonicioli remonstrated with him so
unpleasantly that even the spectators were dismayed.

The major disturbance arose when the conductor wanted the orchestra
to start again from bar 77 and expressed it in a way which, through his
evident familiarity with its terminology, suggested that he was a devotee
of the lottery. With baton raised, he made his request:

Let us start again, Gentlemen, from ..... as they used to say, the legs of the
beautiful ladies, seventy-seven.

As he sat in Gambrinus, writing a notice for - on this occasion -
Mattino, Bracco disclaimed any knowledge of whether there attached to
the number 77 any arcane significance or calumny that transcended

---

43 (1853-1933) Real name Frühmann, Bonicioli was also a composer of operas and symphonic poems.
44 *Paese*, Jan. 12 1893.

mere indelicacy.[45] Whether or not there was, the phrase itself - on top of the general irritation - was enough. A murmur of female outrage was heard. Villani asked Bonicioli to refrain from gratuitous remarks. A few crisp comments ensued. The interchange grew heated. Among the spectators in the shadows arose cries of apprehension. The more courageous applauded to cheer the faint-hearted. A cry of 'Enough! Down with Bonicioli!' was heard as a band of gallants surrounded him. On the stage, wrapped in his mantle of *divo* tenor, De Lucia remained aloof as singers and chorus voiced their indignation. Amid pandemonium, Bonicioli was jostled by the shoulders of excitable Neapolitans, enraged by this apparent insult. He rose from his seat and left the theatre. Fifteen minutes later, excited *sicofanti*, publishers, critics, and theatre personnel were persuading a reluctant Vincenzo Lombardi to take over the opera. Other spectators, Neapolitans first and last, after lengthy conclave concluded that such an omen made the sequence, 14 22 48 77, an excellent lottery prospect.[46]

At the première, Procida noted that, after a reserved start - through the activities of a foolish and imprudent *claque* - the public was slow to approve. An encore of the prologue, with three calls to the composer, was less than spontaneous. It predisposed the audience so badly that, when the *claque* wanted an encore of the chorus of villagers, the general public disapproved strongly and the chorus, which had returned for the repeat, had to make a hasty retreat. This was a difficult moment; the duet passed in silence and so, almost, did Nedda's aria. Not until Canio's agonising scene, given with vigour and with vehement passion by De Lucia, did Procida feel the opera's fortunes rise. In the second act:

> ... Harlequin's serenade was given with admirable grace and colouring but, in an absurd, most culpable interchange, by De Lucia. It was repeated and gave two more calls to Leoncavallo, but it is none the less grotesque that Harlequin [Raffaele De Rosa] should sing with the throat of Puncinello ...
>
> The strong, coarse characters in solid colours satisfy [De Lucia's] undisciplined, changeable disposition, and he therefore assimilates such passionate types easily. [He] is not a lofty, varied, multiform artist, who can give life, as can Maurel and ... Bellincioni, to contrasting characters. He does not possess this force of objective method, this precious and rare secret of representative creation. He has only dramatic intuition and an admirable ability to assimilate it into his spontaneous sensations as a man.
>
> But these sensations are frequently magnificent, always vibrant, sometimes, as in *Carmen*, irresistible. And so, also, is crude Canio, impassioned, thoughtless in love and in pleasure, expressing anguish and fury in an extreme outburst. His beautiful voice is of the timbre of a noble metal, melodious as the sweep of a viola, accurate, warm and coloured, full of a sweet resonance which causes sudden flickers in the emotions and rouses the stalls with a spontaneity which makes the *claque* superfluous: this [is a] beautiful voice, fresh and used with skill, of a tone which, even when the note is swelled and threatens to burst

---

45 *Mattino*, Jan. 12/13 1893. The article is signed 'Baby', Bracco's pen-name. Usually, he reviewed for *Corriere di Napoli* or *Fortunio*.

46 The writer has not established whether it won.

its banks, is well adapted to this dramatic part and depicts well enough the agony of the lst act aria, 'Vesti la giubba'. [He] was no less effective in the final scene, forcing his face - a little inexpressive - into fiery mien and rapid changes. ... If advice is not unpalatable to singers, I would recommend to De Lucia that he dilute the [vocal] colours, which would soften some rather unrefined effects in the recitative.

The theatre and life are not the same thing; less impetuosity, but more sadness [are due] to the phrase: *'E ognuno applaudirà'*.[47]

Uda was not enamoured of the opera:

Only at Canio's aria, after the brief and effective tirade against Nedda, did we enter into drama from which we did not escape again, in so far as the emotion was not ended by the double stabbing of the tragedy ... The enthusiastic applause for the aria, sung by De Lucia with profound emotion, mixed with irony and sadness, marked the point at which convention ended. From that moment all public indecision vanished; unanimous applause broke out, the success was great and genuine ...

More than singing a part he created a character. He sang the part delightfully, as he sings everything, with that warm and sweet voice of his; but the character was portrayed complete with the proper physiognomy; with expression, with the accent of that voice, made to speak with passion; it took shape in the face, in the gesture, in every movement of the body. After the ferocious, demented phrases of the deceived husband, now avenged, with what heartache, in what moral and physical prostration, he said: *'La commedia è finita!'* We all shuddered, and acclaimed the actor revealed in the triumphant tenor.[48]

Leoncavallo had ten calls at the end. He looked tired, pale, and disturbed by the fleeting prospect of failure. It was generally agreed that it was De Lucia who had saved the opera.

And still *Lohengrin* was delayed, and still the devotees of the Holy Grail anxiously awaited the arrival of the swan. Meanwhile, on January 22nd 1893 the subscribers saw the première of *La Favorita*. The public, eager for Battistini's mellow tones in one of his most celebrated parts, was also curious to hear De Lucia in a Donizettian rôle, 'the old *Favorita*, so melodious, so dramatic, its artistic sinews still vigorous enough ... to rout the protagonists of modern realism'.[49]

As Procida remarked, it would be absurd and unjust to suppose that with the death of Gayarre - for the Neapolitans, unapproachable and irreplaceable in *La Favorita* - the opera itself would die at the San Carlo. But part of the audience was hostile, and the first two acts were greeted somewhat coldly. De Lucia was thought to have

... emerged triumphantly from the difficult test, without subordinating the highly strung effectiveness of his action, the irreproachability of his method

---

[47] *Paese*, Jan. 15 1893. The 'interchange' had been well rehearsed.

[48] *Pungolo*, Jan. 15/16 1893.

[49] *Mattino*, Jan. 23/24 1893.

[and] the genuine originality of his talent to the imitation of other peoples'
effects. ... The voice which he has succeeded in tailoring to the dramatic
inflections of *verismo* has, in *La Favorita*, an impassioned sweetness of
modulation which goes from the ear to the heart, and which words cannot
describe. His singing is always finely chiselled. As the drama unfolds, the
phrases are drawn, sculpted, warmed, and coloured with sentiment. [He was]
rapturously applauded in the duet with Leonora, no less so in the great scene of
the third act, and in all the fourth act, to the beginning of the blissful, literally
paradisal romanza ['Spirto gentil'], which he sang without affectations of
sentimental virtuosity, making one thrill, now with indignation, now with
sadness, now with all the sad memories which it retraced.[50]

Uda praised De Lucia's courage in refusing an encore which would
have damaged the artistic sense. Battistini had been less scrupulous, but
in repeating 'A tanto amor' - where 'he rises like an eagle on the pinions
of art'[51] - he had not recaptured the mood of his first delivery. The effects
of modulation and ironic grace were there, but not the feeling.[52] The
repeat initiated an incident which, in any other theatre, might well have
been comical; at the San Carlo, the *patiti* took it as provocation. De
Lucia, presumably poorly advised by the stage manager and not
anticipating an encore, had re-entered the stage during the applause.
When the encore became inevitable, he withdrew. The baritone, realising
the misunderstanding, behaved courteously, but the pro-Battistini
faction, evidently believing that De Lucia was trying to thwart their idol,
was hostile on the tenor's subsequent reappearance. Their shouts were
swamped by the applause and by the boisterous good humour of the
majority, but the occurrence - which the press duly turned into 'The De
Lucia Incident' - had clearly unnerved him. He could not deploy all his
resources in the finale. Nor could he, in 'Spirto gentil', emulate Gayarre
in the span of '*Ahimè, ahimè*', holding the breath through to the *ripresa*;
but his singing was polished and its sweetness compensated. Mormone
described him as 'a Fernando in the original style (*tono*), an even rarer
art'.[53]

By the second performance De Lucia had relented and he granted
encores of 'Una vergine' and of 'Spirto gentil'. Uda's displeasure was
clear as he condemned the vanity of performers and the perverted taste
of·the public. But he approved of De Lucia:

... in vocal art, in accuracy of intonation, in the caress of the note, he could go
no further; he gave to the romanza 'Spirto gentil' a new expression of heartfelt
grief, and at the phrase '*nelle sue sale il re ti appella*' of the final duet, [he
expressed] the cutting irony that is in the music [but] that was never in the
voice of any Fernando, great or small, who has preceded him.[54]

---

50 *Pungolo*, Jan. 23/24 1893.
51 *Gazzetta dei Teatri*, Feb. 2 1893.
52 *Pungolo*, Jan. 23/24 1893.
53 The several meanings of '*tono*' include both 'style' and 'key'.
54 *Pungolo*, Jan. 28/29 1893.

In *Mattino*, Rocco Pagliara wrote presciently of the tenor:

> ... For my part, I very much enjoyed hearing and seeing Fernando De Lucia employ, finally, his magnificent powers of voice, art, and genius, in a complete part in which, solely through genuine elements of melodious singing, he penetrates the various phases of a passion, rich in events and contrasts, as it unfolds nobly and vibrantly. He is at the finest point of his artistic life, the greatest and the most momentous, which he can sustain without damage only if the throat and the emotion are kept within narrow bounds.
>
> He can and must develop, with all the unrestrained power with which he is endowed, both for himself and for art. Fragmentary parts and bourgeois and rustic little operas have the honour of profiting from his worth, gaining support and a passport to stages of which they are unworthy; but they do not distract him too much from the the great lyric repertoire which, in exchange for all the precious tributes that he can offer with his beautiful artistic gifts, will increase his powers and will speedily complete the development of his finely-endowed voice and of his agile and robust temperament.
>
> Last night he sang his first piece with such great artistic refinement, with such sweetness of voice, and with such pure style that everyone was bewitched ..... In the fourth act he gave to ['Spirto gentil'] a personal interpretation of delicacy and refinement that made it seem a vocal spell, in which echoed the inconsolable sadness of a broken heart, lamenting its love.[55]

De Lucia first recorded 'Una vergine' [No. 20] in 1904, a decade after he last sang *La Favorita* on the stage, and he was by then obliged to transpose heavily. The record is notable for the arresting effect achieved through his observance of Donizetti's *'con anima'* in the phrase starting: *'Ah! mio padre'*. His 1917 recording of 'Spirto gentil' [No. 159] is also transposed; in his fifty-seventh year he was still able - albeit with some effort - to carry the tone over on *'Ahimè! ... Spirto gentil'*. The solid, ringing B flat (with a presumed tone transposition) in full voice shows, however, that such notes were occasionally still within his grasp.

While Sarah Bernhardt gave *Fedora* and *Tosca* at the San Carlo and at the Teatro Sannazzaro the critics grew ever more impatient for *Lohengrin*. Their discontent increased over the number of performances of *Fritz* 'inflicted' on the subscribers.[56] 'Come soon, pure Cavalier of the Swan': in his exhortation Pagliara was echoed by most of the critics of Naples.[57]

De Lucia's appearance with Darclée and Battistini in *Linda di Chamounix* was a last-minute affair. The opera, fifty years old but fresh as ever, had pleasant associations for older opera-goers. For the younger ones, their appetite for Donizetti whetted by *Maria di Rohan* and *La Favorita*, the more intimate work might well have been overpowered in the great spaces of the San Carlo but for the excellence of the principal singers. Battistini had a clear success, though 'his voice cares too much

---

55 *Mattino*, Jan. 23/24 1893.

56 *Corriere di Napoli*, Feb. 7/8 1893.

57 *Mattino*, Jan. 23/24 1893.

for vocal effects, sometimes undermining the dramatic expression, which is lost in a sweet monotony of caressing modulations'.[58] Darclée sang, trilled, and embellished the themes with grace. With De Lucia she sang the love duet 'so delightfully that it seemed new'. The tenor was well-suited by the part; in the first act duet it was noted that his love of *sfumature* was particularly valuable in a uniformly tender intonation. But, though he fascinated the audience, the part was an insignificant one.[59]

In a *mattinata musicale* at the Sala Tarsia, De Lucia joined Battistini, Darclée, and the Portuguese mezzo-soprano Maria Judice.[60] The tenor's programme, which included Enrico Bossi's 'Ave Maria', seemed to reveal some artistic rivalry, a certain *amour-propre*:

> This 'Ave Maria', of purest inspiration in the extreme simplicity of its form . . . is not helped by an insistent, almost petulant sound of violins predominating over the vocal line and, at times, ruining its expression. Yesterday we witnessed a contest so much more dangerous in that the violin was played by Angelo Ferni [brother of Virginia Ferni-Germano] and the singer was Fernando De Lucia, two extremely fine masters who strove for supremacy without either winning and, at the same time, cooperated with affectionate artistic camaraderie in the triumph . . . [61]

There was great interest in a single performance, on February 20th 1893, of *Crispino e la Comare*, last performed in Naples in 1884-5 at the Teatro Fondo. The part of Mirabolano was to be sung by the well-remembered veteran, the Neapolitan *buffo* Luigi Colonnese.[62] Clearly, some critics felt such music to be beneath their dignity, and inappropriate to the San Carlo. The suggestion was treated, first, as a joke, then with amazement as Villani persisted. But the public did not share the critics' stiffness. The columns of *Corriere di Napoli* gleefully noted that the tickets were almost sold-out. When the names of Darclée, De Lucia, and Battistini appeared as interpreters, everyone smiled. In Carnival every joke is worthwhile:[63]

> Can you imagine [Darclée] singing the 'Song of the Pancake' in Venetian? Can you imagine De Lucia singing of his love among the mortars of the druggists pounding theriac? And can you imagine Battistini . . . ?[64]

Even Procida agreed that, though hardly worthy of the critics' effort, provided that it was a *single* performance, *outside* the subscription, the cobbler's bench and the fairy's well should be seen.[65]

---

58 *Pungolo*, Feb. 12/13 1893.

59 Ibid.

60 Often spelt Giudice. Her full surname was Judice Da Costa.

61 *Pungolo*, Feb. 14/15 1893.

62 The tenor part of Mirabolano is often adapted for bass.

63 *Carnevale* (Carnival) is specifically the period of merrymaking before the self-denial of Lent.

64 *Pungolo*, Feb. 15/16 1893.

65 *Paese*, Feb. 21 1893. There is some inconsistency in the distribution of rôles, as reported in local

The opera was accepted in a happy spirit by an elegant public. Simplicity, the *Corriere* declared, was always a beautiful and a pleasing thing, asking neither intellectual power to be understood, nor excessive attention to be appreciated:

> Ah, Santo Dio! It is so charming to hear *ariette, cabalette, duettini*, [and] *arie alla tarantella*, suffused with a period, roguish grace. [It is] so unusual in our times, where all is tragic, to hear characters who speak to one another singing: 'Crepa, crepa, tu di bile creperai etc.'[66] A modern author, instead of such apostrophes, would have had to contrive a stabbing . . .
>
> But the San Carlo - some would observe - is made for sombre musical dramas, for profound Wagnerian conceptions. Stuff and nonsense! . . . Don't the jokes of waggish managements count for anything? *Crispino* and its company were very happily received.[67]

The work struck Uda as gaily satirical, witty and full of simple, fresh, graceful, and pleasing melodies. The audience obviously enjoyed its evening tremendously despite a performance by singers who were unaccustomed to this kind of music and who could not do real justice to its *brio*. The duet between Crispino and Annetta was both sung and danced, allowing Darclée to display her vocal and athletic graces.[68] Procida's review, however, barely permitted itself a smile:

> It would be ingenuous to praise De Lucia [as Del Fiore], who sang an aria with easy grace; Battistini, who sang his part with *brio*, gaining applause for Fabrizio's only piece; Colonnese, the glorious veteran baritone . . . was witty in the doctors' trio . . . [69]

Even Mormone, in spite of himself, was forced to reflect that it was surely better that the San Carlo should give an *opera buffa*, seriously sung, than some lyric tragedy 'sung God knows how.'[70]

Much of the critical severity was probably a sign of the impatience for *Lohengrin* which, on March 1st, was finally imminent and the subject of fascinated conversation in every *caffè* and *salotto*. It had first been heard at the San Carlo in 1881, with Sani as protagonist. However, Naples had been one of the last major Italian cities to lend an ear to Wagner, and *Lohengrin* had been his only opera to have been accepted without disapproval by the conservative Neapolitans. Some would have preferred something shorter, others something of greater effect, yet others something more dazzling, but most had by now accepted *Lohengrin* as 'truly one of the most marvellous creations of human genius'.[71]

---

newspapers. That given in the Chronology has been preferred to the cast supplied by Carlo Marinelli Roscioni, *Il Teatro di San Carlo*, Vol. II, p. 425.

66 'You will burst of ill-temper.'
67 *Corriere di Napoli*, Feb. 21/22 1893.
68 *Pungolo*, Feb. 21/22 1893.
69 *Paese*, Feb. 21 1893.
70 *Roma*, Feb. 21 1893.
71 *Mattino*, Mar. 2/3 1893.

For some critics this was the real point of the season:

At the San Carlo the music season began yesterday. The frame has its picture, the great theatre has its music ...
The performance contained a surprise: there was no comparison with that day twelve years ago ... specifically because of the talent of De Lucia, who gave us an ideal interpretation of the protagonist. His voice was never so tender: a tenderness of musing song. Golden-haired in his silver armour he bestrides the stage, a brilliant vision. The mystic knights-errant of Tennyson's 'Idylls of the King', evoked by the magic of Tennyson's verse, must have moved, struck postures, and smiled as he does, and spoken as he sings. Perhaps his preoccupation with avoiding everything which, vocally, even remotely recalled the violence of melodramatic passion, was unnecessary; and a more exciting movement and a warmer inflection would perhaps have thrown the human side of the character into sharper relief in the contest scene and also in the nuptial duet. But the farewell to the swan and the declaration of love for Elsa, the marvellous narrative and the resigned sadness of departure could not, in singing, acting, and characterisation, have more closely approached the ideal interpretation that we long for.[72]

Procida wrote:

The lively curiosity of last night was for De Lucia. This tenor [who] cannot free himself from loving contemplation of those volcanic characters, inflamed with passion and movement ... which serve the flashes of his southern temperament ... has had to immerse himself in the mystic purity of the Cavalier of the Holy Grail, and he has been inspired.
It was audacious, and De Lucia, with the concentrated will that is in his nature, has attempted it. He still has a weighty task; he must complete the attempt; he will need, in posture, in stride and in expression, to give Lohengrin greater majesty, a more ethereal, supernatural rapture, [and to reduce] the excessive use of affected *falsetti*.
Last night that was not possible. De Lucia was restless, anxious; he seemed to feel that, given his talents and his tender, sweet, and delightful voice, he should render the character in full; when he himself is not entirely satisfied it provokes a laudable self-criticism.[73]

His were not the only reservations. Not everyone was impressed by De Lucia's costume; one critic, in reference to his armour, was said to have written: 'This was Turiddu, dressed as a mullet.' But the representative (almost certainly the poet Roberto Bracco) of *Corriere di Napoli*, the salute to the swan still resounding in his ears, had no reservations. For him, De Lucia - an impeccable figure, glittering in silver and girdled in gold - had overcome all the difficulties. He had 'idealised the character, moulding his voice with all the delicacy he possesses ...[with] the delightful half tones with which he breathed his pieces, his words, his final *racconto*'.[74]

Pagliara, also, observed that De Lucia seemed preoccupied and

72 *Pungolo*, Mar. 2/3 1893.
73 *Paese*, Mar. 2 1893.
74 'Da voi lontan' ('In fernem Land'). *Corriere di Napoli*, Mar. 2/3 and Mar. 5/6 1893.

disturbed. Despite this,

> ...whoever understands the figure of the mystic Cavalier cannot but admire the loftiness with which De Lucia has felt his part and the nobility of understanding that he has brought to it. Marvellously costumed and idealised, in the blondness which gave greater projection to his radiant glance, he was as if surrounded by a poetic halo. And his singing was of the most delicate poetry, so sweet, so tender, verging on the dreamy. The audience has never heard such elegance: no matter! The artist has shown that he is capable of acute insight and of the subtlest sentiments. He could so easily have drawn on those effects that fascinate and conquer the stalls; that his sense of art has not permitted them will increase his standing with anyone of good taste. ...All should understand the rare elegance, the tender harmoniousness of the farewell to the swan, and of the first passage with Elsa, culminating in that ineffable *'Io t'amo'*, in which the bewitching timbre of one of the most beautiful notes rings and soothes. One ends by understanding completely the value of the vocal mastery employed [in the Bridal Chamber scene] in the heavenly passage of the flowers ... [in] the longing of the *racconto* - a magic invocation - and [in] the loving sadness of the farewell, where his accents are worthy of the divine melody.[75]

Carrera (who had substituted at short notice for Darclée) sang Elsa with ringing tones and correct production, but was detached and inexpressive to the point of coldness, apparently unconscious of the progress of the action. Magini-Coletti was convincing as Telramund. The noisy applause for the chorus obliged Maestro Nicoli to take a rare curtain call.[76] In such preoccupation with the singers the orchestral forces were not forgotten, and especially the contribution of Vincenzo Lombardi, whose care and perseverance had contributed so much.

The second performance, when subscribers also saw the ballet *Coppelia*, did not finish until 2 am. Six hours without a hint of boredom. The performance surpassed even that of the première. Emotions ran riot, the applause was prodigious. Of De Lucia, Uda wrote in glowing terms:

> Thanks to the art of his transitions, attained by *sfumature* of the most delicate subtlety, the figure of the Knight of the Grail appeared at the same time both gentle and virile. From the farewell to the swan to the sublime *'T'amo'*; from the challenge to the love duet; the progression of human sentiment was intensified in voice and gesture, to the point when Elsa broke her vow and he was filled with the sorrow of noble resignation, and of happiness that has fled; to the last Farewell, vibrant with pity and sadness.
>
> Last night, De Lucia made us understand all this; thanks to his talent - part study, part observation - the legendary personage lost the unchanging sweetness of uniform expression. From the moment in which Lohengrin leaves Monsalvato to the moment when he returns is the brief period in which he loves and suffers. In this period we have the drama as Wagner created it and as we love it. De Lucia has the intelligence, the voice and the art to make us feel these passages; it seemed to me that he was striving for perfection ... From the *Faust* of his début to the *Lohengrin* of the artist in all the fullness of his [vocal] means, what a journey![77]

---

75 *Mattino*, Mar. 2/3 1893.
76 *Pungolo*, Mar. 2/3 1893.
77 Ibid., Mar. 5/6 1893 and Uda, op. cit., Vol. II, pp. 210-11.

In comparison with the première, *Mattino* reported:

> De Lucia disperses any small cloud as he pours forth his splendid golden voice
> and the graces of his most refined art. To me, there seemed an even greater
> feeling for the poetry of the mystical figure of the Chevalier of the Grail.[78]

By the fifth performance of *Lohengrin* there was no longer any chatter
in the boxes, the stalls had lost their habit of shouting for encores, and
the usually tempestuous gallery was like a church:

> De Lucia has never sung as last night, with a sweet and yet virile voice, now a
> light caress delighting the ear, now warm and vibrant, touching the heart.
> Among the many in which he is pre-eminent his interpretation of *Lohengrin* is
> that which brings him most honour.[79]

From March 13th the rôle was taken over by Viñas; in his first
performance he was overcome by nerves at the prospect of facing a public
accustomed to the modulations of De Lucia. And the critics indeed found
some graceless inflections and undisciplined passages in an imperfectly
polished voice.[80]

Lohengrin was an opera in which Gayarre, Masini, and Stagno, De
Lucia's predecessors and models, had each had notable successes over
several years. But for De Lucia this excursion into Wagner was never to
be repeated after that season. He evidently felt some sympathy with
views such as those of the tenor Giuseppe Anselmi, who described
Wagner as 'foremost murderer of voices', or of the baritone Giuseppe De
Luca, who wrote that Beckmesser was one of the 'parts which ruin the
voice'.[81]

An analysis of when such a massacre of the singing voice might have
begun must consider both the gradual rise in pitch, from A = 422 or
below in the time of Mozart, to the modern A = 440 or even higher (a rise
of almost a semitone), and a corresponding increase in size of the
orchestra. In the eighteenth century, few orchestras numbered more
than forty. By 1825, that of La Scala had reached 66 and, by the middle
of the century, the Paris Opéra orchestra included 75 players. By the
beginning of the twentieth century numbers had reached and exceeded
one hundred, causing serious difficulties for singers trapped in an
increasingly demanding repertory.[82] Thus, the struggle between the
orchestral forces and one human throat became ever more unequal.

Wagner evidently attached great importance to the clear and
emphatic enunciation of the words, and to those vocal qualities essential

[78] *Mattino*, Mar. 5/6 1893.
[79] *Pungolo*, Mar. 10/11 1893.
[80] *Paese*, Mar. 14 1893.
[81] (BLS) De Luca - D'Ormeville (undated). Anselmi's letter (BLS, Coll. Casati 28), probably to the same agent, is dated Feb. 9 1906.
[82] Gara, 'Cantanti mascagnani', loc. cit., pp. 203-4.

in the performance of Bellini's operas, to wit:

> ... rounded coloratura ... genuine, unaffected, soul-stirring portamento ... complete equalisation of the registers ... steady intonation through all the varying shades of crescendo and diminuendo ... [83]

His operas, he told Manuel Garcia II, should be sung using the methods of 'the great old Italian opera ... with complete mastery of voice technique'. To Angelo Neumann, he exclaimed: 'They think that when they stand there and shout at the top of their voices, this is the "Wagnerian" style.'[84]

It is difficult to believe that nuances of the delicacy of De Lucia's could be heard to advantage above a Wagnerian orchestra even in a theatre such as the Bayreuth Festspielhaus, where the design of the pit reduces the risk that the voices might be overpowered. Five performances at the San Carlo, which lacks such refinements, were perhaps enough to convince him that to continue with the part was to risk vocal damage and, if his head voice and more refined effects were in any case inaudible, to no good purpose. On the flyleaf of his score of *Lohengrin*, De Lucia wrote:

> 'An opera that I sang with adoration but abandoned because it ruins the voice.'

Fortunately, he recorded much of the part of Lohengrin, with several versions of some extracts. By modern standards they are almost infinitely drawn out and, as Steane remarks, he '... is impossible, no doubt. But how he makes us listen!'[85] Some writers have criticised his interpretations in terms such as 'Crooning *Addio* to the *cigno*.' Others, though, have noted:

> Though *Lohengrin* is the most Italianate of Wagner's operas, it is hard today not to frown a little on hearing this tenor spin and linger over the vocal line. Yet few singers can have turned the phrases of the swan knight's music so exquisitely and delivered the admonition to Elsa with such conviction.[86]

Elsewhere, we read:

> The Farewell to the Swan ... will be a shock to those accustomed to the bull-necked roarings of the usual Wagnerian tenor: it contains tonal modulations of fantastic delicacy. [87]

The same extract, with its 'infinite tenderness and regret'[88] has been

---

[83] Wagner, in 1834, under the pseudonym '*Canto Spianato*', Weinstock, *Vincenzo Bellini*, p. 446.

[84] Blanche Marchesi, op. cit., pp. 19-20, reports her own conversations with Garcia and Neumann.

[85] John Steane, Notes to lp issue: 'The Tenors', GEMM 252/6.

[86] John Stratton, Notes to lp issue 'Fernando De Lucia', Rococo R39.

[87] Edward Sackville-West and Desmond Shawe-Taylor, *The Record Year*, p. 351.

[88] Charles Osborne, *Opera on Record*, (1979), p. 359.

described as

> ...unconventional in style, [it] is far more poetic and intimate in feeling than
> the standard German interpretation; it contains some wonderful long-drawn
> diminuendos and the final phrase, on the words 'cigno canor', is exquisitely
> turned.[89]

Of the love duet, one critic writes that for all its extravagant rubato '...it
is doubtful whether any other version ...is more lovingly sung than by
Fernando De Lucia and Josefina Huguet' [No. 45].[90] In performances of
such unsurpassed, spellbinding, poetry an Italian Lohengrin seems
entirely natural. As De Lucia sings 'Di non t'incanta' (Atmest du nicht)
[No. 26], we may almost smell the fragrance of the garden which lies
beyond the window of the Bridal Chamber.

From the Scheldt to the Guadalquivir. In a typical Sunday
performance De Lucia returned to the familiar rôle of Don José in a
Carmen whose première saw another indecent uproar between the *patiti*.
Applause vied with disapproval; encores were requested and countered;
frenzied insistence from the gallery met reaction from the stalls. In the
midst of this din the mood of the audience was felt on the stage, where
Judice's gestures, as Carmen, were more typical of operetta;
Magini-Coletti, as Escamillo, was enfeebled, as if 'gored by too many
bulls', and a loss of pitch completely ruined the quintet. But the faults
were not evident in De Lucia, 'a singing angel, dressed as a soldier':[91]

> Last night the actor competed with the singer and gave us a real, complete
> singer in the most noble sense of the word. Tenors who really enter into the part
> that they are playing and live by its passion are few and far between, and De
> Lucia is among the best of these ...The dissenters in the gallery and those in
> the stalls had only one opinion of Don José; a leading article would say that De
> Lucia was a kind of No Man's Land, where Neapolitans meet to unite in a
> single, enthusiastic manifestation.[92]

The criticism of Judice is worth closer examination; it mentions

> ...a deficiency in the lower notes ...perhaps because the lively cigarette girl of
> Seville had not imagined that the great Maestro ...would impose certain vocal
> *abbassamenti* on her.[93]

Artistic criticism must sometimes be interpreted. Ambiguity is
inherent in Italian musical writings, which are characterised by

---

89 Shawe-Taylor (1955), p. 434.
90 Michael Scott, *The Record of Singing: To 1914*, p. 18.
91 *Corriere di Napoli*, Mar. 13/14 1893.
92 *Pungolo*, Mar. 14/15 1893.
93 *Corriere di Napoli*, Mar. 13/14 1893. '*Abbassamento*' can mean 'lowering' (transposition) or
'deterioration' e.g. through illness. An '*abbassamento di voce*' is a common reason for cancellation of a
performance or for asking the audience's indulgence. Since there was no evidence that Judice was ill the
unidentified critic clearly refers to transposition.

obliqueness and by use of words with several meanings.[94] Doubtless, it was sometimes the critic's intention to be vague and so soften some unpalatable truth. To the opera singer and, it appears, especially to the tenor, few things are more distasteful than the suggestion that he needs to transpose. It was, and remains, a delicate matter, a serious question of self-respect for tenors, who almost all maintain that they 'always used the original keys'.[95] Discussion of it takes place *sotto voce*. Fully forty years after his death, such of his friends who did not indignantly deny that De Lucia ever transposed would - in public, at any rate - utter the words *'mezzo tono sotto'* ('semitone down') only in a whisper. The critic's remark - which he did not amplify - was probably the nearest approach that he felt he could make to such a truth. It may be the first traceable hint, since the *Cimbellino* fiasco, that De Lucia, now a celebrity and the undisputed tenor monarch of the San Carlo, was having difficulty with the *tessitura* of certain pieces and that transpositions made for his benefit were inconveniencing his partners. In later years the press would be more forthright.

Meanwhile, however, the critics praised his versatility and self-possession as he passed from Donizetti's Fernando to the mystic ideals of the Holy Grail, and to the passions of Don José.[96] Criticism, when it came, was of his preoccupation with the details of his rôles, sometimes to the detriment of the total concept. Procida, however, again joined those who warned of the damage that rôles such as Don José might do to his voice:

> ... still under that overpowering spell, I take issue with the delightful tenor [and advise him] to pay attention to certain sonorities of the middle register which injure his beautiful and harmonious voice.[97]

Particular interest attached to a new opera, *Il Profeta Velato*, whose Neapolitan composer, Daniele Napoletano (1872-1943), was a former student of San Pietro a Maiella. The work had been entered for the same Sonzogno competition in which *Cavalleria Rusticana* was the victor.[98] Napoletano had returned to his studies and had continued to work on his opera, which was finally presented to the public at the San Carlo on April 1st, 1893. The way had been paved by Villani and, perhaps mindful of the promise made to Mormone at the time of *Cimbellino* (and possibly even as early as 1889), by De Lucia. The artists - De Lucia, Carrera, Di Grazia, and Magini-Coletti - gave of their best, but the opera, though already shortened by about a third during rehearsals, was still too long

---

94 For example, *'prezioso'* has a range of meanings fully as wide as has 'precious', and just as susceptible to ambiguity.

95 Such practices and denials are not confined to singers of the past, nor to tenors.

96 *Mattino,* Mar. 13/14 1893.

97 *Paese,* Mar. 13 1893.

98 *Corriere di Napoli,* Apr. 3/4 1893.

not to create boredom.[99] The première was marked by confusion in the production and by the audience's slowness to applaud. The second performance was more successful, Napoletano receiving at least twenty calls at the end. Most of the critics' ink was used, however, on describing the lavish presents - including an engraved gold watch from De Lucia - given to conductor Lombardi to mark his saint's day.[100] Unreported was De Lucia's momentary discomfiture when, at one point of the performance, his trousers started to fall.[101]

During the flurry of farewell performances he took part in a concert in honour of the now partially paralysed Maestro Beniamino Cesi, of San Pietro a Maiella. The tenor chose music by two other former Conservatory pupils; Enrico De Leva's 'Sull'alba', was followed by Tosti's 'Serenata' and 'Bacio'. In them his voice was shown as '. . . vibrant with ardour, with which he expressed the slightest inflection of sentiment, guided by perfect artistic intuition'.[102]

The *Lohengrin* of April 22nd was given 'with quintuple illumination' for the celebrations of the Silver Wedding of King Umberto and Queen Margherita of Italy.[103] Next day, at the Quirinale Palace in Rome, De Lucia and Alice Barbi took part in a court concert. The splendid spectacle, preceded by a fireworks display, was attended by Emperor Wilhelm and Empress Victoria of Germany, Italian and foreign princes and princesses, ladies and gentlemen of the court, Papal dignitaries, and the diplomatic corps, who had driven to the palace past fountains illuminated with Bengal lights as the city paid homage to the two royal families. Starting at 10.45 pm, the long programme, which included orchestral music by Beethoven, Massenet, Rossini, Veracini, and Verdi, continued until the early hours. De Lucia's singing is reported to have brought the Emperor to his feet, exclaiming, 'He is the glory of his country!' During the performance the King made De Lucia a Cavalier of the Order of the Crown of Italy. The Queen presented the singers to the German ruler; after he had personally congratulated De Lucia the Emperor remarked to Marchetti that at Berlin there was 'no conception of such tenors'.[104]

At Naples, meanwhile, excitement was growing over the forthcoming visit by the royal families of Germany and Italy. There were extra performances at the San Carlo and a programme of songs in Piazza Plebiscito. It seemed that hardly a Neapolitan, of whatever station, could resist the latter. The weather was calm, the streets were splendidly

---

99 *Mattino*, Mar. 27/28 1893. The rôle distribution of the chronology is taken from a theatre programme and differs from that given by Marinelli, op. cit., Vol. II, p. 425.

100 *Pungolo*, Apr. 6/7 1893.

101 Riccardo Ricciardi, in conversation with the writer, 1968. The publisher Ricciardi was, from 1944 to 1958, President of San Pietro a Maiella.

102 *Pungolo*, Apr. 11/12 1893.

103 *Mattino*, Apr. 22/23 1893.

104 *Corriere di Napoli*, Apr. 24/25 1893.

illuminated, and the King and Queen were their guests. Already,

La luna nova 'ncoppa lu mare
stenne 'na fascia d'argiento fine . . .

and other recent successes resounded in the streets long before the band struck up.[105] Entire neighbourhoods deserted their homes for the evening to cram the great open space in incalculable numbers. And there, beneath a moon bright enough to mock the lamps, they listened to the songs and greeted their visitors as, for an hour or more, they made their appearances on the central balcony of the Royal Palace. As the music at last died away, and the distinguished guests retired to their apartments, the gas flames shortened and the mantles took on the roseate colour of the alabaster lamp globes of the monastery of San Martino. The square slowly emptied beneath the silver gleam of the lantern in the sky. And it had all seemed a dream.[106]

On April 28th there was a gala performance at the San Carlo for the Emperor and Empress of Germany. From 8 pm onwards the crowds were kept moving by the red-liveried city officials as the procession of carriages moved slowly past the three doors under the lofty stone portico of the theatre. But, when the performance began at 8.30, only the boxes, each eventually crammed with at least ten people, were occupied. Not until the end of Act I of *Il Profeta Velato* did the stalls start to fill with the socially-prominent citizens whose names - with descriptions of the ladies' gowns - occupied many columns of the newspapers the next day. All around were the glitter of decorations and the gleam of bare shoulders. The theatre was resplendent. All that it lacked was the royal party.

Hardly had the curtain risen on Act III of *Lohengrin* when a servant spread over the parapet of the Royal Box a crimson cloth, edged with gold. The audience rose and turned in expectation. The music continued, but all opera glasses were trained elsewhere. During the ensuing fifteen minutes, attention was shared between the entry of the Court into neighbouring boxes, and the continuing music of *Lohengrin*. Not until 10.35, when Viñas was almost at the end of his 'racconto', did a whisper from the stage spread through the theatre and the opera stop as the royal party entered, to be received by officers of the city and by the Assessor of Theatres, Cav. de Bury. As Lombardi conducted the two National Anthems the Queen, at the front of the box, acknowledged the applause.

Lohengrin recommenced from the beginning of the 'racconto'. But the music was an irrelevance: the newspapers noted the clothes, jewels, and

---

105 Di Giacomo and Costa, 'Luna nova'. ('The new moon spreads a ribbon of fine silver on the sea.')
106 *Corriere di Napoli*, Apr. 28/29 1893.

decorations; the lively gestures employed by the Emperor, oblivious to proceedings on stage, to emphasise his animated conversation with the Duke of Abruzzi; the conversations between the other members of the royal party; the Queen's opera-glass with its tortoiseshell handle; and the interest taken by the Prince of Naples in the aristocratic ladies in other boxes.[107] Even so, the San Carlo would have surprised those accustomed to going there every night and to treating it almost as a club or an enormous *caffè*. Voices were relatively subdued. None of the usual pranks were played on friends or fellow subscribers. The gilding, paintings, and graceful lines of the old building took on something of their former respectability around the human tapestry, where beauty, elegance, and the representatives of the highest strata of society were shown in a solemnity quite unlike the atmosphere of a subscription evening.

As Act III of *Lohengrin* ended, all turned to look at the Royal Box; the National Anthems were heard again, to great applause. Fifteen minutes before midnight the curtain fell on Act IV of *La Favorita*, heard in relative quiet, and the royal party left. During the performance a sapphire tie-pin, mounted with brilliants, and the insignia of the Order of the Crown of Italy, to which the King had himself nominated him, were sent to De Lucia's dressing-room. With them went a letter recalling His Majesty's pleasant memories of the concert at the Quirinale.[108]

April 30th 1893 marked the closure of the season at the San Carlo. As cannon fire announced the departure of the sovereigns of Italy and Germany *Carmen* was given for the last time, but so great was the crowd around the Royal Palace that all the theatre doors were obstructed and the performance was delayed for an hour:

> De Lucia, the triumphant tenor of the whole season, was revealed in all his glory ... they listened to him with delight, all eyes fixed on the stage. It was most enthusiastic applause ... his warm voice resonates passionately from one end of the crowded theatre to the other; the audience missed nothing - the finesse [and] the dynamism of the voice were fully appreciated.[109]

And so ended what, in almost fifty performances of eight widely different parts, would prove to be De Lucia's most ambitious and, as Pagliara had foreshadowed, probably his most successful season at Naples. Two years passed before he sang there again. And he was then more selective of his rôles.

---

107 Ibid., Apr. 29/30 1893.
108 *Mattino*, Apr. 29/30 1893.
109 *Pungolo*, May 1/2 1893.

10

A Man of Unusual Temperament

We prolong by ornaments the expression of emotions on which the mind is
willing to linger.   Manuel Garcia, *Hints on Singing*

In May 1893 De Lucia returned to London as part of a company which
included Emma Albani, Ancona, Arnoldson, Bispham, Calvé, the De
Reszke brothers, Dufriche, Melba, Nordica, Plançon, and the Ravogli
sisters. In the nineties, the colony of peripatetic operatic performers was
a convivial one in lodging houses, hotels, and the houses of expatriate
Italians and French in London. There, in homes away from home, they
met on rest nights for cards, camaraderie, and such important matters
as the exchange of favourite measures against the *jettatura* or maladies
of the throat. De Lucia and Ancona evidently lodged at a Pensione
Ravogli, where the tenor's valet demonstrated his ability to fish bottles of
wine out of the cellar, through a small window. History does not relate
whose idea it was, or who emptied them.[1] At other times they lodged
with their friend Pietro Mazzoni, at 15, Charlotte Street, Bedford
Square;[2] there, once, by the hand of Calvé's maid, came a note for
'Monsieur Ancona, *Célèbre Baryton* ami du non moins célèbre Ténor de
Lucia'. It was from a 'suffering' Emma, who asked Ancona to copy from
De Lucia's book an influenza remedy based on aconite, ammonia, extract
of cherry bark, and other efficacious substances, and to recommend a
French pharmacist.[3]

Harris, for whom *Punch* devised ever more fanciful nicknames, had
arranged for the New Italian School to be represented by Leoncavallo
and Mascagni, both visiting London for the first time. Great interest was
shown in the Royal Opera Season, which opened with *Lohengrin* on May
15th. Socially, it was a season of *bals masqués* and gala nights. The sums
lavished by Harris on flowers for State performances turned Covent
Garden into a rose bower.[4]

De Lucia made his début as Canio; Melba sang Nedda, a part which

---

[1] G.R. Ancona.

[2] De Lucia's visiting cards sometimes carry Mazzoni's address. Both number and street name were
changed on Nov. 20 1894; the house is now 50, Bloomsbury St.

[3] (A) Letter E. Calvé - M. Ancona, undated.

[4] Klein, *The Golden Age*, p. 183.

she had promised the composer that she would create in London. Leoncavallo obviously thought her very suitable; a letter from him to an unnamed impresario asked that Melba, 'if she is to be engaged (for your next spring season)', could be offered the rôle of Nedda.[5] Ancona, the Silvio of the world première, was cast as Tonio.

The London première of *Pagliacci* was on May 19th. Covent Garden was crowded. The opera had been preceded by its fame, and the expectancy of the audience was that associated only with special occasions. Few, if any, were disappointed. Ten years later, Hermann Klein wrote:

> I have rarely seen an audience so breathless with excitement over the development of an opera plot. The effect of the little tragedy was augmented by the burning intensity of De Lucia, whose portrayal of the hapless Canio's anguish and suffering was a triumph of realism. His touching soliloquy at the end of the first act was delivered with an abandonment of feeling that completely carried away his auditors. Very fine, too, was Ancona's rendering of the already famous Prologue; deliciously pure and sweet was Melba's vocalisation in the *ballatella* for Nedda ... while Mancinelli's conducting left not a point undiscerned throughout.[6]

Earlier, the house had roared with laughter at the entrance of Melba, energetically driving a somewhat unwilling donkey, while De Lucia blew his cornet and belaboured his *grosse caisse* at the rear. The tenor's half-serious reply, 'Un tal gioco', to the chaffing remarks of the crowd drew added impact from Melba's facial by-play.[7] There was surprise at De Lucia's acting as Klein's 'strong, sympathetic *pagliaccio*'[8] at the close of the first act, where the fervour and the pathos of the scene made the most powerful impression. He gave 'Vesti la giubba' with a passion and abandon that carried every note straight to the hearts of the audience. Nothing that he had previously done in London, especially his 'light, graceful acting in *L'Amico Fritz*', had prompted anyone to imagine that he could command such force and emotion.[9] Even *Punch*, which scarcely ever took opera seriously, proclaimed him a great actor.[10] *The Times*, describing the tenor's consummate dramatic skill in the same scene, wrote of the ensuing 'fine piece of pantomime' which was, however, spoiled by applause and by an ill-timed lowering of the curtain. In suggesting that the encore (of 'Vesti la giubba') afforded a better opportunity to appreciate the piece, *The Times* was alone in finding compensation for its damaging effect on the drama. The composer and singers took many calls at this point, and also at the end:

---

5 Milan, Mar. 10 1893, a date that suggests the imminent London season. (Letter offered for sale by Richard Macnutt, 'Quarto 11', undated.)

6 Klein, *Thirty Years*, p. 378.

7 *Sunday Times*, May 21 1893.

8 *Gramophone*, Sept. 1924.

9 *Era*, May 27 1893.

10 *Punch*, May 27 1893.

But here the chief applause was for Signor de Lucia, and it was well bestowed. The very qualities which to some extent mar his efforts in music of a purely lyrical kind are turned to the best account here, and the part and the performer are exactly suited to each other.[11]

In Act II, De Lucia was a Canio in deadly earnest. Both he and Melba rose to the occasion as the music alternated between gaiety and gravity. The ending

... was just as it should have been, like a flash of lightning. The whole business of killing Nedda and pinning Silvio to the earth with a dagger occupied as much time as it took Tonio to say *'La commedia è finita.'*[12]

The attention of the audience was captured. Particular interest was shown by the Duke of York (the future King George V) who had accompanied his father, the Prince of Wales, to the theatre. In his box on the lowest tier, near the stage, he leant forward to avoid missing a note.[13] Only Mascagni seemed unimpressed by the tenor; after one performance, he wrote: '... De Lucia sang very well but that music is not for him.'[14]

Unlike Mascagni, Leoncavallo did not care to conduct his own operas. He had full confidence in Mancinelli, whose interpretation was, he declared, the closest since Toscanini's to his ideal. After leading the demands for an encore of the *ballatella*, the usually undemonstrative composer rushed backstage to embrace Melba before the end of the act.[15] From the purely vocal standpoint the performance surpassed all that he had previously heard:

This was no mere flattery on the composer's part. The music of Nedda was exquisitely sung by Melba. Mario Ancona was admittedly the best Tonio of his day and made a tremendous hit with the prologue. De Lucia, despite his tremolo, was just the kind of passionate tenor for the rôle of Canio.[16]

The unassuming composer was dragged repeatedly on to the stage at the end of the performance to acknowledge applause of an intensity that Klein had rarely experienced. The news of the success of the maestro and tenor was duly telegraphed to Naples and to the theatrical agencies of Milan which, on this occasion, had no need to exaggerate the success of their clients. At his breakfast table next morning Ancona - as, probably, also the other principals - received a letter of thanks from the grateful Leoncavallo.[17]

---

[11] *The Times*, May 20 1893.
[12] *Sunday Times*, May 21 1893.
[13] *Sketch*, May 31 1893.
[14] Pompei, op. cit., p. 178.
[15] Klein, *Great Women-Singers of My Time*, p. 146. Toscanini conducted the world première of *Pagliacci*.
[16] Klein, *The Golden Age*, p. 177.
[17] W.R. Moran, 'Mario Ancona (1860-1931)', *Record Collector*, Vol. XVI, No. 5-6, Apr. 1965, pp. 101-2.

Pagliacci was the great triumph of the season. The morning after the première De Lucia and Ancona were engaged by Henry Abbey and Maurice Grau, with whom the Covent Garden management was closely linked, for the coming winter at the Metropolitan Opera of New York. On June 29th, Ancona wrote to Leoncavallo from London:

> ... the success of *Pagliacci* is constant: enthusiasm every night like the first, and a full theatre. (A)

Two acts of *I Pescatori di Perle*, on June 3rd, brought renewed reference to De Lucia's 'constant tremolo and his habit of forcing his voice'.[18] In a poorly-received work, Calvé received the credit for having done all that was possible with an opera so empty of dramatic interest.

The success of the season justified its costly scale and vindicated the modern repertory at Covent Garden. Unprecedented subscription prices did not deter audiences who were offered three Mascagni works. When, on June 19th, Mascagni conducted *L'Amico Fritz* he had a noisy and enthusiastic welcome from an audience which, in near-intolerable heat, packed the theatre. So many were the royal personages that the Royal Box could not hold them all. Mascagni's reading of his work was closely scrutinised. The *tempi* were generally slower than Enrico Bevignani's, and 'no less effective for being so'.[19] *Punch* remarked that 'he had warm work waving the baton and beating time into fits with both hands'; Mlle Joran played the violin with taste and finish, but a fiddle was scarcely required given that there was 'so much bowing and scraping interchange between the singers and Mascagni on every possible opportunity'.[20]

Melba had assured Mascagni that she would sing in the London première of *I Rantzau*.[21] After delays while Ancona and others learned their parts the work was given on July 7th, another oppressively hot night. Mascagni's new opera fared less well than Leoncavallo's. Klein found the plot 'inadequate for a four-act opera', though portions of the work were 'strong, rugged, original and clever'.[22] *The Times* concluded that 'for continuous ugliness unredeemed by any possible dramatic force or expressiveness, *I Rantzau* would be very hard to beat'.[23] The sole contribution of Luisa (Melba) to the action was thought to be when she was knocked down by her father, Gianni (Ancona). De Lucia, 'singing with even more energy than usual' worked hard for a success that was not achieved: he alone met with Mascagni's approval.[24] The only general

---

18 *The Times*, June 5 1893.

19 *Illustrated London News*, June 24 1893.

20 *Punch*, July 1 1893.

21 John Alan Haughton, 'Melba's Career a Long Succession of Triumphs', *Musical America*, Mar. 1931, quoted in Moran, *Nellie Melba*, p. 259.

22 Klein, *Thirty Years*, p. 385.

23 *The Times*, July 10 1893.

24 Pompei, op. cit., p. 186.

enthusiasm arose when Mascagni took his place in the orchestra; otherwise, applause was sustained almost entirely by Mascagni's 'friends in front'. Despite its impressive cast the new opera was given only once. There could have been but little rejoicing at the Savoy, where Melba gave a party for Mascagni after the performance.

In all other respects, the composer's first visit to London had been a triumph from the moment when Ancona, De Lucia, Harris, Mancinelli, and Tosti met him at the station and when, on his arrival at Covent Garden, the orchestra stood to applaud him.[25] He quickly became the lion of the season both in fashionable London and in the Italian colony. Many old friends were there that spring, and the *cachet* of his company was eagerly sought. His displeasure that restaurants closed so early was assuaged by the many invitations to dinner, to a reception for a thousand guests in the gardens of 'The Elms' (Harris's residence in St. John's Wood), and to Windsor Castle, where he had a great personal success when he conducted *Cavalleria* and Act II of *Fritz* for Queen Victoria. At a charity matinee Harris achieved the coup of persuading him to conduct the *Cavalleria* 'Ave Maria', a music publisher's adaptation of his music that Mascagni detested, sung - adding insult to injury - by Calvé.[26] She, as if to mollify him, forgot past differences to the extent of entertaining him at a soirée at her house.[27] De Lucia gave a dinner for him at Mazzoni's house, where the guests heard the composer recall the events of the first production of *Cavalleria Rusticana*, and also his amusing mimicry of Stagno. It is illuminating to compare Mascagni's version, as related by Klein, with Bellincioni's account of the same events.[28]

De Lucia's engagements finished in mid-July. Naples was in the grip of yet another outbreak of cholera and, as soon as possible, he sought the cool and safety of Cava. There, the agreeable customs of the *villeggiatura* took their unchanging course. At a fair in aid of a Hospice he joined a crowd eager to compete for the gifts presented by the Queen, the Prince of Naples, and members of the summer colony, and had the satisfaction of winning one of the best prizes of the day.[29]

But, as a letter to Ancona makes clear, he was preoccupied:

Cava dei Tirreni
August 7th 1893

Dearest Mario,

Your letter saddened me very much, since I did not think that you judged me to have so little regard for you, whereas I swear to you, by the love I have for my children, that I have always loved and esteemed you like a brother. If I have not

---

25 Ibid., pp. 175-6.

26 James M. Glover, *Jimmy Glover His Book*, p. 120. Glover was for years an associate of Harris at Drury Lane, Covent Garden, and elsewhere.

27 Pompei, op. cit., p. 178.

28 Bellincioni, op. cit., pp. 97-103 and Klein, *Thirty Years*, pp. 381-4.

29 *Fortunio*, Sept. 29 1893.

written to you it is because I have suffered a thousand misfortunes since arriving in Naples and I find no peace.

However, if you believe me guilty of so little affection for you, I ask your forgiveness. Regarding America, we shall reach agreement in due course. I shall come to America alone, that is to say with Enrico; my wife will not come because she is pregnant and ill. I have many things to tell you when we are together.

I am not stirring from here through fear of the *cholera*.

Enough, I kiss you with affection and I am always your affectionate,

Fernando De Lucia[30]

For yet another domestic crisis had developed. Its precise chronology and course are obscure in the tangled skein of De Lucia's marriage. However, in essence it had started during his absence in London in 1892 when, it will be recalled, Itala - pleading illness after an allegedly acrimonious quarrel with his family - had moved to her mother's house.

On his arrival from England, De Lucia had sought to have her return to him. However, instead of going in person to escort her to the matrimonial home, he sent Enrico. Though this may simply have been insensitivity it is more likely that he considered that to go himself would be seen by Itala and others as weakness on his part. Whatever the reason, Enrico's 'discourteous and boorish' manner and, especially, his insinuation that her illness was feigned, outraged her. She declined to accompany him, and awaited her husband. On his arrival he presented himself not to embrace her, or even his sons, but to call her 'adulteress, prostitute, and whatever worse was possible'.[31]

The precise reasons for this extraordinary denunciation by the usually placid and good-natured De Lucia are not entirely clear. However, the evidence indicates that the explosive violence which he could display on the stage stemmed not only from long study but also from a powerful identification with his rôles, and that stage emotions overflowed into his personal life. His correspondence reveals that conjugal relationships with Itala - a product of her times - were less than satisfactory to a man of his hot-blooded temperament. Years later, he would write that he had never known a caress from her.[32] Whether her indifference was the cause or the effect of his philandering is a fine point for debate. In his eyes her very coldness was ample proof of her infidelity. His accusations suggest that he believed the innuendoes that Nadir was not his child, and his reaction was not uncharacteristic of an impetuous, passionate Neapolitan, defied by a woman whom he considered was now a wife only in name and, moreover, one whose family he was supporting.

Itala had prepared to sue him for defamation. However, calmer

---

30 (A) De Lucia uses the form 'Cava dei Tirreni'.
31 De Roberto, op. cit., pp. 16-17.
32 Letter to Nestore Siciliano, Venice, Jan. 21 1908.

counsels prevailed, and he asked forgiveness. This Itala was prepared to agree to only in exchange for some financial independence. Thus, in a private legal contract, in 1893 he made over to her the dividend on a capital sum of 120,000 lire in State Bonds, of whose income she would retain 100 lire monthly, and he the balance. In the event of separation she would have the entire yield, some 6,000 lire per annum. For the present, some kind of peace was restored and, as suggested by his letter to Ancona, some intimacy also.[33] Eventually, Itala decided to leave the children in Italy and to accompany him, first to America for the 1893-4 season, and then to England.

On November 19th 1893 he reached New York on the *Champagne*. With Calvé, Melba, and Plançon he was to join the De Reszkes, Emma Eames, Lassalle, Nordica, and Sofia Scalchi - the favourites of 1891-2 - in the first Metropolitan Opera House season since the fire of August 1892.

Odell described the ambience as the season opened:

> My reader knows with what expectant bliss I climbed the unending stairways to my place in the upper regions of the house, and with what interest I examined the changes the architects had effected in the interior of the temple ... the rich red and gold as the colour scheme of the new auditorium ... I watched the ... slow filling of the 35 parterre boxes with their magnificently clad and jewelled ladies from the ranks of that decorative social aristocracy whose names were known throughout the land. [34]

Under the terms of his agreement, Abbey was obliged to include in each presentation at least two from a stipulated group of six performers.[35] He scarcely needed encouragement. At a period when the 'star-system' reached its highest development, Abbey's 'ensemble' was simply a group where every singer was of the first class. There were, however, differences of prestige and salary. It could not be maintained that Ancona, Arnoldson, and De Lucia commanded the following of Jean de Reszke, Lassalle, and Melba.

The notices of De Lucia's appearances in the United States are the first really detailed reviews from a non-Latin country. They are some of the most informative and suggestive to be found on his voice, style and, above all, his acting. They have something of the enthusiasm of the Latin critic, together with decidedly closer observation, and they avoid the aloofness of many contemporary London critics. As such, no apology is needed for quoting some of them at length.

He made his début in the first New York performance of *Pagliacci*, on December 11th 1893. The opera was preceded by a poorly-received performance of Gluck's *Orfeo*. However, at Mancinelli's first beat for the

---

33 If Itala was in fact pregnant she either miscarried or the child was stillborn, for Armando and Nadir were the only children of the marriage to survive birth.

34 George C.D. Odell, *Annals of the New York Stage*, Vol. XV, p. 664.

35 Irving Kolodin, *The Story of the Metropolitan Opera*, p. 122.

prelude of *Pagliacci*, the mood changed for music which had a properly modern ring of truth and passion and which 'seized hold of the listener involuntarily'. But first there was unintentional comedy, again involving an ass: while the peasant chorus filled the stage, to much cracking of whips, jingling of bells, and commotion among the people, a somewhat portly donkey came on stage, drawing the cart bearing Nedda (Melba) and Canio. When De Lucia began to beat his drum the donkey sat down and firmly refused to move. In vain Melba pulled at the reins. He would not budge. Stout villagers picked him up but, when put down, he was, although limp, still exceedingly obstinate, and Melba and De Lucia had eventually to dismount.[36]

The *New York Times* (December 12th) described De Lucia's voice as 'white', and used with 'an exaggerated opera method'. His strength lay in his acting and in the emotional force of his singing. An 'earnest artist', his work - considering the limitations of his voice and vocal method - was expressive and full of effort. Of the *Pagliacci* of December 22nd the same paper wrote (December 23rd) that he was '... at his best in the rôle of Canio. He acts it with a fine intelligence and with a wonderful variety of expression ... He aroused a great deal of enthusiasm.'

Another critic wrote:

> De Lucia ... is an artist of temperament. He evidently feels the passions of the rôle he assumes and is always tremendously in earnest.
> It is this quality, no doubt, that makes his vocal efforts more acceptable than they would be were he more superficial of feeling. His frame and his tones vibrate with the intensity of his passion, and so for the moment you actually believe in the deceived jack pudding you see before you.[37]

The *New York Daily Tribune* (December 12th) loftily described De Lucia and Ancona as 'of a higher order of capability than any of their colleagues in the second rank of the company's singers'. Their performance was interrupted a dozen times in the course of the evening to the frantic applause of their professional and other friends. Though De Lucia's voice was thought pallid and light 'there is a good deal of it'. Interestingly, Mancinelli encouraged him to give an encore of 'Vesti la giubba' when De Lucia himself was obviously not eager to oblige.

Pagliacci was not a great success at the Metropolitan that season, and it achieved only four performances. The *verismo* works did not appeal to everyone. Krehbiel wrote of the basic similarity of their plots, of their

> ... piquant contemplation of adultery, seduction, and murder amid the reek and stench of the Italian barnyard. ... It is their filth and blood which fructifies the music, which rasps the nerves even as the plays revolt the moral stomach.[38]

---

36 *New York Herald*, Dec. 12 1893.
37 Ibid.
38 H.E. Krehbiel, *Chapters of Opera*, p. 223.

Cavalleria Rusticana fared somewhat better; however, De Lucia sang only one Turiddu when, on December 15th 1893, he shared the stage with Calvé, who was repeating the rôle in which, with Viñas, she had made her shattering début there. Krehbiel wrote of that occasion, November 29th, 1893: 'She held her listeners so completely captive and swayed them so powerfully that she compelled [the *claqueurs*] to hold their peace. ... There was as little conventionality in her singing as in her acting ... she saturated the music with emotion ... in moments of extreme excitement one scarcely realised that she was singing ... The two expressions, song and action, were one.'[39] Now,

> ... Signor de Lucia assuming the part of Turiddu ... Mascagni's opera at last came in for its proper perspective. ... [and] proved incomparably more inspiring than on previous occasions. How that duet in the latter half of the first [*sic*] act stirred the audience! Vocally and dramatically it was equally convincing!
>
> In point of temperament, not as a singer, Signor de Lucia reminds one of Campanini in his best days. His voice is of the whitest, but his acting is so full of color that you rarely, if ever, think of his vocal defects.[40]

New York cared little for De Lucia in concert when, on December 17th, he appeared with Ancona, Arnoldson, Plançon, and others in his first Sunday evening gathering at the Metropolitan. One critic wrote:

> If Signor de Lucia is at all jealous of his artistic reputation he should ... never again appear in concert.
>
> At the Metropolitan Opera House he last evening experimented on 'Il mio tesoro' from *Don Giovanni*. He also played havoc with 'La donna è mobile' from *Rigoletto*. Both efforts proved conclusively that Signor de Lucia is essentially a singing actor, not a fine musician, not a singer of taste, not an artist of culture or refinement. He delivered the chaste measures of Mozart much as he would the drinking song in *Cavalleria Rusticana*, paying not the slightest regard to time, rhythm or tradition. His voice, moreover, was rarely true to pitch, the ornamental passages were slurred and the sentiment was not Mozartian. And the singer violated all rules of good taste by gesticulating vehemently and throwing his heart at the audience's feet when he was recalled. Everybody laughed heartily at the demonstrativeness of the Signor, who is not long enough in the country to know that such things as the throwing of hearts and kisses excite our risibilities.[41]

On December 19th the company made one of its regular visits to Philadelphia's Academy of Music, a charming theatre decorated in cream, red, and gold, where a small audience heard *Orfeo* and *Pagliacci*. The *Evening Bulletin* (December 20th) described De Lucia's voice as

> ... quite light and yet strong, vibrant and capable of emotional expression in no small degree; he is also an actor of quick and deft touches and his portraiture of

---

39 Ibid., p. 238.
40 *New York Herald*, Dec. 16 1893.
41 Ibid., Dec. 18 1893.

the agonized actor tormented by jealousy and hate over the infidelity of his heartless Nedda was a distinct success.

According to the *Philadelphia Record* (December 20th), he sang with intensity and true artistic feeling in *Pagliacci* although his voice had scarcely the vibrant quality required for the complete rendering of the music. His acting was highly effective. For the *Philadelphia Inquirer* (December 20th) it was a 'pale lyric voice, but ... a pure tenor'.

The *Public Ledger* (December 20th) wrote of

> ... a new singer who won the cordial applause he met with, Fernando De Lucia, the Canio, who has a tenor voice of the real tenor quality, light but telling, and of unusually good range, and is, moreover, one of the best actors the Italian operatic stage has sent this way in recent years. His one important solo, at the close of the first division of the opera, was so well and so passionately sung that the audience compelled him to reappear after the curtain dropped and repeat the song - a violation of the dramatic unities ...

In a dreadful winter for the singers' throats, the management of the Metropolitan had to bring in performers from outside the company for the *Don Giovanni* of December 27th. Kate Rolla, who had not sung Donna Elvira for three years, had no rehearsal; Emmy Fursch-Madi assumed the part of Donna Anna, with Arnoldson as Zerlina, Lassalle as the Don, and Edouard de Reszke as Leporello. The performance was unsuccessful. A small audience showed no enthusiasm. It was reported that a stout dowager was heard to ask her husband: 'How do you think it goes?' - to which he replied: 'I don't think that there is any go in it.'[42]

As one, the New York critics disparaged De Lucia's Ottavio. The *Sun* (December 28th) was, perhaps, the most charitable of the newspapers. It noted that he 'sang with less acerbity than usual' and that he

> ... proceeded to cover his tones, put a large quantity of the vowel 'o' into them, and in consequence the two large arias ... were more consistently agreeable to hear than most of his vocal work has so far proved.

The *New York Times* (December 28th) was scathing:

> Ottavio was Sig. de Lucia, a tenor who has a remarkable facility for jumping from very good to very bad. His performance of Don Ottavio was of the latter variety. Dr. Hans von Bülow once said that a tenor was not a man but an illness. He must have heard Signor de Lucia sing 'Dalla sua pace'.

The *New York Herald* (December 28th) agreed that he

> ... really was very bad as Ottavio, his voice trembling until certain passages were positively unrecognizable and his style of singing being in every respect exactly the opposite of all that is pure, classical and Mozartian.

---

[42] *Sun*, Dec. 28 1893.

The *New York Daily Tribune* (December 28th) observed that he

> ... caricatured his music from beginning to end. Don Ottavio is a milksop at best, but when his representative knows how to sing he is, as someone has said, a divine milksop. The divine attributes were not in last night's performance.

De Lucia made only two records [Nos. 51 and 53] of pieces from *Don Giovanni*: they are performances of his times, phrased with ardour but with no hint of a Mozartian style as presently understood.

In the Metropolitan *Rigoletto* of December 29th the Duke, as De Lucia portrayed him, was described by the *New York Times* as not the sort of man who would walk away with a young girl's affections at first sight. His singing was described as - 'as usual' - pallid in colour and lackadaisical in style; his acting was 'burdened with affectations'.[43] He was accused of forcing his voice and advised that less frequent use of *la voix blanche* would allow his taste and subtle discrimination in expression to be better discerned.[44]

Prices of $3 and under at Brooklyn left some wondering how Abbey and Grau could transport productions across town and still charge $2 less than at the Metropolitan. The Brooklyn *Faust* of December 30th 1893 was notable for Plançon, whose 'superb, authoritative style made him dominate the stage'.[45] This was probably the performance after which De Lucia evidently thought that the audience deserved a reward for its enthusiasm. Since the orchestra had already left the pit he sang the 'Siciliana' from *Cavalleria Rusticana*, unaccompanied.[46]

For the Philadelphia *Carmen* of January 2nd 1894 the theatre had all the gaiety and animation of a real grand opera night, with possibly its largest and most fashionable audience for years. Predictably, the press wrote of Calvé's 'wonderfully expressive' dark eyes and of her make-up, a 'decided departure' of hair and costume, a *negligé* sauciness entirely in keeping with the character.[47] She dominated the notices. The *Evening Bulletin* (January 3rd 1894) limited itself to describing De Lucia as

> ... an admirable actor, but his thin, 'white' tenor in this part has not sufficient of the robust quality, which he cannot make amends for in his tense straining for effects.

For others he was

> ... stiff in manner and uneven in his singing. .... Praise, however, is due him for his expressive rendition of the [Flower] song, while in the last act he did make an earnest attempt to infuse energy into the rôle.[48]

---

43 *New York Times*, Dec. 30 1893.
44 *Sun*, Dec. 30 1893.
45 *New York Times*, Dec. 31 1893.
46 Quaintance Eaton, *Opera Caravan*, p. 90.
47 *Philadelphia Record*, Jan. 3 1894.
48 Ibid.

The *Public Ledger* (January 3rd) felt that Arnoldson, with her 'pretty little Dresden china voice', was overweighted with the music of Micaëla. De Lucia's Don José was notable for ardour and, though he misused 'an exceptionally good voice', his very vigour made a good impression.

A Metropolitan *Faust* on January 6th was damned as 'somnolent'. De Lucia's 'Salve, dimora' was given 'at a funereal pace and with a voice as "reedy" as an indifferent oboe'.[49]

On January 9th Philadelphia heard *Rigoletto*, with Melba, who had already caused much interest as Lucia. Signor De Lucia was

> ... a spirited young gentleman but his tenor voice, which is at times highly agreeable and at other times highly disagreeable, was not effective or satisfying in many of the passages. There was ... the inevitable encore for the old warhorse 'La donna è mobile', which he sang with fantastic affectations.[50]

The critic of the *Philadelphia Record* (January 10th) was, though, of different mind, writing of

> ... a happy selection for the character of the amatory Duke. He was in most excellent voice and gave all of his music with gracious expression and clearness. In the early love duets with Gilda [Melba] his singing was capital while he sang 'La donna è mobile' with spirited breeziness and dash that won for the effort a triple encore. His acting was more decided in purpose than usual and there was an air of confident intention in everything he did.

The *Public Ledger* (January 10th) considered that

> ... Sig. De Lucia proved a fine Duke except that he showed a tendency to misuse his agreeable tenor and flatten his tones whenever he wished to express strong emotion. This is, so far, only a bad habit and, as he is so good a singer and so impressive an actor, it is to be hoped that he will overcome it. He came here unheralded by the insinuating voice of the press agent, but he is already established as a favourite, of whom it would be gratifying to see much more.

The Metropolitan première of *L'Amico Fritz* on January 10th 1894 disproved the view that the public attended simply to hear Calvé. It required a stronger work than the 'pretty and idyllic' *Fritz* to fill an opera house in New York. De Lucia had a mixed reception; for one reviewer '... the objections to his peculiar voice were not removed by last night's performance ...'.[51] For Odell '... the useful De Lucia, did not let us down'.[52] Some thought him better in *Fritz* than in any other work this season except *Pagliacci*; others judged him 'at sea when he has no passionate part to enact'.[53]

---

49 *New York Herald*, Jan. 7 1894.
50 *Evening Bulletin*, Jan. 10 1894.
51 *New York Times*, Jan. 11 1894.
52 Odell, op. cit., p. 671.
53 *New York Herald*, Jan. 11 1894.

De Lucia's reviews had been decidedly varied and inconsistent, but a change was now at hand. It came when he began to sing the part of Don José regularly. Calvé, saying that she would never perform the part in anything except French, had implacably resisted the efforts of Abbey to persuade her to sing *Carmen* in Italian. At the Metropolitan on December 20th 1893 she sang the work with Jean de Reszke, in New York's first opportunity to hear the work in French.[54] These two singers subsequently gave it there on six further occasions that season, the last being on February 7th 1894,[55] and again on tour.[56] But it appears that, although the De Reszke brothers would enthusiastically sing, as an unaccompanied duet, their own arrangement on the refrain of the Dragoon of Alcala, the Polish tenor was not enamoured of the part.[57] Rather than a general dislike of it he was probably becoming exasperated with Calvé's capriciousness and by her love of new stage 'business': such 'novelties' included her pushing a rose into his mouth as he was preparing to deliver a love song, or obliging him to pursue her around the stage before a difficult piece of singing.[58] She was known to require her partners to transpose for her at a moment's notice.[59] It is said that there was disagreement between Calvé and Jean de Reszke at rehearsals; the tenor 'felt reduced in stature' and De Lucia was asked to substitute.[60] This reasoning - implausible in view of their numerous appearances together - has been put forward as a reason why, for the matinée of February 3rd, De Reszke was 'indisposed'. Now, Ancona, Arnoldson, and De Lucia replaced the more expensive singers of the earlier casts. And the *Sun* (February 4th) found that the Neapolitan, in an ornate velvet costume,

> ...with his impulsiveness, intensity and keen dramatic instincts, gave more local color to the rôle and that his delineation served as a better matched companion piece of passionate ferocity to Carmen than the more gentle, cooler methods of De Reszke. The question may be raised, however, whether the brilliancy of Calvé's impersonation does not gain from contrast. Though she can act up to De Lucia's vehemence with more freedom, it is not certain that her figure stands out so boldly in prominence with him in the background.

Increasingly, the critics shared this opinion as they wrote of De Lucia's 'emotional personification', 'realistic passion', and of the 'whole-souled manner in which he flung himself into the part'. In 1930, Emma Calvé told Max de Schauensee that she greatly preferred De Lucia to

---

54 It seems to have passed almost unnoticed that Calvé and De Lucia formed a bilingual partnership in *Carmen*.

55 William H. Seltsam, *Metropolitan Opera Annals*, pp. 54-61.

56 Eaton, *Opera Caravan*, p. 203.

57 Klein, *The Golden Age*, pp. 159-60.

58 Clara Leiser, *Jean de Reszke*, pp. 180-1.

59 Eaton, *The Miracle of the Met*, p. 164.

60 *International Lyric Courier*, Oct. - Nov., 1947.

Jean de Reszke as Don José, for the more fiery and elemental features of his characterisation, which better complemented her Carmen.[61]

On February 15th 1894, when the poor of New York benefited from a charity performance at the Metropolitan, the usual society audience was supplemented by many who rarely attended the opera. The jewellery was conspicuous: necklaces, tiaras, and every variety of diamond ornament flashed from the boxes. After 8 pm, those with admission tickets only were standing four deep at the back. Latecomers, unable to reach their seats, either returned, crestfallen, to their homes or enjoyed the music as best they could with opera glasses and straining ears. The event raised $20,000. De Lucia sang Act II of *Il Barbiere di Siviglia* and Act IV (*sc.* Act III) of *Rigoletto*, where he 'sat carelessly on the corner of the table and announced in waltz time "La donna è mobile", or "The Lady from Mobile", as it is sometimes called, with B flats and much applause.'[62]

Late in February, the company began a six-week tour: 'a milky way of stars, rolling along in nine or ten Pullmans ... with good food, good drinks, good laughs ... and a table of poker at which I sat from six to eight hours daily', as Andres De Segurola wrote of the 1899 tour.[63] With gallic concern for her comfort and nourishment, Calvé painted a less attractive picture of touring with Grau: of small quarters; of trains which did not always include a dining car; of artists who carried their own food in order to be independent of station buffets; but of jolly times at impromptu suppers.[64]

The first stop was at Boston, where there was intense interest in the singers. The newspapers carried accounts of their hotels. Dutifully, they reported that a proprietor of the Copley Square Hôtel had made his own private suite available to Sofia Scalchi and her husband, Signor Lolli. Assiduously, they reported on the raw eggs consumed by Emma Eames for the benefit of her throat. The greatest interest of all was reserved for the non-English-speaking Calvé and her companion, Mme Lozeron, and for the French waiter specially hired for them by the Brunswick Hôtel.

The performances were given at the Mechanics' Institute Auditorium in Boston, a theatre capable of seating some 7,000. Its reputedly poor acoustics and unfashionable location did not deter enormous crowds from attending the opening performance - *Faust* - on February 26th.

De Lucia made his Boston début in *Carmen* on February 27th 1894. In the usual preoccupation with Calvé there were many reminders of her first performances of the part of the protagonist, and of the associated interest in her petticoats. She immediately came under the scrutiny of the redoubtable Philip Hale (1854-1934), critic of the *Boston Journal*. He was an erudite, brilliant, but opinionated writer who, with equal facility,

---

61 Max de Schauensee, letter to the writer, 1967.
62 *New York Times*, Feb. 16 1894. The mention of B flats implies a semitone transposition.
63 Andres De Segurola, 'Through My Monocle', unpublished MS, quoted in Eaton, *Opera Caravan*, p. 80.
64 Calvé, *My Life*, p. 122.

directed his savage notices at incompetent performers or at composers whose only crime was to be modern. He judged her Carmen '... original, inexorably consistent, intensely dramatic, abounding in the broadest effects and in the most cunning detail, wild and free, passionate without exaggeration, with tones that clutched the heart or chilled the marrow'. But the impression that she made was equalled or surpassed:

> De Lucia, a tenor born apparently for the new operatic school, gave a remarkable representation. ... When the curtain rose for the third act Don José was a murderer at heart. How irresistible the contrast between the honest, good-natured soldier at the beginning and the crazed man who crept before the audience like a wild beast.[65]

His voice was judged unsympathetic but reliable, used in an honest and straightforward way. Histrionically, though, his abilities were first-rate, the final scene ranking with the best work of the dramatic stage.[66] So used was the critic Louis Elson (1848-1920) to tenors whose only gestures were to wring their hands when in despair or to feel for the chest-protector when experiencing love that, he wrote, 'a man of brains and intelligence was a grateful novelty'.[67] For the *Boston Evening Transcript* De Lucia's acting, initially lifeless, from the last scene of the second and on through the third and fourth acts became

> ... more and more superb with every moment. Curiously enough, many of his finest and most impressive moments were when he was practically doing nothing and his enormous dramatic force came from mere facial expression and an essentially dramatic presence. ... But the picture he gave of the gradual moral deterioration and crumbling away of Don José's character under the influence of baulked passion and jealousy, his ever-growing abject misery of soul, and frantic desperation, was admirably fine, powerful, and artistic. In the third act and the final scene of the fourth he carried everything before him. ... He, too, has temperament and to spare![68]

His next appearance was on March 2nd, when *Pagliacci*, followed by *Cavalleria Rusticana*, drew an audience of more than three thousand. The critics were unanimous that *Cavalleria* - Calvé notwithstanding - was a somewhat superfluous and not entirely welcome 'bit of fury' after De Lucia's Canio. They also agreed that not even four recalls ought to have persuaded De Lucia to repeat 'Vesti la giubba', to the grave damage of the drama. And they agreed on the power of his acting and singing:

> His voice is full, vibrant and musical, and is of particularly good quality in the lower and middle register. In many respects he is one of the best dramatic tenors ever heard here.[69]

---

65 *Boston Journal*, Feb. 28 1894.
66 *Boston Herald*, Feb. 28 1894.
67 *Boston Daily Advertiser*, Feb. 28 1894.
68 *Boston Evening Transcript*, Feb. 28 1894.
69 *Boston Daily Globe*, Mar. 3 1894.

The critic of the *Transcript* wrote:

Sig. De Lucia's Canio is, dramatically and musically, one of those impersonations of which one instinctively says little; it is utterly superb from beginning to end, one is tempted to call it one of the 'events' of the year. Intelligence, skill, enormous force, and complete artistic measure marked it throughout. [70]

Hale was moved to write:

No singer in opera has so stirred a Boston audience in late years as did Fernando De Lucia last evening by his remarkable exhibition of natural temperament and dramatic skill. His voice, which might not always be sympathetic in purely lyric opera, is adapted admirably to the realistic operas of the day; for the peculiar characteristics lend a poignancy, a wild fervor to his declamations. Though apparently a man of unusual temperament, he has learned the use of it. As in 'Carmen' so in 'I Pagliacci' [*sic*] he is a master of his resources. Dramatically, as well as vocally, he knows the value of a crescendo. After witnessing such an exhibition of combined nature and skill, it is difficult to speak coolly, to weigh words and to balance sentences: but is it too much to say that in the history of opera here for the last dozen years no operatic tenor has so deeply moved an audience as did De Lucia by his delivery of 'Vesti la giubba' and by his marvellous frenzy in the last act. I use the word 'frenzy'; and yet the actor did not lose control of himself; there was no vulgar ranting or mouthing. In that vast hall the individuality of one man, not remarkable in distinction of body or resplendent beauty, shook the audience. [71]

His Canio drew the word 'sensational' from the critic of the *Boston Herald* and created a furore such as few natives could recall in their city; it was, at several points, difficult to realise that 'staid Bostonians occupied the hall'. Any impression that the city had seen the opera before was 'a mistaken one'. De Lucia's voice

... does not bear critical comparison in some ways but for the rôle of last evening there has not been a better one heard here for a generation. It has the true dramatic quality demanded by the music ... and Sig. De Lucia threw himself into the action of the rôle with an abandon seldom seen in the work of the greatest artists of the dramatic stage. His voice met the demands he put upon it without apparent effort, and he simply carried his audience beyond all control over their emotions by the grand vocal work he gave in the rôle.
    ... last night - a Calvé night, too - De Lucia swept the audience away into a state of rapture. The palm remains to the new tenor, for a most glorious Canio he was. The feminine element in the great assemblage went all to pieces, and not even the hideous dress of the mountebank quelled the ardor his superb singing aroused. His triumph was genuine. Every musical person, and the house was eminently that, cheered him again and again. [72]

Hale, too, remarked on De Lucia's particular appeal to the women of

---

[70] *Boston Evening Transcript*, Mar. 3 1894.
[71] *Boston Journal*, Mar. 3 1894.
[72] *Boston Herald*, Mar. 3 1894.

Boston; his pictures were selling like wildfire, and it was doubtful whether more were to be had. 'He has the hearts of the girls, as well as the hands and voices of the Boston public, and when the season is over no one will be remembered with the heart throbs excited by the name of De Lucia.'[73]

The jubilant tenor wrote to Tosti, who had written to ask when he would arrive in London:

Dear Maestro,

I answer your kind letter immediately so that you may know that I have received it.

I am very happy to learn that your wife is completely recovered ... My wife is with me and she also is looking forward to meeting your wife after all I told her about her. . . .

My success here, both in *Carmen* and in *Pagliacci* has been triumphal, they talk of nothing but De Lucia. Let us speak no more of me since I hope that your friends will tell you about me. The entire press praises me to the skies.

Here real merit receives just rewards.

Tonight I shall sing *Mignon* and hope to acquit myself well.[74]

In fact, *Mignon* was more of a low-key affair. At the outset, the hall was thought much too large for so intimate a work. Then De Lucia's voice, the *Boston Herald* decided, lacked something of the romantic nature necessary for the part of Wilhelm Meister. Hale pronounced that the unpleasant qualities of the voice and method of this 'creature of passion' stood out in bold relief in the part of the 'walking gentleman', Meister, whose singing should be characterised by sweetness. None the less, the Neapolitan enunciated and phrased his recitatives delightfully and he often gave pleasure in a lyrical outburst.[75] Signor De Lucia, 'is every inch a man and tends instinctively to put all his manhood into his work ... over-doing things a little'.[76] Others thought that his intonation was sometimes at fault, certainly by comparison with Plançon, who sang Lothario with a beauty previously unknown to Bostonians. The performance had, at any rate, one notable feature in the form of a dog, introduced among the gypsies for the sake of realism. He listened to the quintet critically and, being convinced that he could sing higher than any of the soloists, attempted to turn the ensemble into a sextet. He did not appear with the singers in their curtain calls.[77]

On March 7th, Ancona, Arnoldson, De Lucia, Guercia, and Melba visited Sleeper Hall, of Boston Conservatory, at the invitation of the managers and of the well-known song composer, Augusto Rotoli, who taught there. Rotoli's request for a little music met a ready response

---

73 *Boston Journal*, Mar. 7 1894.
74 (JC) De Lucia - Tosti, Boston, Mar. 6 1894.
75 *Boston Journal*, Mar. 7 1894.
76 *Boston Evening Transcript*, Mar. 7 1894.
77 *Boston Daily Advertiser*, Mar. 7 1894.

from Ancona and De Lucia; the ladies were not prepared to give an impromptu recital, but agreed to return in a day or so.[78]

The Boston season ended on March 10th with a third *Carmen*, given to wild applause and a refusal of the audience to disperse until Calvé, De Lucia, Lassalle, and conductor Bevignani had come out again and again. Soprano and tenor, unaccompanied, rewarded them with songs which further fuelled the enthusiasm.[79] At 2 am next morning the scenery and properties left Boston for Chicago by special train. The artists left at noon in a second special, comprising drawing rooms and sleeping cars.

In his summary of the Boston season Hale, with remarkable prescience for later vocal deterioration, described De Lucia as

> ... a singer of remarkable individuality. ... How he frets and tears his voice in passionate outbursts, as Canio or as Don José! Do you say the man is foolish, a spendthrift, that he destroys his voice just for the excitement and triumph of another night? But in the artistic life of an opera singer a week is like unto a year; yea, the whole life is but a fleeting shadow. In that one memorable night of 'I Pagliacci' the singer packed the glory of a year of the calm, precise, correct, conventional tenor, who neither perspires nor disarranges his linen.[80]

Hale was one of the few who saw that De Lucia was not the dramatic tenor that he appeared, and who realised the price that the spellbinding virtuoso of the early years would pay to become the singing actor of such vitality, his voice shrill with the passion of Canio and Don José. In 1912 he would include De Lucia's Canio among the creations which, over the years, had stood out for him: De Reszke's Roméo, Milka Ternina's Isolde; Calvé's Carmen; Jeanne Gerville-Réache's Dalila, and Maurel's Iago.

In Chicago, the company was to appear at the Auditorium, that remarkable edifice intended to reflect the city's aspirations to cultural eminence, built on its wealth and power at the railway crossroads of the nation. It was the largest and most complex building in Chicago. The lobby and foyers were of the most expensive marble, with intricate mosaics. Balustrades were of bronze. Onyx and fine woods abounded. The elaborate stage mechanism could simulate any desired effect. The acoustics of the ivory and gold interior were said to be the finest in the world. It seated at least 4,000 but, in accordance with the egalitarian views of the President of the Auditorium Association, it had only forty boxes.[81]

Notwithstanding the economic depression of that winter, receipts during the Chicago spring season of 1894 were the highest of the decade. A company including Calvé, De Lucia, the De Reszke brothers, Eames, Lassalle, Melba, Nordica, and Plançon proved irresistible to Chicagoans.

---

[78] *Boston Herald*, Mar. 8 1894.
[79] *Boston Evening Transcript*, Mar. 12 1894.
[80] *Boston Journal*, Mar. 11 1894.
[81] Ronald Davis, *Opera in Chicago*, pp. 41-2.

Advance sales exceeded all expectations. Ticket speculators were making profits of one hundred per cent.

Faust, with Eames and the De Reszkes, opened the season on March 12th. The following evening, De Lucia made his début in *Carmen*. His advance description as 'a singer who has steadily surmounted the many difficulties [associated with] limited means' gave no hint of what Chicagoans would witness. Perhaps only those who had read the Boston papers were prepared for the dramatic power of that evening at the Auditorium, where - though not all critics were impressed - he inspired one of the most glowing and detailed reviews of his entire career. The Chicago critic and vocal teacher Karleton Hackett (1867-1935) wrote:

Art-loving Americans have this year been stirred to their utmost depths by the power of a young man who has come to us for the first time. So great is the interest he has awakened and so little is he known here, that a sketch of his career has become necessary. Fernando De Lucia is a Neapolitan and the burning lava of his native Vesuvius was not more irresistible than is the overmastering force of his art. ... No great artist ever came to Chicago more simply or unheralded. But, when the time comes, he goes to the theatre with his 'Mind, voice, and heart' - and the public speaks. ...

Let us come to what we ourselves have seen here with our own eyes. ...

What was Don José? A Spaniard ... a sergeant of dragoons, the son of a peasant, in love with a peasant girl, and at last goaded to madness and murder by the devilish fascination of a gypsy cigarette-maker. A man of the people, moved by the simple, violent passions of the people. It requires a man of peculiar temperament and exceptional voice; - and such a one is De Lucia. His interpretation is ideal. From the soldierly entrance with the dragoons to the last broken ejaculation over Carmen's dead body, a supreme creation. 'Ideal', but what sort of ideal! That of Don José as he was, as Bizet imagined him. Not a dainty picture for my lady's boudoir, but the laying bare of a throbbing, suffering human heart; the pitiful story of a simple dragoon turned deserter, wrecking the life of the gentle girl who loved him, leaving his heartbroken mother to die alone of shame until he, a brigand and an outlaw, touches the depth of despair, and slays her who was the cause of it all. Bizet has demanded truth, and in each phrase from the first soldierly statement to the frenzy of the climax De Lucia gives it, - naked, pitiless, overpowering truth. It is startling. Never on the operatic, scarcely on the dramatic stage, has anything like it been seen here. While under its spell the audience cannot restrain its enthusiasm; still it is so strange, so wonderful, that they hardly know what to think; there seems to be no criterion by which to judge. It must be seen many times and thought upon before its full proportions may be grasped.

... Perhaps the most marvellous thing in all the performance is the vocal command that is shown. De Lucia's pallet is supplied with every color. He not only suits 'the word to the action, the action to the word', but for each word and action he has just the *tone quality* to express the full meaning of the sentiment. In the first act it is the soldier who loses his mother, Micaëla, and his profession, but who has never been stirred to his depths, knows nothing of what life may mean. When Carmen appears he scarcely has interest enough to look up from the sword cord he is braiding and ask who she is. When Micaëla enters he greets her with joy, and remembers Carmen no longer. When he sings to her, and of his mother his voice speaks only gentle affection, and the *color* is such as belongs to the careless soldier who has never known a sorrow. In the second act the seed of evil has taken root, but as yet all is love. His singing of the romanza of the flower is the apex of merely vocal beauty. The tone color is exquisitely tender, yet passionate with love, a shade reproachful but without a trace of anger. In point of dramatic effect the first two acts belong to Carmen. There she 'sows the Wind'. In the third act ... the Whirlwind bursts forth. She becomes but a wisp of straw tossed hither and yon by the boundless fury of that love turned to hate. She knows her fate, she knows that Don José will kill her. ... But what may be said of De Lucia in these last two acts? The audience sits in breathless silence while he struggles between love, hatred and remorse. When Micaëla tells him that his mother is dying and he knows that the debt of filial love must be paid before he can avenge his own wrongs, after that warning has come from his lips, 'Carmen, I go - but we shall meet again!', the audience echoes the relief of the smugglers as he turns to go up the rocks, even though they feel the catastrophe is but postponed. Then the last act. The doomed man slinks on the stage like a hunted animal. What agony in those eyes! What supplication in every movement! Now it is that the wonders of his art are shown. Every chord of the heart is touched. Heartache, pleading; devoted love; entreaty that they may begin life again in some other place. Anything will he do. No task is too hard, no degradation so great but he will explore its uttermost depths if only she will love him. But she cannot - and the joyful shout 'Victory' rising from the amphitheatre rings in his ears. Then the pity, the wickedness of it all drives him mad. 'Dost thou deny thyself to all my hopes? Shall I live to see thee, wicked, infamous devil, in *his* arms, laughing at me?' She hurls the ring at him. That cry of anguish is torn from his heart, 'then all is over', - there is a flash of gleaming steel, the crazed man, tiger-like, leaps for the neck. - It is too terrible. We are suffocated; we cannot speak. Let us out into the fresh pure air, we can stand it in there no longer. That is Fernando De Lucia.[82]

After Chicago the company gave eight performances in St. Louis. It returned to New York on April 16th 1894, for a two-week season before departure for Covent Garden. The *Carmen* of April 17th was not a harmonious occasion. Hostility had smouldered between Calvé and Eames during the tour, and it now became clear to New Yorkers, too, that they were 'not exemplars of mutual affection'. Calvé's animosity erupted when she declined to come before the curtain at the end of Act III, although Eames beckoned to her. Calvé later took a solo curtain call. When all the artists appeared Ancona attempted to join their hands, but Calvé refused to touch Eames, or even to look at her.[83] When Calvé dropped some combs and scarves the gallant De Lucia retrieved them; when he returned with one scarf he 'received such a fierce glance that he dropped it and ran as if pursued by the bull'.[84] His season ended on April 27th, with Act II of *Carmen* in a miscellaneous programme.

For the critics and for many citizens of Boston, Chicago, and New York, not even the advent of Caruso effaced the memory of Fernando De Lucia in the two rôles which fitted him best: Canio and Don José. It has been suggested that his failure to be re-engaged was attributable less to the overwhelming success of Jean de Reszke, since their repertoires scarcely overlapped, than to his vibrato, a quality which was

---

[82] *Music*, Vol. 5, Apr. 1894, pp. 763-8.

[83] *New York Herald*, Apr. 18 1894.

[84] Eaton, *Opera Caravan*, p. 73.

objectionable to American ears and which also signalled the dismissal of Stagno and of Kaschmann (who, though, managed two seasons). Yet the critics seldom mentioned that feature of De Lucia's voice.[85]

Since he never sang again in North America it is appropriate to end this account of that single season with the testimony of an enthusiastic opera-goer, a certain John J. Smith, who heard De Lucia at the Metropolitan; almost fifty years later he described his impressions:

> In 1893 and 1894 there came to the Metropolitan a little Italian tenor who had absolutely no technique, a shocking lack of style and a contempt for *tempi* so complete that both conductor and orchestra groaned whenever he appeared. In the course of an operatic performance he committed every sin in the vocal calendar; his breathing was faulty, he strained for and forced (and how!) his high notes to which he hung on as though he wished to burst wide open and end it all. But, my God, how the man could act! If he'd been a speaking actor he might have been one of the greatest of all time, but as a singer he was a complete and utter financial failure, drawing to half-filled houses and critically killed by the 'Death Watch' (The newspaper critics Henderson, Huneker, Krehbiel etc.)
>
> Yet as Canio and Don José he never had an equal, though in the very frenzy of his passion he was inclined to forget that he was singing in opera, and one felt sorry for Nedda or Carmen. One night I thought he actually had killed Carmen (Calvé, of course) and for the interminable moment after the curtain fell there was an expectant and funereal hush throughout the house. But there came no tragic announcement and the audience sighed with relief. Calvé survived to taunt many another Don José but I doubt whether she was ever again 'murdered' with such realistic violence as on that unforgettable night.

This account of De Lucia, with its very Anglo-Saxon views on his technique, was sent for comment to the baritone Emilio De Gogorza, who undoubtedly heard the tenor many times, and perhaps in this very season.[86] In June 1941 he wrote:

> The criticism of this very special artist by one who heard him at the 'Met' is interesting. At that period Italian tenors were 'anathema' to critics and public. Jean de Reszke was King and as he sang in perfect style with a voice of barytone quality the Italian voice was sissyfied in comparison and this style, approved and demanded in Italian opera houses, was frowned upon by both British and American critics. De Lucia sang in Italy, Spain and Portugal with phenomenal success, for the Masini mannerisms which he had acquired in lyrical rôles, and his astonishing vocal security, graceful acting and musicianship captured his exacting publics. In Madrid, where he followed Gayarre, he was idolized and carried in triumph. When 'Cavalleria Rusticana' and 'Pagliacci' were produced, De Lucia changed his style and became a dramatic artist. He imbued Turiddu and Canio with a real peasant atmosphere and tore passion to tatters, adapting his voice to the characters he was impersonating. His Canio was never approached because he lived the part and understood the effects demanded as well as the orchestration, which means that he gave where he

---

85 His strongly-rumoured engagement for the 1900-01 season at the Metropolitan did not materialise.

86 De Gogorza (1874-1949) was one of the most polished and refined singers to make records. From 1903 to 1908 he was in charge of contracting artists for the Red Seal series of the Victor Talking Machine Company. His opinions command respect.

could be heard and never attempted the impossible. There were difficulties in the De Lucia voice and vowels had to be changed to effectively focus the very highest notes, viz in *Tosca* you will see that Puccini has changed *'Mi costasse la vita'* in the first act to *'La vita mi costasse!'*[87] This was one example and it was done for De Lucia. As a voice pure and simple this tenor did not possess a velvety organ. As I said before he resorted to mannerisms of the period in his early career - *smorzandi*, sudden *crescendi*, tremendous long breaths and the vibrato that more than pleased his European audiences. In *Carmen* he was hardly French, either from atavism or style, for *Carmen* is not Spanish. He was Italian pure and simple; the flavor of the music was lost, while the little man ranted, cried and really felt that it was happening. *Rigoletto* was a masterpiece, for his impersonation of the Duke had distinction and he sang it in the approved Italian tradition and not in the metronomic style of today. Signor Mancinelli, precursor of Toscanini, raved about the subject we are discussing, so there was at least one authority who was competent to judge - but then he was an Italian who wanted his music sung with the flavor of the language and not covered up with barytone tints so as not to offend Anglo Saxon ears.

To judge a singer by records reminds me of two remarks: Nellie Melba, while listening to the numbers she had recorded a few days before, quietly interrupted in the following manner: 'I say, if I sang like that they wouldn't pay me!' Plançon was more pungent. 'Emilio, this is a bad joke, for while allowing that it is my style the voice is pitched too high and to be frank it is a caricature of a very good singer seen through the wrong side of an opera glass.' That goes for De Lucia. His records are curious and the execution in 'Ecco ridente' is astonishing, but one had to feel the effluvia of this man in the theatre to understand his message. Pertile in recent years was hardly noticed at the 'Met', in Italy he was a God. At first Caruso was not understood for he was accused of possessing a white voice of small size and volume. Enrico immediately decided to darken his tones and to enlarge his lyric voice which he accomplished to the detriment of his *mezza voce* and his easy flowing production. One has to pay to please managers and public.

To sum up, Fernando De Lucia was *sui generis*. He would not change his style and vocal mannerisms. He was a student and a fine musician but like pianists of the older school his liberties were accepted, in lyric rôles, because they belonged in the period he lived in. It was a voice of great carrying power; his piano tones reached the very ends of the theatre; his enunciation was faultless, tinged with a slight breeze from Naples where his song and word were law. Like Tamagno he belonged to Europe, not America or England.

Amen[88]

---

87 De Gogorza was not quite correct. The original text was *'Ne andasse della vita'*; the alteration causes the high B to fall on the open 'a' of *'costasse'* instead of on the closed 'i' of *'vita'*.

88 The material was prepared by Smith and De Gogorza for use by Stephen B. Fassett, who kindly made it available, stipulating that, if used, it should be quoted complete.

11

The Singer not the Song

All the same there are people in history as well as in art who do not seem to be born at the right moment.   Blanche Marchesi, *Singer's Pilgrimage*

The troupe left New York for London on April 28th 1894, on the vessels *La Touraine* and *Aurania*. After a long season, the *Touraine* artists still managed to give a shipboard concert on May 4th, with Calvé, Coquelin, De Lucia, the De Reszke brothers, Domenech, Lassalle, Melba, and Plançon. It was a stellar occasion, on which Jean de Reszke showed his skills as accompanist.[1]

The 1894 Covent Garden season saw seven new works, including *Falstaff*, Bemberg's *Elaine*, Massenet's *La Navarraise* - specially composed for Calvé and for Covent Garden - and *Manon Lescaut* which, in the composer's presence, opened the season. On May 16th, De Lucia - his billing now as prominent as Melba's - once again made his début in a Mascagni opera, *Cavalleria Rusticana*; again, the reviews were overwhelmingly oriented towards Calvé. Indeed, *Punch* (May 26th) suggested that Harris might well advertise it as *Calvé-leria Rusticana*.

The following night, *Pagliacci* was given with *Philémon et Baucis*. Nedda was sung by Sigrid Arnoldson, whose 'tiny voice' was judged inadequate in a performance whose most striking points were the well-known characterisations of Tonio and Canio. Shaw wrote that the performances of *Cavalleria* and *Pagliacci* 'derive an altogether exceptional dramatic force from the acting of De Lucia and Ancona in parts that are in constant danger of being handed over to a second-rate tenor and baritone'.[2]

On May 19th came the first Command performance of the season, when Queen Victoria witnessed *Faust* at Windsor Castle. It was given in the Waterloo Chamber, prepared under the supervision of Harris. The dais, draped in crimson, was approached by a red-carpeted passageway from St. George's Hall. Her Majesty's State Chair and an inlaid round table occupied the centre of the platform, with chairs nearby for the

---

[1] Leiser, op. cit., p. 133.
[2] *World*, May 23 1894.

other members of the royal family. To the rear, a sloping gallery seated about one hundred spectators. Displays of maidenhair ferns, white gladioli, and orange blossom adorned the platform.[3] The desks of the musicians were surrounded by azaleas and ferns.

Present were the Duke and Duchess of Connaught, Prince and Princess Henry of Battenberg, Prince Christian and Princess Victoria of Schleswig-Holstein, and many other members of the royal houses of Europe. The librⴰtto was especially printed for the occasion.

The players, chorus, and orchestra, about 160 strong, had travelled from Paddington to Windsor by special train of the Great Western Railway Company. Royal carriages waited to take them to the castle, where rooms had been provided for the company to make its preparations. De Lucia, Ancona, Plançon, Villani,[4] and the *régisseur*, Castelmary, had accommodation at the west end of St. George's Hall. The throne room was converted into a ladies' dressing chamber, and the ante-throne room into a Green Room. High tea was provided at 7 pm, after which the artists were free to roam around many parts of the buildings and grounds before the performance.[5]

Just before proceedings were to start it was discovered that Faust's first-act robe was missing. On his arrival - he had been dining with the Royal Household - the resourceful Harris quickly set to work with knife and scissors to improvise something suitable from a robe appropriated from the chorus. The matter did not, however, escape the notice of Queen Victoria, who observed that the venerable doctor did not undergo the usual transformation from old age to youth. It was explained to her that the adapted cloak was not so fitted that the trick could be done.[6]

On stage, blooms from the royal gardens and glasshouses were ranged alongside the artificial sunflowers in Marguerite's garden. Eighteen men of the Coldstream Guards took part in the scene of the Soldiers' Chorus. The opera ended at midnight, when the Royal party retired to the private apartments. Harris, Albani, and Bevignani were summoned to be presented to Her Majesty in one of the drawing rooms. The manager was then asked to present Ancona, De Lucia, and Plançon. This last, in anticipation of an excursion on the Thames with Harris, was already dressed in a light tweed suit, which was considered unsuitable attire for presentation. The Queen, however, on being informed of the difficulty, insisted on waiting for his appearance. Refreshments were provided for the guests in the Dining Room, for Harris and the soloists in the Audience Chamber, and for the chorus and orchestra in the Presence Chamber and Vandyke Room. Except for the few who stayed the night at the White Hart the company returned by special train to London.

---

3 *Era*, May 26 1894.
4 Probably Giovanni Villani.
5 Klein, *The Times*, Oct. 10 1931.
6 Klein, ibid., Oct. 14 1931.

In her journal, the Queen recorded the event:

May 19th 1894

... at 9 we went over to the Waterloo Gallery where the stage was arranged as usual, & we witnessed an admirable performance of Gounod's most beautiful opera 'Faust', every note of which is lovely beyond words. Albani took the part of Marguerite, Mlle. Pauline Joran that of Siebel, Mlle Bauermeister that of Martha ... Plançon was magnificent, both as to his appearance and splendid voice & acting. Ancona and Villani are also good; de Lucia, though I admire his voice, I thought not quite as good as he ought to have been. Albani sang most beautifully, & acts so touchingly, particularly in the Garden Scene. I saw her, her husband, Mr. Gye, Sir A. Harrison [*sic*] afterwards, & in the corridor spoke to M. Plançon & the other performers.

It was the sovereign's custom, ten days or so after a Windsor 'command', to send each principal artist a diamond pin or other ornament. On May 28th De Lucia duly received from the Queen's private secretary, Sir Henry Ponsonby, a solitaire stone, sent to him by command of Her Majesty as a souvenir of the performance.[7] On one such occasion Ancona was much agitated that, after the usual period, his memento had not yet arrived; so much did he complain that some of the company decided to play a prank on him. During the dress rehearsal of *La Navarraise*, with the stalls full of singers and pressmen, Ancona among them, a Hussar in full-dress uniform entered, calling out: 'Signor Hancona'. To the joy of the baritone, and amid cries from the onlookers of 'What is it?', 'Do let us see', and 'How charming of the Queen', he was handed a box, tied with red ribbon and carrying a Royal Seal which had actually been retrieved from one of the invitation cards sent to the artists. Having rewarded the messenger, Ancona anxiously tore off the string and encountered a dozen paper wrappings covering the supposed jewel - a paste-glass chandelier drop, tied with pieces of red ribbon.[8]

The frequency of Command performances rather worried Harris, since the fee allowed by the Royal authorities usually fell several hundred pounds short of the cost of special trains, scenery, and dislocation of casts. So, when Her Majesty commanded three performances within two weeks, Harris wrote a note of explanation to the Queen's secretary. Armed with Sir Henry's sympathetic response, Harris sadly explained to Calvé that her fee of some £80-100 was too high for him to count the Royal Command as one performance in her contract; since the Command was for *Cavalleria Rusticana*, with no artists specified, he was obliged to minimise the expense by using artists paid by the month and not by the performance. Calvé protested. Harris was sorrowful but firm. Finally, he 'relented', and suggested that she write to Sir Henry, stating that the honour of participating was so great that a fee would be unthinkable.

---

7 Letter Sir Henry Ponsonby - De Lucia, May 28 1894.
8 Glover, op. cit., p. 179.

Harris knew the vanities of opera singers. Calvé quickly wrote the note, which he undertook to deliver. Then, he went in turn to Ancona, De Lucia, and Plançon - all of whom had also been 'Commanded' - and repeated his performance. Their despair was 'awful' but, Harris slyly added, 'if they cared to do as Calvé had done it would be a pretty compliment'. Soon, then, he had four letters of homage, which he took immediately to Buckingham Palace. Thus, he saved £300 on this command performance.[9] He also saved fees by care in the use of 'per performance' artists during his opera seasons.[10]

Meanwhile, the season at Covent Garden, with Leoncavallo, Mascagni and, above all, Puccini, was proving a success that astonished Shaw. On May 23rd he wrote: 'I have been to the Opera six times; and I still live. ... an unlooked-for thing has happened. Italian ópera has been born again.' Perhaps, he mused, in providing it with a home Harris was less of an enemy of humanity than he had supposed.[11]

On May 25th 1894 De Lucia sang his first London *Faust*, with Zina de Nuovina, Ancona, and Plançon. The tenor was, *Punch* remarked facetiously, 'passable ... but not *Faust*-rate, a trifle too small for the gay and gallant rejuvenated professor'.[12] *The Times* wrote that his singing had improved 'wonderfully' since last year. A new horror was given to Plançon's 'unsurpassed performance' as Mephistopheles when, as he stood beside Marghérite in the cathedral, he was visible through the painted columns of the back scene.[13]

Despite a strike of hansom-cab drivers the house was crowded when, on June 2nd, *Faust* was repeated with Melba as a Marguérite whose French, thought Shaw, rather resembled his own. Her perfect intonation, though, reminded him of how wide was the gap between the ordinary artist, who simply avoids singing out of tune, and the one who sings really and truly in tune. De Lucia, as an Italian Faust, might well have been over-weighted by his part had not his dramatic instincts helped him through it. 'Several times in the garden scene he found the right musical treatment with exceptional success.'[14] Plançon, as Mephistopheles, sang in French in the Church and Walpurgis scenes, giving the rest in Italian.

---

9 Glover, op. cit., pp. 113-14, who does not specify the year (almost certainly 1894) of this supposed *coup* by Harris, confuses several events. The cartoon of Plançon (facing p. 122) relates to the Windsor *Faust* of May 19, and not July 6. The Royal Archives confirm that the 'three [Windsor] command performances in ten days' mentioned (somewhat inaccurately) by Glover were in fact: *Philémon et Baucis* with *La Navarraise* (not with *Cavalleria Rusticana*, as implied by Glover and perpetuated by Rosenthal, op. cit., p. 263) (July 6); the State Concert, which was actually at Buckingham Palace and was not attended by the Queen (July 9); and extracts from Cowen's *Signa* (July 17), all of 1894. The four singers named were, however, all commanded that year, some of them more than once. *Se non è vero, è ben trovato.*

10 Glover's claim, op. cit., p. 113 that Harris saved fifty guineas by having Melba perform *Lucia di Lammermoor* with a stock tenor rather than with De Lucia is clearly wrong, since the latter never sang Edgardo. If the story actually involved those two singers it probably relates to 1895 and to *Rigoletto*.

11 *World*, May 23 1894.

12 *Punch*, June 2 1894.

13 *The Times*, May 28 1894.

14 *World*, June 6 1894.

The admirable, *'utilissima'* Mathilde Bauermeister, with supreme versatility, used the language preferred by the artist whom she was addressing at that moment. Bevignani, as was his custom, beamed from the orchestra. Harris appeared delighted.

The *Rigoletto* of June 9th had, 'By special desire', Melba, 'in admirable voice' as Gilda, while De Lucia was first rate as the wicked Duke.[15] Shaw thought Ancona's Rigoletto a disappointment for his failure to display the full dramatic possibilities of the part; for him, the honours of the performance went to Giulia Ravogli, who played Maddalena very cleverly; to De Lucia who, 'over-parted as he was, got through with the Duke's music adroitly and pluckily'; and to Melba.[16] *The Times*, in describing De Lucia as 'not ill-suited to the part', seemed to agree.[17]

On June 24th the President of France was assassinated by an Italian. It so happened that the Covent Garden chorus was half Italian and half French or Belgian; three Italian conductors - Bevignani, Mancinelli, and Armando Seppilli - controlled the Italian repertory, and Philippe Flon, who was half French and half Belgian, the French repertory. Subsequently, none of the French choristers would perform with the Italian conductors, nor the Italian choristers for Flon, who abruptly left London for fear of 'a homicidal encounter' with Bevignani.[18]

On July 12th one of London's most famous galleries, the Grafton Gallery, was the scene of a concert in which many of the company from Covent Garden participated. De Lucia sang the romanza from *Romeo e Giulietta*, Tosti's 'Sogno', a duet from *Marta* with Plançon and, with Melba, Scalchi, and Ancona, the quartet from *Rigoletto*, while Mr. Waddington Cooke provided valiant support at the pianoforte.[19]

In reviewing the season so far, the *Sketch* (July 4th) remarked that:

> It is the example, too, of so careful an actor and so conscientious a singer as Signor De Lucia which has contributed not a little to this portentous novelty of Covent Garden taking itself seriously. In 'Pagliacci' this artist, of course, made his chief reputation; but, although he has never again reached the particular height of achievement which won him fame in that opera, he has also never failed to show his fellow artists how much can be done with a tolerably fine voice and fine histrionic powers in combination with conscientious endeavour.

After the London season the De Lucias returned to Italy, where they stayed for some two months at Cava de' Tirreni. There, Itala could be with her family. Each day, she and her mother would play cards as they took the air in an open carriage. Her sister Flora would visit the villa almost nightly, to Fernando's obvious pleasure. Spontaneously, Flora

---

[15] *Punch*, June 16 1894.
[16] *World*, June 20 1894.
[17] *The Times*, June 11 1894.
[18] Glover, op. cit., pp. 116-17.
[19] Programme, G.R. Ancona.

would go to the piano and play, and the tenor would start to sing. So engrossed did he become with his singing on those warm summer evenings, and so great was his physical effort, that he could lose a kilogram in weight.[20]

On October 22nd, closing the series of pleasant social evenings which characterised the *villeggiatura*, there was a *serata musicale* at the De Lucia villa. It was no impromptu private concert. Almost two months earlier, *Fortunio* (August 30th) had announced that its song for Piedigrotta of 1894 would be Nunzio Cosentino's 'Ammore è tuosseco', dedicated to De Lucia, and that the tenor would sing it at a party at his villa. The occasion was a tribute to Cosentino, a Florentine by birth but now well-established in Naples as a writer of *canzoni* and romanzas. It was attended by a select audience, mostly Neapolitans who had not yet returned to the city. Flora De Giorgio sang 'Vorrei' and her sister, Pia, gave Cosentino's setting of Pagliara's 'Sogni e rose'.[21] 'Povera stanza mia' was sung by Ninì Frascani; then only sixteen years old, and a pupil of Cosentino, she was still a decade away from sharing the stage of the San Carlo with her celebrated host. But the highlight of the evening was naturally Fernando De Lucia, singing 'Ammore è tuosseco', with a chorus which included Flora, Pia, and Ninì, and the Signori Frascani and De Giorgio (probably Alfredo). To great applause it was repeated twice; both singer and composer, the latter radiant with pleasure, had to present themselves many times to the audience. At around midnight, to the music of a small local orchestra, the dances started. The evening closed with an 'exceedingly lavish' buffet.[22]

Beneath the peaceful surface, however, the domestic cauldron was again starting to simmer. On July 28th 1894 Itala, alleging ill-treatment which included physical violence, had again gone to law. The root of the matter was an attempt, actual or threatened, by her husband to annul the financial arrangements of the previous year. She, however, held that her life was intolerable; she was, she claimed, no longer mistress in her own house, where her every word was contradicted by her husband's mother and sisters. Legal wrangling continued into the autumn. The court eventually ordered that, in addition to the private financial arrangements - which yielded 6,000 lire annually before tax - the tenor should pay his wife 150 lire monthly in the event of separation.[23] On December 5th 1894, Itala later alleged, he had locked her into her bedroom to try to force her to rescind the financial settlement and, on her refusal, he had struck her. She again went to live with her mother.

---

20 Giuseppina Giordano.

21 Since the reports specifically attribute all the other programme items to Cosentino it is probable that, although no Cosentino version has been traced, the 'Vorrei' was his rather than Tosti's song of the same name.

22 *Corriere di Napoli*, Oct. 26 1894.

23 The monthly total, 650 lire, is in 1988 terms equivalent to about £2,600. At the time, Itala's lawyers stated that De Lucia earned 3,000 lire per performance.

Fernando brought a suit alleging desertion, and Itala responded with a request for a personal separation.

Their tedious squabbles, recriminations, and refutations need not concern us here. They relate to the terms of maintenance; to clothes, jewels, and even furniture which, she insisted, he had taken away; and to the custody of Armando. Though the picture painted by Itala's lawyers is a sordid one, there is more than a hint of paranoia in her repeated suggestions that her husband, his family, and the servants were conspiring to persecute her. Her claim that, to deprive her of the boy, De Lucia's mother and sisters - the tenor was away at the time - had passed him from one house to another via the roof, with risk to life and limb, showed that the squalid business also had its theatrical side.

De Lucia's next operatic appearances were on the familiar stage of the Teatro Real of Madrid. His booking seems to have been a late one, since the season was already some two months old. Giuseppe Borgatti had sung *La Gioconda*, and he and Masini had shared *Lohengrin* with Viñas. Masini, who had already reduced his initial commitment from 40 performances at Fr. 3000 per night, to 24, had sung in *Il Barbiere di Siviglia*, *L'Elisir d'Amore*, and *La Sonnambula*; by mid-December, however, he had declared that he wanted to reduce the number still further, in order to leave for St. Petersburg. As he took his controversial departure, a spiteful press wrote of 'the melancholic twilight of a fading day'.

Instead of the Masini rôles, in which Madrid knew him in all except the Wagner, De Lucia took the opportunity to sing his first *Carmen* there, on December 26th 1894. The Queen and the Infanta were to have attended, but shortly before their departure for the theatre came the news of the death of the ex-King of the Two Sicilies, the last Bourbon ruler of Naples. They were spared a début for which, if one may believe 'Nelusko' - the joint correspondent, with 'Oremor', of *Gazzetta dei Teatri* - the choice of Don José was not a wise one. It was a night over which most critics thought it best to draw a veil. De Lucia was afflicted by nerves which one critic found 'improbable and incomprehensible'. It is possible that he was still affected by the recent disturbances in his private life. Certain local newspapers provided plenty of adulatory comment, little of it specific enough to throw new light on his performance. The *Correspondencia de España* remarked that his middle register had been strengthened and that the high notes presented no difficulties. Several papers described Don José as the part that best threw into relief his exceptional gifts as actor and singer.[24] *Epoca* (December 27th), however, was more specific:

---

[24] (SPM) All undated reviews from this Madrid season are quoted from a compilation: *Fernando De Lucia: Madrid - Milano, 1895*. They are undoubtedly selective and they exhibit a certain uniformity of metaphor which suggests, if not unanimity among the critics, at least some licence by the translator into Italian.

I doubt whether last night's public would have gone as far as kissing the hands of Bizet's interpreters because, to tell the truth, they were not generally up to the level of *Carmen*; but it is also true that to let out a strident bellow (I hope my readers will pardon the expression) because the tenor De Lucia, in attacking a high note, was for a second a fraction out of tune, seemed to me excessively sensitive and a serious lack of consideration ...

De Lucia was much applauded in the Flower Song and in the final duet. ... in the remaining scenes he was short of breath and sometimes sang in the head register what should have been placed in the chest; despite this, he phrased in a masterly manner ...

When the brutish opposition of a certain part of the audience does not, as it did last night, stifle his abilities, one hopes that [he] will easily regain lost ground.

Despite some organised dissent, *Mefistofele*, with the popular Eva Tetrazzini, allowed him to redeem his reputation.[25] Again came the comparisons with Gayarre and Masini; *Liberal* suggested that he convincingly won the comparison, at least with the former. *Epoca* (January 7th 1895) wrote:

De Lucia, who had overcome the rage of the enemy camp in the performances of *Carmen*, fighting bravely, last night attained a new and important victory. ... he imbued the garden quartet with its singular air of comic opera. ... In the epilogue he was a Professor of Singing, phrasing the romanza magisterially and giving to this page, immortalised here by Gayarre, the poetic and poignant expression of the unforgettable tenor of Navarre.

The performances of *La Gioconda* had been spectacular, not least because of the jewels, reputed to be worth 60,000 lire, worn by the Laura, Emma Leonardi.[26] On January 26th 1895 De Lucia, who had not sung Enzo for three years, replaced the indisposed Borgatti at short notice. The fourth act trio, the delicate treatment of the duet with Laura and, naturally, 'Cielo e mar' all served to illustrate to *Resumen* that he was

... a singer of the first rank, a profound connoisseur of his art and of his vocal organ, and a correct and intelligent actor, who can give his character realism and effectiveness.

Of his appearances in *Cavalleria Rusticana*, whose première was on January 22nd 1895, special note was taken (*Figaro*) of his mode of decoration of the 'Siciliana', 'sculptured with a refined exquisiteness beyond human capacity to surpass'. *Nacional* observed that the little duet with Alfio was given 'without the excessive hate and rage that always mar it'. Calvé, the Santuzza, was evidently out-of-tune when attacking certain high notes. It seems that the press was losing patience with that once-irresistible source of copy: one day lost amulets; another, a fainting fit on stage; yet another, a stolen handbag, containing

---

25 *Cosmorama*, Jan. 18 1895.
26 *Gazzetta dei Teatri*, Jan. 3 1895.

talismans without which failure in Madrid was certain. The theatrical mercury fluctuated violently as *Calvétitis* afflicted the public. There was more than a hint of satisfaction in the success recorded by Eva Tetrazzini when she took over the rôle of Santuzza.[27]

The novelty, both for De Lucia and for the Real, came with *Manon* on February 23rd 1895. Some of the listeners thought the proportions of the theatre were ill-matched to those of the opera, whose more delicate effects were appreciated only in the stalls. None the less, the work was received with overall pleasure, and much was made of De Lucia's suitability for the part, notwithstanding what *Epoca* (February 24th) termed the 'terrible *tessitura* of the romanza ("Ah! dispar vision")'. *Resumen* wrote:

> Had Maestro Massenet had a thorough knowledge of the exceptional qualifications, the very flexible voice, [and] the talent of De Lucia, he could not have written a score better adapted to put them into relief. De Lucia, through voice, figure, and bearing realised the true Des Grieux conceived by the Abbé Prévost, and with his exceptional talent as a singer gave animation, colour, and effectiveness to . . . the score.

The public was cold during Act I. The first indications of enthusiasm came when De Lucia sang the 'Sogno' ('En fermant les yeux'). In the duet in San Sulpice, when Des Grieux feels the rebirth of his love for Manon and cries: '*Io vivo solo del tuo amore*', he gave to the outburst such passion that the audience burst into an ovation. For *Liberal*, the part fitted him 'like a ring on a finger'. *Pais* declared that no tenor since Masini could rival De Lucia in this opera; space did not permit them to indicate all the *filate* and all the difficult phrases that he gave with taste and sincerity. The critic of *Eco Militar* proclaimed that 'of his kind, De Lucia is unsurpassable'.

It was *Nacional* that produced the famous quotation:

> There are four first-rank tenors who dominate the stages of today: I is De Lucia, II is De Lucia, III is De Lucia, IV is De Lucia.
> In Manon, they applauded the romanza, exquisitely sung by De Lucia, tenor number one, two, three and four.

The Real management tried to reconfirm him until the end of the season, but he was able to offer only a few more performances and the promise - never fulfilled - of another season.[28] Madrid had seen the last of De Lucia, of 'a star which blazes to its zenith, in all the splendour of its dazzling light . . . never obscured by even the lightest cloud'.[29]

His proposed engagement in a Sonzogno season in Paris had not

---

27 Ibid., Mar. 7 1895.
28 Ibid.
29 G.A.B. in *Fernando De Lucia: Madrid - Milano, 1895*.

materialised. Instead, he was now involved with a new Mascagni work, *Silvano*. It was to be performed at La Scala, Milan, where Sonzogno was at that time impresario.

In the 1890s Milan was the unquestioned centre of Italian lyric activity. The major music publishers were established there. Scenery built in Milan was shipped from Genoa to theatres throughout the world. The principal theatrical costumiers would measure their patrons as they passed through Milan *en route* from London to Palermo, and fit them as they returned, heading for Moscow and Tiflis. Theatrical agents, though active in Florence, Naples, Rome, and Venice, and still to be found in Bologna, were now concentrated in Milan which, in 1897, had at least thirty.[30] From Lombardy, they despatched their clients to every theatre where Italian opera was to be heard.

In the city centre, a stone's-throw from La Scala, was the Galleria, that great crucible of Milanese musical life. Here, protected from sun and rain, the young recording engineer Fred Gaisberg sat during his first visit to Milan, in 1899, watching, among the chattering throngs, the reigning composers and singers holding court amid their admirers. Franchetti, Giordano, Leoncavallo, Mascagni, Puccini, and Tamagno were to be seen on their way to their mid-day aperitif, for that was when the artistic community converged on the Galleria, when artists met their managers, and when *comprimarii, professori d'orchestra* and *coristi* were engaged in this clearing house of the operatic world.[31] Negotiations between librettists and composers, publishers and impresarios moved from the contract-strewn offices of Ricordi and Sonzogno to the cafés and restaurants of the Galleria. Milan had, though, a more sinister side. Masini warned the young Chaliapin to stay away from the Galleria, this 'nest of all evil, ... this promenade for *cani*'.[32] For here a *claque* could be bought or a singer's reputation compromised by vicious talk. However, though exceptions were known - Masini himself never sang there - a successful appearance at nearby La Scala was arguably the most prestigious of all recommendations, a prerequisite for a singer who wished to be taken seriously.

Silvano was not the only Mascagni novelty at La Scala that season. On February 16th 1895, after lengthy litigation with Ricordi, who had claimed that it was contracted to him, Sonzogno had mounted the first performance of *Guglielmo Ratcliff*, the opera on which Mascagni had been working since his student days. Only weeks later, La Scala gave the world première of his *Silvano*, with De Lucia in the title rôle and with other principal parts performed by Giuseppe Pacini (Renzo) and Adelina Stehle (Matilde), and conducted by Rodolfo Ferrari.

---

30 *Cosmorama*, Aug. 12 1897.
31 Jerrold Northrop Moore, *A Voice in Time*, pp. 35-6.
32 Maxim Gorky, *Chaliapin*, p. 154. The actual authorship of this work is disputed: See Borovsky, *Chaliapin*, pp. 22-3.

'If *Silvano* ever has any value, it will be that of having shown Mascagni his duty to improve himself.'[33] So wrote one of Mascagni's biographers. For it is now considered his weakest opera, a work born for no reason - if one excepts his reputed financial problems at the time - other than expediency. Its *raison d'être* was the insistence of Sonzogno who, doubting the viability of a work as advanced for its time as *Ratcliff*, had wanted to provide himself with a *verismo* opera, along the lines of *Cavalleria Rusticana*, to recoup his anticipated losses.[34] But it was written in haste and Mascagni invested little in it except, as D'Ormeville sadly pointed out, his reputation.[35] Only three months before the première Mascagni wrote to Galli: '*Silvano* is like death: *it is late in coming!* But even it will come in the end.'[36] As it turned out, *Ratcliff* was a qualified success whose subsequent career has been impeded principally by the difficulty of casting its protagonist, and *Silvano* was an acknowledged failure. The miracle could happen only once.

The libretto of *Silvano* was by Targioni-Tozzetti, based on a novel by Alphonse Karr. It is a slender story of Silvano, forced by poverty to become a smuggler. When unmasked in his work he escapes and becomes a highwayman. On his eventual return to his native village he discovers that his fiancée, Matilde, has become the mistress of Renzo, a violent and uncouth fisherman. When her love for Silvano reawakens Renzo threatens to kill him. In an assignation, Renzo and Matilde are surprised by Silvano, who shoots his rival dead and then, taking flight, again leaves Matilde desolate.

The part of the protagonist had been written by Mascagni for De Lucia, who was clearly anxious to have the music before he left for Madrid. Mascagni wrote to reassure him:

Livorno, November 28th 1894

My dear Fernando,

Don't be exasperated if you have not yet had the part of Silvano: don't worry about anything - it is a part written for you by your Pietruccio . . . . . and I will say nothing else to you.

In four days you can go on stage -

The opera is in two acts; the protagonist is the tenor; the part of the tenor is extensive enough; in the first act there is:

Love duet (with the soprano)

Scene with aria and a *duettino* with the mother -

Some recitative

In Act 2

Scene with the mother -

Little romanza -

Recitative with some chorus ladies -

---

33 Giannotto Bastianelli, *Pietro Mascagni*, p. 80.
34 Gianandrea Gavazzeni, 'La Musica di Mascagni, Oggi', in Morini, *Mascagni*, Vol. I, p. 24.
35 *Gazzetta dei Teatri*, Mar. 28 1895.
36 Letter Mascagni - Galli, Dec. 22 1894, quoted in Morini, *Mascagni*, Vol. I, p. 300.

Serenade -
Scene -
Finale -
In the second act there are no artists (except the mother): there is only the tenor!
Are you satisfied? . . . . .
You will hear what I have prepared for you! . . . . .
Write to me and tell me when you leave, what you are doing, etc. . . . . .
The opera will be complete before Christmas - if you want the second act, which is the more important, I can send it to you in three or four days.
Write to me -
I embrace you,

P. Mascagni (RE)

On March 25th 1895 one of the season's most crowded and fashionable audiences was disappointed by an opera which lasted less than two hours, including a long intermezzo. It also lacked appeal. Even Galli, writing in Sonzogno's own newspaper, was obliged to recognise the fact. While applause was not lacking, neither were hostility, and *zitti*.[37] At the second performance it was plain that the enthusiasm shown by a few hundred spectators, even though it was not always uncontested, was contrived.[38]

Opinions on the singers were a different matter. Stehle and Pacini were applauded despite their colourless parts. De Lucia encountered some of the reserve shown at the Costanzi. More even than the Romans, the Milanese of La Scala considered themselves to be the supreme arbiters of all matters operatic. Singers coming with the accolade of the Teatro San Carlo of Naples were scrutinised especially closely. However, the critics were almost unanimous. Galli wrote:

In this duet ['Torno, adorata mia'] resounded, for the first time at La Scala, the very beautiful voice of the tenor De Lucia. At his first notes the entire public was moved to immediate admiration.

De Lucia, [his voice] responsive to the most delicate gradations and musical shadings, ready to produce the most varied effects, has an enviable ability to rouse his audience to enthusiasm. . . . the famous tenor sang with his whole soul, . . . The cry of *'Bis'* exploded from every part of the theatre . . .

The quarrel scene, with Silvano's apostrophe:

'Ah, m'hai detto bandito?'

is the culminating point of the first act. . . . De Lucia appeared . . . not only as a singer of the first rank, but also full of passion as a dramatic interpreter and of superior intelligence . . .

De Lucia is the *tenore di grazia*, the interpreter of sentiments which breathe gentleness; he sings love songs as Giuglini sang them; in him live the traditions of Italian singing, intact and splendid, but modified according to the tastes of the new art, which substitute dramatic expression, inspired by truth, for virtuosity of the throat.[39]

37 The cries used to silence a noisy audience.
38 *Perseveranza*, Mar. 28 1895.
39 *Secolo*, Mar. 26-27 1895.

In *Gazzetta dei Teatri* we read:

> Here is the true, the only hero of the evening. Woe to Mascagni, had he not had this truly exceptional artist.
>
> The echo of the triumphs attained by De Lucia in all the principal theatres of the two worlds had reached us but this great reputation had not been confirmed by the sovereign verdict of the Milanese public. Confirmation there was ... spontaneous, unconditional confirmation. A rushing wave of enthusiastic acclaim broke out at the celebrated tenor's first phrases, for his mellow and fluid voice and for his impassioned and irresistible intonation. And they immediately wanted an encore of a passage in the duet with Matilde in the first act, as also of Silvano's second act 'romanza.' This they even wanted three times.
>
> It was a glorious battle waged by De Lucia on this occasion. Without his great, unquestionable worth there would have been ample reason for being overwhelmed by the terrible struggle with a public like that of the Scala, annoyed and embittered by its disappointment with the opera. And De Lucia sensed the wind, understood the atmosphere, and felt all the grave responsibility that rested on him. But he did not lose his courage. Rather, it seemed to redouble. He wanted to conquer and he conquered; he wanted to triumph and he triumphed. Honour to him! ... Glory and laurels to him! ...
>
> De Lucia's stock, already highly quoted on the theatrical Bourse, shows a phenomenal rise today. He represents a most remarkable individuality in contemporary lyric art.[40]

G.B. Nappi wrote:

> I am happy to associate myself with the admiring paean of praise directed at the tenor De Lucia during the performance. ... every phrase of his predominant part was approved [and] saluted by lively and insistent applause. He has amply justified his fame. His voice is one of radiant splendour, mellow, fluent, coloured, trained to the subtlest refinements of modulation. The delivery is easy, intense, the accent always warm and impassioned. Pure diction, facility of *portamento*, elegant figure, [and] ease and effectiveness of dramatic action, are the results of conspicuous gifts which must be the envy of many and which will justify the brilliant career of the young artist.[41]

Achille Tedeschi ('Leporello') asserted:

> All the qualities called for in a singer's voice are found united in him: the mellowness, the freshness, the security of intonation, and the spontaneity which conceals any effort; and he does not lack the gifts of a good actor: stage-mastery, clear and precise diction, dramatic expression.[42]

Most critics agreed with *Italia del Popolo*:

> De Lucia was a true sheet anchor ... The voice [is] free, extended, brilliant in the top register.[43]

---

40 *Gazzetta dei Teatri*, Mar. 28 1895.

41 *Perseveranza*, Mar. 26 1895. Nappi (1857-1932) was a writer, composer, and one of the most influential and authoritative Italian critics of the time.

42 *Illustrazione Italiana*, Mar. 31 1895.

43 *Italia del Popolo*, quoted in *Gazzetta dei Teatri*, Apr. 4 1895.

He was judged to be

> ... among the few who show what was, what ought to be, the true Italian style
> of singing. In the voice, in the action, in his passionate accents he reveals his
> native Naples. It is impossible not to be enslaved.[44]

Others drew attention to his 'extraordinary range'; to the power of his
delivery in the phrase '*Io non ti vo' più mesta, o mio tesoro*', which he had
to repeat;[45] and to 'an exquisite *barcarola* ["S'è spento il sol lontano"] in
which Mascagni's melodic invention sparkles like a jewel'.[46] The critic of
Tribuna rhapsodised:

> And Silvano sings to the night, to love, and to the sea, and his song is repeated
> amid great pleasure.[47]

One reviewer after another noted that only the 'extraordinary
communicative powers' of Fernando De Lucia saved the opera from utter
failure. It is ironic that, in the year in which he was, arguably, at the
height of his fame and prestige, he should have been associated with so
feeble a work. The one dissenting voice belonged to Ricordi and was not
without validity. After complaining of 'a large and villainous *claque*,
whose presence is scandalous', he continued:

> Signor De Lucia has a good and extended tenor voice and clean, clear, and
> effective delivery, and he provoked enthusiasm. Speaking frankly, I do not
> share this enthusiasm, as I cannot convince myself that the manner of delivery
> of this artist can be called, as some have called it, *bell'arte di canto*. It certainly
> makes an impression, produces an effect, that great facility of vocal emission
> which he reduces in an instant from a *fortissimo* to a *pianissimo*, and no less an
> effect is produced by the tender elongation of the notes, swelled as when the foot
> increases the pressure of the bellows with the word '*expression*' on the
> harmonium; but when such effects do not always find aesthetic justification in
> the essence of the music, when the melody is disfigured by the abuse of
> repeated *corone*, then truly I cannot call this *bell'arte di canto*, but I will call it a
> true artistic artifice, calculated to wring applause from the public. And the
> applause of the La Scala audience was the more justified because the entire
> season has condemned it to mediocre voices.[48]

These were telling words from Ricordi. Later, he would argue against
the engagement of De Lucia for the world première of *La Bohème*.[49]
Nevertheless, Ricordi would later use him on occasions as important as
the first La Scala performance of *La Bohème*, and the world première of
Iris. Given the power of the music publishers and their right of veto it

---

44　*Perseveranza*, Mar. 28 1895.
45　*Lombardia*, quoted in *Gazzetta dei Teatri*, Apr. 4 1895.
46　*Fanfulla*, quoted in *Gazzetta dei Teatri*, Apr. 4 1895.
47　*Tribuna*, quoted in *Gazzetta dei Teatri*, Apr. 4 1895.
48　*Gazzetta Musicale di Milano*, Mar. 31 1895.
49　Letter Ricordi - Puccini, Oct. 1895, see Gara, *Carteggi Pucciniani*, pp. 129-30.

hardly seems possible that he could have been chosen without Ricordi's approval. It has been suggested that the tenor might by then have changed his style, discarding the affectations which so irritated the publisher.[50] There is, though, no evidence that he had, and much that he had not.

On April 7th the eighth performance of *Silvano* closed a season where quantity was thought to have prevailed over quality. To the end of the run there was continual enthusiasm for De Lucia,

> ... who knows the art of electrifying the public with the fascinating modulations of a priceless voice and with ardent, sometimes exuberant, dash ... [51]

From Milan he returned to Naples, where the San Carlo was again in turmoil. In 1894, the regular summer contest for the concession had seen bids by Anna Stolzmann and by Nicola Daspuro who, for the past year, had held that of the Teatro Mercadante. This, the old Teatro Fondo, had been restored and modernised at Sonzogno's expense and had reopened on December 6th 1893. The cost involved had justified the award of the concession for the unusually long period of twenty-five years. The first season was one which, fifty years later, was still remembered in Naples: Daspuro engaged twenty-one prima donnas, including Bellincioni, Darclée, Frandin, and Stehle, and nine first tenors, including Masini, Stagno, and Tamagno, to say nothing of three prima ballerinas.[52] By April 1894 the Municipality seemed certain to favour Daspuro for the San Carlo; it later changed its mind and awarded the concession to Stolzmann, who offered a programme which included works from both the Ricordi and the Sonzogno stables.

Stolzmann soon met insuperable difficulties. She was roundly damned by the Neapolitans, with cries of 'Down with Stolzmann' and 'Back to Rome!', and she gave only a few operas before abandoning the theatre. By mid-January 1895 the San Carlo had been closed for ten days, with the chorus and orchestra 'resting' and the singers unpaid. A month later it was reported that the Magistrate had affixed the seals of bankruptcy, but that a Società Anonima, though unwilling to assume Stolzmann's liabilities, had offered to assume the continuance of the season.[53] The theatre finally reopened at the end of March, under the management of Villani, to give *Silvano* and *Guglielmo Ratcliff*, conducted by Mascagni, and other Sonzogno operas, including *Manon* and *Werther*.

Many seats and boxes were empty on April 30th 1895, when only a few subscribers paid the supplement to hear *Silvano*. There were grumbles at the cost of a performance that had still not started at almost

---

[50] Gara, in 'Cantanti Mascagnani', Morini, *Mascagni*, Vol. I, p. 224.
[51] *Perseveranza*, Apr. 8 1895.
[52] Daspuro, 'Memorie', ch. XLIV.
[53] *Gazzetta dei Teatri*, Feb. 14 1895.

10 pm. The opera was condemned more or less explicitly by the principal critics. In a satirical article two imaginary subscribers debated whether it was original or contained reminders of other works. It was a pity, they concluded, that the note of sartorial elegance struck by Mascagni, resplendent in a smart new waistcoat, did not extend to De Lucia's costumes.[54] Procida, calling the opera 'grotesque', reflected that it had, though, the merit of displaying the voice of De Lucia, 'its timbre like the ringing of a metal bell'. The review continued:

> ... in his middle register he displays warm and ample notes, because its volume has noticeably increased without, for the moment and also, I hope, for the future, having suffered damage to the higher register. His art is yet more evident in *filature*, in dexterity of shading, in the *tenderness* of the *mezza voce*, in his intonation. His singing is a joy to the ear.[55]

By now, Mascagni was not surprised by the verdict on his opera, and he was probably not greatly disturbed by what he - by his own admission, a relentless reader of newspapers - found in the press. Instead, he contented himself with writing a letter to *Don Marzio*, wittily pointing out the folly of taking notice of critics who could seldom be relied upon to agree about anything.[56]

De Lucia, however, had enjoyed a triumph that was certainly preordained. In his honour the management staged a performance of *Cavalleria Rusticana*. The theatre was full to overflowing. 'In Naples', remarked Uda, 'the singer is the most effective invitation to buy an opera ticket.' He continued:

> The singer's success was immediate, and noisy; ... we might even say that success came before [his] appearance, so saturated was the atmosphere with his triumph. ... the 'Brindisi' was encored as usual, to the satisfaction even of those who might have observed the inopportunity of certain *puntature*, [and] an obvious tendency to virtuosity. What, on the other hand, De Lucia emphasised in excellent fashion was the 'Addio alla madre', where the sense of doom passed into Turiddu's soul ...[57]

As the tenor left for London, however, jubilation may have been somewhat tempered by the outspoken views of Procida:

> Fernando De Lucia has scored another brilliant success ... above all in the 'Addio', sung ... without recourse to ingenious cadenzas, to interpolated *gruppetti*, or to *volatine* [little runs]. De Lucia is an élite singer, who has uncovered all the secrets and exploited all the resources of his art. He has a soft, melodious, and beautiful voice, a penetrating and polished *mezza voce*, perfect syllabification, and secure intonation; his dramatic interpretation is not

---

54 *Don Marzio*, May 1/2 1895.
55 *Fortunio*, May 5 1895.
56 *Don Marzio*, May 2/3 1895.
57 *Pungolo*, May 5/6 1895.

always correct, since frequently he exceeds, or ignores, the finer points of the character but, for his effective colouration and penetrating *accent*, it would be unjust to be ungrateful. He is still one of the very few artists of the lyric stage who move and delight one but who aim, rather than at one's intellect, at one's heart ... one of those rare singers who has made a *cult* of the education of his voice. With such precious and exceptional gifts, then, why must he become enraptured of this same success and be eager to exceed its confines? The capricious interpretation of the 'Brindisi', to which he joined *puntature*, *gruppetti*, and *volatine*, the interminably held note at the end of the 'Siciliana', and here and there, especially in *Silvano*, several [notes] melting away too affectedly, induce me to warn the friend and marvellous singer, to whom my voice, amid the celebrations prepared for him in London, may not come much in tune, that this adds nothing to the grace and *sweetness [dolcezza]* of his singing; rather, it fossilises it with the wearisome affectation of the *virtuoso*. Return to the spontaneous virtues, ... leave the task of moving [us] to the *sweet* and tender voice without inflicting [on us] that which astonishes, and success will remain equally constant and artistically more convincing.58

---

58 *Fortunio*, May 11 1895.

12

A Handful of Delights

It is not easy to dream in the Opera House - blazing with diamonds, brilliant
with beauty, buzzing with the soft sibilation of Society small-talk - even to the
soothing cadences of Mascagni. Yet a night at the Opera is always a time of
memories. . . . It is at the Opera that the men and women of the day gather in
fullest force.   *The Sketch*, May 15th 1895

The 1895 Royal Opera Season at Covent Garden saw important changes,
for the De Reszke brothers were missing from the roster. It was Jean's
first absence from a London summer since 1886. In partial
compensation, Tamagno made his début at Covent Garden, as Otello, a
part in which London already knew what Shaw termed his 'magnificent
screaming', from his appearances at the Lyceum in 1889.[1] There was a
great resurgence of interest in Italian opera which, a few years earlier,
many had pronounced dead. The old encores were shouted for with
boundless enthusiasm. But this was no ordinary season. The great *coup*
for Harris was the return, ten years after her last performance at Covent
Garden, of Adelina Patti, whom London had not heard in opera since her
single appearance for Mapleson at Her Majesty's Theatre in 1887. In a
company that included Emma Albani, Ancona, Bellincioni, De Lucia, De
Lussan, Eames, Maurel, Melba, Plançon, and Sembrich, it was the 52-
year-old Patti who undoubtedly fascinated London society.

Otello opened the season on May 13th. De Lucia made his *rentrée* on
May 14th, with Macintyre and Plançon, in *Mefistofele*, as 'a rather
timorous and bashful Faust, with one eye for Maggie and the other for
Nellie [Mancinelli] as if praying the latter to conduct him safely and keep
him from temptation to go wrong'.[2] *The Times* (May 17th) thought that
he sang 'with much earnestness, and in the last scene his vocalisation
was entirely free from the peculiarities of tone usually indulged in by
him'. Two nights later he repeated his 'triumphant' success as Canio.

On May 20th, *Fra Diavolo* was revived at the particular request of the
Prince of Wales, and was performed by De Lucia, David Bispham, and
Marie Engle. The crowded house, delighted with almost everything to do
with the opera, was startled when some enthusiast, apparently ecstatic,

[1] Shaw, *London Music in 1888-89*, p. 171.
[2] *Punch*, May 25 1895.

threw a leather lorgnette case which missed the Prince only by inches. For a moment, it was thought that it might be a bomb. Bevignani's baton paused in mid-air; singers and orchestra were stricken with horror. Then they realised what it was and continued.[3] Bispham, resplendent in blue swallow-tailed coat with gold buttons, frilled shirt, top boots, and mutton-chop whiskers, was very much admired. His memoirs, which describe De Lucia as 'admirable in the title rôle' are not supported by critical opinion, which thought him 'disappointing'[4] and 'tame'.[5]

On May 22nd De Lucia sang Fenton in *Falstaff*; though the *Star* thought that he sang and acted 'capitally', others judged him somewhat self-conscious.[6] On May 24th, in a sparsely attended theatre, came his first London *Carmen*, with Zélie De Lussan, Marie Engle, and Mario Ancona. His Don José was 'extremely dramatic', second only to his Canio;[7] his fervour in the 'Flower Song' almost startled the house.[8]

After *Rigoletto*, his next appearance was on June 11th in *La Traviata*, with Patti as Violetta. It was, for many, the whole point of the season. For Patti was a nonpareil. Even ten years later, at the age of 62, she still occupied

> ... an unassailed position as the greatest singer in the world, and she had held that position for so long that not only had she left behind all the petty jealousy and jockeying for place that enlivens her progress through the pages of Colonel Mapleson's Memoirs, but she herself was universally admired and respected by her colleagues.[9]

It had not been easy to induce the *diva* to return to Covent Garden. The intermediary between Harris and the soprano, who was reluctant to sing in opera - especially in Europe - when concerts offered higher fees, had been the indefatigable Hermann Klein, who had known her since 1885 and from whose writings the story may be pieced together.[10] We learn of Harris's visit to Craig-y-Nos Castle in 1891; of Klein's preliminary soundings of Harris and of Percy Harrison, the manager without whose consent she could not appear in opera in Great Britain; of Klein's conversations with Patti during strolls in the conservatory at the castle at Christmas 1894; of Harris and Klein, waiting at Paddington Station for the express from South Wales on the bleak evening of January 12th 1895; and of her meeting with Harris in a private sitting-room at the Great Western Hôtel.

3 Ibid., June 1 1895.

4 *Musical Standard*, quoted in *The Year's Music, 1896*.

5 *The Year's Music, 1896*.

6 *Illustrated London News*, June 15 1895.

7 Ibid., June 1 1895.

8 *Sketch*, June 5 1895.

9 Michael Aspinall, 'Adelina Patti', Introductory essay to an edition of Patti's records, EMI set RLS 711, 1973.

10 Klein, *The Golden Age*, pp. 210-13; *Thirty Years*, pp. 323-4; *The Reign of Patti*, pp. 321-5.

Now, all was arranged. As far away as Montevideo the press reported the high premium commanded by tickets in London, where frenzy had replaced apathy among opera-goers.[11] Commented Klein:

> [It] was a vivid reminder of old times; the prices paid ... recalled the extravagant figures recorded in connection with the famous bygone Patti nights. Society was fairly agog with anticipation of an experience now regarded almost as a tradition - an experience whereof the most brilliant Melba and de Reszke nights never furnished more than a faint replica. While, therefore, every seat was sold days beforehand, the 'old guard' began forming its queue at the gallery entrance before midday on the morning of the performance.[12]

For Patti, the reappearance after so long was nerve-racking. Talking to Klein after the performance, she admitted:

> 'When I made my entry, when I looked across the footlights at the familiar picture, as I went on bowing again and again, while the storm of applause seemed as if it would never cease, I felt more like breaking down and crying than singing. But after we had sat down to the supper-table and De Lucia ... had begun the "Libiamo", I suddenly regained my confidence and courage. I never lost them again. I think I never sang my "Libiamo" better!'[13]

For the Ball Scene Patti wore a white dress encrusted with almost four thousand stones, including some 'hundreds of large diamonds, dismounted for the occasion from some of her finest jewels. This mass of coruscating brilliants gave the effect of a veritable blaze of light.' Her husband, Nicolini, gave its value as £200,000.[14] For security, two detectives from Bow Street police station mingled with Flora's guests.

It was a genuine event, the return of a singer who, for a quarter of a century, had held near-undisputed dominion, and who, after a decade's absence, had reappeared with almost undiminished powers and arguably still at the head of her profession. *The Times* was not, perhaps, entering into the spirit of the occasion by reporting that it was

> ... impossible to blink the fact that even with Mme. Patti time has not stood still. In spite of every device by which trouble and exertion might be spared, it was evident in each scene that the singer was within measurable distance of reaching the limit of her powers. [However] the exquisite quality of the middle register made itself felt, and the beautiful timbre of these notes could not but be recognised as a thing unapproachable in the present day. ... For the night, a return was made to the old order of things ... and after the third act the once familiar spectacle was witnessed of Mme. Patti standing behind a screen of bouquets. ... Signor De Lucia was a capital Alfredo and Signor Ancona altogether admirable as the elder Germont.[15]

---

11 *Montevideo Times*, July 13 1895.
12 Klein, *The Reign of Patti*, p. 327.
13 Ibid., p. 328.
14 (SLC) Letter Patti - Kingston, Aug. 29 1895.
15 *The Times*, June 12 1895.

Patti, *Punch* trenchantly agreed, was quite

> ... in her 'best tra-la-la-viata'. The knowing ones observed high keys politely transposed to suit Adelina, but what manager could refuse to *put down the notes* when Adelina agrees to sing.[16]

Many cartoons lampooned her fees which were, in fact, only half those paid to her by Mapleson in 1887. The *Musical Times* wrote of her portrayal as 'a magnificent lesson on the mightiness of small things' and of De Lucia as indulging in a 'persistent vibrato, which greatly marred his efforts'.[17] *Punch*, dismissing him as 'first-rate as poor, spoony little Alfredo',[18] was at odds with Klein, who wrote that his suitability lay in the possession of passion rather than vocal charm.[19]

During the London season, tardy confirmation had arrived that Ciacchi would, after all, be mounting opera in Argentina and Uruguay. His company, though not in the very top flight, nevertheless included De Lucia, Saffo Bellincioni,[20] Inès De Frate, Giuseppe Pacini, and Elisa Petri. It left Genoa on June 22nd 1895 on the *Nord America*, arriving on July 11th at Montevideo which, that winter, could boast not only three opera troupes (for both Ferrari and Beccario were also bringing out companies) but also precedence over Buenos Aires in savouring what was arguably the best of them. Ciacchi was to enjoy a subsidy of £4,000 and Ferrari one of £1,000, a controversial distribution, described by some as 'discreditable', which was probably not unconnected with the feeling that the Ciacchi company had come specially for Montevideo, where 'Society' was often deeply conscious of taking the leavings of the Argentine capital.[21] The press was sharply divided: newspapers sympathetic to Ferrari ignored Ciacchi, his company, and its performances entirely.

Even in fashion-conscious Buenos Aires, which somewhat disparaged Montevideo, interest in the season was considerable. There was earnest discussion of the etiquette of the theatre dress-coat and the ball-coat. Great indignation was aroused by a Montevideo newspaper, *Razon*, when it decreed that morning costume and not the 'frac' (evening dress) should ordinarily be worn, declaring: 'What would be left to us to wear on Gala occasions if we wore our "fracs" every evening?' Critics who made their way from Buenos Aires to Montevideo to hear one *La Gioconda* immediately noticed the effect of the article, since

> ... the Brazilian Chargé d'Affaires ... was the only man properly dressed in a theatre dress-coat. In the Plate they probably ignore such distinctions ... [22]

---

[16] *Punch*, June 22 1895.

[17] *The Musical Times*, July 1 1895.

[18] *Punch*, June 22 1895.

[19] Klein, *The Reign of Patti*, p. 329.

[20] Sister of Gemma B. and wife of Giuseppe Frigiotti.

[21] *Standard*, July 17 and *Montevideo Times*, Aug. 13 1895.

[22] *Standard*, July 26 1895.

However, their writings were not now the only source of information for those unable to make the overnight journey to 'the Mount', as Montevideo was colloquially known. The Theatrophone, based on Edison's Loudspeaker Telephone, had already been employed to allow up to 1,000 people to listen to a concert 250 miles away. By 1893, some fifteen Parisian theatres were connected to private subscribers and to listening stations in public places, such as the salons of the larger hotels.[23] By such means the rehearsals of *Mefistofele* at the Teatro Nuevo Politeama were clearly received in Buenos Aires.

The Ciacchi company made its début at the Politeama on July 16th 1895, with *Mefistofele*. Not a seat was vacant; the fashionable audience included President Borda and many Ministers. The audiences were no different from European in chattering, reciting the words, and humming. One performance of *La Gioconda* was hardly audible above the private affairs of noisy neighbours.[24]

As Faust, De Lucia was now

> ... something very different from the immature but promising singer of some eight years ago. He is not of the 'bellowing bull of Bashan' order of which Tamagno is the chief exponent, but rather follows in the delicate and sentimental school of Gayarre and Masini, and will well bear comparison with the latter. His voice is delightfully clear and sweet, rich in the lower register and bell-like in the upper notes, while he has attained a mastery and delicacy of modulation, especially in the upper notes, that we have not heard surpassed in any man's voice. In addition ... he acts his part with admirable dramatic appreciation. ... He is certainly one of the most notable tenors that has visited us for several years and we look forward with interest to his appearance in a more showy part.[25]

Other critics thought that although he used the *falsetto* overmuch he had extremely felicitous moments when he sang in full voice, which was 'very extensive and powerful' and whose 'fresh, sweet [and] harmonious [tones] went to one's very soul'.[26] Yet others took to hyperbole:

> [He] is not one of those great tenors who impress first with their powerful notes; but he is one of those great tenors who sing like the angels. ... each of his notes is a work of art.[27]

Elisa Petri, as Margherita and Elena, showed 'a rich, full voice and correct style'.[28] She had 'all the airs of a very good actress, and her voice had considerable flexibility.'[29] The duet 'Lontano, lontano' was exquisitely given.

23 De Vries, *Victorian Inventions*, p. 134ff.
24 *Siglo*, Aug. 4 1895.
25 *Montevideo Times*, July 18 1895.
26 *Tribuna Popolar*, July 19 1895.
27 Unidentified Spanish language newspaper, July 19 1895.
28 *Montevideo Times*, July 18 1895.
29 *Tribuna Popolar*, July 19 1895.

On July 17th the President gave a Grand Reception in which some of Ciacchi's secondary artists sang.[30] For the gala function the following night, *Mefistofele* was repeated; fully 2,000 crowded the house, which was attended by the President, Ministers, and the highest echelons of the military and judiciary. De Lucia's singing, it was noted, was characterised by passing from the tones of the half voice to *falsetto*, and to the full and vigorous chest voice, while always retaining its fluidity and sweetness.[31] The Solis theatre, which also gave a gala, was sparsely attended, evidence that the theatre-going public of the city could not support two companies.

De Lucia did not win undivided approval. Certainly, his 'angelic' singing won much exuberant (and uncritical) acclaim. But, within a week of his début, the *Montevideo Times* noted that some of its contemporaries, 'apparently better judges of noise than of singing', were already expressing disappointment with the eminent tenor

> ... because he does not bawl and bellow like an infuriated bull. Much the same happened when Patti visited us seven or eight years ago. There were not a few then who were openly disappointed because this greatest of vocalists did not yell and shriek at the top of her lungs and to the utter destruction of her vocal organ after the vicious style so dear to River Plate gallery audiences. It will evidently require another generation of great singers to teach such *critics* as these the difference between shouting and singing.[32]

The contrast with Valentin Duc, who sang the part of Eleazar in *L'Ebrea* was plain. The latter was

> ... the very antithesis of De Lucia, a voice of little effect in the middle and lower registers, but of extraordinary power and brilliancy in the high notes ...

Condescendingly, the same critic commented on local taste:

> ... This is exactly what pleases a River Plate audience ... several *bravura* passages raised the house to what our native contemporaries call 'delirious enthusiasm'.[33]

On July 23rd the Ciacchi company gave *La Gioconda*. The *Montevideo Times* noted a performance in which, quite unusually, the minor parts were satisfactorily performed. De Lucia, the 'hero of the evening', seemed determined to rid himself of the 'quite inappropriate' charge made against him in *Mefistofele*, namely that his style was 'too effeminate and lacking in robustness'. Such accusations could certainly not be made in *La Gioconda*, for

---

30 *Standard*, July 19 1895.
31 *Nación*, July 20 1895.
32 *Montevideo Times*, July 21 1895.
33 Ibid., July 23 1895.

... he issued note after note of great potency and of exquisite clearness and sweetness, ringing through the large theatre like the sound of a silver clarion. Still, fine as these effects were, we prefer him in his softer passages such as the romance 'Cielo e mar' [which] he delivered with a beauty of expression and sentiment beyond all description, ending on a superb high note of such beauty that it fairly electrified the house. This was the gem of a brilliant evening and produced such an ovation as we have rarely seen, though he was equally faultless in other passages of the opera, developing beauties in the music hitherto unknown. It was generally agreed that no such interpretation of the part of Enzo has been heard in Montevideo, and it is to be doubted if any living tenor could surpass it.[34]

Nación returned to the question of adapting the means to the need:

If De Lucia does not make a parade of his vocal facility it is because he believes, rightly, that the human voice should show the various feelings of the soul and therefore should, according to the situation, be powerful or delicate, sweet or rough, so that it can reveal the range of human feelings. ...

In the first act duet of Enzo with Barnaba the famous tenor brought the audience to enthusiasm, but when he sang the sentimental romanza in the second act ['Cielo e mar'] the enthusiasm of the theatre reached its highest point ... One needs to have been there to realise the wonderful art and the really extraordinary ability with which De Lucia sang this passage ... De Lucia, in *La Gioconda* ... proved that he is not only a *tenore di grazia* as everyone had supposed, but that he can also be *di forza*, with the difference nevertheless that he knows exactly when to use the one style and the other, which goes to show that he is a masterly interpreter.[35]

Tribuna Popolar (July 24th), one of the papers which had described him, in *Mefistofele*, as having 'hidden his voice in order to delight the audience with his *falsetto*', remarked that he used his full vocal resources

... to show that he can do so when and where he wishes, and he attacked the most difficult high notes and interpreted with feeling the most delicate passages in the score. Last night De Lucia sang with the full force of his lungs, and electrified the public ... with his clear and powerful notes, which sometimes stood out over the chorus and orchestra.

In 'Cielo e mar' he was superb. He began it gently, decorating the notes and drawing them out delicately so as to finish on a glorious, powerful high note, which was splendidly sustained.

In later performances, critics noted his 'magnificent B from the chest' to end the air,[36] and a sublime burst of feeling and despair in the last act.[37]

He sang B flats much less often by 1917, when he first recorded 'Cielo e mar' [No. 113]. He recalls the decorations of his stage appearances; the climactic A (assuming a semitone transposition) is followed by a delicate *mezza voce* attack on the next phrase; it is an inventive, imaginative display of virtuosity even if - it must be said - decidedly a mannered one.

---

34 Ibid., July 25 1895.

35 *Nación*, July 25 1895.

36 *Tribuna Popolar*, July 29 1895. The note is properly B flat.

37 *Siglo*, Aug. 4 1895.

Towards the end of July the Beccario opera troupe arrived in Montevideo, to appear at the Teatro Cibils. Despite this competition and the imminent arrival of Ferrari's company, the Ciacchi *Rigoletto* of August 1st was well attended by an over-enthusiastic audience which, with bursts of ill-timed applause, twice in succession drowned the final cadenza and culminating high note of De Lucia's arias. The tenor himself, it was noted, could hardly restrain a smile at the interruption.[38]

He was in splendid voice. The notes flowed from him harmoniously and limpidly; 'Questa o quella' was delivered with taste and great ease. He gave 'La donna è mobile' four times, and it might well have been five:

He sang better than he did the *Gioconda* although, as he performed the famous aria the third time, he flagged a little in the *fioritura* at the end. . . . He sang the whole work excellently, dividing his production between the chest voice and the *falsetto*, both of which he manages with equal mastery.[39]

He was, *Nación* (August 3rd) remarked,

. . . quite exceptional, and we can say only that so far as the purity and sweetness of the voice and interpretative artistry are concerned he was comparable with Masini, who sang like a nightingale. De Lucia . . . sings the same musical passage three or four times in different ways and each different interpretation is received with enthusiastic applause. He has exceptional natural advantages, supplemented by his excellent artistry, and these were displayed in the popular fourth act [*sc.* third act] song . . . which last night seemed new again, and most beautiful, an exquisite, artistic rendering. . . . De Lucia sang 'Questa o quella' with such richness of tone and such facility that the applause was unanimous at the end of the second verse, which he willingly repeated, he himself pleased to be singing so well.

The duet with Inès De Frate (Gilda) 'electrified' the audience; the critic wrote that he had never before heard it sung with such richness of feeling, taste, and passion.

Razon, in a long review, noted that whereas Masini had sung the part, and Stagno had acted it, De Lucia did both. 'Our public', it wrote, had

. . . seen the best Dukes of Mantua, from [Raffaele] Mirate to [Enrico] Tamberlick, and it is now persuaded that De Lucia is today the ideal tenor for *Rigoletto*. We shall never have a Duke of Mantua who delivers with such lively self-possession the cynical phrases of the first act aria, nor performs such miracles of the throat while appearing to concentrate his attention on donning white gloves. . . . In a word, the philosophy of the young Duke can be reduced to 'I detest love, which is a preoccupation, and I adore pleasure.' and [it is] delivered by De Lucia with incomparable realism and effectiveness. And this same frivolity, blended with burning tenderness, rises in the introductory phrases to the famous quartet, which De Lucia gives with irresistible expression.[40]

---

38 *Montevideo Times*, Aug. 3 1895.
39 *Tribuna Popolar*, Aug. 2 1895.
40 *Razon*, quoted in *Cosmorama*, Oct. 3 1895.

He sang, remarked a critic at a later *Rigoletto,*

> ... better than ever last night; it was something quite splendid, something that
> one hardly ever hears and which one remembers all one's life ... He showed
> himself worthy of a monument on whose pedestal one might inscribe: 'To the
> most talented tenor of our lifetime.'

But, continued the writer, he was not well supported, and an austere
spirit would have found it entirely natural that he should seduce his
courtiers' wives and his clown's daughter.[41]

A frequent visitor to the theatre in Montevideo was ex-President
Herrera. He was famed for his opera-glasses, which were a household
word in the city since they were reputed to be the largest on earth. They
were like twin telescopes and were capable of detecting the rings of
Saturn. In the theatre, their orbit was almost always confined to
wandering from the ladies of the *corps de ballet* to those of the *cazuela,*
backward and forward all evening.[42] When the Teatro Nuevo Politeama
was totally destroyed by fire in October 1895 all Montevideo was relieved
to know that Herrera's opera-glasses were safe. However, probably
because of past political assassinations there, even at the opera he
carried a small revolver in his pocket. During a performance at the Solis
he slipped when leaving the box of the Reyes family, and the gun went
off, wounding him in the leg. In the confusion, the handsome weapon was
appropriated by a souvenir-hunter.[43]

By the end of Acts I and IV (*sc.* Act III) of *La Traviata,* which preceded
Cavalleria Rusticana on August 8th 1895, a fairly large audience had
built up for the Mascagni work, which was the principal attraction. As
Turiddu, De Lucia, playing to a Santuzza - Petri - who was condemned to
wear a most unbecoming wig, and to the handsome Lola of Borlinetto,
was a 'revelation'; it was a part giving ample scope for

> ... the extraordinary variety of expression of which he is master, and of this he
> took full advantage, displaying in several passages all the resources of his
> marvellous art, and giving them new meaning and beauty. ... In the drinking-
> song he introduced some exquisite vocal effects.[44]

Nación (August 10th) suggested that he was a 'very good dramatic actor;
as such he can compete with the best, and he pays great attention to
detail and verisimilitude'. *Tribuna Popolar* (August 9th) stressed the
vocal powers through which he 'played with the audience as he pleased,
... sending them mad with the prodigies of his throat'. Only at the
climactic points did he imprint real dramatic passion on his singing. For
the most part, he displayed the lyricism of *Rigoletto* as he delighted the

---

41 Unidentified Spanish language newspaper, Aug. 16 1895.
42 *Standard,* Oct. 13 1895.
43 Ibid., Aug. 13 1895.
44 *Montevideo Times,* Aug. 10 1895.

audience with *fioriture* and replaced drama with delicate phrasing and with a magnificent head voice. The 'Brindisi' drew particular applause; he sang it *a piacere*, varying the tempo and converting the 'allegro' of the score into a rhythmic 'andante'. While it was agreed that this reduced the merit of the passage, he achieved wonders with the facility with which he held a long-drawn chest note and reduced it to *falsetto*.

Despite the active and unconcealed opposition of the President and his faction, the subsidy had been guaranteed by the Directors of the Solis and the subscription had been taken up with a will. On August 10th Ferrari's dramatic company there was replaced by his operatic troupe - including Carmen Bonaplata-Bau, Regina Pinkert, Virginia Guerrini, Emilio De Marchi, Francesco Signorini, and Arcangelo Rossi - which opened the season the following day, with *Aida*. It was followed by *Manon Lescaut*, with De Marchi as Des Grieux. The choral work and the orchestra, conducted by Edoardo Mascheroni, were excellent, but the audience was benevolent to a degree which, thought some, the overall artistic merit of the company did not warrant. The newspapers quickly took sides, though, as one pointed out, an hour of Mascheroni's orchestra or of De Lucia's vocalisation was worth a year of politics.[45]

De Lucia's season continued with *Faust*. The brightness of his white suit, contrasting with clerical purple, was thought admirably suited to the transformation which was effected by the cocktail offered to him by Mephistopheles. He sang his part

> ... with the extraordinary novelties of his *bel canto* [and] revealed a passion so spontaneous that we almost thought that the archetypal seducer of Goethe had been inspired by a golden brown inhabitant of Casamicciola.[46]
>
> The 'Salve dimora' ... was interpreted solemnly ...
>
> To us, Faust has never seemed more voluptuous than last night; never have we felt ... Goethe's poem so vividly traced, over a wretched background of human misery.
>
> Passion and art, the volcano and the ideal, stood out equally in those love duets, inspired by night, the smiling accomplice, with its perfumes and phosphorescence, and the eternal romance of scandalous adventure.[47]

Meanwhile, Montevidean society was preoccupied with the President's choice of theatre for the official gala function of August 25th, which was also the anniversary of the inauguration of the Teatro Solis. Matters had taken a decidedly political turn. For whatever reason, His Excellency had promised Ciacchi that the Politeama would receive the official patronage. Then, as it became clear that society - as it had for thirty years - would be attending the Solis that night, he vacillated. Two weeks

---

[45] The Milanese composer and conductor Edoardo Mascheroni (1857 (or 1859)-1941), who had conducted the world première of Verdi's *Falstaff*, would again cross De Lucia's path in the preparations for Mascagni's *Iris*, in 1898.

[46] A resort much frequented by Neapolitans on the island of Ischia.

[47] *Siglo*, Aug. 28 1895. The review is of the second performance.

before the occasion, citizens were scandalised by the suggestion that the government was selling the seats which, in recognition of the subsidy, had been reserved for it at the Politeama; reporters were sent to note the occupants of such places. However, on August 15th, the President finally decided on the Politeama, whose public seemed more sympathetic to him. The next day there was a musical *soirée*, with De Lucia and other (unspecified) artists from the Politeama. The press construed it as a *llapa*[48] to His Excellency for having kept his promise to Ciacchi.

On August 25th the fashionable attended *La Gioconda* at the Solis. So also did the principal critics, ignoring the Politeama and the first South American performance of *Manon*. And so the wits of Montevideo were able to ponder on the paradox: the Solis, where society contemplated an empty state box, and the Politeama, where the President, Ministers of State, and diplomatic corps, gorgeous in full dress uniforms, rubbed shoulders at an important musical première with a contingent ' "mixed" to a degree we have never seen before at an official function in this gay capital'.[49]

The day had been an exciting one: the parades; the newly-formed Corps of Guardias de Seguridad, in their flaming new uniforms and plumed, gilt helmets; the *Te Deum* at the cathedral. The only contretemps had been when an ill-aimed rocket wandered playfully and harmlessly among the men of the President's escort. Later, it was a brilliant evening at the Politeama. The theatre - Montevideo's largest - was full, thousands had been turned away, and the police were needed to impose order at the box-office. Ciacchi himself sat taking in the money. When all the tickets were sold, they began to change hands at up to fifty gold dollars a seat, as Argentines who had made the river trip to join the Uruguayan national celebrations swelled the demand for seats.

Ciacchi had spared no expense to justify the President's confidence and had provided the very best in costumes, scenery, and hospitality. The champagne flowed freely at the Politeama that evening. By the end of the performance of *Manon* Ciacchi was the most flattered and congratulated man in Montevideo. Enthusiasm reached delirium: men and women, on their feet, carried away by the performance, forgot authority and officialdom and threw bouquets on to the stage. At the end there were seven calls for De Lucia and Petri; for the soprano, as for the tenor, it had been a memorable success.[50] At a first hearing, though, that success was felt to reside more in the performance than in the opera, which had '...some splendid passages ...but also passages that are trivial and tedious'.[51]

---

48 'Llapa', a word peculiar to South America, has different meanings in different countries. As used here it is a gift to smooth the path for a sale, but less a bribe than a 'sweetener'.

49 *Montevideo Times*, Aug. 27 1895.

50 *Standard*, Aug. 27 1895.

51 *Montevideo Times*, Aug. 27 1895.

The Ferrari season at the Solis closed, apparently early, on August 26th. Mascheroni alone had escaped the critics' censure. The performances had not been of the quality expected at such high prices. 'If Sr. Ferrari comes here again on his unaided merits he will have to do something better than this', declared the *Montevideo Times*.[52]

On August 30th the Politeama staged another gala, with *Manon*, to give society the chance to hear the opera in less politically-charged circumstances. *Siglo* commented on the power of De Lucia's voice:

> It is simply a fact that, wherever De Lucia is, he is prince, duke and gentleman. To tell how he characterised the passionate Des Grieux, with what expression and delicacy he sang, is impossible. Each day he shows greater faculties, and grows in stature. . . . he produced notes so powerful, so broad and long-held that even Tamagno could not do better.[53]

The tenor was popular with the public and, by and large, with the press, for whom he gave a banquet at Charpentier's restaurant on September 3rd.[54] On September 9th the Politeama was again crowded when, for De Lucia's benefit, *Manon* closed the season. The ladies' gowns gave the auditorium the appearance of 'a meadow, full of flowers'. Never had De Lucia and Petri, 'lively, graceful, refined as a Sèvres figure', sung better, asserted *Siglo*, as it congratulated 'the great tenor and his most intelligent companion'. After Des Grieux's soliloquy in St. Sulpice the performance was interrupted for the presentations. Among De Lucia's gifts were a solitaire diamond from the President and a tie-pin, adorned with a large pearl, from Herrera.[55] He also received jewelled matchboxes, walking sticks, a gold watch and, from Elisa Petri, a jewelled tie-pin. Neapolitan compatriots gave him a picture by Di Noncio; painted on silk, the richly-framed painting showed the Bay of Naples and included his own portrait. Several hundred enthusiasts, mostly Neapolitan, later accompanied De Lucia's carriage to the Hôtel Oriental, bearing torches and Bengal lights, cheering lustily, and shouting '*Viva!*', all to the accompaniment of an excruciating brass band. It was 1 am and the tenor was almost too exhausted to be able to express his thanks.[56]

Of the abundant Latin exuberance of the occasion, and of the age, what follows was typical:

> Ah! De Lucia, De Lucia! If you make us feel thus, you strike at the window of our most intimate feelings and you bring them into the light, turned into tense shudderings, stifled exclamations, sighs and tears; who can surpass you, where is the artist who, like you, can move us with such deep and sublime emotions?[57]

---

[52] Ibid.
[53] *Siglo*, Aug. 31 1895.
[54] *Montevideo Times*, Sept. 5 1895.
[55] *Siglo*, Sept. 10 1895.
[56] *Montevideo Times*, Sept. 11 1895.
[57] Unidentified Spanish language newspaper, Sept. 10 1895.

Even as De Lucia left for Buenos Aires, on September 10th, it was announced that Ciacchi had signed a contract - in the event, unfulfilled - with him for the following year at $3,000 per month and other benefits. Socially, he left behind impressions of a well-educated, cultivated, and polite man, and of a distinguished and pleasant guest.[58]

The company played Buenos Aires at the end of the traditional opera season, after another political crisis and after Ferrari's company had already performed there. The Ghigliani company at the Teatro San Martin included Luisa Tetrazzini, who was already nearing her fiftieth *Lucia di Lammermoor* and who was accumulating a considerable collection of jewellery, presented to her during her tour through the provinces.[59]

The Ciacchi company made its début at the Politeama on September 12th, with *La Gioconda*. De Lucia's appearance on the stage was greeted with a burst of applause which 'almost made the theatre shake'. *Nación* (September 13th) devoted much space to him:

> We knew nearly all the singers, ... [including] De Lucia. That is to say, De Lucia - it seemed that we did not know him, such was the surprise that he caused us with his first displays of voice, in which he showed a power and even a timbre which sounded completely new to us.
>
> In the principal phrases of his duet with Barnaba in the first act he let forth such a torrent of voice and shaped the phrases in such a way that he brought forth a terrific burst of applause ...
>
> During the course of playing his part he seemed to take delight in showing all the colours, and even all the timbres of his voice, for indeed he has several and, if the truth be told, not all of them equally pleasant. One could call him the Mosaic if this did not seem rather disrespectful with an artist of such worth.
>
> Through his singing one sees pass all the styles and best-known schools, for he knows how to assimilate the best of two or three celebrities and on the basis of this form himself into something different, something of his own of which one can say only that we must call it the 'De Lucia style'. His best moments ... appeared in the celebrated romanza in the second act, in which he poured out colouring and details in the most original and capricious style, which greatly refreshed this well-known piece.
>
> ... In the third act ensemble his voice was, at times, able to dominate the whole mass of voices. Is this pure artifice? Are these genuine faculties? The public did not waste its time arguing about it, occupied as it was in applauding it.[60]

It was a flattering greeting for the company, and one shared by Ciacchi as he was dragged by the coat-tails on to the stage.

Of De Lucia's Duke of Mantua, on September 17th, the *Standard* wrote that to describe him as equal to Masini all round would be unfair to both, but that in this rôle he was certainly Masini's equal, if not his superior, 'and that is saying a great deal'. His voice, which he never

---

58 *Nación*, Sept. 11 1895.
59 *Standard*, Sept. 13 1895.
60 *Nación* (of Buenos Aires), Sept. 13 1895.

forced for an instant, and his gestures conveyed meaning which compelled the audience to applaud. His 'original and masterly rendering' of 'La donna è mobile' was repeated three times.[61]

On September 24th 1895, *Mefistofele* had its première. The critic of the *Standard* (September 26th) seemed at a loss for expository comment on De Lucia, who seemed 'to have adopted a style of singing entirely different from anything we have yet heard'. *Nación*, however, provided an extremely detailed and informative notice:

> . . . we will say only that he offered one more example of that handful of delights with which he decorates and builds the interpretation of every rôle; by this we mean that, in the variations which, from time to time, he introduces into the length of notes or into the colour of vowels which do not suit him, and through the liberties which he is wont to take in the name of personal taste, when he does not entirely succeed in satisfying, at least he interests and, therefore, everything always turns out to be pleasant. 'Let's see how he will say this, how he will take that one.' This is the sort of talk which goes among his listeners, and which attracts their attention. This is not to do him any discredit, rather the contrary. The simple fact of inspiring this kind of curiosity is sufficient praise of Sr. De Lucia; an ordinary, common-or-garden singer would not interest us in this particular way.
>
> He always sang with the greatest possible expression and, on occasion, with very great taste as in the andantino 'Forma ideal purissima', in our judgement the best that he did, inasmuch that the romanza in the epilogue was not exactly an example of good style and unity of character. Almost the whole of it was beautiful, but there were at least two moments which were, at best, doubtful. In the phrase *'dell'esistenza mia'* he doubled the 'a' in the word *'mia'*, altering the length of the notes and producing a *'mia-a'*, whose beauty is not easy to see; and in the final cadence, he introduced a *'gruppetto'* which was completely against the style and character of that intense melody, a reflective melody, we might say, one which is not conducive to any kind of *fioritura*.
>
> Nevertheless, since the actual performance was very good, it earned great applause. . . . We point out these little details by way of illustration, because it seems fair to do so since we are dealing with an artist of the renown and great quality of a De Lucia. [62]

So great was the interest in the Argentinian première of *Manon* on September 27th that tickets were unobtainable for days beforehand. Most of the boxes were occupied by members of the Stock Exchange, the Volunteer Militia (*Freiwilliger*), and the beauties of the English and German contingents of the city. The occasion, proclaimed the *Standard*, cast the performances in Montevideo completely into the shade:

> The sympathetic Miss Petri rendered her rôle as Manon in a most artistic style. Her vocalisation, her acting and her graceful movements showed her as one of our most prominent stars. The same may be said of De Lucia in his part of Des Grieux, who together with her brought the house to its feet. The applause was something stupendous, shaking the walls of our old favourite the Politeama.[63]

---

61 *Standard*, Sept. 17 and 18 1895. It is not clear whether the critic means three performances or three encores of the aria.

62 *Nación*, Sept. 25 1895.

63 *Standard*, Sept. 28 1895.

It was a memorable occasion, entirely successful in every respect according even to so stern a judge as the critic, probably Freixas, of *Nación*. He agreed that the admiration aroused by De Lucia's Des Grieux in Montevideo had been not at all exaggerated:

> Constantly identifying himself with the character, ... and always possessed of that elevated and persistent amorous sentiment which is the moving force of all his acts, good or bad, during the course of the action ... he produced a great effect upon his listeners.[64]

Manon continued to draw the public. Petri continued to be 'perfect in the tenderness and love which she shows to the long-suffering De Lucia in his part as Des Grieux',[65] and the press continued to urge Ciacchi to ensure that, like the Neapolitan tenor, she should return next season. Ciacchi's immediate concern, however, was to extend the current season - which should have ended with *Manon* on October 3rd - and to profit from the popularity both of his company and of Massenet. Since the Politeama was required for other events he opened a new subscription of six performances at the Teatro Nacional, Sr. Basualdo's beautiful theatre in Calle Florida, the most fashionable street of Buenos Aires.

Still other 'extra' performances were given of *Il Barbiere di Siviglia*, combining the Ciacchi and Ghigliani companies. The first of them was attended by an audience in an 'excessively critical spirit', as might be expected for a performance that had been announced as exceptional, a model:

> Sr. De Lucia showed not his mastery of singing in general, which there was no need to demonstrate, but sufficient of the Rossinian style and the decorated form for him to figure as one of the best interpreters of the part of Almaviva. To recognise him as such it would have sufficed to hear how he outlined, shaded in and then decorated the 'Ecco ridente in cielo', which brought him thunderous applause. In many places he sang passages, in *mezza voce* and *a fior di labbro*, truly delicately and with similarly correct execution but, because he found himself without perfect control of his vocal organ, he had to make rather too much use of his *forte* than the character of the song permitted.[66]

Luisa Tetrazzini, as Rosina, was criticised for stylistic contradictions, the use of ornament in the first statement of the principal theme of her aria, and the long top notes scattered profusely throughout her performance.

Meanwhile, from Milan came the news that Ferrari had engaged Tamagno for next season. The news caused an immediate fall in the local price of gold, raised everyone's spirits, and was expected to put up the price of 'Argentines', an astonishing example of the importance of a piece of good musical news to the economy of the Argentine.[67]

---

[64] *Nación*, Sept. 28 1895.
[65] *Standard*, Oct. 6 1895.
[66] *Nación*, Oct. 12 1895.
[67] *Standard*, Oct. 1 1895.

The artists also had time for charitable good works. On October 13th De Lucia, Petri, and other lyric and dramatic artists participated in a garden fête at the country house of a Sr. Varela, at Palermo. The guests moved among the flower stalls and kiosks in the grounds to the strains of a band. In one theatre, conveniently close to the sweetmeat stall, there was entertainment for the youngsters. In the other, twenty musicians provided an accompaniment for De Lucia and his colleagues. Three days later, he and Tetrazzini again sang arias for charity, in the Teatro San Martin.

On October 17th he took his benefit, in *Manon*, on the last night of the Nacional season. It was a nostalgic occasion as the Buenos Aires public took leave of 'the two great operatic stars', De Lucia and his partner, Elisa Petri.

13

Noontide in Bohemia

Indeed the mere possession of a voice and the ability to sing songs is but little, unless behind that there is an informing spirit, which with its magic touch irradiates everything that an artist subsequently does before the public.

David Bispham, *A Quaker Singer's Recollections.*

De Lucia was now at the very zenith of his career. He had doubled D'Ormeville's prediction that he would earn 2,000 lire per performance. It was said that within a few years of his début he had amassed a fortune of three million lire.[1] Pursued and fêted by the managements of the major opera houses, he could now choose his engagements and could virtually dictate his own terms, especially for an important première.

As the troupe sailed for Italy, the possibility - or even probability - of creating the part of Rodolfo in Puccini's *La Bohème* certainly preoccupied De Lucia. The opera was now nearing its first performance. In the composer's mind, De Lucia's prestige and reputation made him the obvious choice for Rodolfo and, before the Neapolitan left for Montevideo on June 22nd 1895, they had discussed the matter.

From the steamer *Nord America* De Lucia wrote to Puccini:

Carissimo Puccini,

Excuse me for this late reply. I shall be happy to create your new opera and I imagine that you are making me a real part [*costume*].[2]

For my part, I will do everything I can to satisfy you. I promise you that I shall accept no contracts, I place myself at your disposal - let me know anything positive.

If you are willing, send me my part so that I can study it with heart and affection.

Write to me at Montevideo, Teatro Politeama.

I thank you very very much for the recollections that you hold of me, and believe me your great admirer and friend.

Fernando De Lucia (PC)

---

1 Daspuro, 'Memorie', ch. XXII. In 1988 purchasing power, about £12 million.

2 The two were evidently on friendly terms, since he uses the familiar and not the formal mode of address. Both here and in his letter of Sept. 9 De Lucia obviously refers to the part of Rodolfo but, perhaps in a contemporary theatrical colloquialism, now obsolete, he uses the Italian word *'costume'* ('costume', 'dress', but also 'contained within a figure or mode of conduct').

On August 9th, Puccini wrote to Carlo Clausetti, Ricordi's energetic representative at Naples:

Pescia, August 9th 1895

Caro Carlino,

What a time eh!? I am banished here and I work in a black fever. We shall certainly see one another at Naples. Rome also wants *Bohème*, Turin the same, Warsaw the same, Trieste etc. But we shall certainly do it at Naples, Turin and Rome (in this last city depending on who has the theatre).[3] I have written to (he has written to me) De Lucia, who represents my ideal Rodolfo, and we are already in agreement. Bellincioni is ideal for Mimì (but how to get her?). I am distressed over Musetta, I do not know where to find her. I am thinking (fancy!) of Blanche Lescaut for the elegance, the polish, the *brio* necessary, but I do not know whether the voice would be adequate.[4] But then a 'chanteuse' of the *caffè concerto* at the San Carlo, or at the Regio [of Turin], would be monstrous enough to bring a blush to the beautiful, aristocratic shoulders of the noblewomen of Turin and the duchesses of Naples![5]

Puccini's letter to De Lucia has not been found, but the tenor's reply has survived. Evidently, he had not seen enough of the part to convince himself of its suitability, and he was hesitant:

Montevideo, September 9th 1895

I have received your letter and I thank you for the most beautiful part [*costume*] that you have made, and I hope to be able to wear it well.

On the very day that I arrive in Italy, I will come expressly to Milan to gauge this exceptional part [*costume*].

I assure you of a great desire to hear my part, and of an even greater desire to perform it.

I will put into the opera all of that small talent and voice, given to me by God, to present it as well as I can.

I am certain that you will have written absolutely sublime things.

Unless I hear your opera I shall arrange nothing for the winter.

Meanwhile I embrace you with all my heart, and believe me your friend and ardent admirer.

Fernando De Lucia

PS Many respectful greetings to Commendatore Ricordi. (PC)

In October, Puccini wrote to Giulio Ricordi asking him, *inter alia*, to think of the singers, and expressing disappointment that the première should be arranged for Turin. His reasons were that the theatre had a muffled sound; that (after *Manon Lescaut*), *non bis in idem*; that the

---

[3] Ricordi often granted performance rights for an opera only if he knew who was to sing in it.

[4] Real name Emma Sorel. Lescaut had recently had a great success at the Circo delle Varietà of Naples. After a considerable and profitable career as a *canzonettista* at Naples she sang, under the name Bel Sorel, in *La Bohème, Manon,* and *Mignon* at the Teatro Lirico, Milan, in Massenet's *Cendrillon* at Rome, and at Bucharest, Warsaw, and elsewhere.

[5] Gara, *Carteggi Pucciniani*, No. 127, pp. 116-17.

director was an ill-bred man; and that it was too close to the 'snapping curs' of Milan.[6] Naples and Rome, he considered, should be first. He expressed a hope that the work could have simultaneous premières at Naples, Rome, and Turin.[7]

It is appropriate at this point to examine a figure who was not only central to Italian opera in the late nineteenth century but who would also play an important part in De Lucia's musical activities for the next several years. Giulio Ricordi (1840-1912) was a man with an excellent classical education; he spoke English, French, and German, was a competent poet, and wrote music under both his own name and the pseudonym J. Burgmein. His informed musical criticisms were a feature of the Ricordi house publications *Gazzetta Musicale di Milano*, *Musica e Musicisti*, and *Ars et Labor*. As the third generation of a family that had built up what was by then the most important music-publishing house in Italy, he was also a man of immense theatrical experience. And, as he encouraged, humoured, and cajoled his librettists and composers he showed all the qualities of the professional diplomat. Though he was willing to use his firm's money to back his judgement and to support gifted and promising composers, he was financially cautious.[8] In a revealing letter, earthy and direct, he replied at length to Puccini on the matter of the casting:[9]

Comerio, October 12th 1895

...I see the De Lucia letter: fine words, but in practice they mean nothing!! Because they will not diminish the demands by a penny, and the theatres, now reduced to the most paltry subsidies, cannot ruin themselves through these so-called stars, my bollocks.[10] Neither is it in our true interest to involve the managements in insupportable expenses: true success lies in the earnings of the impresario!!! The opera is a masterpiece! And regarding the performers, [and] the observations that you make to me, permit me to to tell you, with my usual frankness, and do not take it badly, dear Puccini, that they are uncalled for and unfair! Oh!.....at one time, yes, when all depended on real virtuosity in the throat, one needed specialists: thus, in *Sonnambula* and *Norma* and the like. Now, opera needs a homogeneous cast, and as intelligent as possible!! It is not the artist that causes an opera to please, but truly the opera itself!! What the deuce did it do for the fortunes of Mascagni, who had De Lucia in *Silvano*!! Did the opera please, did it live? By no means, and De Lucia wasn't worth a fig!! And the other one, Leonasino [Leoncavallo], what did he gain from having even

---

6 (R) Gara, ibid., No. 137, p. 125, omits Puccini's objections to the '*direttore*' of the Teatro Regio of Turin, a reference either to the manager, Luigi Piontelli, or, more probably, to the conductor, Arturo Toscanini. Gara also excises the vulgarities of the original, which reads: '... *troppo vicino ai botoli milanesi che mi fotteranno sicuramente*'. ('... too near to the snapping curs of Milan, who will surely screw me').

7 *Fortunio*,   ʟ 1895.

8 For an excel'ent o cise account of the influence of Giulio Ricordi in the late nineteenth century the reader is referred to Marc'., op. cit., pp. 64-8.

9 Many correspondents of the period use four, five, or more dots to convey the delicacy of a situation or to leave matters suggested but unstated. Ricordi's punctuation has been retained to avoid confusion with the customary three dots of ellipsis.

10 Despite broadly similar sentiments, to translate it as the more usual '... stars, my foot!' is to lose the idiomatic ribaldry of Ricordi's '... *divi de' miei minchioni*'.

Tamagno as a *Medico*?..... Even with him that masterpiece died!!..... and all
the doctors could not save it. ... 11

In your *Bohème* the only real problem will be Musetta ... Let us assemble a
homogeneous cast, willing, motivated by enthusiasm, and we shall have what is
needed. Let us take heed that the opera house is going to certain ruin; let us not
commit managements to impossible expenses ... now that subsidies of 100 or
200 thousand lire are no more!! Let us remember that a fat cow is weakened
and made unproductive by too much milking. Do not think that I speak through
consideration for the impresarios!! Quite the reverse: I speak as a businessman
of long experience! ...

Bohème is now fixed for Turin and Rome. Nothing is known of Naples, and I
no longer want to dwell on the uncertainties of those famous impresarios! ...

But to complete the company definitively you must confer with the
managements: I can do it up to a certain point; but it is a new opera and
everyone wants to hear the Composer on the subject, and they are right!! It is
also urgent that you hear the Mimì whom I see as number one for Rome:
[Angelica] Pandolfini - [like a] true artist, she wants you to be the judge. She is
being considered by 3 theatres, so the decision is urgent. No matter how sure I
am that she is an ideal Mimì, I also want your opinion: who knows, she might
also be a Musetta ... 12

On October 18th Ricordi again wrote to Puccini, thanking him 'for the
great trust that you have in me'.13 However, Puccini must have insisted
on De Lucia, or perhaps it proved more difficult than Ricordi had
supposed to find a reputable but not excessively expensive tenor. In any
event, on November 5th Puccini again wrote on the subject of singers. On
behalf of his father, Tito Ricordi replied:

November 7th 1895
Carissimo,

Papa, at present very busy and troubled by headaches, has asked me to reply to
your recent letter of the 5th. ... I wish you a good trip and good hunting at
Montecristo. ...

Regarding the Garbin business,14 Papa is surprised by your absolute veto:
were Piontelli not to accept De Lucia's demands, what would happen? *Bohème*
would be without a tenor at Turin, because Garbin is negotiating with Palermo
and must soon give a reply: if he is allowed to escape, good night! Piontelli will
be at Milan within about a week: we must find a way of detaining Garbin until
then and, if it is not possible to have De Lucia, Papa believes that the *only* good
Rodolfo for Turin is Garbin. Cremonini15 and [Umberto] Beduschi are already
engaged: Pandolfini is an unknown.16 Write to us if you have seen De Lucia, if
he will *deign* to accept the part and if he will *not ask* too much. ... 17

11 Ricordi is joking. Leoncavallo's *I Medici*, in which Tamagno had created the tenor part, is not about
doctors but about the Medici family.

12 Translated from Gara, *Carteggi Pucciniani*, No. 142, pp. 129-31, who dates it October 1895. Marek, op.
cit., pp. 148-9, who quotes only part, specifies Oct. 12th. The original has not been located.

13 Marek, op. cit., p. 149.

14 Edoardo Garbin, first Fenton in *Falstaff*.

15 Giuseppe Cremonini, first Des Grieux in *Manon Lescaut*.

16 Franco Pandolfini, son of the baritone Francesco and brother of Angelica P.

17 (R) *Copialettere* 1895-96/8/39. Ricordi maintained two separate correspondence files. One was for
private, or 'Reserved' correspondence. The other, intended for general business letters, nevertheless contains
much material of a delicate nature.

Puccini's insistence confirms De Lucia's then pre-eminence. Clearly, to a greater extent than any other tenor of the time except Masini, the Neapolitan was given to embellishments and variations of all kinds. If we may believe Specht, interpolated flourishes by singers roused Puccini to fury.[18] Ironically, possibly the most flagrant and unmusical departure from the score in De Lucia's entire recorded legacy is to be found in 'Che gelida manina', from *La Bohème* [No. 125]. But such absurdities are rare. For all that they throw phrases into relief, only infrequently do his decorations disrupt the vocal line. Puccini presumably recognised his mitigating virtues: a tenor with a great popular following and one with whom success was likely. At any rate, at least in the composer's view, De Lucia continued as a possible or even probable tenor for Rodolfo and Puccini appears to have asked that Ricordi send the tenor part to the singer. The publisher's reply was uncompromising:

Wednesday

...You are.....really too kind. His Majesty [*S.M.*] De Lucia does not know, then, if the 3rd act is high, or not?.....Why have you not taken an examination to see if you are capable of writing for the tenor voice?.....
...Give out a part?.....never again.....and still less to a De Lucia at Naples, where half an hour later the entire Camorra will know the fact and the opera!!.....
At the appropriate time I will send the parts to the management, with the obligation to guard them: and they will do it, because it is in their own interest: that is how it was done with *Falstaff*. We do not need to make *La Bohème* public.[19]

De Lucia had, meanwhile, returned from Buenos Aires and had gone to visit Puccini at Viarreggio.[20] Once again Giulio Ricordi wrote to the composer:

November 18th 1895

...All the best engravers are occupied entirely on *Bohème*.....there are many hundreds of plates!!.....and now we are counting the hours. I am sorry to dwell so - I am very sorry but it is your fault, because I am not accustomed to having, as with this *Bohème*, the first 3 acts at great speed, one after the other.....
...We are agreed so far on Mugnone for Naples - I have already advised that the 1st condition for giving *Bohème* is to have Mugnone: in this we are very much in agreement. I do not believe that De Lucia will reduce his fee sufficiently to make his engagement possible - further, it seems that he would want to be engaged for only 8 performances: this would interfere with other plans.[21]

---

18 Specht, op. cit., p. 84.
19 (R) *Copialettere*, Reserved correspondence, Vol. I, No. 382, undated. Marek, op. cit., p. 150, ascribes a date of Nov. 13 1895.
20 *Gazzetta dei Teatri*, Nov. 14 1895.
21 (R) *Copialettere* 1895-96/8/355-358. Clearly, Ricordi wanted a longer run; in fact, the twenty-four performances at Turin overlapped with the first performances at Naples, for which De Lucia was engaged.

A week later came the final chance of reaching agreement with De Lucia, as he paused in Milan, *en route* for St. Petersburg. On November 26th, Ricordi telegraphed Puccini:

> ... Be confident for Turin, where De Lucia impossible because of demands, and fruitless, but very practical for Naples. ... (R)

For arrangements were now well advanced for giving *La Bohème* at the San Carlo, whose concession had been awarded to Musella for five years, with an annual subsidy of 60,000 lire.[22] On December 3rd Ricordi approved his roster of artists, including De Lucia.

The choice of tenor for Turin had still to be made. In a letter to Illica, January 6th 1896, Puccini wrote of awaiting the tenor Evan Gorga, 'to decide things'.[23] Rehearsals with this singer finally started in mid-January, and the première took place at Turin on February 1st 1896. Puccini wrote to his wife:

> My real worries are Gorga and Wilmant [Marcello]. The first hasn't got such a bad voice, but I doubt whether he will last. ... The baritone is full of good will but a terrible actor.[24]

> ... I foresee a great and sensational success - if the artists will do their part. I had to transpose almost the entire part of the tenor.[25]

Ultimately, Ricordi was vindicated. The continuing popularity of *La Bohème* proved that it did not need a distinguished cast. Since, however, De Lucia later created Rodolfo in several major theatres, including La Scala and the San Carlo, where his fees may have been more moderate than for a world première, it seems that both he and Ricordi eventually realised the mutual benefits of compromise.

Compromise was also being imposed on Fernando's personal life. From his correspondence from Russia it emerges that Itala was again travelling with him. Later, they went together to South America and to England, accompanied by their two sons. Once more, there had been a reconciliation.

In her memoirs, Minnie Hauk paints a vivid picture of travelling in Russia in the 1870s. At the end of October, when the weather was already cold, the unheated trains carried neither sleeping nor restaurant cars. Refreshments were obtained periodically at wayside stations. Each waiting-room had its brass samovar over a charcoal fire, and hot drinks

---

[22] *Occhialetto*, Nov. 16 1895.

[23] Gara, *Carteggi Pucciniani*, No. 150, p. 137. When the Regio roster was published on Dec. 12 1895 it already included Giovanni Evangelista Gorga, who does not seem to have been engaged specifically for *La Bohème*.

[24] Marek, op. cit., p. 153.

[25] Ibid.

were prepared from boiling water, a slice of lemon, and essence of tea from a tightly-corked bottle. Food was rarely more ambitious than a crust of bread. Hauk lived mainly on dry biscuits.[26] In 1900, Mascagni found sleeping cars, but little else had improved. Writing to his wife, he complained:

> Goodbye fine carriages, goodbye luxury, goodbye comfort. Russian railway compartments are special. Bare, empty, tasteless, with small, fixed, double-glazed windows, no electric light, no gas or paraffin, lit only by wax candles; all this - they say - to reduce the possibility of fire: because if there were a fire in that snowy desert the poor passengers would be as good as dead.
>
> The beds [have] no sheets of blankets; only a hard and narrow mattress. One sleeps clothed. The dining car is worse than our third-class carriages. Here, also, every table has its candlestick. An inexpressible drabness.[27]

From Milan to St. Petersburg involved five days and four nights of travel. The rigours of the long journey were, however, endured for the sake of the hospitality and the rewards that lyric artists enjoyed in Russia. Most Italian singers of repute made at least some appearances in provincial cities such as Kharkov, Kiev, Odessa, and Tiflis, pausing at Warsaw on the way. Artists such as Battistini, Cotogni, Marconi, and Masini spent winter after winter in St. Petersburg and Moscow. Emma Calvé writes persuasively if, we suspect, somewhat romantically of St. Petersburg, of the chivalry of the Grand Dukes, and of the other members of a refined Czarist aristocracy as they threw their cloaks on to the snow in the path to her troika. We learn of the jewels given in appreciation of her performance at a concert at the Winter Palace, and of the sumptuous feasts that she enjoyed in the company of Cossack officers and of Battistini, who was thoroughly at home in the *haut monde* of St. Petersburg. 'Had it continued', she muses, 'I think I would have lost my head.'[28]

The journey could also be endured for the generous fees that the Imperial family could pay for the best artists. The Imperial Dramatic Theatres, the Opera, and the Ballet were all handsomely subsidised, giving their artists and staff a comfortable standard of living free from financial worries. Every care was taken to safeguard the health of the artists as coaches whisked them from door to door, with elaborate measures to preserve them from draughts.[29] On the days for payment the Imperial Treasurer would call on the principal singers and pay them from a large roll of notes.[30] Chaliapin describes the settings of opera and ballet as '... magnificent. Nothing was stinted, no expense spared. The prodigality in costumes and décor far exceeded the wildest dreams of

---

[26] Minnie Hauk, *Memories of a Singer*, p. 60.
[27] Pompei, op. cit., p. 284.
[28] Calvé, *Sous tous les ciels j'ai chanté*, p. 125.
[29] Glackens, op. cit., p. 73.
[30] Mapleson, op. cit., Vol. I, p. 83.

other managements.'[31] Well might the singers feel that, for such
conditions, a theatre etiquette which forbade applause except by the
example of the 'Little Father' was a small price to pay. Gaisberg writes of
having seen 'opera performances on a scale unbelievably lavish. Only the
wealthiest family in the world, the Romanoffs, could support them. I had
heard and negotiated with a bevy of the greatest and perhaps most
spoiled artists of that epoch.'[32] Years later, De Lucia would tell his
children of the opulence of the Imperial table, glittering with gold and
jewellery. At the splendours of a ball at the Winter Palace we can now
only hint.[33]

St. Petersburg was built on water, nineteen islands connected by
many bridges and penetrated by a skein of canals. Its *sobriquets* included
'the Venice of the North' and 'the Babylon of the Snows'. It was
characterised by wide streets, richly-endowed churches, and an
abundance of gardens. The architecture of its great baroque palaces, in
red, yellow, pale green, and white, reflected the taste of the Italians who
had designed them. Ornamented windows and columned doorways
disguised the tremendous size of its buildings.

Many of St. Petersburg's institutions and much of its culture would
have seemed familiar to an upper-class Parisian, who would blend easily
into a society which regularly spoke French and read the *Journal de St.
Pétersbourg*. It was a society which bought its luxuries from Paris, spent
its evenings at the Maryinsky Theatre or at the Théâtre Français, and
supported a refined musical life outside the theatres and Imperial
circles.[34] Artists considered it an honour to perform in the famous soirées
of personages such as Tertii Filippov, Minister of State Control, who
provided one of the early opportunities for St. Petersburg society to hear
the boy-prodigy Josef Hofmann and the little-known bass Feodor
Chaliapin.[35]

On December 9th 1895 De Lucia made his début at the Theatre of the
Aquarium in *La Gioconda*, with Adalgisa Gabbi and Mattia Battistini.
He was immediately compared with Marconi and Masini, who had
together dominated this repertoire for many years. Masini, especially,
was idolised by Russian theatre audiences. He was much admired by the
Tsar and his family, and he was a regular guest at the Imperial
palaces.[36] Since his Russian début in 1876 he had been the tenor against
whom all others were measured there. In 1895-6 he was singing with the
Lago Italian Opera which, after a season in Moscow, appeared at the
Maly, or Petit Théâtre, in St. Petersburg.

[31] Feodor Chaliapin, *Man and Mask*, p. 67.
[32] F.W. Gaisberg, *Music on Record*, p. 38.
[33] Robert K. Massie, *Nicholas and Alexandra*, p. 8.
[34] Eugenio Pirani, 'Pietroburgo Musicale', *Gazzetta Musicale di Milano*, Apr. 15 1888.
[35] Chaliapin, op. cit., p. 66.
[36] Michele Raffaelli in *Angelo Masini: Il tenore angelico*, pp. 24-5.

Platon de Vaxel, of the *Journal de St. Pétersbourg*, wrote of De Lucia:

One was, above all, curious to hear the tenor who is said to replace, with us, Messieurs Masini and Marconi. From his first phrase he conquered the public, which exploded into applause. ... He had to repeat the duet with [Battistini][37] ... Monsieur De Lucia has great qualities of which the principal, in our opinion, is knowing, as do few of his predecessors, how to throw a phrase into relief, to modulate it, and to shade it to infinity, with a gradation of effect. His high notes are sonorous, but of a vibrant metal that puts too much of an edge on the body of the voice which, at times, is also spoiled by a somewhat nasal emission, but these natural faults are more than compensated by the art and phrasing of the eminent artist, whose true domain is the lyric field, which he has proved as Enzo. Despite the brilliant success attained with his great dramatic *élan* ... we give the palm to the more restrained passages, or those touched by sentiment. ... Here the artist was charming, and very personal, with no fear of comparison.[38]

His next appearance, in *La Sonnambula*, was less successful:

The music needs a surpassing virtuosity, together with charm. ... M. De Lucia has them, in his fashion, but his type of voice and, above all, his method, so suitable for Ponchielli and Mascagni, are not ideal for Bellinian *bel canto*. Above all, the *cantabile* [passages], delivered in a weary voice and with listless *tempi*, leave much to be desired. ...

Vocalising with facility (a good omen for *Il Barbiere*), M. De Lucia has the fault of composing Verdian cadences that have nothing in common with Bellini. Now and then, our tenor also abuses the *fermate* [pauses] but not to the extent of Mlle Pacini, who seems to believe that length is a substitute for intensity.[39]

In *Il Barbiere di Siviglia*, one critic, while commending a beautiful voice and undoubted vocal ability, disliked some of his open notes, which did not create a pleasant impression.[40] However, he received a flattering review from De Vaxel, with an interesting reference to the talent for comedy that is so apparent in his recordings of this music, and especially in the *Il Barbiere* set made for Phonotype in his last years:

Signor De Lucia, our new Almaviva, has eclipsed all his immediate predecessors from the point of view of the action. From the duet with Figaro, in which he leaves the critic nothing to say, his interpretation puts his scenes into relief with animation and truly perfect taste. Even in the drunken scene, while making everyone laugh a great deal, he never goes too far.

In Italy, the Neapolitans are celebrated for their comic talent, their popular stages always holding some screamingly funny comedians; ah well, Monsieur De Lucia is one of them, to a degree that far surpasses the usual level of tenors. Having a sufficiently well-developed vocalisation, he always sings his part very well, showing proof of great security in the ensembles. In the duet: 'Qual trionfo', after Sembrich's phrase, given with the detail that only she can achieve, he produced a true effect by his repetition of this phrase, sensibly

---

37 The review erroneously gives Cotogni as the Barnaba.

38 *Journal de St. Pétersbourg*, Nov. 29/Dec. 11 1895 (os/ns). In the text, all Russian dates are given in new style.

39 Ibid., Dec. 1/13 1895

40 Unidentified cutting, possibly *Novoie Vremia*, Dec. 1895.

modified, but not inconsistent with Rossini. In the first act he had to repeat the two serenades, the second overall being delightfully phrased, better even than by Monsieur Masini, although not with the latter's beauty of voice.[41]

The triumph was shared by Sembrich[42] and Battistini. At the end, the ovation lasted a good half-hour and the *diva* was overwhelmed with flowers; two footmen were needed to carry one colossal display. The impresario, Ughetti, was beset by requests for a repeat performance.

De Lucia's Duke of Mantua was thought almost as good as his Almaviva, 'even better from the vocal point of view, since it seems that Verdi's music is his true province'. His diction and acting were praised. He repeated 'Questa o quella' and the duet with Sembrich. Especially, he shone in the scene in the inn where he sang 'La donna è mobile' three times, like a true Don Juan, 'each time with new nuances and ornaments; a phrase given in *mezza voce* was very pretty'.[43]

He wrote to Pagliara of his success:

> Grand Hôtel Pétersbourg
> December 19th 1895
>
> Even from so far away, I write to wish you a happy Christmas and a very happy New Year, with your dear family.
> I wish you luck, eternal good health, and everything one could wish.
> Are you happy??
> After *La Gioconda* and *La Sonnambula*, I sang *Il Barbiere* and *Rigoletto*, to great enthusiasm. In *Barbiere* I repeated the two serenades, and all the rest of the opera went very well.
> From the article that I enclose you will see that they judge me superior to Masini. In *Rigoletto* I repeated the 1st act *ballata*, the 2nd act duet with the famous Sembrich, and I sang 'La donna è mobile' *three* times. As you see, here too I have achieved a solid *success*.
> My wife sends greetings, and I send you a kiss of true affection.[44]

The correspondent of *Gazzetta dei Teatri* reported in the usual terms of battles won, in this case convincingly:

> Superior to any comparison, he has by this time no need to fight, but only to win and triumph. ... he had to give four repeats of 'La donna è mobile' ... giving to each repeat a new and different *cachet* of diction and interpretation. The public had only one cry - '*Viva De Lucia!*'[45]

As *Faust*, he was judged 'less good than as Almaviva or Mantua'.[46] At the second performance, he sang rather limply through Act I but

---

41 *Journal de St. Pétersbourg*, Dec. 5/17 1895.

42 The Polish soprano Marcella Sembrich (1858-1935).

43 *Journal de St. Pétersbourg*, Dec. 7-8/19-20 1895.

44 (SLC) The performance statistics were duly published in the Neapolitan press.

45 *Gazzetta dei Teatri*, Dec. 26 1895. As before, the meaning of 'four repeats' is not clear.

46 *Journal de St. Pétersbourg*, Dec. 12/24 1895.

...blossomed in Act III, especially in the duet with Margherita and again in the duel scene, which was repeated. He is an outstandingly sensitive artist and singer and ... we are somewhat surprised that in the dramatic parts he often produces open notes, which are not at all dramatic in themselves but spoil the effect.[47]

Then came a *Mignon* where

...he put an Italian warmth into Meister - the French play it more temperately. It would be difficult to sing the second act romance ['Addio, Mignon'] as De Lucia did. The phrase on the knees, before Mignon, ending with a note spun in a *diminuendo*, was of the first order, such as one rarely hears. This reminds us of Naples, of *Carmen* and *Cavalleria Rusticana*, and certain phrases that we have never forgotten.[48]

His records from *Mignon* exhibit many such charming touches. In the words of Hurst, the 'Addio, Mignon' [No. 30] is

...sung with such exquisite expression and taste as to turn it into great music. It is in a pathetic appeal like this that De Lucia outshone all his rivals ... [49]

However, for all its self-indulgent virtuosity, perhaps the most felicitous of his *Mignon* extracts is 'Ah! non credevi tu' [No. 32]; the words *'Almo april'* are given with a sensuous languor which, in a less self-assured singer, would border on indolence. The record shows to perfection his ability, by freedom 'boldly and beautifully exercised', to capture and hold a moment.[50] And the reviews of his Wilhelm Meister, both in 1896 and in 1906 (p. 358), refute the suggestion that such moments were possible only in the recording studio, with an acquiescent Sabajno at the piano. Quite clearly, they characterised his stage appearances.

De Lucia's success in St. Petersburg had been great enough for the management to reconfirm him for next season.[51] *Romeo e Giulietta* was announced for his benefit and farewell performance, but, owing to Sembrich's illness, it was replaced by *Il Barbiere di Siviglia*, with Regina Pacini.

He had been scheduled, next, to sing *Carmen*, *Silvano*, and Massenet's *La Navarrese*, at La Scala.[52] But, for some reason, Garulli assumed the part of Araquil in the Massenet work. In a luckless season for Sonzogno, Garulli, however, fell ill; the première was postponed twice before, on January 28th, he finally declared himself unfit. Money was already being returned to the irate subscribers while Massenet was still attempting to

---

47 Unidentified cutting, possibly *Isvestia*, Jan. 6 1896 ns.
48 *Journal de St. Pétersbourg*, Dec. 22 1895/Jan. 3 1896.
49 Hurst, *Gramophone*, April 1934, p. 458.
50 Steane, *The Grand Tradition*, p. 32.
51 *Journal de St. Pétersbourg*, Jan. 2-3/14-15 1896.
52 *Gazzetta dei Teatri*, Dec. 5 1895.

persuade Garulli to sing, suggesting that, in a not unusual practice, the 'romanza' could be played by the 'cello, to orchestral accompaniment.[53]

On De Lucia's return to Milan, he was immediately advised of the problem and, at short notice, agreed to essay the part of Araquil. It was not, critics noted sympathetically, a work to be learned in a moment. Nevertheless, after delays while De Lucia, in his turn, was indisposed, the opera went on stage on February 6th 1896.

So disparate were the reviews that they might relate to different operas. Galli, in the Sonzogno newspaper *Secolo*, noted the fashionable audience; he analysed the musical and dramatic features of this work of the 'fascinating melodist, Massenet'. Turning to the performance, he expressed himself unable to imagine anyone who better identified with the protagonist than Frandin, who gave to every word its required importance, and who possessed a psychological insight which was rare in lyric artists. However, he confessed, the same could not be said for her singing, for she was nervous and, also, somewhat indisposed. Then:

> With true pleasure we heard the tenor De Lucia again. He is one of the very few who today hold high the honour of the Italian school of singing, that school that is founded on perfect delivery of the most melodious sounds of the language; on instinctive emission of a voice of the purest metal; that school which preserves the most exquisite methods of singing and which carries sentimental expression to supreme perfection.
>
> In the duet with Anita; in the romanza, which he repeated; in the death scene; De Lucia was equal to his fame: to hear him is to understand how music can be considered the most moving of the arts.[54]

Significantly, Galli said nothing of the reception of the work; there was no chronicle of applause and calls, the *sine qua non* of a success. Even a mere *succès d'estime* for a composer whose work was destined to vanish into oblivion usually merited such an account. Of *La Navarrese* there was nothing, and it was ignored in the next issue of the Sonzogno publication *Secolo Illustrata della Domenica*.

It failed not because the non-musical sounds, the tremendous fusillade in the opening scene, the smoke, or the smell of gunpowder offended the Milanese. The opera was a victim of theatre politics and was almost certainly doomed before the curtain rose. The audience did not actually hiss: it remained 'serenely implacable' and indulged only in some restrained shouts, which were the 'Requiem'. The reasons for the hostility of press and public may be read in the self-righteous indignation of *Gazzetta dei Teatri*:

> To present *La Navarrese* at La Scala as one of the important novelties of the season makes a mockery of the good taste, good sense and . . . culture of the Milanese public.

---

53 *Secolo*, Jan. 29/30 1896.
54 Ibid., Feb. 7/8 1896.

The correspondent commented smugly, as a foregone conclusion, on the hostile demonstration which, he asserted, expressed censure of the management and a protest against

> ... this overflowing of foreign operas, increasingly dangerous and damaging to the national product, of which a subsidised theatre should be the jealous custodian. ... *La Navarrese* may please Signor Sonzogno: *de gustibus non est disputandum* but, if he wanted so much to transplant it to Italian soil he should have done it at the Teatro Lirico Internazionale, his private and absolute property. There he is the master, to do and not to do, and any pleasure is licensed in his laws. At the Scala it is quite another pair of shoes. The repertoire must, first of all, be Italian ... and foreign works ... should be those few undisputed masterpieces which all recognise and appreciate.[55]

In a long, xenophobic review the critic roundly damned the opera as a 'hotch-potch which would hardly pass for a pantomime in a theatre of the third rank'. Most of the singers were poor, he claimed, singling out Frandin for special criticism, possibly because of her status as one of Sonzogno's *amanti putative*.[56] Her vocal means, 'never overwhelming', were no longer sufficient for La Scala.

Turning to De Lucia, the critic remarked that it was futile to engage artists of fame and indisputable worth for such unworthy operas:

> The public yearned to hear again the fascinating tenor who had left such a warm and intense impression of himself; De Lucia, for his part, longed to reappear before this public, and to move it once more with the irresistible enchantment of his vibrant accents and of his passionate singing. But the one and the other were sacrificed; certainly, De Lucia found the means of making something of that miserable *romanzina*. The public, seizing on a single slab of pleasure, made him repeat it, but neither the artist nor his admirers should remain fully satisfied, and to say that Signor Sonzogno has operas such as *I Pescatori di Perle* and *Manon*, in which De Lucia is great in the widest sense of this glorifying adjective! ... But no, these operas had to remain on the shelf, and De Lucia had to be burned on the altar of *La Navarrese!*..... And now I do not think that any further hope exists of hearing him again this season![57]

Almost certainly, the author of this was D'Ormeville who, by this time, was probably De Lucia's agent; certainly, he published extensive extracts from the tenor's reviews in Italian and foreign newspapers. His views may not, therefore, be impartial. A more disinterested witness was Umberto Giordano, who was in Milan preparing for the première of *Andrea Chénier*. From the Gambrinus café in the Galleria he wrote to Illica:

[February 6th 1896]

I have just come from the Scala - (*prima* of *Navarrese*) - never have I seen so

---

55 *Gazzetta dei Teatri*, Feb. 13 1896.
56 Daspuro, 'Memorie', ch. XLI.
57 *Gazzetta dei Teatri*, Feb. 13 1896.

unjust an audience. The opera was a colossal fiasco. And to say that both the opera and the performance merited a real success. Frandin was extraordinary. De Lucia capital, and so we go on, but (I don't know why) the opera was thrown into an abyss from which it will not emerge. You can imagine how I suffered. Shame, a real shame![58]

Frandin refused to appear again, and Sonzogno declined to replace her.[59] *La Navarrese* was not repeated and, when *Carmen* was given, two weeks later, it was sung not by Frandin and De Lucia but by Ida Rappini and Francisco Viñas.

From the disappointments of Milan De Lucia returned to Naples where, after yet another hiatus, the San Carlo was reopening. '*Inneggiamo, il San Carlo non è morto!*', wrote the correspondent of *Gazzetta dei Teatri* in parody of Santuzza's phrase in *Cavalleria Rusticana*.[60] For the 1895-6 season Musella, no doubt to ease negotiations for *La Bohème*, had offered a programme strongly based on Ricordi works. The roster included Elisa Petri, whom De Lucia had warmly recommended to Pagliara:[61]

Milan, November 27th 1895

Carissimo Pagliara,

I write you from here to recommend to you *very very much* Signorina Elisa Petri, distinguished singing artist.

This is her first appearance at the San Carlo, and I am sure that she will arouse fanaticism, because she is an artist of real merit, as I have told you.

I recommend her to you because you will be able to do much for her. I am sure that you will please me, and I shall be most grateful to you for this.

I embrace you with true affection. (SLC)

De Lucia was at last to sing Rodolfo. The piano rehearsals for principals and chorus started late in February. Early in March, Puccini and Tito Ricordi arrived to help the conductor, Vittorio Vanzo, prepare the work. From Naples, Puccini wrote to Mascheroni:

We are rehearsing with piano here. ... De Lucia will be excellent, as will Signorina Petri.[62]

Suggestions that De Lucia was ill were quickly denied. For all the experience of a notable career he seems always to have suffered from nerves.

---

58 Biblioteca Comunale di Piacenza.

59 Letter Giordano - Illica, Feb. 7 1896, Morini, *Umberto Giordano*, p. 287.

60 *Gazzetta dei Teatri*, Feb. 13 1896. 'Rejoice, the San Carlo is not dead!'

61 The *raccomandazione* (recommendation), while not a uniquely Neapolitan institution, may well reach its highest pitch of development there as a favoured and well-accepted method of advancement. Even today, little of substance is accomplished without one.

62 Puccini - Mascheroni, Mar. 2 1896. (Letter offered for sale by Altman, May 1978).

The Naples première of *La Bohème* took place on March 14th 1896, before an audience that was surprisingly fashionable for so late in the season. The critics immediately praised the *mise en scène*. They enjoyed the illusion of the nocturnal *festa*, and wrote enthusiastically of Act III. Dawn in the snowy landscape and the whitened trees against the pearl-grey sky caused shivers even in the comfortable warmth of the theatre.

It was a triumph for all concerned. The applause rumbled into an unbroken series of ovations, a crescendo of applause for Puccini, and some thirty calls for him and for the artists. There were repeats of the Act I and Act III finales. In *Corriere di Napoli* the critic wrote:

> Puccini has depicted splendidly, in musical form, the true nature of the Bohemians, a surface of luminous and tender sea below which threatens a roaring tempest. Its interpretation is made more perfect and picturesque by the addition of an exquisite artist such as Fernando De Lucia . . .
>
> De Lucia, unrivalled interpreter of passionate scenes, has a singular gift of revealing, with the voice, a state of mind, [and] of expressing caresses and sighs with his infinitely soft vocal timbre, with certain passages, and with modulations of irresistible sweetness.[63]

Procida, in *Pungolo*, described De Lucia's work as:

> . . . A valuable contribution, . . . an invaluable contributor, almost - for Puccini may never again find so admirable an interpreter to make Rodolfo's entreaties stand forth - was Fernando De Lucia: sweet, ingratiating and touching where tenderness overflows; sturdy and vigorous where impulse erupts and vibrates in the spirit of the artist. A wonderful vocal skill and a profound artistic sentiment fuse together to produce an enchanting ecstasy . . . an echo which will last in the senses for as long as the memory lasts in those who heard the artist. Of the three *bis* . . . one was due entirely to his merit, as were, in part, the other two.[64]

By the time that he wrote his notice for *Fortunio*, Procida had had time for mature consideration. After lengthy discussion of the opera and of all the other singers, he came to the Rodolfo:

> But the solemn note of this performance was De Lucia. The *divo* who, through capriciousness, had allowed himself to believe that he had a head cold, displayed all the graces of his throat, from the sweet and penetrating *mezza voce* to tender shadings and to warm and lacerating impulses. Perhaps he emasculated Rodolfo a little, wrung from him more tears that *La Bohème* merited, but in those whispers, the inflections that accompany such sweetness of delivery, a little licence is permitted. . . . .
>
> De Lucia is a refined cultivator of singing; he has left unexplored not one of the faculties that lie in the depths of his throat. The long, shaded B flat in *falsetto* is, in *La Bohème*, one of the most marvellous things to be found in his singing. By now, his art has surpassed even his natural qualities of pure timbre, of secure intonation, of trenchant execution, and that is good. Now, do not lapse into affectation, descend into mawkishness, or be in a tearing hurry: stay thus.[65]

---

63 *Corriere di Napoli*, Mar. 15 1896.
64 *Pungolo*, Mar. 15 1896.
65 *Fortunio*, Mar. 26 1896.

1. Portrait, c. 1890. (De Lucia family)

2. As a pupil of the Conservatorio di San Pietro a Maiella, Naples, with (right) an
   unidentified fellow-student. (De Lucia family)

Ai miei affezionatissimi genitori

~ Fernando ~

3. Portrait in clean-shaven days. (De Lucia family)

4. The young concert artist.
(De Lucia family)

5. The young concert artist.
(De Lucia family)

6. As Faust in his operatic début, 1885. (William F. Porter)

7. As Faust in his operatic début, 1885. (De Lucia family)

8. A Falk portrait, c. 1893.

9. The man-about-town, c. 1893.
(Giacomo R. Ancona)

10. A Falk portrait, c. 1893.

11. The dandy, c. 1886.
(De Lucia family)

12. As Turiddu, c. 1891-2.
    (De Lucia family)

13. De Lucia as Turiddu and
    Emma Calvé as Santuzza,
    London, c. 1892. (Georges
    Girard)

14. A fiercely-dramatic Turiddu. (Desmond Shawe-Taylor)

15-20. As Canio in *Pagliacci*, with
Mario Ancona (Tonio) and
Nellie Melba (Nedda),
London, 1893. (Giacomo R.
Ancona) *continued overleaf.*

21. De Lucia (right), with Mario Ancona and Luigi Mancinelli, London, 1893. (Giacomo R. Ancona)

22. *En famille* at Cava de' Tirreni, c. 1894. Recognisable in the second row are Penelope De Giorgio (2nd from left), Itala (centre), a morose Fernando, and Flora De Giorgio (right). Centre is Rodolfo De Giorgio (with white pocket handkerchief), with Armando at his left shoulder. Nadir is at his father's feet. (Giuseppina Giordano)

23. Portrait dedicated to Carlo
    Clausetti, 1893. (Museo
    della Scala)

24. Sketch from the period of
    his New York début,
    December 1893. *(New York
    Herald)*

25. Cartoon showing De Lucia and Calvé as Fritz and Suzel at Covent Garden. (*Punch*, June 4th 1892).

26. Cartoon showing De Lucia, Mascagni, and Calvé at Covent Garden. (*Punch*, July 1st 1893).

Alla mia adorata madre, Fernando ed i tuoi figli. Armando - Nadir.

Roma 10 - 12 - 98 —

27. The father: De Lucia with Armando (left) and Nadir (centre), 1898. (De Lucia family)

28. Portrait from the period of the La Scala premiere of *La Bohème*, March 1897. (Ricordi)

29. *Iris* at La Scala, January 1899. Standing, left to right: Guglielmo Caruson, Tilde Milanesi, and Fernando De Lucia. Giuseppe Tisci-Rubini is at the extreme right. (Ricordi)

30. Portrait inscribed to Elvira Giommi. (De Lucia family)

Qui De Lucia dalla canora gola,
sommo signor dell'altissimo canto,
che sovra gli altri com' aquila vola.

32. De Lucia, who sent the newspaper to
    Elvira Giommi, has written 'baci'
    ('kisses') on this cartoon in *Rastignac*
    (August 29th 1905). The verse reads:

Here, (is) De Lucia, of the melodious throat,
supreme master of most heavenly singing
who soars above the others like an eagle.

Questo a un dipresso è il divo De Lucia
ch'è stato fatto pur Commendator
e ognuno che lo sente si nni pria
se la romanza canta di Fedor.

31. Cartoon in *Papiol* (April 24th 1902).
    The verse reads:

This, more or less, is the *divo* De Lucia
who has even been made *Commendatore*
and everyone is intoxicated when they hear
him sing the romanza from *Fedora*.

33. Portrait, c. 1905. (De Lucia family)

34. Elvira Giommi. (De Lucia family)

35. Portrait, c. 1905. (Stuart-Liff Collection)

36. Portrait, c. 1900. (Ricordi)

37. Portrait inscribed to Antonio Caggiula, dated 1908 but probably of earlier date. (Luigi Caggiula)

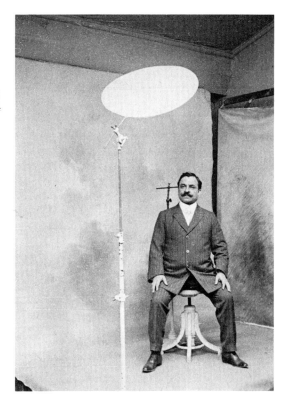

38. De Lucia, photographed by
    Alfredo De Giorgio while sitting
    for a portrait by Felicetti, Rome
    November 8th 1908. (Biblioteca
    di Storia Moderna e
    Contemporanea, Rome)

Cava dei Tirreni - Villa Maria (Villaggio Rotolo)

39. View from the terrace of the De Lucia villa (now 'Villa Maria') at Cava de' Tirreni.
    (Sergio Pepe)

40. The father: with Rosa and Vanni, c. 1911. (De Lucia family)

41. As Almaviva with (left to right) Feodor Chaliapin (Basilio), De Lucia, Rosina Storchio (Rosina), Antonio Pini-Corsi (Bartolo), and Titta Ruffo (Figaro), Monte Carlo, 1907. (Royal Archives, Monaco)

42. Portrait, c. 1908. (De Lucia family)

43. On holiday, c. 1906, with Elvira, Vanni, and (probably) Amalia Galanti.
    (De Lucia family)

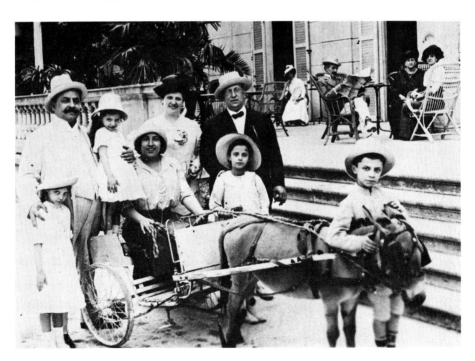

44. On holiday at Salsomaggiore, c. 1910. Fernando, Elvira, the children (left to right:
    Giuseppina, Amalia, Rosa, and Vanni), and two unidentified family friends.
    (De Lucia family)

45. The teacher (probably Naples, c. 1910). (De Lucia family)

46. On the terrace of Villa Maria, Cava de' Tirreni, with an unidentified visitor (possibly one of the Michaëlis brothers.) (Michael Wyler, from the estate of Fred Gaisberg)

47. De Lucia listening to a record (probably Milan). (Michael Wyler, from the estate of Fred Gaisberg)

48. At the front, c. 1917. (De Lucia family)

49. At the front, singing a mass for the dead, c. 1917. (De Lucia family)

50. With his accompanist and a group of pupils, c. 1916-17. (De Lucia family)

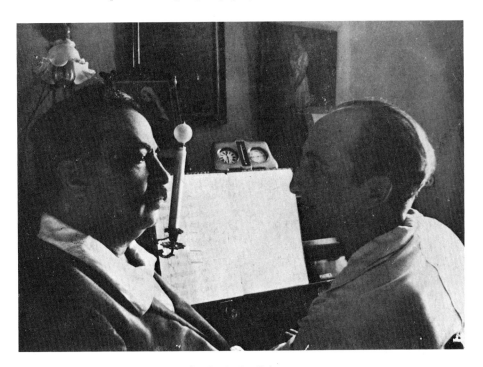

51. Fernando and Nadir De Lucia. (De Lucia family)

52. The last known portrait. (Felice Forino)

His work pleased Puccini, who wrote to his friend Alfredo Caselli: '... here we shall go as God wills - De Lucia is excellent.'[66]

The success was marked by a luncheon given for Puccini by Tito Ricordi in the recently-opened Sala Ricordi in the Galleria. On March 16th 1896 some thirty authors, musicians, and journalists gathered to honour the composer.[67] Thanks were expressed to Ricordi, to Clausetti, and to the artists. During a noisy, festive *après-diner*, Salvatore di Giacomo improvised a sonnet, 'A Giacomo Puccini', which was published in the newspaper *Don Marzio* that very day.[68] De Lucia sang Tosti songs, to Vanzo's accompaniment. Musella spoke for many when he expressed the hope that *Tosca* would be given first at the San Carlo.

In 1910, looking back on many San Carlo performances of *La Bohème*, De Lucia wrote in his score: 'I am sure that my fellow Neapolitans will always remember my Rodolfo.' His belief was probably well founded. The houses continued good, and *'Tutto esaurito'* notices were posted from midday even on the day of a 'last' *La Bohème*, then of a 'final' and then of the 'definitely last' performance, which closed the season on April 15th. Musella proudly exhibited telegrams of congratulation from Ricordi and from Puccini, who had also telegraphed thanks to some of the artists.

From Naples, the tenor returned to Covent Garden. Jean de Reszke, after a season's absence, opened the 1896 season as Roméo, on May 11th; later, he sang Lohengrin and Tristan in German. By comparison with these much-anticipated novelties all else paled. De Lucia sang *Cavalleria Rusticana*, his Turiddu 'so tremendously in earnest that he stepped once or twice out of the reaches of the sublime into - shall it be called? - the paths of light comedy'.[69] *Fra Diavolo*, *Pagliacci*, *Rigoletto*, and *La Traviata* were his other works.[70] Only his Canio escaped some - however slight - adverse comment or being damned by faint praise. In *Rigoletto*, *Punch* described him as

> ...a gallant but deceitful Dook. ...De Lucia [was] rather hard for such an amorous dog of a dook, yet his great song 'La donna è mobile' he gave in such a careless, reckless style, which is the very keynote of the character. However, conductor Bevignani did not have many bouquets to hand up onto the stage.[71]

His small stature continued to intrigue *Punch*, for whom he was

> ...uncommonly good as *Alfredo mio*, *'le petit bonhomme plus petit que ça'*. Except Manon's lover, is there any lover in operatic history who is such a nincompoop of a character as this 'Alf-and-'Alf-redo?'[72]

---

66 (PC) Mar. 17 1896.
67 *Paese*, Mar. 16 1896.
68 Schlitzer, op. cit., No. 640, pp. 310-11.
69 *Sketch*, May 20 1896.
70 The *Mefistofele* billed for May 23 may not have taken place.
71 *Punch*, May 30 1896.
72 Ibid, June 20 1896.

De Lucia had already completed his performances when, on June 22nd, came news of the death of Harris. According to Sir Augustus's wish, the theatre remained open and the season continued without interruption.[73]

The proposed season in South America had come to nothing. His next traceable engagement was still months away, in the cold of St. Petersburg. There was time to spend a leisurely summer and autumn at Cava de' Tirreni. But even on holiday he visited the theatre. He is reported to have driven to nearby Salerno specifically to hear the young tenor Enrico Caruso, in *I Puritani*. De Lucia is said to have visited him in his dressing-room, to offer his congratulations and to urge upon him his own philosophy of continual study.[74]

73 Rosenthal, op. cit., p. 271.
74 Key and Zirato, op. cit., p. 399 give August. Thomas G. Kaufman, in Scott: *The Great Caruso*, specifies Sept. 10 for the première.

14

Dreams of Starlit Nights

'Ses fioritures? Comment les dépeindre? Je ne sais si elles étaient plaisantes mais elles étaient extraordinairement bien faites!'   Georges Thill[1]

En route for St. Petersburg, De Lucia was taken ill in Milan and his first two operas, *L'Elisir d'Amore* and *Romeo e Giulietta*, scheduled for December 30th and January 1st respectively, were cancelled. The embarrassed management of the Imperial Conservatoire was obliged to call on the unfortunate Augusto Brogi, the only available tenor, to sing *La Traviata*, *Tannhäuser*, *Lucia di Lammermoor*, and *Un Ballo in Maschera* in rapid succession.

Even when De Lucia arrived he was, as he explained to Pagliara, not fit to sing:

> Grand Hôtel, Pietroburgo
> [undated]
>
> Carissimo Rocco,
>
> Here I am, finally arrived here in this land of snow, after my miserable illness suffered in Milan, and while I still feel weak I hope to be able to sing in a few days, otherwise I shall return to Naples.
>
> I have received a letter ... asking me to sing *Doña Flora*, and I have naturally replied that my present state of health does not permit me to learn a new opera.[2]
>
> My vocal organ must not be overworked, especially after a grave illness.
>
> I wish you a happy New Year, with all your family, and specially that old saint your father.
>
> Write me sometimes, and think of one who wishes you so well. Give my regards to Napoletano, and accept a kiss from your affectionate friend. (SLC)

Only partly recovered, he joined Sembrich and Battistini in the fourth *La Traviata*, on January 9th 1897.[3] The critic De Vaxel reported an encore of the 'Brindisi' and a success that grew continuously after the card scene, which he 'rendered like a great artist'. Older connoisseurs

---

[1] 'His *fioriture*? How can one describe them? I don't know whether they were pleasant but they were extraordinarily well done!' Letter to the writer, October 1967, when Thill, a De Lucia pupil, commented on his teacher's style.

[2] *Doña Flor* (Van Westerhout) had been given at the San Carlo, Naples, on Feb. 15 1896.

[3] Russian dates are given in new style in the text.

declared that they had never before heard 'Parigi, o cara' sung with such blending of voices, and with such an artistic interpretation.[4]

He now discovered the power of the *masinisti*. Masini, who had recently appeared at the Petit Théâtre in St. Petersburg, had already left for Moscow; De Lucia's illness brought him back to St. Petersburg, specifically to sing *L'Elisir d'Amore* and *Rigoletto*.[5] From his travels back and forth between the two cities, and the fatigue of singing every other night, Masini had apparently caught cold. In any event, he was indisposed, and his supporters tried to prevent De Lucia from deputising. They staged their protest at a performance of *Rigoletto* on January 14th.

De Lucia wrote to Elvira Giommi:

> Pietroburgo
> [January 19th 1897]
>
> Carissima Elvira,
>
> After my very serious illness I have, by God's grace, started to sing. I expect clamorous successes. Here, there are two other tenors, Tamagno and Masini. With Tamagno I get on very well, and we have respect, one for the other, but Masini has declared war on me. But the glory is mine, and I hope to triumph in the end. My adversary is very powerful because he has sung here for twenty-five years and he has a very strong army in his defence. I will do what Galliano [an Italian patriot] did, resist with just a few men. A few evenings ago he had to sing *Rigoletto*, but before the opera was due to start he said that he was ill and that the performance could not take place. The impresario came to me to save the situation, to sing *Rigoletto*. When Masini heard that I had accepted, battle orders were issued. The struggle took place as you can see from this article that I have sent you. Triumph was mine: just imagine - I sang the *ballata* three times, 'La donna è mobile' four times, and the duet with Gilda twice, and the quartet twice. Last night I had another triumph with *Romeo e Giulietta*.
>
> I am sorry that your mother has been ill. I hope that God will always guard her. Regards to your mother and to your grandmother. Regards to your friend, and I send you a kiss on your head.
>
> Your friend,
> Fernando (PC)

The article in question tells of a lively evening indeed at the theatre of the Conservatoire:

> The first act started with a semi-scandal, Monsieur Masini having made an excuse at the last moment because of having caught cold. The *Masinisti*, who were at the theatre in great numbers, wanted to prevent Monsieur De Lucia, who had replaced his colleague without prior notice, from singing. The true public intervened and the excellent tenor had a great success.[6]

Another critic remarked that the timbre of De Lucia's voice very much

---

4 *Journal de St. Pétersbourg*, Dec. 31 1896/Jan. 12 1897.

5 *Cosmorama*, Jan. 29 1897.

6 *Journal de St. Pétersbourg*, Jan. 4/16 1897.

recalled Masini's,

> ... especially in the *piano*, which is, however, more noble and more metallic [than Masini's]. The breathing is masterly and the action always well considered, rendered with talent [even] in the more insignificant details of the rôle.[7]

In *Romeo e Giulietta* there were reports of forty calls, including thirty for De Lucia and Sembrich. The tenor 'bewitched the listener with his heavenly singing and aroused enthusiasm with his fervour'.[8] Elsewhere, though, while there was approval of his phrasing, the 'somewhat tremulous' quality of the voice was not thought to be well adapted to the recitatives.

His engagement should have kept him in St. Petersburg all February.[9] However, after singing only a few times, he left for Naples, his contract broken. Ostensibly, it was for reasons of health. Privately, he was said to be angry that, having recovered from his illness, he had not been allowed to take over the rôle of Nemorino from Masini.

In Naples there were performances of *Carmen* and *Cavalleria Rusticana* and the usual eulogies for the passion and the power of his Don José. The critic of *Paese* (March 5th) described two German opera-goers

> ... who - cold, restrained, serious, and composed in appearance - little by little allowed themselves to be transported, seduced, fascinated by that magician of singing Fernando De Lucia. And when, in the third and fourth acts, rage breaks out in the drama, in all its terrible, savage effectiveness, they could not take their eyes from him, and repeated: *'Bravo! Bravo!'*, gesticulating and applauding like a couple of *claqueurs*.

But there was also criticism of mannered singing, and renewed concern over the damage that might possibly result from his vocal methods. Procida wrote of him:

> ... Turiddu was - *chapeau bas!* - De Lucia. The miracle was due to [him]. .... However, I do not believe that [the rôle] is particularly suited to his singing, [which is] velvety, sometimes mannered. He insists on modifying and lingering over certain passages, which deforms the character of the music in a manner which is anything but elegant. For example, [he] - I have written this on other occasions - adds to the 'Brindisi' certain *diminuendi*, certain contrasts in *piano*, certain grace notes which, without attenuating the lack of refinement, falsify its character. ...I believe that De Lucia gives the 'Addio' too much sentiment ...One may note that the middle register has by now reached its maximum robustness and mellowness, but I wish that the great singer would not so abuse this, to the detriment of his high notes.[10]

---

7 *Novoje Vremia*, quoted in *Gazzetta dei Teatri*, Feb. 4 1897.

8 Ibid.

9 *Gazzetta dei Teatri*, Nov. 26 1896.

10 *Pungolo*, Feb. 11/12 1897.

On March 5th 1897 the tenor signed a contract with Musella to return to the San Carlo in 1897-8. Two days later he arrived in Milan and immediately started rehearsals for the first La Scala production of *La Bohème*. The Mimì was Angelica Pandolfini, whom Ricordi had heard in the part at Rome and who, he reported to Illica, 'left Ferrani far behind'.[11]

The night before the première, Puccini wrote to the tenor:

Milan, March 14th 1897

Dear De Lucia,

On the eve of the staging of *Bohème* at the Scala, I feel the need to express to you once again my admiration and my gratitude for all the zeal and love that you continually show for my work. Looking forward to having you as interpreter of my future works, I am happy to tell you that, as I write *Tosca*, I think of you as my Mario, [a rôle] which I hope that you will be the first to create.[12]

The whole performance was a colossal success, a 'radiant evening, the apotheosis of light'.[13] The critics seemed deserted by any invective. Pandolfini, De Lucia, and Mugnone swept them from their feet to join the wildly enthusiastic audience in an astonishing display of emotion. The famed and feared critic G.B. Nappi described attendance at the theatre as 'splendid', and the success as 'magnificent'. He detailed almost twenty calls; the encores of 'Che gelida manina' and the third act quartet; the enthusiasm for Camilla Pasini, the original Musetta, in her waltz song; the conducting of Mugnone.[14] Indeed, his comments on the performers started with praise - in which he was not alone - for the work of the conductor, whom others described as having 'transformed the orchestra; ... a true and accurate collaborator of Puccini. The insistence of composer and publisher on having Mugnone was well justified.'[15]

Angelica Pandolfini, making her La Scala début, had a great triumph. Her intelligent and exquisite singing epitomised, for Nappi, all the feminine virtues. Her voice 'thrilled last night in the surroundings of the Scala, resounded, died, revealing ... a refined modulation and exquisite phrasing. It seemed to me that the character of Mimì finds, in her, its most complete incarnation.'[16]

Significantly, Nappi's description of De Lucia accepted the tenor's liberties with the score as a legitimate means to an interpretative end. And it was no sycophant but an influential and widely respected critic who wrote of the Rodolfo:

11 Letter G. Ricordi - L. Illica, Feb. 15 1896, Gara, *Carteggi*, No. 157, p. 143. Cesira Ferrani was the original Mimì.
12 (RE) Published in facsimile in *Illustracion Sud-Americana*, 1897, p. 235.
13 *Gazzetta dei Teatri*, Mar. 18 1897.
14 *Perseveranza*, Mar. 16 1897.
15 *Gazzetta dei Teatri*, Mar. 18 1897. Puccini had heard Mugnone at Florence and had recommended him to Ricordi for La Scala (Gara, *Carteggi*, No. 170, p. 153).
16 *Perseveranza*, Mar. 16 1897.

...De Lucia has shown ...a splendour of brightness, of sweetness, of passionate intensity. It is a dazzling voice, which fascinates and ravishes when at the disposal of a talented artist, who can flex it with a refinement that has few counterparts among modern singers.

His *mezza voce* is heavenly; it recalls that of Gayarre. He sang the first act aria in a way that electrified the listener. One could do no more, nor do it better. Some accentuation peculiar [to him], to seek greater intensity of expression, is condoned for the quite remarkable results, even if it does not wholly correspond to the spirit of the work. Neither was the actor less worthy and effective than the singer. He gave the final scene with evident and moving anguish.[17]

It seemed, remarked *Italia del Popolo*, that the public, hearing De Lucia's voice, gave a great sigh of satisfaction; it seemed to say:

This is a tenor! This is a voice!

And, in fact, De Lucia's voice, retaining all its vibrancy and its intensity of expression ...seemed to have gained in robustness: facile and ingratiating, it reached the high C with ease. The public was fascinated by ...his *portamenti*, by his *smorzature*: a master of the throat, whose equal is difficult to find.[18]

The *Gazzetta dei Teatri* waxed even more lyrical:

And the performance? Simply marvellous.

De Lucia, the great De Lucia, has made of the character of Rodolfo what, in theatrical parlance, is called a creation. What incisive declamation, what effective phrasing, what exquisite singing. To hear him is to experience a sense of inexpressible well-being, a sweet delight to the enraptured soul. The fame that precedes him makes the listener exacting and ...almost doubtful. But the expectations are met, doubts disappear, and approval grows spontaneously ...

He possesses ...the gift of bewitching the public and of forcing it to pay him the most religious attention. He conquers it, he seduces it, he hypnotises it. The heavenly magic of his singing captivates the most intransigent critic ... [19]

To others, his singing evoked Naples:

His warm, ingratiating voice reawoke in the listener who heard him the dream of starlit nights and of soft love-songs floating over the sea of the Sirens.[20]

Some time later, D'Ormeville wrote:

And still echo the triumphs of sixteen evenings at our Scala theatre by this magician of the lyric art. ...

And will it be possible to attain a more colossal triumph?

To Fernando De Lucia and to his fascinating genius everything is possible.[21]

---

[17] Ibid.

[18] *Italia del Popolo*, Mar. 16/17 1897. The reference to the high C is unequivocal. Though not all critics are knowledgeable or precise in such matters, neither this nor any other traceable review *of this performance* suggests transposition of 'Che gelida manina' or of any other piece.

[19] *Gazzetta dei Teatri*, Mar. 18 1897.

[20] Carlo Gatti, *Il Teatro alla Scala*.

[21] D'Ormeville, 'Ricordi recenti', introduction to a pamphlet, *Fernando De Lucia*, by Achemenide De Giorgio, Milan, 1897.

It was one of De Lucia's most incontrovertible successes. At the end of the performance Puccini embraced and kissed his Rodolfo, and 'few times, I believe, can there have been more spontaneous an embrace and more sincere a kiss ...the expression of just and heartfelt thanks'.[22] While the public called the tenor repeatedly on to the stage, a group which included Gatti-Casazza, Duke Visconti di Modrone, and Giulio Ricordi gathered in the wings, happy at the success but with the seriousness that befitted their status. Suddenly, De Lucia's valet, Enrico, burst upon the group, announcing himself by landing a mighty slap on Ricordi's back, and shouting: '*Commendato*', did you see the Neapolitans wipe the floor with the Milanese?!' For this high-spirited onslaught, at first taken as an assault, Enrico was arrested and only De Lucia's intervention freed him.[23]

The performances continued, to undiminished success and enthusiasm. After the seventh, De Lucia's reconfirmation for all sixteen was announced. Personally, he was less popular in some circles; in a letter to Puccini, Tito Ricordi described him as 'behaving like God almighty, five hundred times over'.[24]

Such arrogance was unusual. As we have seen, Fernando De Lucia was not without his weaknesses. He was polite to the point that some thought him patronising.[25] However, by common consent, he was a genial, whole-hearted, and simple Neapolitan, whose ingenuous pleasure in his own fame had a deep underlying modesty. He loved his native city and he valued his celebrity chiefly for the recognition that it gave him among his fellow citizens. Brotherly and warm, his manner was the same for the King as for his bootblack friend, Vincenzo. Though he moved in the highest circles he was no snob. With Neapolitans he always spoke the local dialect. Even the most humble came to his door to ask for help, a *raccomandazione*, a testimonial. At such times '*Il Commendatore*', as he was always known, would not hesitate to leave his guests or the dinner table. That he also had his share of humility was shown in the interest he took in Itala's seamstress, Vincenza Senatore, the daughter of a poor family at Cava. He considered her to have a promising voice and he went in person to see her parents, in a vain attempt to persuade them to allow her to follow a vocal career.[26]

He was known as a humorous man, full of fun and high spirits. Affectionate towards his nephews and nieces, he would unrepentingly indulge them both with money and with the chocolate of which he himself was so fond. Felice Forino, who married his niece, Edwige Amato, recalled meeting him for the first time when the singer was

---

22 *Gazzetta dei Teatri*, Mar. 18 1897.

23 R. Celletti, *Musica e Dischi*, April, 1955, p. 15. Gatti-Casazza was not yet in post at La Scala.

24 (PC) Tito Ricordi - Puccini, Mar. 29 1897.

25 Rodolfo Mele, in conversation with the writer, 1968.

26 Vincenza Senatore, in conversation with the writer, 1967.

about 60 years old. De Lucia entered the room as if making a stage entrance, his jolly face beaming. He bounded over to his nephew-to-be, lifted him clear of the floor, and sat down with the amazed Felice on his knee.[27]

All the evidence suggests that his natural bonhomie and his talkative, exuberant nature changed under the intensity of his characterisations. During his artistic life, they were an obsession through which his personality was transformed. His mood, on returning home after a successful performance, was anything but jubilant; he could not, by night, forsake the characters whom he had embodied so intensely a few hours earlier. On such occasions he was very different from the effusive, spirited extrovert. The vividness of his portrayals suggests that, of all his rôles, he identified most closely with Canio and Don José. And as each, before our eyes, changes from the affectionate to the passionate and to the uncontrollably violent, so it seems could De Lucia.

His final performance of the season took place at La Scala on April 13th 1897. Two days later, with his wife and sons, he was with the Ferrari company on board the steamship *Sirio*, bound for the Teatro de la Opera, Buenos Aires. The troupe also included Bonaplata-Bau, Ferrani, Guerrini, Arcangelo and Giulio Rossi, Mario Sammarco, Antonio Scotti, and Toresella. The principal conductor was Mascheroni.

They arrived in the River Plate on May 5th, to find that many habitués of the opera had not renewed their subscription. In Queen Victoria's Diamond Jubilee year many of the wealthy British community were crowding the steamers to Europe. The season opened on May 11th, with *La Gioconda*. Mascheroni, a firm local favourite, received a great ovation on his appearance, as did the Enzo, Gioconda (Bonaplata-Bau), and Cieca (Guerrini). De Lucia, commented *Nación*, could not be said to have sung the part with the same excellence as two years ago, because

> ... among the peculiarities of this singer, full of initiative and eager for progress, is that of seeming never to do the same. Even in the rôles in which he is best known, one always expects something new from him, and the truth is that one never hopes in vain, for his studious spirit and his instinct for variety continually suggest further novelties to him, albeit of detail, which increase the interest that he continually inspires. ... He sang the duet with the baritone in a dramatic style, singing it from the chest, displaying a full and powerful sonority, from which it could be observed that he has considerably strengthened the centre of his voice.

The critic noted that he poured out the first part of 'Cielo e mar', filled with nuances and cadences, in a way that could be termed celestial; the last phrase, '*sogno d'amor*' (presumably the final repetition of '*sogni d'or*'), was an absolute marvel of beauty. Had the audience accorded him what he deserved, a single burst of applause, or even a '*Bravo!*', at that

---

[27] Felice Forino, in conversation with George S. Shepherd, 1967.

point - standard practice in Italy - it might have had an encore:

> It was a cause for shame that the audience waited until the last high B [flat]
> before showing its approval; what must De Lucia have thought of the deep
> silence that greeted the finest thing that he did during the evening?[28]

In a flowery review, replete with imagery, the critic of *Diario* likened
the De Lucia voice to

> ... the most precious of metals in the hands of the goldsmith. [It] responds to all
> his whims, and it is carved, shaped, and moulded, obedient to his most
> audacious and esoteric fantasies.[29]

For *Italiano*, De Lucia - the 'true *divo*' - had

> ... left behind his affectations, his exaggerated stances and gestures, and
> disagreeable attitudes of head and mouth, abuse of held notes, of *appoggiature*
> and variations. De Lucia has reached perfection, and no tenor can compete with
> him today in the art of *bel canto*. ... While, at times, he reaches maximum
> power in the high register, at times he delights us with *smorzature*, the *mezza
> voce* almost sighing in a way no longer heard since Gayarre.
>   His dramatic prowess equals his musical. Nor - unlike other celebrities -
> does he content himself with emerging at one or two places in the opera;
> De Lucia is always great. He neglects not a word, a phrase or a beat of the
> entire score. Conscientious, ardent, he makes the audience vibrate with the
> emotions and the burdens of the character whom he incarnates and reveals ...
>   [In the duet with Laura] the phrase '*Coi baci in fronte e colle vele al vento*', in
> which De Lucia very tenderly spun down the A sharp of the word '*vele*', to fall
> with the maximum power on to the C sharp - A sharp of the word '*vento*',
> aroused enthusiasm in every connoisseur, and won him an ovation.[30]

After a 'hastily-prepared' *Aida*, which confirmed Mascheroni's own
misgivings at having to produce three operas within a week of arrival,
the next event was the première of *La Bohème*, on May 15th 1897. It took
place under what the critic of *Nación* described as 'the happy star' that
always seemed to shine on the work:

> Last night [it shone] more than ever, thanks to the performance of the tenor
> De Lucia. He alone would have been sufficient, and was sufficient, to spread
> such an atmosphere of life, of intimate feeling and, above all of novelty, through
> Puccini's work that at certain times we seemed to hear something that we did
> not yet know. And this in fact happened: the creation that De Lucia makes of
> the part of Rodolfo is so completely his that one could do a complete tour of the
> world in the absolute certainty of not finding any either equal or in any way
> similar. This creation cannot be reduced to a simple personal achievement, to
> an isolated effect, but it seems to pervade the entire work and shed its light
> through all the action and all the characters. ...
>   [In the first act], what admirable tone De Lucia employed to characterise the
> impression made on him by the unexpected presence of that young woman in

---

28 *Nación*, May 12 1897.

29 *Diario*, quoted in *Gazzetta dei Teatri*, June 24 1897.

30 *Italiano*, quoted in *Gazzetta dei Teatri*, June 24 1897.

his room! What a marvellous way of reflecting, in the control of the voice, the joy that so unexpected and delightful a conquest caused in him! What a marvellous gradation of audacity in his advances towards the gentle interrupter of his tasks! Then, with what effusion in the *racconto*, what varied and opportune inflections, what art of seduction does the Bohemian poet put into the definition of his life, from the words '*Sono un poeta*'! This was the great moment of the work . . . 31

'Always', wrote *Patria Italiana*, 'he gives us something new'. For *Italia al Plata*, De Lucia

> . . . was simply great. . . . At one moment his voice laughs; at others it frolics, weeps, sobs, or sighs. It speaks to us with the gallant cheerfulness of the thoughtless bohemian, the sharpened passion of the enamoured poet, the tears of the lover . . . and with the agony of the heart, lacerated by anxious agony. It makes us laugh and weep, it is impossible to do more or better. The 1st act *racconto* 'Talor del mio forziere' had to be repeated . . . and was sung again in a completely different, but no less perfect way.
> Cesira Ferrani has what the French call *le physique du rôle*, refined, delicate, subtle. . . . What soul, what passion, what sincere and heartfelt sorrow shake and possess that fragile little body, and how the song and the eyes express what is spoken by the word!32

La Bohème was followed by *Rigoletto* and by a much-abbreviated *Manon*. One critic heard his Des Grieux with some impatience:

> [He] would have been a perfect Des Grieux had he not abused his main fault: to sing *mezza voce*, *smorzare*, *filare*, is all right, but in God's name, *falsetto*, always *falsetto* is a little too much.33

As June 20th approached, the English language press of Buenos Aires and Montevideo was preoccupied with the jubilee. Poems in the Sovereign's honour appeared. The outfitters Gath & Chaves launched the 'Victoria cravat'.34 The balls and banquets went on for weeks and doubtless kept still more opera-goers away from the theatre. Ferrari had eventually to launch a new subscription, at reduced prices.

Mefistofele was given on June 24th. De Lucia's conception of Faust was different from Goethe's and he should study the part more carefully, remarked one critic severely.35 But the miracles of *mezza voce* and *portamento* in 'Forma ideal purissima' pleased the Latin taste.36

On July 17th came the novelty, for De Lucia and for the Argentine, of *Werther*, which he sang with Livia Berlendi, Ferrani, and Sammarco. It was his first performance of a part in which he had been interested for

---

31 *Nación*, May 16 1897.

32 *Italia al Plata*, quoted in *Gazzetta dei Teatri*, June 17 1897.

33 *Theatralia*, quoted in *Cosmorama*, July 16 1897.

34 In later years Gath & Chaves also marketed records under their own label.

35 *Standard*, June 25 1897.

36 *Italiano*, in *Gazzetta dei Teatri*, July 29 1897.

some time and which he had studied during summers at Cava. He had visited Vienna and Paris, where he heard the great interpreters, above all Van Dyck.[37] Nor was his study limited to the score and to a libretto which, especially in translation, appeared to him an unrefined copy of the original. And, as the works of Dumas and Mürger helped while away long train journeys and illuminated his performances as Alfredo and Rodolfo, so was his portrayal of Werther based on a study of Goethe.[38]

He impressed by his conception of the part. Indeed, so much of the character did he reveal that, according to some critics, it was difficult to believe that this was his first performance of it. However, the pages of enthusiastic, not to say euphoric, reviews tell us little about specific points of performance. The representative of *Italia al Plata* was, first of all, carried away by the orchestra:

> Sublime, sublime, sublime! The orchestra was superb. Sig. Mascheroni has surpassed himself...
> De Lucia is enamoured of the part of Werther ...To say that he makes a creation of it is to state the truth, he is as great an actor as a singer; he enters the spirit of the personage, he makes flesh of his flesh ...
> I would like to see him without his moustache, and in a wig. It is a small fault, literally a mole, but it mars.[39]

As he finished Ossian's aria the audience exploded into long and noisy applause. But artistic taste prevailed, and he refused the encore which would have broken the spell: '... he was sublime, it is the only word.'[40]

De Lucia's own Sonzogno Italian vocal score of *Werther* bears many handwritten annotations, generally designed to ensure that high notes fall on the vowels which are the easiest ones to sing. A cut of ten bars, from '*I libri!*' (p. 174), leads to Carlotta's '*Ed ecco i versi d'Ossian*', which is marked 'semitone down', a transposition which continues beyond the end of the aria 'Ah, non mi ridestar' ('Pourquoi me réveiller'). In this aria, the phrase '*Di già spuntar il dì.....Del soffrire*' becomes '*Il giorno già vien delle pene*'. The repeat of '*Ah, non mi ridestar*' adds '*Ahimè*' on the high A (p. 177). The phrase '*più che lutto*' is replaced by '*più che tenebre*', replacing '*u*' by '*e*' on a long-held F (p. 179). At '*Capito ho ben?*' (p. 180) score pitch resumes.[41]

The date of the alterations is not shown. However, his 1902 recording [No. 2] of 'Ah! non mi ridestar', which omits the second verse, reflects the first of the textual changes, and the 1917 recording [No. 112] shows all of them. Both versions exhibit a heavier transposition than the indicated

---

37 *Patria degli Italiani*, in *Gazzetta dei Teatri*, Sept. 2 1897. Ernest Van Dyck had created the part (in German) at the world première, Feb. 16 1892.

38 De Lucia family.

39 *Italia al Plata*, in *Gazzetta dei Teatri*, Aug. 26 1897.

40 *Patria degl'Italiani*, in *Gazzetta dei Teatri*, Sept. 2 1897.

41 In mentioning individual notes the marked transposition has been taken into account.

semitone. His score presumably reflects his performances, which spanned 1897-1904, since modifications are marked in passages that he did not record.

Since critics have noted his tendency to make them, we may remark that modifications to cause certain vowels to fall on particular notes have a respectable provenance. Blanche Marchesi, for instance, writes at length on the subject, advising women not to attempt to sing 'u' or 'i' above F sharp, or men to sing an open 'a' on a top note if either wishes to avoid vocal damage.[42] Her own answer was camouflage and, for example, to sing 'Sagfrad' instead of 'Siegfried' on the high A flat of the final scene of *Götterdämmerung*. De Lucia's best-known example - not even as high as F sharp - is possibly *'Tosca sei te!'* instead of '. . . *sei tu!'*, at the end of 'Recondita armonia'.

Werther was the work given for his benefit, on August 5th 1897; after the second act the élite of Buenos Aires demanded five solo curtain calls before presenting him with a remarkable array of gifts: an antique miniature, set in jewels; antique gold studs; a set of diamond and ruby-mounted studs from some habitués of the *cazuela*; a diamond and emerald ring from Ferrari; a gold pencil from Giuseppe Tisci-Rubini; a tie-pin, set with a black oriental pearl; a tie-clip in brilliants and rubies; silver-gilt cuff-links, set with diamonds; silver-mounted walking-sticks; a fur coat; baskets of flowers; a laurel wreath from Mascheroni. The gifts and the applause recognised his part in saving an undistinguished season.[43] There was pleasure in the news that he and Ferrani were expected to return in 1898. He wrote to Pagliara:

August 12th 1897

My dearest Pagliara,

I have written you three letters, with this one, and I have not yet received any reply, while I would have been happy to receive your news.

I received Napoletano's two romanzas, and thank him very much for me. Last night I sang 'Sola, sola' and aroused fanaticism. This romanza was the success of the evening, to my satisfaction. I enclose an article that speaks of the concert and especially of 'Sola sola'.[44] I also enclose an article that speaks of my *serata d'onore* and of my triumphal season here, where I alone bore all the responsibility of the season.

You would do me a great favour if you would report in the newspaper *Il Mattino* all the part of the article which refers to me.

On the 16th of this month we go to Montevideo and on September 16th or 18th we shall leave for Italy. . . .

My Signora salutes you, my sons kiss you, and I embrace you dearly. (SLC)

---

42 B. Marchesi, op. cit., pp. 200-1.

43 *Patria degl'Italiani, in Gazzetta dei Teatri*, Sept. 2 1897.

44 The concert location has not been traced. The several settings of Pagliara's verses 'Sola sola!' include the poet's own, as Mario Perla (see *Fortunio*, Apr. 7 1889), published in *Numero Unico Piedigrotta*, Tipi Bideri, 1889. It was also set by Costa (1890). Daniele Napoletano's setting was one of the *Fortunio* songs for Piedigrotta, 1896 and the reference to him strongly suggests that this was the version sung by De Lucia. Settings of Pagliara's 'Sola!' include versions by Denza and by Van Westerhout (1886).

The company gave its last performance in Buenos Aires on August 15th and, the following day, embarked for Montevideo on the *Venus*. Dining-room, saloons, and cabins glowed with flowers, the parting tribute of the audiences of the Argentine. On board, as on land, the artists formed their cliques: on one side were the basses and baritones; on the other the tenor Mariacher chatted to Ferrani, Guerrini, and other sopranos and contraltos. Alone and silent stood De Lucia, 'the only artist who has led an independent life in the capital'.[45] Arrival in Montevideo was met with similar press interest, some distinctly malicious. The newspapers knew why he had not joined in the customary social life of a visiting operatic troupe. *Siglo* welcomed the return of so many friends. Its reporter did not, as he waited at dawn by the wharf, expect to see De Lucia who 'seemed to sleep a great deal when on board.' He professed surprise that the tenor had come with his wife and two children:

> So. . . . . la Petri?
> Here, we stopped the dialogue, because it was not going very well, and we decided that it was better, with artists, not to ask family questions.
> And, so far as his voice is concerned, how is the great singer?
> Better than ever. His powerful art has overcome every difficulty. . . . It is a matter of waiting . . . to acclaim him as the most passionate tenor of the lyric stage truly merits, the only tenor who, in mastery of delicacy and feeling, has proved a worthy successor to Stagno.[46]

Such mischievous references did not, though, prevent De Lucia from renewing old friendships with members of the press.[47]

Montevideo's appetite for opera had been affected by the heavy fighting of yet another revolution, whose repercussions rumbled on through the winter. When, on August 19th, the company opened in *La Gioconda*, the house was barely two-thirds full of what was termed a 'frigid' audience. A notable absentee was President Borda; he, having proved to be no less corrupt than his predecessor, Herrera, and perhaps recalling events at previous performances of *La Gioconda* in Montevideo, had judged it politic to be elsewhere.

Few of the notices reveal anything new about De Lucia's performance. The *Montevideo Times* (August 21st) remarked that it had to disagree with its contemporaries, whose opinion was that De Lucia had improved since 1895; its own view was that his increased power had been gained at the expense of sweetness and of the 'almost feminine flexibility for which he was remarkable'. He was also criticised for pandering to what was termed the 'degraded River Plate taste for exaggerating the high notes and shouting them *alla* Tamagno'. Both complaints were retracted after *Manon*, but his Enzo did not make the same impression as formerly, nor

---

45 *Nación*, Aug. 19 1897, quoting *Diario*, of Buenos Aires.
46 *Siglo*, Aug. 17 1897.
47 *Nación*, Aug. 18 1897. Newspapers regularly reported visits by singers to their offices.

did it gain the same applause. Even 'Cielo e mar' failed to win an encore but that, the paper conceded, could be blamed on the coldness of the audience.

La Bohème was much better received. De Lucia's performance in it, it was noted, made it easy to understand how the work had brought him, in only eight months, the respectable sum of 250,000 francs.[48] A feature of his singing of 'Che gelida manina', 'interpreted in a manner all his own', was the way in which, unlike other tenors, who sang the phrase '*Talor dal mio forziere*' in full voice, he strongly stressed the words '*L'anima ho milionaria*', starting the ensuing love song very tenderly. At the end of the piece, at '*Deh! parlate...vi piaccia dir*', he took an E flat 'with a long-held thread of voice, in a ravishing *smorzando* which accompanied a deep bow before the trembling girl'.[49] Elsewhere, it was noted that,

> ...[in a] character that does not demand notes, notes and simply notes, nor demand that it be sung at the top of one's voice, the fact that he sometimes exaggerates his methods, as in the duet with Marcello - where he uses too much energy and is a little excessive in expression and gesture - was a small blemish that disappeared in the general excellence of his interpretation.[50]

As the Ciacchi company arrived from the opposite bank of the river, *La Bohème* continued to achieve good notices for Ferrari. The air of revolution persisted, however. When, on August 25th, Borda was shot while leaving the Cathedral after the *Te Deum* to mark the Independence Fêtes, many recalled that De Lucia had been singing in the Cibils Theatre when Santos was shot in 1886. Street disturbances briefly confined the Neapolitan and his family to the hotel, but the assassination had a salutary effect on audiences, who thereafter refused to allow politics to interfere with opera and who thronged the theatres.

On August 28th, the day of De Lucia's début as Werther, one of his sons was taken ill. As it turned out it was not serious, but the anxious tenor went on stage unsure of how soon the good Dr. Borghini, summoned by telegraph, could arrive from Buenos Aires.

Werther did not please everyone. Some termed it monotonous, a long series of solos and duets.[51] More kindly critics admitted that its musical beauties were not easy to find at the beginning.[52] What praise there was came primarily for the performance, for the 'magnificent duet sung by De Lucia and Ferrani ... two souls which pulse with powerful vibrations of love and which communicate ... through notes of extraordinarily dramatic vigour'.[53] De Lucia's family anxieties no doubt impaired his

---

48 *Razon*, in *Gazzetta dei Teatri*, Sept. 30 1897.
49 *Italia al Plata*, in *Gazzetta dei Teatri*, Sept. 30 1897. E flat implies score pitch.
50 *Siglo*, Aug. 23 1897.
51 *Montevideo Times*, Aug. 31 1897.
52 *Siglo*, Aug. 30 1897.
53 Unidentified newspaper, probably *Tribuna Popular*, Aug. 30 1897.

performance; few times, as now, could an audience have remained immobile after Werther's 'romanza'.

Manon followed, and then *Mefistofele*, which seemed to cast a spell on the troupe. Ferrari had an attack of asthma, and was 'coughing and spitting like a Turk', and his singers fared little better. De Lucia had a cold and had no real desire to sing; Giulio Rossi, in putting on his false nose, left inside it a fragment of cardboard that kept him sneezing for half an hour; and that 'flower of youth and beauty' Berlendi had to cover her splendid bosom with a porous plaster to alleviate certain pains. All in all, the Solis resembled a hospital and it was perhaps unsurprising that the opera was poorly received. The circumstances lent a slight air of frivolity to the performance. When, in the scene of the classic Sabbath, the action requires Faust to bow to Helen, De Lucia knelt at Ferrani's feet, where he proceeded, during the 'outpourings of exquisite sweetness and sentimental expression' ('Forma ideal purissima'), to scratch his head and smoothe his hair, provoking the comment that, in those insignificant details, he had decided to tease the public. Yet, even so, *Siglo* remarked, with Stagno dead and Masini in decline, there were

> ...few tenors who possess the exceptional gift of moving us, of weeping while singing, of making us feel in such a deep and extraordinary manner as does this Neapolitan devil, in whose artistic spirit there is as much fire and lava as in the crater of Vesuvius in full eruption.[54]

Opinions on the tenor were mixed that season. *Nación* reported his private diffidence and his conviction that he could never sing well enough for River Plate audiences, whom '...he would like to inspire as he himself is fired by the characters whom he interprets': it remarked that the singer did not realise how well, in fact, he achieved his aims.[55] *Siglo* evidently disagreed when it described the repeat of *La Gioconda* on September 9th as notable only for the duet for Gioconda and Laura in the second act, sung splendidly by Bonaplata-Bau and Guerrini. The rest was

> ...lukewarm, except the '*Tu sei morta*' theme, which De Lucia sang with the feeling and delicacy that he is wont to stamp, at intervals, on his parts.
>
> The 'romanza', for which this tenor is celebrated, and Enzo's other themes were simply stuttered and truncated without the public's finding any general fault. But the audience is inclined to indulge the mutilations and caprices of an artist provided that he *gratifies the ear* with *fioriture* and interpolations which informed criticism condemns and which even reasonably discriminating audiences will not stomach.[56]

Sharpening its claws, *Siglo* claimed that *Revista Artistica* and

---

54 *Siglo*, Sept. 3 1897.
55 *Nación*, Aug. 19 1897.
56 *Siglo*, Sept. 10 1897.

Montevideo Musical shared its views on the artist

> ... who, vainglorious today, doubtless believes himself to be a luminary of the first magnitude, while we consider him to be merely an acceptable singer. De Lucia should not have made excuses to a society that has elevated him ... to a height that, in any rigorous discussion of his worth, without any sort of conventionality, he does not deserve artistically.[57]

This outburst by *Siglo* - contrasting with earlier, complimentary, notices - reflected the fact that De Lucia, pleading indisposition, had excused himself from a benefit performance on September 20th for the musical society 'La Lira'. South American audiences, perhaps in the belief that they were considered an operatic backwater, seemed very sensitive to such things; years after the event, Buenos Aires had neither forgotten nor forgiven Patti for having declined to sing in a benefit in 1889. But there was to be no need - or opportunity - for De Lucia to redeem himself with River Plate audiences, for he never sang there again.

In Naples, the San Carlo, under Musella's management, opened on St. Stephen's Day, December 26th, with *La Bohème*. The opening, to judge from the applause and the calls, was a triumph; in the lobbies the discussion was somewhat more analytical than at the work's first performance there, in 1896. For *Pungolo* it was a reminder both of its inspired and of its insignificant pages.[58] The Marcello, Mario Roussel, was admired for a fine voice and sound technique; Angelica Pandolfini obtained an undoubted success for her

> ... limpid, pealing, exquisitely educated voice [which] possesses fluidity, ductility and warmth ... [She] does not forget that she is Mimì and not a superior melodramatic creature. Her gesture and her attack do not conflict ... with the mediocrity of her condition and the poverty of her dress.[59]

The *Pungolo* critic wrote that 'she relies on the gracious and cultivated singing of well-shaped phrases, and on a refined and true interpretation of the character rather than on purely vocal art. She prefers to be a soul rather than a throat.'[60] But for this Neapolitan audience the promise of their great - now indisputably great - tenor would alone have brought them to the San Carlo. Above all, they agreed that

> ... 'Il Commendatore', as now suffices to identify him, improves, maturing like a generous wine. Neither could the excesses of his numerous friends in the theatre last night diminish the fascination of that soft melodiousness, of that exceptional mellowness of voice, of that tenderness of vocal inflection that make him the most acclaimed tenor of the solar system.[61]

---

57 Ibid., Sept. 22 1897, quoting *Montevideo Musical*.
58 *Pungolo*, Dec. 27/28 1897.
59 *Corriere di Napoli*, Dec. 27 1897.
60 *Pungolo*, Dec. 27/28 1897.
61 Ibid.

Mattino pondered on whether De Lucia owed a debt to Puccini, or *vice versa*. The tenor's refinement of the part was such that he could well be forgiven 'several minuscule blemishes, and some small liberties':

> The timbre of the voice . . . is always of a crystalline limpidity, the intonation is always impeccable, the method admirable, and the artist lavishes his treasures *a gran signore* without ever the public's being able to notice a moment of uncertainty or exertion, an expedient, a doubt . . . And as I have already admired the fidelity of Fernando De Lucia to the musical text (even the two insignificant *transpositions* observed by some pedants are permitted by the composer, such that they appear in the score) I cannot recommend him earnestly enough to guard against . . . poetic tampering, such as *'mio ben'* substituted in the first act for *'Chi son'*, perhaps for ease of syllabification.62

Pungolo criticised effects which were often in bad taste, but nevertheless noted that 'the bewitching quality of his voice won over the audience'.63 A comment on the second performance is revealing:

> . . . why the silence . . . at the end of the second act? . . . [It is] because the tenor sings little or, one should say, De Lucia sings little; he has a small part, and for Neapolitans nothing counts when De Lucia's part does not reflect him alone.64

Pungolo was less severe when, on February 20th, he sang his first Naples Alfredo, in *La Traviata*. He was greeted with applause: he was

> . . . a charmer of ears . . . . His vocal colouring is always correct. In the last act one observed all the impetuous, southern feeling that is one of the most-appreciated characteristics of De Lucia's dramatic art. This part is, indeed, rather a hard one for [him]; the tenor parts of Verdi's second period are often a challenge to the lungs, especially when a tenor has De Lucia's type of voice. But . . . [he] seems to be able to sing full-bloodedly while retaining the modulated grace that typifies him, and he is indeed an ideal . . . Alfredo.65

Tribuna Sport commented that, now that Nicolini and Stagno were no more, De Lucia alone preserved the traditions of the rôle. *Don Marzio* observed that, like those two,

> . . . when their periods as *virtuosi* were over: *he sang*. And he sang exquisitely and magisterially.66

However, both De Lucia and the intelligent and tasteful baritone Eugenio Giraldoni were overshadowed by Pandolfini.67

---

62 *Mattino*, Dec. 27/28 1897. Though the transpositions are unspecified, one was probably the optional B which replaces the high C of 'Che gelida manina'. The *'mio ben'* appears in neither of his recordings of the piece.

63 *Pungolo*, Dec. 29/30 1897.

64 *Cosmorama*, Jan. 9 1898.

65 *Pungolo*, Feb. 21/22 1898.

66 Quoted in *Rassegna Melodrammatica*, Apr. 23 and Apr. 1 1898, respectively.

67 Michael Henstock, 'Some notes on Angelica Pandolfini', *Recorded Sound*, No. 38, Apr. 1970, pp. 622-5.

De Lucia's records of *La Traviata* have been much analysed. The 1906 version of 'De' miei bollenti spiriti' [No. 38] lasts some 2 minutes 40 seconds (in D flat), of which perhaps half is pianissimo singing; it is spacious enough to permit him, on *'dell'amor'*, to insert a rapid *gruppetto* and to observe the written *ppp*. And yet we never feel that the tempo is sluggish. By contrast, Jan Peerce, conducted by Toscanini, requires only 1 minute 35 seconds; most of his singing is *mezza forte*, and he conveys little of the sense or sentiments of the aria.[68] In 1932, Hurst invited his readers to listen to De Lucia's recording and to '. . . say whether you have heard anyone else put so much beautiful singing into it; from the softest *pp* to the full power of a perfectly equipped voice he shows complete control of every detail of singing'.[69] What Shawe-Taylor has called a 'subtle and spirited performance' is remarkable for its rhythmic hesitations, for two wonderful *morendi* on the high G flat (the piece is transposed by a tone), and for the way that his

> . . . vivid enunciation of the text (how memorably he declaims the words *Dal dì che disse 'Vivere io voglio a te fedel'*) captures all the ardour and youthful happiness of Alfredo.[70]

Steane, too, draws attention to the record for its illustration of the legitimate dramatic possibilities of imaginative departure from the score. This

> . . . marvellous piece of singing . . . brings our listening on to a different plane. Here we have someone who can do wonderful things with the voice - things I suppose he would never be allowed to do today. Yet this art, free as it is in its handling of the score, does in fact *serve* the music, so that although Verdi has given no such directions, De Lucia's fine spinning-out of the climax sustains the moment as a magical, precious thing . . . . This is no mere vocal exhibitionism, for De Lucia's style is actually more 'inner' than any of the [other recordings of the piece]: I mean that at the opening of the solo we feel ourselves listening to a soliloquy, sung here with rapt tenderness that takes one close to the singer as a dramatic character. There are innumerable places where we could catch De Lucia out if we believe in absolute fidelity to the score: but this record seems to provide a good example of those rare instances of inspired deviation which in fact *add* a delight.[71]

De Lucia's 1904 recording of 'Un dì felice' [No. 19] takes 2 minutes 10 seconds (in E). It is, for some tastes, too long-drawn. But the portamento to *'Di quell'amor'* is magical. When he sings of the power of love as the heartbeat of the universe, *'Di quell'amor . . . ch'è palpito . . . dell'universo intero, misterioso . . . '*, it sounds like the passionate declaration that it is. Peerce and Toscanini take 59 seconds; they ignore Verdi's *'con grazia'*; the sense of mystery has fled.

---

68 Crutchfield (1983), p. 13.

69 Hurst, *Gramophone*, Dec. 1932, p. 305.

70 Shawe-Taylor (1955), p. 437, and *Gramophone*, July 1953, p. 33.

71 Steane, op. cit., pp. 581-2.

Two weeks after the première of *La Bohème*, Michele Uda examined De Lucia's progress in the twelve years since his début at the San Carlo. This second San Carlo *Bohème* was, he felt, less good than its predecessor. The exception was its Rodolfo. This season, *La Bohème*

... comes before the public and critics re-baptised with the name of its success; this year's *La Bohème* is called De Lucia.

De Lucia is not only a marvellous tenor; he is, above all, impassioned of his art, a subtle seeker after the secrets of expression, a refined moulder of the musical phrase, whether of grace, sentiment or passion. From time to time, first as Turiddu, then as Fritz, then as José, then as Rodolfo, he loves to return to the great stage, to the public which, in its acclaim, first detected the dawn of his glory. And he returns to submit, for our verdict, a hitherto-unknown side of his talent as an interpreter: the patient study for a new effect, a vocal audacity not previously attempted, a long-desired polish, a summit of aesthetic expression fully attained. And he returns ... with the strength of the Neapolitan of Naples reinvigorated by the northern triumphs of St. Petersburg, of New York, of London; with a more robust, more extended, warmer voice - the voice which, in the new Rodolfo, surprised the other evening and sustained, after the final duet of the third act, such an ardent, insistent, roaring rapture of applause ... Have you still in your ears, as I have, the delicate, pale, almost sexless sweetness of that first *Faust* at the San Carlo? And, thinking again of it, are you not surprised at the rapid transformation of the *tenorino* of that time who, after *Cavalleria Rusticana*, after *I Pescatori di Perle*, after *Carmen*, after the Spanish enthusiasm for *L'Elisir d'Amore* and for *La Sonnambula*, returns to the San Carlo, risks *Lohengrin*, and is confirmed as an artist of *grande repertorio* in five famous performances?

Today, in *La Bohème*, the part of Rodolfo is the only one that has new colour in a musically and scenically perfect interpretation. Another step would be exaggeration; one further, mannerism. He knows that the ideal has been attained. You will see that the nervous restlessness of his search will pause, going forward in another opera - *Tosca*, perhaps. Meanwhile, with talent well balanced by study, with impulses born of passion, enriched by a wonderful voice that is not a trick of a throat patiently and mechanically educated in singing, ... he makes the music of others his own property; he is exalted by the talent of the composer: he feels its ardour breaking forth from the inspiration; he creates - as a subordinate, but he creates - the dramatic personage; he gives it flesh, blood, sinews, action, life, with such an illusion of truth as to make two very different successes - one is that of the maestro, the other is that of his interpretation - into a single success, as much for the spectator who submits to his spell as for the critic who discusses it. The spectator jumps to his feet and proclaims the triumph. The critic hurries to the newspaper and sings his praises there. The artist, in the full maturity of a youthful talent, resourceful, strong, ambitious, gazes on high, even beyond the sky where *La Bohème* glitters, and he smiles in the spotlight of apotheosis.[72]

The season did not, however, finish happily for De Lucia. On December 30th 1897, after a day when he had seemed to be in good health, he had suffered an *abbassamento di voce* at the start of the performance of *La Bohème*. He had completed the first act and his brief phrases in the second before the opera was abandoned. The theatre had then remained closed until January 5th, when Gorga, whom Musella had

---

[72] Article dated Jan. 10 1898, in Uda, op. cit., Vol. II, pp. 151-3.

engaged at short notice, had sung Rodolfo. On January 6th De Lucia declared himself fit to sing again. Musella, however, was in no hurry to restore him to the cast, and it was January 13th before the San Carlo audience was able to welcome him back to the stage. Subsequently, he shared the part of Rodolfo with Gorga and, still later, with other tenors.

There was then a disagreement with Musella over fees. De Lucia's contract with him provided for twenty-four performances in the period December 26th 1897 - April 10th 1898, with no two on consecutive days, and a fee of 2,100 lire per appearance, payable on the morning of the performance.[73] Instead, apart from non-subscription performances and gala occasions outside his contract, he had sung only twenty times. The two men were unable to resolve the matter amicably and on April 9th 1898 De Lucia took his case to the courts, initially over the fee for the curtailed performance. Later, he claimed a further 6,300 lire for the other performances by which he had fallen short of the agreed number. The Court found in his favour, and ordered Musella to pay 8,400 lire, interest, and all the costs.[74]

But the rift would keep De Lucia from the boards of the San Carlo for the next two seasons. Musella appealed, pointing out that he had agreed to extend the season to make good the shortfall and had also offered De Lucia a rôle in De Leva's opera *La Camargo*. Neither course had been acceptable to the tenor. The case turned on whether De Lucia's contract entitled him, *in the stated period*, to the agreed number of performances *of operas acceptable to him*, or whether Musella was within his rights to schedule operas and singers for his own convenience. The season was quite long enough, it was argued, to give three additional performances of *La Bohème*, had Musella so wished. De Lucia, hinted the press, had a *de facto* monopoly of the part of Rodolfo at the San Carlo;[75] he and some of the subscribers may well have been annoyed that Gorga had replaced him. The Court of Appeal drew a distinction between the performance curtailed through illness - for which the artist was responsible - and the three performances for which Musella had not called upon De Lucia. It decreed that the manager should pay only 6,300 lire and three-quarters of the legal costs of the previous and present cases.[76] Musella took the case to the Supreme Court of Naples, which overturned the original verdict.[77] The matter was not resolved until 1901, when the Court of Appeal again upheld Musella.[78]

---

[73] De Lucia's agreed complimentary tickets were: two boxes in specified rows, 18 stalls, and 10 gallery places, with a total of 30 *ingressi* (general admission fee) in all.

[74] Tribunale di Napoli, No. 473, June 24 - July 1 1898.

[75] 'Why is De Lucia the only Rodolfo, and why is the San Carlo public deprived?' (Despatch from Naples, Jan. 2 1898, in *Cosmorama*, Jan. 9 1898.) For whatever reason, it is certainly true that, until De Lucia's illness, no other tenor had sung the part at that theatre.

[76] Corte di Appello di Napoli, No. 1757, Aug. 24 - 29 1898.

[77] Corte di Cassazione di Napoli, No. 558, Dec. 19 1898 - Jan. 21 1899.

[78] Corte di Appello di Napoli, No. 109, Jan. 25 - 30 1901.

Domestically, matters were again deteriorating. Since her attempt, in 1895, to gain a legal separation, Itala and the children had accompanied Fernando on some of his travels. Clearly, it was no more than an armed truce, imposed by circumstance. The taciturnity and solitariness noted in South America were uncharacteristic of the singer. There was no love lost between him and Itala's family, either, and the rift had deepened in 1891, when the death of Eduardo De Giorgio had obliged his widow, Penelope, to borrow from her son-in-law. Relations must have been in a parlous state by May 1898, for his reaction, when the De Giorgio family defaulted on its repayments, was an uncompromising threat to foreclose on the loan.[79]

---

[79] Precetto 16386/6251, Conservatoria Registri Immobiliari, Naples, May 11 1898.

15

Hams and Mortadella

... it is better to return to the modest conductors of earlier times ... When I began to scandalise the musical world with my misdeeds there was the calamity of the Rondo of the *prima donna*; today there is the tyranny of the conductors! Bad, bad! But the former is the lesser evil!!   Giuseppe Verdi[1]

The year 1898 brought De Lucia once again into contact with Mascagni, who was working on *Iris*, his only opera for Ricordi. Like that of almost all Mascagni's affairs, its progress was convoluted. His direct dealings with Ricordi went back as least as far as May 1890 when, while the composer awaited Sonzogno's decision on whether to take up *Cavalleria Rusticana* - which the terms of the *Concorso Sonzogno* did not oblige Sonzogno to do - he had offered *Cavalleria* to Ricordi should the rival publishing house decline it.[2]

Subsequently, Mascagni - probably after a disagreement with Sonzogno - contracted with Ricordi to publish his opera *Guglielmo Ratcliff*. In December 1892, with the manuscript long overdue, Ricordi asked Eugenio Checchi to intercede 'delicately' to establish the status of the work.[3] Mascagni claimed to have misunderstood the date for completion. Ricordi, although clearly angry, agreed to defer *Ratcliff* until 1893. Subsequently, Sonzogno contested Ricordi's contractual right to publish it. After some bickering it was agreed that Sonzogno should have the rights both to *Ratcliff* and to certain future Mascagni operas. *Zanetto* (1896) was the first of these. Mascagni remained under an obligation to write an opera for Ricordi, who began to search for a subject. The composer - whose relationships with both publishers were, to say the least, volatile and inconsistent - thought that his contract with Ricordi had been almost extorted, calling him, in a bitter letter of September 1896, his 'imposed publisher'.[4]

Mascagni was initially attracted by Zola's *Nanà*, and even obtained permission to use it. The idea of *Iris* came about through a meeting, at

---

[1] Verdi - Giulio Ricordi, Mar. 18 1899, in Franco Abbiati, *Giuseppe Verdi*, Vol. IV, p. 638. He referred to Toscanini.

[2] (R) Mascagni - G. Ricordi, May 19 1890.

[3] (R) G. Ricordi - Checchi, Dec. 9 and 15 1892.

[4] Letter Mascagni - Illica, Sept. 26 1896, Morini, *Mascagni*, Vol. I, pp. 312-13.

Ricordi's instigation, with Luigi Illica. The poet had originally thought of it for Franchetti who, however, had put it aside in favour, first, of *Tosca* and then of *Germania*.[5] At any rate, the subject was in Mascagni's mind in late 1895 or early 1896, and by March 1896 he was finally in agreement with Ricordi.[6]

In addition to his new responsibilities as Director of the Liceo Rossini at Pesaro, Mascagni had now to deal with two publishers simultaneously, and every day brought the risk of alienating one or the other. His contract with Ricordi required *Iris* to be ready for inclusion in the manifesto of a major Italian theatre in the winter of 1896-7. In fact, his obligations elsewhere gave him no hope of completing it in time; his next opera for Sonzogno was due before the end of 1897. Sonzogno, on learning the details of Mascagni's contract with Ricordi, demanded that *Iris* should not be delivered before his own opera was ready or, at least, that the works should be despatched contemporaneously so that his own new Mascagni work could compete with *Iris*. Thus, Mascagni was engaged on two operas for publishers who were at odds with one another.[7] Indeed, in June 1898 Sonzogno accused him of breach of contract. As he had done three years earlier to Leoncavallo,[8] he suspended his monthly advances and withheld quarterly royalties.

The choice of tenor for the première of *Iris* was not straightforward. As early as April 1896 Illica seems to have favoured Garbin for the part of Osaka.[9] By September 1897, however, a Buenos Aires newspaper was reporting that, 'in a few months', De Lucia would create both Osaka in *Iris* and Cavaradossi in Puccini's *Tosca*.[10] Notwithstanding, in May 1898 the tenor De Marchi[11] accompanied Illica to visit Mascagni and much impressed the composer, who wrote to Ricordi:

> The short visit by Illica and by De Marchi ... was a real pleasure: the opera seems to have made a good impression on De Marchi; the part fits him like a glove; he has sung me the *Serenata* of Jor in full voice and I can guarantee that it is a piece of a secure effect (sung thus) ...
> De Marchi will come to you to discuss *Iris* - to me he seems well disposed. By now there is no longer any doubt for the *prima* at the end of September.[12]

The proposal of De Marchi did not last for long since, on June 24th 1898, at the end of a 12-page letter (in which he excused himself for his

5 Contract dated Jul. 24 1894, Mario Morini, 'Iris e i progetti non realizzati', in *Pietro Mascagni nel 1º Centenario*, p. 195.
6 Letter Ricordi - Illica, ibid., p. 203.
7 The Sonzogno work, *Le Maschere*, was not in fact performed until Jan. 1901.
8 Letter Giordano - Illica, Apr. 1895, Morini, *Giordano*, pp. 280-1.
9 Letter Illica - G. Ricordi, Apr. 1 1896, Morini, 'Iris e i progetti', p. 204.
10 *Patria degl'Italiani*, quoted in *Gazzetta dei Teatri*, Sept. 2 1897.
11 De Lucia was evidently on good terms with De Marchi (1861-1917), whom he had visited during the latter's illness at Naples in March 1898.
12 (R) May 16 1898.

haste) largely concerned with the instrumentation of *Iris* and the choice of conductor for Rome, Mascagni wrote to Ricordi:

> And now there seems nothing else to say - Ah! - The *tenor* - They speak to me of De Lucia: certainly he is a great artist but his voice is short: one needs to alter the entire opera. Who is this Colli? . . . 13

However, by July 1898 De Lucia had been confirmed for the part.14 Clearly, the rôle of Osaka was not written for his voice, a practice that was by then almost obsolete. This view is reinforced by the fact that, at the première, he transposed the 'Serenata', so setting a precedent which has been followed by many a grateful tenor to the point at which it might be termed traditional. If, indeed, the part was tailored to any particular tenor it is likely to have been De Marchi. An analysis of the *tessitura* of the tenor part indicates its demands. The 'Serenata' ('Apri la tua finestra'), marked *'dolcissimo ed espressivo'*, although woven on the notes most favoured by lyric tenors, is onerous because of its phrasing. We observe, at the words *'a me, fanciulla'*, a prolonged A natural, falling to F sharp. The 'andante' *'Iris, son io! Io sono Osaka, Jor'* (Ricordi vocal score pp. 237-8) is taxing, with the solid and increasing pressure of the orchestra. In the final cry of *'Iris ancor, ancor ti voglio!'* (pp. 243-4), only a voice with vigour and penetration in the region between F and A flat can make itself heard.15

Naples and Rome were the principal contenders for the honour of staging the première. Mascagni, while accepting that Musella, at the San Carlo, would provide excellent *mise-en-scène* and first class singers, evidently had reservations about the Neapolitan public.16 Rome was obviously his favoured city, and there was little real question that the Costanzi would ultimately be preferred.

After his holiday at Salsomaggiore De Lucia was in Rome early in October to start rehearsals.17 On October 21st Mascagni arrived to continue preparations for the première. The orchestral readings were to start on the 26th and orchestral rehearsals on November 7th under the direction of the composer.18

Tension arose during rehearsals. There were gibes by Mascagni who, determined to have his intentions observed both on the stage and in the pit, did battle with first one, then another of the artists. Darclée, it was rumoured, no longer wished to sing in the new opera.19 Illica wrote to Giulio Ricordi, who had returned to Milan to avoid the unpleasantness that attended the Costanzi in the days before the première:

13 (R) Mascagni refers to the Sicilian tenor Ernesto Colli (d. 1928), teacher of Hipólito Lazaro.
14 *Cosmorama*, July 10 1898.
15 Gara, 'Cantanti Mascagnani', loc. cit., p. 225.
16 (R) Mascagni - G. Ricordi, Oct. 6 1897.
17 *Rassegna Melodrammatica*, Oct. 1 1898.
18 (R) Mascagni - Ricordi, Pesaro, Oct. 21 1898.
19 *Cosmorama*, Nov. 21 1898.

... One incident finished and closed, another starts; and these incidents are not the usual gossip, ill-humour, nerves, etc. Here all is lunacy. Such an atmosphere has been created that Tito [Ricordi] has lost six kilograms and I am already almost prostrate with running from one to another, placating this one, calming that. Minds have become poisoned with that accursed influence that is in the air of all stages. Insults, rages, fur flying, wives in a fury like cats, outbursts of anger, harangues (these are what annoy most of all) that are as long and interminable as they are vain and empty, threats, unlikely adjectives, uproar over a glance, fantastic interpretations if someone breathes a little too hard. This is the stage; the orchestra below is a volcanic land ... in expectation ... if you oblige me to make a judgement I would say that *Iris* is an opera of the mad-house ... 20

Amid such inconsequential incidents was a more serious altercation, between Mascagni and the conductor Edoardo Mascheroni who, as musical director of the Costanzi, was to conduct *Iris*. Mascagni was clearly outraged by this prospect. Months before the première he had complained to Ricordi that Mascheroni - who had long enjoyed the publisher's confidence in many matters - had given *Cavalleria Rusticana* at Barcelona with insufficient rehearsal, bringing him and his work into ridicule. One passage of his long and detailed letter is most significant:

Pesaro, June 24 1898

... *Iris* will have the performance that I want, and Signor Mascheroni will have to bow to the wishes of the composer. One must remember that [at Rome] ... Toscanini was engaged to conduct *I Rantzau*: but Toscanini remained simply a listener and spectator, while I myself conducted *I Rantzau*. I state this to avoid future misunderstandings: *Iris* is very difficult in its orchestration and above all in its interpretation: I do not believe M⁰ Mascheroni capable of understanding it ... 21

What ensued was inevitable. At the third rehearsal (November 10th) Mascagni - no longer the unassuming youngster - made lively interjections. There were frequent differences of opinion on points of interpretation. The rehearsal had almost finished when Mascheroni asked Mascagni:

Well, how does it seem to you?
Yes. I am not dissatisfied, quite the reverse, in fact! but.....
But?
But *it lacks personality!*

Into this equivocal phrase Mascheroni read an insult! Rising from his seat, he handed the baton to Mascagni and was gone.22
The orchestra sent Mascheroni a letter of support, stating that only

---

20 Illica - G. Ricordi, Rome, Nov. 10 1898, Morini, '*Iris* e i progetti', p. 222.

21 (R) Two years later, Mascagni would say the same of Mugnone and the première of *Iris* at Bologna.

22 *Corriere dei Teatri*, Nov. 20 1898. More dramatic accounts have it that he snapped his baton and threw the pieces at Mascagni.

duty had prevented it from following him.[23] *Tribuna* published an open letter from the conductor to Mascagni:

> Rome, November 11th
>
> Dear Maestro,
>
> Wishing to allow you the pleasure of directing your new opera *Iris*, I willingly relinquish my post, wishing you the splendid success for which I have worked until today, with the orchestral preparation with which you had been very ready to declare yourself satisfied, as much with me as with the members of the Roman Orchestra.[24]

It is not impossible that Mascagni, with his almost obsessive desire to conduct his own works and so to enjoy the added acclaim that his presence conferred upon them, had deliberately provoked the whole affair. However, although an acrimonious public exchange of letters took place over several days, the only apparent effect was to delay the première slightly. The composer, now unarguably in charge, was pictured as he worked in the half-light of the theatre, his face 'illuminated as if the glowing images of the music are transmuted into visible reflections'. Cigar in mouth, he prowled nervously from one orchestral desk to another, or jumped on to the stage to alter a piece of scenery, or to move a fan or piece of furniture.[25]

On November 11th there was a quarrel between Mascagni and De Lucia. To this day, its cause and nature are uncertain. It has been suggested that De Lucia, an old friend of Mascheroni, resented Mascagni's treatment of the conductor. More probably, it arose from the composer's unhappiness with aspects of the performance: it is no secret that, after the première, he expressed anger at the demands made by the singers and at the concessions made to their 'deficiencies and poor taste'. Gara identifies the transposition of the 'Serenata' as the root of the disagreement.[26] It appears that during the rehearsals of *Iris* De Lucia slapped Mascagni, and that the composer accepted it, not wishing to lose the tenor's services.[27] However that may be, the following morning De Lucia unequivocally declined to sing the opera.[28] Despite entreaties from Tito Ricordi, Illica, and the other singers, he remained resolute, and for a day or so the performance seemed seriously compromised. However, theatrical storms are often brief, and by November 13th - notwithstanding mischievous gossip that had the two *Commendatori* squaring for a fight - De Lucia was back at his post as Mascagni prepared to direct the first rehearsal with singers and orchestra.

---

[23] *Corriere della Sera*, Nov. 15-16 1898.

[24] *Tribuna*, Nov. 12 1898.

[25] *Fanfulla*, Nov. 21 1898.

[26] Gara, letter to the writer, July 1969. His source was not stated.

[27] Francesco Canessa, 'Un grande tenore liberty', *Mattino*, Feb. 21 1975. This *'incidente degli schiaffi'* has passed into operatic folklore.

[28] *Lombardia*, Nov. 12 1898.

Rehearsals finished amicably on November 19th. The *prova generale* took place the next day. As he left it, Jean de Reszke is reported to have said, with a preoccupied air: 'It is a formidable and magnificent masterpiece.'

Iris had focused the interest which always surrounded Mascagni at Rome. For weeks the city had been full of advertisements in the Japanese style, as its musical press printed indiscretions and anecdotes from the 'well-informed'. Much was made of the authentic oriental sounds achieved with specially-made *tam-tam* cymbals and wind instruments. A special edition of the newspaper *Don Chisciotte* included photographs of Darclée, De Lucia, and Mascagni. For a select group, De Lucia, with Mascagni at the piano, sang the 'Serenata' from the new opera.[29] Such publicity ensured that, despite extremely high prices, the theatre - especially the amphitheatre and the 'gods' - was crowded for the première on November 22nd 1898. So great was the demand for favourable gallery positions that the waiting throng forced entry three hours before the normal hour for the sale of tickets.

An excited audience, including Jean de Reszke, Giulio Gatti-Casazza, Siegfried Wagner, and the principal critics of Europe and the Americas awaited the new work. At precisely 8.30 pm, Queen Margherita and the Prince of Naples[30] entered the Teatro Costanzi. After Mascagni had conducted the Royal March there was great applause and a cry of *'Viva Mascagni!'* Then the house darkened and the hubbub ceased.

'The symphonic prelude "The Hymn to the Sun" seemed', commented Pompei, 'to have been designed deliberately to enrapture the audience.' That night, the first section passed almost in silence; only at the Dawn theme, 'its tender, spacious phrase echoed in the chords of the unseen chorus and closing in the majestic key of D major, did the throng that packed the theatre explode in clamorous and interminable applause'. The 'Serenata', sung by De Lucia, was repeated. There were twelve calls for Mascagni.

The second act, judged better than the first, was an unbroken triumph both for composer and singers. Darclée had to repeat her *racconto* and De Lucia the phrases *'Or dammi il braccio tuo'*. In the following scene he touched new heights of excellence.[31]

In the opinion of some the drama ended with this act, where the opera itself might well have finished. The critics noted a certain monotony in the 'musically empty' third act, which was shortened for the second performance. The mood of the public changed. Within a few minutes the thermometer of interest dropped to zero. An epidemic of 'asinine' coughing rapidly developed in the theatre. It was an unpleasant quarter

---

29 *Corriere di Teatri*, Nov. 20 1898.

30 The future King Vittorio Emanuele III.

31 *Fanfulla*, Nov. 24 1898.

of an hour until the public's curiosity overcame its tyranny and calm was restored.[32] The act closed exultantly with the Hymn to the Sun.

If critical opinion was harsh towards the libretto it was generally favourable towards the music and its interpreters. Its orchestration was 'sublime'. Mascagni had shown himself 'a master of harmony and melody. . . . *Iris* is a lofty work of art, and will endure.' For Checchi, *Iris* was Mascagni's best work, Italian in form, style, and melody. Others, through the manner in which the instruments predominated over the voices, detected a concession to the theories of Wagner. If hardly as marketable as *Cavalleria Rusticana*, the new work was judged superior to it, although requiring a theatre and artists of the first rank. Darclée and De Lucia were 'not the singers of the opera but the composer's collaborators'.[33]

The disagreement with Mascagni had, perhaps, taken its toll of De Lucia's nervous energy. At any rate, he was judged to have sung 'less well than his vocal means and his artistic intelligence had made one anticipate'.[34] Elsewhere, we read:

> De Lucia is today one of the most acclaimed tenors: his means are not powerful but more than sufficient, and his timbre [is] among the most beautiful: most skilful in joining the head notes to the others, his ascents are never perilous, although he sang in E the first 'serenata', written in F; we would take no exception to that did he not, as Osaka, by now tend too evidently to certain formalities, not to say to certain affectations of guttural singing which, in his last years, had become the hallmark of Roberto Stagno.[35]

Another critic wrote:

> . . . of [great impact] was the *romanza*, the *canzone*, the *serenata* - all in all that beautiful thing that De Lucia, half-concealed by a puppet theatre, sang to a marionette. . . . I do not know whether the greater effect was due to the inimitable grace of De Lucia's singing or to the opportunity - truly remarkable in a modern opera - of being able to hear a simple and gracious melody expressed by a human voice, without its being complicated or overpowered by a monstrous orchestra.
>
> Mascagni owes much of his success to his collaborators. . . . Signora Darclée, together with De Lucia, truly a tenor musician, *rara avis*, form a couple that it would be difficult to equal. . . . Both had to battle against the not inconsiderable demands of the *tessitura*, and overcame them with aplomb.[36]

This was not the only review to suggest that the main success of the 'Serenata' was due to De Lucia. Critics noted his *smorzature*, the 'effects

---

[32] Morini, '*Iris* e i progetti', p. 227.

[33] *Corriere dei Teatri*, Nov. 30 1898.

[34] *Corriere della Sera*, Nov. 23-4 1898.

[35] *Natura e Arte*, Dec. 5 1898. Gualerzi, 'Cavalcata canora', loc. cit., p. 361, states that De Lucia transposed the 'Serenata' by a tone. His source is not given.

[36] *Tribuna*, Nov. 24 1898.

which are special to him', the inimitably recondite feeling that he gave to
the phrase of the kiss (*'E questo il bacio!'*),[37] and that:

> ... He is always the *God* of tenors. He drew miraculous effects from his part
> and enchanted the listeners with his celestial voice.[38]

Leopoldo Bandini wrote:

> And De Lucia? He is always the *tenore di grazia*, the tender artist of sweetest
> voice, of crystalline purity, who intoxicates you and forces you to applaud, so
> great is the fascination and power [which] vibrate in his warm and passionate
> phrases.[39]

Even for Mascagni's old friend Checchi the opera owed much of its
success to the principal singers; in particular 'the beautiful, ringing,
exquisite voice of Fernando De Lucia held flatteries and caresses,
fascinating suppleness ...'.[40]

Credit went to the orchestra, which Mascagni was adjudged to have
conducted in most worthy and distinguished fashion. For the composer's
serata d'onore on December 13th *Iris* was accompanied by the Cherry
Duet, from *L'Amico Fritz*, sung by De Lucia and Darclée, and by some of
his other works. This programme was repeated two nights later, the
closure of the season, for the benefit of the two singers.[41]

Mascagni and his music also featured prominently in the celebrations
of the Circolo Artistico of Rome on December 9th, when many of the
distinguished gathering, unable to get in, had to listen from the corridors
as Caruson,[42] Darclée, and De Lucia sang, accompanied by Mascagni at
the piano. A similar concert took place at the Grand Hôtel on December
16th, with Cotogni, Darclée, and De Lucia.

The troubles which bedevilled *Iris* at the Costanzi were as the cooing
of doves compared with the events at La Scala two months later. Their
appreciation requires some retrospection. Even at the time of *Cavalleria
Rusticana*, Mascagni had considered that transposition damaged the
tonality of his work. No doubt he had then thought it politic to
accommodate Stagno and to transpose two pieces for the famous tenor.[43]
His correspondence, though, makes it clear that the interpreters of *Iris*
at Rome had made transpositions which he found unacceptable. Those

---

37 *Rassegna Melodrammatica*, Dec. 1 1898.
38 *Cosmorama*, Nov. 27 1898.
39 *Rassegna Melodrammatica*, Dec. 5 1898.
40 *Fanfulla*, Nov. 24 1898.
41 *Tribuna*, Dec. 17 1898.
42 Guglielmo Caruson, the first Kyoto in *Iris*.
43 Mascagni - Lina Mascagni, Rome, May 5 1890. 'Tonight I have had to stay up to work on the score.
Since Stagno transposes two pieces, I have had enormous toil to make this transposition and then return to
pitch, without the audience's being aware of it.' (Pompei, op. cit., p. 79.) Mascagni's irritation may have been
increased when Stagno, claiming that the original text was not Sicilian, changed the words of the 'Siciliana'
and overrode the composer on points of interpretation. (Ricci, *34 Anni con Pietro Mascagni*, pp. 25 and 31.)

same principals were also to perform *Iris* at La Scala, and by now he felt able to protest. Through a theatrical irony, the conductor at Milan was to be Toscanini, whom Mascagni had so slighted during the preparation of *I Rantzau* at the Costanzi, six years earlier. Now, the morning after the première of *Iris* at Rome, the composer met the conductor and some mutual friends in a small room at the Caffè Aragno. Mascagni plainly conveyed his dissatisfaction with the performance. He requested Toscanini to prevent the singers from 'lacerating the music', and to oblige them 'to perform it ... as written'.

To this Toscanini replied:

> My dear Maestro, how can you expect me to impose my will on [those same] singers who, within a month or so, will be at the Scala and who will be able to retort that they have performed the opera [at Rome], in this way and with this freedom, under your direction? [44]

Eventually, the two men agreed that Mascagni would write a letter, 'obliging' Toscanini to perform the music exactly as written; further, at the request of the publisher, he would send the letter to Ricordi, so that it might serve also to admonish other conductors.

However, the impetuous Mascagni had, on reflection, decided that this approach was insufficiently direct; instead, he would express his disapproval by absenting himself from the rehearsals at Milan. Thus, on December 21st 1898, Ricordi - who, even before the première at Rome, had declared to Illica that he had had enough of *Iris* - was answering at length a letter (which has apparently not survived) from Avvocato Dario Cassuto, evidently Mascagni's lawyer, of Leghorn. Mascagni, wrote Ricordi, had 'mysteriously' changed his attitude to him, and to his company, and had even suggested that 'Casa Ricordi, after the Mascagni - Sonzogno reconciliation, wanted *Iris* to fail'. In fact, he wrote, for three years he had striven to satisfy Mascagni's requirements, and his conscience was perfectly clear. The publisher continued:

> Regarding the performance of the opera, the Maestro was entirely free to make, undo, try [and] retry as he thought fit: if the performance did not wholly meet his expectations, what fault is it of ours!

There was a danger, he felt, that Mascagni's constant complaints that the work had not been performed as written might sway the public's judgement.

Further, Ricordi went on, Mascagni had requested that the autograph score should be sent to him at Rome, and he now refused to return it. This was a commercial embarrassment, since it was needed for the preparation of copies, and also infringed Italian law, which required it to be registered with the authorities for copyright purposes. Ricordi's

---

[44] Letter Walter Toscanini - Luigi Oldani, Apr. 17 1967, Barblan, *Toscanini e la Scala*, p. 323n.

exasperation is plain:

> ... In 36 years of dealings with composers I have never found myself in such an uproar! ... I cannot conceal from you that I received with satisfaction the news that M⁰ Mascagni will not attend the rehearsals at the Teatro alla Scala, [instead] confining himself to coming to the *generale* and to being present at the first performances. - For me, it is sad to write in this vein, but on the other hand the experience of Rome would make me fear the sudden, dreadful avalanche which, as well as impairing the undisturbed study of the opera, would create a hostile current towards the Maestro in the Milanese public. ...
>
> I know perfectly well that the *creator* can never, in the depths of his soul, hear his own work interpreted according to his ideals! - I know very well that some .....*celebrated!* artists sing and interpret a little too much in their own fashion!⁴⁵..... but all this is a part of human imperfection which one will never succeed in correcting. On the other hand, let us be practical: to protest, to withdraw the opera?..... who will take that seriously?..... the great general public, which is not attracted by subtlety, will conclude that the Maestro is unwilling to subject *Iris* to fresh judgement!..... it will find it ridiculous that artists, [now] judged inadequate, were applauded for 10 nights at Rome, and even repeated pieces..... (R)

Ricordi's relief that Mascagni would not be attending the rehearsals at La Scala was, however, represented by Cassuto to his client - or perhaps the irascible composer misconstrued the lawyer's words - as a formal or, in Mascagni's own phrase, 'absolute ban' on his presence. At any rate, for more than a month he sulked intractably at Pesaro and Leghorn while various family illnesses provided him with good reasons - or excuses - for not coming to Milan. Not until January 19th, the very eve of the première, was the matter clarified.

Meanwhile, on December 28th 1898, Ricordi wrote to Mascagni, requesting that he send to the publishing house the prearranged letter requiring it

> ... to inform M⁰ Toscanini that, starting from the piano rehearsals, he should insist that the artists perform the music as written: that is to say without inappropriate *corone*, or *rall.* [*rallentandi*, i.e. slackening of tempo] - or alterations of expression etc. etc. - In *Iris* all is indicated, with particular detail - there is nothing to do except to follow the composer's indications - (R)

Thus, after the easy familiarity of earlier correspondence, the unaccustomed formality of the letter in question:

Leghorn, December 31st 1898

Sig. G. Ricordi e C.

> ... It is my duty to advise you that, for the imminent performances of *Iris* at Milan, I strongly desire that, right from the beginning of the rehearsals, the music should be performed in its entirety, because in the first performance at Rome too many concessions were made to the caprices and [the] deficiencies of the artists.

---

⁴⁵ A clear reference to De Lucia.

Therefore, I declare that the transpositions tried at Rome are absolutely damaging to the opera which, in the orchestral ensemble, loses the imprint of the original. The only concession that I can make is the transposition of the 'Serenata' in the first act. Further, I require that the colours and all the effects that I indicated in the score should be respected *absolutely*, and without the inappropriate and deplorably tasteless licence that the artists were permitted at Rome. ... The sorrow that I felt at Rome for such a *deficient* performance was immense; and I beg that, at least at Milan, *Iris* will be performed as I have written it and with the effects explicitly marked by me. - Every and any other effect would damage, would impair my concept -

Had I a score to hand I could mark all the artists' errors, and so assist the Conductor. (R)

Confirming receipt of the letter, Ricordi telegraphed Mascagni assuring him that it would serve to 'achieve everything possible'.[46] It was immediately copied and sent to Gatti-Casazza, with instructions to communicate it to Toscanini.

As rehearsals continued, Ricordi sought to mollify Mascagni. He telegraphed Cassuto, soliciting a reply to his letter of December 21st. He kept the composer informed of the progress of rehearsals. On January 9th 1899 he wrote Mascagni a conciliatory, even generous, letter, taking courage from the distance between them to make suggestions - for 'small cuts' - that a fear of 'incurring thunderbolts from Jupiter' had prevented his making at Rome.[47] However, as the première approached, his fears increased that the composer did not intend to be present; telegrams went daily from Milan to Pesaro, almost imploring him to attend.

Meanwhile, Mascagni was writing to Toscanini:

Pesaro, January 16th 1899

Maestro carissimo,

Regarding the agreement that we reached at Rome ... I have had a word with Comm. Giulio Ricordi.

And Comm. Ricordi wrote to me at the beginning of the year asking me to send to the company of Ricordi and Co. a letter with a request to safeguard the performance at Milan, and to ensure that ... what happened at Rome does not happen at Milan; that is to say that the opera should not be performed contrary to the idea of the composer; and that each piece should be performed in the original 'key'; and that the artists should not improvise (as at Rome) *corone* or *puntature*, special colourations, and thousands and thousands of other things.

I believed, and still believe, that such a letter was requested by Ricordi in full agreement with you, and that such a letter was to reflect the purposes prearranged between us at Rome, and therefore I wrote the requested letter, conceding 'only' the transposition into 'E' of the 'Serenata' of the first act.

Reading now in the newspapers that the Milan performance will totally restore my opera, I ask if you were given sight of my letter to the firm of Ricordi, before asking that company what use has been made of my writing.

The 'absolute ban' imposed by Comm. Ricordi on my coming to Milan for the rehearsals and first performances justifiably makes me a little suspicious.

---

46 (R) Ricordi - Mascagni, Jan. 1 1899.
47 (R) Ricordi - Mascagni, Jan. 9 1899.

> If you, dear Toscanini, are still of the opinion so courteously expressed at Rome, you should do me the kindness of informing me, and perhaps advising me in time to permit me a little excursion to Milan to be present ('in the most perfect *incognito*') at the *prova generale*.
>
> From a third person (since Casa Ricordi lets me know nothing) I know that you are putting your entire soul into conducting and directing *Iris*. This is a great comfort for me. . . . 48

Mascagni was being less than fair to Ricordi's almost daily letters and telegrams. As late as January 18th the publisher telegraphed with news of lighting trials, and repeated his warm invitation to attend. However, the telegrams said nothing regarding what clearly irritated Mascagni most of all: the caprices of De Lucia, on whom the maximum influence was now being brought to bear by conductor and publisher alike.

On Thursday January 19th, the day of the première, a telegram - which has not survived - from Mascagni finally alerted Ricordi to the damage done, knowingly or otherwise, by Cassuto. Ricordi's telegraphed reply was almost painful in its frankness:

> Surprised and sorry your telegram. Surprised that Cassuto could have represented to you something so contrary to the truth. Sorry that you could believe impositions on the composer [that are] simply ridiculous. Absolutely necessary [that we have] communication [regarding] my letter 21 December to clarify things. I wrote that, Mascagni having advised [that] he did not intend to be present [at] rehearsals, it saddened me to say I preferred [it] thus fearing renewal [of] Rome troubles. By which [I felt that it was] better that the composer should be present at the *prova generale* and at the first few performances. . . . I do not understand [to] which deficiencies you allude. If you really mean Osaka rather than deficiencies, the incomprehensible and known - well known - abuses never appeared during rehearsals but were kept as a pleasant surprise for Tuesday evening. Today I will go expressly to make serious remonstrances with him. For the rest magnificent performance. Your refusal [of the] invitation to come if not surprising [is] saddening because it proves that there exists neither faith in our friendship nor artistic faith. Meanwhile I inform you that about five hundred people besieged [the] box-office from five o'clock this morning. (R)

The publisher had then to honour his undertaking to 'remonstrate' with De Lucia, newly nominated Commander of the Order of the Crown of Italy.49 Instead, though, of going in person - a course that, in his exasperated state, might have made things worse - Ricordi drafted a letter:

January 19th 1899

To the celebrated artist Comm. Fernando De Lucia

Since I have always been your faithful friend and cordial admirer, I feel myself qualified to write this letter, and also to discharge what I believe to be my

---

48 Barblan, op. cit., pp. 322-3.
49 The nomination is dated Jan. 8 1899.

absolute duty -

If you, dear Comm., are a most talented and enchanting interpreter of the part of Osaka - it cannot be denied that, at certain points, the passion and the vigour of the artist correspond neither with the intentions of the composer nor with the demands of scenic reality! - There is more! - because rather than adding effect they reduce it!..... And clearly, frankly, I say to the artist:

1o Why add to the serenade a *gruppetto* which has nothing to do with the style of the piece?

2o Why finish the serenade by singing it 'at the footlights'?..... creating the most nonsensical scenic absurdity, putting Osaka in full view of Iris and of the chorus!!..... which has no further connection with the rest of the action?.....

3o Why repeat the advance to the footlights in order to say *'Danzatrici alate'*?..... what are all those people around the little theatre doing?..... they might as well get up and come around the singer in order to hear him!!..... 50

4o Why change the notes of the last beat of the kiss, to produce a vocal delivery that means nothing, when the effect of a *mezza voce*, all voluptuousness and delight, was magnificent?.....

These observations were made and repeated at Rome! - made and repeated here!..... and we all believed that we had fully convinced you - the more so since they do not spoil the effect at all; on the contrary they increased it very much when the Comm. De Lucia had the courtesy to perform it as we had requested -

I cannot, therefore, conceal from you the displeasure that I felt on Tuesday evening, seeing that you no longer took account of these absolutely necessary recommendations. Knowing your great talent as singer and actor it seems impossible that you believe that all this is useful and of good effect: when you have an exquisite, absolutely delightful voice, such as yours, you find expressions which go to the heart, with no need to do what I have already indicated.

Through duty, then, and through friendship, I urge you - I add nothing more, because I have complete faith in the word of Comm. De Lucia, and in the skill and sensibility of the artist, and I am sure that all will contribute, according to their strengths and abilities, to ensure the full success of Mascagni's opera ...

I hope that you will not take offence at this: I have always been accustomed to express my opinions frankly, especially with friends - and I want you always to count me among your most faithful and sincere, as I am already among your most enthusiastic admirers. (R)

Thus Ricordi wrote, and perhaps he even intended to send the letter. But it never reached De Lucia.[51] Instead, Ricordi asked Toscanini to address the problem and to repeat, yet again, the strictures of composer and publisher.[52]

The outcome at La Scala on January 19th 1899 was prejudiced from the outset since, in order to perform the opening scene to its best advantage, the theatre was plunged into total darkness as soon as

---

[50] The action requires Osaka to be concealed in the puppet theatre while singing Jor's serenade and the ensuing phrase noted by Ricordi.

[51] At the head of the copy letter, in a different hand, appear the words: *'Non spedita d'ord. Sig. Giulio.'* ('Not sent by order of Sig. Giulio').

[52] Ricordi bore some animosity towards Toscanini (see Carner, op. cit., p. 50n); it is not inconceivable that he saw the humorous side of imposing this task on the conductor.

Toscanini had taken his place. Though warned in advance, the disgruntled public - especially in the 'Gods' - was audibly discontented.[53] However, the 'Hymn to the Sun' brought an encore; they were not yet forbidden, Toscanini notwithstanding. The first stanzas sung by Iris 'soothed with the warmth of the sun. Osaka's appearance with Kyoto, and a cadenza which De Lucia sang with clarity and facility, drew approval.' At the end of Act I there was one call, compared with five at Rome. The 'Serenata',

> ... a melody born at the foot of Vesuvius and sung, with much elegance, *alla napoletana*, by De Lucia in a Japanese landscape was repeated, but with lively opposition. Never was I persuaded as I was last night of the futility of *bis* which, instead of increasing the prestige of a success, threatened to pervert and, often, to compromise it. Toscanini was admirable ... able to put the slightest details into relief. Darclée, who could not have given a better account of herself at the Scala, with that stupendous voice, always fresh and impassioned, emerged from a part with so little dramatic relief thanks [only] to her dramatic temperament. De Lucia, exquisite modulator, master of phrasing and of colouring his delightful voice, was perhaps a little affected in accent at times.[54]

Cosmorama, observing - ambiguously - that 'De Lucia sings the "Serenata" with a grace that recalls Piedigrotta', also noted that half of the audience wanted an encore, while the other half thought that once was already more than enough.[55] D'Ormeville, too, felt that the opera could more appropriately have been set near Vesuvius than Fujiyama. To Iris and Kyoto he preferred Santuzza and Turiddu. But the performance was 'absolutely ideal ... De Lucia [was] a highly finished sculptor'.[56]

The interval discussion in the boxes and corridors was lively and not generally favourable. At the end of the second and third acts benevolence had given way to hostile severity. But public opinion gradually improved at successive performances. Two days later Puccini wrote:

> For me, this opera, which contains so many beautiful things and most dazzling and coloured instrumentation, has the defect of its origin: an action which does not interest and which is diluted and languishes for three acts. In consequence, if God himself had set such a libretto he would not have made more of it than has Pietro. ... What I have said about the libretto etc. is *inter nos*, you understand?[57]

The house of Ricordi moved to inform its agents in other cities. To the Palermo branch Ricordi wrote that the outcome 'was not bad, but somewhat contested because of the excessive severity of a public which

---

53 *Perseveranza*, Jan. 19 1899.

54 Ibid., Jan. 20 1899.

55 *Cosmorama*, Jan. 28 1899.

56 *Gazzetta dei Teatri*, Jan. 26 1899.

57 Letter Puccini - Alberto Crecchi, Jan. 21 1899, Gara, *Carteggi Pucciniani*, No. 201, p. 173. Illica was librettist for Puccini's *Manon Lescaut*, *La Bohème*, *Tosca*, and *Madama Butterfly*.

was disgusted with the malicious *claque* organised by some artists'. To Naples, he telegraphed that De Lucia was 'excellent'.

To Mascagni, on the night of the première, he launched a telegram after each act to inform him of the positive aspects of the opera's reception. No one knew better than Ricordi that nothing succeeds like success. No doubt he hoped to bring the wayward composer to La Scala where his presence would be the spark to ignite a triumph which would fill the papers with flattering reviews and Ricordi's books with orders. Still, for family or other reasons, Mascagni procrastinated. Ricordi's telegram of January 21st reported to him on the singers. De Lucia was, it appeared, unrepentant:

> ...Darclée performs wonders third act. Buti extraordinary Kioto [sic]. Osaka prince [and] traitor.... (R)

By telegraph, the composer continued to carp at the performances, while the publisher soothed, placated, cajoled, and defended. Ricordi's reactions to an especially petulant outburst prompted yet another diatribe from Mascagni:

Leghorn, January 26th 1899

From your last telegram it appears that you have taken my observations about the Milan performance in bad part. But you must excuse me: from persons (in whom, without exception, I have complete faith) I have had astounding reports; but the articles on the matter in *Don Chisciotte* were already enough. What surprised me more than anything was the fact that Toscanini ruined all the *tempi*. What the Devil? And you and Tito have not corrected him?.\.... It rather seems that you correct only the composer! - Or perhaps you felt obliged to agree with the *critic* Ponchielli[58] who declared in his newspaper that Toscanini's interpretation is far superior to that of the composer himself?..... Hurrah! Hurrah! -

But let us talk no more. My dignity certainly suggested that I should come to Milan in case I were invited to conduct a performance of *Iris*. I would gain nothing from coming to endorse a deficient (and so described by me in advance) performance. And further: I asked Toscanini to advise me of the day of the *prova generale*, so that I might be present *incognito*. Well then: he does his utmost to ensure that I do not know the day of that rehearsal, preventing me from exercising a sacrosanct right.[59]

Regarding De Lucia, I had arranged everything with that letter to the firm of Ricordi, a letter requested by you and previously arranged with maestro Toscanini. What use has been made of that letter?..... (R)

It was doubtless a weary Ricordi who replied to this latest litany of complaint, which had already been joined on his desk by yet another telegram from the composer:

---

58 Annibale Ponchielli, son of the composer.

59 Mascagni was later to claim that Ricordi had failed to notify him of the date of the première of *Iris* at Turin in December 1899. In a letter to Illica, Dec. 22 1899, he wrote: 'For the sake of conductors, who do not want me at rehearsals, an opera is ruined.' (Quoted in Morini, *Mascagni*, Vol. I, p. 329).

January 28th 1899

Shall we speak - or rather write - frankly as good friends ...?

You write to me about absolutely *astounding* reports: of articles in *Don Chisciotte*, [and] of entirely contrary evaluations in the *Sera*. I am in the habit of not listening to the more or less official reports of friends and non-friends, and of not reading newspapers! - And if, for reasons of..... business, they are put before my eyes, similarly I have the habit of paying no attention, because I know how much journalistic articles are worth. In this case, then, I have read neither *Don Chisciotte*, nor *La Sera*, and not even *Perseveranza* and *Corriere* - precisely as I did at Rome with their newspapers, since if in the management of my affairs, if in the shaping and conduct of my artistic and industrial concepts I were to allow myself to be guided, or merely affected by, all the wiseacres of the newspapers, we should be in a mess. I look only at the facts! - And the facts are these: that they were working skilfully to prepare an atmosphere hostile to *Iris*, in every way!..... even mobilising the clerical element to prevent attendance at a scandalous spectacle, like that of the exhibition of a ..... naked woman!..... in the 2nd act. Finally, the day of going on stage, there was a general rumour that the opera would not be allowed to finish!!..... But we cocked a snook at them: the attempts at sabotage were not lacking, the outbreaks of coughing, skilfully done here and there, *et similia*. *Iris* imposed herself: imposed silence, attention, interest, and won!..... These are the facts: the rest is the rabid slaver of the impotent. - And the 2nd, 3rd, 4th performances had an excellent outcome and, what counts most, great gatherings of the public, attentive and applauding - reducing to silence the usual stubborn subscribers, among whom, if I am not mistaken, you number several..... friends! - and what friends! -

... Regarding the performance, everyone has his own view, and certainly no judgement is more authoritative and correct than that of the composer himself: but, needless to say, [only] when there are no prejudices, or excessive and dangerous tenseness. And do not take it badly, dear Mascagni, (because I am not making a criticism but noting a psychological fact deriving from a very excitable nature) if I say that, reminding myself of Rome, you could not be calm!!..... But since I always respect the composer I could not ridicule what you write to me, which can be summarised in this collective judgement:

We [are] *asses*, for the production - even noting that Illica was present at one rehearsal and approved everything.
Toscanini [is an] *ass* - who cannot conduct.
The scenery painters are *asses*.
The performers are *asses!*.....

Altogether, a certificate of asininity which is acceptable in the composer's letter, but one which, repeated by the voice of Mo Mascagni, could create only friction, disgust, displeasure - things which, as well as breaking bonds which it is good and desirable to keep intact, would damage common interests, *Iris* most of all.

And it is also time to concern ourselves with these common interests, since it does not seem to me that either Mo Mascagni nor my company would benefit from throwing everything into the fire. And it was precisely for these common interests that I thought it most advisable for the composer to be present at one of the first performances of *Iris*, a presence that would have stirred the affection that the public has for you, a presence that would have lent a special interest to the evening, to the obvious advantage of the opera itself. But it was necessary that the composer should not come with the preconceived idea of carrying out an inspection of his interpreters, and then perhaps of saying to everyone: absolute trash!!..... Goodbye benefit!!

With resignation, the venerable publisher lectured his disputatious composer on their respective rights and obligations, and on the commercial needs of an opera. Passing to the performance, he continued:

> As far as your letter that I requested for the Firm is concerned, I must remind you that, on the whole, it went further than I had asked, to which I replied by telegraph that whatever was *possible* would be done. And everything possible was done regarding Sig. De Lucia, who at rehearsals accepted all the observations, [and] performed as required: only at the last rehearsal had I the - fleeting - suspicion that he was placating us! I intended to go to him myself: but for fear of causing trouble, since I was very exasperated, I sent Toscanini to repeat to him all the recommendations made a hundred times at rehearsals. - And the first night De Lucia played a dirty trick and did it in his own way!. . . . . What should we have done?. . . . . Dragged him out through the wings?. . . . . or fired a revolver shot at him?. . . . . Unfortunately these are the miseries which one must endure in the theatre, they are not the first, nor will they be the last - and, unless we are prepared to be philosophical about it, [it would be] better to shut up shop and become sellers of hams and *mortadella*. Besides, in conclusion, what were you yourself able to achieve with De Lucia at Rome? (R)

Mascagni eventually relented, coming to Milan early in February to accept belated acclaim at what still remained of the ten performances of *Iris*. Two months later the opera was given at the San Carlo, Naples, where Ernesto Colli sang the part of Osaka. Elvino Ventura sang it there in 1900-01, when De Lucia was in the company. Indeed, in 1900, when Fernando was involved managerially with the theatre, Ricordi had agreed that *Iris* could open the season.[60] Negotiations were at that time complicated by the proposal that Naples should stage the new Mascagni opera, *Le Maschere*, published by Sonzogno. Since the latter had recently withdrawn - at the last moment - permission for *Le Maschere* to be given in a season which included two Ricordi works, one may easily agree with Mascagni's misgivings and his expressed sentiment: '. . . it is a very delicate [matter]. . . . . '[61] However, there was never any public suggestion that De Lucia should sing it at Naples; he seemed content that his memories of the rôle should be confined to his scrapbook. From *Iris* he recorded only the 'Serenata' [No. 355].

Within three years of the La Scala production *Iris* had been given in a further nine Italian cities with - perhaps significantly - eight different tenors. None of them was De Lucia, whom Ricordi, before the imbroglio at Milan, had himself recommended to his Palermo representative for the production there.[62] It was planned to give it in London, with the same cast as at Rome and Milan, and conducted by Toscanini, or, if he

---

60 (R) Telegram Ricordi - De Lucia, May 11 1900.

61 (R) Mascagni - Ricordi, Pesaro, June 2 1900.

62 On Jan. 28 1899 the publisher reported to Mascagni that negotiations for Palermo were bedevilled by the 'absolutely impossible' demands of the artists, one of whom was presumably De Lucia (R). Eventually, Ventura created Osaka there.

refused, by Mascagni.[63] In the event, it was not given at Covent Garden until 1919.

Coincidentally or otherwise, De Lucia never again sang with Toscanini. Something of the conductor's later views about him may be adduced from an incident in 1947, when he used one of the tenor's *Rigoletto* records to demonstrate how he had distorted phrases.[64]

It remains to examine Mascagni's relationship with De Lucia. Before leaving the theatre on the night of the Rome première of *Iris*, Mascagni is said to have visited the tenor's dressing room to express his gratitude for his valuable contribution.[65] Whether they were genuine or *pro forma* thanks is speculative. Perhaps only with the arrival of the morning papers did his exhilaration start to be replaced by the old hostility to his collaborators in general, and towards De Lucia in particular.

Many of the reviews of *I Rantzau* and *Silvano* remark on the disasters that might have befallen Mascagni had he not had De Lucia for those now almost forgotten operas. The proposition that they might have achieved greater success with another singer fails on the evidence that no later tenor has succeeded in breathing life into them. The day before the première of *Iris*, Checchi had stressed the debt that his old friend Pietro owed the tenor. The wistful *'Mi ci vorrebbe il De Lucia!'* of many a composer mounting a new opera had, he noted, become a reality for Mascagni.[66] And, as has been seen, Mascagni's temperamental inability to share his acclaim with others, whether singers such as Bellincioni and Stagno, conductors such as Mugnone, or librettists such as Verga, had been noted since at least the period of *Cavalleria Rusticana*.

The available evidence hardly permits us to compare in great depth the personalities of De Lucia and Mascagni. We may, however, observe certain similarities: highly individualistic in their artistic lives, their affability, great personal charm, and expansive bonhomie could quickly give way to violent passions. Such resemblances made them, perhaps, so alike in some respects that friction between them was inevitable. The composer's hostility towards the tenor had been noted at the time of *I Rantzau*. Clearly, De Lucia - after the fashion of a previous era - was capricious and wilful, and he interpreted and embellished works in a way perfectly in character with his training in the older repertoire but out of keeping with the music of Mascagni, whose vexation bordered on outrage. But De Lucia had by now a great public following. Had it been otherwise, Mascagni would probably not have accepted him to create his rôles. It cannot have been less than galling for the composer to read

63 *Corriere dei Teatri*, Mar. 12 1899.

64 The context of the discussion was evidently 'singers with nothing but voices', an accusation which certainly could not be levelled at De Lucia. (B.H. Haggin, *Conversations with Toscanini*, p. 61.)

65 Antonio Salvucci, *Confidenze e aneddoti*, pp. 95-108. The chapter is based on a meeting with De Lucia in August 1921, when the tenor reminisced on the early performances of *Iris* and showed Salvucci a collection of relevant press cuttings.

66 'Would that I had De Lucia!' *Fanfulla*, Nov. 21 1898.

criticisms which, rightly or not, attributed the success of *Iris* to De Lucia, and even to his singular characteristics. The evidence indicates that the storms which characterised the early performances of *Iris* reflected Mascagni's fierce and enduring resentment of the degree to which, since *Cavalleria Rusticana*, his triumphs had depended, or had been judged to depend, on the abilities - and on the whims - of a tenor who was by now a law unto himself, Fernando De Lucia.

16

'Mid Pleasures and Palaces

In every career there comes a day when the decline of the human capacities begins to show its tragic face. On that day man must be able to put down even a crown.   Blanche Marchesi, *Singer's Pilgrimage*

Before the time of *Iris*, De Lucia had renewed old friendships with Umberto Giordano (1867-1948), seven years his junior and, from 1880, a fellow student at San Pietro a Maiella.

Giordano's admiration for De Lucia clearly emerges in a letter to D'Ormeville, regarding the first Naples production of *Andrea Chénier*:

[Naples, probably 1896]

You will have received my telegram regarding Petri. I, as you know, do not know her, but knowing her to be an intelligent and conscientious artist, I believe that she herself will know whether the part of Maddalena is adapted to her register.

Here, De Lucia has created much interest in *Chénier*. He has let it be heard in several gatherings in Naples, and has stimulated the desire to hear him in it at the San Carlo.

I, *for my part, you understand, express no preference*, but were it possible to arrange for De Lucia to do it here and for Borgatti to fulfil his engagements here in some other way, I would be very happy at having satisfied Borgatti and the wishes of many Neapolitans. . . .

PS Do me the courtesy of writing to tell me whether Borgatti has been engaged for Genoa. (BLS)

At the world première of *Andrea Chénier* at La Scala, in March 1896, the title rôle had been sung by the 25-year-old Bolognese, Giuseppe Borgatti. In expressing a discreet, but distinct, preference that De Lucia - who, possibly, could not by then match Borgatti for vitality and ringing top notes - should sing the part at the San Carlo, Giordano was certainly aware of the advantages of having 'Don Fernando', the influential local favourite, in the cast. In the event, Borgatti created Chénier at Naples, with Mary d'Arneiro, in March 1897. De Lucia never sang the part on stage. His opportunity to create a Giordano rôle arose with *Fedora*.

The principal parts in Giordano's first opera, *Mala Vita* (1892), had been created by Bellincioni and Stagno, who had subsequently befriended the composer.[1] There is no reason to doubt the soprano's statement that Giordano wrote the part of Loris, in *Fedora*, in the expectation that Stagno would create it. The Sicilian tenor was, though, well past his prime, his brilliant top register now only a memory. Giordano's music recognises the fact: with only one B flat in the entire work, and the famous 'Amor ti vieta' rising only to A natural, the *tessitura* is generally undemanding.

Stagno's sudden death, in April 1897, started the search for a replacement. De Lucia, the most famous and prominent tenor of the period and for long the 'House Tenor' for Sonzogno, Giordano's publisher, was the obvious choice. Giordano negotiated personally with his old school friend. Clearly, too, he still wanted him to sing Chénier and, as his letters make clear, he was prepared to go to some trouble to achieve this:

Milan, February 1st 1898

Dear De Lucia,

I cannot at present send you the part of Loris in *Fedora* because it is not complete. Although he is the important character of the three act drama he sings only in the 2nd and in the 3rd - in the 1st he is silent.

As I have already told you, the part is *written for you*, and if the opera, as I hope it will, achieves success, it will be one of your war-horses.....You will achieve great effects without the slightest exertion -

At present, I am thinking a great deal about hearing you in *Chénier*. [Charles] Delmas has recently sung it at the Lirico, scoring a triumph. Imagine what you yourself could do!.....I have lowered the whole part and, if you will send me the score on which we made the transpositions together, I will write the other transpositions on it - as in the first act aria where the transposition in the recitative *'Colpito qui m'avete ov'io geloso celo etc'* is made on the word *'celo'*; instead of rising to D natural it stays on D flat - and the transposition continues thus for the whole piece.[2] I will also indicate it for the final duet....(RE)

Negotiations with De Lucia for *Fedora* eventually came to nothing; according to Bellincioni, his commitments with other theatres prevented his undertaking the work, whose première took place just five days before that of *Iris* at Rome. However, as we have seen, his involvement with *Iris* - if we except the 1897 reference in Buenos Aires - was a tardy one; as late as June 1898 Colli was still under consideration for Osaka in the première. At the time of Giordano's letter De Lucia had not been engaged for *Iris*; there is no evidence of commitments so far ahead as November 1898, and Bellincioni's explanation seems implausible. Her daughter is more emphatic, writing that De Lucia had been capricious in the matter and that Sonzogno, almost at the last moment, had found himself without a tenor.[3] In the shifting sands of the operatic world any

---

1 Bellincioni, op. cit., pp. 124-6.

2 Modern scores of *Andrea Chénier* show this as an optional transposition.

3 Bianca Stagno-Bellincioni, *Roberto Stagno e Gemma Bellincioni Intimi*, p. 104.

one of several reasons could have been decisive. Whichever it was, Giordano requested Bellincioni to go to Leghorn to hear Caruso, who had already created the part of Vito in *Il Voto*, as the shortened and modified *Mala Vita* had now been renamed, and it was Caruso who was the first Loris; De Lucia did not sing it until more than a year later. Nevertheless, it was a part which, as Giordano had predicted, gave him some of the most clamorous successes of his career.

Meanwhile, however, he was engaged for his first season at Lisbon, to sing Turiddu, Rodolfo, and Boito's Faust in a company that included Ancona and Eva Tetrazzini. The Teatro Sao Carlos of Lisbon still maintained all the traditions of an international theatre of the first rank. The long winter seasons attracted the most eminent artists who were paid handsomely for their work before a severely critical audience, with factions not unlike those of the theatre's namesake in Naples. A note of pomp and elegance was conferred by the frequent attendance of the King and the Court. The subscribers customarily attended all the orchestral rehearsals and crowded on to the stage between acts, to compliment their idols. Bellincioni, who sang some of her earliest engagements there, recalled the theatre:

> The Lisbon public had a particular way of showing its disapproval in the theatre.....it beat, in fury, with its walking-sticks or its feet and, when this proved insufficient, it also used the moveable seats which, on the stormiest nights, were completely smashed! The public [on such occasions] struck terror, because it sometimes became savage, and I have seen, in that season [1883] *all the Gods of the S. Carlos Olympus* tremble, just like leaves on a tree, before going on stage for an important première.[4]

The impresario was José Pacini, brother of the soprano, Regina. Pacini saw the opera house as an extension of the ballroom of his personal friend, the King. He ran the theatre like a dictator whose despotism was directed as much towards the audience as the artists. His methods were to offer cheap subscriptions so that, in addition to a full theatre, there were always a hundred would-be subscribers. When a subscriber displeased him by his conduct a replacement was easily found. Progressively, he had reduced the size of the gallery until what was left accommodated a group of thirty seats to which Napoleon, the leader of the *claque*, and his followers had free access. Such close control by the management freed the artists from the tiresome custom and expense of dealing with a *claque*.[5] None the less, Lisbon was well recognised as one of the most turbulent places in the operatic world; its greatest theatre was the centre of famous fiascos or exhilarating triumphs, and was known to be a particularly difficult *piazza* for tenors.

---

4 Bellincioni, op. cit., p. 47.
5 Carelli, op. cit., p. 86.

Somewhat delayed by *Iris* at La Scala, De Lucia arrived on the Sud Express on February 20th 1899, after five days of travelling. He made his début in *Cavalleria Rusticana*, to tremendous applause and to a reported twenty calls. On March 3rd he sang Rodolfo at a performance attended by the King and Queen, and by the Prince of Monaco. A critic noted that:

> He must be considered an interpreter *hors ligne* of Puccini's beautiful opera.
> ... As for his voice, if it is not very extensive, it is of the easiest emission and the artist knows how to draw from it all the effects of colouring.[6]

His *festa* was in *La Bohème* on March 8th, a performance of 'truly marvellous perfection, grace and enchantment. The malleability ... of his voice is unrivalled.' In the interval between Acts II and III he received many handsome gifts, for which he expressed his thanks by singing the serenade from *Iris*, 'A suon di baci', and 'La donna è mobile'.[7]

On March 4th the tenor was received in audience by the King. Subsequently, during his farewell operatic performance, *Mefistofele*, the King bestowed on him the insignia of Official of the Order of Santiago.[8] He had many calls and was persuaded to sing several romanzas at the piano. His success earned him reconfirmation for the following year, while a contented Pacini received the royal party's congratulations.

After a short stay in Naples, De Lucia and his family left for his first London season since the death of Harris. Covent Garden was now in the hands of the Grand Opera Syndicate, formed expressly for the purposes of managing the summer seasons at the theatre, but the influence of Harris was to last for many years through Neil Forsyth, Frank Rendle, and Maurice Grau. The patronage of Lady de Grey, so long exercised through her friendship with Harris, continued through her brother-in-law, Higgins, Chairman of the Syndicate.

Many subscribers were disappointed that the appearances of Jean de Reszke were again limited by ill-health. However, the season saw the return of Lilli Lehmann, the débuts of Johanna Gadski, Félia Litvinne and Antonio Scotti, and the first Grand Opera Syndicate performance of Puccini's *La Bohème*. The mixture of nationalities was the despair of Sidney Homer, who wrote of the continual changes of artist in *Aida*, where his wife, Louise, sang Amneris to three different sopranos and two or three tenors. 'Diction went by the board. Artists from a dozen countries sang in Italian, French, and German, and their diction mattered little. Few in the audience understood them, in any case. Various methods of singing would be jumbled in one performance, but that disturbed no one except, perhaps, the orchestral conductor. What he

---

[6] *Diario de Noticias*, Mar. 4 1899.

[7] Ibid., Mar. 9 1899.

[8] *Corriere dei Teatri*, Mar. 26 1899. This decoration, which is also noted in De Lucia's file at San Pietro a Maiella, cannot be confirmed from official Portuguese sources.

thought did not count; his job was to manage the orchestra.'[9] Puccini, too, was scathing about Covent Garden management, to whom the words *ensemble* and *mise-en-scène* meant nothing.[10] A struggle was also being waged against the *claque* which some Italian artists had attempted to establish for their own greater glory.[11]

By now, De Lucia, Ancona and their artistic cronies had numerous friends in London. Typical of a rest-night dinner was that of May 7th 1899, at the Monico Egyptian Saloon, where they relaxed in the company of Arditi, Bevignani, Cowen, Denza, Manuel Garcia, Edward German, Mancinelli, Martucci, Parry, Randegger, Seppilli, Stanford, and many others, including De Renzi, the Italian ambassador.[12]

Two days later, De Lucia made his début as Canio, the rôle that he had by now made his own at Covent Garden. He then gave *Rigoletto*, with Melba and Scotti.[13] On June 30th, with Emma Albani, Bispham, Marie Brema, and Emma Nevada he appeared in a State Concert at Buckingham Palace. The Prince of Wales presided in the absence of Queen Victoria, who was at Windsor Castle.

Even Bispham, the austere Quaker, was impressed:

> This occasion was attended by a most gorgeous array of dignitaries - no other words describe it. All the diplomatic corps from every country in the world were present, every one in full regalia. . . . amongst all the royalty, the Indian princes, the great nobles, and fair, coroneted ladies present, the one figure that stands out in my mind is that of Lord Kitchener, who, head and shoulders above almost any one in the room, was one of the most striking personalities in that incomparable assemblage.[14]

The programme included songs by Arditi and others, and solid Victorian fare by Stanford and Sullivan. Albani and Bispham sang 'Là ci darem' from *Don Giovanni* and Nevada gave the 'Bell Song' from *Lakmé*.[15] De Lucia sang 'Ecco ridente' from *Il Barbiere di Siviglia*, at the special request of the Prince.[16]

On July 1st, Puccini was present for the performance of *La Bohème*. It was Melba's first appearance at Covent Garden in a part which she was almost to monopolise there until the Great War. The audience included the Princess of Wales, the Duke of York, the Duke of Cambridge, and the Grand Duke and Duchess of Mecklenburg-Strelitz, 'drawn together by the superlative attraction of Melba, the sweetest songstress in the world,

---

9   Sidney Homer, *My Wife and I*, p. 95.

10   Vincent Seligmann, *Puccini Among Friends*, pp. 112-13.

11   *Corriere dei Teatri*, June 10 1899.

12   G.R. Ancona.

13   Rosenthal, op. cit., omits the performances of *Rigoletto* this season.

14   David Bispham, *A Quaker Singer's Recollections*, p. 265.

15   Royal Archives.

16   *Corriere dei Teatri*, July 30 1899.

as Mimì'.[17] Curiously, her appearance and acting made more of an effect than her singing, where

> ...her limpid purity of *timbre* and faultless skill of vocalisation and musical phrasing seemed almost to contradict, by their suggestion of radiant health and youthful freshness, the idea of the frail flower-maker ...For this reason the first act, with its delicious duet in the dark with Rudolpho [sic] was, vocally, the most satisfactory, and its conclusion, one of the prettiest ever invented, was a marvel of pure singing.
>   ...As the four students Signori De Lucia and Ancona, MM Gilibert and Journet were inimitably funny ...and the singing of the first two was marked by high artistic qualities.[18]

For the *Illustrated London News*, Melba identified marvellously with the part, 'without attempting to make any show of her magnificent voice. ...Signor De Lucia's Rodolfo was energetically sung, if he did not altogether prove himself to be the sweetest tenor of our times.' Dufriche, as Benoit and Alcindoro, and Zélie De Lussan, as Musetta, not to overlook 'Mr. Stedman's choir of boys', completed a well-found cast under the intelligent direction of Mancinelli. Ricordi telegraphed his congratulations to De Lucia, 'friend and splendid Rodolfo'.

Three days later came another Command Performance at Windsor Castle, where *Pagliacci* was given with Adam's *Le Châlet*. Queen Victoria recorded the event in her diary:

July 4th 1899

> A little after 9 went over to the Waterloo Gallery, where we had a very successful operatic performance. It began by a small 'Opéra Comique' 'Le Châlet' by Adam, composed about 60 years ago. Plançon and Mlle Leclerc & a Mr. Cazeneuve performed in it. The music is pretty and lively, much of it I remembered. But there is hardly any story in it & as Plançon said it is '*un peu naïf*'. He sang and acted admirably as usual. Then followed Leon Cavallo's [sic] celebrated opera 'Pagliacci', which he was to have conducted himself but was prevented, from ill health. It is eminently dramatic & very tragic & full of passion. The music is beautiful, very descriptive but chiefly sad, the orchestration very fine. I still prefer the 'Cavalleria', though this is perhaps a more powerful composition. It was admirably sung and acted by Mme Suzanne Adams, Signor de Lucia, as the Pagliaccio, & Signor Ancona as 'Tonio'. Mancinelli conducted. - Afterwards the invited guests passed by & at the end, the performers, who were presented by Ld. de Grey.[19]

The Queen's remarks to De Lucia conveyed how moved she had been by his '*Ridi, Pagliaccio*'.[20] The artists' gifts included a diamond bracelet for Adams, a silver inkstand for Grau, and gold cuff-links, with the royal

---

17 *Illustrated London News*, precise date unknown.

18 *The Times*, July 3 1899.

19 The mistake in Leoncavallo's name is not necessarily the Queen's; Princess Beatrice, in fulfilment of her mother's wish, copied out the journal before destroying the original.

20 *Corriere dei Teatri*, July 30 1899.

arms and monogram in diamonds, for Forsyth.[21] From the hands of
Princess Beatrice De Lucia received a cigar casket in silver and gold,
with the inscription: 'Fernando De Lucia from R.I.V. Windsor Castle.'[22]

He sang only a few performances at Covent Garden that season. Much
of his time was spent with his family; Nadir suffered an attack of
bronchitis, causing the tenor to decline pressing invitations from the
Italian community.[23] There were meetings with agents and managers, as
impresarios such as Raoul Gunsbourg, director of the Monte Carlo opera,
sought to assemble companies for yet other seasons. But there were
private engagements, where the wealthy sought to entertain one another
with events such as the musical 'At Home' beloved of late Victorian social
life. The dapper and fashionably dressed figure of Ancona was almost as
well-known off-stage as on it. A courtly, charming, and delightful
raconteur and conversationalist, he was much in demand for such
functions, at which De Lucia sometimes joined his friend. At a soirée at
the Haig residence, on July 19th 1899, Ancona, De Lucia, De Lussan,
Nevada, and others appeared. The silk programme recalls an evening
when De Lucia sang 'Ancora' (Tosti), 'Addio, Mignon' from *Mignon*, and,
with Emma Nevada, the duet from *Romeo e Giulietta*.[24]

The summer was spent in the peace of Cava de' Tirreni, in drives,
visits, and conviviality. Evenings at the De Lucia villa were usually in
the open air of the broad terrace, like the deck of a ship. They were
evenings of warm, scented air, of old wine, and of impromptu music-
making. Seventy years later, elderly *Cavesi* would still recount how the
songs of the host - who gave generously of his voice - enthralled the
uninvited listeners who assembled, sometimes in hundreds, around the
low boundary wall; on still evenings the voice would echo down the
flowered slopes of the valley, beyond Rotolo, to disperse among the trees.
The merest breeze, perfumed with citrus or pine, would carry it to Cava
itself. Attilio Della Porta reminisced:

> These memories ... lived again for me in the 1940s, as I went each Sunday to
> Villa Pepe [the former De Lucia villa]: passing through the wooded lanes, with a
> view of the valley, suffused with green, in the enthralling summits of the hills,
> in the caressing harmony of nature, I seemed to see again the statuesque figure
> of the illustrious artist and, in the peace and tranquillity, to hear again the
> notes of his enchanting singing.[25]

On July 28th 1899, in the sanctuary of Santa Maria dell'Olmo at
Cava, De Lucia sang in celebration of the saint's Feast day as her effigy
was carried in procession from there to the cathedral. It is reported that

---

21 (E) Unidentified newspaper cutting, July 8 1899.
22 *Corriere dei Teatri*, July 30 1899.
23 (BLS) De Lucia - Federico Balesta, June 2 1899.
24 (A) At 65, Brook Street, London.
25 A. Della Porta, *Incontri*, p. 230.

the tenor was accompanied at the piano by his son. When, on September 11th, the journey took place in reverse, members of the San Carlo orchestra and chorus participated in the ceremony. In the cathedral, with its pillars covered in red velvet and the portrait of the saint in a halo of brocade and gold, they performed Perosi's *Messa*. Then, they accompanied De Lucia as he sang 'Pietà, Signore'. An eye-witness recalled that, as the tenor's clear, mellow voice delivered the words: *'Pietà, Signore, di me dolente'*, a wave of emotion, intensified by the mystery being celebrated at the altar, spread through a congregation which remained almost breathless for as long as the notes echoed between the walls.[26] After the solemnity came the merrymaking when, to the sound of famous bands, displays of fireworks lit the night sky.[27]

Days at Cava were also absorbed by his lifelong obsession with the study of singing, of interpretation, and of new music. Thill wrote of him:

> De Lucia's singing was nothing but the result of unimaginable work, for he was the least gifted of singers of yesterday. He lived only for his singing . . . [28]

Time and again critics wrote of his studiousness and of his refusal to rest on his laurels. Only by unremitting study had he increased the volume of his voice - cultivated and impassioned, but initially small - to bring it to the degree of perfection achieved at his peak.[29] But even then the work continued: the Milanese critic who in 1897 wrote that '[he] has found a way of remedying a defect in some notes by study that does his wonderful talent credit' was describing an established artist who still continued to develop his methods.[30] Study, perseverance, and genius, united with energy and imagination, and driven by iron determination, rare intelligence, and eclectic imitation were judged to underlie the success of a singer who lacked an exceptional natural voice.[31]

His assimilative powers enabled him both to profit from the vocal techniques of the singers whom he heard in his youth and to learn, with notable speed, the music of new parts. While working with Giordano on *Andrea Chénier* one reading of a passage sufficed for him to absorb the elements of it for later refinement.[32] But this facility, useful as it was in an emergency, was not his way, which was first to study a score at a desk. He would read out phrases, shortening or lengthening each in turn.

26 Canonico, op. cit., Vol. III, p. 71, erroneously gives 1895. This 'Preghiera' is variously attributed to Rossini or to Stradella (1644-1682); the 'Doubtful and Supposititious Works' section for the latter in the British Library Catalogue lists more than fifty items which attribute it to him. According to *The New Grove*, Vol. 13, p. 221, it is thought to be by L.A. Niedermeyer (1802-1861); no source is cited.
27 Della Porta, *Il Santuario*, p. 85.
28 Thill, letter to the writer, Oct. 1967.
29 D'Ormeville, *Gazzetta dei Teatri*, Apr. 11 1895.
30 *Cosmorama*, Mar. 19 1897.
31 *Occhialetto*, Jan. 18 1890.
32 Achemenide De Giorgio, *Fernando De Lucia*.

He wrote out the words as an *aide-mémoire*.[33] Only then would he go to one of the three pianos: he had one even in the bedroom. Sometimes, his emotion in a piece that he was practising would bring him to tears.[34] Perhaps this was why he referred to the *filature* as *'lacreme'*.[35] In the theatre the perfect execution of a *'lacrema'* was judged by the public but, when studying, the arbiter was Enrico, to whom he would say: *'Errì*, listen to this *lacrema!'* And the valet, enamoured of his master's singing, would exclaim, with all his southern enthusiasm and impetuous sincerity: 'What a *lacrema*, *Commendatore!* What a beautiful *lacrema!'*

The churches of Naples could always call upon De Lucia's services. Each Holy Friday, he would sing the Pergolesi *Stabat Mater* at the Church of San Ferdinando, and each October there was the Niedermeyer 'Preghiera', in the Church of Santa Brigida. Each year, two months before the event, he would get out the score, which would then be kept on his desk, at his bedside, or by his favourite chair, where he would often study it. To his family, he would say: 'This year, I must sing a better "Preghiera"; this year it must be a little different.'[36]

It was not unusual for him to work intermittently for two years on the interpretation of a 'romanza' before he sang it in public. Once, he refused a request by Matilde Serao to sing Tosti's 'Ideale' at one of her parties, because he had only a few days in which to renew his conception of it.

His vocal régime was unalterable. Edward Petrillo, who lived on the floor above the tenor in the Palazzo Cirella in Naples, recalled that he would sometimes come on to his balcony while practising, and his voice would fill the quiet cul-de-sac of Angiporto Galleria.[37] And the routine continued during holidays at Cava: as Pasquale drove Itala's dressmaker to the villa on summer mornings they would hear vocalisations or the tenor's favourite 'romanzas'. All sources agree that, to the end of his life, he strove unceasingly to research and expand his vocal resources. Social visits to Carelli or Lombardi always developed into an examination of some facet of singing. After performances which fell short of his standards he would contrast his own dissatisfaction with the pleasure of an applauding public, which he thought too easily contented.

From Cava he wrote to D'Ormeville of new contracts and projects:

> Villino De Lucia
> August 29th 1899

Carissimo Carlo,

> In London, Gunsbourg told me that I would sing *Bohème* - In the event that this opera is not done I shall be happy to sing *Barbiere*, especially with Pinkert. You know my demands, since it is the good season, and then only for three

---

33 De Lucia family.
34 Franz Gleijeses.
35 Neapolitan dialect for *'lagrime'* (tears).
36 De Lucia family.
37 Now Piazzetta Matilde Serao.

performances, I would prefer it that you made the offer, but always providing that it were in the second half of March - 1900 -

Performing *Bohème*, I would like to be the *creator* at Monte Carlo. It is easy to understand that, singing for the first time at Monte Carlo, it is my sole desire to sing an opera where I can again display my qualities.[38]

His eagerness to create Rodolfo was, perhaps, the greater now that it was clear that he was not, after all, to be the first Cavaradossi.

As early as 1889, Puccini had thought of setting Sardou's *Tosca*; in 1891 it was announced that Casa Ricordi had acquired the rights to the play and, within days, that Puccini would write an opera on it, to a libretto by Illica. For whatever reason, however, Puccini did not start on the project immediately, and in 1893 Franchetti signed a contract with Ricordi for an opera based on it.

The subject did not surface again in Puccini's mind until 1895, when he went to Florence specially to see the play. Specht suggests that he had been deeply impressed by Sarah Bernhardt, with her slim, graceful figure, her cloud of fair hair, and the impassioned, clarinet-like timbre of her voice.[39] Her striking costume - the rustling silk dress, plumed hat, bouquet of flowers, and long, slender cane - is preserved in the performing traditions of *Tosca*. When it was clear that Puccini was again interested in the work, Ricordi - by means altogether questionable - first persuaded Franchetti to relinquish the rights to it and then contracted with Puccini to set the existing Illica libretto.

As we have noted, as early as March 1897 Puccini had expressed the hope that De Lucia would create Cavaradossi. Subsequent cordial correspondence between the two does not suggest that he was any less enthusiastic.[40] Indeed, the news that De Lucia would create the part was noised as far abroad as Buenos Aires.[41] Another confident tenor among those engaged for the 1899-1900 season at the Costanzi, Rome, where *Tosca* was to have its première, was Caruso. He had impressed Puccini at Torre del Lago and he, too, hoped to create Cavaradossi.[42] In fact, his contract stated that in addition to the repertoire operas - *Iris*, *La Gioconda*, and *Mefistofele* - he would be entrusted with the tenor rôle in a new opera by a well-known composer.[43] But Caruso, despite his incontestable gifts, was young and his voice was sweet and flexible rather than round and vibrant, a lyric rather than a dramatic voice. The decision seems to have been Puccini's, and he selected Emilio De Marchi.

---

[38] (BLS) Bonci and Marconi are only two of the other eminent singers who, in correspondence with D'Ormeville, express a wish to sing with Regina Pinkert, who was clearly a close friend of the agent.

[39] Specht, op. cit., p. 154. The source does not specifically state that Puccini saw Bernhardt in Florence. She had first performed *Tosca* in 1887.

[40] Letter Puccini - De Lucia, Pescia, Aug. 9 1897, quoted in Phonotype Celebrity Catalogue (undated, post-1925).

[41] *Patria degl'Italiani*, quoted in *Gazzetta dei Teatri*, Sept. 2 1897.

[42] Ybarra, op. cit., p. 45.

[43] Key and Zirato, op. cit., pp. 112-14.

Almost certainly, the reason for his choice lies not in vocal matters but elsewhere. Clearly, he had first wanted De Lucia for the part. He might also have thought highly of Caruso's credentials. But in Milan it was widely believed that, above all, Puccini - always susceptible to female beauty - wanted Hariclea Darclée for the part of Tosca. Darclée, arrestingly elegant and an excellent actress, was then probably the finest dramatic soprano in the Italian lyric field. In musical circles and in the lightly-veiled references of the press it was no secret that Darclée and De Marchi were lovers who, since 1896, had made many appearances and tours together.[44] Darclée is thought to have made De Marchi's engagement as Cavaradossi a condition of her own acceptance, and so important was her cooperation that Puccini did not hesitate for long. De Marchi was, in any case, obviously a singer of merit, more experienced than Caruso and probably better able to put vocal fire into the A sharps of the second act than was De Lucia, whose voice, after years of singing Canio and Don José, was showing signs of wear.

By August 1899 the final choice of artists had been made and the première of *Tosca* set for January 1900, with Darclée, De Marchi, and Eugenio Giraldoni, conducted by Mugnone. The artists and conductor would gather as soon as possible at Puccini's home at Torre del Lago to agree on the interpretation of the opera.[45] Not until six weeks before the eventual première was De Marchi sent his part, with instructions to guard it 'most jealously'.[46]

De Lucia was, meanwhile, scheduled to sing *Werther* at the Costanzi in December, and *La Bohème* later in the same season. In between was the Lisbon reconfirmation, an engagement that included his first performance as Loris Ipanov, in *Fedora*.

On December 30th 1899 the Costanzi impresario, Carlo Superti, offered Italy its first opportunity to hear De Lucia in *Werther*, and Rome its first glimpse of the opera. Though the audience was well enough disposed some critics observed an excessive severity, characteristic of the first production of a work. The reception was warmer at the second and subsequent performances. Even at the première, however, there was enthusiasm for De Lucia, 'the great sorcerer of Italian singing',[47] though, in the fashion of the line-by-line evaluations of Italian audiences, it came piecemeal as *'Bravo!'* underlined his more felicitous or ambitious phrases.

The critic of *Tribuna* eulogised the tenor's singing. 'Very beautiful' was Werther's outburst in the duet with Carlotta *'Ah questo primo bacio'*:

---

44 Ricordi had to ask De Marchi for her address in order to send her the part of Tosca. Of her performance in *La Bohème* at Buenos Aires in 1896, *Siglo* (Aug. 23 1897) wrote that she had 'had at her side the stimulus and incentive of the enamoured De Marchi'.

45 *Corriere dei Teatri*, Aug. 14 1899.

46 (R) Ricordi - E. De Marchi, Dec. 1 1899.

47 *Gazzetta dei Teatri*, Jan. 4 1900.

... here, De Lucia's art is consummate. ... All the relief of the character of Werther was given by the performance; woe if the protagonist is weak! ... De Lucia has equalled, if not surpassed, the fame that preceded him. Last night's *Werther* was his triumph ... a true artist, or rather a true and great master of the art of singing.[48]

Messaggero dwelt on his sensitive portrayal of the character:

The delicate and refined score, entrusted to gifted performers such as De Lucia and to a conductor like Mugnone, had an excellent interpretation in every detail, such as to justify the expression: above all praise ...

The major merit certainly belongs to De Lucia, who has studied the part with love and great understanding, succeeding in delineating the character with outlines which are precise and fully effective, with all the impetuosity of fervid passion, with all the sad and desperate moments of unrequited love.

On the stage, he carried not only the priceless treasures of his vocal art but also a dramatic action through which, with transparent lucidity, the psychological studies of the unhappy love-lorn poet are drawn, and beneath whose every phrase vibrates passion - powerfully - as his soul throbs in his singing.

And his artistic soul has coloured the melodic content to the greatest effect ... thanks to a voice, [which he] modulates with talent, and to the most refined gradations, whereby he moves from violent outbursts of passion to the finest of attenuations.[49]

Attention was now centred on *Tosca*. Against all tradition, the abrasive Tito Ricordi had banned journalists and other non-participants from the *prova generale* of the new opera. Would Puccini himself be permitted to enter, wondered some correspondents. De Lucia delayed his departure for Lisbon long enough to hear the first performance, with its many calls for the composer. It was soon announced that the work would be given in the spring season at London, with De Lucia and Melba.[50]

At Lisbon, De Lucia made his début as the Duke of Mantua. The *Gazzetta dei Teatri* reported a success 'without precedent', with multiple encores of the usual pieces. The calls were described as 'absolutely kilometrical' and his manner of singing as '*fantasista*', with five performances of 'La donna è mobile', each quite different from the others,[51] but 'always agreeable and elegant'.[52] He then gave *La Traviata*, *Fedora*, *La Bohème*, and *Pagliacci*, in which Nedda was sung by Lina Cavalieri, the beautiful ex-*canzonettista* of the *caffè-concerto*; later in the season she was to leave Lisbon hurriedly after her performance was loudly hissed.

In his memoirs the bass Andres De Segurola writes that, for eventfulness, no performance in his entire theatrical career could

---

48 *Tribuna*, Jan. 1 1900.
49 *Messaggero*, Jan. 1 1900.
50 *Corriere dei Teatri*, Feb. 1 1900.
51 *Gazzetta dei Teatri*, Feb. 15 1900.
52 *Diario de Noticias*, Feb. 9 1900, which gives four performances of 'La donna è mobile'.

compare with one *La Gioconda*, in which he sang with De Lucia, Elena Teodorini, and Delfino Menotti at Lisbon. It was a performance which, from the outset, seemed beset by misfortune: first, it was enlivened by the antics of a large bat which had somehow entered the theatre and hidden in the recesses of the carved ornamentation. By the second act the creature was thoroughly awake and flew hither and thither, to the great alarm of the fashionable ladies. Entering the Royal Box it became entangled in the *coiffure* of the Queen Dowager; escaping the swords of the King and of the Duke of Oporto it then fell helplessly and met its end at the feet of a trombonist. The second act recommenced, and the audience prepared to enjoy 'Cielo e mar!' De Lucia delivered the recitative 'with great authority' from the prow of his brigantine but, in descending the gangplank to sing the aria from the stage, he fell, twisting his ankle so badly that the dashing Enzo, the 'good-looking and graceful De Lucia', as De Segurola described him, was thereafter reduced to a most unromantic limp.

During the following interval, a magnificent basket of flowers arrived for each principal singer. Identical cards read: 'Farewell, from one who is leaving.' Over the applause at the third act finale a pistol shot rang out in the first gallery. There was pandemonium. When Teodorini fainted and was carried off by bass and baritone some thought that she had been assassinated. It emerged, however, that it was a suicide. In the dead man's pocket was the receipt for five baskets of flowers.[53]

But the artistic landmark for De Lucia was his first *Fedora*, on February 13th 1900. That it was an unqualified triumph was generally agreed. An emotional public went wild with enthusiasm for Bellincioni and De Lucia. For a detailed account of how they sang it, however, we look in vain among the notices of the Lisbon critics. There were, though, to be many other De Lucia performances of this work elsewhere over the next fifteen years, some with Bellincioni who, in her memoirs of twenty years later, prudently avoids making a judgement between Caruso (the creator of the part of Loris) and De Lucia:

> Each of the two great artists had his own very personal and different expedients, and it was a case of remembering the age of *Gli Ugonotti* of Stagno ..... Masini..... and Gayarre. The Loris of Caruso was not the Loris of De Lucia..... and the Loris of De Lucia was very different from that of Caruso. It was a true triumph, that *Fedora* at Lisbon ... [54]

---

53 Andres De Segurola, 'Through my monocle', pp. 78-81. These memoirs, which are most emphatic about this dramatic incident and refer to it several times in later pages, do not document the occasion. Without specifying the date De Segurola clearly implies the 1899-1900 season. Da Fonseca Benvenides, *O Real Theatro de S. Carlos*, p. 140, does not give *La Gioconda* for that season and includes neither Teodorini nor Menotti in the roster of the Teatro S. Carlos. It is possible that the opera was included in the short extra season, which started on Mar. 10 1900, or in a command performance outside the subscription; however, it seems likely that the memoirs - which date from almost fifty years later - confuse the occasion with the Lisbon *Gioconda* of the following season when, on Jan. 3 1901, De Segurola, Teodorini, and Menotti sang it with the tenor José Palet. Menotti was later replaced by Giuseppe De Luca.

54 Bellincioni, op. cit., pp. 127-8.

Loris would become one of De Lucia's most famous rôles and he, in turn, would be one of what Celletti has termed the 'poets of "Amor ti vieta" ', for the fame and success of a Loris has so often been based on this brief *arioso*.[55] When the Neapolitan critic Luigi De Lillo heard De Lucia in this fragment, as it may be termed, in 1914, he sang it in a way

> ...that no one has repeated, in its refinements, and its *fioriture*. He passed from sweetness, from the exceptional refinement of the famous *romanza*, to the dramatic accents - possibly even to excess - of the second act *racconto* [Mia madre], where, though in his latter years, he really *was* Loris.[56]

For the last night of the *carnevale* it was traditional for the Sao Carlos to indulge in some foolishness, for women to appear in male garb, children as serious artists, and so forth. That year, Bellincioni entered the field of *zarzuela* and took the part of the tenor Giuseppini, in *El Duo de la Africana*. She interpolated into the work some familiar operatic pieces, showing much talent as a mimic of other celebrated artists.[57] One scene, set in the Sao Carlos itself, gave great amusement when she sang 'La donna è mobile', imitating De Lucia.[58]

The tenor returned to Rome, to sing Rodolfo to the Mimì of Giorgina Caprile. The first performance was to a theatre full as could be wished. *Tribuna* attributed it to the 'simple recipe of ... choosing a score of secure appeal and entrusting it to good artists, at least one of whom can exercise an irresistible fascination on the public.'[59] In general, the performance owed its calls and encores not to its quality but to a noisy *claque*. However, De Lucia,

> ...whom we cannot praise sufficiently for his *Iris* and *Werther*, last night sang admirably..... another opera. In fact, - although delighting the ears of the audience - he succeeded in altering and transforming Puccini's music in such a way, and to give such a tragic stamp to the character of Rodolfo, that neither was perfectly recognisable. But he is always the most exquisite singer, his voice has such limpid notes [and] such delightful suppleness and gradations ... [60]

The fidelity to the score noted by the Neapolitan critic in 1897 had clearly been eroded. By the time that De Lucia came to record portions of the rôle, in 1917-20, his individualism was probably even more marked. On the words 'Che gelida manina' [No. 125], instead of remaining on the same note, he sings the rising orchestral phrase; a delicate attack on 'Cercar che giova?' includes a turn on 'che'. A further decoration, on 'notte' in 'è una notte di luna', has the mobility of quicksilver. The later

55 Celletti, 'Gli interpreti giordaniani', in Morini, *Giordano*, pp. 214-16.
56 In conversation with the writer, April 1968.
57 *Gazzetta dei Teatri*, Mar. 8 1900.
58 Da Fonseca Benvenides, op. cit., p. 141.
59 *Tribuna*, Mar. 22 1900.
60 *Messaggero*, Mar. 22 1900.

version [No. 314] is less eccentric. The rarely-recorded 'Quest'è Mimì' [No. 335] has many delightful touches: the playful turn on *compagnia*; the *morendo* on *'sboccia l'amor'*, and the eloquent delivery of *'Perchè son io il poeta'* combine in a charming, quite individual interpretation.

After *La Bohème*, Massenet's *Saffo* was given with Bellincioni but not, as had been announced, with De Lucia; no explanation was offered.[61] A few days after leaving Rome he was in Seville, to join several of the singers with whom he had latterly appeared at Lisbon. His duties there were to start with Eslava's *Miserere*, to be given in the cathedral for the first time in twelve years. An official informed De Lucia and De Segurola that they were to wear formal dress with white tie. The tenor was aghast for, not supposing that tails would be necessary for so short a stay in Seville, his were with his heavy luggage in Italy.

What was to be done? Ready-made suits were evidently unheard-of in Seville. Tense and nervous, he begged De Segurola to accompany him to see José Pacini, the company's manager. Friends began to scour the city for tails which would fit De Lucia's by-now stocky figure. At the very last minute he was able to hire a suit from a modest dramatic company, with no time even to attempt to make it fit him any better.

To compound his fears, De Lucia had learned that when Gayarre had sung the *Miserere* at the cathedral he had added a high C at the end of the tenor's final piece, and that the general public would certainly expect to hear this note. De Segurola and other members of the company who had occasion to go to the theatre would hear De Lucia trying, again and again, at different times, that famous high C.

A few minutes before they took their places in the cathedral De Lucia, his expression serious, said to De Segurola:

'Andres, I am very nervous. These damned tails and this damned high C have me worried. I wish I could run away.'

'It would', recalled the Spanish bass, 'have been better for a superstitious Neapolitan tenor like him to run away.' To De Lucia it fell to sing the final solo. De Segurola described the moment:

From my place I could see the fingers of his left hand twisting nervously. His phrasing was beautiful as usual but when, at the end of the motet, he wanted to sing that high C on the last syllable of the word 'Mi-se-re-re', he took a long deep breath, opened his mouth wide, made a supreme effort and..... an awful shrieky sound came out instead of the splendid high C of Julián Gayarre that the people expected. I heard, too, at that time the exclamations of surprise from the audience ... The distressed De Lucia attributed all to the hoodoo of his damn unfitting [sic] tails.[62]

61 Ibid., Mar. 31 1900.
62 De Segurola, op. cit., pp. 110-13 states that the *Miserere* was given on Maundy Thursday - when, he claims, De Lucia's vocal failure occurred - and Good Friday (Apr. 12 and 13 1900), with rehearsals on Apr. 10 and 11. However, the reviews (*Porvenir*, Apr. 12 and 13) reveal that (Ernesto) Colli sang both performances,

The short season at the Teatro San Fernando of Seville coincided with the Festival of the Bulls, lending topicality to the first words of a review of the opening opera, *La Bohème*, 'a work that is as modernist as the posters for the Feria'. De Lucia, the critic continued, 'was good and praiseworthy, despite certain visible deficiencies'.[63]

In *Il Barbiere di Siviglia*, on April 18th 1900, De Lucia's first act duet with Giuseppe De Luca, as Figaro, brought thunderous applause. But the critic José Sanmartino wrote with a pen more deeply analytical than most. He had, it seems, not heard the tenor before. His impressions of the voice as it was in 1900 may, for that reason, be more objective than those of critics who had heard him a decade or longer ago, and whose views were now coloured by nostalgic memories of what had been. At any rate, it is a significant description of a singer only thirty-nine years old:

> The tenor De Lucia, of whom the most enthusiastic eulogies have been made, reaches Seville in the eventide of his powers. Despite this he made himself warmly applauded in the *Barbiere*. What talent this man has!
>
> At the beginning of the cavatina 'Ecco ridente in cielo' I observed a curious manner of voice production, [when] the artist sings completely on the air, without any support, so that the sounds emerge opaque and colourless, without nuance. He goes from this *pianissimo* to his natural, supported, voice which results in a harsh contrast, lacking in gradation, in half-colour, in light and shade. So that it can clearly be seen that the artist knows how to use his vocal resources, he performs miracles which cause some to burst into thunderous applause and enthusiastic 'Bravo!', and others, like myself, are led into a sort of amazement and admiration. What a pity! Artists like De Lucia deserve to be young for ever and to have the gift of preserving their voice fresh all their life long, but..... there is no talisman with such properties and one must suffer the grief of time. Despite these reflections one cannot allow it to pass when the necessary notes are not given in ensembles, those corresponding to the chords written by the composer; for example, the G, which did not come from De Lucia in the quintet, leaving it maimed and colourless. ...I still believe that the famous tenor could have achieved a better harmony of the andante 'Ah!, qual trionfo inaspettato' with the cadenza 'Son vicino a delirar'. It is necessary to open less in the finale and give more substance at the beginning.[64]

The occasion may have caught him in one of those *abbassamenti* through which he sang in order not to disappoint a public that was hearing him for the first time. Yet singers are usually swift to ask an audience's indulgence, and no such plea was recorded. De Segurola, however, reported a complete success, in which De Lucia regained the laurels which he had lost with the high C of the *Miserere*. 'Of course', added the bass, 'he did not wear those accursed tails!'

---

without reported incident. Since De Segurola's account is otherwise consistent both with the known circumstances and with the difficulties that De Lucia was by then experiencing with high notes the failure that he describes presumably occurred at rehearsal (probably the second, since De Lucia was in Rome until Apr. 8) and caused him to withdraw from the engagement.

63 *Porvenir*, Apr. 17 1900.

64 Ibid., Apr. 19 1900.

After a short stay in Milan, De Lucia's next engagements were in
Fedora and *La Traviata* at the Imperial Theatre, Vienna. He shared in
the acclaim for Giordano; in the presentations; and in the banquet given
for the composer by Mahler, artistic director of the theatre. He was
presented to the Emperor Franz Josef. But, while travelling more
intensively than ever, his professional ambitions lay not in short seasons
in foreign capitals, but closer to home. Specifically, he wanted to resume
his career at the San Carlo, where he had not sung since his quarrel with
Musella in 1898. The means of achieving this had now emerged.

For the five winter seasons since the Stolzmann fiasco of 1894-5 the
San Carlo concession had been held by Musella and, after their
disagreement, it seemed unlikely that De Lucia could return to the
theatre during his tenure, which was due to end in March 1900. By
November 1899 the Board of Directors of the theatre had already offered
to extend Musella's contract for five years but, directed by the City
Council, it had laid down certain conditions regarding improvements at
the theatre that Musella found unacceptable.[65] Hence, he withdrew his
original proposal and resumed negotiations with the Board, obviously
hoping for a capitulation. De Lucia saw his chance: on March 27th 1900
it was reported that he and Carlo Superti, impresario of the Costanzi,
had presented to the Mayor of Naples a request for the San Carlo
concession for five years.[66]

In fact, Musella seems to have got wind of the new bid well before it
became public knowledge; on March 10th, probably fearful of losing the
theatre, he had declared himself ready to accept the conditions insisted
upon by the Board, and had signed an agreement.

But the De Lucia bid had aroused the interest of those Council
members who had previously been content to leave the matter to the
Board. There was uproar when, at the Council meeting of March 30th,
Alderman Adinolfi announced that the Board had already decided to
grant the concession to Musella, and that this new submission by
De Lucia and Superti had been admitted only 'as a sign of respect to the
illustrious signatories'.

Defying the clamour for an open contest, the City Council discussed
the matter behind closed doors. Count Caracciolo accused Musella of
having undermined the prestige of the theatre. Another councillor
pointed out the inconsistency of endorsing one proposal while admitting
another. The Mayor sought to calm the excited councillors. The San
Carlo concession, he pointed out, had never been decided by open
competition. Moreover, the De Lucia proposal offered no improvement
over Musella's bid. In fact, it was particularly vague and imprecise. It
was agreed, however, that the decision of March 10th should be held in

---

65 *Corriere dei Teatri*, Nov. 26 1899.
66 *Pungolo*, Mar. 27/28 1900.

abeyance to give De Lucia and Superti time to provide a more detailed description of their plans.[67] An autocratic time limit of five days was laid down for submission of the proposal and for payment of a bond in the substantial sum of 15,000 lire.

The situation was complicated by the absence of De Lucia, first in Rome and then in Seville. It came as no surprise that Superti soon withdrew from the lists, disliking the idea of being left with all the responsibility while the tenor undertook his tours of Europe and elsewhere. Thus, when De Lucia's lawyer Laliccia, who held power of attorney for him, paid the deposit to the Council on April 10th, the submission was from De Lucia alone. *Pungolo* remarked out that it held nothing that all impresarios did not offer: a Neapolitan conductor, a world-famous conductor, artists of international repute, and undertakings to maintain the numbers in chorus and orchestra. The only well-received new idea was that for a choral school. The proposal, 'though praiseworthy, is still too vague'.[68]

On April 12th, amid rumours that De Lucia was favoured, the Board met to consider the rival bids. Adinolfi, remarking that Superti's withdrawal left De Lucia unable to provide adequate guarantees to carry out the contract, contended that the singer's proposal represented no advance. Therefore, the Board intended to recommend to the Council that Musella's contract should be renewed. Several councillors who did not normally attend spoke in favour of De Lucia, pointing out that the San Carlo chorus was not enamoured of Musella, who had not scrupulously respected points of his previous contract. After many other contributions it was agreed to accept, more or less as they stood, the De Lucia proposals. The Board was invited to open detailed discussions with him immediately.[69]

Then, possibly because of De Lucia's absence in Seville, Vienna, and London, there was delay in formal confirmation of the Council's decision; not until the summer did it authorise the Board to undertake final negotiations with the singer.[70] There was a spate of articles in the theatrical press of Milan, including simulated interviews with Musella, confident that justice would prevail and declaring that De Lucia would not sing at the San Carlo while he managed the theatre. Commentators on the tenor's peripatetic life noted that, after Vienna, he proposed to rest until the time of his departure for North America for a season that would last from November until April: 'And the San Carlo of Naples? Will the management perhaps direct it by telegraph from New York?'[71] De Lucia, remarked *Gazzetta dei Teatri*, would earn applause if, without

---

67 Ibid., Mar. 31/Apr. 1 1900.
68 Ibid., Apr. 10/11 1900.
69 Ibid., Apr. 13/14 1900.
70 *Corriere dei Teatri*, June 12 1900.
71 *Gazzetta dei Teatri*, May 3 1900.

losing money, he could follow Musella, who could justifiably claim to have surpassed his predecessors. It should not be forgotten that it was through Musella - now accused of clouding the splendour of the San Carlo theatre - that Neapolitans had so often been privileged to enjoy the art of De Lucia.

Meanwhile, De Lucia was again in London, for the final Grau season. It started without its usual air of gaiety: no one could escape the pall of the war in South Africa. But soon the mood improved. The news that Mahon had relieved Mafeking took almost the entire audience for *Lohengrin* at Covent Garden on May 18th out into the streets for a victory celebration.

In a season which offered many evenings of Wagner, operatic London again heard only five performances from Jean de Reszke in what would prove to be his farewell there. It saw, however, the début of the diminutive lyric tenor Alessandro Bonci.

Salignac had already sung Canio in a performance that was evidently highly praised.[72] When, on June 14th, De Lucia made his début in *Pagliacci*, he was judged to be 'as strenuous as ever'.[73] The performance took place on Ascot Gold Cup day, *Punch* reminded its readers:

> ... but few of us were lucky enough to *lay* on the right *cavallo*. ... The first event was a walkover for Canio, De Lucia up, but he has been ridden to victory so often by this jockey that his win was a foregone conclusion.[74]

Don Giovanni followed. Then came the Royal Command to a State Concert at Buckingham Palace on June 25th 1900.[75] With De Lucia appeared Suzanne Adams, Louise Homer, Pol Plançon, and the chorus and orchestra of the Royal School of Music. In the absence of Queen Victoria, who was at Windsor, the Prince and Princess of Wales presided over a gathering of Empire. The fourteen hundred guests were said to represent ownership of three-quarters of the lands of England, Scotland, and Wales. The event gave Sidney Homer, watching from the organ loft, a 'tremendous impression of the concentration of power in Great Britain'.[76]

Despite their previous experience of such events it was the male singers who were least at ease: Plançon seemed nervous and De Lucia 'far from home'. The women, by contrast, were composed: Adams seemed quite unconcerned and Homer appeared calm. There was a hush as the chamberlains appeared, bowing low as they walked backwards in order not to turn their backs on the royal family. After 'God Save the Queen'

---

72 Rosenthal, op. cit., p. 291.

73 *Graphic*, June 23 1900.

74 *Punch*, June 20 1900.

75 Royal Archives. Anne Homer, *Louise Homer and the Golden Age of Opera*, p. 179, incorrectly gives the date as July 25.

76 S. Homer, op. cit., pp. 105-8.

the concert started. Each item closed in silence, in the immutable tradition that forbade applause. De Lucia sang the aria and, with Suzanne Adams, the duet from Act I of *La Bohème*.[77] Later, they were joined by Homer and Plançon in the quartet from *Rigoletto*. After the performance the Prince and Princess of Wales thanked the artists. The singers received forty guineas apiece and, at a midnight supper, 'were served a marvellous array of rare delicacies on gold plates, by an impressive array of footmen and waiters in resplendent uniforms'.[78]

The following evening there was a visit to Windsor Castle for a command performance for Queen Victoria, who recorded the event in her diary:

At 9 we all went to the Waterloo Gallery, which was arranged as usual, with lovely flowers in front of the stage, and a performance of the 1st act of *'Carmen'* followed by *'Cavalleria Rusticana'* was given. Calvé was more charming and wonderful than ever, her voice even more beautiful and powerful than before. Suzanne Adams was delightful as Micaëla. Saléza as Don José did very well and the whole *mise en scène*, chorus and orchestra were very good. Needless to say, Calvé was perfection in my favourite *'Cavalleria'*, but was not well supported by de Lucia, who bawled in all the most pathetic parts, in a distressing manner. After receiving the guests who had been invited, in the Green Drawingroom [*sic*], saw all the 'artistes', Mme Calvé coming first, wrapped in a long black cloak. Lord de Grey presented them all, as well as Mr. Grau and the 2 conductors Mr. Fleau [Flon], and Signor Mancinelli. I thanked Calvé for her kindness in coming over, as she had done, on purpose to sing before me, and she repeated that it was *'un très grand honneur que la Reine ait voulue m'entendre encore une fois'*. I gave her a sapphire and diamond pendant, and Lenchen and Beatrice gave the other presents.

At Covent Garden, Bonci had made a favourable impression, as Rodolfo to a 'frail heroine' (Melba) who dwarfed him. On July 6th De Lucia took over the part, alongside Melba and Fritzi Scheff (Musetta). His tremolo was thought 'far less noticeable than in many other operas'.[79] Puccini dismissed the performance, with Gilibert, Dufriche, and Journet, as

... so-so ... De Lucia reasonable, Musetta excellent, Mancinelli good, the others *cani*, real *cani*...[80]

In this 'amusing little opera', remarked *Punch*, 'with the exception of the duet - in which a first-rate tenor like De Lucia has the best of it - there is nothing great enough for Melba'.[81]

---

77 The wording of the programme suggests, but does not confirm, that De Lucia and Adams each sang an aria from Act I of *La Bohème*.

78 A. Homer, op. cit., p. 180.

79 *The Times*, July 9 1900.

80 (PC) Puccini to unidentified correspondent, July 6 or 7 1900.

81 *Punch*, July 11 1900.

To his familiar repertory De Lucia now added the new Puccini opera, *Tosca*, apparently the main reason for his engagement. Puccini, who had come specially to superintend the final rehearsals, wrote to his wife:

> The theatre is completely sold out. I hope to have a great success because the artists are very good ... better than at La Scala ... In the tragic moments Ternina is extraordinary. In moments of love and lightness, she has little *charme*. The second act, however, she does wonderfully, except the 'Vissi d'arte', which she sings a little like a German ... Scotti marvellous; bad voice, but talent, and of a grand stature in the part.[82]

Giulio Ricordi, meanwhile, was writing encouraging letters to the composer:

June 15th 1900

> And how is the Commendatore De Lucia performing the part?..... where does he go down?..... where does he go up?..... [83]

On June 18th, Puccini wrote:

> ... today I had the 1o rehearsal. De Lucia whom I had thought worst seemed to me the best.[84]

On July 10th, he confided:

> ... today most excellent rehearsal. I foresee a good success here. Tosca is the best of all! Splendid scenery De Lucia most excellent unrecognisable Ternina tragic enough to make one shiver, Scotti good, Mancinelli all right.[85]

At the première of the new piece, on July 12th 1900, there was disagreement on its musical value. Certainly, Puccini was dragged before the curtain, hand in hand with his singers and conductor. *Punch*, though, declared that the theatres of Italy and South America, where *Tosca* had been so successful, were welcome to keep it to themselves as an opera. Klein admitted to having had doubts concerning both the work and its heroine, though the latter were swiftly and unreservedly withdrawn before the commanding merits of Milka Ternina.[86]

The singers received much praise. Klein considered that Antonio Scotti had created the ideal presentment of the subtle and malevolent figure of Scarpia. De Lucia was a 'first-rate Cavaradossi', who gave Ternina excellent support. Here, he was thought to have a character that

---

82 (Undated), Marek, op. cit., p. 194.

83 (PC) Giulio Ricordi - Giacomo Puccini.

84 (PC) Puccini to unidentified correspondent.

85 (PC) Puccini to unidentified correspondent. Though the lack of punctuation obscures the meaning, 'unrecognisable' probably refers to De Lucia.

86 Klein, *The Golden Age*, pp. 231-2 and *Thirty Years*, pp. 455-6.

was well-suited to him, and in which he used his opportunities to great effect.[87] Particular note was taken that

> ...in his soliloquy on the strange harmony of contrasts he addressed his remarks to the picture he was painting, and, while painting it, sang in the quiet reflective way ... which the scene requires. Can any other tenor be recalled who has had the courage to do this, and avoid the urge to turn his back on his work and address the audience?[88]

His 1902 recording of 'Recondita armonia' [No. 8] is similarly quiet and reflective as he uses the head voice to observe Puccini's *pp* on the high G (presuming a tone transposition) of *'te'* in *'E te beltade ignota'*. In *'E lucevan le stelle'* [No. 313], though he separates *'languide'* from *'carezze'*, he conveys, in touches such as the two-note slide on *'veli'* in *'le belle forme disciogliea dai veli!'*, all the contemplative yearning of the condemned man. As he plays with the voice, we might imagine a San Carlo audience catching its breath before leaping to its feet, roaring its approval.

According to *The Times*, he was a 'very earnest lover, although he rather spares his listeners the terrors of the torture chamber'.[89] The vocal honours of the evening belonged, however, to Ternina. The Croatian soprano had first won Klein's encomiums as Isolde to the Tristan of Jean de Reszke in 1898: 'glorious to look at on the stage, [and] "uncommon tall" ' was how he described her.[90] Since she almost matched De Reszke for height she must have towered over De Lucia. Sidney Homer wrote of her: '...a grander artist I have never known. Her soul was in the clouds; nothing existed for her but art. ....Whenever she sang ...a large part of the company would gather in the wings and watch her.'[91] Bispham, too, described her majestic appearance, splendid voice, and great histrionic power.[92] It was largely thanks to her genius that many of the beauties of *Tosca* revealed themselves that season.[93]

On July 23rd, a night verging on the tropical, Covent Garden gave *Il Barbiere di Siviglia*. 'Light airs refresh us!', quoth the critic of *Punch* who, his heart weighed down by so much Wagner, broke into verse:

> Weary of Wagner, Meyerbeer, Puccini
> We welcome sweet, melodious Rossini.

Melba was as sprightly a Rosina as any young lady of Spain not yet out of her teens could be, singing so perfectly that 'not one young lady of Spain, Italy or Australia etc. could come within measurable distance'.

---

[87] *Musical Times*, Aug. 1900, p. 537.
[88] P.G. Hurst, *The Age of Jean de Reszke*, p. 180.
[89] *The Times*, July 13 1900.
[90] Klein, *The Golden Age*, p. 230.
[91] S. Homer, op. cit., p. 157.
[92] Bispham, op. cit., p. 291.
[93] Klein, *Thirty Years*, pp. 455-6.

As for Signor De Lucia, *his* singing as Count Almaviva, if not so honey-sweet as the serenade and the love music demand, is otherwise perfect; it is not his fault if he is not the ideal Count; Almavivas are born not made, and can't be 'made up'.[94]

In the Lesson Scene, Melba sang the Mad Scene from *Lucia*; then, heartily applauded by De Lucia and Baldelli as well as by the audience, she accompanied herself at the piano in Tosti's 'Mattinata'.[95]

For the *Musical Times* the performance was 'brilliantly spirited'; Baldelli gave a very humorous and finished picture of senile decay and fatuity; De Reszke's 'inimitably unctuous fooling as Don Basilio' clearly gave him as much pleasure as it did the audience. His singing of 'La calunnia' was considered a 'masterly exhibition of pomposity'. Melba 'revels in the hoydenish pranks of Rosina'. De Lucia was 'full of fervour and also not devoid of humour; his singing of florid music was not above reproach'.[96] *The Times* termed him a 'capital' Almaviva, despite the fact that the 'somewhat strident quality of his voice suits the modern Italian music far better than it does that of the period of the *bel canto*.'[97]

In mid-July, De Lucia telegraphed from London that he would be in Naples by the end of the month to sign the contracts prepared by his lawyer.[98] On his return, he calmly went about his business, announcing that he had released himself from his American contract for the coming winter in order to devote himself entirely to the management of the San Carlo. Laliccia advised the Mayor of an intention to sue for damages, expenses, and interest associated with the delay in awarding the concession.[99] De Lucia was, however, startled to discover the paucity of scenery and costumes remaining in the theatre. Cartoons depicted him scouring the cellars for properties. As was his right, the departing Musella had taken almost everything that was movable.[100]

The tenor's fastidiousness in his dress continued to intrigue the satirical *Monsignor Perrelli*, which reported a *signorino bassotto elegant* who had visited Salvi brothers' shop in the Toledo, leaving with evident contentment and a large quantity of their most tasteful shirts and ties.[101] De Lucia, the paper explained, considered them far superior to those obtainable in London. He continued to order suits from Caggiula. Luigi had recently died, and his son, Antonio, was now in charge. De Lucia was

---

94 *Punch*, Aug. 1 1900.
95 Ibid.
96 *Musical Times*, Aug. 1900, p. 537.
97 *The Times*, July 24 1900.
98 *Corriere dei Teatri*, July 27 1900.
99 Ibid., Aug. 10 1900.
100 *Monsignor Perrelli*, Aug. 12 1900. The page layout of this twice-weekly satirical and humorous publication is variable (and characteristically eccentric) and, since the binding of the only available file precludes separation into individual issues, some doubt attaches to the dates. The dates given are considered to be the most probable ones but, except when the item in question appears on the title page, they can be specified only to within four days.
101 Ibid., Aug. 9 1900. A *bassotto* is a Bassett Hound and also a nickname for a short man.

worried that no one would take the same care over his suits as had Luigi. Antonio reassured him: 'I promise you that I shall maintain the same standards as my father.' The singer was sceptical: 'Oh, you are young and do not have the experience. Still, let us choose a suit as a trial.'

The young tailor, intent on impressing such a good and influential client - for whom his employees would sometimes work all night in an emergency, and who would give them tickets and boxes for the opera - decided to finish the suit immediately. When De Lucia arrived for what he thought would be a fitting Caggiula confessed to his actions: the suit was ready. Grumbled De Lucia: 'These young people - so full of themselves, but understanding nothing. Better see what you have made for me!' He put on the suit, which was perfect. Embracing Caggiula, he exclaimed: 'Now I understand what you wanted to prove.'[102]

His jackets had always had a tolerance of 12 cm rather than the 2 cm allowed for a normal chest expansion. But he was no longer a slim young man, and before one Royal visit he found that his tailcoat was uncomfortably tight. He sent for Antonio's son, Luigi - whom he always jocularly called '*Il Bersagliere*', from having once seen his photograph, as a boy, dressed in their distinctive regimental uniform[103] - to measure him for a new one: 'And, also, I have tried on the trousers. I realised that I was getting fatter, but not that I was getting shorter - they are 10 cm too long.' He had not realised that stoutness shortens the distance from fork to ground, making trousers too long; he was still the same height. But stouter he certainly was. He enjoyed good food, albeit simple dishes. A favourite was the *pizza*, a culinary speciality of Naples, and he would sometimes send Enrico out at night to bring some back to the house. He did, apparently, try to control his weight by eating salads. Nadir would tell of the occasion when the waiter was taking their order in an exclusive Paris restaurant. De Lucia said that he required only fresh celery and some salt. When the waiter looked suitably scornful, Nadir said: 'Papa, everyone is looking at these two well-dressed men who order celery.' De Lucia snorted: 'I don't care a fig! I want celery!'[104]

But it was a losing battle, for he had an exceedingly sweet tooth. Some home-made cakes from a friend brought the tribute from him: 'These *dolci* are so good that they sing!'[105] Above all, he was addicted to chocolate. Whenever young Caggiula came to his house, he would say to him: '*Vieni ccà, bersagliè, miett'a man'intu u tiretto, e pigliati tutto chello che vuò.*'[106] In the desk there was invariably a large box of the richest products of the confectioner's art.

---

[102] Luigi Caggiula.

[103] The *Bersaglieri*, the crack troops of the Italian army, are recognisable by the green cock feathers that trim their hats and by their characteristically rapid march. '*Bersagliere*' is also a sobriquet for a bold young man.

[104] De Lucia family.

[105] Franz Gleijeses.

[106] Luigi Caggiula. 'Come here, *Bersagliere*! Open the drawer and take as many chocolates as you wish.'

Throughout the autumn of 1900, during the most agreeable weather for years, he relaxed at Cava with Marghieri, De Bury, and other friends among the *villeggianti*. They enjoyed the concerts given by the many musical groups, such as the Società Mandolinistica of Cava. Social events rather than musical, they were well-attended by Itala, Pia - now Signora Ricco - and by friends such as the Frascani family.[107] It was a carefree time, one to be savoured before returning to the troubles of Naples.

For the press now carried cartoons of cobwebs gathering over the stage of the San Carlo. De Lucia had reconsidered his wish to be an impresario: he wanted to retract his bid for the theatre. A satire in *Monsignor Perrelli* has him arriving by train from London, to be met by hundreds of people seeking either employment or a theatre pass. Similar numbers, each with a recommendation, greet him at the Palazzo Cirella. Calling cards await him from theatre officials, ranging from the inspector of drains to the obstetrician to the *corps de ballet*. A delegation from the San Carlo chorus asks for more money, free tickets, or help with medical bills. A building contractor suggests that for a mere 100,000 lire - of which the Council would provide half - the new impresario could create a proper foyer. Unsubtle jibes have him singing baritone rather than tenor. Even at night, in the peace of his bedroom, the wretched man is visited by the critic Mormone, seeking a post for his son.[108] One cartoon implies that subscribers were not plentiful, even at bargain prices.[109] Another suggests that De Lucia had 'been to try the water, but had retreated in time'. The moment of decision had come and gone.[110]

On September 18th 1900 the Council met *in camera* to authorise a lawsuit against the tenor. 'But whom', asked *Corriere dei Teatri*, 'would it benefit, once the theatre had reopened?' If it opened without major loss to the city, what magistrate could morally confiscate the deposit? One law-suit, more or less, mattered little to a Council that had been litigating since 1860. It certainly would not ruin De Lucia who, in the coming season, was sure to find artistic triumphs which would amply compensate him for this frustration of his managerial ambitions. The applause of the Neapolitan public would, it was suggested, soon make him forget the bailiffs' orders served on him by its civic representatives.[111]

Less than two weeks later, the San Carlo concession was awarded to a joint stock company, of which De Lucia was a member and Alberto Marghieri and Roberto de Sanna were Chairman and Managing Director.[112] It busied itself with the task of preparing for the new season.

---

107 *Corriere di Napoli*, Oct. 8 1900. Pia had married Giovanni Ricco of an aristocratic family of Naples.
108 *Monsignor Perrelli*, Aug. 9 1900.
109 Ibid., Aug. 26 1900.
110 Ibid., issues of Aug. 9 - Sept. 2 1900.
111 *Corriere dei Teatri*, Sept. 30 1900.
112 Report from Naples, Sept. 30, in *Corriere dei Teatri*, Oct. 10 1900.

The theatre was controlled by such bodies until the Great War. Although it was then taken over by Augusto Laganà, who would run it for seven years, the era of the old-fashioned impresario was, for better or for worse, already over at that theatre.[113]

On November 22nd Marghieri presented to the Town Hall a demand from De Lucia for the return of his deposit on the basis that, as a paid-up shareholder in the company controlling the theatre, he could not be deemed to have defaulted on a request made in his own name. This was only the latest twist in litigation by De Lucia for the return of his money while the Council, for its part, counter-claimed for the payment of damages and interest.[114]

Ironically, the company's choice of artistic director a year later was Carlo Superti.[115] Three months after that, De Lucia renounced his interest, in favour of the other members.[116]

His despondency over the concession was followed by personal tragedy when, on November 25th 1900, his son Armando died. His health had always been frail and now, a few days after his fourteenth birthday, he succumbed to typhoid. The death of this precocious, intelligent, and handsome boy did not bring his parents together. Instead, it made the relationship more bitter than ever.

[113] *Cento Anni di Vita del Teatro San Carlo.*
[114] *Mattino,* Nov. 23/24 1900.
[115] *Corriere dei Teatri,* Aug. 10 1901.
[116] Report from Naples, Oct. 12 1901, in *Corriere dei Teatri,* Nov. 8 1901.

17

And then - Naples... is Naples!!

> In fact, an artist who always sings loudly will impress at first, but he will eventually displease the ears, while one who can use the *mezza voce* judiciously, passing from *piano* to *forte*, will obtain a double effect, and the voice will seem more robust than it is in reality.   Vincenzo De Giorgio, *Canto e Cantanti*[1]

As the fashionable season drew nearer in the autumn of 1900 the gossip columns filled with news of the *villeggianti*, of '... the beautiful swallows, whom the heat had driven away, [as they] return to their winter nests from the country'. The name of Salvi Brothers, tailors of Via Toledo (*sic*), reappeared discreetly in those columns as chic young men ordered their evening dress for the opening of the San Carlo. In anticipation of the Naples première of *Tosca*, Carlo Clausetti planned to honour Puccini with a banquet at the Caffè Calzona. Not to be outdone, Daspuro announced a dinner for Mascagni and his friends at the Grand Hôtel, to celebrate the anticipated success of the season's Sonzogno novelty, *Le Maschere*. Almost daily came hints of the gastronomic and post-prandial delights to be offered, as each publishing house sought to outdo the other. Most of the Neapolitan critics declined to attend either.[2] The newspaper that noted, without comment, that the game-shooting season would open on December 18th, was doubtless warning subscribers that Puccini, an indefatigable hunter, might well be elsewhere.

The San Carlo was sold out when Marino Villani opened the season on December 20th 1900 with *Tosca*. The splendours of such openings could always be taken for granted. This one, however, combined the promise of a new management, the presence of De Lucia and Pandolfini, and the new opera of a composer who was dear both to the *grandes dames* and to the daughters of middle-class families. They were to be disappointed when Puccini telegraphed Mugnone, regretting that 'commitments in Milan' prevented him from attending. All the principal critics were there. The imposing figure of Matilde Serao, armed with her lorgnette, occupied a box of the second row. Pia Ricco-De Giorgio was noticed; if Itala, who was registered as a subscriber, attended her face escaped the columnist.

---

[1] Vincenzo De Giorgio had no apparent connection with Itala's family.
[2] *Monsignor Perrelli*, Dec. 16 1900.

At 9.10 pm, Mugnone raised his baton. A few bars, and the curtain rose in a silence quite as religious as that on the stage. It was a silence that lasted for most of the evening. The most that could be said, perhaps, was that the work intrigued its public, especially in the scene of the Roman dawn. However, if the audience could not be called enthusiastic, at least no one seemed actually discontented. The *sicofanti* deserved special mention for their restraint. They applauded only occasionally, when the principal singers merited the exception, but 'with what style the *sicofanti* contained themselves last night'.[3]

Those editors who devoted more space to Pandolfini's dresses than to analysis of the new opera reflected the attitude of society to the opera. But *Pungolo* had no doubts of the musical importance of the event. Exceptionally, its review started on the front page. Procida - Uda had died in April 1898 - shared some of the reservations, ranging from perplexity to hostility, regarding *Tosca* in those early years. However, he was decided in his views of the singers:

> We must not forget the caressing, almost angelic voice [in the prelude to the third act] of a young boy, Vincenzo Medina. ... In the part of Cavaradossi, a conqueror, De Lucia, the ever-delightful tenor, the ever-fascinating singer. Yesterday, he uttered everything with burning impetuosity, with honeyed but inexpressible grace. De Lucia is a master of the art of singing; he is a virtuoso of modulation and a supreme actor. ... His was the triumph in the final aria; the bewitching quality of his voice won over the audience, and it is just because he is such a distinguished singer, so rich in the intensity of his sentiment, that I would prefer him to avoid exaggerated gesture, accent or mood, all examples of an exuberant Southern temperament, [and] some examples of unrefined inflection which spoil the character of Mario.
>
> Pandolfini displayed her usual *bravura*, cultivated intelligence, dramatic gifts, and refined singing. At the height of the drama she showed exquisite histrionic powers, even if her singing was not always of the same standard. She seemed, to me, to be rather uncertain of her secure, flexible, educated voice. [However] she gave the character the boldness and passion that it demands [and] sang with rare polish where the musical line was not the principal one.[4]

At the second performance De Lucia repeated his two arias and had a remarkable artistic moment in the outburst '*Ah! C'è un Dio vendicator!*'[5] On later occasions, the critics noted how he embellished and illuminated his two arias.[6] He was a '*charmeur*',[7] singing with the smoothness and penetrating grace that had made him the favourite of the stalls![8]

A comic element invested one finale when, two of the musketeers having fired before the signal, Cavaradossi delayed his fall until the regulation volley had been discharged. Not everyone, in any case, took

3 *Corriere di Napoli*, Dec. 21 1900.
4 *Pungolo*, Dec. 21/22 1900.
5 *Corriere di Napoli*, Dec. 24 1900.
6 *Pungolo*, Jan. 9/10 1901.
7 Ibid., Jan. 29/30 1901.
8 Ibid., Jan. 9/10 1901.

Tosca seriously. Ugo Ricci indulged himself in some lines of doggerel:

Tosca arrives and cries: Where is the *Commendatore?*
- But he is coming - But what are they doing? No, nothing, a folly. . . . .
Give me a kiss! Give me De Lucia![9]

It was a part which gave full scope to De Lucia's histrionic abilities. One night, at the phrase *'Io muoio disperato'*, he pulled out a lock of hair which he afterwards kept in his wallet, sometimes showing it to his friends. Though cynics suggested that only a wig had suffered the story attained the currency that is reserved for true celebrities.[10]

The latest Mascagni opera, *Le Maschere*, was to be staged at Naples as one of seven simultaneous premières. As he toured the theatres involved, the composer came to Naples on January 12th, for a rehearsal which took all afternoon, and left for Rome the same day without answering the question about which speculation was rife: was Florindo to be sung by Alessandro Ravazzolo or by De Lucia?[11] The latter had read the part, with which he was said to be impressed, but had not committed himself because of the very high *tessitura*. Procida loftily announced later that *he* had known, on the morning of the 13th, that De Lucia had accepted the rôle but had reserved his opinion of the *tessitura* as it related to his own voice. Intimates of the tenor expressed the same opinion. But, after rehearsals, De Lucia's doubts returned, and this time he did not vacillate. Ignoring the mischievous suggestion that no one would notice if the part were sung by a baritone, the management searched for another tenor. Anselmi was quickly confirmed for the part; though his singing of Elvino at the San Carlo had drawn criticism, much of it had been tongue-in-cheek, such as 'his attempted emulation of De Lucia in singing *La Sonnambula* with the same style as he used for *La Bohème'*.[12] However, it was too late to match Genoa, Milan, Rome, Turin, Venice, and Verona, and to give the première on January 17th 1901. Characteristically, Naples was two days late.

On January 27th 1901 Giuseppe Verdi died and the San Carlo was closed in homage. A commemorative performance was soon in preparation. De Lucia's suggestion, it was said, was that it should include extracts from *Falstaff*. *Monsignor Perrelli* declared that this was not - 'as malicious gossip had it' - because the principal part was for baritone, but to allow Naples to hear an exquisite performance of Fenton's aria.[13] A month later, the concert took place at the San Carlo. The first applause broke out as a bronze bust of Verdi was placed on a column in the centre of the stage. The programme included the overture

---

[9] *Monsignor Perrelli*, Dec. 20 1900.
[10] F. De Filippis, *Napoli Teatrale*, pp. 135-7.
[11] *Pungolo*, Jan. 13/14 1901.
[12] *Monsignor Perrelli*, Jan. 3 1901.
[13] Ibid., Feb. 3 1901.

from *Luisa Miller*; from the same work Anselmi gave 'Quando le sere al placido'. Extracts from *I Lombardi, Nabucco, Rigoletto, Ernani, Macbeth,* and *La Forza del Destino* followed. The programme ended with Act IV of *La Traviata*, sung 'most movingly' by De Lucia, Pandolfini, and Camera. Even *Monsignor Perrelli* could find nothing more to criticise than the tenor's morning coat, the colour of tobacco, 'which gave the great Fernando the aspect of half a cigar'.[14]

Mugnone, who had received royal recognition when the King himself had nominated him Cavaliere of the Ordine Mauriziano, one of the most prestigious of Italian orders, was well appreciated at Naples that season. His transformation of the San Carlo orchestra and his conducting, especially in *Tosca*, had gained warm praise from his native audiences and critics. It was regarded as a major achievement that, despite the attendant difficulties, he had put *Le Maschere* on stage only two days late. With *La Bohème*, on January 31st 1901, the accolade grew still more cordial:

> This unrivalled score of Puccini was greeted with the most enthusiastic applause; . . . the orchestra has never displayed such refinement, colouring and fire in an atmosphere of overwhelming sound, which the conductor succeeded in transfusing last night, thanks to his energetic gestures and fiery glances. . . . Our great audience conferred its recognition on this happy worker of miracles in the form of loud acclaim at the end of every act.[15]

He was well supported by his singers: Pandolfini's Mimì was 'a gentle creation; her fresh, caressing voice, her exquisite acting, the deep sentiment of her interpretation gave the poetic figure of Mimì a rare element of grace'; De Lucia displayed 'strength as a most sensitive artist and sincere actor - never was his charm so undeniable as last night'.[16]

Mugnone may not have appreciated this 'charm'. He could not always bring himself to approve of De Lucia's vocal effects, which frequently amounted to alterations to the score. The two were often in dispute over them, but Mugnone could not gainsay their popularity. When De Lucia sang a *filata* the voice died away to a thread until, when it seemed that no breath could be left, he produced a *gruppetto* and the audience erupted in wild enthusiasm. They were effects which, while orchestras paused and conductors fulminated, drove audiences frantic. At the San Carlo, Mugnone could impose his authority up to a point, but no further.

As he returned from Palermo, early in April 1901, Puccini paused at Naples. After a banquet at the Vesuvius observatory he attended the San Carlo *Tosca* of April 1st. His presence provoked even fiercer demands for encores. What the composer thought of them, especially the repetition of

---

[14] Ibid., Feb. 28 1901.

[15] *Pungolo*, Feb. 1/2 1901.

[16] Ibid.

the 'Roman dawn' scene, is not recorded. The 'absolute explosion' of applause and calls at the end of the opera formally confirmed his triumph. He was called fully twenty times, and received many gifts. But a cartoon, featuring Puccini and Mugnone, put the event in perspective:

> Puccini: What a pleasure to receive so many gifts. I shall keep them as souvenirs [*ricordi*].
> Mugnone: Don't bother! It is really Ricordi who has paid for them.[17]

There was special interest in Giordano's *Fedora*, also new for Naples, since both the composer - a pupil of San Pietro a Maiella - and the librettist, Arturo Colautti, had strong local connections. Even so, since it had already been given elsewhere, both in Italy and abroad, there was the usual resolve not to endorse too readily the verdict of other audiences, especially those of Milan.

In a satire on the *prova generale, Monsignor Perrelli* lampooned the local reverence accorded De Lucia. Especially sycophantic were Averolino and Agamennone De Giorgio. They, it wrote, stoutly maintained that '*Il Commendatore* always behaves like God - even when he is not singing.'[18]

At the première, on April 8th 1901, the opera was received coolly. The first act ended without applause. Some hisses came from on high. There was an immediate, perverse, reaction from those who felt their position as judges to be usurped, and even the orchestra joined in the applause that followed. Yet all knew that this was not acclaim for the work - still being assessed by the *cognoscenti* - but a message to the *anti-claque* to give it a fair hearing. The whole affair was deplored by the *sicofanti*. Cavaliere Monaco and Prince Castagneto, gesticulating expressively, were incensed by the action of the orchestra, whose applause should, they considered, be reserved to honour the work of a great maestro. 'In our time,' they exclaimed to younger subscribers, 'such a thing would never have happened.'[19]

Backstage, the Fedora, Angelica Pandolfini, began to panic. Giordano, almost frantic, paced about nervously. De Lucia, who was not required until Act II, kept to his dressing room, his throat protected by a scarf. At his call, he met Giordano, who expressed his anxieties. The composer's words were despairing: 'It's finished, they don't like it!' In broad Neapolitan, De Lucia's reply was blithely self-confident: *'Umbè, 'nun te piglià collera: famme'ascì a 'mme e t'acconcio tutte cose io!!'*[20] Giordano, thinking that he meant to go on stage prematurely, to appeal to the audience, caught him by the lapels: 'No! For pity's sake!' But the *divo*

---

17 *Monsignor Perrelli*, Apr. 4 1901.

18 Ibid., Apr. 7th 1901. Averolino was a professor at San Pietro a Maiella. He was, almost certainly, closely related to Achemenide and Adelgonda De Giorgio and, therefore, to De Lucia by marriage. No Agamennone De Giorgio is known; the reference may be a joke against the pompous Achemenide.

19 *Corriere di Napoli*, Apr. 9 1901.

20 'Umberto, don't upset yourself: let me go out there and I will settle everything!' *Mezzogiorno*, Feb. 24/25 1925.

calmed him, and awaited his cue. Nor was his assurance misplaced. The review in the *Corriere di Napoli* was as though the performance were still in progress, all its urgency conveyed in the present tense. In the second act duet with Fedora, De Lucia

> ... is simply bewitching. A hurricane of applause greets the *divo* at the end of the *strofa* 'Amor ti vieta'.
>
> It is an extract of sweet and fascinating melody. The public leaps to its feet and calls unanimously for ... Giordano. De Lucia has to give an encore ...
>
> Angelica Pandolfini sings ... with great warmth and with most fascinating sweetness. When Loris confesses to having killed Vladimir, Pandolfini has an outburst of terrifying dramatic intensity. Sustained applause rewards the two unapproachable interpreters of Giordano's music.....
>
> De Lucia carries away the immense crowd when, with all the dramatic power of which his temperament is capable, he sings, in an outburst full of ardour and sorrow, 'Vedi, io piango, ma se piango'.[21]

Procida noted five calls after the second act, and eight after the third:

> Last night, Fernando De Lucia sang wonderfully. With exquisite passion in the romanza, with impressive diction in the dialogue at the reception, with varied inflections, ample humour and vocal colour in the narrative and, finally, with spirit and with bold melodious force at the close of the duet ... [Let him] stay in that idiom, make it perhaps a little more sober in action and gesture, and Loris may then be placed among his masterly parts. Change only one thing: the cravat in the third act. It is the only thing that.....jars, in De Lucia.[22]

The precise meaning of the words with which Giordano is said to have congratulated his Loris must, in the context of De Lucia's known embellishments and caprices, forever remain a conundrum: 'Fernando, it was as though the romanza had been written by you, not by me!'[23]

Whatever he meant, Giordano was clearly delighted. He doubtless shared the views of *Mattino* on De Lucia's 'complete triumph, ... magnificent in the second act, ... complete mastery of his vocal powers, ... [his] irresistible, penetrating sweetness, his honeyed tones ...'[24] Even *Monsignor Perrelli* described the tenor as 'divine'. *Fedora* was a work which would continue to win De Lucia acclaim until his final years on the operatic stage. His score is marked:

'Like *Carmen*, [an] opera that made me tremble.'

At Mugnone's *serata d'onore* - the *Fedora* of April 11th 1901 - the list of gifts was impressive: from the theatre administration, from the

---

21 *Corriere di Napoli*, Apr. 9 1901.

22 *Pungolo*, Apr. 9/10 1901.

23 Luigi de Lillo.

24 *Mattino*, Apr. 9/10 1901.

orchestra, and from singers Rina Giachetti,[25] Edoardo Camera, Raffaele De Rosa, Costantino Thos, and Ettore Borelli.[26] To all these marks of esteem the satirists added some imaginary ones: from De Lucia an embalmed top C from the chest; from Pandolfini a French 'r', translated into Italian; from the tenor Schiavazzi a silver *stecca*;[27] from Rina Giachetti 'a portrait of herself in *décolleté* (a gift that caused uproar in the maestro's house)'.[28]

On April 12th there was a benefit concert at the San Carlo. On such a good-humoured occasion the press again paid special attention to Giachetti's well-developed physique and the possibilities for word-play offered by her name.[29] De Lucia, announced to sing the 'romanza' from *Tosca*, sang instead a *romanza da salone*, then a *serenata di strada*. Then, it seems, it required some effort to dissuade him from singing a disreputable *canzone di mala vita*.[30] More sober reviews wrote of his having 'extemporised' two romanzas of Tosti, and one of Costa.[31]

By now he was a pillar of Neapolitan society. Not only among opera goers had his name no need of 'Fernando', or 'Ferdinando', as some critics insisted on calling him, in reference to the supposed affectation of shortening his name. For many he was a fetish, an object of adoration bordering on idolatry. His fame transcended social class. Di Giacomo wrote of two street urchins, in their street make-believe, as 'a little De Lucia of the tenements, a twelve-year-old Gayarre of the Eden [a local flea-pit]'. However, such fame carried its penalties, and the tenor now found himself the object of some amiable mockery. In an age when the opera was a popular entertainment and its great singers were some of the most prominent and illustrious beings on earth, they endorsed everything from pianos to hair-cream and from liqueurs to soap, sometimes with unintended humour. The 'Pink Pills' praised by Francesco Marconi as an influenza nostrum had - four years earlier, in another newspaper and another city - been promoted as a sovereign remedy for 'all the disorders of the female organism'.

In common with many singers and composers who doubtless made a useful income from the practice De Lucia had lent his name to the sale of 'Sulphurol', a locally-made patent cold and cough remedy, 'very useful for singers'.[32] *Monsignor Perrelli*, which had teased him mercilessly over the shirts that he had, perhaps unwittingly, advertised earlier, now printed

---

25　Sometimes Giacchetti. Rina's sister, Ada Giachetti-Botti, had sung at the San Carlo in 1896-7.

26　*Pungolo*, Apr. 12/13 1901.

27　*stecca* = paper knife, but also a false note.

28　*Monsignor Perrelli*, Apr. 14 1901 mischievously refers to Mugnone's long-standing association with the Giachetti sisters. Press and public were later to take a great interest in Rina's close friendship with Roberto De Sanna, Managing Director of the San Carlo.

29　*giacchetta* = jacket.

30　*Monsignor Perrelli*, Apr. 14 1901.

31　*Pungolo*, Apr. 13/14 1901.

32　See, for example, *Corriere di Napoli*, Mar. 16 1901.

a 'letter' which had him claiming that Salvi's ten-lire shirts, like 'Sulphurol', were 'most beneficial for chills and stubborn coughs'.[33] Another 'letter', supposedly from Salvi Bros, refuted the rumour that they had furnished the ties and shirts of the Russians and French in *Fedora*. Their Russian clientele, they stated, was 'composed simply of the Comm. De Lucia and several Grand Dukes of the Imperial Household'. Reporters supposedly sent to obtain from the tenor the *ex cathedra* biographical information deemed essential for a 'personality of such enormous importance' returned empty-handed from Cava de' Tirreni, their trousers ripped by savage dogs. The banter went on for months.

With *Fedora*, given with the usual festivities, the San Carlo season closed on April 15th 1901. There had been sly references to Musella's replacement at the San Carlo by 'one of his last baritones',[34] but *Monsignor Perrelli* had generally praised De Lucia's singing. No further appearances have been traced for him for that year. He remained at Naples throughout the spring of 1901 while the new management of the San Carlo discussed next season's repertoire and artists with the agent Bergamina. In May it was announced that the company would include De Lucia, Bellincioni, and Caruso.[35] By late June, exceptionally early, he was able to leave for the peace of Cava and for his first lengthy rest for several years. His preoccupation with management rather than singing had enabled *Monsignor Perrelli* to write spitefully - and equivocally - of '...De Lucia, then, who for some time has ceased to be a tenor'.[36]

Despite an outbreak of plague, which had at one time threatened the winter operatic programme, *Lohengrin*, with Viñas,duly opened the San Carlo season on December 21st; local interest, though, was fixed firmly on the début there of the 28-year-old Caruso.

Of all tenors, Caruso's early history needs no rehearsal here except to remark that, from 1894 onwards, he had sung in the smaller Neapolitan theatres, such as the Nuovo, Bellini - where he had gained the accolade that he 'sings *à la* De Lucia' - and Mercadante.[37] Subsequently, he had appeared in major theatres in Italy - latterly at La Scala - Russia, and South America; he could fairly be reckoned a seasoned artist, for whom many Neapolitans felt an engagement at the San Carlo was overdue.[38] Caruso, it seems, anticipated unstinted acclaim in his native city.

His San Carlo début, which took place in *L'Elisir d'Amore* on December 30th 1901, is possibly the most exhaustively analysed of any singer, and it remains controversial. His success there surpassed that of many well-established celebrities on similar occasions. But it was not the

33 *Monsignor Perrelli*, Mar. 17 1901.
34 Ibid., Aug. 12 1900.
35 *Gazzetta dei Teatri*, May 30 1901.
36 *Monsignor Perrelli*, July 7 1901.
37 Key and Zirato, *Enrico Caruso*, p. 74.
38 *Monsignor Perrelli*, Oct. 20 1901.

unqualified triumph that he had expected. The coolness of his reception
has been attributed - with various levels of probability - to high prices
and a short performance; to insufficient deference to the *sicofanti*; to
failing to call on the principal critics; to a style which, after the subtle
modulations of De Lucia, was found unrefined; to the influence of the
older tenor who, in later years at any rate, could be jealous of young
singers, and - probably decisively - to Neapolitan determination not to
endorse uncritically the verdict of Milan.

The reviews by Procida, whom Daspuro claims to have been 'a great
friend and fanatical admirer of De Lucia', are said to have been specially
wounding to Caruso. But were they so damning? For their historical
interest, for their particular relevance to De Lucia, and for the fact that -
to this day - they continue to form the basis for so many accusations,
they are worth quoting at length. Of the première, Procida wrote:

> For the expected ice of the première last night's audience substituted a great
> deal of anticipated benevolence. The name of Enrico Caruso reached us adorned
> by the most refulgent adjectives, and this could not displease the citizens who
> had witnessed the début of the young tenor, no more than five years ago, at the
> Mercadante. . . . But the benevolence did not preclude a jealous independence of
> its own verdict, and our public does not immediately abandon itself to sheep-
> like enthusiasm. First, it wished to judge, then endorse. . . .
> The young, very fortunate *divo* - although I do not believe in the precocious
> use of this word, especially when we remember how great singers of the past
> worked so hard and so long before they achieved greatness - seemed to me last
> night, in the first act, completely terrified by his own fame.
> Even the intrinsic quality of his voice suffered, and also the purity of his
> vocal line and the comic quality of the part, which Caruso slightly exaggerated.
> Later, the applause of the audience seemed to restore the artist a little . . . and
> after the curtain calls, which showed the audience to be very favourable
> towards Caruso, we were able to judge him fairly.
> This is my own, very frank impression: Caruso possesses a voice with
> baritone-like tones: of good volume, equalised, of adequate range, with a ringing
> tone, and all this contributes to his theatrical success.[39] He possesses notes of a
> rare power (his B flat has a full, pealing, silvery tone) but I cannot see that his
> technical knowledge is in the same measure as his voice, [which has been] well
> endowed by nature. Such technical knowledge would enable him to discipline
> these natural gifts and make the voice much fuller, much smoother in vocal
> production, and far more elastic and agile in light and florid singing such as is
> required in *L'Elisir d'Amore*, the changes of register more impeccable, the
> intonation, which (and I hope that it was merely a question of his début) was
> sometimes extremely uncertain last night, more precise; overall, I do not yet
> recognise in Caruso the artist to whom the world already accords such acclaim
> and attributes a voice so pre-eminently endowed.[40]

In Procida's review we find criticism not of the voice but of the style
and of Caruso's obstinacy in singing music of *mezzo carattere* on the

---

[39] Fred Gaisberg, who heard him at that time, also used the term 'baritonal' about Caruso.

[40] *Pungolo*, Dec. 31 1901/Jan. 1 1902. The several editions of the newspaper reflect changes but the
sentiments of the review remain unchanged.

strength of his success as Nemorino at La Scala. He reproached him for the passion that he brought to the part:

> . . . I do not understand why Caruso persists in singing music of *mezzo carattere* such as *L'Elisir*. I know: at La Scala of Milan he had a tumultuous success in this light and frivolous opera . . . . And what does that mean? An artist must realise the extent of his capabilities and not allow himself to be swayed by the mistaken judgements of the audience.
>
> Now, Caruso gives fire and colour to his voice - which is not yet fully educated - he sings with profound accents, and in an impetuous manner; he is indeed a most passionate singer and was loudly acclaimed last night. . . . And is he under the impression that, with such passionate quality [and with] the elements of an clearly dramatic temperament, he can sing this type of music which, on the contrary, requires cold, inexorable, patient vocal discipline? How can one hope to sing equally well the tenor parts in . . . *Il Barbiere* and . . . *Tosca*? To do this would mean spoiling the purity of the natural voice; one would need the mastery of a Stagno. One would need to inure the voice to this kind of singing, so as to avoid the dangers of a double repertory. But Caruso . . . is far from achieving that kind of prodigious art . . . and for now, [he] should choose one of the two genres. I certainly do not commend *virtuosity* to him. It seems to me that he does not have the right style, so much so that Nemorino seems, at times, to adopt gestures and phrasing more typical of Raoul or Enzo Grimaldo. I believe that Caruso must adopt the dramatic genre which, without aspiring to the heroic, conveys the passionate ardour of the contemporary. Last night, in the romanza, the accent of sadness was so warm and so real and he was so involved in certain heroic passages that there was no doubt where his real métier lies.[41]

An eminently sensible view was that of the critic who wrote:

> Caruso's reception - acclaim without delirium or excess - had the excellent virtue of balance. . . . to appreciate him completely the public must hear him in a more vigorous and modern work.[42]

Caruso had many calls. He had not, though, received the unequivocal acclaim that he had thought his due. He may not have been amused when the irrepressible Ricci suggested that the true triumph of the evening of December 30th 1901 belonged to the gleaming fronts of Salvi's shirts. And he may again have been hurt when, a fortnight later, he sang Massenet's Des Grieux. Procida, commenting that he was obliged to treat him with the severity commensurate with his fame and his fee, again admired the voice, which displayed some of the most limpid notes that he had ever heard, but found that Caruso

> . . . lacked the *charme* of the singer, the vocal finesse of the artist, the elegance of the actor, the refined diction derived only from a study of one's vocal organ, a diligent calculation of its colour, and wise vocal technique. Now, his voice is placed too much in the throat rather than in the head, he makes too great a use of passages from loud notes to *mezza voce*, with no shading at all, [sometimes] producing ugly sounds. . . . Caruso either emits notes of a Tamagno-like quality,

41 Ibid.
42 *Mattino*, Dec. 31 1901/Jan. 1 1902.

perhaps because the great tenor was in the audience, or exhibits provincial mannerisms.

The 'Sogno' is a little affected, with no dreamy quality. Caruso's gifts are better realised here than in *L'Elisir* ... but one notes, equally, the defects; we may indeed have a great singer one day, perhaps even an artist. ... he must discipline, refine, instruct himself.[43]

Undoubtedly, De Lucia was popular with the *sicofanti*. Emilio De Marchi was almost certainly referring to him and to his local following when, as early as 1891, he wrote apprehensively of singing at the San Carlo:

'*E poi, e poi - Napoli* . . . . . *è Napoli!!!!!! C'è u commendatore.* . . . . '.[44]

However, as we have seen, De Lucia was not immune from harsh reviews from Neapolitan writers. For all his supposed influence, he had received, and continued to receive, when appropriate, maulings from the local press, including Procida. There is no evidence whatever that the latter favoured him. If these notices on Caruso are not without adverse criticism - and few singers escaped some criticism at the San Carlo - there is also much that is positive. Notably, Procida's reviews of later performances of *Elisir* have been virtually ignored. Thus, his verdict on the second:

Caruso, last night, confirmed all convictions that his voice is one of the most powerful, freshest, most malleable, and [one] which, by study and refinement of its most valuable qualities, [is] found once in a million times. ... Caruso sang ['Una furtiva lagrima'] marvellously, ... with wonderful effects of sonority, accent and colour.[45]

About his Nemorino of January 5th 1902, Procida verged on the ecstatic. The charge of excessive severity with a young singer is unsubstantiated. But the press, then as now, thrived on confrontation and was prepared to manufacture a rivalry if none existed; humorous speculation about the numbers of tickets bought by Caruso's friends or by De Lucia's relatives for the début of the other singer was doubtless thought more amusing than the facts.

There remains the allegation - and it is only that - that at Caruso's first *Manon* at the San Carlo, on January 16th 1902, De Lucia was in a box, very close to the stage, and that he asked his companions, perhaps a trifle more loudly than was necessary: '*Che modo di cantare è questo?*'[46]

---

43 *Pungolo*, Jan. 17/18 1902.

44 (BLS) Letter De Marchi - D'Ormeville, Bologna, Sept. 15 1891. 'And then, and then - Naples . . . . . is Naples!!!!!! There is the Commendatore. . . . . ' The underlining is De Marchi's.

45 *Pungolo*, Jan. 3/4 1902.

46 Angelo Notariello. 'What manner of singing is this?' Notariello heard this from Agostino Roche, his teacher at San Pietro a Maiella. Though De Lucia sang in Budapest on Jan. 19th he could still have been in

True or false, assertions about two such dominant - and incomparably different - vocal personalities continue to make good copy. Through the years, they have been told, retold, and embellished. They have become folklore, along with the comparisons, the controversies, the analyses of whether or not they were friends, and the stories of spaghetti dinners and reputed competitions in singing Tosti's 'Marechiare'.[47]

Meanwhile, De Lucia was finding new audiences in Warsaw and Budapest. Not until late in the season did he return to the San Carlo, to sing his first Almaviva in Italy, on February 27th 1902. Procida wrote:

> De Lucia showed the greatness of his fascination in the first *serenata*, 'Ecco ridente'. The penetrating sweetness of a voice that touches the innermost chords and exquisitely strikes the innate sentimentality of our audience immediately acted like a philtre; De Lucia modulated the sweet melody with a stimulating quality and a sentiment which are in the nature of the distinguished tenor; flexible, smooth, and caressing, his voice seduces by the beauty of its timbre. ... it is astonishing that a singer who is so knowing, and of such a sentimental nature, sustained a rôle in such playful and strongly rhythmic music, which requires so much technical agility, without ever jumping a note, using a voice that is not usually exercised in such technical requirements, but [is] dedicated to *Carmen*, and which has become heavier as a result of his performance of Loris. Enough of all that: [despite] certain technical difficulties it was an extraordinary achievement, and [the applause was for] the exquisite art of the singer and also for his excellent acting and movement as Count Almaviva.[48]

With Ancona, who played Figaro in the caustic and penetrating spirit of the Beaumarchais original, and Pinkert, De Lucia sang Almaviva with good Rossinian style. Polished and animated, he coloured the recitatives with grace and exceptional facility. 'The smoothest among tenors', he displayed all the gaiety and clear diction which are essential in Rossini.[49]

The reviews of *Il Barbiere di Siviglia* are interesting for the light that Procida - an informed judge with a good critical and historical knowledge of De Lucia - casts on the nature of his voice as he neared the end of his operatic career. For listeners today, much of his fame lies in his technical prowess and, especially, in the delicate, flexible singing of his recordings of *Il Barbiere*. Significantly, even before De Lucia made the first of those records, Procida - who was possibly unaware of how often he had sung Almaviva abroad - was writing of 'technical difficulties' and of the extent to which the voice had become heavier. It had been Procida who, a decade earlier, had sounded the first traceable warning of the perils of weighting the centre of the voice, to the detriment of the high notes.

Naples on the 16th.

[47] See, for example, 'Una sfida [contest] memorabile fra Caruso e De Lucia', *Corriere di Napoli*, Jan. 12 1964; 'La voce di Napoli si chiama De Lucia', *Mattino*, Jan. 8 1987; 'Ma con Caruso Napoli non è ingrata', *Mattino*, Mar. 25 1988; 'Napoli e Caruso', Letters in *Mattino*, Apr. 14 1988.

[48] *Pungolo*, Feb. 28/Mar. 1 1902.

[49] Ibid., Mar. 3/4 1902.

De Lucia had not sung with his old friend Mario Ancona since 1899. The baritone, whose urbanity had earned him the nickname of Baron de Ancona, particularly enjoyed the social life of the season. Most nights, when not on stage, his 'superb blonde beard and impeccable *smoking English* [smoking jacket]' were to be seen in the stalls of the San Carlo, at the Caffettuccio, along Via Chiaia, or at Santa Lucia.[50]

There were complaints about the mediocre presentation of *Carmen*, De Lucia's next opera, and about the prices. Nevertheless, a capacity audience was drawn by the magnet of one who was 'still the great Don José'. Procida wrote of one performance:

> It is impossible - for anyone who was not present - to imagine what a tender, burning, enraged, desperate Don José De Lucia was last night. ... In the third act [there was] delirium, in the fourth an endless ovation. Seldom has De Lucia been so inspired and rarely has his sweet voice so arrogantly ravished the audience. ... From the first row of the stalls to the last row of the pit, people were on their feet, cheering.[51]

But other reviewers concerned themselves with the voice, rather than the interpretation:

> Others, perhaps, will praise him and extol his virtues as usual. I am not so disposed. He sang with passion ... but I did not recognise in him the De Lucia of one time, of the sweet and seductive voice ... He is now too baritonal, and not attractively so. Compared with Caruso, he seems a tenor of the third rank.[52]

His next work was *Fedora*, with Bellincioni, 'that glittering gem of the lyric stage', whose exquisite gowns - which were different for each performance - were much discussed in the *salotti* and the cafés as well as the San Carlo boxes. What a shame, murmured some, that she did not change the voice and, especially, the intonation![53] But others, despite her now restricted vocal range, took pleasure in the dramatic powers, the graceful womanliness, and the magnetic interpretation of one

> ... whose aristocratic personage has lost nothing of its fascinating grace, whose face retains the same profound expression, whose art still resonates with that dramatic quality ... as it becomes animated in the accentuation of the words, in the electrifying diction, in her mobile bearing, whose Fedora is unlike any other, precisely because the character lives with a dramatic fire all its own.[54]

Of De Lucia's Loris of March 29th 1902 *Sud* wrote

> Fernando De Lucia who, in his dramatic art, becomes ever more insuperable, still obstinately wants to sing as a *tenor*. This is a truly strange demand, which

---

50 *Monsignor Perrelli*, Jan. 1 1902.
51 *Pungolo*, Mar. 18/19 1902.
52 *Sud*, Mar. 13 1902.
53 *Monsignor Perrelli*, Apr. 1 1902.
54 *Pungolo*, Mar. 31/Apr. 1 1902.

contrasts with his talent as musician and distinguished artist. The drama and the action very much help the *ex-divo* in his prodigious art but, despite his efforts, not a limpid, sonorous note comes to illuminate the beautiful music of *Fedora*.[55]

The tenor had cancelled a number of performances during that season and, possibly as a result of years of singing rôles which were too heavy for him, he may have been in poor vocal health.[56] Various critical references show beyond question that (like many other singers[57]) he transposed on stage. De Segurola, remarking that the deterioration in recent years of De Lucia's high notes had compelled him to transpose some of his pieces to lower keys, noted that conductors 'generally consented to this' in consideration of his exceptional reputation and undisputed artistry.[58] It is said that, as Mascagni and some friends, De Segurola among them, strolled about Naples after a generous luncheon, someone pointed out De Lucia's house to them:

'Santa Madonna, it must be worth a million or more! ... that is the only piece that my friend De Lucia can never transpose.'

exclaimed the quick-witted composer.[59]

In 1902, however, few would have agreed with the judgement of *Sud*. Though, as Bellincioni recalled, the practice inconvenienced his partners in *Fedora*,[60] not everyone recognised De Lucia's transpositions or felt that they were important compared with his commanding merits. The audience applauded continually and frenziedly. During the second and third acts the tenor was called at least twenty times to the footlights.

The *Fedora* of April 10th 1902 was his farewell and the occasion for presentations of garlands and, from Bellincioni, his portrait in a magnificent silver frame.[61] Perhaps, speculated the satirists, he was going to fulfil that famous American engagement at 200,000 lire - 'unless this information is also..... a tone down!'[62]

---

55 *Sud*, Mar. 30 1902.

56 Notwithstanding the difficulties (discussed in the Introduction to the Discography) of determining the correct playing speeds for De Lucia's records, some of his 1902 series seem to be more heavily transposed than are his later recordings of the same pieces.

57 For some comparatively recent and well-documented examples see David Hamilton, *Record Collector*, Vol. 34, Nos. 5-7, July 1989, p. 144.

58 (LCML) De Segurola, op. cit., p. 113.

59 (LCML) De Segurola, op. cit., pp. 113-14. The incident occurred during De Segurola's season at the San Carlo, in 1907-8. Other versions of this story are still current in Naples; one of them attributes the remark to Mugnone, in conversation with the bass Melchiore Luise. Mascagni, a noted punster, doubtless used the verb 'trasportare' (to remove or transport, but also to transpose; the same range of possible meanings also gave rise to one of De Lucia's nicknames, 'Gondrand', after the old-established Italian removals company.

60 Franz Gleijeses.

61 *Pungolo*, Apr. 11/12 1902.

62 *Monsignor Perrelli*, Apr. 1 1902. The American engagement did not materialise; however, an unexplained curiosity is a programme of *Guglielmo Ratcliff*, scheduled for Philadelphia, Oct. 15 1902, as part of the Mascagni tour of the United States, which gives an (unspecified) De Lucia in the minor part of John (LCML). The performance was cancelled, evidently for financial reasons; see *Boston Traveler*, Nov. 6 1902.

Five appearances at Palermo offered Sicilians the opportunity to congratulate Giordano and to hear De Lucia, Pandolfini, and Giuseppe De Luca in *Fedora*, conducted by Mugnone. It was also their first exposure, since the pre-début days of 1885, to De Lucia's *'mezza voce*, an enchantment of tenderness; his high notes limpid, bell-like, penetrating; his elegance of the highest. . . . he has come to startle us and move us to tears.'[63] The enthusiasm was 'delirious', wrote another critic, stating with '[our] habitual sincerity that anyone who hears De Lucia is moved and bewitched'.[64]

He refused confirmation at Palermo in order to sing two performances of *Manon* at Naples. He had to change at short notice from the drama of Loris to the miniatures, the delicacy, and the gentle vocal modulations of Massenet. And he succeeded well enough:

> . . . expert singer of every blandishment and of every tenderness, he sang the first duet with insight, the 'Dream' with singular dexterity, . . . [and] caressed the *gruppetto* with splendid incisiveness.[65]

The San Carlo season over, there was eager anticipation of a benefit concert organised by the great Neapolitan comedy actor Edoardo Scarpetta for the Theatrical Association. It had already been postponed for a week through the illness of De Lucia, who was to have sung songs. On the eve of the performance he again declined to sing, on account of 'chronic catarrh' and other indispositions 'caused by slight atmospheric changes'. In summer temperatures the excuse was considered to be a poor one, and the resulting financial losses caused no little ill-feeling. Perhaps the tenor had caught cold riding in the horseless carriage - then very much a preserve of the affluent - that he had recently purchased.[66] But, as one writer remarked, 'do you not think that a *divo* - and the press has always enthusiastically agreed that he is such - has the right to his caprices, and that the chivalry which bows to minor female hysterics applies also to the minor derangements. . . . . of the divinities?'[67]

---

63 *Papiol*, Apr. 24 1902.
64 *Paese* (of Palermo), Apr. 20/21 1902.
65 *Pungolo*, May 16/17 1902.
66 *Monsignor Perrelli*, June 17 1902.
67 *Settimana*, unidentified date.

18

Immortality in Wax

> In order to form some notion of the blithe, self-confident way in which cadenzas and changes were once improvised by the old singers, we must study the gramophone records of Fernando De Lucia.
>
> Desmond Shawe-Taylor, *Fernando De Lucia*[1]

In his strolls past the shops of Via Chiaia, De Lucia had certainly seen recording equipment, such as the Graphophone, 'the most perfect talking machine, with which anyone can record', offered for 37 lire in Jaforte's music shop in 1900.[2] No doubt he had thought about the artistic and financial possibilities of recording. The revenues were probably still trifling, but the famous Gaisberg payment of £100 for ten recordings by Caruso would change that. Operatic colleagues who were already making or purchasing records may have helped to convince De Lucia of the artistic possibilities: one such was the tenor Russitano, whose house in Milan was filled with the records that he bought on his tours.[3]

Whatever the stimulus and wherewithal, De Lucia's first titles for the Gramophone and Typewriter Company Ltd. (G&T) were made by Will Gaisberg in Milan, late in 1902. Since their serial numbers (2861-2870) are contiguous with those of the Caruso session (starting at 2871) of that month they were made either the same day, Sunday, November 30th or, at most, a day or two earlier. On December 7th Alfred Michaëlis, the company's Milan representative, wrote to the Managing Director, W.B. Owen, in London remarking that 'Mr. Gaisberg finished his work here yesterday and has left for London.' Commenting on the celebrity work completed by De Lucia, Caruso, De Luca, Ferrani, Garbin, Giraldoni, Russitano, and others, he described De Lucia as having

> ... held the last ten years the undisputed position of [the] greatest master of Italian tenors as far as delicate singing is concerned. ... If his records are silent in proportion to the tests heard here, they will form the apex of the Gramophone so far as fine singing is concerned. We have been able to hear that his most delicate nuances have been taken in by the machine. De Lucia is the

---

1 Shawe-Taylor (1955), p. 433.
2 *Pungolo*, Dec. 13/14 1900.
3 Otto Müller in conversation with the writer, 1969.

tenor who was offered 20,000 Francs for a few records by a certain Martini of New York, who you are like [sic] to know and who was arrested for publishing records under the name of De Lucia, who had refused to sing for him. He has come to sing for us all the way from his country house near Naples, not for the money we paid him, but because he wants the world to judge between his records and Caruso's.[4]

With endorsements by Caruso and Toscanini, Michaëlis held a letter from De Lucia, commending the products of the Gramophone Company. It was subsequently used in advertising:

Fernando De Lucia writes:

Milan, December 3rd 1902

I must in truth attest that only the Gramophone of the Gramophone Co. has allowed me to hear my voice with all the charm of the Italian art of 'Il bel canto'.[5]

The records of De Lucia's first series retain their fascination to this day. Thirty years later, Hurst, who termed him 'a particularly bright ornament to the most brilliant operatic epoch of our age',[6] caught the imagination of a generation of those prepared to listen intently:

The early records of De Lucia were veritable gems. They were a ten-inch series made in Milan in 1903 [sic], and appearing in the London celebrity catalogue of that year. They were generally unusually brief, but so remarkable were they that one listened with the greater concentration. The 'La donna è mobile' actually gave the first verse only, and showed the oddly unconventional style which the singer often affected.[7]

Their brevity, recalled Russitano, brought on De Lucia the nickname *'tenore di telegramma'*.[8] Some of them show heavy transposition. But there will be many who, with Duval, will agree that he 'has left us some exquisite records, no more perfect or amorous exist'.[9] His 1902 'La donna è mobile' [No. 3] was one of the group used in 1904 to persuade Massenet to endorse the Gramophone and, a year later, to induce Patti to record.[10]
De Lucia was among the singers who, in December 1902, had accepted one-year agreements to record only for the Gramophone and Typewriter Company.[11] He was, however, alive to his own value and to the prospect of playing off one recording company against another. His first G&T

---

4 (EMI) Contemporary company stationery gives the name as Michaëlis, not Michelis.
5 *Tribuna*, Apr. 6 1903.
6 Hurst, 'Collectors' Corner', *Gramophone*, Dec. 1932, p. 305.
7 Hurst, *The Golden Age Recorded* (1946), pp. 82-3. Issue of these and other records was delayed by a shortage of shellac at the Hanover pressing plant.
8 Otto Müller.
9 J.H. Duval, *Svengali's Secrets*, p. 81.
10 Jerrold Northrop Moore, 'Recording Patti', Notes to EMI RLS 711, 'Adelina Patti', p. 9.
11 (EMI) A. Michaëlis - W.B. Owen, Dec. 7 1902.

records could hardly have reached the shops when negotiations opened - or perhaps resumed - with the Anglo-Italian Commerce Company (AICC), of Milan and Genoa. Michaëlis wrote to Owen:

April 16th 1903

I sent you yesterday the following telegram:-
'Please wire decision Zonophone for guidance. Urgent'
The Anglo Italian are offering large sums to De Lucia. He is engaged with us for another 6 months, but writes in an ambiguous way and is quite capable of breaking his engagement.
The opposition is hard at work all round and I ought to know your decision about the Zonophone in order to shape my plans.[12]

Indeed, by May 1903 the AICC was advertising Zonophone Talking Machines and 'celebrity discs of Tamagno, Caruso, De Negri, De Lucia, Bendazzi, Garulli, Magini-Coletti, Wulman, Paoli, Wermez, and Salvini'.[13] After a few weeks, De Lucia and Tamagno disappeared from AICC publicity, but the former's name persists in the advertising of retailers such as Jaforte, who - as late as January 1904, at least - included him in publicity which related largely to Zonophone products. Certainly, none of the loosely worded and punctuated announcements states positively that De Lucia and Tamagno had made Zonophone records nor even, in most cases, that the records offered were exclusively Zonophone products. However, since all the other artists mentioned by AICC recorded for Zonophone, and some for no other company, the inference is very strong that the intention was to promote Zonophone discs which currently or prospectively featured these two tenors. The Jaforte advertisement is less significant, since it also includes Rosa Caligaris, a G&T artist who apparently made no Zonophone records.[14]

The AICC, however, was then using G&T records, obtained through unofficial channels, to promote Zonophone machines, and the advertisements may simply reflect that fact.[15] Clearly, De Lucia flirted with Zonophone but there is no evidence that he recorded for them, and no Zonophone record of De Lucia (or Tamagno) has been reported.

More tangible were De Lucia's negotiations with Alfred Michaëlis who, in the summer of 1904, had left the Gramophone Company to become, it seems, the Italian agent for the International Talking Machine Co., of Berlin, the manufacturers of Odeon records. With others, Michaëlis also founded the Società Italiana di Fonotipia.[16] It was on

---

12 (EMI). AICC was the Italian agency for the International Zonophone Company which, until 1903, was a formidable rival to the Gramophone and Typewriter.

13 See, for example, *Tribuna*, May 28 1903.

14 *Mattino Illustrato*, issues of Dec. 25 1903 - Jan. 10 1904. Tamagno is not mentioned.

15 (EMI) A. Michaëlis - W.B. Owen, Dec. 24 1902: 'The most serious harm the opposition [Zonophone and AICC] is doing us comes from the fact that they manage to get our Celebrity records and sell their machines with them, even supplying retailers if necessary, with very small or no profit at all.'

16 H. Frank Andrews, 'A Fonotipia Fragmentia', *The Talking Machine Review-International*, No. 40, June

September 30th 1904 that Kenneth Muir, who now occupied Michaëlis's former position in the Gramophone Company (Italy) in Milan, both telegraphed and wrote to Theodore Birnbaum, Owen's successor as Managing Director in London:

> ... De Lucia has just come up from Naples to sing for the Odeon having made a loose contract with Michaëlis which he is prepared to break. We have sounded him on the question of terms ...
>
> In view of the importance of this artiste to our Celebrity-Catalogue, and that we require either him or Caruso, who would be much more expensive, for the romances composed for us by Cilea, Puccini, Mascagni, and others which we now have ready for recording, I am strongly in favour of accepting this offer. After Caruso and Tamagno, De Lucia is undoubtedly the best male voice on our catalogue, and his records, before the matrices began to wear, have commanded a good sale here and, as far as I know, everywhere else ...
>
> At present we hold Tamagno and Caruso under exclusive contracts, and I would not like to see De Lucia on the competition catalogues as long as we can make a good profit out of him as we certainly ought to on the present offer. De Lucia can only leave this offer open until tomorrow 1st of October evening, so please wire me your instructions ...[17]

In reply to a telegram from Birnbaum, Hanover advised that, up until October 1st 1904, a total of 15,187 copies of De Lucia's 15 recordings had been pressed.[18] Muir confirmed to Birnbaum that the records were selling especially well in Russia, and that De Lucia had not yet sung for Odeon. Birnbaum authorised him to conclude an exclusive contract with De Lucia for five years. On October 3rd Muir was able to reassure him:

> On Saturday evening [October 1st] I concluded contract with De Lucia after a tremendous struggle with him as he evidently wanted to put himself up for auction. This artiste is a particularly slippery customer, and I insisted on his signing the contract at once as I was afraid that he might first sing for Michaëlis and then make his contract with us subsequently. He tried to gain time by saying that he must first notify Michaëlis formally; that he considered his contract with him as non-existent because it was made with the 'Società Italiana di Fonotipia', which company, not yet having been registered, has no existence in law.
>
> Finally, I got him to sign the contract late in the evening, and arranged with him verbally that we would exchange new contracts on Monday with the new date on them destroying the Saturday contracts, but I do not intend to do this without getting a written undertaking from him that he has not sung for Michaëlis in the meantime.
>
> Michaëlis has been making capital over getting hold of De Lucia, and intended to make him the *'pièce de résistance'* of his new catalogue.
>
> As we already have exclusive contracts with Tamagno and Caruso, I thought it important for the Company not to let such a well-known singer as De Lucia slip though our fingers.[19]

1976, pp. 691-2.

[17] (EMI) Letter Kenneth Muir - Theodore R. Birnbaum, Sept. 30 1904. De Lucia wished to make ten records immediately, for 10,000 lire, followed by a five-year contract for five pieces per year at 1,000 lire each.

[18] (EMI) 'Ideale' (52410, [No. 1], 1,725 copies) had been the most and 'Sei morta ne la vita mia' (52438, [No. 14], 415 copies) the least popular titles.

[19] (EMI) Letter Muir - Birnbaum, Oct. 3 1904.

On October 6th 1904 De Lucia signed the contract. He declared in writing that he had made no records whatsoever since October 1st, and agreed to appropriate penalties should the Company be able to prove to the contrary.[20] The same day, Muir informed London that the tenor had

> ... already sung eight records for us, and will probably sing the remaining two this evening. He has asked us to pay his travelling expenses and the expense of his legal consultation which ... amounts to 1000 Francs, which we thought it best to agree to under the circumstances. He also expressed the wish to be presented with a Gramophone, and we presume that there is no objection to this.

Muir added that the financial backers of the new Società Italiana di Fonotipia (among whom the tenor Francesco Tamagno was, at the time, rumoured to figure prominently) had made the recruitment of leading artists a precondition for their investment in it; the loss of De Lucia would no doubt be a blow to them. Michaëlis was, Muir warned, now trying to recruit Battistini and the soprano Maria Barrientos, and was almost certain to make a bid for Bonci and Anselmi.

London lost no time in conveying displeasure over the payment of De Lucia's expenses. Muir, though, pointed out that he had had

> ... great trouble with this artist, and as his travelling expenses were promised to him by Mr. Michaëlis it was difficult for us to get out of these. The legal expenses we might have refused, but it was very important to get De Lucia to sing these records without delay, and we induced him to do so partly by keeping the question of these charges dangling. He is frightfully capricious and a difficult character to handle.[21]

No written agreement - if, indeed, there was one - for De Lucia's 1902 records is now to be found. That of October 1904 was his first known formal contract with the Gramophone Company; it provided for him to make ten records in 1904, for which the Company agreed to pay 10,000 lire (£400), half on signature and half on the completion of recording.[22] The fee of 1,000 lire per piece, though far short of the 5,000 lire per piece and 5 lire for each copy sold that Tamagno had negotiated in 1902, was twice what Aristodemo Giorgini would be paid in 1906 and - a measure of the remarkable changes since 1902 - already four times the 2,500 lire which Gaisberg had then thought such a vast sum for Caruso to earn for ten records. Caruso, by November 1904, received 2,000 lire per piece. De Lucia, who agreed to record only for the Gramophone Company, was

> ... if necessary to repeat, until thoroughly satisfactory to both contracting parties, musical pieces to be selected by common consent.

---

20 (EMI) Declaration signed by De Lucia, Oct. 6 1904.

21 (EMI) Muir - The Gramophone and Typewriter Ltd., Oct. 13 1904.

22 (EMI) The existing copy of the contract bears its original date of Oct. 1 1904.

A further 25 pieces were to follow, recorded at the rate of five per year, in the five-year period from January 1st 1905, for an annual remuneration of 5,000 lire (£200), payable after recording. The tenor's penalty for infringement was set at 10,000 lire (£400), without prejudice to any further action for damages resulting from such infringement.[23]

The 1904 session, supervised by Franz Hampe, produced De Lucia's first recorded duet (with Celestina Boninsegna) and also the celebrated 'Ecco ridente' from *Il Barbiere di Siviglia* [No. 25], probably his most famous recording, and one which has attracted much interest and admiration.[24] Two recordings of Cilea's music drew authenticity from the composer's presence at the piano. At first, Milan regarded the records as very satisfactory;[25] two months later, however, Muir wrote to London regarding 39 Red Label records which he had returned to the factory:

> The sample we received of [Cilea's] 'Lontananza' sung by De Lucia was really good but the records are very imperfect, and as they are they could not possibly be placed on the market.
>
> We wrote to Hanover on the subject, and hope that they may find their way to obtain a perfect record especially as the same is sold along with the printed notes by Cilea, and is consequently of the highest importance to us.[26]

For whatever reason, the 1904 records are decidedly the least clear of those that De Lucia made for the Gramophone Company; 'Lontananza' was remade in 1906, but not issued. Only one other [No. 45] is known to have been remade. Technically and vocally most are highly satisfactory. Following his recording session late in 1905 London wrote authorising Milan, 'in view of the excellence of the De Lucia samples', to take ten

---

23 (EMI).

24 See p. 353.

25 (EMI) Unsigned letter Oct. 31 1904.

26 (EMI) Letter Muir - The Gramophone and Typewriter Ltd., Nov. 25 1904. Muir's letter to London, May 1 1906 (see pp. 327-8), states that De Lucia had recently remade this record. In fact, all known pressings of it carry a 1904 matrix number, 2159L, without the '1/2' suffix which normally denotes a second take. Though it is conceivable that the 1/2 was accidentally omitted from the 1906 retake, both matrix and catalogue numbers of all pressings inspected by or reported to the writer are in the style typical of 1904, with larger characters than those used in 1906, and they have the aural fogginess characteristic of De Lucia's 1904 records. Such evidence suggests that existing pressings are from the 1904 matrix, and that the retake was unpublished. This is consistent with the listing of *published* matrices by Kelly, *His Master's Voice/La Voce del Padrone*, p. 29, which makes no mention of a 'Lontananza' in the De Lucia session of 1906. The possible reasons for continuing to use the 1904 matrix are speculative. Unless Cilea participated in the 1906 re-recording - and there is no evidence that he did - it would lack the cachet of having him accompany a song which, as the label proclaims, was 'written expressly for the Gramophone [Company]', and this consideration possibly transcended the technical imperfections of the 1904 version. The retake would also lack the distinction of Cilea's signature, which his contract (dated June 7 1904) with the Gramophone Company required to be cut into each record made under his supervision. All reported pressings of 'Lontananza' have such a signature; curiously, some pressings from the adjacent matrix 2160L (*Adriana Lecouvreur*) which, like 'Lontananza' is labelled as 'accompanied by the composer', do not carry the signature. Alternatively, Cilea might have insisted that his own recording of his song be issued, not least because he received 200 lire for each piano-accompanied record that he arranged and supervised. All the 25 cm matrices with numbers close to those of De Lucia's 1906 recordings are attributable; by contrast, the 30 cm series shows six unknown matrices in the range 615-638c, and one of these seems likely to have been the second, unpublished, 'Lontananza'.

pieces instead of five, which would cover the company's contractual obligations for two years.[27] They must also have been a commercial success for, after barely a year of his five-year agreement, De Lucia was able to negotiate an expanded contract. In December 1905, Muir wrote to London:

> When passing through Naples about a fortnight ago I heard through a third party that an attempt had been made ... to get De Lucia to break his contract with us. A few days ago I received a letter from De Lucia saying he wished to see me very much on an urgent matter connected with his contract, but that it was impossible for him to leave Naples as he was singing at the S. Carlo theatre. I therefore sent on our Bookkeeper to see what the matter was. De Lucia informed him that Ricordi had been down there and heard the five new records which he sang for us, whereupon he asked De Lucia to break his contract with us and to make a contract with the Fonotipia, over which Company, by the way, Ricordi is taking more and more control.[28]

This - as we are tempted to believe De Lucia knew perfectly well - took place at a time when the Gramophone Company was vulnerable to pressure. Its records were meeting competition from the splendidly realistic and forcefully promoted products of Fonotipia; furthermore, since October 1904, Fonotipia had attracted to its banner Arkel, Carelli, De Luca, Garbin, Maurel, Russ, Sammarco, Schiavazzi, Ventura, Viñas, and Zenatello, all former Gramophone Company artists. According to De Lucia, the offer from the rival company was 20,000 francs (20,000 lire, or £800) in cash; 10,000 francs would pay his indemnity clause with the Gramophone Company, and the Fonotipia would assume any further liabilities for his infringement of the Gramophone and Typewriter contract. The remaining 10,000 francs was to be a cash payment on signing his contract; in addition, he would receive a 10% royalty on his records, with a minimum guarantee for five years of 15,000 francs per annum. Muir continued:

> Of course, it is impossible to believe the truth of this offer, especially coming from a clever and slippery Neapolitan like De Lucia; at the same time, it seems pretty clear that some offer has been made to him. He then wished to know what offer we could make him, but our Bookkeeper said he had no power to make any offer, and would therefore like to know what De Lucia wanted, so as to submit the proposal to Head Quarters.

After 'a long conversation and considerable bargaining', Muir added, De Lucia had eventually 'moderated his ideas' and agreed to ask that his

---

27 (EMI) Letter The Gramophone and Typewriter Ltd. - Muir, Nov. 9 1905.

28 (EMI) Letter Muir - The Gramophone and Typewriter Ltd., Dec. 27 1905. In 1906 the firm of G. Ricordi was the fourth largest shareholder in Fonotipia Limited, with 3,400 of a total of 41,000 shares. Tito Ricordi held a further 909. When, in July 1911, Fonotipia was taken over by Carl Lindström AG, of Berlin, Ricordi was still a prominent shareholder (see H. Frank Andrews, 'A Fonotipia Fragmentia', *The Talking Machine Review-International*, No. 41, Aug. 1976, pp. 756-7, and No. 44, Feb. 1977, pp. 909-10).

contract be expanded to sing, over the next four years, forty pieces instead of twenty, at 1,000 francs per piece:

> ...We have already agreed to let him sing the five pieces of 1907 in the year 1906, i.e. ten pieces in 1906. If the Company accepts his proposal he is willing to make a new contract increasing the indemnity clause from ten thousand to fifty thousand francs, and would agree to sing at least one half of all the pieces with orchestral accompaniment, and also to agree to all such pieces, provided they are in his repertoire, as the Company may desire, whether solos, duets,. terzets etc. He asks, however, that the Company should pay his travelling and hotel expenses in coming up from Naples to Milan to sing. ...I would [also] suggest insisting on a clause under which De Lucia engages to renew his contract on the same terms for another three years at the Company's option before engaging himself elsewhere at the expiration of the contract. I think there is very little risk in accepting these terms beyond the usual risk that we run with all artistes of his losing his voice and even in this case a clause might be put to obviate that eventuality, which is frequently done by theatres and their contracts with artistes. De Lucia is in remarkably good voice at present. In fact, people in Naples say his voice is now improving again rather than going off. He ...takes great care of his voice and being a very finished artiste with correct voice production he is very unlikely to strain his voice when singing at theatres. I feel very much in favour of accepting this agreement, which will always be a profitable one in itself and also because it will enable us to oblige De Lucia to sing the pieces which we require and of which there is a large sale instead of leaving the choice partly to him. Also because it ties him absolutely to us.[29]

Muir then listed ten records to be made by De Lucia in 1906, including titles which, in fact, he never made for G&T, such as *La Favorita*: 'Spirto gentil' and the duet 'Fia vero lasciarti' with mezzo-soprano; a duet with mezzo-soprano from *Mignon*; and tenor-soprano duets from *Linda di Chamounix* and *Romeo e Giulietta*. A suggested duet with soprano from *Faust* was not made until 1907. Instead, in 1906 there appeared 'Numero quindici' [No. 31] and 'Ah! qual colpo' [No. 39] from *Il Barbiere di Siviglia*; 'Mi par d'udir ancora' [No. 34] and a duet [No. 37] with Huguet, both from *I Pescatori di Perle*; the duet from *Rigoletto* [No. 40]; and 'De miei bollenti spiriti' [No. 38] from *La Traviata*. The others included *Mignon*: 'Ah! non credevi tu' which, Muir noted, had already been 'sung by Bonci for the Fonotipia'. Finally, he observed that De Lucia, under his contract, had already sung fifteen pieces for 15,000 francs; should he break it and pay the indemnity the Company would effectively have

> ...received fifteen pieces for five thousand fcs. and should still have a claim for infringement of contract, and this claim we could prove by our sales to be a very large one, but of course the action would drag out a considerable time during which the Fonotipia would have the benefit of the records he made for them. Please inform me as quickly as possible whether I am to accept or refuse the new terms as, in view of the offer from Ricordi, De Lucia is anxious to have a reply as soon as possible.[30]

---

29 (EMI) Letter Muir - The Gramophone and Typewriter Ltd., Dec. 27 1905. Mention of an improvement in the voice supports the thesis that his previous records had been made during a period of poor vocal health.
30 Ibid.

The Gramophone and Typewriter replied immediately that the matter was one which should come before the Board of Directors. The Company was clearly anxious not to lose De Lucia. Meanwhile, however,

> ...you should be able to get better terms than those which De Lucia has expressed himself willing to accept from us.
>
> As the next Meeting of the Board does not take place until the 10th January we would wish you to keep in very close contact with De Lucia until after that date in order that he may not slip through our fingers. In the meantime we would wish you to endeavour to modify the terms ...; for instance, we think you should be able to get him to agree to sing ten songs during [each of] the first two years and five per annum afterwards, all at the same rate of 1,000 lire each.
>
> We think if you cannot get De Lucia to modify his demands that the Board will most probably give way and pay what he asks rather than lose him ... [31]

These terms were duly proposed to De Lucia. He was, felt Muir, unlikely to accept what amounted only to ten extra records, or a sum of 10,000 francs, because the inducement was not very great to a man who

> ...is worth between three and four million francs, and also because we feel sure that the offer which he received from the Fonotipia will at least be on the lines of the contract they made with Bonci after their first contract with De Lucia fell through, which, as you will remember, brought about our present contract with De Lucia.[32]

Bonci's Fonotipia contract, which Muir had seen, provided for a cash advance of 15,000 francs for 20 records and a 10% royalty on net sales world-wide, and guaranteed a minimum annual royalty of 10,000 francs for the first five years. The tenor was free to sing, exclusively for Fonotipia, as many more records as were mutually agreed, for a 10% royalty. Fonotipia was subject to a penalty of 20,000 francs 'in the event of Bonci proving that there are any records of his with duplicate serial numbers on sale'.[33] There was no penalty should Bonci break his contract:

> In this way Bonci received 15,000 fcs. cash and was guaranteed 50,000 fcs. in royalty over the first five years, and it may be taken for granted that the offer to De Lucia will in any case not be inferior to this. It must be remembered that De Lucia is considered by the Fonotipia people, and rightly, a more valuable artiste for talking machine purposes than Bonci, and accordingly they first tried to secure the [former] singer and only turned to Bonci when they failed with De Lucia. Lastly, I do not think in my first letter that I made quite clear that the terms submitted eventually by De Lucia were the result of hard bargaining with us ... The cleverness of De Lucia in negotiating has always shown itself in his not overshooting the mark as other artistes usually do. He has the intelligence to offer terms which are likely to be accepted ... [34]

---

[31] (EMI) The Gramophone and Typewriter Ltd. - Muir, Dec. 30 1905.

[32] (EMI) Muir - Fassett, Jan. 5 1906. Bonci's first records for Fonotipia were made in Feb. 1905, some four months after De Lucia signed his 1904 contract with the Gramophone and Typewriter Ltd.

[33] The individual pressing number on the label of each Fonotipia disc indicates the size of the edition.

[34] (EMI) Muir - Fassett, Jan. 5 1906.

On January 9th Muir telegraphed that, as expected, De Lucia was resolute. At the Board meeting next day the Company's directors learned that sales of his records for the last 15 months were 7,282.[35] They resolved to authorise him to make ten records yearly for four years at a fee of 1,000 francs each, but urged Muir to secure the option to renew the contract for three years. Travelling expenses were, they complained, an unreasonable addition to such handsome sums, but

> ... if he absolutely holds out on this point we think you will have to meet him to
> some extent, fixing a reasonable limit, however ... [36]

Muir again sent his representative to Naples, only to learn that De Lucia was now demanding an agreement for five years instead of four. He hoped to prevail on the tenor to settle for four years, because

> ... the competition have a very big proposition before them to offer anything
> better, and before signing away to the competition De Lucia is sure to haggle
> with them a long time and to come back and reopen negotiations with us as an
> offset.[37]

Meanwhile, he requested authorisation to increase, if unavoidable, the term of the new contract. Again, Head Office reacted swiftly:

> In view ... of the importance of this Singer we wired you today as follows: - 'Do
> not lose Lucia [sic] by refusing five-year contract if he absolutely insists.'[38]

In his letter of January 18th 1906 the systematic Muir announced that, just before the telegram arrived from London, a wire from Naples had confirmed that the contract had been signed. De Lucia undertook not to record, in the four-year period to January 15th 1910, for any company not possessed by the Gramophone Company,

> ... as the hire of his voice is considered an absolute and exclusive cession in
> favour of the company.[39]

The contract provided for ten records per year, the pieces to be

> ... chosen and fixed by the Company, taking into account the quality of voice of
> Comm. Fernando De Lucia and the repertoire he has performed or will perform
> during the present contract.

---

35 (EMI) Minutes of Board Meeting, Jan. 10 1906. On Nov. 9 1906 Hanover confirmed to London that, from July 1 1904 to June 30 1906, 16,633 copies of De Lucia records had been pressed, compared with 57,062 for Caruso.

36 (EMI) The Gramophone and Typewriter Ltd. - Muir, Jan. 11 1906.

37 (EMI) Muir - Fassett, Jan. 15 1906.

38 (EMI) The Gramophone and Typewriter Ltd. - Muir, Jan. 17 1906.

39 (EMI) A typographical error in the contract, dated Jan. 15 1906, causes it to state that its *four-year* term expired in *1909* instead of 1910.

De Lucia agreed to sing 'ensemble' pieces, such as duets, trios, and quartets, with orchestra if so required. This was certainly in response to Fonotipia, whose advertising then made much of its recordings of concerted pieces.[40] His emoluments were 10,000 lire yearly, plus travelling expenses of two first-class railway tickets and hotel expenses for the 'whole time in which Comm. De Lucia will be at the disposal of the Company for the execution of the pieces'. The company could renew the contract for three years, under the same terms, by notice given six months before the expiry of the present contract. It also agreed to give De Lucia, annually, a gramophone and fifty records. As before, the records, masters, and exclusive rights for their reproduction were to belong to the company indefinitely.[41] For infraction of any clause De Lucia was liable to pay to 'the Gramophone' the sum of 50,000 lire (£2,000) which, as Muir remarked with satisfaction, '...makes it practically impossible for any Company to take him away from us'.[42]

Head Office, too, was in contented mood:

> ... we can now congratulate ourselves on having absolutely secured De Lucia in such a manner that no other competing company will be able to get at him, at any rate for seven years.[43]

Except that the second contract ended six months early, these contracts are consistent with De Lucia's known recording activity for the Gramophone Company.[44] But the tenor himself made a proposal which, had it been taken up, would surely have yielded some of the most interesting of records. Following De Lucia's recording session of 1906 Muir wrote to London:

> We have made eleven new records of De Lucia of which one was our song 'Lontananza', which De Lucia repeated for nothing as Hampe's record [of 1904] was not a very good one. I have succeeded in making three records accompanied by orchestra after a struggle, as De Lucia is very much against this. He promised, however, that he would not raise difficulties to orchestral accompaniments in future if the present ones turn out a success.
> I have been fortunate in getting him to sing a considerable proportion of duets on this occasion and these were all admirably rendered, so that if the recording is all right we ought to have a very fine set of records this time, and I have tried to select some subjects with a view to sales in other countries, such as the duet ... of *Rigoletto* with the soprano Huguet, 'Salve! Dimora' from *Faust*, [and the] 'Parigi, o cara' duet with soprano from *Traviata*.
> De Lucia has requested me to try and arrange for him to sing four or five duets with Adelina Patti, suggesting the following subjects: The two duets from *Romeo & Juliette*, the duet 'Un dì felice, eterea' from *Traviata*, the duet 'Tardi si fa' from *Faust*, and the duet from *Linda di Chamounix*. He has sung in many theatres together with Madame Patti and Gaisberg tells me that she has the

---

40 *Mattino*, Dec. 20/21 1905.
41 (EMI) Contract dated Jan. 15 1906.
42 (EMI) Muir - Fassett, Jan. 18 1906.
43 (EMI) The Gramophone and Typewriter Ltd. - Muir, Jan. 23 1906.
44 Henstock (1985), pp. 149-58.

highest opinion of him as an artist and singer. Certainly, as an artiste De Lucia is [by] a long way the best lyric tenor as Adelina Patti is [by] a long way the most perfect artiste of all sopranos, and I think such duets would make a tremendous hit. They would help the sale of the other De Lucia records in England and would increase the sale of the other Patti records in Italy. I think it is a magnificent combination as both are perfect artistes and their voices are about equally balanced in strength for recording purposes. De Lucia would be ready to go to Wales to make these records and as I have just received a letter from London advising me that a new series of Patti records is - *sur le tapis* - I wish to communicate this offer to your consideration.[45]

Alas! this fascinating suggestion came to nothing. Irrespective of other possible obstacles, there was probably too little time to arrange matters before, in June 1906, Fred Gaisberg returned to Craig-y-Nos castle for Patti's second, and final, recording session.[46] We can but speculate on what we might have heard from two such extraordinary singers.

William Michaëlis, Alfred's brother, was the Gramophone Company's agent in Naples. There, on May 21st 1909, Fred Gaisberg recorded De Lucia in romanzas and Neapolitan songs which, for their lightness of touch and beguiling vocal quality, are some of the most enchanting of all his records. Ironically, they ended his association with the Gramophone Company. A letter to the Victor Talking Machine Company confirms that his contract was cancelled on June 15th 1909.[47] Carlo Sabajno, evaluating the principal artists still under contract or - as, presumably, in De Lucia's case - option, advised the Company's Sydney Dixon, in London, that the De Lucia contract was 'exhausted', with no royalty:

> It is not advisable to renew the contract with this artist because his method of singing, though very artistic, abounds with falset [*sic*], a thing which the public does not like.[48]

Another, from Dixon to Sabajno, remarked that De Lucia, who had just agreed to record for Fonotipia,

> ... can hardly be in as good voice to-day as he was when we recorded him five or six years ago. I am only so sorry that we made a new contract with De Lucia instead of with Anselmi.[49]

After his final Gramophone Company session, almost two years elapsed before De Lucia recorded for Fonotipia. The thirty-two records,

---

45 (EMI) Muir - Birnbaum, May 1 1906.

46 (EMI) The Gramophone and Typewriter Ltd. - Alfred Clark, June 18 1906: '... the Baroness is to sing some further records this week and Mr. Birnbaum has arranged to go down to Craig-y-Nos castle when these records are made.'

47 (EMI) Jan. 21 1911.

48 (EMI) Aug. 20 1909. Sabajno (1874-1933 or 1934) was house pianist, conductor, and operatic scout to the Gramophone Company in Milan. De Lucia's contract was due to run until Jan. 15 1910. On it, a handwritten annotation reads 'See letter ending 26/5/08'. This letter, which cannot now be found, might explain why De Lucia's contract had already been cancelled before the date of Sabajno's letter to Dixon.

49 (EMI) Nov. 7 1910.

made in Milan on five consecutive days, January 10-14th 1911, were all of songs.[50] Two of them, 'Serenata a Maria' and 'Comme 'a na fronna', both by Gambardella, were unsatisfactory and remain unpublished.

Nowhere were the Fonotipia records more impatiently anticipated than in Naples, where proud citizens were eager to pay their 6 lire for each double-faced disc. For the records had great local interest and they were lavishly advertised by the principal music shops there - Jaforte, Emilio Gennarelli & Co., and Fratelli Esposito di Raffaele.

Raffaele Esposito (1865-1945) had started his commercial life with a harness and saddlery business in Via S. Anna dei Lombardi, Naples. He prospered as he gained the custom of Neapolitan society and of the royal house. He attained the status associated with summer villas at Capodimonte and Pozzuoli, the title of 'Cavaliere', and a local prominence which brought singers from the San Carlo to his parties. In the closing years of the nineteenth century he indulged a strong musical interest by buying a cylinder recording machine, with which he would record his guests. When Berliner records by operatic artists, such as Ferruccio Giannini, began to circulate, these same guests suggested to Esposito that he should manufacture records. Eventually, he purchased German recording and processing equipment and, in 1901, set up business in a former stable in Via Enrico De Marinis, at the corner of Via Mezzocannone.[51] There, he founded the Società Fonografica Napoletana, one of the earliest Italian record houses. He recorded local artists such as the great Nicola Maldacea, a *macchiettista*, that untranslatable stage term embracing both comic and character actor, with a suggestion of Harlequin and Pantaloon. Then came the *divi* of the Neapolitan song: Elvira Donnarumma, Armando Gill, Gilda Mignonette, Salvatore Papaccio, Vittorio Parisi and, considered the greatest of all, Gennaro Pasquariello. Operatic records featured artists such as Angela De Angelis, Franz Gleijeses, Giuseppe Godono, and Giorgio Schottler. Typical conditions were those of a Pasquariello contract of March 29th 1909, specifying a payment of 1,600 lire for 24 records.

The *posteggiatore* Giorgio Schottler recalled visiting the small ground-floor studio in about 1902, when he was ten years old. He had accompanied his uncle, the operatic baritone of the same name, who was there to make records. His most enduring memory was of the proprietor, Raffaele Esposito, a short, thick-set man in a grey overall. Round his neck was a cord from which swung an enormous pocket watch, almost like an alarm-clock, which he continually checked during recording.

The tiny recording 'laboratory', as it was then termed, was run frugally. Unable to afford the luxury of a musical director, Esposito

---

[50] (EMI) Fonotipia registers. Fonotipia, too, presented him with one of their instruments.
[51] Paliotti, 'C'è un Esposito nella Storia del Disco', *Il Mattino Illustrato*, Anno 4, No. 5, Feb. 2 1980, pp. 14-17 and 19-25, and *Napoletani si nasceva*, pp. 207-17.

employed the half-time services of Robert Felsman, the German conductor of the Salone Margherita orchestra. Many were the improvisations of those days, when singers, famous and unknown alike, yielded their artistic freedom to the authority of Don Raffaele's formidable watch. The recordings steadily improved as Raffaele and his son Americo (1890-1956) travelled to Germany twice yearly in search of new ideas and improved equipment.

The retail side of Esposito's business was also expanding. He advertised Fonotipia, Odeon, and Zonophone discs in the local press alongside his own records. By 1914 he had other shops in Naples. Americo's brothers, Luigi and Vincenzo, joined him in the business. They manufactured and sold - sometimes on instalments - 'Toreador' and 'Phonodart' talking machines; 'Phonodart' was also the title of a magazine published by the family. The year 1911 saw came a more international image for the recording 'studios', with a change of name to 'Phonotype Record'. The name was that of one of the shops, founded in 1905 by Vincenzo and Francesco Esposito, and acquired by Americo and Raffaele in 1910.[52] In 1921 Francesco founded the publishing company Casa Editrice Partenope, and in 1924 Americo and Vincenzo launched Casa Editrice Musicale Marechiaro.[53]

By 1917, Americo was in effective charge of Phonotype Record. He was now ready to extend his recording activities beyond the songs and music-halls of Naples. His ambition lay in operatic records made by singers more celebrated than the artists on whom he had previously depended. His opportunity came when De Lucia made his farewell performances at the San Carlo in 1917, showing, at the age of fifty-six, that his voice and technique were in fine state and that he retained his local following.

The Esposito family had known De Lucia for many years; indeed, the singer's influence with the Italian royal family is said to have saved Americo from conscription in 1915. In 1917 the time was propitious for the tenor to record for them, and Americo achieved the coup of engaging him. Probably, the tenor's then domestic and financial circumstances made the offer a tempting one. Correspondence also suggests that he was almost pathetically grateful to be asked to record, and for the chance to preserve more of his repertoire than had previously been possible.

Much has been made of the fact that De Lucia made more than three hundred records - some of them decidedly eccentric - for Phonotype. The freedom with text and music, the very abundance of recorded titles, and the fact that he is almost the only operatic singer of note found on the Phonotype label was possibly what gave rise to the popular fiction that he founded, owned, or at least had a financial interest in the company.[54]

52 Roberto Esposito, in conversation with the writer, 1985.
53 De Mura, *Enciclopedia*, Vol. I, pp. 467 and 471.
54 Stephen B. Fassett, 'Some notes on the De Lucia Phonotypes', *Hobbies*, Oct. 1946, p. 23.

Another rumour has it that the company was founded by the tenor's family, to record the last remnants of his voice.[55] Yet another fascinating hypothesis is that he formed it himself, to recoup gambling losses.

None of this has any factual basis. Certainly, De Lucia knew Raffaele and Americo socially. But Phonotype existed long before there was any professional contact between them. Not only is there no evidence whatever of any financial involvement by the tenor - a suggestion refuted by Americo's sons, the present owners of the company - but documents existing in the company's archives place the matter beyond doubt.

De Lucia first recorded for Phonotype on May 24th 1917, and by September 16th that year he had already made eighty titles. Three receipts from that period survive. They are in his own hand, and are for fees received from Americo and Vincenzo Esposito. That of April 8th 1917 is for 5,000 lire, representing half his remuneration for 20 records 'to be made in Naples on days to be agreed'. The other half was to be paid after recording, and another (undated) receipt relates to such a balance of 5,000 lire, on completion of a group of 20 records. The third (undated) acknowledges receipt of 20,000 lire for forty records already made. Together, they are consistent with his known output of eighty selections in that period, and they imply total payments of 40,000 lire.[56] Such arrangements hardly suggest ownership of the company. Neither, despite the fact that the tenor evidently sometimes waived advance payment, is the formal, legalist phrasing of his receipt for 20,000 lire consistent with proprietorial rights; in it he declared that he was satisfied with the arrangement and that he had

> . . . no other claims, either directly or indirectly, and [that] Signori Americo and Vincenzo Esposito have the right to put them on sale . . . [57]

Record sales obviously justified something more durable than this *ad hoc* arrangement for, in the autumn of 1917, in his own bold, untidy, but clear hand, De Lucia wrote a letter-contract:

> September 24th 1917
>
> Dear Signor Americo Esposito of Raffaele and brothers -
>
> I accept the contract that you offer me to sing three pieces per month, to be chosen from romanzas, duets, trios, quartets, concerted pieces from opera, *romanzas da camera* or songs, for the duration of three years from October 1st 1917 to October 1st 1920, for the total sum of *thirty-six thousand* lire, payable bi-monthly in arrears, of *two thousand*, commencing November 30th 1917.

---

55 Hurst, *Gramophone*, Jan. 1937, p. 362.

56 Later, he would simply sign a standard form of receipt. These are surprisingly large emoluments for a small recording company whose products had such a localised and restricted distribution; certainly, they were very handsome sums compared with De Lucia's salary of 4,000 lire per annum at San Pietro a Maiella, where he was by then a professor of singing.

57 (RE) Undated.

Of my own volition, I undertake not to sing for any other manufacturer of talking machines for the duration of the contract, giving you exclusiveness of recording my voice. Similarly, still of my own accord, I shall be at your disposal whenever you have need of my work, as artistic adviser of your company.

> With all my affection, Sincerely,
> Fernando De Lucia (RE)

This, then, was their business agreement. Esposito could expand his catalogue. For De Lucia, the remuneration - though somewhat less per record than he had previously received from Phonotype - was regular and, as 'artistic adviser', he no doubt had some influence over what was recorded. He duly received 2,000 lire on November 30th 1917, and every two months thereafter. In practice, neither party rigidly observed the contract. The *Rigoletto* and *Il Barbiere di Siviglia* sets were evidently outside the agreement; for the latter he received 3,000 lire. But, even without these, during the contract period he made 126 records, significantly more than the number specified. Esposito, for his part, continued to pay De Lucia for eight months when the tenor was too ill to record. The growing cordiality is reflected in their correspondence. Typical was a letter to Raffaele and Americo at Milan:

> October 11th 1917
>
> Dearest Don Raffaele, Don Peppino[58] and Americo,
>
> Your postcards bring me great joy, and I cannot tell of the pleasure that I feel.
>
> Assuredly, I rejoice also because I learn that you also must be happy. Here, they speak only *of you*, always missed, whose absence we feel so much, and of the records.
>
> I live in anticipation, and every day that passes increases my desire to hear all the records.
>
> I hope that all my records are to your complete satisfaction, this alone will make me doubly content. I have also received the [olive] oil, and I do not know what to say to you and to the kindly Don Peppino ...
>
> I am happy that my great recordist is showing the Milanese how to record the human voice, and they will certainly be enchanted.
>
> I live with you, my spirit is always with you.
>
> Accept all my thoughts - with a kiss and embrace.
>
> A kiss of gratitude to my great recordist, whom I wish so well.
>
> All are well at home, and all goes well.
>
> Affectionately,
> Fernando De Lucia
>
> P.S. I have also telegraphed this morning.
> Also the girl [who] sells the records sings constantly, and is always kind. (RE)

Nowhere is there any mention of royalties. De Lucia was already receiving, nominally, 330 lire per record, compared with the 125 lire paid

---

58 Don Peppino was the master electroplater.

to Angeles Ottein who, with Pasquale Amato and Benvenuto Franci, completed the roster of Phonotype's celebrity catalogue.[59] In November 1920 his contract was renewed under the same conditions as before; by early 1921, however, his bi-monthly payments had risen to 2,500 lire.

De Lucia's correspondence clearly shows that he was fascinated by his work in the studio. Even during a stay at Rome to visit his son Nadir, who had been wounded in action during the Great War, he wrote to Raffaele of his records:

> Hôtel Quirinal
> October 21st 1917
>
> I live struggling with a child still ill at Naples, and a son of 25 years who must return [to being] a soldier if God does not help him.
> You will thus be able to judge my state of mind.
> With such sad thoughts, I rejoice only when I think of the beauty of my records, and with what sadness I wrenched myself away from them. Dear Signor Esposito, to find myself so far from you, from Americo, from Vincenzino, after being so kind to me, proves a double penalty, and I cannot imagine when I shall see you again. . . .
> Write to me at length when you have time and, if I merit [it], speak to me of my records - (Only thing that I live for today.)[60]

Business and personal relationships with Americo seem to have been excellent. However, as might be expected, the singer was somewhat more anxious than the businessman to repeat a recording that was judged less than satisfactory. When, on occasion, Esposito demurred De Lucia would say: 'Americo, either we do it my way, or we will not do it at all!' But his feelings are clear in a letter from which all formality is absent:

> December 26th 1919
>
> Dearest Americo,
>
> I am still affected by the thrilling emotion and still feel the tears of joy that I shed hearing my record - *O dolci mani* - recorded with your new soundbox, [that] you have so successfully devised, and I must again, and with [even] greater enthusiasm, repeat to you that you are the greatest recordist of the human voice in the whole world, because only you have been able to let me hear all the charm, all the gradations, all the colours and all the graces that art has been able to inspire in me.
> Now, to mark the date of this new event, I have decided to give you a present, small but very great for me, because it was the first gift that I had in my first concert, when I experienced the very *first* emotions of art and public.
> I have kept it as a relic because it was a talisman to me throughout all my glorious career, and as such I have decided to offer it to you, on this occasion, because nothing else could have such sentimental value and noble sentiments for a kind and artistic soul - for all its modesty - such as yours.
> Accept it with an embrace, full of affection and of great admiration.[61]

---

59 Amato's records were pressed from Homocord masters, recorded in Germany. (See *Record Collector*, Vol. XXI, No. 1-2, Mar. 1973, p. 37.)

60 (RE) 'Vincenzino' refers to Vincenzo Moschetti, the factory manager.

61 (RE) The present remains unidentified.

De Lucia always travelled to the studio in a horse-drawn cab, the *carrozzella*, then so characteristic of Naples. Before a recording session, a young Phonotype employee, Luigi Russo, would go to his house to fetch the case containing his music. When he later returned it the tenor would tip the youth a sum larger than his normal daily wage. At the Via Roma house Russo met singers such as Benvenuto Franci, who would be rehearsing with the tenor. De Lucia spent much time in and around the Phonotype premises, even when not himself recording. On March 30th 1920 Angeles Ottein was in the studio. She recalled the occasion:

> It was ... while recording Violetta's aria from the first act of *Traviata* that I was surprised by hearing this gentleman, whom I did not yet know, launch into the tenor's part. I was rather nonpleased [*sic*] since we had rehearsed it without the tenor's part, nevertheless I went on with the recording and it came out beautifully. Afterwards I was introduced to Señor De Lucia by the conductor, and I was really delighted to meet such a famous artist. ... He was an elderly, rather portly gentleman, of great charm.[62]

His pleasure in his records, which he would play with pride to family and friends, arose partly from the opportunity of hearing his own vocal colouring, inflections, and modulations, and partly from the admiration that they inspired in others. But should anyone talk, he would instantly stop the record, close the lid of the gramophone, and the recital would be over. It was probably on one such occasion that the poet Giovanni Capurro put pen to paper in praise of Esposito and De Lucia. If - even in its original dialect - it is hardly a distinguished example of his verse it must be one of very few sonnets to be inspired by an acoustic record:

A Record of Esposito

There is a record of *Rigoletto*,
'Quest'e quella', sung by De Lucia.
A marvellous and perfect record,
That makes one's mouth water, upon my word.

What grace, what embroidery, it is like lace.
More than a record, it is a poem.
It so inspired me, just imagine,
That I had to write a sonnet.

This record, superior to all others,
Is truly a masterpiece;
Hear it, and then pass judgement.
Bravo Esposito, sincere congratulations.
This has come off splendidly,
A thread of voice, delighting everyone.[63]

---

62 Letter (in English) to the writer, July 1967. Ottein (real name: Nieto) had a successful operatic career 1914-1942. See *The Record Collector*, Vol. XVII, No. 7, Aug. 1967, pp. 147-54.

63 Giuseppina De Lucia. The poem is undated. Capurro died in January 1920.

With the exceptions of Franci, Ottein, and, possibly, Luis Muñoz and Antonio Armentano, his partners on the Phonotype records were not distinguished. There is no evidence that, as has been suggested latterly, his association with the palpably mediocre Angela De Angelis extended beyond the studio which they so frequently shared. Olga Perugino was probably related by marriage to his brother, Federico. The soprano Maria Resemba and the baritones Francesco Novelli and Giorgio Schottler sang at the San Carlo but were not of major operatic importance. Sergio Viterbini was professor of violoncello at San Pietro a Maiella.

The distribution of Phonotypes was not extensive, even in Naples. Certain dealers in Rome sold them (it is said), but they were almost unknown elsewhere in Europe. They were probably never sold in England. Sets of the *Rigoletto* and *Il Barbiere di Siviglia* are rare enough to qualify for the adjective 'fabled', possibly because the records were available separately, thus allowing a purchaser to select only the more popular pieces. The circulation of De Lucia Phonotypes in the United States is due, apparently, to one man, Benny Manno, the almost legendary barber of New York City. He, it appears, had long been an admirer of De Lucia, and he claimed to have been the sole importer of his Phonotypes into the USA, where he sold them from the back of his barber's shop.[64] It is a fittingly bizarre note on which to end an account of Phonotype Record, a company whose name, outside Naples, lives on largely through its associations with Fernando De Lucia.

There is, though, a remarkable postscript to the story. During World War II Italians were called upon to collect metals, particularly copper, for the war effort. Raffaele and Americo Esposito knew that their matrices were threatened. Secretly, largely at night, they built a concrete bunker under the garden behind the factory in Via Enrico De Marinis, and there many of the matrices - of the records of De Lucia, of Donnarumma, and of the other great ones of Naples - passed the war years. A few reappeared when peace was renewed, but most remained underground. Raffaele died in 1945 and Americo in 1956. Astonishingly, neither ever revealed to the family the secret of the garden.

In 1961, during work to enlarge the factory, a workman's pick struck the edge of the bunker. As Americo's sons Fernando, Raffaele, Roberto, and Vincenzo watched, the vault was opened, and the matrices once again saw daylight.[65]

As we have seen, De Lucia was still recording prolifically and satisfactorily in 1920: Caruso (1873-1921) would soon be no more, Bonci (1870-1940) had much deteriorated, and Anselmi (1876-1929) had made no records for almost a decade. It is easy, then, to think of De Lucia as a member - albeit an idiosyncratic and atypical one - of this generation of

---

[64] Fassett, loc. cit.

[65] Roberto Esposito, in conversation with the writer, 1968.

much more straightforward singers. Analysis of his records must, however, recognise that his artistic roots and training belong to an era in which the singer was the *sine qua non* of opera and not simply one element of it. Study of their ornamentation of Verdi, for instance, suggests that Battistini (1856-1928) and De Lucia, far from being the 'glorious eccentrics' that they at first appear, actually represent an older and less amply recorded generation, that of Patti (1843-1919), Tamagno (1850-1905), Kaschmann (1850 or 1852-1925), Marconi (1853 or 1855-1916), and Valero (1854-1914).[66] Further, any comparison of De Lucia's records with those of others must note their respective ages at the time of recording. Among tenors, a fair basis for comparison with his 1902 series, when he was forty-two, would be Bonci in 1912, Caruso in 1915 - each, by then, well past his best - Pertile in 1927, and Gigli in 1932.

Contemporary reviews clearly indicate that De Lucia had for some time been in vocal decline when, in 1902, he made his first recordings, and suggest that he was, perhaps, also in poor health; by late 1905 his voice was said 'to be improving again'.[67] In the first of his 1902 groups he transposed arias such as 'Ah! non mi ridestar' ('Pourquoi me réveiller'), which he sang a minor third down on a record which plays at about 66 rpm. In such pieces it was a practice which has often gone unremarked, for two reasons: firstly because at or around the 78 rpm which later became the standard record speed many of the arias emerge at or near score pitch, and secondly because many of them seem unlikely candidates for transposition. 'Ah! non mi ridestar', for example, does not, as written, rise above A sharp. However, since speed and pitch are related, years of playing his records of transposed pieces at that standard speed or at score pitch have - to the extent to which 78 rpm or score pitch are wrong in any particular case - inculcated an entirely false notion of his timbre. His transpositions are, moreover, variable: in some 1902 records, for example 'Mercè, cigno gentil' from *Lohengrin*, transposition appears to have been heavier than in the later G&T recording of the piece, made in 1907, when his voice may have benefited from longer periods of rest between operatic engagements. Some of his Phonotypes, made after several years of virtual retirement from operatic work, may also show smaller transpositions than the corresponding G&T records.[68] However, those were times when recording engineers did not adjust their machines systematically and when most listeners, including some singers, were too delighted by the novelty of hearing a mechanically-reproduced voice to worry about whether the pitch was correct.[69] Amid

---

[66] Crutchfield (1988), p. 14.

[67] See letter Muir - The Gramophone and Typewriter Ltd., Dec. 27 1905, quoted above.

[68] The speeds are crucial in the evaluation of De Lucia's records. The subject is examined in greater detail in the Introduction to the Discography, pp. 438ff, which also contains an analysis of the speeds and keys used in his early sessions and a discussion of why much uncertainty still attaches to the extent of his transpositions.

[69] An evident exception was Marcella Sembrich, who expressed lively displeasure when she heard her

such arbitrariness, key changes for their convenience were taken for granted by artists and were obviously regular features of recording, as they were of the operatic and concert stages. One of Fred Gaisberg's routine responsibilities before a recording session with any singer involved making sure that the transpositions were available, if needed.[70]

The hazards of keys and turntable speeds for the De Lucia records were pointed out by Hurst in 1937, if not earlier, and Gaisberg himself provided the clue to pitching them when, forty years after recording him, he wrote of 'the wealthy, generous and likeable De Lucia':

> He had what they call a short voice, a highest note of barely an A natural. To hear him sing 'A te, o cara' and 'Spirto gentil' gave one unforgettable delight.[71]

This, with Mascagni's comment (1898) on De Lucia's 'short' voice, Giordano's transpositions for him the same year, and satirical references (1900-05) to 'the baritone De Lucia', supports Carelli's account: 'a *vocetta*, based on a few notes, carried to glory by study and passion'.[72] Such evidence readily explains what Daspuro was telling Sonzogno in that famous letter of 1897, in response to the latter's charge that Caruso (whom Daspuro had engaged for him) was not a tenor but a baritone:

> ... if Caruso is a baritone, De Lucia, whom I also engaged for you, is a *basso profondo*.[73]

However, we have noted (p. 153) that the heavy transpositions of the 1902 records, to bring top notes down to A flat, or even lower, were not always necessary. On some occasions he evidently felt in better voice than on others, and in records such as 'Spirto gentil' [No. 159] or 'O bei lochi' [No. 166] he reaches B flat in apparent comfort.[74]

A systematic review of De Lucia's very numerous records is outside the scope of this biography. We may, however, examine some of the many critical observations on their historical importance and on what they tell us of the tenor and of the vocal customs and style of his times.

From at least as early as 1890 it was generally agreed that this was not an exceptional natural throat, and that 'study, perseverance, and genius have prepared this miracle that audacity and energy have

---

records played at the wrong speed. See, for example, Fagan and Moran, *The Encyclopedic Discography of Victor Recordings, Matrix Series: 1 through 4999*, pp. xxxiii-xxxvi.

70 F.W. Gaisberg, *Music on Record*, p. 40.

71 F.W. Gaisberg, 'Enrico Caruso', *Gramophone*, Jan. 1944, pp. 117-18. It is not clear when or under what circumstances Gaisberg heard him sing these arias.

72 Carelli, op. cit., p. 15.

73 Daspuro, *Enrico Caruso*, p. 22.

74 Such instances are not uncommon. It is reported that a below-par Melba had decided to sing 'Depuis le jour' from *Louise* with a tone transposition, and rehearsed it at the lower pitch. By the night of the performance she had recovered, and reverted to score pitch. (See Moran, *Nellie Melba*, pp. 293-4.)

completed'.[75] What the records show, at the correct speeds, is a voice produced predominantly in the head, with a fine-grained, regular vibrato and - even allowing for the inability of acoustic recording to capture the higher frequencies - of remarkably dark tones for a tenor, as judged by today's criteria. They are wholly consistent with numerous contemporary references to baritonal timbre. It is arguable, noting the similarity of timbre in the late acoustic and the early electrical records of those singers who recorded by both processes, that the Phonotypes, at least, give a tolerably accurate idea of his vocal quality at the time.

What is unarguable is the evidence of his style and technical powers. In a masterly *legato* words flow smoothly from one to another as they advance on an even stream of breath. There is a now-rare quality in male singers: a full dynamic range, an audible difference between forte and fortissimo, or between piano as it becomes pianissimo and, in turn, the delicate thread of a *filata*. There is the *messa di voce*, the swelling of tone from piano to forte, and back again to piano. Such an ability

> ... gives the heady feeling that the voice is the instrument of the singer's will - that it can go in any direction, at any speed, any dynamic, on command.[76]

There is a complete command of *portamento*: smooth as satin, the voice is uniformly vibrant as it floats seamlessly and without apparent effort between notes. There is a flexibility which enables him to imbue the ornaments of Bellini with an inimitable tenderness. With an agility in florid music which earlier generations took for granted he avoids the intrusive aspirate, the only means whereby lesser singers can negotiate rapid scale passages or even reach one note from another on the same syllable. Above all, we hear the art of display: in almost every record he embellishes phrases with grace notes, pianissimi, *filature*, *gruppetti*, and phrases in *mezza voce*. His fluency and his *morbidezza* are proverbial, and so are his *smorzature*, all serving the legitimate cause of expression:

> The finely produced tones were held, swelled or retracted, dwelt on as elements of expression and beauty in and of themselves. The legato line was molded not just with highly coherent rhythmic fluidity, at that time characteristic of romantic performance, but also with the sculpting curve of portamento. Detailed dynamic nuances shaped the phrases (making them, as it were, three-dimensional, as opposed to the flat quality of a phrase shaped only by rhythm and pitch). Florid ornaments, executed too fluently to be disruptive, gave the lines texture and finish.[77]

The records also display a wide variety of vocal ornaments. An analysis of 207 examples of ornamentation in acoustic recordings of

---

[75] *Occhialetto*, Jan. 18 1890.
[76] Conrad L. Osborne, quoted by Crutchfield (1987), p. 11.
[77] Crutchfield (1988), p. 11.

Verdi includes 24 by De Lucia, second in number only to Battistini.[78] Beyond ornaments such as the *acciaccatura*, the slide, and the *gruppetto* are the larger cadenzas and improvisations. Beyond them, we hear decoration which varies from one recording to another of the same piece, in much the same way as his stage interpretations varied from one performance to another. They exemplify the singer's world of other days. For their number, scope, and variety, the De Lucia records are a unique repository of information on nineteenth-century operatic practice.

Georges Thill, his most famous pupil, has written disparagingly of them:

> What I can tell you is that it is impossible to appraise the singing, as it was, of De Lucia. The records give no idea of his voice, nor of his vocal art. One had to have heard him![79]

Indeed, Thill claimed that only with difficulty could he recognise De Lucia's voice from recordings. When his teacher sang in his presence he displayed a tonal beauty which the French tenor did not discern in the records. It is possible - probable, even - that he heard them at the wrong speeds. At any rate, what is audible under optimum conditions is quite remarkable. We may easily concur when Hurst describes the voice as

> ... equally well produced from the softest *pianissimo* to a *fortissimo* of tremendous power. Besides these great though not unusual gifts, he had developed a control of his vocal mechanism that was probably unique in any other male singer excepting Battistini, and he was able to colour his tones in a seemingly miraculous manner. In him the true meaning of the term *bel canto* becomes clear, for no more sensitive and expressive singing has been heard in the memory of anyone now alive. To some this style may seem effeminate in some degree, but these should not overlook that it required a technical ability far beyond that employed by the *tenore robusto*.[80]

The singing teacher Vincenzo d'Alessandro heard him in the première of *Iris*, again in Palermo early this century, and in *Fedora* in 1916; De Lucia's singing of 'Amor ti vieta' was, he recalled, one of the greatest feats of vocalism that he had ever heard. The records 'represented the singing exactly, although the voice sounded much more beautiful and the vibrato was less apparent in the theatre; the *mezza voce* carried to the farthest reaches of the hall'.[81]

It has been suggested that De Lucia's reputation as a 'paragon of bel canto ... hardly squares with the record'.[82] From some - but by no means all - of the London reviews (whence the writer in question largely selects his evidence) we might well believe this. Given Anglo-Saxon dislike of

---

[78] Crutchfield (1983), pp. 21-49.
[79] Letter to the writer, May 1967.
[80] Hurst, *The Golden Age Recorded* (1946), p. 82.
[81] In conversation with Michael Aspinall, 1968.
[82] Scott, *The Record of Singing: To 1914*, pp. 123-6.

vibrato, then held as a 'modern' trait and acceptable only in modern
music, it is not surprising that his voice was thought suitable only for
contemporary works. In Latin countries 'the record' was another story.
However, *contemporary* references to the 'strident quality' for which he
was supposedly 'so much criticised' seem, on examination, to be confined
to a few London reviews.[83] The alleged 'excessive recourse to the long
"ee" [the Italian "i"] vowel to try and focus the tone and keep it forward'
arises in the writings of modern critics, who can know the voice solely
from records.[84] De Gogorza (p. 186) and other contemporary writers
make it clear that De Lucia would, in performance, change texts to cause
high notes to fall on more congenial vowels. The tenor's records
sometimes reflect this. We should, however, distinguish between change
of vowel and change of emphasis of the vowel: though there are sporadic
references to various vocal flaws, none of the many hundreds of reviews
scrutinised, even of De Lucia's last performances, makes any mention
whatever of such undue emphasis of the 'i'. Though, as in the *Il Guarany*
duet [No. 148], he sometimes employs it for effect, the illusion almost
certainly results from playing the records too fast, presumably in the
reasonable belief that the pieces were sung at or near score pitch. At
what are now thought to be the correct speeds the 'ee' sound and the
unpleasantly rapid vibrato largely disappear, to be replaced by a more
natural enunciation of vowels and a vocal quality which can convey,
when appropriate, an astonishing dramatic power.

On the subject of vibrato, the same writer (Scott) continues:

> The pronounced vibrato or tremolo which we hear in the recordings of de Lucia,
> Valero, Bonci and Giraud . . . was a decadence in technique as well as style; it is
> impossible to separate the two, for the obtrusive vibrato had its origins in the
> abuse of an affecting device.[85]

Here the critic is at odds with Ben Davies, Zélie De Lussan, Emma
Eames, Blanche Marchesi, and Emma Nevada, competent judges who
considered that vocal vibrato and tremolo were quite different.[86] And,
though the thesis is ingenious, no authoritative evidence is adduced for
the extraordinary assertion that the vibrato 'facilitated De Lucia's skill

---

83 Shaw, *Music in London*, Vol. II, p. 104 (June 1 1892) and *The Times*, July 24 1900.

84 Scott, *The Record of Singing: To 1914*, p. 125. The earliest traceable references to the 'ee' sound are
found in the writings of Celletti, starting in the mid-1950s.

85 Ibid.

86 *Gramophone*, Jan. 1936, pp. 349-50. (See above, pp. 61-2.) However, there is always the potential for
confusion between them owing to the different usages (of which some singers seem unaware) of the terms
'vibrato' and 'tremolo' in different types of music: in vocal music 'vibrato', certainly in De Lucia's time, was an
alternate partial extinction and reinforcement of a note, producing almost its apparent reiteration, while
'tremolo' ('almost exclusively an acquired habit in this age (c. 1910) of "intensity" ') was a rapid change of
pitch. In the parlance of stringed instruments, however, notwithstanding some indiscriminate usage which
persisted from earlier times, 'vibrato' was generally the pitch variation brought about by a quick oscillation of
the hand while the finger is stopping a note, whereas 'tremolo' was the rapid reiteration of the same note by
up and down motion of the bow (see, for example, *Grove's Dictionary*, second edition, Vol. V, pp. 147-8 and
268-9).

in fioritura, enabling him, as it were, to run up and down the vibrato, so making florid music relatively easy to accomplish'.[87] Were this so, we might expect his proficiency in such music to be matched by any other of the numerous male singers - Lauri-Volpi, for example - in whom the vibrato is so conspicuous. Finally, the charge of faulty method is refuted by De Lucia's artistic longevity: when, almost forty years after his first professional engagements, he chose to sing he was, in his sixties, still a commanding vocal presence on great public occasions and in the recording studio. For all his transpositions, no singer who - as he did - lacked an outstanding natural voice could have endured so long had his technique been unsound.

Technique and style are the features which so distinguish De Lucia, giving him that remarkable quality of appeal in the most delicate shades of expression, in *mezza voce* and in *rubato* which, as Hurst remarks, places him with the soprano Olimpia Boronat

> ... as a pattern of those achievements so much admired by our forebears - something that blossomed and faded under the fierce light of competition.[88]

Edward Hain asks:

> In what lies De Lucia's incredible charm? I think the foundation of it lies in a complete mastery of his vocal instrument as regards tonal colour and flexibility. So rapidly and so smoothly is he able to vary the shade, pitch or volume of his voice that he is able to convey an extraordinary sense of spontaneity in music of a florid nature or which lends itself to embellishment. ...
>
> The human voice is unique among musical instruments in its ability to change smoothly from loud to soft and vice versa. Nevertheless, the cultivation of this ... *'messa di voce'* ... which endows the art of singing with one of its most effective means of charming the ear, is almost neglected today. The average contemporary Italian tenor ... is generally like a singer with two different voices which he is quite incapable of integrating or blending smoothly with one another. Consequently, a vast range of expression is barred to him.
>
> In this respect, De Lucia excels. The extraordinary expressiveness of 'Addio, Mignon!' and 'Ah! non credevi tu' is undoubtedly made possible by the singer's perfect mastery of *'messa di voce'*.[89]

Desmond Shawe-Taylor, who has termed him 'the last singer of the rococo age', notes

> ... the perfect vocal control and the poignant expressiveness of the phrasing. To quote the old Latin tag, 'everything he touched he adorned', delivering the florid passages of Rossini or Bellini with a variety of colour and a light touch which border on the miraculous.[90]

---

87 Scott, *The Great Caruso*, p. 11.

88 Hurst, *The Golden Age Recorded* (1963), p. 63.

89 Edward Hain, Commentary [on the records of De Lucia], *Record Collector*, Vol. XI, No. 6, June 1957, pp. 129-31.

90 Sackville West and Shawe-Taylor, op. cit., p. 351.

Elsewhere, in a peerless commentary on the qualities - the charm, the variety, and the individuality - which make De Lucia a nonpareil, the same critic has written of

> ... the poignant expressiveness of his phrasing. He makes one think of the old saying 'Plus fait douceur que violence'. His enunciation is distinct and loving, his variety of nuance and tonal coloration unequalled, his treatment of the musical text uncommonly free and supple. He is a master of light and shade; he openly delights in the display of vocal dexterity; he defies the listener to remain indifferent, as he spins out a sustained note in a long diminuendo or throws off a rapid scale or figuration in a casual, apparently effortless way - very much as Pachmann used to do when playing Chopin. To listen to De Lucia in the *Sonnambula* duets is to be reminded of the close link between Chopin and Bellini - a link that seldom occurs to us during the standard Italian performances of today. Everything this singer does is intensely personal; whether the ornamentation he sings is the composer's or his own, he delivers it as though it had just that moment occurred to him. . . .
>
> This extreme tenderness and gentleness - a quality which the Italians call 'morbidezza' - is something which has almost vanished from singing . . . The drawback to De Lucia's graceful, caressing, indolent manner . . . is that it tends to emasculate the rhythm. Nineteenth-century singers seem to have cared little for rhythm as we understand it . . . [91]

De Lucia was unusual even in his own times. Few tenors were so often or so insistently likened to those idiosyncratic singers of the previous generation, Masini and Stagno. His art, wrote Max De Schauensee on De Lucia's centenary, is 'an echo of a world that has ceased to exist. . . . This was a singer who would have brought despair to today's conductors; . . . it would have been well-nigh impossible to fit him into the symphonic approach of the performances of our time.' He continues:

> [In his records] we hear reproduced with almost photographic accuracy a voice characterized by a fast vibrato, a voice sometimes shrill and penetrating, at other times hanging in mid-air - arabesques of dulcet, half-murmured pianissimi. De Lucia knew all the tricks of the trade, all the calculated refinements and artifices his public demanded and expected. Phrases were ornamented with provocative *gruppetti*; long-held, carefully graduated diminuendi seemed to fade into a half-sensed hush. Nor was De Lucia, in his status of *tenore assoluto* of the old school, above altering the melodic line if it suited him.
>
> Thus, his art was a compound of virtues and defects, viewed from today's perspective. He was the denial of such phrases as 'organic cohesion' and 'overall shaping' (so beloved of our younger critics) as applied to operatic performances. Though his coloratura, bubbling along on top of the breath, is a lost art, De Lucia's was not a strictly first-class voice, but one that had been cultivated down to the last dot and dash. Despite such refinements, he could also break into a sudden and apparently spontaneous eruption of vibrant power, much in the manner of his predecessor Stagno. . . .
>
> However we may argue, the recorded fact remains that Fernando De Lucia was a great and fascinating example of the old school. True *bel canto* backed by passionate belief can still be heard in a day when belief is not a watchword.[92]

---

91 Shawe-Taylor (1955), pp. 436-7.
92 De Schauensee, loc. cit.

In the records of De Lucia, maintains Francesco Canessa, one hears precisely the mode of singing adopted by Stagno:

> ... no sooner had Stagno abandoned the swords and plumed hats of *I Puritani*, *Gli Ugonotti*, and *Il Barbiere di Siviglia* than he took up the knife and tasselled hat of the Sicilian peasant. No one should wonder, then, if the reviews dwell on the marvels of his trill, or an archaic flourish above the stave at the end of the 'Brindisi' ...
>
> For all that it is baroque, it is therefore inappropriate to fret about the style of Fernando De Lucia, hearing the recorded evidence of his fabulous successes of those years: it was exactly the mode of singing that pleased. Relaxed *tempi*, open *corone*, stratagems for carrying the high notes on to the most favourable vowels, honeyed shadings, and cadenzas made with hieroglyphics of notes. ... from the hiss of the old records emerge the many secrets of this artist's success. For the affectation equally often reveals tenderness, and the ductility and the fluency of the phrasing make something different of the piece.[93]

The records show many of the nuances and embellishments of the *bel canto* style. One that is missing - from records known to the writer, at any rate - is the trill, or shake. His records, even of pieces such as 'Ecco ridente' or 'Ah! sì, ben mio', where the trill is written, do not include it, certainly in its full-blooded form. The G&T 'Pietà, Signore' [No. 41] and second 'Se il mio nome' [No. 54] contain suggestions, mere hints which might simply be an extension of the vibrato. However, instead of ignoring it, as do most recorded tenors in the *Il Trovatore* piece [No. 150], both there and in the Phonotype 'Pietà, Signore' [No. 201] De Lucia performs a quick, measured alternation between leading note and tonic, corresponding to the 'slow trill' described by Garcia.[94] Singers who knew him were emphatic that he could trill, and they attribute the omissions to his temperament in the studio.[95] It is strange that none of his four recordings of 'Ecco ridente' - where we observe notable changes in ornamentation from one version to another - should have found him ready to attempt the shake. Though it appears unlikely that a singer of his training and accomplishment could not perform it, it seems equally implausible that someone with such inclination towards display would not do so if so equipped, or would have made so curious a substitute.

His interpretations of the *verismo* operas well suggest the intensity of his sensations and the force of his acting. His 'Vesti la giubba', from *Pagliacci* [No. 381], has been described as

> ... a fine-drawn line, vibrant with rage and passion; if this performance cannot equal Caruso's massive outpourings of golden tone, it has one very striking feature which brings the jealous Canio even more vividly before our eyes. The laugh after *Sei tu forse un uom?* sounds wild and a little mad, pitched as it is

---

93 *Mattino*, Feb. 21 1975.

94 Crutchfield (1983), p. 10n.

95 Tom Burke, in 1967, insisted to the writer that De Lucia could 'trill as well as any soprano', and De Lucia's pupil, Angelo Notariello, in conversation in July 1973, even specified that he trilled best in the region of G - A flat.

right up on the high A of the final word; a savage, terrifying laugh, the laugh of a striking actor.[96]

Even in recordings of operas that he never sang on the stage, the spell persists. His 'Bianca al par' [No. 173] from *Gli Ugonotti* impresses for its observance of dynamic markings, and for its elegance and finish.[97] In his score of *Adriana Lecouvreur* the tenor wrote: 'I no longer wish to sing this opera because I hate the third act.' Yet his early version of 'L'anima ho stanca' [No. 23] from *Adriana* - to which he was so clearly unsympathetic - is marked by a remarkable lightness of touch, a feature which is rivalled, and possibly even surpassed, by phrasing which is some of the most arresting that he achieved on record. His handling of the phrase '*ma se amor, se amor cadrà*' lingers in the memory.

Undeniably, his intonation is occasionally uncertain, especially in attack. Moreover, as pointed out by Celletti, some of his bad habits - arbitrary breathing; words or entire phrases substituted for those of the text, to make certain difficult notes fall on one vowel rather than on another, and variations and interpolations of many kinds - characterise his records. For all that,

> ... De Lucia is one of the most individualistic vocal personalities that the record has portrayed from its origins up to the present. One distinguishes and recognises him immediately; and not only for the timbre but also for the diction, the phrasing, the style. His voice shows an astonishing ductility and fluency, it flexes in trills and gradations of all kinds; it has *mezza voce* attacks of incomparable tenderness.
>
> On records, ignoring for the moment the *verismo* repertory, it is the *tenore di grazia* that emerges, investing the extracts from *Il Barbiere di Siviglia*, *La Sonnambula* and *Rigoletto* with baroque *fioriture*, frequently in poor taste, but notable for the way in which, by the clear brilliance of their execution, they relate to us the vocal patterns of an earlier age.[98]

If some of his textual and musical changes hardly enhance the music, many of his alterations strike us as totally in character. His singing of the rising orchestral phrase on the words 'Che gelida manina', from *La Bohème* [No. 125] is perhaps the most striking solecism of all. But in 'Questa o quella' [No. 119] from *Rigoletto* the capricious variations - which can rarely, if ever, have been emulated since his day - seem wholly consistent with the character of the Duke of Mantua.[99] Other ornaments, as they 'prolong the expression of emotions on which the mind is willing to linger', perfectly symbolise and vindicate Garcia's definition of their function.

---

96 Shawe-Taylor (1955), p. 437. With the probable transposition the laugh lies on A flat.

97 Bebb, Richard and Vivian Liff, 'Opera on the Gramophone: "*Les Huguenots*" - Part I', *Opera*, Vol. 20, No. 7, July 1969, p. 584.

98 Celletti, *Le Grandi Voci*, pp. 223-4. His reference to trills (*gorgheggi*) is not specific.

99 Giuseppe Oxilia's record evidently employs identical ornaments (Crutchfield (1983), p. 20).

Celletti has ascribed to him the weaknesses of a great vocalist who, intoxicated with the facility and the delicacy of his own voice, was yet responsive, in temperament and expressive capacity, to the needs of the tumultuous *verismo* repertory. His 'sudden electric surges to high tension, attained despite limited means, gave the full measure of his art and intelligence' just as his alternation of archaicism and modernism revealed an artistic personality torn between romanticism and *verismo*: he was 'half the refined miniaturist, half the voluptuous and ardent street trader'. Often affected and baroque, he was 'one of the tenors who best exemplified the first echelon of the interpreters of the "young school", half *veristi*, half singers *di grazia* and *d'agilità*'.[100]

How far the records reflect De Lucia's voice may never be known. For every claim, such as Martinelli's, that the records (possibly at the wrong speeds) exaggerated the *vibrato*, there may be a legitimate, opposing, view, gained on another occasion. In 1931, Herman Klein was surprised by a 1909 recording of De Lucia, whom he had known well during the Harris era at Covent Garden, but had heard only on the operatic stage:

> The marked tremolo he then indulged had now quite disappeared in a charming rendering of the since-hackneyed ' 'O sole mio'. Doubtless the record was one that had helped to spread the popularity of the song; but as it happened, I had never heard it before, nor had I altogether associated my old acquaintance, except by name, with the tenor whom the H.M.V. list justly described, I see, as 'a delightful and consummate artist in his rendering of Neapolitan songs.'[101]

Modern reproduction can draw from these acoustic records more than could ever have been heard from them when they were made. From them we may appreciate something of the artistry and technical prowess which place De Lucia beyond compare on records, and which 'made [him] an operatic giant even in those days when there were many giants on the earth'.[102] The voice itself can sound sensuously beautiful, with a bewitching sheen. But, faithful as they may be in preserving his style, it is doubtful whether what records capture of the voice would, even under the best conditions, suggest what, in the theatre, one critic likened to 'a hothouse, full of greenery and flowers'. On De Lucia's death, Francesco Dell'Erba wrote:

> Poor De Lucia! What remains of those triumphs, those enthusiasms, those frenzies? What gramophone can render the sweetness and the fascination of his voice which, making us forget mundane cares, carried us into the boundless sky? Nothing remains but the unforgettable memories of those who heard him, of those who loved him, of the generation which was his and which he entranced.[103]

---

100 Celletti, 'Gli interpreti giordaniani', p. 215, and *Musica e Dischi*, April 1955.

101 *Gramophone*, Vol. VIII, April 1931, p. 528. Martinelli heard De Lucia at La Scala in 1905, see p. 62.

102 Louis Migliorini, sleeve note to the Classic reissue 'Fernando De Lucia' (CE 7002).

103 *Napoli: Un quarto di secolo*, p. 175, based on his obituary in *Giornale d'Italia*, Feb. 24 1925.

19

One has to pay to please

The real source of all biography is the confession of the man himself to
somebody.   Ralph Waldo Emerson

After the closure of the San Carlo season in May 1902 and after a
leisurely summer - during which the theatrical papers show him as
available - De Lucia did not sing until January 1903, when he made his
first, handsomely paid, appearances at Genoa, as Loris. Then, traversing
the length of Italy, he sang at Catania, where, after successes in *Fedora*
and *Tosca*, the management reconfirmed him for *La Traviata*.[1] Palermo
followed. The engagement had been arranged by D'Ormeville with whom
dealings had lately been less cordial than in the past:

Cava dei Tirreni
August 19th 1902

Dearest Carlo,

For next year I would like make arrangements for America because I have
convinced the family. For the winter I am still available because the offers
received are unacceptable to me.
   Therefore, think where it would be my turn this year.
   I would return to Palermo for fifteen performances because Palermo
interests me and, since I know that friend Laganà cannot pay, given the
condition of his theatre, I would help on the fees, naturally [assuming] the
operas are agreed.
   Thus I want to put myself once again in good relations with you and to
arrange good business.
   You will know of my latest successes at Naples and Palermo.
   I shake your hand cordially. (BLS)

The agent's offer seems to have been unsatisfactory, for on August
24th the tenor wrote to him again:

Cava dei Tirreni

To avoid wasting time in negotiations, I will tell you immediately my final
demands, taking account of the period and the conditions of the theatre, and
above all through the affection I have for friend Laganà and for you.

---

[1] *Gazzetta dei Teatri*, Mar. 5 1903.

For 15 performances, then, I would accept 25 thousand lire and some tickets, as they gave me last year. I believe that I cannot ask less, given my name, and without taking account of the success that I had last year with *Fedora at that theatre.*

For the operas, I would choose from those that Laganà will arrange. I would willingly sing *Gioconda, Pescatori,* and also *Traviata,* if there is nothing else to choose, but I repeat that we will settle the operas.

Therefore, as you see, I have genuine goodwill to arrange something.

I await the contracts without discussing anything else; Laganà knows how I deal with artistic matters. (BLS)

The performances of *La Bohème* at Palermo were well-received. 'Before the name of Fernando De Lucia', wrote one local critic, 'one can only bend the knee.' He continued:

Who can fail to be subjugated, filled with enthusiasm, and won over by his - we may say - creations? How much art, what analysis of the most insignificant details of the personages whom he incarnates! What compelling fascination in his notes, now sweet, now powerful, but always suffused with the warmth of Naples![2]

At his last appearance, an enthusiastic crowd formed a torchlight procession to accompany the tenor back to the Hôtel des Palmes.

After a concert in Messina there was a single performance of Rossini's *Stabat Mater,* at the Teatro Argentina, Rome. He was judged somewhat frugal of his art, since, after the 'Cujus animam', he left the stage and did not reappear, the public being deprived of an encore of the piece, which he '. . . coloured and modulated with great finesse'.[3]

His domestic situation had again become entangled. Relations with Itala had deteriorated still further. In part, this was because her family - now in reduced circumstances - had been obliged to sell Villa Erminia to him.[4] Thereafter, it seems that Fernando and Itala spent their summers apart, in their separate villas at Cava, but in other respects his social life there continued as before. The former De Giorgio residence was a spacious house, with the ground floor walls so arranged that it could be used for recitals. Local people still talk of the parties and concerts there, when the line of carriages would stretch right back to the bridge at the foot of the hill. Within the De Giorgio family the villas were always referred to as 'Villa Eduardo' and 'Villa Itala'. Alfredo continued to visit both.

Fernando's relationship with Elvira Giommi had deepened. Clearly, she was much more of a kindred spirit than was Itala, and her

2 *Eco Artistico,* Mar. 26-29 1903.

3 *Tribuna,* Apr. 10/12 1903.

4 Private treaty, Naples, Apr. 7 1902. The De Giorgio family had evidently been unable to support the mortgage owing to De Lucia, and their debts had increased. When, in April 1902, they sold the villa to him much of the purchase price of 49,510 lire was already owed to him in liabilities - meticulously detailed, as they had been in the loan documents of 1892 - of 29,691.97 lire. They owed at least 20,000 lire to others.

relationship with the singer had almost certainly originated in shared musical interests. But there were now other links. Probably, Elvira had accompanied him to Catania. The 'sister' with whom he now sometimes shared Villa Erminia in summer was presumably she. She was now pregnant with their first child, who was born at Naples, on June 24th 1903. He was named Ferdinando (Vanni) Giommi. As was customary when the father was unwilling, or not free, to marry, paternity was registered as 'Unknown'. Elvira had left the Giommi family home in Via Partenope for a second-floor apartment at Vico Secondo Corsea, No. 11. And this was probably the point at which her financial support required sums that De Lucia could provide only by a subterfuge, such as his supposed gambling losses.

In July 1903 his mother died. It was a period of turmoil and no engagements are traceable between April and November, when he was listed as 'unavailable'. He was, however, far from being forgotten by the staff of the remorseless *Monsignor Perrelli*, as they held their convivial meetings at Gambrinus. Week by week Ricci and his colleagues launched their darts; in their customary list of Easter gifts, the magazine proposed to send De Lucia a subscription to *La Voce ... della Verità (The Voice ... of the Truth)*, for the year 1902-3.[5] They reported his acquisition of a fine gramophone in order 'to comply properly with the requests of those visitors who wanted to hear him sing'.[6] There were repeated plays on the pretentious names of some of the De Giorgio family: Averolino, Agamennone, and Acapicassio, it was reported, were hoping that Anselmi, who was enjoying a great success as Cavaradossi, would be hissed.[7]

Late in 1903 there was an engagement for De Lucia to sing in *Fedora* at Sonzogno's own theatre, the Teatro Lirico Internazionale in Milan. He was undoubtedly the major attraction of the evening, a *divo* who

> ...had a splendid success, a *maestro* of filigreed singing, of most finished vocalisation, and of irresistible effects. All evening the large audience warmly showed its great rapport and admiration ... [8]

The audience demanded not one but two encores of 'Amor ti vieta'. The enthusiasm of the *Corriere della Sera* was, however, tempered with scarcely-veiled criticism:

> He sang the première of 'Amor ti vieta' and all the duet with the soprano in a way calculated to make applause break out with irresistible violence at each item, it can be said at each phrase. The *bel canto* fanatics almost jumped out of their skins; the others, admiring the perfect art of the singer and the marvellous virtue of a voice that flexes and bends, is rounded off and fades,

---

5 *Monsignor Perrelli*, Apr. 9 1903. No file of *La Voce della Verità* has been located.
6 Ibid., July 18 1903.
7 Ibid., Mar. 17 1903.
8 *Lombardia*, Nov. 22 1903.

passing away smooth and secure through the most delicate and caressing shadings, would have desired more dramatic accents, more vibrant notes, and more harshness in the great tenderness of sounds and slurs - tenderness that is sometimes almost affectation.[9]

From Milan, he again set out across Europe. Elvira, who accompanied him, recalled that he spent the long train journey reading Goethe's novel, in preparation for *Werther* at Florence. But, first, his travels took him to Lisbon, and to the Teatro Sao Carlos. The manager, Pacini, had invited him to sing Loris in a gala presentation of *Fedora*, in honour of the King of Spain. The conductor was an old friend, Vincenzo Lombardi. So pleased was Pacini reported to be with De Lucia's performance that he reconfirmed him for 1904-5; in the event, the engagement was never to be fulfilled.

After this briefest of stays he travelled on to Oporto, where the management of the refurbished Teatro Sao Joao was mounting the season in lavish style. It was the city's first chance to applaud the peripatetic De Lucia. And so it did as, with the Portuguese soprano Maria Arneiro, he inspired scenes of great enthusiasm in *Fedora* and *Tosca*. It was a succession of triumphs, of encores, of calls, of interminable applause for his 'velvety *mezza voce*, scintillating with sound and colour' and for his 'singular brilliance of sound'.[10] In particular, it was noted how his name had become as firmly associated with *Fedora* as had Masini's with *L'Elisir d'Amore* and Gayarre's with *La Favorita*.[11]

The première of *Tosca* at the same theatre featured luxurious programmes, printed on superb paper and carrying the portraits of the principal artists. De Lucia's singing drew expressions of wonder:

[Of 'E lucevan le stelle'] The way in which he shades, the enchanting gloss and embroidery with which he shapes this piece, making it stand out in all its melodic opulence, the easy way in which he passes from the softest *mezza voce* notes to the most powerful ones in the upper register, all this is a real marvel.[12]

Though the production did not match the singing, the audience's distaste for an out-of-tune cellist soon gave way to hilarity when, in another mishap involving firearms and incompetent extras, some of the 'soldiers' fired their weapons before coming on stage for Act III, so that scarcely a round remained to despatch Cavaradossi.

From Oporto De Lucia passed in rapid succession to Lisbon and then to Florence, where he was awaited 'like a Messiah' for *Werther*. The Pergola had not heard him for more than a decade, and Florentines gladly paid unusually high prices to hear performances praised to the

---

[9] *Corriere della Sera*, Nov. 22 1903.

[10] *Commercio do Porto*, Dec. 23 and 29 1903.

[11] *Palavra*, Dec. 27 1903.

[12] *Commercio do Porto*, Dec. 29 1903.

skies by the local press. His old friend the baritone Mario Ancona attended one performance, accompanied by his son, Giacomo, who looked back on the occasion:

> His *filate* and *mezze voci* in 'Deh non mi ridestar' were of surpassing beauty and virtuosity. Of course, he showed the usual tendency of the tenors to overdoing.[13]

De Lucia returned to Naples and to the San Carlo for some performances of *Fedora*, given in honour of Giordano. Equal enthusiasm was, however, shown for the tenor, who was singing there after an absence of two years from that theatre. After 'Amor ti vieta' there was a storm of applause. Procida noted that, in the encore, he changed his style completely: from having been ardent and dramatic,

> ... he sang the repeat of the sweet, fluid melody [with] a mastery that created wonderful, spun-out notes, soft modulations, exquisite phrasing. ... He is, more than ever, a master of song. His diction is wonderful, his resources are endless. ... He has continued to refine the character of Loris; last night, his interpretation of the *racconto* revealed just how great his feeling for the music is ... his sweet, graceful singing reached a hitherto unknown peak. ... After the many tenors ... this season at the San Carlo, De Lucia seemed to us to be in quite a different category; he seemed to represent Truth; accents ... which, transcending any mere interpretation of a piece of music, enter directly into the heart of the sufferer.[14]

Not all were wholly pleased at his return. *Monsignor Perrelli* had to agree that he was always an authentic singer and artist. Earlier, though, true to its acid form, a lengthy piece of doggerel about the state of things in the city had started:

> Over the bowed heads of the Neapolitans
> De Lucia and Novelli hang like a sword of Damocles.[15]

'Is it not time for him to bow out gracefully?' was Ricci's message. More doggerel suggested that his audiences tore their hair in anguish:

> *Sovra gli acuti - De Lucia - più belli*
> *Suole caccia le mani nei capelli*
> *Per cui lo spettatore che lo sente*
> *Lo stesso fa, contemporaneamente*
>
> (On his finest high notes, De Lucia
> Thrusts his hands through his hair
> Causing the spectator who hears him
> To do the same, simultaneously.)[16]

---

13 G.R. Ancona, letter (in English) to the writer, May 1967.
14 *Pungolo*, Feb. 29 1904.
15 'Canzone della Lotteria a Premio Certo', *Monsignor Perrelli*, Feb. 9 1904.
16 *Monsignor Perrelli*, unknown date. Communicated by Domenico Farina.

After De Lucia's departure for Bari, Anselmi sang Loris at the San Carlo. *Monsignor Perrelli* sarcastically asked why he did not put his hands in his hair when he sang, especially since he had an abundance, almost more than De Lucia; why did he not beat the ground with his foot at climactic points of the opera; why was he allowed to sing his music at score pitch; and why did he risk singing a refined cadenza rather than the usual tragic one in 'Amor ti vieta'? He would incur grave displeasure in *Tosca*, the paper warned, unless he sang it as it was generally sung - two tones down and with the hands run through the hair.[17]

But, in cities which had not yet had their fill of De Lucia, or had never heard what many termed his 'matchless' interpretation of Loris, the queues formed the day before the performance and the critics found yet more superlatives to describe the 'perfect schooling and extraordinary diction', the 'most delicate *sfumature* of that prodigious throat',[18] and the ways in which his interpretations changed vocally and histrionically from night to night, creating the part afresh.[19] He was perceived to give 'a special personal quality, a certain *saper vivere* on the stage'.[20] The manager of the Teatro Petruzzelli at Bari took newspaper space, begging to advise his clientèle that they could enjoy the performances confident that specially-arranged tramway trains would run after the opera.

The performances, though, were becoming fewer. Like Puccini, De Lucia preferred the comforts of home, where he was surrounded by the trophies and mementoes of his artistic life. A reminder of happier days, before Fernando and Itala grew apart, lay in Vergil's words, written on the door jamb of their villa: *'Deus nobis haec otia fecit.'*[21] Especially in his later years, he preferred to be somewhere where he could summon his doctor by telephone, a modern convenience that he had adopted enthusiastically. Perhaps he was tired of carrying on his travels the small head cushion which alone assured him of sound sleep. Or perhaps he yearned for the company of Elvira Giommi, who now waited for him in the wings during performances. After Bari he was heard no more in 1904. A trip to Milan to make records was his sole traceable artistic endeavour until the San Carlo season of 1904-5. Even then, he sang only one rôle, that of Yann in Mugnone's *Vita Brettona.*[22]

The world première of Mugnone's work came on March 14th 1905, near the end of a season which had included Battistini, Bonci, Luppi, Maurel, Regina Pacini, and Viñas in its impressive roster. De Lucia was joined by Bellincioni, Ninì Frascani, Francesco Maria Bonini, and Mario Sammarco. The composer conducted.

---

17 Ibid., Apr. 23 1904.

18 *Risveglio Commerciale*, Mar. 26/27 1904.

19 *Corriere delle Puglie*, Mar. 23 and 25 1904.

20 *Risveglio Commerciale*, Mar. 26/27 1904.

21 'God made us this leisure.'

22 Often spelled *Brettone* or *Bretone*. The opera is dedicated: 'To the sublime artist Antonio Cotogni.'

The sensitive, excitable Mugnone, his expression a 'mixture of devilry and ecstasy, at times as gentle as a child, at times as furious as one obsessed' commanded great local affection and an admiration that neared devotion. But, even admitting Mugnone's many talents and his ability to give life to works that had seemed dead, and admitting also that staging, soloists, and chorus could not have been bettered, faint praise in tactful reviews was the best that the critics could manage. De Lucia, who 'felicitously alternated passion with charming affectations ... triumphed once again'.[23]

From Naples, De Lucia returned to Milan, for some performances of *Il Barbiere di Siviglia*. It was a time of civil unrest, when the railways were run by government officials and required protection from attacks by militant strikers. After a tense journey, he registered at the Hôtel Continental for a stay which was later to cause much interest.

The ever-popular Rossini opera (the last production of the season) had not been given at La Scala for some years, and it filled the theatre for six performances. The cast was a fine one, including Maria Barrientos, Giuseppe De Luca, Antonio Pini-Corsi, and Gaudio Mansueto. However, it did not live up to expectations. Cleofonte Campanini allowed too many liberties: one singer would abuse this freedom in the cadenzas, another in the comic action, and another would give the recitatives in his own individual way, such that there was a 'most bizarre variety of declamation'.

The singing of Barrientos was felt to lack expression. Pini-Corsi caricatured the part of Bartolo. It was Giuseppe De Luca, an expressive and self-controlled Figaro, always attentive to the action and funny without exaggeration, who gained the greatest praise. De Lucia, one critic wrote,

> ... was, in other days, an excellent Almaviva. Today, his singing is obliged to make almost continuous use of *mezza voce*, and his grace smacks of mannerism.[24]

To the critic of *La Perseveranza*, the tenor seemed somewhat alarmed by the evident discontent:

> However much applauded after the 'largo' of the *serenata* and the *canzone*, he realised that the assembly was not totally convinced of the intentions of his interpretation. He is always the refined interpreter, who knows all of the more subtle resources of his art, who bends his voice in delightful modulations, in gradations, in beauties of expression, appropriate to those who perceive the beauties of true Italian singing. He has sought to mitigate his tendencies to mannered singing, to *puntature*, to seeking effects by means of artifice, of the *falsetto*, of *corone* etc. But not enough to persuade the public. The two first-act arias, lowered by a semitone, lost their liveliness of colour, and this, too,

---

23 *Pungolo*, Mar. 16 1905.
24 *Corriere della Sera*, Apr. 6 1905.

prevented the listeners from appraising him fully. . . . He can perform Almaviva with noble elegance, with fluency, and with comedy of the highest class. When the excitement is over, he will succeed better . . . by singing the Rossinian text with greater precision. 25

Some accusation of excessive mannerism in modulation, colouring, and phrasing came at later performances. None the less, he remained for the critic 'one of the few who can, today, tackle this kind of music'.26 For Giovanni Martinelli, who heard one of the performances, it was the rather baritonal timbre of De Lucia which, he thought, would better have suited the part of Figaro.27 For the young John McCormack, who heard him several times that season, he was 'a glorious artist'.28

De Lucia's recordings of Almaviva are among those for which 'incomparable' may justly be used. His 1904 'Ecco ridente' [No. 25] shows to advantage the beauty of tone that he commanded in those early years of recording, and which was captured by even the primitive equipment then employed. The ornaments, which start on the second syllable of the first *'aurora'*, are lovingly shaped and flawlessly executed. The agility of the 'allegro' section is breathtaking. His style has drawn the comment:

> Certainly he was the last Almaviva properly to deploy a wholly individual style of ornamentation: ornamentation as effortless, as mysterious yet as ineluctably right, as the play of light in a summer glade. Can the words 'la bella aurora' . . . ever have been painted so exquisitely on the voice . . . ?29

Hain comments:

> When it comes to florid singing, De Lucia has no equal among male singers. His 'Ecco ridente' is the classic example of florid singing by a tenor, with the incredible ease and neatness of the *allegro* divisions, which are like pearls strung on an unbroken thread. No 'intrusive aspirate' nonsense, but an absolutely unbroken line, within which one has the impression of a little velvet hammer tapping out the notes with crystal clarity.30

Steane writes of De Lucia's 'wonderful feeling' for Almaviva's music:

> He seems to have known exactly when to linger, when to soften, when to add an ornament, when to join one phrase to another. In . . . 'Se il mio nome', the embellishments are exquisite . . . His ornamentation of the second verse is exceptionally bold, both in its departure from the written line and in the demand it makes on the performer (it involves, for instance, a downward *glissando* of an octave and a fifth). Yet so naturally and easily is it done that one never feels this is flashy or out of place.31

---

25 *Perseveranza*, Apr. 6 1905.
26 Ibid., Apr. 13 1905.
27 In conversation with the writer, 1967.
28 Key, *John McCormack*, p. 117.
29 Richard Osborne, *Opera on Record*, 1979, p. 146.
30 Hain, loc. cit., p. 130.
31 Steane, op. cit., p. 31.

His recordings of these airs are justly celebrated for their stylishness, unrivalled elegance, and technical brilliance. Other extracts from *Il Barbiere di Siviglia* fascinate for their echoes of the *buffo* style. The comic duets with Pini-Corsi (as Figaro), recorded in 1906, draw added point from the perfect diction of both singers, a feature which much enhances our enjoyment of their perfect timing and subtle nuances, especially in 'All'idea di quel metallo' [No. 35]. The 'Numero quindici' [No. 31] is notable for the light touch in the section starting 'Ah, che d'amore' and is a supreme example of De Lucia's coloratura. The trio 'Ah! qual colpo' [No. 39] with Huguet and Pini-Corsi is an enchanting and impressive display of the tenor's command of light and shade.

After Milan, he made his first appearances in France, when he joined the great Sonzogno company assembled by Daspuro at the Théâtre Sarah Bernhardt in Paris. His colleagues included Amedeo Bassi, Berlendi, Caruso, Cavalieri, Garbin, Kaschmann, Oreste Luppi, Masini, Amelia Pinto, Maurice Renaud, Ruffo, Sammarco, Stehle, and Eva Tetrazzini.[32]

In a season almost entirely of Sonzogno works De Lucia appeared only in the Paris première of *L'Amico Fritz*, on May 9th 1905. 'Its success', wrote *Gil Blas*, 'must largely be attributed to the marvellous tenor Fernando De Lucia.'[33] Another critic described him as

> ... a singer out of the ordinary, who plays with the voice as one plays on a violin. It is an achievement of vocal perfection; it is, probably, the last representation of that admirable Italian school that we once valued - the Fraschinis, the Naudins, and the Monginis.[34]

Returning to London in 1905, he appeared in opera at the Waldorf Theatre.[35] The season, under the management of Henry Russell, ran from May 22nd to July 15th, providing Covent Garden with its first summer competition for years.

The operas, which alternated with appearances of the great actress Eleonora Duse, offered an array of talent that included Ancona, Arimondi, Bonci, Alice Nielsen, and Antonio Pini-Corsi. However, so many expensive singers in a house described as 'elegant' (a euphemism for small) raised ticket prices to levels which deterred audiences. Nearby Covent Garden - with Caruso, Destinn, Gerville-Reache, Kurz, Litvinne, and Maurel - was a counter-attraction. There were plenty of empty seats at the Waldorf. So-called 'rover' tickets were issued, permitting their purchasers to stand wherever they wished; there was never any objection when they settled in choice seats as the lights went down.[36]

---

32 *Musica*, Apr. 1905.

33 *Gil Blas*, May 10 1905.

34 *Petit Journal*, May 10 1905. The critic refers to the tenors Gaetano Fraschini (1816-1887), Emilio Naudin (1823-1890), and Pietro Mongini (1830-1874).

35 Now the Strand Theatre.

36 Riddell Hunter, *Gramophone*, July 1938, p. 55.

Once again, De Lucia opened a London season in *Pagliacci,* to the Tonio of Mario Ancona, and once again they were entirely successful. For the *Sketch,* though not the same De Lucia as in 1893, he was 'extremely passionate, as magnificently histrionic, as he was in the old days'.[37] One *Pagliacci* was witnessed by the young P.G. Hurst, who wrote of De Lucia

> ... of whose performance as Canio I find it impossible to speak too highly. He was so fine an actor that his portrayal of the emotions through which the unfortunate Canio passes were all expressed with complete conviction. His cheerful and lively entry ... with the ravishing Nedda of Irene de Bohuss, with Tonio and Beppe ... in glittering costumes, filled the stage and the eye at once, [and] his familiarity with the rôle ... made one at once aware that De Lucia was a great stage artist.[38]

In 'Vesti la giubba' he underlined pathos rather than fury. His 'delicate art was seen at its best and its most perfect. ... His singing never lost its silvery quality or the perfect melodic line.' Hurst concluded:

> After witnessing a cavalcade of Canios, I find that De Lucia's stands supreme for the unforced pathos of his acting, and the sheer beauty of his singing.[39]

As on other occasions, De Lucia sang Harlequin's serenade from behind the scenes. In one performance, a nervous newcomer took the part of Silvio. His self-consciousness was apparently aggravated by the sound of his squeaky shoes. The several unhappy moments in his duet with Nedda were as nothing, however, compared with his misfortune at the end. De Lucia was 'singing and acting wonderfully'. So realistic was his portrayal of Canio that Silvio, who was quite terrified, jumped back to avoid the knife. Canio, with nothing to strike, lost his balance and fell headlong down the steps of his little theatre. None the less, he composed himself and managed to say his final words: *'La commedia è finita!'* With Silvio still on his feet not all of the audience agreed. History does not record the conversation behind the curtain when, finally, it fell.[40]

De Lucia's other parts were Fritz, Turiddu, and Almaviva. In *Il Barbiere di Siviglia, The Times* rated very highly the

> ... irresistibly comic acting of Signori Pini-Corsi and Arimondi, as a diminutive Bartolo and a gigantic Basilio ... These parts can surely never have been better played.[41]

For ensemble and infectious spirit it was, declared the *Sunday Times* (June 11th), the best London *Il Barbiere* for years. Hurst wrote of

---

[37] *Sketch,* May 31 1905.
[38] Hurst, *The Age of Jean de Reszke,* pp. 208-9.
[39] Ibid., p. 152.
[40] Riddell Hunter, loc. cit.
[41] *The Times,* June 10 1905.

De Lucia's delightful and entertaining stage presence; of how he entered into, or even led, the brisk humour of the *buffo* scenes; and of how his 'polished fooling, with the more robust fun of Ancona' made a 'most artistic combination'.[42] The tenor was greatly entertaining in the fake drunk scene, clearing the floor with a sweep of his sword in his own inimitable way. (The moment may still be savoured in his amusing and unsurpassed record of 'Finora in questa camera ...Ehi di casa' [No. 241].) Sixty years later Hurst still remembered the beauty of a long head note, a *diminuendo*, leading into 'Buona sera, mio Signore' (a touch that is preserved in the Phonotype recording of the piece [No. 245]), and the very Italianate gesture that accompanied it. The comedy was excellent, although entirely free from unvocal horseplay.[43] It was the 'most marvellous exhibition of operatic team-work I have ever seen'.[44]

The poorly-supported season was, however, not a happy one for some of the artists. De Lucia evidently stayed the course, but on June 30th Russell released Ancona from his contract.[45] In a letter to Guy d'Hardelot, the baritone wrote:

> I have finished at the Waldorf..... I have had enough of it. They continue to announce my name but my contract is finished.[46]

As usual, De Lucia spent the summer at Cava, where he was much upset by news of the death, on August 31st 1905, of Tamagno. They had always been good friends, each respecting the gifts of the other. He restored his spirits by sending newspapers with humorous, if hardly flattering, cartoons of himself to Elvira who, while awaiting a second child, was living at her mother's home. There, on October 19th 1905, a daughter was born. She was baptised Adelina but was always called Rosa, after De Lucia's mother.

His next engagement was for the 1905-6 season at the recently refurbished San Carlo, now managed by Roberto De Sanna. Artistic problems arose when, a few days before the scheduled opening, there was a disagreement with Mugnone, and a substitute had to be found at short notice. Eventually, four other conductors were engaged, including Mascagni. His fees and those of the impressive roster of singers raised prices well above last season's, and wonder was expressed at the public's ability and willingness to pay in such numbers every night.

The season opened with Battistini, De Marchi, and Irma Monti-Baldini in *Un Ballo in Maschera*. De Lucia made his season début in *Tosca*, followed by *Il Barbiere di Siviglia*. The latter was conducted by

42 Hurst, *The Age of Jean de Reszke*, p. 209.
43 Hurst, private communication, May 1967.
44 Hurst, *Gramophone*, July 1931, p. 64.
45 (A) Letter Russell - Ancona, June 30 1905.
46 (H) Undated.

Mascagni, who diplomatically wrote to the tenor:

December 24th 1905

Dear Fernando,

The management has fixed the *Barbiere di Siviglia* for Friday next, with my direction and performed by you, Battistini and Pacini. Wanting, before anything else, to exchange some ideas with you, I would be most grateful to you if you would favour me with a meeting tomorrow in the theatre . . .

. . . with the most affectionate greetings, I am always yours,

Mascagni (RE)

Pungolo, after admiring the versatility of Battistini, '*gran signore* of singing', as he lent his refined tones to the gaiety of Figaro, recalled De Lucia's previous appearances as Almaviva at the San Carlo. He seemed

. . . even more subtle, more shrewd . . . more gracefully resourceful in maintaining, in Almaviva's singing, an open, light, ingratiating method, paying attention to the delightful arabesques of agility with the same care with which he had embellished his opening aria ['Ecco ridente'] and the serenade ['Se il mio nome'] of the first act.[47]

Mattino remarked on his animated acting and arresting gaiety, which conformed exactly to the spirit of the character.[48] For *Giorno* he was

. . . full of colour, elegance and *brio*, the personification of the cavalier and of the witty soldier, . . . flaunting all the richness of his palette in the second and third acts, . . . causing shivers, like the gentle caress of a warm breeze on the face. . . . . [49]

However, he was, again, soon the butt of *Monsignor Perrelli*'s humour. Plays on words suggested not only that he transposed but that he could not even reach an A. 'Barber Battistini' had for his clients 'Queen [Regina] Pacini and the baritone De Lucia'.[50] Rossini's tomb was depicted, 'somewhat profaned and transformed into a receiving line':

Rossini: 'And you, Dear Figaro. . . . . that is to say Dear Don Basilio. . . . . or, better to say, what have we in common, you and I?'
De Lucia (imperturbable): 'Nothing in common, but I am Almaviva.'
Rossini (with noisy cordiality): 'Ah! that is true. I had not recognised you.'[51]

Scurrilous poems made further reference to hair-tearing. When Altobelli, a local lawyer much given to operatic hand-gestures, went

---

47 *Pungolo*, Dec. 31 1905.
48 *Mattino*, Dec. 30/31 1905.
49 *Giorno*, Dec. 30 1905.
50 *Monsignor Perrelli*, Jan. 4 1906
51 Ibid., Dec. 30, 1905.

hoarse while conducting an important lawsuit, a double-edged gibe described him as 'like the great Fernando - without a voice'.[52] Such viciousness was not, though, confined to De Lucia, for the entire cast of *Il Barbiere* received similar treatment.

Gennarelli's music shop now advertised 'new celebrity recordings' of De Lucia singing 'Addio, Mignon!' and 'La tua bell'alma'.[53] For he was to appear in *Mignon*, which was new for the San Carlo. He declined to wear a wig. *Monsignor Perrelli* predicted that he would pull out quantities of hair, to give greater force to his singing lessons which, 'quite rightly, the critics exhort the pupils of the Conservatory to go to hear'. Of the performance, it wrote:

> So far as our personal friend Commendatore De Lucia is concerned, we noted immediately that he could not do more. Another artist, for example a tenor, would have been able to sing the part as it is written, but our personal friend Comm. De Lucia, as that master of singing that he is recognised to be, confronted by certain exigencies of the score, has given out a most authoritative 'No!' of protest; for which reason he could not, afterwards, deliver that B . . . . . natural in any self-respecting tenor.[54]

More serious comment noted that the opera faded in the vastness of the San Carlo. The première received exceedingly faint praise. At the second, the replacement of Marta Currelich by the personable Irma Monti-Baldini much improved the reception. With her dark, smouldering 'eyes full of dreams' and her mantle of dark hair she was a lovely creature, who immediately captivated the press.[55]

Pungolo dealt severely with De Lucia's use of ornament:

> De Lucia, who is entirely devoted to extracting from his voice the most complicated decorations, sang the part of Meister with the rarest accomplishments of vocal grace, with effects in *falsetti*, with *filature*, with effective and rapid transitions from *piano* to *forte* . . . so many that I have not even the courage to try to describe the excessive wealth of them.[56]

His other rôles were his well-known impersonations of Loris and Canio. The *Fedora* of March 25th was conducted by Giordano. It was an evening of lessons: while De Lucia taught singing and hair-tearing, the striking Marie Lafargue's *décolleté* had the ladies admiring her elegance and the gentlemen. . . . . simply lost in admiration.[57]

Again, the critics noted De Lucia's ability to change the vocal effects, so that the second performance, with its encores, almost became a

52 Poem 'Il tenore di forza', ibid., Feb. 8 1906.
53 *Mattino*, Mar. 2/3 1906.
54 *Monsignor Perrelli*, Feb. 1 1906.
55 *Giorno*, Feb. 3 1906.
56 *Pungolo*, Feb. 2 1906.
57 *Monsignor Perrelli*, Mar. 27 1906.

third.[58] These oft-remarked variations from one performance to another were not usually spontaneous. They were arranged beforehand by De Lucia, with much deliberation. Like Stagno, he knew his public and how to move it. Sometimes, in conversation with Antonio Caggiula, he would predict the precise moments at which - quite independently of any *claque* - he would bring the audience to its feet, roaring its approval.

The performances of *Fedora* and *Tosca* continued at the San Carlo, but De Lucia's engagements were over in what was to be his last full season there. As it drew to its close, Naples was preoccupied with the eruption of Vesuvius, which had already destroyed several small towns and was threatening others, including Portici and Torre Annunziata. There was near-panic in the more densely-populated quarters of Naples when a terrifying rumble shook the ground. Many people rushed into the streets, shouting '*Un terremoto! Un terremoto!*' Men, women, and children, clothed as best they could manage, prayed in the streets to Santa Anna and, more especially, to San Gennaro, who was said to have saved them so often over many centuries. Through the open doors of the *bassi* could be seen candles, burning before images of saints. At Porta Capuana, weeping women knelt around an image of the Madonna of Pompei. In Piazza Salerno, an enormous crowd gathered to look at Vesuvius, wrapped in dense smoke:

> The sight is marvellous; a blood-red cloud hangs over the mountain. It is a deep red in the centre, rose-pink at the edges, which are lost, little-by-little, in the densest smoke, in the dark clouds of cinders. It seems as though a colossal, monstrous, frightful fire reflects the flashes of its consuming flames from a cover of mist. Almost uninterrupted electric discharges furrow the sky with luminous, serpentine, silvery streaks. In the glimmer of a flash, which rends the clouds of cinders, I see the outline of the cone; it looks an enormous, black mass, at whose top burns a colossal burst of flame, from which fall streams of molten gold, rivulets of incandescent rubies. And the ground shakes, murmurs, boils, as if, in the viscera of the earth, boils some great kettle. The characteristic noise impresses like that of hundreds and hundreds of locomotives which run on rails of molten iron.[59]

As the eruption continued, the King and Queen of Italy arrived to comfort the injured, the bereaved, and the dispossessed. *Pungolo* reprinted *The Last Days of Pompei*. But, gradually, the fury of the volcano abated. On April 20th, news of the San Francisco earthquake and concern for their *concittadino* Caruso finally displaced Vesuvius from the front pages. The theatrical columns reappeared. King Edward VII and Queen Alexandra of England arrived at Naples. A concert was arranged at the San Carlo for the benefit of the victims of the eruption.

For De Lucia, there were no further operatic appearances in 1906. So far as is known, except for recording activities in Milan he remained in

---

58 Ibid.
59 *Pungolo*, Apr. 9 1906.

Naples. Elvira was pregnant with their third child, who was born on November 15th 1906 and was named Giuseppina, in memory of Giuseppe De Lucia.

The San Carlo, managed by Augusto Laganà, opened for the 1906-7 season with Maria Farneti and Eugenio Giraldoni in *Madama Butterfly*, a work that De Lucia, although he loved the opera, refused to sing because, he said, he hated the character of Pinkerton. He made his only appearances of the season in *L'Amico Fritz*, whose première took place on January 6th 1907. It was conducted by Mugnone, who was still able to infuse sparkle into the score. For *Giorno*, Farneti and De Lucia both sang wonderfully. 'All the fresh and perfumed breeze of Spring, all the breath of the flowered fields of April passed last night in the *bel canto* of Maria Farneti.' And De Lucia 'gave the treasures of his golden throat, which has the purity of ringing metal, and inimitable *sfumature*'.[60]

Pungolo remarked:

> There are no summits left for De Lucia to conquer, as an artist of bewitching song. In the duet he conveyed a sensation of subtle joy, by the sweetness with which he opens the 'Tutto tace', and the delicate shading of his *falsetti*, the poetry of his changes of register, which transfigure the closing bars of the Cherry Duet in a dreamlike illusion. . . . in the third act romanza . . . the tenor's voice lingers with a faint rustling of wings . . . [61]

According to *Monsignor Perrelli*, whose cartoon suggested that there had been the occasional hiss, Mugnone took fully half the credit, and what remained went to Farneti. Its treatment of De Lucia reached new depths of scurrilousness.[62]

The opera was repeated on January 8th, with 'quintuple illumination' in honour of the Queen's birthday, and on six more occasions, latterly with Georgina Caprile.

In March 1907 he appeared at the Monte Carlo opera. As early as 1895, Princess Alice of Monaco had expressed interest in engaging him.[63] Actual negotiations may have taken place with Gunsbourg in 1899. Now, the three performances of *Il Barbiere di Siviglia* presented him in a strong cast. Rosina Storchio was a seductive Rosina, pure of voice, of excellent delivery, her acting full of engaging mischief. Ruffo showed his versatility as Figaro. Chaliapin, as Basilio, found great scope for his gifts of facial expression. Antonio Pini-Corsi was a Bartolo of 'impeccable talent . . . of epic buffoonery'. De Lucia was

> . . . shown as an excellent comedian, served by a delightful voice which gives all the accents of a conception [which is] among the most artistic. Need one add that he sang each phrase with superior art? M. De Lucia has long had a

---

60 *Giorno*, Jan. 7 1907.
61 *Pungolo*, Jan. 8 1907.
62 *Monsignor Perrelli*, Jan. 8 1907.
63 T.J. Walsh, *Monte Carlo Opera 1879-1909*, p. 94.

reputation as one of the most remarkable singers, on whom comment is superfluous.[64]

De Lucia's servants accompanied him to Monte Carlo. The singer considered the expense as money well spent for, he claimed, French chefs had little idea of Italian cuisine, and habitually over-cooked pasta; they in turn claimed that De Lucia and his family liked their pasta raw. Each day, around noon, Luciano, wearing his tall white chef's *toque*, would go to the hotel kitchen to cook De Lucia's vermicelli.

The cook was of similar build to his master, who would give him cast-off suits that were scarcely worn. When Luciano completed the ensemble with a straw hat, such as the tenor wore in summer, and went walking with the children he was often mistaken for him. Perplexed, he asked De Lucia for advice:

'What shall I do, when they say *"Bon soir*, M. De Lucia"? They think that I'm you.'

'Well, don't be rude and ignore them. Say *"Bon soir"* in return, and raise your hat.'

From Monte Carlo the company went to Berlin for a single appearance at the Royal Opera House on April 13th. A few days later De Lucia was back in Naples, which was preparing for another visit by the King and Queen of England, who were travelling on board the Royal Yacht 'Victoria and Albert'. While the royal party visited Santa Lucia, the Galleria, and Capodimonte, their ship and its escorts (the cruisers 'Suffolk' and 'Lancaster') occasioned great interest among the citizens of Naples. The visit culminated on April 22nd 1907 when, the King having requested a light and melodious opera, De Lucia sang Fritz in a Gala performance.

There had been no known legal moves between Fernando and Itala since 1895. In 1908, however, the tenor's domestic life moved into a decisive phase: he applied for a separation and - not for the first time - for the revocation of his financial settlements, on the grounds that they were not being used for the purposes for which he had made them. Specifically, he sought control over their villa at Cava de' Tirreni and over a sum of 120,000 lire in bonds of the Italian Public Debt and of the Credito Fondiario of the Banco di Napoli, which, as the price of her dropping her lawsuit for defamation, he had settled on Itala in 1893 to give her some financial independence. The agreement had been that half their yield was for her personal use, and half 'for the family', evidently the De Giorgio family.[65]

---

[64] *Journal de Monaco*, Mar. 19 1907.

[65] (TPN) Fernando De Lucia, in evidence given to Tribunale Penale di Napoli, Naples, June 15 1909. This concerns not Villa Erminia ('Villa Eduardo') but the house purchased in 1891 ('Villa Itala').

The causes of these new developments were, though, much deeper and went back many years. De Lucia's financial support and help of various kinds to different members of the De Giorgio family had, he claimed in 1909, brought him only their contempt; they treated his house as an hotel, damaging the furnishings and using gas and electricity profligately to create a show. Now, at a time when his appearances were becoming fewer and his income lower - the sums asked of Laganà in 1902 were much smaller than the 2,100 lire a performance received from Musella in 1898 - he had clear and increasing financial liabilities towards Elvira and to their children. His increased demands of the Gramophone Company early in 1906 were certainly connected with those financial pressures. The De Giorgio family saw a threat to a life-style that was largely supported by De Lucia. Itala had complained to her lawyer about the enormous sums that he spent on women - including a claimed 50,000 lire to Elvira, whom he maintained in a house 'with every ease' - while being mean with the family.[66] She appears to have threatened a lawsuit against Fernando and Elvira on the grounds of adultery, in those days a criminal offence. In an attempt to avoid a public scandal De Lucia made substantial financial offers to Itala and, when she rejected them, he allegedly banished her from the house. Since she moved only to her family in another part of Palazzo Cirella this was perhaps less dramatic than it appears.

In June 1908, Itala was to claim that only during the past month had she learned of her husband's relationship with Elvira Giommi. Some credibility is lent to this claim by her initial complaint, where she incorrectly names the woman with whom her husband 'notoriously' consorted. However, Elvira was known to the family. Indeed, Armando, who had died in 1900, is said to have been very fond of her.[67] The affair had been an intimate one since at least late 1902, and probably earlier. To anyone who knows anything of Naples and of its social circles it is quite implausible that a relationship involving someone as well-known as De Lucia could have continued for so long, and with the birth of three children, without Itala's knowledge. Further, if the affair were truly notorious, she could scarcely have been unaware of it. It is clear that she not only knew about it but - as with his other peccadilloes - she ignored it while convenient, which was for as long as he continued to provide financial help to her family.

De Lucia attempted to avoid litigation. Various intermediaries, including lawyers, family friends, and even the family physician, the aptly-named Dr. Vigorito, sought to reconcile the parties. De Lucia stated that if Itala declined to return to the family home he would

---

[66] Domenico Scardaccione, in evidence Naples, Feb. 24 1909. Itala certainly refers to the De Giorgio family.

[67] De Lucia family.

increase the 400 lire per month awarded by the Tribunal in 1894 - an award that may never have been implemented because of their eventual reconciliation - to 500-600 lire. He would also allow her the use of the villa at Cava de' Tirreni, 'in order to free her from her anguished state'. One serious obstacle was whether the yield from the bonds should or should not form part of the settlement. These bonds were an obsession for Fernando, probably for the support that they provided for Itala's detested family, and especially for some of her brothers, whom he considered shiftless.

But, meanwhile, with his old colleague Bellincioni he was to create one last part, in Giordano's *Marcella*, which was nearing its première at the Teatro Lirico of Milan.

The composer had written to Illica:

> Villa Fedora, Baveno
> March 16th 1907

> I have been here from early March and it is drudgery from morning till night. I feel that the noose is around my throat. If we do not organise ourselves thus the opera will never be finished. I have arranged for Bellincioni and De Lucia to be engaged. One never knows..... If the opera is not a success, I will say that they have not done it justice. I take them as insurance against disaster.[68]

The reference may have been a joking one but it is a clear allusion to the vocal decline of the two *divi*. On a personal level, however, Giordano is said to have done much to encourage De Lucia, writing: 'All my hopes for *Marcella* are in you. I am so glad that you have agreed to sing it.'[69]

During the summer, Bellincioni, Giordano, and De Lucia worked on *Marcella* at the soprano's villa overlooking the sea at Ardenza.[70] Subsequent rehearsals in Milan stimulated only mild interest in the events taking place in the mysterious depths of the Lirico, without the usual 'indiscretions'. Giordano was silent and withdrawn. However, despite unusually high prices, the tickets sold well. So well did the principals know the opera that a *prova generale* was thought unnecessary. The première took place on November 9th 1907, to an equivocal reception.

> *Marcella* is not an opera of immediate effect; it is neither complicated, nor abstruse, and it does not yield everything, immediately, to the enthusiasm of spectators who are too used to vocal and instrumental violence. The value of the music of *Marcella* is in its delicacy. ...*Marcella* cannot be an opera of great effect. One needs only to read the libretto to be persuaded of the fact. A libretto more vacuous, more devoid of action, more ingenuously simple has never been seen. ... we did not have the impression of hearing truly new music ... [71]

---

68 Biblioteca Comunale, Piacenza.
69 De Lucia family.
70 *Teatro Illustrato*, Aug. 31 1907.
71 *Corriere della Sera*, Nov. 10 1907.

Among expressions of spontaneous satisfaction were others, distinctly unfavourable.[72] The first act contained two episodes which were sung by De Lucia, as Giorgio, 'with infinite grace', and which were marked by outbreaks of applause, sometimes opposed by other factions. The applause, which was far from unanimous, and was accompanied by cries of 'Hush!', was renewed at the end of the act until the singers appeared.[73] Giordano did not present himself. In the foyers the initial impression was benevolent but without crushing enthusiasm.

The second act was better received, especially Marcella's 'Son tre mesi questa sera.' The following duet, between Giorgio and Vernier (Leo Eral), was heard in silence. The success was rekindled and burst into flames with sudden vigour when the love duet between Giorgio and Marcella restarted. Giorgio's song 'O mia Marcella, abbandonarti?' made a shiver of emotion run around the theatre. Spontaneous and deafening applause broke out - with some cries of *'Bravo De Lucia! Fedora! Fedora!'*[74] and an encore was given. One critic wrote that he did not greatly care for De Lucia's mode of singing when he wished to give great intensity of expression to the melody, but admitted that 'the public is not of my opinion'.[75] That public demanded an encore of Giorgio's 'O mia Marcella', which De Lucia sang with 'the special art which moved and conquered'. There were five calls for the singers and conductor.

Also singled out for praise was Giorgio's phrase 'Lascerò per sempre questo nido ove nacque il nostro amore', described as 'very beautiful, delicate, and full of sorrow.' The finale 'Sognammo tra i fiori' was greeted with 'prolonged, vigorous, *convinced* applause' especially for Bellincioni, judged an 'incomparable actress and a singer full of passion' and for De Lucia, who was blandly described as singing 'with exquisite sentiment, lavishing [on it] all the grace and sweetness of his art'.[76]

The poorly-attended second performance saw no change in the overall verdict on the opera. Vocally, De Lucia was judged much better than Bellincioni who, however, remained a most accomplished dramatic interpreter.[77]

> The choice of these artists was ... most felicitous. The face of Bellincioni is, in turn, a poem in joy and in sorrow. All the variations of the soul pass into those great, radiant eyes, that luminous mouth. We comprehend the character through the variations in her physiognomy, in the movements of her body.
>
> Fernando De Lucia renews ... all the vocal qualities that have made him irresistible among the *divi*. It is impossible to find in others all the vocal and emotional fullness that he expresses in 'O mia Marcella!'[78]

---

72 *Sera*, Nov. 10-11 1907.
73 Ibid.
74 Ibid.
75 *Corriere della Sera*, Nov. 10 1907.
76 *Pungolo*, Nov. 11 1907.
77 *Perseveranza*, Nov. 12 1907.
78 *Teatro Illustrato*, Nov. 15 1907.

Later performances of *Marcella* were given with Mascagni's *Amica*, and the programme attracted increasingly enthusiastic houses. The gallery was packed to an extent perhaps never before seen at the theatre and a few intrepid spectators, in order to get a better view, stood upright on the iron rails which partitioned off the seats, holding on to the columns and projections, and almost hanging in space.[79]

Giordano's view of the première was cynical. He wrote to Illica on November 13th 1907:

> You ask me about *Marcella*. No different from all the Milanese 'premières' of those of us who have 'arrived': warmth, coldness, applause, opposition, *bis*, hisses; graceful libretto, music lacking; music delightful, very bad libretto; excellent performance, breathless singers; vital opera, dead opera; success, fiasco. [The critics] shouting as though their corns were being trampled on. From all this chatter only one truth appears [important] to me: the bookings are starting.[80]

As in so many other cases, it is indeed difficult to reconcile the different accounts of this performance. What kind of applause (after the first act) could be at once 'warm' (*Corriere della Sera*) and 'feeble and incomplete, insistent *zitti*, [with] two - opposed - calls' (*Sera*)? We conclude that *Marcella* was a modest success while it was a novelty. And such it was at its next production, two months later, at Venice. De Lucia had never sung there and he was eagerly awaited. There was also great interest in Giordano, who was to attend.

It was, though, all a great anticlimax. The performances at the Teatro La Fenice were marked by a *contretemps* between Giordano and the conductor, Giuseppe Baroni.[81] The *prova generale* was held on January 17th 1908 and the première was scheduled for the 19th. Giordano, who had arrived a week beforehand, was apparently well satisfied with Baroni who, he told the theatre management after the first rehearsal, had revealed previously unheard details of the score. Indeed, he accepted his judgement in all musical matters relating to the opera, including the choice of protagonist.

And this judgement was to be needed, for Amina Matini, the singer engaged to sing Marcella, was taken ill. Baroni invited Lucia Crestani, who had had a good success at Venice in *Le Cid*, to sing the part; she duly learned it in only four days. Meanwhile, however, the impresario, Giuseppe Ragusa, had independently telegraphed for the American Emma Hoffmann. She was a pupil and family friend of Giordano, who had personally coached her in the rôle. Despite his expressed confidence in Baroni's judgement, Giordano favoured Hoffmann for the part.

---

79 *Perseveranza*, Nov. 17 1907.

80 Morini, *Giordano*, p. 243.

81 In his youth this former San Pietro a Maiella pupil spelled his name Barone.

Subsequent differences of opinion proved irreconcilable. Giordano could not make up his mind. In the theatre he favoured Crestani; outside, Hoffmann was his choice. In his indecision he was evidently much influenced by his wife; she took the side of Hoffmann, whom Baroni had reduced to tears and who was threatening to create a scandal.[82]

As late as 3 pm on the day before the première, Giordano repeated his satisfaction and his confidence in the outcome. However, later that day he wrote to Baroni, alleging that certain parts were 'still very unprepared' and stating that he did not intend to stay for the première. Then, before the letter could be delivered, he caught the train to Naples.[83] He took the precaution of repeating his dissatisfaction by telegraph from Bologna to *Corriere della Sera*.

Interviewed next day in Naples, Giordano described the discussion between impresario and conductor as 'a lively altercation'. His solution had been to consult De Lucia, who had concluded that the opera lay within Hoffmann's capabilities. With evident discourtesy, bad grace, and signs and gestures of disapproval Baroni had heard her at the piano. Giordano sat opposite Baroni while the latter - knowing full well that she had been taught by the composer himself - criticised Hoffmann's reading of the part. More than once Giordano had been on the point of tearing up the score. Eventually, he had decided that to impose Hoffmann on the conductor would do her no service; instead, it would be politic to give two or three performances with Crestani before entrusting the part to Hoffmann. Not until the *prova generale*, he claimed, did he realise that Crestani was quite unsuitable.[84]

Such a public pronouncement could only discredit the performance, and it swiftly brought telegrams to *Corriere della Sera* from the Fenice management and from Baroni: each professed surprise, since Giordano had consistently declared himself satisfied with a performance which he had judged superior to its antecedents.[85] There were threats of legal action against him. Baroni, Crestani, and Hoffmann each leapt into print with different versions of events. Claim and counter-claim flew back and forth.

What had happened? How could the composer's enthusiasm have been transformed so quickly? Why had he humiliated artists whose goodwill was so important to him? And why had he protested so publicly, to the detriment of the opera? *Corriere della Sera* concluded that Giordano, uncertain of the outcome of the performances, had sought to prepare plausible excuses for any failure by throwing doubt on the preparedness of the opera as, indeed, he had taken his 'insurance' for possible failure

82 *Corriere della Sera*, Jan. 20 1908.
83 *Gazzetta di Venezia*, issues of Jan. 18-24, 1908.
84 *Corriere della Sera*, Jan. 21 1908.
85 *Gazzetta di Venezia*, loc. cit.

at Milan. Ironically, his action acted as a provocation to theatre habitués, who attended the opening night in imposing numbers and grandeur. On his appearance, Baroni received a standing ovation from the orchestra and from most of the audience. The singers, especially Crestani, were forcefully applauded. It was the typical reaction of an Italian audience to a perceived injustice. Typical also were the whistling and *'Zitti!'* that followed any applause for some especially ingratiating page of the score. But the artists won approval throughout.[86]

De Lucia, on learning of Giordano's departure, had declared himself unwilling to sing, but Ragusa had persuaded him not to be hasty. After two performances, however, he telegraphed the *Corriere della Sera*:

> ... when I was interviewed I said only that I had seen no act of disapproval nor derision, because I was some way from the stage, but from the auditorium I noted some disinclination in Maestro Baroni to accompany Miss Hoffmann, who was discouraged; I also declare frankly that I was convinced that, by the day fixed for the première, the protagonist could not, through shortage of time, be as well-prepared as Hoffmann had been by Giordano.
>
> Regarding the rest of the performance, I was enthusiastic over Baroni. Meanwhile, wearied by this odious polemic, which reflects on *Marcella*, I have broken my contract.[87]

A telegram from Giordano thanked him for his loyalty. In fact, De Lucia might well have wanted an excuse to leave for Naples. For matters with Itala were coming to a head. Despite attempted mediation by Nestore Siciliano - apart from Fernando's old friend Alfredo, Nestore (Itala's uncle) was one of the few members of the De Giorgio family whom De Lucia trusted - they were already living apart.[88] It was evidently in reply to a letter from Nestore, probably an appeal for a reconciliation, that the tenor wrote a long, distraught letter, whose disjointed structure and abrupt changes of direction surely denote a passionate spirit in turmoil:

Venice
January 21st 1908

Dearest Uncle Nestore,

I swear that I suffer in saying to you that I cannot satisfy you.

Itala's *venomous* and *cutting tongue* is robbing me of life, and I can tolerate it no longer, and it is vicious even with her own son.

Now, why should I live for ever with a woman who has always had disdain for her husband and takes pleasure when they speak ill of me and of my son? - A man who has created a position ought to be loved - for 25 years I have tolerated her arrogance and insolence (excuse the expression) and I no longer

---

86 Ibid., Jan. 20 1908.

87 Ibid., Jan. 24 1908.

88 When, in 1907, Nadir entered the Conservatory it was Itala's brother, Rodolfo, who guaranteed his fees and other expenses.

have the health to oppose her. Consequently, I see a separation as the only means of avoiding a scandal, which would entirely damage her interests, I have given instructions to [my lawyer] Comm. De Bury concerning my wishes, and I can now say to you that - so Comm. De Bury writes to me - she also has accepted. I have arranged for my wife an allowance *da gran signora* [to live in style]. If she wants to help 'her own' let her do it as she has always done but not sacrificing me *in a thousand ways* but let her sacrifice herself - she can even spend two lire a day and give the rest to her family, but I repeat that she must not sacrifice me -

I no longer want to sing and I must adjust my budget, and the many sacrifices that I made and tolerated earlier I ought not to and cannot make now, because of the duty of thinking of myself.

I have sacrificed myself for all the De Giorgio family, and have always been repaid with ingratitude.

I have been obliged to terminate their stay in my house because it has become an exasperation. The things they waste - carpets destroyed - they entertain as if in their own house - they use gas and electricity to create an impression - and add to that what my wife said to me, that her family, and especially her mother, had the right to come to my house and to take their ease. This puts me with my back to the wall, and I have let her see that *I alone am the master of my house and no other and I alone in my house decide who shall enter*. Dear Uncle, it is useless to speak to you of Itala because you know her nature - a woman virtuous to the point of excess; but the character overpowers.

To sum up: if she, as agreed, writes me an assurance to calm me, I will return home as soon as my commitments are finished and I will avoid a lawsuit. Otherwise, I will leave home until I have sold my house and then, afterwards, we shall see who will come off worse. That is how I wish it to be and, in time, all will be put in order - if it is worth the trouble and if my wife changes her nature. Dear Uncle, the very day that I left Naples my wife's behaviour and demands, in Flora's [Itala's sister] presence, were disgusting. My wife must respect her husband, because I have worked and work all my life, and ought not to be indifferent.

I assure you that if I even recall her character I tremble and am horrified. You should not listen to the nonsense that they tell you. - I do not call my son to judge, but my son must know how much I have suffered through my wife. My son sees and feels what his mother and her relations say of his father and he burns with sorrow after I have achieved so much.

I am concerned, then, with respect for the mother, I always preach to him that he should love his mother because that is the only way to prosperity.

Now, in accordance with what I have written to Comm. De Bury, I await a declaration signed by Itala, as arranged with De Bury, and then I will return to my house, but to return and again start discussions with my wife - I would prefer to die rather than return to the family. I already have a buyer for my house and I await this declaration from Itala, to break off the negotiations or to sign the contract of sale already prepared.

Understand that I have settled on my wife a position of more than *250,000* between the capital of maintenance of *120,000* lire plus *70,000* lire that the villa (which is hers) cost, and then all the jewels, which could be *60,000* lire. I must think of having at least the same situation, and to attain this we want to sell the house and [after] the division thereof the judge *will arrange the figure for my wife*, who is alone, and for me, who carries on his shoulders so many, many other expenses.

And then, do you not think that my wife is waiting for you to write to me; she and her mother have been to many lawyers in Naples and have heard from persons such as *Scardaccione* and *Pessina* [lawyers] that I have taken a just road, because I do not want to die under the torture of that *terrible* tongue.

Dear Uncle, in 22 or 23 years of marriage, I have never known a *caress from my wife* - consequently I have the right and the need to have a woman -

My wife knew only how to rob me and I have a letter from her that proves what I have said.

But, for goodness sake!, do not speak to me of my wife, she is content always to live deceitfully and with the *chamber-pot* as sentinel - what poetry? What fascination for an artist who returns after a triumph???

What enthusiastic embraces, what transports of joy have I found at home.....

Dear Uncle, do not make me say any more - my wife has the sole merit of being virtuous -

But in this even the prostitute is preferable to the virtuous woman because at least she will have the merit of knowing how to make love to the man to whom she sells herself. I have written you this letter after having given my second performance, and God knows how I suffer now when I sing.

My wife instead thinks of her foolish rights - There will certainly be someone who will respect my hallowed rights, and I weep with sorrow.

You, who have been so good and dear, I pray you to excuse me and I beg you to think of me in your heart to see how I suffer, and I do not know why I am not dead with rage because of my wife.

If you wish Itala well, have her sign the declaration that De Bury will present to her, and thus all will be accommodated for the best. Otherwise, Itala will find herself destroyed, because I am tired of her and tired of suffering.

Wish me well always, as I also wish you, and believe me, your affectionate nephew,

Fernando

It has done me good to unburden myself so.
Excuse the mistakes, it is 2 am.[89]

Some three weeks later, he sang Almaviva at Rome, where the young Mignon Nevada was to make her début. Also present were old colleagues De Luca and Mugnone. On the evening of the première, February 15th 1908, De Lucia was apparently depressed, even more than usually nervous. Mignon, by contrast, was full of eager anticipation. Seeing the tenor, huddled in a cloak and evidently unhappy, she said to her mother: 'Look at Fernando, he is trembling: why?' De Lucia, who had overheard, answered for her: 'This child is on the first step of her career, and I am at the end of mine, with everything to lose, and she wonders why I tremble!'[90]

His misgivings - for the spitefulness of sections of the Neapolitan press was by now unconcealed - are evident. He perhaps feared that the Romans would be similarly pitiless to a failing artist. He need not have worried. The press, charmed by the good humour of the score, recognised a splendid cast which fulfilled its promise and, in Mugnone, a conductor of great finesse and *brio*. De Luca was a 'model Figaro', Adamo Didur a 'consummate artist', Nevada able to overcome 'the most arduous

---

[89] (TPN) Since this letter was later used in evidence, Fernando's trust in Nestore was perhaps misplaced.

[90] Hurst, *The Age of Jean de Reszke*, p. 227, as related to him by Emma Nevada.

difficulties ... a voice of incredible range.' De Lucia

> ... sang Almaviva with marvellous vocal refinement ... [He is] one of the very
> few who keep alive the traditions of Italian *bel canto* ... extraordinary ability as
> a virtuoso.[91]

Mild reproaches over alterations to the character of the music related
not to Almaviva but to Rosina and Figaro. The second performance,
when the audience included Patti and Cotogni, was equally well
received. For *Giornale d'Italia*, De Lucia was 'in full possession of his
vocal means, he sang with singular fascination and with the treasure of
his *mezza voce* ...'.[92]

Rome provided an opportunity to revisit Alfredo De Giorgio, who had
taught music and singing there since 1893. Fernando also received a
visit from Nestore Siciliano, who had come to ask him to regularise
matters with Itala. The singer promised to 'molest his wife no further';
on his return to Naples, there was a supposed reconciliation, celebrated
with a banquet. Peace broke down after ten days, and he banished her
from the house. At this point, Nestore claimed, he realised that they
were irreparably alienated, and he revealed to his niece the truth about
De Lucia's second family.[93] Itala then brought an action against her
husband and Elvira Giommi, on a charge of adultery.

---

91 *Tribuna*, Feb. 17 1908.

92 *Giornale d'Italia*, Feb. 20 1908.

93 Nestore Siciliano, in evidence at Valle di Maddaloni, Mar. 12 1909.

20

Neapolitan Twilight

> There is only one way in which a book such as this can be written, with any
> chance of its possessing some value. ... In so much as either romance or
> suppression enter into the record, its worth is impaired.
>
> H.F. Chorley, *Thirty Years' Musical Recollections*

After *Il Barbiere* at the Costanzi De Lucia made no more stage
appearances until three performances of *Marcella* at the Teatro Adriano,
Rome, in the autumn of 1908. Giordano was present for the première on
November 12th. *Giornale d'Italia* (November 13th) showed enthusiasm
for De Lucia, who truly had 'one of his most felicitous evenings'. But the
opera had no great success in Rome, either. After these appearances De
Lucia's operatic career effectively ended. At the age of 48, a long silence
descended.

The reasons for this hiatus are now clear. Though it was hardly
surprising that a singer with a quarter century of steady work and
intensive travel behind him should wish to sing less often, on August 2nd
1908 the birth of a Elvira's fourth (and last) child, Amalia, provided
another inducement for him to spend more time in Naples. Moreover,
whether through natural changes or, as foreshadowed by Hale and by
Procida, through a long series of too-vigorous portrayals of Canio and
Don José, the period since 1900 had been one of vocal decline.
Transposition was not infrequently noted in his performances. Still
another cogent reason was the complaint for adultery that Itala, urged
on by her family, was building. His letter to Nestore makes it clear that
he no longer wished to sing. His obvious bitterness towards most of the
De Giorgio family suggests that he felt that his earnings would, by what
a judge would later denounce as 'judicial blackmail', end up in their
pockets. Elvira, alarmed at the demoralising effect on him of inactivity,
continually encouraged him to return to the theatre, saying: 'Give her
what she wants, but sing!!'[1]

The year 1909, however, witnessed almost complete retirement from
the stage. A single charity concert in Rome, on January 15th, saw him,

---

[1] De Lucia family.

together with De Luca, Salomea Krusceniski, Marconi, Mascagni, and Charles Rousselière, contributing to the welfare of the victims of earthquakes in Sicily and Calabria. But he remained active in Neapolitan musical circles. Often, when seized by the desire to hear some of the works of his greatest triumphs, he would be seen in the corridors ana boxes of the San Carlo. His eye would turn questioningly to Procida, as if inviting comparisons, as if demanding to know whether the critic was stirred as he had been when, in other days, De Lucia had offered his arm to Mimì, or had related to Fedora the drama of the shooting of Vladimir.[2]

John McCormack, who had several times heard De Lucia at La Scala and who admired him 'extravagantly', engaged him in conversation at the San Carlo one evening in 1909, Lily McCormack recalled:

> Sitting just in front of John was the tenor Fernando De Lucia. . . . John nudged Lily and pointed out De Lucia with great pride. Then he listened carefully to every word which the tenor spoke to his companion.
> During one of the intervals, De Lucia asked his friend what operas were to be performed during the coming week. His friend told him that the only important thing was the début of a young English [sic] tenor - i.e. John.
> Eagerly John leaned forward to hear the great man's comments.
> 'Oh', said De Lucia, 'let us go. At least there will be something to laugh at.'
> For a moment John felt like bursting into tears. Then his sense of humour came to the rescue.
> He leaned forward and tapped De Lucia on the shoulder.
> 'Maestro, I am the poor devil who is making his début next week, and I hope there won't be anything to laugh at.'
> De Lucia was most embarrassed, and was profuse in his apologies and explanations. When John made his début in *Rigoletto*, the great tenor came round on purpose to congratulate him.
> 'I loved him for it,' says John, 'but I did not feel I had earned his encomiums.'[3]

The law, meanwhile, was taking its ponderous course. Itala's complaint of adultery, filed in July 1908, summarised legal actions up until 1895. Her husband, she claimed, had for some time maltreated her and had failed to show respect. More seriously, he had now informed her, 'in a most brutal manner', that he had another woman. Since she 'had never given any cause not to deserve conjugal affection', she had 'not entertained the vaguest of suspicions, other than the chatter of simple insinuation or malign statements of jealous people, or even enemies'.[4]

The woman with whom De Lucia consorted was, she stated, a noted *canzonettista*, accustomed to artistic wanderings in the company of an aunt, also a musician. Clearly, there was some initial confusion with Elvira's mother, Amalia Galanti, or, possibly, her mother's sister,

---

2 *Mezzogiorno*, Feb. 22/23 1925.

3 Strong, *John McCormack*, pp. 113-14. McCormack's début was in *La Traviata* on Mar. 19 1909; on Mar. 25 he sang *Rigoletto*.

4 Tribunale Penale di Napoli, No. 14189 del reg. gen. dell'Uff. del Proc. del Re, 368/909.

Adelina, since Itala gave the name of the woman as Elena Galanti, a native of Rome. However, Itala's statement of July 15th 1908 identifies the 'concubine' as Elvira Giomma (*sic*) and the house where her husband 'notoriously' maintained her as Vico Secondo Corsea, No. 11. According to the police, Giommi sold music and was director of a small orchestra; the theatrical agent Giuseppe Russo testified that, in a life 'perfectly typical of an artist', she had several times come to him for engagements.[5]

The word 'notorious' is significant: more than a mere element in any loss of self-esteem or of public respect for an injured wife, 'notoriety' was a legal prerequisite for any conviction for adultery, and so was of very great importance to Itala's case. It was essential for her to prove both the fact and its notoriety.

Itala's complaint that her husband had tried to deprive her of money and property - the villa - that were rightfully hers was accompanied by some inconsequential whines, such as Fernando's having taken Nadir to the spa of Salsomaggiore without first telling her. She also cited a long list of witnesses in evidence of adultery. Her hairdresser would be able to confirm that relations were not good, and to testify that De Lucia was sometimes discourteous to his wife; that when Itala shut herself in her room he followed to cast abuse at her; that he had told Itala that he had children with another woman, whom he had to maintain; that he had enjoined his wife to leave the matrimonial home, and that he had claimed that only Itala's 'excessive self-righteousness' had provoked him into scandalising her by revealing the existence of his other family.

Many witnesses for Itala repeated hearsay regarding De Lucia's extra-marital relationship. Through several hundred pages of repetitious legal language and crabbed calligraphy are scattered the names of the tradespeople who were alleged to have supplied Giommi with goods for which De Lucia had paid; they included tailors, furnishers, and Amalia Galanti's seamstress. Almost without exception these witnesses, whose evidence the prosecution had so confidently outlined initially, were in the event found to know nothing, or to be unable to remember where they had heard - if, in fact, they ever had - nebulous rumours about De Lucia. Visitors to Penelope De Giorgio's house, years earlier, and to that of Itala's sister, Pia Ricco, remembered vague references to a liaison. The police in Rome assiduously tracked down relatives of Alfredo's wife and carefully recorded their trivial or circumstantial evidence for the judge. Note was taken of crowds, listening late at night under the balcony of Giommi's house, where De Lucia could clearly be heard singing, and of a party for Signora Galanti, with whom he sang duets. Written depositions were summoned from the Hôtel Continental, Milan, where De Lucia had stayed in March and April 1905: to determine what the waiters and chambermaids might have observed; to examine what the register

---

[5] No professional appearances by Elvira Giommi have been traced.

contained, and to establish the truth of allegations that the singer had offered to pay the manager, Sig. Bertolini, to destroy the documentation.[6] All the minutiae and the pettiness of the Domestic Court are there.

The rôles of the mezzo-soprano Ninì Frascani (b. 1878) and of her brother Enrico are, if not mischievous, at least intriguing. For many years the Frascani family had been socially and musically prominent in and around Naples and Cava.[7] In 1894, the young and handsome Ninì had sung at a concert at the De Lucia villa. Her later career had unfolded rapidly. Within two years of her operatic début at the San Carlo in 1903,[8] she had sung at La Scala, Covent Garden and, again at the San Carlo, in the world première of *Vita Brettona* in 1905. Since it is scarcely conceivable that she could so quickly have been accepted in Naples against the wishes of someone locally as influential as De Lucia, we may presume that she was then on good terms with him. How Ninì came to know, as she alleged she did, that in 1905 De Lucia had telegraphed Milan for two hotel rooms; why he should have 'given her to understand that he was taking his mistress', and why - as stated by a witness, Virginia De Tomaso - she announced all this to a group of people at Pia Ricco's house are matters on which we can only speculate.[9]

In evidence, Ninì stated only that Bertolini had told her and Enrico Frascani that De Lucia and his wife were in Milan and, as family friends, they had gone to visit them. As they arrived, De Lucia was leaving the hotel with one elderly and one young woman whom, apart from noting that they were not his wife and mother-in-law, the Frascanis could not identify because De Lucia, hastily coming to greet them, 'did his best' to block their view.[10]

Nestore Siciliano claimed that De Lucia did not conceal his liaison even from Itala's family, but that they always kept it from her. When she refused to renounce the 400 lire per month already awarded, Fernando struck her.[11] A witness from Rome, where the relationship with Giommi was 'known to many', stated that De Lucia had spoken of a need to reduce his expenditure severely in order to support his second family.

Elvira herself stated that she had known De Lucia for thirty years. He had brought her toys as a child, and had later taught her music, whereby

---

6 The handwritten testimony from Milan is decidedly ambiguous but, in view of what is now known of the relationship, its interpretation is irrelevant.

7 The recurring association of the Frascanis with the De Lucia and De Giorgio families is evident but its nature, with no visible link by marriage, is unclear. Neither is it obvious why *Monsignor Perrelli* (Jan. 8 1907), reviewing a *Fritz* in which De Lucia sang at the San Carlo, deemed it relevant and of interest to refer to the presence '. . . of [unspecified] brother Frascani in a stall'. The dilettante bass Menotti Frascani, who was active in the *salotti* of Naples in the 1880s, was probably related to Ninì. Despite the similarity in names he may not be the Menotti Frascona who was billed to sing the minor part of Bell in the projected *Guglielmo Ratcliff* at Philadelphia in 1902, with an (unspecified) De Lucia in the minor part of John (see p. 315n).

8 Some sources incorrectly suggest that Ninì made her San Carlo début in 1899.

9 (TPN) Virginia de Tomaso, in evidence Mar. 2 1909.

10 (TPN) In evidence Feb. 22 1909.

11 (TPN) In evidence Mar. 12 1909.

she now earned her living. For all that it was quite false, her refutation of the criminal charge of adultery rings of sweet reasonableness. Only jealousy, she suggested, could shadow a friendship of such length and honesty as hers with De Lucia. As for his being the father of her children, were they not registered as being by a bachelor? Surely she would not have allowed any child of his to forego any possible rights towards him? She had neither travelled with him nor been with him other than in Naples. The women in Milan would have been some of his many friends in the lyric world. Many witnesses had testified that, since Elvira was a woman of the theatre, people came and went, with playing and singing in her house at all hours. De Lucia visited the house, often twice a day, but so did others. Yes, certainly he sang while there, and no one should be surprised if people gathered to hear him. As witness of her good character they could call on Prof. Averolino De Giorgio (who taught at the Royal College of Music), on the Capurro family, and on others.

De Lucia stated that the quarrels had arisen from his and his wife's respective interests. She was 'impossible' to live with. None the less, he had supported her, their son Nadir, and her 'very numerous' family, who had lived on his shoulders. His generosity to the family had amounted to half a million lire over the years, with a recent gift of 10,000 lire to Flora, to help with the expenses of her marriage in February 1909. Now, at the end of his career, he wanted to put his affairs in order and the De Giorgio family saw its comfort threatened by his pending applications for personal separation and for revocation of the settlements. He had made over the villa, 100,000 lire in jewels, and the bonds on the understanding that half their yield was for family needs. However, Itala had tried to keep the entire proceeds for herself. The true motive for the suit by his wife's family was to oblige him to continue to support them.

It emerges that Itala's brother, Arnaldo De Giorgio, had taken the lead in suggesting a lawsuit. Evidence suggests that he went about Naples 'suborning testimony, hinting at this or that, planting insinuations, and stating allegations as fact'. The defence accused him of trying to induce witnesses to give false evidence - 'an exercise for the sole purpose of damaging the accused'. Arnaldo, by threatening exposure and scandal, had attempted to apply judicial blackmail.[12]

Several lawyers called as witnesses by the prosecution must have disappointed Itala. Luigi Catalano could say only that he had seen Giommi in a box at the opera and that he had heard that 'she could be very well known by De Lucia'. Giuseppe Villani who, the prosecution stated, knew that De Lucia had paid Elvira Giommi 50,000 lire, claimed professional secrecy on the grounds that he had been the tenor's lawyer until the start of this action; he had always advised against litigation, and De Lucia had done everything possible to avoid it. Villani, De Bury,

---

[12] (TPN) Deposition of De Lucia's lawyers, Dec. 23 1908.

Nestore Siciliano, and Dr. Vigorito had all made proposals for an amicable settlement. Riccardo Catalano, who acted for De Lucia in dealings with the Gramophone Company, knew that relations were not good and had heard talk of separation. He had made offers to Itala, on Fernando's behalf, for an amicable division, given their incompatibility, and had no evidence that the offer was made on grounds other than those of equity. Other offers were made after the complaint. But he knew nothing of any offer made to induce Itala to leave Fernando free to continue his liaison. It was not Itala but her brother, Arnaldo, who, when there was a quarrel over the bonds, had first mentioned to him the matter of an affair with Elvira.

Certain pieces of evidence damning to the prosecution's case - and to its motives - emerged from its own witnesses. Elisabetta Cardone, Elvira Giommi's obstetrician, had received visits from men who had inquired into the fatherhood of the children, and who had offered rewards for her help. Arnaldo De Giorgio, claiming to represent De Lucia, had asked the cashier at the furniture shop, Solei-Herbert, for details of addresses to which they had delivered items bought by the tenor in 1902 and 1904 and, when refused, had become abusive. Most telling of all for the judge was the extraordinary testimony of a lawyer, Silvio del Buono. In May 1908 he had been in the company of Vittorio De Giorgio in an establishment which he guardedly described as 'a certain house for the fulfilment of my need'.[13] As Silvio re-entered the salon from the room in which he had been accommodated, Vittorio - who had remained in the salon - had drawn his attention to a picture there of someone who, he suggested, resembled the young De Lucia; he had, he said, learned from the Madam, Nina Deliso, that De Lucia was expected there imminently with the wife of a friend. Some two months later, Rodolfo De Giorgio approached Del Buono and asked him to testify that what he had heard had come not from Vittorio but from the Madam. It would not be necessary, De Giorgio added, to say where he had heard it. A month later, Rodolfo again asked him to testify, this time suggesting that Del Buono might claim to have heard it at the Caffè Gambrinus.

Judgement was delivered on July 9th 1909. The judge, Luigi De Sanctis, alluded to the questionable motives of the De Giorgio family in bringing the case. No one could be certain that the relationship was adulterous. Moreover, certainly at the time of the break between Fernando and Itala, there had been no notoriety. Such as there was, the judge pronounced, had been manufactured by Itala's brothers since the initiation of the suit. He dismissed the case.

Almost certainly, this was not the final legal tussle between husband and wife. But it was the last traceable dispute to be conducted openly, by the full weight of the law. Itala and some of her family continued to live

---

[13] (TPN) In evidence June 26 1909.

at Palazzo Cirella, but their accommodation was now separate from Fernando's. In around 1916, Elvira and the children moved to a flat in that same building, looking out over Angiporto Galleria. It was on the floor above De Lucia's residence, to which it was connected by a short, private staircase. Thus were the proprieties observed.

The law had pronounced that Fernando and Elvira were not criminals. The tenor was subsequently able to recognise Elvira's children as his, though the matter of their legal name was to wait long years for resolution. However, the financial demands continued. There were threats, ostensibly by the *camorra*, against the superstitious singer. Unquestionably, further negotiations ensued in legal offices, and other financial bargains were struck. Between 1908, when he sold a house to his sister, Teresa, and 1916 De Lucia is known to have disposed of property - including the burial vault which he had purchased in the 1890s to contain the remains of his and Itala's father, and all but a small part of the Via Roma residence - to the value of 206,000 lire.[14] There were certainly undocumented sales of assets such as jewellery. And now the gambling subterfuge that formerly had covered his philandering screened arrangements made by the ageing singer to provide financial security for Elvira and the children. For he knew that only his legitimate family - and, indirectly, the detested De Giorgio brothers - could inherit his estate. It is said that, at one hearing over Itala's maintenance, De Lucia said to the judge: *'Eccellenza*, I no longer have a penny.' 'What a shame that there is no audience to applaud!' scoffed Itala.[15]

Meanwhile, the 1909-10 San Carlo season billed him in *Marcella*, with Emma Druetti, and the opera reached rehearsal. But it was not given, and there is no evidence that De Lucia sang there that season. Possibly as a result of the stresses of the trial, he did not sing in public for more than a year. Concert activity resumed in 1910 as, on February 18th, he appeared with Marconi and Emma Carelli in Rome. When, in March 1910, he gave all his operatic scores to Elvira, it must have been in the expectation that he would never need them again. Yet in October that year he made another début when, for the benefit of the Monument Sardou, he sang for the first time at the Paris Opéra, in Act II of *Fedora* with Lina Cavalieri.

Family matters occupied him. Nadir, who had entered San Pietro a Maiella but who had never completed his formal studies, was nevertheless developing into an promising pianist. Later, he moved to Rome to teach singing and to compose songs, the opera *L'Intrusa* and, before the rise of Mussolini, patriotic songs and anthems. He was music critic for *Impero*. He was proving to be a chip of the old block so far as women were concerned. In 1912, at the age of 19, he made an ill-

---

14 Conservatoria Registri Immobiliari, Naples.
15 Franz Gleijeses in conversation with the writer, 1968.

considered marriage to Ofelia Cuccari. She was an accomplished pianist, at least a decade his senior, wealthy, and notably eccentric. Ofelia was given to throwing tomatoes at people whom she believed were staring at her. Once she bit a piece out of Nadir's jacket. Elvira laughingly suggested that she and Nadir met only on an artistic plane. Their first separation, after less than a month of marriage, was followed by many more before they parted for good. Thereafter, Nadir became something of a playboy. It amused him that his father used to retire at an hour when, said Nadir, life was just beginning. He was fond of Elvira and of her daughters, his 'sorelline' (little sisters). With Fernando (Vanni), however, he got on very badly, each protective of the position of his own mother. Their hostility was to come to flash point after their father's death.

De Lucia was a strict father, especially in matters of schooling. All the Giommi children were musical and were educated at San Pietro a Maiella. Rosa played the pianoforte, Amalia and Giuseppina the violin, and Vanni played both. Luigi Caggiula, who was taught the violin by De Lucia's brother, Federico, recalled playing duets with Amalia or Giuseppina, with Rosa at the piano. When Amalia's music teacher upset De Lucia he barred him from the house; subsequently, the teacher gave the lessons at Nina Sabatano's residence, where Amalia would sometimes stay.[16] Giuseppina also had a fine voice, but her vocal studies with her father were interrupted by ill health. De Lucia would sometimes take them with him to the recording studio, where Vanni's violin playing and Amalia's recitation were preserved by Esposito.[17]

It was a well-organised household. Though they had a cook and housemaids, Elvira liked the girls to try their hand in the kitchen. De Lucia would grumble at this waste of time that might better be spent studying but, like any father, he was inordinately proud when any of them cooked something particularly good. Old-fashioned in his view of the rôle of women, he disapproved of the prospect of his daughters' going out to work. But Elvira, looking into an uncertain future, insisted that each must be able to earn a living. It was not a lavish life-style. Holidays were spent mostly at Salsomaggiore and Monte Carlo. They rarely visited Cava de' Tirreni, possibly because of its associations with Itala; in 1916, the former De Giorgio villa was sold to a certain Scaramella who, with fine irony, is reputed to have sold it to pay family gambling debts.[18]

From October 1910 until January 1914 there were no known stage appearances, partly because of the physical discomfort of a bladder infection that sometimes pained him during the last thirteen or so years

---

16 Amalia De Lucia. Sabatano, who recorded for Phonotype, declined to be interviewed; she became De Lucia's teaching assistant and a family friend.

17 Vanni recorded 'Madrigale' (Simonetti) on matrix no. 1849, Nov. 15 1917. On Sept. 12 1920, matrix 2412, Amalia recited an Italian translation of Victor Hugo's 'Guèrre civile'. On an acetate, dating from 1953, Giuseppina sings to Rosa's piano accompaniment.

18 Villa Erminia is now named Villa Rosa. Itala retained her house - now named Villa Maria - until 1922, when she sold it to Avv. Eduardo Pepe, whose family still owns it.

of his life. In January 1911, evidently somewhat apprehensive for the state of his voice, he went to record for Fonotipia in Milan. Anxious friends greeted him at the station on his return. His answer to their concern was to place his hand on his wallet and to say: 'It went well!'[19]

In January 1914 he returned to the stage. At the San Carlo there was a new generation of singers. Instead of Gayarre and Masini there were Aureliano Pertile and Tito Schipa; instead of Bellincioni there was Carmen Melis. But Mugnone was there,[20] and it was apparently he who, despite the great success of Schipa in the 1913-14 season, advised the manager, Laganà, to engage De Lucia for *Fedora*.[21] And thus the older generation of opera-goers had the opportunity of renewing old memories, and the younger of hearing an idol from what already seemed a remote musical world.

The interest in his reappearance was intense. As January 24th 1914 approached, and as affectionate articles in the press welcomed him back, not a ticket was to be had. For here was an opportunity to hear

> ... the Craftsman of the Voice: in his throat, like that of a nightingale, the notes do not erupt violently and impetuously, but sweetly, melodiously, of a tunefulness which brings tears to the eyes. ... the Magician of the Voice: with one of his famous *falsetti*, with a sustained note such as only he can emit, he can set in motion mysterious vibrations which stir the root of every nerve.[22]

The tenor was no longer a romantic figure; indeed, he was by now decidedly portly. Getting into the knee-breeches required by the part presented problems.[23] But prolonged, unanimous, deafening applause greeted him as, pale with emotion, he appeared on a stage which was

> ... so full of memories for him ... Very soon he realised that he had, in the audience - which he can still move and conquer with his resources, his ringing, incisive attack, his passionate feeling, and his dramatic capacity for giving colour to a character - a faithful friend, ready to be roused to enthusiasm.[24]

His first notes betrayed his feelings:

> There were tears within, tears of sweet emotion. Because, when the shiver [of emotion] had gone, Loris repeated 'Amor ti vieta'. Love, in fact, forbade him to remain calm in the face of such a warm and cordial demonstration. But where his passions overwhelmed him, his command of his art imposed itself. De Lucia, unsurpassed in that part, took it up where he had interrupted it, a decade earlier. And, once again, we heard the tender melody breathed with skill and grace, the notes polished as they passed from the weight of passionate accent to the slenderness of an imploring, ever more refined *mezza voce* as they faded

19 Franz Gleijeses.
20 *Stampa Artistica*, Dec. 18 1913.
21 Luigi De Lillo, in conversation with the writer, 1967 and 1968. From Feb. 19 1914 Schipa sang Loris.
22 *Giornale del Mezzogiorno*, Jan. 25-31 1914.
23 De Lillo.
24 *Mattino*, Jan. 25/26 1914.

away. ... In the 'racconto' ['Mia madre'] he was a meticulous analyst: he articulated each narrative phrase with incisive diction, and then unified the final melody, in which he used the most delicate passages of *mezza voce*. And when the drama exploded, the accent erupted with it and, in the entire third act, voices of love and anger combined in the dramatic singing of Loris, to which De Lucia has always given an inimitable stamp.[25]

The final note of 'Amor ti vieta' was a *filata*, the trait so greatly beloved of those who had known him of old, and so eagerly anticipated by those who now heard him for the first time.

Again, the public held its breath when, in the scene where Loris describes the duel, the veteran tenor launched himself across the stage with a vigour such that some feared that the effort might be too much for him.[26] Luigi Caggiula recalled:

> His voice was not, perhaps, as glittering as before, more like a baritone than a tenor, but still he sang. And he still had the high notes in *falsetto*. De Lucia was a *tenore di grazia*, of the type that we had recently admired in Tito Schipa. Schipa was marvellous, but compared with De Lucia he was nothing, nothing. [De Lucia] would sing *filate* ... then, when one thought that he had no breath left, he would finish with a *gruppetto* or a *fioritura.* ...
> When he asked Fedora if the remedy [for every ill] contained in her crucifix was *'Per voi o per gli amici?'* and she replied *'Chi lo sa?'*, his *'Grazie'* was a poem in one word, said in a manner that was unique to him. Anyone can say *'Grazie'*, but not in that way.[27]

Angelo Notariello, then a student of Agostino Roche at the Conservatory but later a private De Lucia pupil, remembered this Loris:

> He had a wonderful magnetic power on the stage, with an ecstatic passion that made you feel what he felt, especially in dramatic scenes ... In the racconto 'Vedi, io piango', he made almost everyone weep.[28]

The second and the remainder of his eight performances were equally well-attended. Giordano wrote to his old friend: 'I read in the newspapers of your triumph and realise that, once again, I should embrace you.'[29]

A few days after his last *Fedora* he appeared in a concert organised by the press at the San Carlo. Five thousand people were there to see gifts distributed to children and to hear a concert that included Schipa, Ester Mazzoleni, and Rinaldo Grassi. The celebrated actor Ruggiero Ruggieri spoke an epic poem by Carducci. When the applause for Ruggieri ceased, De Lucia and Mario Costa appeared on the stage, and the first notes of 'Napulitanata' were heard. Each of Di Giacomo's verses was applauded as soon as De Lucia had sung it, in a 'marvellous interpretation'. Then,

---

25 *Giorno*, Jan. 25/26 1914.
26 De Lillo.
27 Luigi Caggiula, in conversation with the writer, 1968.
28 Angelo Notariello, in several conversations with the writer, 1972-4.
29 *Mattino*, Jan. 30/31 1914.

with the venerable, white-haired Tosti at the piano to play his most celebrated song, De Lucia sang '*Quanno sponta la luna a Marechiaro*':

> ...it was an imposing sight, of dreams and illusions..... That song, which made the hearts of our fathers shiver with love and emotion, which soothed us in our first lamentations of love, which will make future generations tremble as long as the earth has sun and the human mind has light and passion; that song so tender and sweet was evoked yesterday by the hand of the one who, first among all, in the luminous years of his distant youth, felt it in his heart.[30]

Meanwhile, teaching had seized Fernando's interest. His first traceable pupil was Peter Raitscheff, who studied with him as early as 1912.[31] Initially, his students were private pupils. However, in 1915 there were moves to fill a vacant professorial chair at San Pietro a Maiella, where standards in the School of Singing were causing concern. The post had been offered to Giuseppe Kaschmann, who had demanded the same salary - 6,000 lire per annum - as that already enjoyed by Barbara Marchisio. The normal Government stipend was only 4,000 lire, but the college had declared itself ready to find the difference.[32]

A year had now passed since the initial approaches, and Kaschmann had lost interest. A successful approach had instead been made to De Lucia; though he had hesitated on previous occasions he now accepted 'as a sacred artistic mission'. Since there were actually two vacant chairs, Kaschmann could still be accommodated should he later decide to accept the post; this would be an excellent move for a School which 'needed to revitalise itself'. Accordingly, it was agreed that De Lucia should be appointed under the same conditions as those offered to Kaschmann.[33] On October 27th 1915 the President of the Board of Management of the College wrote to the Director, Guido Fano, of having 'overcome the hesitation shown by Comm. Fernando De Lucia on other occasions' and urging that the appointment be finalised. The extra salary, it later emerged, was to be justified by provision of a special advanced course, which would include 'education of the vocal organ, classification of human voices, and physiological considerations for pupils whose limited voice fitted them only for the teaching of singing'.[34]

De Lucia's life on the boards was not, though, quite over. The prospectus for the 1915-16 season at La Scala, Milan, carried his name and he duly made his début on February 5th 1916, replacing Bonci in Puccini's *La Bohème*. The performance was well attended by a deferential public, curious to hear the tenor who, almost twenty years

---

30 *Giorno*, Feb. 21/22 1914.
31 K.J. Kutsch and Leo Riemens, *Unvergängliche Stimmen*, 1975.
32 (SPM) Minutes of the Board of Management, San Pietro a Maiella, Apr. 29 1915.
33 Ibid., Sept. 29 1915.
34 (SPM) Undated (probably Dec. 1916) letter De Lucia - Board of Management, San Pietro a Maiella.

earlier, had sung Rodolfo in the first La Scala production of the opera.[35] And De Lucia, although no longer able to show off a beautiful, ringing voice, phrased with delicacy and was cordially applauded throughout.[36] He was also announced for the centenary celebrations of *Il Barbiere di Siviglia*, but was replaced by Perea.[37]

Three months later, he gave his last performances of *Fedora*, at the Teatro Adriano, Rome. It was his name, decided a critic, that had achieved the miracle of filling the theatre:

> There were old admirers, desirous of hearing once more *chillu Fernandu* [that Fernando] and of reliving possibly unforgettable moments of intense pleasure, through a beautiful *filata*, and through a delightfully-breathed *mezza voce* phrase from the prince of *tenori di grazia*, and there were the young, eager to hear the celebrated singer, even tardily . . . [38]

The public expected few echoes of his splendid prime. But De Lucia, who was applauded on his very appearance

> . . . and who was also overwhelmed by emotion, vanquished this and other fears. His voice is strengthened in the centre; some open notes, and some that exhibit the nasal *appoggiatura* were certainly not pleasant; but these are fleeting blemishes which the astute artist quickly corrects, while his beautiful, velvety *mezza voce* notes, his *crescendo*, and his exceptionally lovely *smorzature* produced the greatest enthusiasm in the listeners. Here, De Lucia insinuated a graceful *appoggiatura*, there he coloured a cadenza with a *gruppetto* that does not disrupt the melodic line, and throws into marvellous relief a virtuosity that does not know the weight of years; his long breaths help him with his supreme effects and miraculous *filature*.[39]

For *Tribuna*, he seemed to be animated by a youthful ardour. And where the voice could not overcome an obstacle, art could.

By official decree of March 19th 1916 he was appointed to the Chair at the Conservatory, with effect from the following October. In an unusual honour, the formality of competitive examination was waived and he was nominated '*Professore senza concorso*'. When, on November 4th, he took the oath of service, it was before a new Director, his old friend and fellow-student, Francesco Cilea.

The new administration soon discovered that the previous Board had assumed heavy financial burdens. It pointed out to the Ministry of Public Instruction that, under wartime financial constraints, De Lucia's supplement of 2,000 lire was insupportable.[40] The Ministry declined to

---

35 *Corriere della Sera*, Feb. 6 1916.

36 *Popolo d'Italia*, Feb. 6 1916. Parpignol was played by the young Francesco Merli who, in a letter to the writer in Sept. 1968, denied ever having sung so small a part.

37 There is no trace of an *Ernani* in which Fred Gaisberg claimed to have heard him.

38 *Messaggero*, May 30/31 1916.

39 Ibid.

40 (SPM) Letter from the President of the Board - Ministry of Public Instruction, Nov. 1916.

make the deficit good and it appears that he did not receive the money.[41] The best that the Board could do was an extra payment, for one year only, of 800 lire for the services of his piano accompanist.[42]

His preference for women students - whom he himself selected with some care - was marked.[43] His earliest Conservatory class, in the wartime year of 1916-17, was entirely female; it included Carolina Caprile and Anna Sabatano.[44] By 1919-20 his class of nine contained two men, neither now of any note.[45] In 1923-4, however, Mikhail Popov and Boris Cristoff were among his first-year pupils.[46] By 1924-5 the size of the class had increased to fourteen, eight of them apparently non-Italians. The fees of one young lady were reputedly paid by Lenin himself.[47] De Lucia described her as having 'come from another world, and the Devil has sent her!'[48]

His influence in the college was shown by the way in which colleagues such as Agostino Roche would sometimes demonstrate how De Lucia would approach a vocal problem. His private teaching continued, sometimes of Conservatory students whom colleagues sent to him for advanced instruction. He went back and forth between Naples and Rome on Government business, assessing students and adjudicating in the serious matter of singing examinations. It was a busy and useful life.

Early in the spring of 1917, the San Carlo *habitués* had one last chance to hear that 'magician of *bel canto* who is Fernando De Lucia', in *L'Amico Fritz*. The opera may have been mounted specially for him. The expectation was enormous for what *Giorno* termed 'the original, the inimitable, the immortal Fritz'. And, on February 22nd, an indulgent audience was happy to be lulled by the 'fragrant dew and sentimental grace' of the score. Even the humorous press refused to carp:

> All is still! O joy of joys! *'Tutto tace!'* The *Commendatore* said it the other evening, and he said it with such sweetness! Oh, with sweetness! A sweetness such as to go to the head of Suzel, and he said it, moreover, with a warmth sufficient to make the cherries ripen on the tree and Suzel mellow on the ladder!
> Away! Let us not make poetry. Here we talk of music. And Mascagni's music again found its way to the heart of a large audience . . . [49]

Notariello never heard vocal coloration like De Lucia's at this time. Top, middle, and low notes, the *legato*, and the feeling for words, were all

---

[41] (SPM) Letter from Ministry of Public Instruction - Director of San Pietro a Maiella, Dec. 13 1916.

[42] (SPM) Minutes of the Board of Management, San Pietro a Maiella, Mar. 24 1917.

[43] Notariello.

[44] Better known as the *comprimario* Nina Sabatano.

[45] The class sheets for 1917-18 and 1922-3 cannot now be found.

[46] Not to be confused with the much later Boris Christoff.

[47] *Carnet de la Semaine*, Jul. 23 1922, quoting Mario Podesta.

[48] De Lucia family.

[49] *Monsignor Perrelli*, Feb. 24 1917.

of remarkable quality. And his acting and stage appearance were those of a much younger man. Only in the 'Cherry Duet' did his age and bulk betray him; when his Suzel (Nera Marmora) handed him the cherries, he dropped some of them. Bending to recover them, he lost his balance and only the tree saved him from falling, while Suzel smiled down at this unrehearsed scene. 'He was a perfect artist, and the one thing that he did not think about was this overbalancing' was the view of one spectator.[50]

Giorno summed up the ambience of the occasion:

> The history of the theatre cannot untie the two names bound by a single triumph - Fritz and De Lucia. Across the time that has passed, the Cherry Duet and the '*Tutto tace*' of De Lucia were always remembered as examples and models. The great tenor's singing last night showed masterly modelling in his individual enchantments and in those murmured *sfumature* which, in *Fritz*, are the heavenly passages '*alla De Lucia*'. One of these wonderful moments was at the close of the famous duet, where the entire audience excitedly acclaimed him and his Suzel, who so admirably supported him in his *filature*. To conclude, De Lucia is always De Lucia, and his Fritz is a great thing.[51]

From the gallery there came a shout: *'Don Ferdinando, ci avete consulato!'*[52]

On March 5th 1917, in the Sala Maddaloni of Naples, a concert took place in memory of Tosti, who had died three months earlier. It attracted a distinguished audience, drawn by many affectionate memories of music which had so often touched the heart, 'like the delicate perfume of flowers, luxuriant in meadows in the fullness of the spring awakening'. The hyperbole of the press echoed that of the orator, Ettore Moschino, who spoke gravely and eloquently on 'The Music of Tosti'. Tina di Angelo sang 'Ancora', 'Dopo', and 'Ninna-Nanna'; De Lucia, who gave 'Ideale' and, as an encore, 'Aprile', was followed by Graziella Pareto in 'Tristezza', 'Ridonami la calma', and 'Nonna, sorridi'. After Sammarco had sung 'L'ultima canzone', De Lucia responded to insistent calls for more and, with the other three singers as chorus, concluded the programme with 'Marechiare'.[53]

Italy was now a belligerent, having declared war on Austria in 1915. Despite De Lucia's efforts to dissuade him from enlisting, Nadir joined the army and refused to allow his influential father to obtain a safe post for him; Alfredo De Giorgio was present to photograph the young man as he left Rome for the front in June 1915. Eventually, Nadir was wounded in the head; he was found in a faint, hanging from the tree where he had been blown by shell-blast on the Austro-Italian border.

---

50 Luigi Caggiula.

51 *Giorno*, Feb. 23 1917.

52 'Don Ferdinando, you have made us happy!'

53 *Roma*, Mar. 6 1917. *Mattino*, Mar. 4/5, stated that De Lucia would sing 'Amour! Amour!' and 'Ideale', while Sammarco's programme would include 'Aprile'.

As soon as his father heard the news he set out for the front. Whenever obstacles arose, as inevitably they did in wartime, he used his name and celebrity. More than once he had to sing a few notes of identification from a railway carriage window to persuade officials to let him pass. When he arrived at the front, the commanding general asked him to sing at a mass for the dead. And, while around him he could hear explosions and the whistling of shot, he sang 'Pietà, Signore'.[54]

He sang this piece also in a Conservatory concert of sacred music in 1918. The other tenor was to be Roche's pupil, Angelo Notariello, who remembered De Lucia's singing:

> He sang it beautifully, with a perfect *legato* and elegance and a perfect emission of voice, without scooping. It sounded like an Amati cello. I will never forget it. It seemed as if he never took a breath from one phrase to another.

But he was not in the best of humour. At rehearsal, he turned to the orchestra after the first phrase and, in a disagreeable voice, said: 'Rispondete al mio dolore!'[55] When he had finished, the young man diffidently offered his modest congratulations. De Lucia replied: 'My dear Notariello, the greatest artists are always delighted, and appreciate the smallest compliment from anyone.'

Next day, Roche informed him that De Lucia had declined to sing if Notariello appeared. Understandably, the young tenor was upset. He could not sing for weeks. Some time later, the two had a chance meeting in a corridor of the college:

> With great courage, I said 'Good morning' to him. He stopped, and said: 'Oh, Notariello, how are you? I want to tell you that I am very sorry for what happened. I know how great a disappointment it was for you. It was not me - only an old, jealous singer. Please do not worry. You are young and your success will come.' After this we became great friends.

The singer's health, formerly robust, was now deteriorating. Obesity and flabbiness were now very evident. Though even his last records, made when he was over 60, show remarkable breath control, his cigar smoking and increased weight made him somewhat breathless and this, as he admitted to Notariello, sometimes obliged him to break phrases.[56] In 1918 came the great influenza pandemic, known in Naples as 'Spanish influenza' and elsewhere as 'the Captain of Death'. De Lucia, with the singer's obsessive concern for his health, did not go out at all until it appeared that the worst was over. Each morning, he would want to know

---

54 De Lucia family.

55 'Respond to my grief!'

56 Letter to the writer, June 1974. Some doubt exists over the extent of his smoking. His children and certain friends claim that he did not smoke, and that he gave cigars to his valet, Enrico, so that he might enjoy the aroma without himself smoking. Since this reference is a firm one, and one photograph shows him, in the open air, holding a lighted cigarette, it is possible that he did not smoke at home.

the number of fatalities during the previous day. However, in October 1918, even he contracted it; it developed into pneumonia, then double pneumonia which lasted until early in 1919.[57] Soon after being allowed to leave his bed his bladder condition recurred and a panel of three eminent physicians prescribed a further two months of treatment and rest at home. Elvira wrote to Cilea:

January 10th 1919

Only today can I assure you that Fernando is out of danger, but very weak after the great haemorrhage; we do not know when his doctors will let him leave his bed. Consequently, I enclose a medical certificate.

With thanks and affectionate greetings from Fernando. I join him in greetings.

Elvira Giommi - De Lucia

P.S. The school, says Fernando, can continue with Maestrina Labassano and Centi, and Maestro Sormiento at the piano. (SPM)

For eight months he made no records. Then, in the Neapolitan spring, he began to regain strength and to look forward to recording. He wrote to Americo Esposito:

May 16th 1919

My dear Americo,

It would be a great misfortune to me not to do the recording on Sunday, and it would appear like a *jettatura* not to sing again, after my detestable illness -

Entreat the maestro not to deal me this misfortune, in the name of friendship.

Accept my greetings of friendship and admiration.

Affectionately,
Fernando De Lucia

I enclose the songs for the maestro. (RE)

On May 24th 1919 he resumed his recording, which then continued, with intervals of no more than a month or two, until November 1921. He had, though, been weakened by the influenza, which had left broncho-pulmonary complications. In 1920 he was stricken by acute prostatitis, and rest was prescribed. The condition worsened until a surgical operation was deemed necessary. So weak was his general condition that a prostatectomy could not be attempted, and the less-drastic alternative - an operation for which he was said to have obtained competitive quotes[58] - of the indwelling catheter was instead adopted.

Subsequently, he was able to continue singing, not in the opera house

---

[57] De Lucia family.
[58] Otto Müller.

but in church. Always a devout Catholic, 'religious and mystical to the core', as he was once described, he carried a purse containing images of saints. Every Sunday, elegant and fastidious as ever, a red carnation in the buttonhole of his black suit, he attended High Mass in the church of San Ferdinando. He was always the first to enter the church, through the sacristy, to occupy the red velvet chair placed for him in the front row. When he sang Pergolesi's 'Vidit suum' there it was in fulfilment of a religious vow taken in a period of ill-health. Latterly, his condition obliged him to leave immediately his part was over, and with him, to the displeasure of the Bishop of Naples, left the less-devout worshippers. On subsequent occasions, though in pain, De Lucia remained at the altar until the bishop left. One or other of his doctors was, however, always within call in case of emergency.

He still attended concerts, especially those involving his pupils. One such was a 'Mattinata' of the newspaper *Giorno* at the Circolo Artistico, in February 1921. Francesco Cilea, the cellist Sergio Viterbini, and others lent their services. De Lucia's baritone student, Brenner, sang. The old tenor must have known that the audience would call for him. And, in 'Amor ti vieta', which was encored, he evoked memories of his finest evenings at the San Carlo.[59]

After his illness, he was permitted to hold some of his Conservatory classes at home. His studio (the former ballroom) held the souvenirs of a distinguished musical career. By the door was his cello, garlanded with tricolour ribbons. One wall was covered with photographs of singers, composers, and conductors. The opposite wall carried those of his pupils. About the room were the jewelled cigarette boxes from the royal houses of England and Italy; the ring from the King of Spain; a glass case with the ornate belt he wore as Lohengrin; another with his decorations. At one end was a podium and the piano on which his eldest daughter, Rosa, accompanied during lessons. Occasionally, his pupil Gianna Pederzini, an excellent pianist, would assume the task. The tenor himself never accompanied. Ever punctual, he would arrive expecting all to be ready for his work. For lessons he wore a black suit, white shirt, and white cravat with a jewelled gold ring near the knot, With a cordial greeting, he would seat himself at a circular black table, where he would take his morning coffee and a cake. He followed the lessons attentively, every so often correcting something that displeased him. He beat time with an ebony and ivory baton. There was no sign of his failing health. His air of dignity, prestige, and authority never left him.[60]

He was not, it seems, the perfect instructor. He had little interest in teaching the rudiments of voice production, and he preferred accomplished pupils, with settled voices and sound musicianship, whom

---

[59] *Mezzogiorno*, Feb. 4/5 1921.
[60] Mikhail Popov, letter to the writer, June 1973.

he could teach interpretation and the finer points of singing. With these, more especially with the girls, his patience was boundless. His views on vocal ornamentation were simple: 'If you cannot do it properly, do not try to do what I do!'[61] He taught by example, never using the arcane language of singing. To his pupils, he would say: 'With one note, you must be able to indicate a mood, such as happiness, anger, or grief.'[62] With some pupils he would sing phrases, transposing where necessary; with others, he would use the gramophone. Popov only rarely heard him sing, usually to demonstrate effects that students found difficult; for a joke, he once attempted to sing the F below the stave, to see how low his range extended. Popov recalled one occasion when he sang an entire piece, as he worked with a student on the tenor aria from *Werther*. De Lucia had first explained the sentiments which move the hero, and the expression necessary at that moment. The student had tried several times, but all remained stilted, without inner conviction:

> Dissatisfied, the Maestro began to lose patience. Suddenly, he rose, went to the podium, and sang the entire aria. It was a miracle! The voice was fresh, sonorous, mellow, with a youthful timbre, and it filled the studio. The aria had a vibrant magnetism, and impulses of real emotion. Phrase followed phrase, with clear pronunciation and good *legato*, expressed with intense sentiment and the richest of colours. Everyone was hushed with admiration and surprise. Even at the first sounds uttered by the *Divo*, all the family and servants had rushed towards the studio; opening the doors, they followed this brilliant moment with breathless emotion, with tears in their eyes and with looks of veneration.
> This was perhaps the final creation of the great singing artist.[63]

Popov described him as a 'great master of *mezza voce* and of spinning out the sound. He had developed to perfection the art of attacking a note *pianissimo*, of swelling it to *forte*, and diminishing it again, all with equal resonance and expression.' De Lucia would recall how, as Nadir, he had made his *mezza voce* heard in the furthest parts of the theatre. It was this ability, particularly, that brought pupils from many countries to his door.

Georges Thill, while studying at the Paris Conservatoire, had been much impressed by the improvement that less than one year of study with De Lucia had wrought in the singing of his friend Mario Podesta.[64] Warned that the Neapolitan was most exacting, Thill and his mother left for Naples in January 1921. A stop in Nice and an 'audience' with Battistini brought the baritone's verdict on De Lucia:

> 'It is not a great voice, but [he is] a skilful singer and endowed with uncommon vocal intelligence.'[65]

---

61 Notariello.
62 De Lucia family.
63 Popov.
64 Podesta taught Mado Robin and Alain Vanzo.
65 Mancini, *Georges Thill*, p. 16.

A later version of the meeting has it that, when asked about De Lucia, Battistini replied:

> 'Oh! De Lucia, very good! A singing musician, intelligent, and certainly an excellent teacher. You could not have made a better choice, young man . . . '66

In a still-later version, Battistini is said to have pronounced him 'the best (teacher) in the world'.67

On arrival at Naples, Thill presented himself to De Lucia, who seated himself at the piano to hear him sing. His eyes quickly brightened and he nodded his head approvingly. Mme. Thill asked the essential question: 'Maestro, do you think that my son has a tenor voice?' De Lucia replied, in his correct French:

> 'Madame, rest assured. No one was ever more of a tenor than he is.'
> 'But do you think that he can attain the perfection of his friend Mario Podesta?'
> 'Oh! Madame. . . . . Mario has the voice for *musica da camera* but your son has a voice for the theatre. No comparison is possible between the two.'68

So began two years that Thill would never forget. Later, he would say that everything that he had achieved was due to De Lucia, to 'this wonderful human being, who was not only immensely generous to his pupils with his time, energy, patience, and understanding, but who knew the infinitely different problems of each voice, and who always found the way to solve them'.69 Each day, weekends included, he went to De Lucia's home or, as an observer, to the Conservatory, sometimes morning and night; he had his lesson and left

> . . . to await, with impatience, the following day. I was 23-24, and he was more than 60. But I know that he had much regard for me as a pupil, for I was extremely attentive and he lived only for singing, for his singing.

The lesson always started with the ritual of the pupil's saying: 'Maestro, per cantare, bisogna aprire la bocca e pronunziare chiaro.'70 Thill attributed his own success wholly to training which taught the nuance of every phrase and the importance of every word. He described De Lucia's methods:

> He had no set system of teaching: he had a horror of the chest voice and of the nasal voice! For him, the teaching of singing consisted primarily of removing the faults and subsequently of fixing the sounds well in the head. He ceaselessly gave examples and enforced an extreme pronunciation and articulation. In the

---

66 Segond, *Georges Thill*, p. 26.
67 Lanfranco Rasponi, *Opera News*, Jan. 19 1985, p. 36.
68 Segond, op. cit., p. 27.
69 Rasponi, *Opera News*, Jan. 19 1985, p. 36.
70 'Maestro, to sing, one must open the mouth and pronounce clearly.'

studies, he made one open one's mouth to an exaggerated extent; he made me put a cork between my teeth, in the lengthwise direction which, the first [few] times, almost dislocated my jaw, but which did me a very great service for the future.[71]

One of his teacher's maxims was:

'Beautiful high notes are like valuable jewels, which women take out rarely, only on great occasions.'[72]

Exercises and *solfeggi* were followed by work on airs, starting with 'Donna non vidi mai' from *Manon Lescaut*. Sometimes De Lucia would sing an *aria* for his pupil, or a Tosti song: 'I remember his interpretation of 'Ideale'. I hear it still.....'[73]

His teacher's demonstrations, his unequalled mastery and amazing breath control often left Thill astonished and, sometimes, disheartened:

'Why insist, Maestro, I shall never be able to sing like that.'
'But, my boy, what you hear is the result of a life of singing and work. I had originally a baritone voice, limited at the top, and of unsympathetic timbre, with a disagreeable vibrato. Only daily exercise and permanent practice of *solfeggi* have given me what you admire: mastery of nuance, breath control, and power. Thus, I have been able to sing, without obvious difficulty, Donizetti and Bellini, but equally the *verismo* composers, and even *Lohengrin*! Nature has given you admirable raw material and you have ample time to make progress. If you persist in your efforts, you will soon sing this air from *Manon Lescaut*, which now terrifies you, better than anyone.'[74]

He taught even when illness confined him to bed, listening attentively to his pupils from his bedroom, near the salon. At Thill's final lesson he is said to have called him to his side and, with emotion, confided:

'You are my son..... I know them all, there is no other like you, and, after you, there never will be again.'[75]

Gianna Pederzini was another pupil who looked back with gratitude to her lessons with De Lucia:

I shall be in his debt forever. He taught me not only what singing was all about, but impeccable diction, which he claimed - and how right he was! - made the difference between a singer and an artist. When he sang to illustrate a passage, his tones were still pure gold.[76]

71 Thill, letters to the writer, May and Oct. 1967.
72 Mancini, 'Portrait de l'artiste en 30 ans de chant', *L'Avant Scène Opéra*, Sept. 1984, p. 10. (Supplied with EMI set 2901933: 'Georges Thill'.)
73 Angelo Pradier, 'Conversation avec Georges Thill', ibid., p. 20.
74 Segond, op. cit., p. 29.
75 Mancini, 'Portrait de l'artiste', loc. cit., p. 17.
76 Lanfranco Rasponi, *The Last Prima Donnas*, p. 299.

He did not often reminisce with students about his career. When in good health and temper he showed a lively wit, and he much enjoyed jokes, though his humour was occasionally somewhat unkind. At Cava de' Tirreni he used to be visited by a friend who, though not a singer, was musically inclined. Nevertheless, De Lucia would encourage him to sing, saying afterwards: 'Tonight we were a little less out of tune.'[77]

Neapolitan dialect offered him many opportunities for teasing foreign pupils. He knew a somewhat effeminate English singer who understood little Italian. De Lucia would tease him in Neapolitan, calling him Donna Luisella. He would ask his daughter to start playing, by saying: 'Now, accompany Donna Luisella.' As she burst out laughing, the bewildered man would ask: 'What are you saying, Maestro?' To a Bulgarian singer who sang a wrong note, he said: 'If you sing like that I'll give you a *carocchia.*' The student went away perplexed and returned next day, no less puzzled, to report that *'carocchia'* (a blow given with the knuckles) was not to be found in his Italian dictionary.

He would advise pupils on their way of life and on the preservation of good vocal health. 'If you want to keep your voice in order', he told Notariello, 'eat well, the finest food and the finest wines.' Frequently, he would press pupils to dine with him at home after the lesson, and this was especially welcome to foreign students on scholarships. When Luciano was away he would often cook their meal, demonstrating no mean culinary skill.[78]

The Hungarian soprano Maria Németh studied privately with him from October 1924 until his death the following February. Her hope was to acquire refinement and facility in *pianissimo* singing. The lessons afforded ample opportunity to note his

> ... *wonderful singing technique,* which was absolutely perfect and unique, especially in his artistic mastery of *piano* and *pianissimo* notes as well as in the various modulations of particular notes and phrases. This kind of perfection and the *euphony* of the voice can indeed be described as matchless.[79]

She found him 'an extremely likeable man, full of understanding for his pupils and devoted to his studies - quite incomparable'. His attention to detail was prodigious:

> I took a lesson with him every day, if he did not cancel or postpone it because of his health, which was already poor. ... The singing lessons were always an experience for me. Sig. De Lucia sang the *pianissimi* to me himself, with the most varied nuances. He always explained to me exactly how I must master the *pianissimo,* and I do not exaggerate if I say that we sometimes practised one note perhaps a hundred times before he was satisfied with it. We always began with the scales, and here he had the opportunity of having every note I sang

---

77　Franz Gleijeses.
78　Notariello.
79　Maria Németh, letter to the writer, Oct. 1967.

modulated as he wanted it and until it pleased him. ... I sometimes told him that I was anxious about the *pianissimi*, to which he always relied: 'Mme. Maria, with that voice you need never be afraid.'

I also worked up the 'Nile aria' [with him]. Each phrase was practised a hundred times. He went on filing and polishing. We worked at this aria for months. First I sang only a few phrases, and then a further phrase was added till the master was satisfied with it all. For the outsider it is almost incredible that one should sing a single aria for months, day after day, and always improve something in it, but the master was striving to achieve a perfection of performance with me that he did achieve in the end.[80]

Almost without exception, his pupils and young friends knew him as a pleasant, congenial man, full of exuberant cordiality and small kindnesses, such as sending them tickets for the opera. He could inspire deep affection in those who knew him. Of his traceable pupils, only one, Rodolfo Mele, did not get on with him, finding him 'pompous, polite - perhaps over-polite and with a tendency to talk down to one'.[81] The young tailor Luigi Caggiula worshipped him. Recalling his own emotions when he last heard him sing, in 1921, he ended with a simple tribute: 'And I loved De Lucia, not like a client but as something that was between the heaven and the earth.'[82]

Though De Lucia could become irritated at the many importunate aspiring singers who came to his door, he was sympathetic to real talent and advised many who were not his pupils. It was after an audition with him that Ada Bruges decided to study for a lyric career.[83] The English tenor, Tom Burke, who met him in Naples around 1916, described him as a punctilious man who demanded constant repetition until something was perfect. He did not study with the older singer who, however, acted as his mentor in artistic matters.[84]

Other pupils who have achieved at least some success were Gennaro Caracciolo, Ciro Formisano, Alfredo Matteotti, Ivan Petroff, and the tenor Enzo Aita who, forty years later, himself taught singing a stone's throw from his former teacher's house in Via Roma. On first hearing Enzo sing, De Lucia immediately showed him how to open the throat to produce much more sound with less effort. This and the old singer's marked intelligence greatly impressed Aita, who persuaded his father to allow him to study with him. The lessons were expensive: one year's tuition would then have bought an apartment in Naples. However, once the financial arrangements had been concluded De Lucia never watched the clock.[85]

---

80 Németh, letter to the writer, July 1967.
81 Rodolfo Mele, letter to the writer, June 1968.
82 Luigi Caggiula, in conversation (in English), Apr. 1968.
83 Bruges later married Salvatore Papaccio, the lyric tenor who was one of the greatest exponents of the Neapolitan song. Papaccio (who declined to be interviewed) recorded prolifically for Phonotype.
84 Tom Burke, in conversation Sept. 1967.
85 Enzo Aita, in conversation April 1968.

On August 2nd 1921, in the Grand Hôtel du Vésuve, Naples, Enrico Caruso died. The entire city went into mourning. As the news spread throughout Italy and beyond, wreaths, telegrams of condolence, and other expressions of sympathy arrived. While permission was sought to hold the funeral rites in the Church of San Francesco di Paola, hitherto reserved for members of the royal family, the body lay in state and what Daspuro described as 'a river of humanity passed by, its silence broken only by weeping'.[86]

It was announced that De Lucia would sing at the funeral service. Though the two tenors had never been close friends they had always maintained the civilities and there is no evidence of any enmity between them. Nevertheless, some suggested that De Lucia, recalling Caruso's début at the San Carlo, had agreed to sing only to salve his conscience. A reporter, seeking to discover what he would sing, found him at home, almost overcome by emotion. The eyes were veiled with tears in the open and expressive face. The restless hands trembled slightly. For a moment even the journalist hesitated to intrude. But the singer then confided that his friends had urged him to give the 'Preghiera' ('Pietà, Signore'), which he forthwith sang to the astonished reporter 'with such sweet accent, such exquisite singing and such heartfelt sadness, that deep emotion overcame the listener'. And, when he held out his hand in silent admiration, De Lucia said:

> 'My soul will speak to his soul. I believe that my voice must reach him as a solace. And I hope that I, who have consecrated all my life to art, shall not be found wanting.'[87]

On the day of the funeral, August 4th 1921, the door of the church of S. Francesco di Paola was curtained in black velvet, fringed with gold. Above it, against a background of crimson velvet, was a great inscription, shrouded in black: '*Ad Enrico Caruso*'. Within, large palms, interwoven with oak boughs and garlands of roses, guarded the entrance to the central colonnade. At either side, pyramids of carnations, chrysanthemums, dahlias, roses, and jasmine stood in two gilded baskets. The catafalque, covered in velvet damask, was flanked by four tall silver candelabra, each with fifteen wax candles.

From 9 am the crowds had struggled to enter the packed basilica. It took soldiers a good half-hour to clear a path for Caruso's family to join the group of dignitaries, diplomats, and lyric artists, some of whom had been waiting for hours. De Lucia also, on his way to the rostrum, had to pause until the crowds deferentially made way for him.

At 11.45 am, the requiem mass started. The writer Antonio Salvucci recalls hearing, over an orchestra of two hundred, a voice singing the

---

[86] Daspuro, *Enrico Caruso*, p. 72.

[87] *Mezzogiorno*, Aug. 4/5 1921.

prayer, 'Pietà, Signore'. Unable to see the singer, he asked Titta Ruffo who it was:

> 'It is the unmistakable voice of old De Lucia. ...In fact, the committee organising the funeral asked me to sing the 'Preghiera', but the unexpected death has so upset me that I had to refuse.'[88]

It seemed, wrote one observer, as though

> ...the voice of the renowned tenor had rediscovered all the freshness of its best days, when it fascinated the public of the greatest theatres of Europe and America to frantic ovations, provoking delirious enthusiasm. When the sublime notes of the *'Gran Dio, Signore, pietà'* echoed, there arose a great murmur of approval, which only just avoided becoming applause, was restrained only with difficulty, and was prolonged like an ever more distant echo.[89]

Daspuro recalled:

> '...that magical voice was full of tears. ...At every new phrase of the great tenor the lump in the throat grew larger, and the emotion more uncontrollable.'

Another observer wrote:

> [He] modulated that emotional and mystic passage with heavenly inflections and accents. Only the singing of De Lucia could be worthy of Enrico Caruso.
> No more noble homage could be rendered to the memory of the great tenor. When Fernando De Lucia fell silent, the public still remained under the spell of the melody, showing its desire to hear more, [and] more. Heavy in heart, it slowly left the church.[90]

As a memento, Caruso's family presented De Lucia with a heavy gold and turquoise snuff-box that had belonged to the dead singer.[91]

After the service, Salvucci asked Ruffo to present him to De Lucia, surrounded as usual by admirers and pupils. Though visibly and deeply moved by the occasion the tenor seemed, from the outset, expansive and genial. As Ruffo took his leave the two singers embraced hoping to meet again in happier times. The hope was, it seems, unfulfilled.

All pretence over, Itala left Naples to live near Nadir in Rome in December 1923. In these last years it was Elvira Giommi who cared for De Lucia, and the warmth of that period endures in many affectionately inscribed scores and photographs. His score of *Manon* bears the words:

> Dear Elvira: Here is your Manon. She will make you remember him
> who thinks of you and who wishes you well

---

88 Salvucci, op. cit., p. 96.
89 *Mattino*, Aug. 5/6 1921.
90 *Giorno*, Aug. 5/6 1921.
91 The richness of this box made a great impression on the young Mikhail Popov.

And that of *Cavalleria Rusticana*:

> My Elvira: I offer you the opera 'Cavalleria', so that
> you may remind yourself of that Turiddu
> who knows only how to love you.

And that of *Faust*:

> My Elvira: here for you the opera which constituted the first link
> in the chain of my triumphs.

A few years before his death, he sang in a benefit concert at the Teatro Politeama in Naples, where he gave Neapolitan songs and the aria 'Amor ti vieta'. Though 'the voice was not as it had once been, sweet and velvety as a caress', the enthusiasm recalled his best days. During a lull in the ovation there came a cry from the gallery: *'Ferdinà, sei sempe tù!'*[92]

In 1922 came his last appearance before a great Neapolitan audience. That year, the festival of Piedigrotta had particular significance: by order of the Chamber of Commerce the festivities took place in daylight. The procession of carriages and floats was the most splendid in years. It brought into the Toledo - by then renamed Via Roma - such enormous crowds, most of them armed with that ferocious weapon, the tin trumpet, that parts of the route were impassable and the procession had to halt.

Almost forty years after the publication of their most famous song, Naples had decided to honour Di Giacomo and Tosti with a memorial in the form of a tablet at the village of Marechiaro.[93] Two rafts, bearing soloist, chorus, and mandolin orchestra, were to cross the bay, round the cape of Posillipo, and moor under the window depicted in the poem. There, while the tablet was unveiled, 'Marechiare' would be performed for the pleasure of thousands of people gathered on the beach and rocks. The press was fulsome in its praise of the song and, especially, of Tosti, a native of Ortona but a former pupil of San Pietro a Maiella. In the eyes of Neapolitans that made him theirs.

De Lucia, who was to sing at the ceremony, wanted the orchestra and chorus to know how the song came to be written. He himself told the story to a gathering in his house of the twenty mandolinists, ten guitarists, six mandora players, and four harpists, with twenty ladies from the San Carlo chorus. Their conductor was Raffaele Calace, a local manufacturer of lutes and mandolins.[94]

One evening in the 1880s - De Lucia recounted - Tosti, Di Giacomo, and some friends went, as they often did, for supper at Marechiaro near

---

[92] Lancellotti, op. cit., p. 191. 'Ferdinando, you are always yourself!' The occasion cannot be documented precisely; it was probably one of the famous *'Mattinate'* organised by Matilde Serao for the subscribers to her newspaper, *Giorno*.

[93] Formerly Mare Chiano, a corruption of 'mare planum'.

[94] Carlo Annunziata. The firm of Calace is today the only remaining maker of mandolins in Naples.

Posillipo. In those days, it was a tiny fishing village, known to few outsiders. It was twilight, the moon was silvering the sea, and the brown-haired Carulì (Carolina) now and then enjoyed the scent of the carnations in a vase on her window-sill. Di Giacomo was inspired. Seizing pencil and paper, he wrote the verses of the song which, for countless people who have never been there, epitomises Naples.[95]

The poem was published in 1884, as 'Varchettiata'; when, however, Tosti's setting of the poem - for which he is said to have paid Di Giacomo the then equivalent of one pound sterling - appeared in the periodical *Capitan Fracassa* of March 25th 1885, it was as 'Marechiare', a title hallowed by its enduring fame.

The event had been fixed for September 5th 1922, when the moon would be full. Unfortunately, by the afternoon of that day the weather was so uncertain that the Italian navy declined to risk the two tugs which it had promised to the committee, and all was postponed. That evening, while it rained at Naples, a radiant moonlit night at Marechiaro was enjoyed only by a few journalists, as they ate the local fish soup at the restaurant 'Rosiello', and by those who had not heard of the postponement. Particularly indignant were the innkeepers, who had been busy all day preparing dishes that remained unsold in the kitchens.

The ceremony finally took place on September 9th. The procession of decorated motor boats, massed with flowers and adorned with lamps in the Venetian manner, left the harbour at Naples for its short journey. Two steamers followed, crammed with spectators. As the convoy passed Via Caracciolo and Posillipo more craft joined the flotilla. Two powerful searchlight beams silvered a path across the water. From the great floating chorus, scattered over the waves, rose the old songs of Naples.

At Marechiaro, an estimated ten thousand people had pushed their way down the narrow, twisting road that led from the cliff top to the seashore that had inspired so many poets. By 7 pm the crowd was an impressive sight. The minutes, quarter-hours, and hours passed, and still the multitude waited patiently. It grew to such proportions that tragedy seemed possible. Close in, the sea was almost covered with hundreds of gaily decorated boats, some providing refuge for onlookers caught between the water and the surges of new arrivals.

The occasion inspired even the journalists:

In the azure sweetness of the September night, in the fragrance of a thousand gardens scattered by the hills of Posillipo, last night there unfolded the poetic ceremony of the glorification of Marechiaro, and of the Neapolitan soul.[96]

---

[95] The writer hopes to conceal in a footnote the sad fact that this delightful story is a fable. When he wrote his poem, Di Giacomo had never been to Marechiaro. (See Schlitzer, op. cit., Nos. 535, 643, and 1407, and Salvatore di Giacomo, *Napoli: Figure e Paesi*, Mondadori, pp. 467-73.) The poet admitted as much in an article in *Mezzogiorno*, July 16-17 1922. The inauguration of the stone seems to have been the justification for some tactful efforts to make Marechiaro conform more closely to the song that had immortalised it.

[96] *Giorno*, Sept. 10 1922.

Another chronicler recalled:

> In the mirror of the water all the boats had stopped. It was a magnificent sight. The great raft bearing Maestro Calace's orchestra was positioned, ... illuminated by a thousand small electric lights, a little in front of the other vessels. Then there was a line of craft of every size and type. . . . A little further back were the two large ships.
>
> The ceremony had been prepared on the beach . . . teeming with Neapolitans. There was a cannon shot. It was followed by a moment of . . . the most profound and almost religious silence. . . .
>
> From the orchestra came the first notes of the famous melody, lost in the immensity of the sea. Sweetly rose the song of Fernando De Lucia, in the languid and passionate tune:
>
> 'A Marechiaro nce sta na fenesta'
>
> A shiver of intense emotion went through the crowd. It seemed to spread in the air. All were absorbed in the sublime illusion . . .
>
> When the voice of Fernando De Lucia fell silent, everyone seemed to awaken from a dream. A great cheer echoed over the sea . . . Then the ovation - interminable, enthusiastic, the delirium of the crowd, the sadness for a song too quickly over. De Lucia was obliged to repeat it twice more.[97]

Such was the impression from the boats. The spectators at the shore-line might also have heard the music. But the event had been what one writer termed 'a triumph of disorganisation'.[98] Weeks earlier, it had been scheduled for 6.30 pm. No one realised that, on September 9th, the moon would not give useful light until after 9 pm; that night, clouds obscured it until 10.30 pm. Worst of all, few on land heard anything over the noise of the crowd. No official unveiled the plaque. Only as the boats prepared to move away was it realised that the ceremony was already over. The crowd, patient and restrained until then, became hostile. Shouts and curses flew in the direction of the window. Hands attacked the veil, which fell amid general uproar. But weariness overcame violence. Resignedly, the crowd drifted away. At Marechiaro only the window, the inscribed stone, and the vase with its red flowers remained. To this day, fresh carnations always grace the window-sill, recalling Carulì.

Two weeks later, on September 24th 1922, De Lucia made his last record for Esposito. It was of 'Marechiare'; though the voice now shows more definite signs of age, the embellishments - more elaborate and audacious than those of 1902 or 1911 - are astounding. His relations always remained cordial with Americo - whom he addresses as 'doubly dear *compariello*' (little godson)[99] and describes as 'truly an angel of a son' - and his fiancée, Elvira, who met the singer for the first time in 1924, when he sang in the church of Santa Brigida. After the service he

---

[97] *Mattino*, Sept. 10/11 1922.

[98] *Mezzogiorno*, Sept. 9/10 1922.

[99] (RE) De Lucia - Americo Esposito, Aug. 13 1923.

sent her a large box of cakes. Each Sunday Americo would accompany De
Lucia to mass, and the tenor would always send some gift for Elvira.

He wrote from Rome to Raffaele Esposito, saddened that

> . . . tomorrow is your anniversary and I am not among you to join your family in
> drinking your health.
>
> A thousand - thousand - affectionate greetings and a long life of peace and
> all good fortune. By an almost mysterious force, I feel myself bound to you by a
> friendship that will end only if death calls me.[100]

He may have sung the Pergolesi *Stabat Mater* on Good Friday, 1924;
otherwise, the last occasion on which he is known to have performed in
public was on March 1st 1924, when Casa Editrice Marechiaro was
inaugurated by Americo and Vincenzo Esposito. Before an audience of
publishers, impresarios, agents, and other artists, De Lucia joined
Donnarumma, Papaccio, Parisi, and Pasqualillo in a programme of
Neapolitan songs.[101] On May 23rd 1924 he was present at a concert at
the Sala Maddaloni, where Nina Sabatano sang Nadir De Lucia's 'Il
marinaro canta'; the tenor's youngest daughter, Amalia, described as '*un
Duse bambina*' then recited Marvasi's 'Il mutilato'.[102] A few days later, in
De Lucia's own studio, a group of friends and critics heard Sabatano sing
'Ninna-nanna' (Nadir De Lucia); daughter Rosa played two piano pieces
and Amalia recited Leopardi's 'A Silvia'. Then, persuaded by the
onlookers, De Lucia sang another of Nadir's songs and 'Amor ti vieta'.[103]

Symptoms of kidney failure were now noted by his doctors.
Nevertheless, he was out and about in the streets of Naples, always
smiling and cheerful, until a few days before his death, though he
appears to have given up his Conservatory classes two months earlier.

The final illness began on February 12th 1925, when he had to curtail
a lesson with Németh because of a haemorrhage that the doctors could
not staunch.[104] On February 17th his condition seemed desperate and his
three physicians decided on surgical procedures. This time, however, his
condition did not improve. The serious symptoms of uraemia began to
appear. All medical attention was in vain as he lapsed into a coma.

Rallying briefly, he asked Nadir and the priest to read him some
prayers. As Elvira and the children gathered around in the final
moments his thoughts were of times long ago in the theatre, and of the
death of Mimì, as he murmured some lines from Act IV of *La Bohème*:[105]

> '*Tutti qui! Tutti qui!*
> *Sorridenti a Mimì.*'

---

100 (RE) Oct. 23 1923.
101 De Mura, *Enciclopedia*, Vol. I, p. 467. The programme has not been established.
102 *Roma*, May 26 1924.
103 Ibid., May 30 1924.
104 De Lucia family.
105 Amalia De Lucia. 'Everyone here! Smiling at Mimì.'

At 9.10 pm on February 21st 1925 Fernando De Lucia drew his last breath.

According to custom, the body was laid out amid flowers and candles in his studio. On one side was his 'cello, on the other a piano. His score of *Faust* lay open on a lectern. Thousands filed past or signed the register in the lodge at Palazzo Cirella. The vigil was kept by Nadir and the four younger children, four nuns, and his pupils. A guard of honour was sent by the City of Naples. The first wreath to arrive was from Angelo Masini.

In the general belief that gambling losses had impoverished him the funeral was paid for by the city. The music was the responsibility of the Conservatory. In the wet greyness of February 23rd, his pupils carried the coffin from the church of San Ferdinando to a vast, ornate hearse, its coachmen and eight black horses decked in the colours of the city. It was an imposing spectacle, for the number of onlookers and for the profound emotion of the occasion. The Sub-Commissioner of the Commune of Naples spoke movingly of the tenor's art, of his career, and of his love for his native city, a love that had made him spurn easy triumphs and greater monetary rewards elsewhere. For all these, but especially for the fact that he had always lived in Naples, his memory would be indelible in the hearts of Neapolitans. 'Today, Naples will mourn the death of Fernando De Lucia, with the anguish of a mother', wrote Procida.[106]

The cortège was preceded by detachments of soldiers, the civic band, and a group of Franciscan monks. On the coffin were sprays of flowers from the children and a wreath of mimosa and carnations, the tribute of Naples. Behind it, Nadir, cousins, and nephews were followed by his pupils. Then came a crowd estimated at four thousand friends, admirers, and citizens, paying their last respects: Bovio, De Leva, Denza, De Rosa, Papaccio, Procida, Schottler - the columns of names are a roll-call of artistic Naples. Among the wreaths, which occupied three carriages, were those from Bellincioni, Cilea, Daspuro, Laganà, Pederzini, Sonzogno, the Esposito family, and the De Giorgio family. The route along the Toledo - as Fernando would undoubtedly have called it - to the Museum was crowded with Neapolitans. Shops closed their blinds at the passage of the cortège. Flowers were thrown from balconies on to the hearse. For he was truly a son of Naples.[107]

Since the family tomb at Poggioreale had been sold he lies in a niche in the chapel of the Congrega di S. Filippo Neri di Chiaia, one of the burial fraternities whose astonishing edifices dominate the necropolis. On the dignified, plain marble front of the tomb are the words:

E il suo canto si mutò in preghiera.[108]

---

[106] *Mezzogiorno*, Feb. 22/23 1925.

[107] In 1961 a new road was named Via Fernando De Lucia. In 1984 Piazza Fernando De Lucia was inaugurated in Rome.

[108] 'And his singing became a prayer.'

The night after the funeral, Nadir sat in De Lucia's apartment all night long, playing his father's records. Next day he had the private staircase walled up and the apartment cleared.

We need not dwell on subsequent family disputes. De Lucia's will, made in 1921 and leaving everything to Elvira and Nadir, expressed the hope that Nadir would not contest it. It did not come to light until after the death, in 1926, of Itala. When, in 1931, his estate was aggregated its value was 85,700 lire.[109] Nadir died in 1927, and Ofelia Cuccari in 1945. By Royal Decree of 1934 Elvira's children won the right to use the name Giommi-De Lucia; in 1942 they were able, largely through the efforts of Cilea, to call themselves De Lucia. Elvira herself lived until 1952.

Saverio Procida, who had witnessed so many of his triumphs, observed in his obituary:

> His career was triumphal, but brief. Too often he destroyed his heart [and] martyred his body in living the characters whom he felt as though [they were] beings woven with his own nerves. Few artists loved their own region [and] the theatre of their native city as did this highly sensitive embellisher of melody.[110]

Reporting the news, *Giorno* grieved:

> He was the last. Ah yes, we still possess tenors today who, by virtue of a slight gift of nature, flock broad-chested and pretentious to the lyric stage, who think that they have reached the summit of the parabola when their high register has been preserved on a gramophone record. But he who died last night belonged to quite a different school, and possessed quite a different nature. . . . Others have had or may have more beautiful voices than his, but with his death we have lost the greatest *dicitore lirico* [lyric orator], an artist who, through a fervent love and knowledge of the music, created his art within his will to be [the character], and who expressed himself coherently and with extreme sensibility. His was a triumphal march. . . .
>
> In a chance meeting, a week ago, we talked about the lyric theatre and about certain interpretations. The Maestro was smiling and mild-mannered as usual, and he had only good words to say: but all at once, with that kind of Neapolitan suddenness, placing his hands on my shoulders, he exclaimed:
>
> > 'A singer who comes on to the stage to sing [only] a few words
> > must have a trembling heart if he is a true artist.'
>
> There was, in those few words of confession, all that he had been able or would have wished to preserve of his own wonderful art.
>
> Fernando De Lucia . . . passed away in the same manner as did the artist on the stage. His radiant day has ended without slow agony; he died like the tenor who, struck by a bullet in the last act of an opera, staggers and falls, as the curtain comes down.[111]

---

109 Ufficio Registri Successioni, Naples. At the then exchange rate, about £1,000 sterling; a three-bedroomed house then cost about £500.

110 *Mezzogiorno*, Feb. 22/23 1925.

111 *Giorno*, Feb. 22 1925.

Chronology of Appearances

> Every other author can aspire to praise; the lexicographer can only hope to escape reproach, and even this negative recompense has been granted to very few.
>   Samuel Johnson

If Dr. Johnson's remark be true for the lexicographer then it is no less so for the chronologer, for neither can guarantee completeness or total accuracy.

While a listing of season premières and principal accompanying artists yields the essentials of a singer's career, a proper appreciation of its progress and tempo requires a knowledge of the number and sequence of performances. However, since the potential for error necessarily increases with the degree of detail attempted, some caveats are necessary here. This chronology documents by date every De Lucia appearance traced. Its source materials - newspapers, musical magazines, and some theatre annals - are generally reliable for dates and principal performers for the season première of a work, but are far less so for secondary artists and for the repeats. As press coverage waned during a season or run of performances the opera could be ignored for periods of weeks, and repeat performances become correspondingly difficult to document. Advertised performances were often cancelled at short notice, albeit usually with confirmation the following day. Dates sometimes present other problems: in a newspaper dated, for example, March 15th, 'yesterday' may mean 14th or 13th, according to edition. One source may detail a performance which another states was cancelled. Changes of cast during long seasons are often noted in reviews; however, after several repeats of an opera, reviews frequently omit singers' names, and discrepancies may then be irreconcilable from accessible sources. Thus, even if the fortunate chronologer has access to a complete file of a newspaper, or even of more than one paper from a given city, complete documentation may still be illusory. Concerts are even more difficult to document, since many undoubtedly took place in private houses and others, even where announced, were unreported.

This chronology includes both reviewed events and those advertised performances which were not subsequently noted as having been cancelled. It uses contemporary sources wherever possible. Where they exist, theatre annals - with which the present work is sometimes in disagreement - are used primarily as confirmation.

I have have always been much vexed by chronologies which (doubtless because cast lists often ignore minor artists) include only principal singers and omit the rôles sung. Several artists may share a surname, e.g. Rossi or Scotti. The Fabbri sisters, Guerrina and Vittorina, often appeared in the same season and notices seldom distinguish between them, and the same is true for Lina and Rosa Garavaglia and for Giulia and Sofia Ravogli. Variant spellings abound: Adele Gazul may be spelled Gasul, Gasull, Gazull, or Gazzull, and Giuseppe Di Grazia may appear as di, de, or De Grazia. While each is clearly identifiable in most variant spellings we cannot, for example, be certain that Ernesto Giordani and Ernesto Giordano were actually two different people, as is implied in indices of some reference books. Even major singers are not immune from repeated misspelling, such as San Marco (for Sammarco). Hence, for completeness and clarity, a considerable effort has been made to identify De Lucia's colleagues by forename on their first appearance in the chronology, and by initial thereafter. Their rôles are also given whenever it has been possible to discover them. In some cases we may reasonably suggest a forename where the source does not provide one. Thus, the

Sig. Ferraguti who appeared in *Cavalleria Rusticana* on February 17th 1897 at Naples, Teatro San Carlo (*Paese*, February 18th), but who is not shown in the theatre annals, seems certain to have been Vittorio; however, the doubt is indicated with a question mark. Reviews which supply no forename may still provide a voice type, abbreviated as: sop (soprano), ms (mezzo soprano), ten (tenor), bar (baritone), and bs (bass). Even where no forename is supplied and the rôle is not identified the review or its language may sometimes indicate the sex of the singer: in this chronology, 'il' denotes a male and 'la' a female artist for whom neither forename nor rôle is available. 'Teatro' has throughout been abbreviated to 'T.' and, in the names of churches, 'S.' signifies 'Saint' or its equivalent. Roman numerals refer to acts of operas given in benefit or gala performances.

Opera titles are given in the language used. Rôles sung by De Lucia are enclosed in square brackets. No consistent policy has been applied to the abbreviation of other rôles other than to facilitate identification of the part sung. In any season only De Lucia's appearances are noted, and the dates given relate solely to his activity; further performances of a given opera may have taken place, on dates other than those given here, with a different tenor. No attempt has been made to document those eccentric occasions on which one singer used, for example, French, and the others Italian. Where known, changes of cast are marked: a solidus (/) between the names of two singers signifies that the first was replaced by the second, but it is impracticable to document them for every date or for every instance where an artist who sang one rôle in a season première later assumed another in the same opera. For concerts, only De Lucia's programme is given, but the names of other artists are supplied when performing with him in concerted items. Accounts of such events often report only, for example, 'Duet from *Don Sebastiano*'.

With such limitations, no chronology of this type can ever be considered complete. The following represents the best information currently available on De Lucia's performances. It is believed that it faithfully outlines his career. However, for the reasons set out above, the writer - uneasily aware of the limitations of his sources and, therefore, of his data - is conscious that, despite his best efforts, errors and omissions will certainly remain.

Naples: Casa Ruta	Concert	Sept 23	Commemoration of Bellini: *La Straniera*: Duet (w. Anna Ruta, sop); *I Puritani*: Quartet (Probably the (offstage) Act I 'Preghiera', 'La luna, il sole, le stelle') (w. A. Ruta, Luigi Colonnese, bar & Alfredo De Giorgio, bs).
Naples: Location unknown	Concert	c. Sept 25	Concert Vincenzo di Napoli: 'Serenata' (Braga); Francesco Daddi, pf.
Naples: Casa Ruta	Concert	Oct 13	*Tornata musicale*: Programme unknown.
Naples: S. Potito	Concert	Nov 11	Concert Vincenzo di Lorenzo: Unidentified pieces, probably of music by Di Lorenzo.

1884

Naples: Società Filarmonica	Concert	Jan 25	'L'Alba' (Rotoli); 'Medje' (Gounod).
Naples: Circolo Partenopeo	Concert	Feb 9	'Addio' (Carelli); *Don Sebastiano*: Duet (w. la A. Gucci).
Naples: Circolo del Commercio	Concert	Mar 1	Concert Niccolò Van Westerhout: Three unidentified songs (Van Westerhout); (One, a 'serenata' to words by Rocco Pagliara, was possibly 'Mesta barcarola'); 'L'Alba'(Rotoli); 'Ideale' (Tosti).
Naples: Sala del Quartetto	Concert	Mar 16	Concert Giuseppe dell'Orefice: Programme unknown.
Naples: Sala del Quartetto	Concert	Mar 18	*Faust*: Duet (w. Carmelina Montefusco, sop); two unidentified romanzas (Tosti).
Naples: Sala dei Nobili, Vico Nilo	Concert	Apr 22	Concert Maria Migliaccio: *Lucrezia Borgia*: Trio (w. M. Migliaccio, sop & G. Marini, bar); 'Aprile' (Tosti); 'L'Alba' (Rotoli); Unidentified duet (Rossini) (w. M. Migliaccio); Angelo Siani, pf.
Ortona a Mare:	*I Turchi in Ortona* (De Nardis)	c. May 7	w. Nobiglioni, bar; Zenone Bertolasi; Camillo De Nardis cdr.
Naples: Sala Flavio Gioia, S. Domenico Maggiore	Concert	May 18	*Mattinata musicale* Vincenzo De Vivo: 'Ideale' (Tosti).
Naples: Conservatorio San Pietro a Maiella	Concert	May 18	*Don Giovanni*: 'Il mio tesoro'.
Castellammare: Hôtel Quisisana	Concert	Aug 19	*Serenata* for Minister Grimaldi: 'L'Alba' (Rotoli).
Naples: Sala Tarsia	Concert	Aug 24	'Aprile' (Tosti).

Naples: Casa Lombardi	*Mefistofele*	Dec 20,23,27,30	[Faust]; Elisa Marzolla (Marg/Elena); Annunziata Lombardi (Marta/Pantalis); Adolfo Calenda (Mef); Eduardo Talamo (Wagner); Vincenzo Lombardi, pf & cdr.
Naples: Sala Vega	Concert	Dec 21	Concert Margherita Tagliacozzo: In aid of cholera orphans: Programme unknown.

1885

Palermo: R. Teatro S. Cecilia	Concert	Feb 6	*L'Africana*: 'O paradiso!'; *La Favorita*: 'Spirto gentil'; 'Serenatella' (Costa).
Palermo: Sala della Filarmonica	Concert	Feb 9	Filarmonica Bellini: 'L'Alba' (Rotoli); 'Amor fa morire!'(Rotoli); 'Ideale' (Tosti); 'Stornello' (probably Tosti, but possibly by De Lucia.) *Faust*: 'Salve! Dimora'.
Naples: T. San Carlo	*Faust*	Mar 9,11,13,15, 21,26	[Faust]; Virginia Ferni-Germano (Marg); Sofia Krammberger (Siebel); Giuseppe del Puente (Val); Francesco Vecchioni (Mef); Bona (Wagner); Magi (Marta); Nicola Bassi cdr.
Naples: Sala Vega	Concert	Mar 16	In aid of cholera victims. *L'Africana*: 'O paradiso'; 'Aprile' (Tosti); 'Mira la bianca luna' (Rossini)(w. V. Ferni-Germano, sop); V. Lombardi, pf.
Naples: Casa Cassaro	*Stabat Mater* (Rossini)	Mar 23	w. Menotti Frascani, bs; V. Lombardi, pf; Salvatore (or Francesco) Quaranta, harmonium; Luigi Filiasi cdr.
Naples: S. Ferdinando	*Stabat Mater* (Pergolesi)	Mar 28	w. Giuseppe Kaschmann, bar.
Naples: Casa Otway	Concert	Apr 1	Programme unknown.
Naples: Casa Otway	Concert	Apr 8	'Ideale' (Tosti); *Un Ballo in Maschera*: Final duet (w. Eliza Otway, sop).
Naples: Location unknown.	Concert	Apr 11	Concert Sancio Blanco: Programme unknown.
Naples: Sala del Quartetto	Concert	Apr 18	Concert Metauretta Torricelli: Unidentified romanza (Bériot); N. Van Westerhout, pf.
Naples: Sala del Quartetto	Concert	May 1	Concert Niccolò van Westerhout. 'Quando co' tuoi celesti occhi'; 'Sulla mia guancia'; 'I divini occhi tuoi' (all Van Westerhout).
Naples: Casa Lombardi	*Mefistofele*	May 19,21	[Faust]; E. Marzolla (Marg/Elena); A. Lombardi (Marta/Pantalis); A. Calenda (Mef); E. Talamo (Wag); V. Lombardi, pf & cdr.
Naples: Sala Vega		May 24	Mattinata Musicale for H.M. Queen Margherita: *Il Duca d'Alba*: 'Romanza'.
Hôtel de la Rivière	Concert	May 28	Concert Maria Smitti: 'Ideale'; 'Aprile' (both Tosti).
Naples: Sala Vega	Concert	May 29	Concert Carlo Lombardi: *L'Africana*: 'O Paradisol'; *Mefistofele*: 'Giunto sul passo'; 'I Mulatieri' (Francesco Masini) (w. Giuseppe Rapp, bar).

Venue	Opera/Event	Dates	Programme
Naples: Casa Edoardo Sottolana	Concert	Jul 26	Programme unknown.
Bologna: T. Comunale	La Traviata	Oct 27,29,31, Nov 1,3,8,10, 15,17,19,21, 22,Dec 5,8	[Alfredo]; Gemma Bellincioni (Viol); Virginia Karnay (Flora); Senatore Sparapani (Germont); Argimiro Bertocchi (Gas); Federico Rappini (Baron); Cesare Cavazzoni (Marchese); Luigi Mancinelli cdr. (Nov 21 Act IV only; Dec 8 Bellincioni Benefit.)
	Dinorah	Nov 24,26,28, 29,Dec 2,3,6	[Correntino]; Ermestina Bendazzi-Secchi (Din); Teresa Angeloni (Capraio); Maria Amadei (Capraia); Ettore Borucchia (Cacciatore); Leandro Dal Passo (Mietitore); Agosto Gnaccarini (Hoël); L. Mancinelli/Giovanni Bolzoni cdr. (Dec 3 Benefit Bendazzi-Secchi: Dinorah Acts I & II; Faust: 'Love duet'.)

1885-6

Venue	Opera/Event	Dates	Programme
Florence: T. Pergola	Mignon	Dec 26,29,30, 31,Jan 9,10	[Meister]; Lison Frandin (Mig); Carolina Smeroschi (Fil); Maria Paolicci-Mugnone (Fed); Carlo De Probizzi (Lot); Romolo Dolcibene (Laerte); Leopoldo Mugnone cdr.
T. Pagliano*	Margherita (Pinsuti)	Jan 16,17,20,21, 23,24,31,Feb.2*, 4*,6*,Mar 5*	[Ermando]; C. Smeroschi (Mar); M. Paolicci-Mugnone (Inf); C. De Probizzi (Grand Inq); Gaudenzio Salassa (Don Rodriguez); L. Mugnone cdr.
	Carmen	Feb 11,13,16, 18,20,21,23,27, 28,Mar. 2,4,7	[Don José]; L. Frandin (Carmen); C. Smeroschi (Micaëla); Matilda Ricci (Frasquita); M. Paolicci-Mugnone (Mercedes); G. Salassa (Escamillo); C. De Probizzi (Zuniga); R. Dolcibene (Dancairo & Morales); L. Mugnone/ Matini cdr. (Feb 27 De Lucia benefit: 'L'Alba' (Rotoli).)
	Mignon (2nd cast)	Mar 13,14,16, 18,19,21,23,29	[Meister]; Costanza Donita (Mig); Elena Theriene-Karganov (Fil); Bice Savoldi (Fed); Alessandro Bottero (Lot); Enrico Giordani (or Giordano) (Laerte); Spreafico (Giarno); Catalanotti cdr.
Florence Società Filarmonica Fiorentina	Concert	Jan 4	Mattinata musicale: Il Duca d'Alba: 'Angelo, casto e bel', L. Mugnone, pf.

1886

Venue	Opera/Event	Dates	Programme
Buenos Aires: T. Politeama Argentino	Faust	Apr 29,May 1,2, 8,Sept 7,8,14, May 11,24*	[Faust]; Eva Tetrazzini (Mar); Clara Negrini (Siebel); F. Vecchioni (Mef); Achille Medini (Val); Arnaldo Conti cdr.
T. Colón*	Lucrezia Borgia	May 26*,29,30,	[Gennaro]; Lina Cerne-Wulman (Lucrezia); C. Negrini (Orsini); F. Vecchioni (Alfonso).
	L'Ebrea (La Juive)	Jun 1,8,10,24, 26,29,Jul 1, Sept 11,12	[Leopoldo]; E. Tetrazzini (Rachel); Benedetto Lucignani (Eleazar); F. Vecchioni (Cardinal); Alessandro Polonini (Ruggiero); Ferretti.
	La Favorita	Jun 17,19,20,22	[Fernando]; E. Tetrazzini (Leon); Ernesto Sivori (Alf); Ettore Brancaleoni (Bal).

	Opera	Dates	Cast
	La Gioconda	Jul 3,4,7,8,9, 11,14, Sept 28,30	[Enzo]; E. Tetrazzini (Gioconda); Clotide Prampolini/M. Preziosi (Laura); E. Sivori (Barnaba).
Montevideo: T. Cibils	*L'Ebrea*	Jul 17,18	[Leopoldo]; E. Tetrazzini (Rac); Elvira Gambogi (Eud); B. Lucignani (Eleaz); A. Polonini (Rugg); Rocco Franzini (Alb); Aristodemo Zanon (Aral); F. Vecchioni (Card); A. Conti cdr.
	La Gioconda	Jul 22 or 23, Aug 17	[Enzo]; E. Tetrazzini (Gio); L. Cerne-Wulman (Lau); E. Brancaleoni (Alv); C. Prampolini (Cieca); E. Sivori (Bar); A. Zanon (Zuane/Singer); Ernesto Bonesini (Isèpo); Pellegrini (Piloto).
	La Favorita	Aug 7,12	[Fernando]; E. Tetrazzini (Leon); Cristina Sprugnolli (Inez); Oreste? Benedetti; A. Medini (Alf); E. Brancaleoni (Bal).
1886-7			
Madrid: T. Real	*Mignon*	Nov 2,4,13,21, Dec 12,Jan 26, Feb 18	[Meister]; Giuseppina Pasqua/Garcia Condé (Mig); Clémentine De Vere (Fil); Guerrina Fabbri (Fed); Antonio Baldelli (Laerte); Giovanni Beltramo (Giarno); Francisco Uétam (Lot); L. Mancinelli cdr.
	Mefistofele	Nov 16,18,24,28, Dec 9,11,18, Jan 6,22, Mar 2,6,26	[Faust]; Ludmilla Kupfer-Berger (Marg/Elena); G. Fabbri (Marta/Pantalis); Giovanni Ziliani; F. Uétam (Mef); L. Mancinelli cdr.
	Linda di Chamounix	Dec 14,16,19, Feb 6,14	[Charles]; C. De Vere (Linda); G. Fabbri (Pierotto); Mattia Battistini (Antonio); F. Uétam; Manuel Pérez cdr.
	Il Barbiere di Siviglia	Dec 28,30,Jan 1, 5,9,13,18,Feb 10	[Almaviva]; Giuseppina Gargano (Rosina); M. Battistini (Figaro); A. Baldelli (Bartolo); F. Uétam (Basilio); M. Pérez cdr.
	Dinorah	Jan 20,25,27, Feb 5,8	[Correntino]; G. Gargano (Din); G. Fabbri (Capraio); Adele Gazul; M. Battistini (Hoël); G. Beltramo (Cacc); G. Ziliani (Miet); Conti; L. Mancinelli cdr.
	Fra Diavolo	Jan 31,Feb 3, 4,20,Mar 3,9	[Fra Diavolo]; C. De Vere (Zerlina); G. Fabbri; A. Baldelli; G. Beltramo; Giovanni Villani (Brigand); Antonio Ponsini.
	La Traviata	Feb 16,21, Mar 8*	[Alfredo]; G. Gargano (Viol); Eugenio Labán (Germont); L. Mancinelli cdr. (* One act only, in Mancinelli benefit, which included *Isora di Provenza*, Act I (Mancinelli), sung by Kupfer-Berger, Pasqua, De Lucia, Battistini, Beltramo, & Martin Verdaguer, with a chorus comprising C. De Vere, G.? Fabbri, Pilar Garrido, A. Gazul, & Bibiana Pérez.)
	L'Elisir d'Amore	Mar 29	[Nemorino]; C. De Vere (Adina); M. Battistini (Bel); A. Baldelli (Dul) (Baldelli benefit).
1887			
London: Theatre Royal, Drury Lane	*La Traviata*	Jun 14	[Alfredo]; Lilian Nordica (Viol); Dora Galba (Flora); Foresta (Annina); G. del Puente (Ger); Giovanni Paroli (Gast); A. De Giorgio (D'Obigny); Vittorio Navarrini (Baron); L. Mancinelli cdr.

Don Giovanni	Jun 18,23, Jul 1,7	[Don Ottavio]; L. Nordica (Elv); Medea Borelli/Hélène Crosmond/Amelia Groll (Anna); Minnie Hauk/Sigrid Arnoldson (Zerlina); Victor Maurel (Don); Edouard de Reszke/Francesco Navarrini (Lep); Giuseppe Ciampi (Mas); Miranda (Comm); L. Mancinelli cdr.[1]
Il Barbiere di Siviglia	Jun 20,24,28, Jul 5,9,22	[Almaviva]; S. Arnoldson (Ros); M. Battistini/Francesco Pandolfini (Fig);[1] Carlotta Desvignes (Berta); E. de Reszke (Bas); G. Ciampi (Bart); A. De Giorgio (Fior); Parisotti (Off); Alberto Randegger cdr.

1887-8

Madrid: T. Real

La Traviata	Oct 5,12,20,22, Nov 8,16,29, Feb 16	[Alfredo]; G. Gargano/Adelina Patti (Viol); Giovanni Bianchi/Giovanni Vaselli (Ger); L. Mancinelli cdr.
L'Ebrea	Oct 26,27, Nov 5	[Leopoldo]; Abigaille Bruschi-Chiatti (Rachel); Boni Lizárraga (Eudoxia); Leopoldo Signoretti (Eleazar); F. Uétam (Cardinal); L. Mancinelli cdr.
L'Elisir d'Amore	Oct 31,Nov 10, 13,27,Dec 6, Jan 21,Feb 7,23	[Nemorino]; G. Gargano (Adina); Ramón Blanchart (Belcore); A. Baldelli (Dulcamara); L. Mancinelli cdr.
Il Barbiere di Siviglia	Nov 19,20,23, Dec 7,Jan 19, Feb 9,26*	[Almaviva]; G. Gargano/A. Patti (Ros); R. Blanchart (Fig); A. Baldelli (Bart); F. Uétam (Bas); M. Pérez cdr (* Act III, in Patti gala).
La Gioconda	Dec 1,3,20,25	[Enzo] (after L. Signoretti); E. Tetrazzini (Gioc); G. Pasqua (Lau); G. Fabbri (Cieca); G. Bianchi/G. Vaselli (Barn); Alessandro Silvestri (Alv).
Mefistofele	Dec 10,13,17,19, 22,24,Jan 5,28, Feb 5,11,Mar 8	[Faust]; E. Tetrazzini (Marg/Elena); G. Fabbri (Marta/Pantalis); A. Silvestri (Mef.); L. Mancinelli cdr.
La Favorita	Dec 29,Jan 7, 11,Feb 28	[Fernando]; G. Pasqua (Leon); R. Blanchart (Alf); A. Silvestri (Bal); M. Pérez cdr.
La Stella del Nord	Jan 4,15,17, 25,27,Feb 13, Mar 3,6,11,13	[Danilowitz]; G. Gargano (Caterina); Bibiana Pérez (Prascovia); F. Uétam (Pietro); A. Baldelli (Gritzenko); Diego Giannini-Grifoni (Giorgio);[2] B. Lizárraga; A. Gazul; A. Ponsini; Francesco Cabrer; Leopoldo Jourdán; G. Ziliani; L. Mancinelli cdr.
Linda di Chamounix	Feb 4	[Carlo]; A. Patti (Lin); G. Fabbri (Pier); G. Vaselli (Antonio); A. Baldelli (Marquis); F. Uétam (Prefect); M. Pérez cdr.

---

1 Though billed to do so, there is no evidence that Pandolfini actually sang Figaro.
2 Among at least seven singers named Giannini it is not certain - though highly probable - that this one was Diego, the younger brother of the dramatic tenor Francesco Giannini.

Rigoletto	Feb 21	[Duke]; A. Patti (Gil); G. Fabbri (Madd); G. Vaselli (Rig); A. Silvestri (Spar); A. Ponsini (Mont); L. Mancinelli cdr.
T. Real Concert	Nov 4	Centenary of *Don Giovanni*. 'Il mio tesoro'; Trio (w. G. Gargano & C. De Vere); Sextet (w. E. Tetrazzini, C. De Vere, G. Gargano, A. Baldelli, & A. Silvestri).
Madrid Royal Palace Concert	Before Feb 18	Programme unknown.

1888-9

Madrid: T. Real *La Gioconda*	Nov 10,11,17,24, Dec 8,Jan 2,4,9, Feb 23,Mar 30	[Enzo]; Elena Teodorini/M. Borelli (Gioc); Emma Leonardi/G. Fabbri (Laura); G. Fabbri/? (Cieca);[3] Delfino Menotti (Barn); Vincenzo Megia; L. Mancinelli cdr.
La Sonnambula	Nov 25,27,29, Dec 2,4,6,9,11	[Elvino]; Emma Nevada (Amina); A. Gazul; P. Garrido; F. Uétam/Giovanni Tanzini (Rodolfo); Pietro Urrutia cdr.
Il Barbiere di Siviglia	Dec 16, Mar 10,17	[Almaviva]; E. Nevada/G. Gargano (Ros); Vittorio Carpi (Fig); A. Baldeli (Bart); F. Uétam (Bas); L. Mancinelli cdr.
Mignon	Dec 29,31,Jan 5, 10,13,22,30 Feb 22,27,Mar 1	[Meister]; L. Frandin (Mignon); B. Lizárraga/Marie van Zandt (Fil); G. Fabbri (Fed); A. Baldelli (Laerte); G. Tanzini/F. Uétam (Lot); L. Mancinelli cdr.
L'Elisir d'Amore	Jan 23,Mar 25	[Nemorino]; G. Gargano (Adina); V. Carpi (Belcore); A. Baldelli (Dulcamara).
Semiramide	Feb 2,21, Mar 16,24	[Idreno]; M. Borelli (Semiramide); G. Fabbri (Arsace); V. Megía (Assur); G. Tanzini (Oroe); A. Ponsini; L. Mancinelli cdr.
Dinorah	Feb 7,10	[Correntino]; M. van Zandt (Din); B. Lizárraga (Capraia); G. Fabbri (Capraio); Scipione Terzi (Hoël); A. Ponsini (Cacc); Enrico Giannini (Miet); L. Mancinelli cdr.
I Promessi Sposi (Petrella)	Mar 21	[Renzo]; Bibiana Pérez; G. Fabbri; D. Menotti; G. Tanzini (Don Cristóforo); A. Baldelli; L. Mancinelli cdr.

1889

Buenos Aires: T. Politeama *La Gioconda*	May 2,5, 12 (part)	[Enzo]; E. Tetrazzini (Gioc); V. Fabbri (Laura); G. Fabbri (Cieca); R. Blanchart (Barn); Giulio Rossi (Alv); Cleofonte Campanini cdr.
Il Barbiere di Siviglia	May 7,24, Jun 22,Jul 22	[Almaviva] (after Alberto De Bassini); A. Patti (Ros); Arturo Marescalchi (Fig); Samuele Reggiani (Bart); Ettore Marcassa (Bas); Romualdo Sapio cdr.
Don Giovanni	May 14	[Ottavio]; Elvira Colomnese (Anna); Vera Domelli (Elv); A. Patti (Zer); R. Blanchart (Don); E. Marcassa (Lep); A. Conti cdr.
Mefistofele	May 21,Jul 4	[Faust]; E. Tetrazzini (Marg/Elena); G. Fabbri (Marta/Pantalis); G. Rossi (Mef); C. Campanini cdr.

---

3 The replacement Cieca is unidentified.

Venue	Opera	Dates	Cast / Notes
	Romeo e Giulietta (Gounod)	Jun 13,16,27, Jul 11,18	[Romeo]; A. Patti (Giul); G. Fabbri (Page); R. Blanchart (Mer); E. Marcassa; Vittorio Arimondi.
	La Sonnambula	Jul 2,9,20	[Elvino]; A. Patti (Amina); E. Marcassa (Rodolfo).
Montevideo: T. Cibils & T. Nuevo Politeama*	La Gioconda	Jul 25,28, Aug 13+,24*	[Enzo]; E. Tetrazzini (Gioc); V. Fabbri (Laura); G. Fabbri (Cieca); R. Blanchart (Barn); G. Rossi (Alv); R. Franzini (Zuane); Natale Cervi (Singer); Vincenzo Pozzi (Isèpo); C. Campanini cdr. (+ Acts of Mefistofele & La Gioconda).
	Mefistofele	Aug 1,4,13+	[Faust]; E. Tetrazzini (Marg/Elena); G. Fabbri (Marta/Pantalis); G. Rossi (Mef); Roberto Vanni (Wagner/Nereo); C. Campanini cdr (+ Acts of Mefistofele & La Gioconda)
	Romeo e Giulietta	Aug 10,15,22*	[Romeo]; E. Tetrazzini (Giul); G. Fabbri (Page); R. Blanchart (Mer); E. Marcassa; C. Campanini cdr.
	La Traviata	Aug 19	[Alfredo]; E. Colonnese (Viol); A. Marescalchi (Ger).[4]
Montevideo: Society La Lira	Concert		Programme unknown.

1890

Venue	Opera	Dates	Cast / Notes
Naples: T. San Carlo	I Pescatori di Perle	Jan 15,16,22, 28,29, Feb 1,2, 6,8,12,16,18, 20,27, Mar 2	[Nadir]; Emma Calvé/Fanny Toresella (Leila); S. Terzi/Leone Fumagalli (Zurga); Camillo Fiegna/Donato Rotoli (Nourabad); Alessandro Pomé cdr.
	Carmen	Mar 8,10,13,16, 20,23,26,29,31, Apr 6,8,10	[José]; Giulia Novelli (Carmen); F. Toresella (Mic); S. Terzi (Esc); D. Rotoli (Capitano); Enrichetta Guarnieri; Inès Patalano; Ruggero Buongiorno (Mor); Enrico Guarnieri; Antonio Rinaldini; A. Pomé/Antonio Siragusa cdr.
Naples: Filarmonica	Concert	Feb 7	Il Figliuol Prodigo (Ponchielli): 'Romanza'; I Pescatori di Perle: 'Della mia vita'.
Naples: Casino dell'Unione	Cristo all'Oliveto (Christus am Ölberge) (Beethoven)	Mar 24	[Christ]; F. Toresella (Seraphim); S. Terzi (St. Peter); Il Duca d'Alba: 'Romanza'; 'Voghiam!' (Tosti) V. Lombardi cdr.
Buenos Aires: T. de la Opera	Mefistofele	May 24,28, Jul 5	[Faust]; Adalgisa Gabbi (Marg/Elena); Irene Borlinetto (Marta/Pantalis); Paolo Wulman (Mef); Marino Mancinelli cdr.
T. Politeama*	La Gioconda	May 26,Jul 20*, Aug 10*	[Enzo] (after Emilio De Marchi); A. Gabbi (Gioc); Amelia Stahl; I. Borlinetto; G. Kaschmann (Barn); P. Wulmann (Alvise).
	La Favorita	May 30,Jun 14	[Fernando]; A. Stahl (Leon); G. Kaschmann (Alf); F. Navarrini (Bal); G. Paroli; M. Mancinelli cdr.

---

4 This advertised La Traviata has not been confirmed.

	Rigoletto	Jun 1,5,17	[Duke]; Zina Dalti (Gil); I. Borlinetto/A. Stahl (Madd); V. Maurel/G. Kaschmann (Rig); P. Wulman (Spar); M. Mancinelli cdr.
	Faust	Jul 26*	[Faust] (after E. De Marchi); E. Colonnese (Marg); I. Borlinetto; G. Kaschmann (Val); P. Wulman (Mef).5

1890-1

Naples: S. Giuseppe di Chiaia	Nuptial Mass	Dec 11	Ave Maria (Gounod), Carlo, Eduardo, & Vincenzo Lombardi (cello, harp, and harmonium.)
Naples: T. San Carlo	*La Gioconda*	Dec 17,20,21,25, 26,Jan 1,5,10, Feb 19,22, Mar 16,28	[Enzo]/Edgardo Bernardi-Zerni; Aurelia Cattaneo (Gioc); G. Novelli (Lau); Alice Cucini/Elvira Ceresoli (Cieca); Eugène Dufriche (Barn); G. Rossi (Alv); S. Terzi (Zuane/Singer); Borghi; V. Lombardi cdr.
	Cavalleria Rusticana	Jan 14,17,18,20, 24,28,30,Feb 2, 4,8,14,15,21,23, Mar 7,8,10,14, 19,24,30,Apr 1, 4,6,12,17	[Turiddu]/E. Bernardi-Zerni; E. Calvé (Santuzza); A. Cucini/Annetta Guli (Lola); I. Patalano (Lucia); E. Dufriche (Alfio); V. Lombardi cdr.
	Rigoletto	Feb 7,10	[Duke]; Carolina De Rossi-Trauner/A. Cattaneo) (Gil); G. Novelli/I. Patalano (Madd); V. Maurel (Rig); Giuseppe Di Grazia (Spar); I. Patalano/? (Countess Ceprano);6 V. Lombardi cdr.
	Carmen	Feb 28,Mar 1,3, 12,15,22,Apr 3, 5,8	[José]; G. Novelli (Carmen); Italia Del Torre (Mic); Salvatore Vinci/E. Dufriche (Esc); I. Patalano; E. Ceresoli; S. Terzi (Capitano); Vincenzo Morghen (Smugg); Oreste Bimboni/V. Lombardi cdr.
Hôtel West End (formerly Nobile)	Concert	Feb 6	In aid of Queen Margherita Orphanage: 'Sera' (Tosti); 'Scetate' (Costa); Fenesta che lucive' (G. Cottrau); Riccardo Barthélemy pf.
Sala Filarmonica	Concert	Mar 4	*Il Duca d'Alba*: 'Romanza'; *Faust*: Duet (w. A. Cattaneo); V. Lombardi cdr.
Casa Uda	Concert	prob. Mar 23	Programme unknown.
T. San Carlo	Concert	Apr 7	In aid of Assoc. Universitaria: *Cavalleria Rusticana* (w. E. Calvé, A. Cucini, E. Dufriche, I. Patalano).

1891

Rome: T. Costanzi	*I Pescatori di Perle*	May 5,7,9	[Nadir]; E. Calvé (Leila); G. Salassa (Zur); G. Di Grazia (Nur); L. Mugnone cdr.

5 This advertised *Faust* has not been confirmed.
6 The replacement Countess Ceprano is unidentified.

410

	rusticana	19*,21*,23*,24 Oct 31,Nov 1,3, 5,7,8,10,12, 14,15,17	(Lucia); L. Mugnone/P. Mascagni cdr (* w. *Pescatori* I; + w. *Pescatori* II).7
	L'Amico Fritz		[Fritz]; E. Calvé (Suzel); Ortensia Synnerberg (Beppe); Lina Parpagnoli (Caterina); Paul Lhérie (David); Giuseppe Cremona (Hanezò); Guglielmo Bessi (Federico); Rodolfo Ferrari cdr.
Florence: T. Pergola	*L'Amico Fritz*	Nov 28,29,30, Dec 1,3,5,6,8	[Fritz]; Hariclea Darclée (Suz); Ester Soarez (Bep); L. Parpagnoli (Cat); P. Lhérie (Dav); G. Cremona (Han); G. Bessi (Fed); R. Ferrari cdr.
T. Pagliano*	*Cavalleria Rusticana*	Dec 14,17, 19*20*	[Turiddu]/P. Garibaldi; Virginia Damerini (Sant); L. Parpagnoli (Lola); Radicchi (Lucia); Francesco Pozzi (Alf); R. Ferrari cdr.

1891-2

Madrid: T. Real	*La Sonnambula*	Dec 30,Jan 1,7, 11,27,Feb 3, Mar 2*	[Elvino]; Regina Pacini (Amina); F. Uétam (Rod); M. Pérez cdr. (* Act III, with *Cavalleria Rusticana*).
	Il Barbiere di Siviglia	Jan 6,14,17,24	[Almaviva]; R. Pacini (Ros); Antonio Cotogni (Fig); E. Borucchia; A. Baldelli (Bart); F. Uétam (Bas); M. Pérez cdr.
	Faust	Jan 20,31, Feb 28	[Faust]; E. Tetrazzini (Marg); Giuseppina Zeppini-Villani (Sieb); Antonio Scotti (Val); F. Uétam (Mef).
	I Pescatori di Perle	Feb 7	[Nadir]; R. Pacini (Leila); Ignazio Tabayo (Zur); L. Mancinelli cdr.
	L'Elisir d'Amore	Feb 10,14,21	[Nemorino]; R. Pacini (Adina); A. Scotti (Bel); A. Baldelli (Dul).
	Cavalleria Rusticana	Feb 17,18,24, Mar 2	[Turiddu]/E. De Marchi; E. Tetrazzini (Sant); A. Scotti (Alfio); G. Zeppini-Villani; P. Garrido (Lucia); L. Mancinelli cdr.
	La Favorita	Jan 13	[Fern] Gala in memory of Gayarre: Act I G. Pasqua (Leon); P. Garrido (Inez); E. Borucchia (Bal); L. Mancinelli cdr. (w. *I Puritani* II and *L'Africana* IV)

1892

London: Covent Garden & Drury Lane*	*Cavalleria Rusticana*	May 16,17,19, 26,Jun 1,6,18, 24,29*,Jul 6*, 12,18,21,23*	[Turiddu]; E. Calvé (Sant); Giulia Ravogli/Marie Brema (Lola); Mathilde Bauermeister (Luc); E. Dufriche (Alf); L. Mancinelli cdr.
	L'Amico Fritz	May 23,28, Jun 9,14, Jul 1,9,16*	[Fritz]; E. Calvé (Suz); G. Ravogli (Bep); M. Bauermeister (Cat); E. Dufriche (Dav); Iginio Corsi (Fed); Antonio De Vaschetti (Han); Enrico Bevignani cdr.
Windsor Castle	Concert	Jul 2	Excerpts from *L'Amico Fritz* & *Cavalleria Rusticana*, w. E. Calvé, F.P. Tosti pf.

---

7 Frajese, op. cit. states that the performance of May 24 was given with Act II *Pescatori*.

Venue	Opera	Dates	Cast
Vienna: Internationales Ausstellungs Theater	*L'Amico Fritz*	Sept 15,16, 22,28,30	[Fritz]; F. Toresella (Suz); Maria Zanon (Bep); Emilia Rossi (Cat); Luigi Fiesoli (Fed); Edoardo Sottolana (Dav); G. Cremona (Han); Pietro Mascagni cdr.
Rome: T. Nazionale	*L'Amico Fritz*	Oct 5,7,9,18	[Fritz]; F. Toresella (Suz); M. Zanon (Bep); E. Rossi (Cat); E. Sottolana (Dav); G. Cremona (Han); L. Fiesoli (Fed); R. Ferrari cdr.
Florence:	Concert	c. Nov 7	Associazione della Stampa Toscana: *Cavalleria Rusticana*: 'Siciliana'; *I Rantzau*: 'Romanza'; P. Mascagni, pf.
Florence: T. Pergola	*I Rantzau*	Nov 10,12,13, 15,17,19,20	[Giorgiol/Francesco Baldini; H. Darclée/F. Toresella] (Luisa); Anna Cecchini (Giulia); G. Paroli (Lebel); M. Battistini (Gianni); Luigi Broglio (Giacomo); E. Sottolana (Fiorenzo); R. Ferrari cdr.
Rome: T. Costanzi	*I Rantzau*	Nov 26,27,29, Dec 1,3,4,6,8	[Giorgiol; H. Darclée (Luisa); A. Cecchini (Giulia); M. Battistini (Gianni); L. Broglio (Giacomo); E. Sottolana (Fiorenzo); G. Paroli (Lebel); P. Mascagni cdr.

1892-3

Venue	Opera	Dates	Cast
Naples: T. San Carlo	*L'Amico Fritz*	Dec 17,18,20,22, 25,26,Jan 1,3, 28,Feb 16	[Fritz]/Federico Corrado; H. Darclée/Maria Stuarda Savelli (Suz); M. Zanon (Bep); Carlo Buti (David); Ninfa Molinari (Cat); Carlo Walter (Han); Dante Zucchi (Fed); R. Buongiorno; P. Mascagni/V. Lombardi cdr.
	Pagliacci	Jan 14,15,17, 19,Feb 7	[Caniol/Georg Ahrens/F. Corrado; M. Savelli (Nedda); Ottorino Beltrami (Tonio); C. Buti/Enrico Pignataro (Silvio); Raffaele De Rosa (Beppe); V. Lombardi cdr.
	La Favorita	Jan 22,27,29, Feb 1,2,4,9, 22,23	[Fernando]; Maria Judice Da Costa (Leonora); M. Battistini (Alfonso); G. Di Grazia (Balthazar); V. Lombardi cdr.
	Linda di Chamounix	Feb 11,12,14, 18,26	[Charles]; H. Darclée (Linda); M. Zanon (Pierrot) M. Battistini (Antonio); Giuseppe Frigiotti (Boisfleury); G. Di Grazia (Prefect); N. Molinari (Madeline); R. De Rosa (Sirval); D. Zucchi (L'Intend); V. Lombardi cdr.
	Crispino e la Comare	Feb 20	[Count Del Fiore]; H. Darclée (Annetta); M. Judice (Fairy); M. Battistini (Fabrizio); G. Di Grazia (Don Asdrubale); Luigi Colonnese (Mirabolano); G. Frigiotti (Crispino); R. De Rosa; V. Lombardi cdr.
	Lohengrin	Mar 1,4,5,7,9	[Lohengrin/Francisco Viñas; Avelina Carrera (Elsa); M. Judice/Irma Di Spagny (Ortruda); Antonio Magini-Coletti (Tel); G. Di Grazia (King Henry); Antonio Sabellico (Herald); V. Lombardi cdr.
	Carmen	Mar 12,14,19, 22,26, Apr 3,6,8,9, 26,30	[José/Vincenzo Maina/F. Corrado; M. Judice/Irma Monti-Baldini/E. Teodorini (Carmen); Adele Antinori (Mic); I. Patalano/Clotilde Verdi (Fras); N. Molinari (Merc); A. Magini-Coletti/E. Pignataro (Esc); V. Morghen (Dan); D. Zucchi (Remen); V. Morghen/R. Buongiorno (Mor); G. Di Grazia (Zuniga); V. Lombardi cdr.
	Il Profeta Velato	Apr 1,5	[Azim]; A. Carrera (Zelica); M. Zanon (Mirzala); A. Magini-Coletti (Abdar); G. Di Grazia (Mocanna); I. Di Spagny; V. Lombardi cdr.

Sala Tarsia Naples	Concert	Mar 3	'Ideale' (Tosti), *Cavalleria Rusticana*: 'Siciliana'.
T. San Carlo Naples: prob. Sala del Quartetto	Concert	Mar 8	Concert Luigi Colonnese: 'Sognai' (Tessarin); two unidentified romanzas; V. Lombardi pf.
Naples: Sala Romaniello	Concert	Apr 10	Concert V. Ferni-Germano: 'Serenata'; 'Lasciali dir'; 'Rosa' (all Tosti); *Mefistofele*: 'Lontano, lontano' (w. V. Ferni-Germano). Concert Beniamino Cesi: 'Sull'alba' (De Leva); 'Serenata', 'Bacio' (both Tosti).
Rome: Quirinale Palace	Court Concert	Apr 23	'Un bacio solo' (Marchetti); *Luisa Miller*: 'Quando le sere al placido'; *Cavalleria Rusticana*: 'Siciliana'; 'Ideale' (Tosti).
Naples: T. San Carlo	Gala	Apr 28	*Il Profeta Velato* I (w. I. Di Spagny, A. Magini-Coletti); *La Favorita* IV (w. E. Teodorini, G. Di Grazia) (w. *Lohengrin* III).

1893

Venue	Work	Date	Cast
London: Covent Garden	*Pagliacci*	May 19,23,31, Jun 9,13,16,22, Jul 10	[Canio/Gaetano? Morello; Nellie Melba (Ned); Mario Ancona (Ton); Richard Green (Sil); Claude Bonnard (Bep); L. Mancinelli cdr.
	I Pescatori di Perle	Jun 3	[Nadir]; E. Calvé (Leila); M. Ancona (Zur); A. De Vaschetti (Nour) (2 acts, with *Cavalleria Rusticana* (Viñas))
	Mefistofele	Jun 16	[Faust]; E. Calvé (Marg); Sofia Ravogli (Elena); Olimpia Guercia (Mart); G. Ravogli (Pant); Pol Plançon (Mef); A. Rinaldini (Wag/Ner); L. Mancinelli cdr.[8]
	L'Amico Fritz	Jun 19, Jul 11	[Fritz]/Viñas; E. Calvé (Suz); I. Corsi (Fed); M. Bauermeister (Cat); Pauline Joran (Beppe); E. Dufriche/M. Ancona (Dav); P. Mascagni cdr.
	Rigoletto	Jun 29	[Duke]; N. Melba (Gil); G. Ravogli (Madd); M. Bauermeister (Giov); Luigi Pignalosa (Rig); Armand Castelmary (Spar); Cernusco (Marul); A. De Vaschetti (Mont). I. Corsi (Borsa); A. Rinaldini (Cep); E. Bevignani cdr.
	I Rantzau	Jul 7	[Giorgio]; N. Melba (Luisa); I. Corsi (Lebel); M. Bauermeister (Giulia); M. Ancona (Gianni); David Bispham (Fiorenzo); A. Castelmary (Giacomo); P. Mascagni cdr.
St. James's Hall	Concert	Jun 22,29	Matinée: Programme unknown.

1893-4

Venue	Work	Date	Cast
New York: Metropolitan Opera House	*Pagliacci*	Dec 11,22, Jan 26,Apr 24	[Canio]; N. Melba (Ned); M. Ancona (Ton); Pedro Guetary (Beppe); Victor De Gromzeski (Sil); L. Mancinelli cdr.
	Cavalleria Rusticana	Dec 15	[Turiddu]; E. Calvé (Sant); O. Guercia (Lola); M. Bauermeister (Lucia); Jean Martapoura (Alf); E. Bevignani cdr.

8 Both *Pagliacci* and this *Mefistofele* and were advertised for June 16. Though no review of either has been traced they are included for completeness

Don Giovanni	Dec 27	[Ottavio]; Emmy Fursch-Madi (Anna); Kate Rolla (Elvira); S. Arnoldson (Zer); Jean Lassalle (Don); E. de Reszke (Lep); Agostino Carbone (Mas); A. De Vaschetti (Comm); L. Mancinelli cdr.
Rigoletto	Dec 29,Feb 12, Feb 15*	[Duke]; N. Melba (Gil); Sofia Scalchi (Madd); M. Bauermeister (Giov); M. Ancona/E. Dufriche (Rig); A. Castelmary (Spar); Lodovico Viviani (Marullo); A. De Vaschetti (Mont); A. Rinaldini (Borsa); Cernusco (Ceprano); E. Bevignani cdr. (* Act IV only.)
Faust	Jan 6	[Faust]; L. Nordica (Mar); S. Scalchi (Siebel); M. Bauermeister (Marta); J. Martapoura (Val); P. Plançon (Mef); E. Bevignani cdr.
L'Amico Fritz	Jan 10,20*	[Fritz]; E. Calvé (Suz); S. Scalchi (Bep); M. Bauermeister (Cat); M. Ancona (Dav); A. De Vaschetti (Han); Stanislao Mastrobuono (Fed); E. Bevignani cdr. (* Act II only)
Il Barbiere di Siviglia	Feb 15 (Act II)	[Almaviva]; S. Arnoldson (Ros); M. Bauermeister (Bert); M. Ancona (Fig); A. Carbone (Bart); E. de Reszke (Bas); S. Mastrobuono (Official); L. Mancinelli cdr.
Carmen	Feb 3,10,19, 22,24, Apr 17,27*	[José]; E. Calvé (Car); S. Arnoldson/E. Eames/Anna Maria Pettigiani (Mic); Grete Risley/M. Bauermeister (Fras); Anita Ibles (Merc); M. Ancona/J. Lassalle (Esc); V. De Gromzeski (Morales); A. Carbone (Dan); A. Rinaldini (Remend); L. Viviani (Zun); L. Mancinelli/E. Bevignani cdr. (*Act II only).9
La Traviata	Feb 9 (Acts I,IV)	[Alfredo]; L. Nordica (Viol); M. Bauermeister (Annina); A. Ibles (Flora); E. Dufriche (Ger); S. Mastrobuono (Gast); L. Viviani (Douphol); A. Rinaldini (D'Obigny); A. De Vaschetti (Grenvil); E. Bevignani cdr. (Benefit concert).
Metropolitan Opera House — Concert	Dec 17	*Don Giovanni*: 'Il mio tesoro'; *Rigoletto*: 'La donna è mobile'.
New York: Carnegie Hall — Concert	Jan 7	*Rigoletto*: 'Quartet' (w. E. Calvé, Consuelo Domenech, M. Ancona).
Concert	Jan 14	*La Gioconda*: 'Air'; Unidentified romanza (Tosti).
Concert	Apr 23	*Cavalleria Rusticana*: 'Siciliana'; *Rigoletto*: 'La donna è mobile'.
Brooklyn: Academy of Music — *Faust*	Dec 30	[Faust]; E. Eames (Mar); S. Scalchi (Sieb); M. Bauermeister (Martha); J. Martapoura (Val); P. Plançon (Mef); A. De Vaschetti (Wag); E. Bevignani cdr.
Carmen	Jan 16,Feb 17, Apr 21	[José]; Jan 16, Apr 21: as for Philadelphia, Jan 2. Feb 17: A.M. Pettigiani sub. S. Arnoldson.
Pagliacci	Jan 30	[Canio]; Rita Elandi (Ned); E. Dufriche (Ton); V. De Gromzeski (Sil); E. Bevignani cdr.
Philadelphia: Academy of Music — *Pagliacci*	Dec 19	[Canio]; Marie Tavary (Ned); M. Ancona (Ton); P. Guetary (Bep); V. De Gromzeski (Sil); L. Mancinelli cdr.
Carmen	Jan 2,18	[José]; E. Calvé (Car); S. Arnoldson (Mic); M. Bauermeister (Fras); A. Ibles (Merc); L. Viviani (Zun); M. Ancona (Esc); V. De Gromzeski (Morales); A. Carbone (Dan); A. Rinaldini (Remend); E. Bevignani cdr.

...); M. Bauermeister (Madd?), M. Bauermeister (Giov?), A. Idles (Countess Ceprano); M. Ancona (Rig); A. Castelmary (Spar); A. De Vaschetti (Mont); L. Viviani (Mar); A. Rinaldini (Borsa); Cermusco (Ceprano); E. Bevignani cdr. (w. *Hamlet* IV)

Boston: Mechanics' Institute Auditorium	*Carmen*	Feb 27	[José]; As for Philadelphia, Jan 2, except A.M. Pettigiani sub. S. Arnoldson;
		Mar 8	As for Philadelphia, Jan 2, except S. Arnoldson sub. E. Calvé; A.M. Pettigiani sub. S. Arnoldson.
	Pagliacci	Mar 10	As for Philadelphia, Jan 2, except J. Lassalle sub. M. Ancona.
	Mignon	Mar 2	[Canio]; As for Philadelphia, Dec 19, except S. Arnoldson sub. M. Tavary.
		Mar 6	[Meister]; E. Calvé (Mig); L. Nordica (Fil); S. Scalchi (Fed); A. Carbone (Laerte); P. Plançon (Lot); A. De Vaschetti (Giarno); Cermusco (Antonio); E. Bevignani cdr.
Chicago: Auditorium	*Carmen*	Mar 13	[José]; As for Philadelphia, Jan 2, except A.M. Pettigiani sub. S. Arnoldson.
		Mar 17,Apr 7	As for Philadelphia, Jan 2.
	Mignon	Mar 23	[Meister]; As for Boston, Mar 6, except S. Arnoldson sub. E. Calvé.
	Rigoletto	Mar 27	[Duke]; As for Philadelphia, Jan 9, except E. Dufriche sub. M. Ancona.
	Pagliacci	Mar 28	[Canio]; As for Philadelphia, Dec 19, except S. Arnoldson sub. M. Tavary.
St. Louis:	*Carmen*	Apr 3	[José]; As for Philadelphia, Jan 2, except A.M. Pettigiani sub. S. Arnoldson.
		Apr 10	[José]; As for Apr 10, except J. Martapoura sub. M. Ancona.
		Apr 14	[Canio]; As for Metropolitan, Dec 19, except S. Arnoldson sub. N. Melba.
	Pagliacci	Apr 12	On board steamship *La Touraine*: *Cavalleria Rusticana*: 'Siciliana'.
At sea:	*Concert*	May 4	[Turiddu/G.? Morello/Joseph O'Mara; E. Calvé (Sant); P. Joran/G. Ravogli (Lola); M. Bauermeister (Lucia); M. Ancona/E. Dufriche/G. Maggi (Alfio); L. Mancinelli/E. Bevignani cdr.
London: Covent Garden	*Cavalleria Rusticana*	May 16,22, Jun 22, Jul 11	[Canio/Philip Brozel; S. Arnoldson/Lucille Hill/N. Melba(Ned); M. Ancona (Ton); R. Green (Sil); C. Bonnard/I. Corsi (Bep); L. Mancinelli/E. Bevignani cdr.
	Pagliacci	May 17,26,30, Jun 4,12, Jul 6,21	[Faust]/Emile Cossira/Albert Alvarez/Jean de Reszke; Zina de Nuovina/N. Melba (Marg); G. Ravogli (Siebel); M. Bauermeister (Marta); M. Ancona (Val); P. Plançon (Mef); A. De Vaschetti; Giovanni? Villani (Wag); E. Bevignani cdr.
	Faust	May 25, Jun 2,6	[Duke]; N. Melba (Gil); G. Ravogli (Madd); M. Bauermeister (Giov); M. Ancona/E. Dufriche (Rig); A. Castelmary (Spar); A. De Vaschetti (Mont); A. Rinaldini (Mar); I. Corsi (Borsa); G.? Villani (Cep); E. Bevignani cdr.
	Rigoletto	Jun 9,21,24*	(* Commencing Act II, with *Signa* (Cowen)).
London Queen's Hall	*Concert*	Jul 7	Extracts from *Cavalleria Rusticana*, w. E. Calvé, P. Joran, M. Bauermeister, R. Green, E. Bevignani cdr.

Venue	Work	Date(s)	Cast
Windsor Castle	Faust	May 19	[Faust]; Emma Albani (Marg); P. Joran (Siebel); M. Bauermeister (Marta); M. Ancona (Val); Giovanni? Villani (Wag); P. Plançon (Mef); E. Bevignani cdr.
London Grafton Galleries	Concert	Jul 12	Marta: Duet (w. P. Plançon); Romeo e Giulietta: 'Romanza'; 'Sogno' ('Tosti); Rigoletto: 'Quartet' (w. N. Melba, S. Scalchi, & M. Ancona); Waddington Cooke pf.
Cava de' Tirreni: Villa De Lucia	Concert	Oct 22	In honour of Nunzio Cosentino: 'Ammore è tuosseco' (Cosentino).

1894-5

Venue	Work	Date(s)	Cast
Madrid: T. Real	Carmen	Dec 26,29, Mar 2	[José]; E. Leonardi (Car); Elena (or Luisa) Fons (Mic); G. Mario Sammarco (Esc); A. Gazul (Fras); P. Garrido (Merc); Carlo Ragni (Dan); Julian Oliver I (Reden); M. Verdaguer; L. Mugnone cdr.
	Mefistofele	Jan 6,10,13, Feb 7,10,12,16	[Faust]; E. Tetrazzini-Campanini (Marg/Elena); Cloe Marchesini (Marta/Pantalis); F. Navarrini (Mef); Maurizio Bensaude; L. Mugnone cdr.
	La Gioconda	Jan 26,Feb 21, Mar 14	[Enzo] (after Giuseppe Borgatti); E. Tetrazzini-Campanini (Gioc); E. Leonardi (Lau); C. Marchesini (Cieca); D. Menotti (Barn); Giovanni Scarneo; M. Verdaguer; C. Campanini cdr.
	Cavalleria Rusticana	Jan 22*,24+, Feb 17@,20#	[Turiddu]/G. Apostolu; E. Calvé/E. Tetrazzini-Campanini (Sant); C. Marchesini (Lola); M. Sammarco (Alf); L. Mugnone cdr. (* w. Otello; + w. Manon Lescaut I & II; @ w. Faust III & IV; # w. Faust II & IV).
	Manon	Feb 23,24,27, Mar 5	[Des Grieux]; E. Tetrazzini-Campanini (Man); C. Marchesini; Emma Cisterna; A. Gazul; P. Garrido; D. Menotti (Les); M. Sammarco (Brétigny); M. Verdaguer; J. Oliver I; V. Megìa; L. Mugnone cdr.

1895

Venue	Work	Date(s)	Cast
Milan: T. alla Scala	Silvano	Mar 25,27,30,31, Apr 2,4,6,7	[Silvano]; Adelina Stehle (Matilde); Giuseppe Pacini (Renzo); Nilde Ponzano (Rosa); R. Ferrari cdr.
Naples: T. San Carlo	Silvano	Apr 30,May 1	[Silvano]; Giuseppina Falconis Della Perla (Matilde); Gina Neviani (Rosa); G. Pacini (Renzo); P. Mascagni cdr.
	Cavalleria Rusticana	May 4,6	[Turiddu]; L. Frandin (Sant); G. Neviani/Stefania Colamarini (Lola); E. Dufriche (Alfio); V. Lombardi cdr.
London: Covent Garden	Mefistofele	May 14	[Faust]; Margaret Macintyre (Marg/Elena); P. Plançon (Mef); L. Mancinelli cdr.
	Pagliacci	May 16,21	[Canio]/P. Brozel; Fanny Moody/M. Macintyre (Nedda); M. Ancona/Antonio Pini-Corsi (Ton); Jacques Bars (Sil); C. Bonnard (Bep); Armando Seppilli cdr.
	Fra Diavolo	May 20, Jun 4,14	[Fra Diavolo]; Marie Engle (Zer); D. Bispham (Cockburn); Amadi (Pamela),[10] J. O'Mara (Lor); A. Pini-Corsi (Bep); V. Arimondi (Giac); A. De Vaschetti (Mat); E. Bevignani cdr.

Date	Opera	Cast
Jun 10		(M. Ford); G. Ravogli (M. Quickly); Arturo Pessina/V. Maurel (Falstaff); A. Pini-Corsi (Ford); V. Arimondi (Pistol); I. Corsi (Caius); Pelagalli-Rossetti (Bard); L. Mancinelli cdr.
May 24	Carmen	[José]/A. Alvarez/C. Bonnard/F. Viñas; Z. de Lussan/E. Calvé/G. Bellincioni (Car); M. Engle/N. Melba/Florence Monteith (Mic); M. Ancona (Esc); E. Bevignani cdr.
Jun 1	Rigoletto	[Duke]; N. Melba (Gil); G. Ravogli (Madd); M. Bauermeister (Giov); M. Ancona (Rig); A. Castelmary (Spar); V. Arimondi (Mont); A. De Vaschetti (Cep); I. Corsi (Borsa);11 E. Bevignani cdr.
Jun 11,15	La Traviata	[Alfredo]/G. Mauguière; A. Patti/Marcella Sembrich (Viol); M. Bauermeister (Annina); Cecile Brani (Flora); M. Ancona/A. Pessina (Ger); J. Bars (Douph); I. Corsi (Gast); Charles Gilibert (Grenvil); L. Mancinelli cdr.
Montevideo: T. Nuevo Politeama		
Jul 16,18, Sept 7	Mefistofele	[Faust]; Elisa Petri (Marg/Elena); Saffo Bellincioni-Frigiotti (Mart/Pant); Gaetano Mazzanti (Wagner/Nereo); Angelo Tamburlini (Mef); Bassano; A. Conti cdr.
Jul 23,27, Aug 3	La Gioconda	[Enzo]; E. Petri (Gioc); I. Borlinetto-Conti (Lau); S. Bellincioni-Frigiotti (Cieca); G. Pacini (Barn); Joaquin Wanrell (Alv); Felice Foglia; A. Conti cdr.
Aug 1,10,15, Sept 9#	Rigoletto	[Duke]; Inès De Frate (Gil); S. Bellincioni-Frigiotti (Madd); Massimo Scaramella (Rig); J. Wanrell (Spar); Francesco Spangher; A. Conti cdr. (# One act only in De Lucia benefit.)
Aug 8,13	Cavalleria Rusticana	[Turiddu]; E. Petri (Sant); I. Borlinetto-Conti (Lola); Emma Crippa (Lucia); M. Scaramella (Alf); A. Conti cdr. (Given with extracts from other operas.)
Aug 18,27	Faust	[Faust]; E. Petri (Marg); Londina Orlati (Sieb); E. Crippa (Mart); G. Pacini (Val); F. Foglia (Wag); A. Tamburlini (Mef); A. Conti cdr.
Aug 25,30, Sept 1,6,9#	Manon	[Des Grieux]; E. Petri (Man); Osanna Quarenghi; Mary Melsa (Javotte); L. Orlati; G. Pacini (Les); F. Spangher (De Brétigny); J. Wanrell (Count); Michele Olivieri (Mortfontaine); A. Conti cdr. (# Sept 9 De Lucia benefit, with three acts Manon, one act Rigoletto.)
Buenos Aires: Aug 16	Concert	Presidential Musical Soirée: Programme unknown.
T. Politeama Sept 12, Oct 14*#	La Gioconda	[Enzo]; E. Petri (Gioc); I. Borlinetto-Conti (Lau); S. Bellincioni-Frigiotti (Cieca); G. Pacini (Barn); J. Wanrell (Alv); (# Act III only, with Il Barbiere di Siviglia.)
T. San Martin * Sept 17,20	Rigoletto	[Duke]; I. De Frate (Gilda); S. Bellincioni-Frigiotti (Madd); M. Scaramella (Rig).
T. Nacional + Sept 24	Mefistofele	[Faust]; E. Petri (Marg/Elena); S. Bellincioni-Frigiotti (Marta/Pantalis); A. Tamburlini (Mef).

---

11 Some sources ascribe the rôles of Monterone to Gilibert and Ceprano to Pelagalli-Rossetti.

Location	Opera	Date	Cast / Notes
	Manon	Sept 27,29, Oct 3,5+,17+ Oct 11+,14*	[Des Grieux]; E. Petri (Manon); M. Melsa (Javotte); G. Pacini (Les); J. Wanrell (Count).
	Il Barbiere di Siviglia		[Almaviva]; Luisa Tetrazzini (Ros); G. Pacini (Fig); Agostino Lanzoni (Bas); Pietro Cesari (Bart) (On both occasions *Il Barbiere* was presented complete, accompanied by scenes from other operas.)
Palermo (Arg.): Quinta Varela	*Cavalleria Rusticana*	Oct 9+	[Turiddu]; Inès De Frate (Sant); I. Borlinetto-Conti (Lola); M. Scaramella (Alfio); (with extracts from other operas.)
Buenos Aires: T. San Martin	Concert	Oct 13	Benefit of San Francisco nuns: Unidentified romanza.
	Concert	Oct 16	Benefit Circulo de Cronistas: *Cavalleria Rusticana*: 'Siciliana'.

1895-6

Location	Opera	Date	Cast / Notes
St. Petersburg: T. Aquarium	*La Gioconda*	Dec 9,25	[Enzo]; A. Gabbi (Gioc); A. Stahl (Lau); Clelia Cappelli (Cieca); M. Battistini (Barnaba); G. Rossi (Alv); Vittorio Podesti cdr.
	La Sonnambula	Dec 11,16	[Elvino]; R. Pacini (Amina); G. Rossi (Rodolfo).
	Il Barbiere di Siviglia	Dec 15, Jan 3,12	[Almaviva]; M. Sembrich/R. Pacini (Ros); C. Cappelli (Berta); M. Battistini (Fig); A. Silvestri (Bart); G. Rossi (Basilio); V. Podesti cdr.
	Rigoletto	Dec 18,27	[Duke]; M. Sembrich (Gil); A. Stahl (Maddalena); M. Battistini (Rig); G. Rossi (Spar); A. Silvestri; V. Podesti cdr.
	Faust	Dec 21, Jan 4	[Faust]; M. Sembrich (Marg); A. Stahl (Sieb); Théa Doré (Marta); M. Battistini (Val); G. Rossi (Mef); V. Podesti cdr.
	Mignon	Jan 1,7	[Meister]; M. Sembrich (Mig); Giulia Biondelli (Fil); A. Stahl (Fed); A. Silvestri (Lot); R. Dolcibene (Laerte); G. Rossi (Giarno); V. Podesti cdr.

(Russian dates are new style.)

1896

Location	Opera	Date	Cast / Notes
Milan: T. alla Scala	*La Navarrese*	Feb 6	[Araquil]; L. Frandin (Anita); G. Roveri (Garrido); Michele Wigley (Remigio); G. Giordani (Ramon); E. Broggi-Muttini (Bustamente); R. Ferrari cdr.
Naples: T. San Carlo	*La Bohème*	Mar 14,15,18, 21,24,28, Apr 4,7,12, 13,15	[Rodolfo]; E. Petri (Mim); Lina Pasini-Vitale (Mus); A. Magini-Coletti (Marc); Luigi Lucenti (Coll); Michele de Padova (Schaun); Dante Bolis (Benoit); Narciso Serra (Alcin.); Bux (Parp); Giovanni Alberti (Sergeant of Customs); Vittorio Vanzo cdr.
Naples: Sala Ricordi		Mar 16	Luncheon for Giacomo Puccini: Three unidentified romanzas (Tosti), V. Vanzo, pf.
London:	*Cavalleria*	May 12,21	[Turiddu/Giuseppe Cremonini; M. Macintyre/D'Alma (Sant); Fernanda Brazzi

Opera	Dates	Cast
Rigoletto	Jun 1,17 May 18	J. Bars/R. Green (Sil); B. Piroia (Bep); E. Bevignani/A. Seppili cdr. [Duke]/G. Cremonini); E. Albani/N. Melba) (Gil); Eugenia Mantelli (Madd); C. Brani (Countess Cep); M. Bauermeister (Giov); M. Ancona (Rig); V. Arimondi (Spar); I. Corsi (Bor); A. Rinaldini (Mar); A. De Vaschetti (Mont); Cernusco (Cep); E. Bevignani cdr.
Fra Diavolo	May 20,26	[Fra Diavolo]; M. Engle (Zer); P. Joran (Pamela); D. Bispham (Cockburn); A. De Vaschetti (Mat); A. Pini-Corsi (Bep); V. Arimondi (Giacomo); B. Piroia/J. O'Mara (Lor); E. Bevignani cdr.
La Traviata	Jun 8	[Alfredo]; E. Albani (Viol); C. Brani (Flora); M. Bauermeister (Annina); A. De Vaschetti (Douphol); M. Ancona (Ger); I. Corsi (Gast); C. Gilibert (Grenvil); E. Bevignani cdr.
Mefistofele	May 23	[Faust]; M. Macintyre (Marg); E. Mantelli (Mart/Pant); P. Plançon (Mef); I. Corsi (Wag/Ner); L. Mancinelli cdr.[12]

1896-7

St. Petersburg: Imperial Conservatoire

Opera	Dates	Cast
La Traviata	Jan 9	[Alfredo] (after Augusto Brogi)/A. Masini; M. Sembrich (Viol); M. Battistini (Ger); V. Podesti cdr.
Rigoletto	Jan 14	[Duke]/A. Masini; M. Sembrich (Gil); Anatilde Carotini (Madd); M. Battistini (Rig); G. Rossi (Spar); V. Podesti cdr.
Romeo e Giulietta	Jan 18	[Romeo]; M. Sembrich (Giul); G. Rossi (Lot); A. Silvestri (Capulet); Vittorio Brombara (Mercutio).

(Russian dates are new style.)

1897

Naples: T. San Carlo

Cavalleria Rusticana	Feb 10,14,17,23	[Turiddu]/Franco Pandolfini/Pietro Ferrari; Ada Giachetti-Botti (Sant); Livia Berlendi (Lola); Teresa De Simone (Lucia); A. Pini-Corsi/Vittorio? Ferraguti (Alfio); A. Conti cdr.
Carmen	Feb 27,Mar 1,4	[José]/F. Pandolfini; Virginia Guerrini (Car); G. Biondelli (Mic); L. Berlendi (Merc); Anna Carigiet (Fras); A. Pini-Corsi (Esc); Roberto Casini (Dan); G. Mazzanti (Remend); N. Serra (Zun); Giuseppe Bergamaschi (Morales); A. Conti cdr.

Milan: T. alla Scala

La Bohème	Mar 15,17,19,21, 23,25,27,28,30, Apr 1,3,5,7,9, 11,13	[Rodolfo]; Angelica Pandolfini/Emilia Merolla (Mimi); Camilla Pasini (Mus); Edoardo Camera (Mar); Ruggiero Galli (Schaun); Gennaro Berenzone/A. Polonini (Coll); Arcangelo Rossi (Ben); A. Polonini/? (Alcin);[13] L. Mugnone cdr.

Buenos Aires: T. de la Opera

Opera	Dates	Cast
La Gioconda	May 11,25, Jul 22	[Enzo]; Carmen Bonaplata-Bau (Gioc); L. Berlendi (Laura); V. Guerrini (Cieca); M. Sammarco (Barn); G. Rossi (Alv); Edoardo Mascheroni cdr.

12 This advertised *Mefistofele* has not been confirmed.
13 The replacement Alcindoro has not been identified.

La Bohème	May 15,18,20, 23,Jun 29, Aug 7	[Rodolfo]; Cesira Ferrani (Mimì); F. Toresella (Mus); M. Sammarco (Mar); Amilcare Monchero (Coll); Giuseppe Tisci-Rubini (Schaun); A. Rossi (Ben. & Alcin.); E. Mascheroni cdr.
Rigoletto	May 29,Jun 1, Jul 6,25, Aug 12*	[Duke]; F. Toresella (Gil); L. Berlendi (Madd); M. Sammarco (Rig); G. Tisci-Rubini (Spar); E. Mascheroni cdr. (* Act III only.)
Manon	Jun 8,12,15, 19,Jul 9	[Des Grieux]; C. Ferrani (Man); M. Sammarco (Les); G. Tisci-Rubini.
Mefistofele	Jun 24,26, Jul 11	[Faust]; C. Ferrani (Marg/Elena); L. Berlendi (Marta/Pantalis); D. Zucchi (Wagner); G. Rossi (Mef); E. Mascheroni cdr.
Werther	Jul 17,20, Aug 5,14	[Werther]; C. Ferrani (Carl); L. Berlendi (Sofia); M. Sammarco (Alb); A. Rossi (Pod); Camillo Tanci; A. Monchero (Joh); D. Zucchi (Schmidt); A. Gazul (Bühlmann); B. Zani (Käthchen); E. Mascheroni cdr.
Cavalleria Rusticana	Aug 12	[Turiddu]; C. Bonaplata-Bau (Sant); L. Berlendi (Lola); A. Gazul (Lucia); M. Sammarco (Alfio); E. Mascheroni cdr. (Given with extracts from other operas.)
Concert		'Sola sola'.14

Location unknown
Montevideo:
T. Solis

La Gioconda	Aug 11 Aug 19, Sept 9	[Enzo]; C. Bonaplata-Bau (Gioc); L. Berlendi (Lau); V. Guerrini (Cieca); M. Sammarco (Barn); G. Tisci-Rubini (Alv); E. Mascheroni cdr.
La Bohème	Aug 22, Sept 4	[Rodolfo]; C. Ferrani (Mimì); F. Toresella (Mus); M. Sammarco (Mar); A. Rossi (Ben. & Alc.); C. Tanci (Parp); A. Monchero (Coll); G. Tisci-Rubini (Schaun); Rocco Francini (Sergeant of Customs).15 E. Mascheroni cdr.
Werther	Aug 28	[Werther]; C. Ferrani (Carl); L. Berlendi (Sof); M. Sammarco (Alb); A. Rossi (Pod).
Manon	Aug 31	[Des Grieux]; C. Ferrani (Man); A. Gazul; M. Sammarco; A. Monchero; A. Rossi; G. Tisci-Rubini; E. Mascheroni cdr.
Mefistofele	Sept 2	[Faust]; C. Ferrani (Marg/Elena); L. Berlendi (Marta/Pantalis); G. Rossi (Mef); E. Mascheroni cdr.
Rigoletto	Sept 7	[Duke]; F. Toresella (Gil); M. Sammarco (Rig).

1897-8

Naples:
T. San Carlo

La Bohème	Dec 26,28,30, Jan 13,17,22, 27,Feb 5,10, 13,16,Mar 29, Apr 5	[Rodolfo/Evan Gorga/Quadri/Ernesto Colli; A. Pandolfini/Amelia Karola/ Lina Montuschi (Mimì); Maria Passeri (Mus); Mario Roussel/E. Sottolana (Mar); Leopoldo Cromberg (Coll); Michelangelo Rossini (Schaun); N. Serra (Ben. & Alcin.); Ferdinando Califano (Parp); Edoardo Vitale/Gaetano Scognamiglio cdr.

14 Almost certainly by Daniele Napoletano, to words by Rocco E. Pagliara (see p. 247).

Venue	Work	Dates	Details
Naples: T. San Carlo	*La Traviata*	Feb 20,22,26, Mar 1,6,11,14, 25,Apr 9,11	[Alfredo]; A. Pandolfini/M. Passeri (Viol); Adele Loporto (Flora); Rosina Bonafous (Annina); Eugenio Giraldoni/M. Rossini (Ger); Alfredo Font (Letorières); Ugo Ciabò (Douphol); Giacomo Giannelli (D'Obigny); L. Cromberg (Grenvil); E. Vitale cdr.
Naples: T. Bellini	Concert	Feb 7	*Mattinata*: Programme unknown.
Naples: T. San Carlo	Concert	Mar 3	Concert Colonnese: 'Sognai' (Tessarin).
1898			
Rome: T. Costanzi	*Iris*	Nov 22,24,26, 29,Dec 1,4,7, 10,13*,15*	[Osaka]; H. Darclée (Iris); Tilde Milanesi (Guècha); Fausta Labia; Guglielmo Caruson (Kyoto); G. Tisci-Rubini (Cieco); Eugenio Grossi (Merciaiulo); Piero Schiavazzi (Cenciaiuolo)16; P. Mascagni cdr. (*w. *L'Amico Fritz*: Cherry Duet (De Lucia and Darclée.))
Rome: Circolo Artistico	Concert	Dec 9	*Iris*: 'Serenata'; *Cavalleria Rusticana*: 'Siciliana'.
Rome: Grand Hôtel		Dec 16	*L'Amico Fritz*: Cherry Duet (w. H. Darclée); three unidentified romanzas.
1899			
Milan: T. alla Scala	*Iris*	Jan 19,21,24, 26,29,31, Feb 2,5,12,14,	[Osaka]; H. Darclée (Iris); Cesira Pagnoni (Guècha); Carlo Buti (Kyoto); G. Tisci-Rubini (Cieco); Celso Bertacchini (Merciaiuolo); Riccardo Sillingardi (Cenciaiuolo); Arturo Toscanini cdr.
Lisbon: T. Sao Carlos	*Cavalleria Rusticana*	Feb 23,25, Mar 1	[Turiddu]; E. Tetrazzini-Campanini (Sant); L. Berlendi (Lola); Lina Garavaglia (Lucia); Giovanni Polese (Alf); C. Campanini cdr. (w. acts of other operas.)
	La Bohème	Mar 3,6,8	[Rodolfo] (after Fiorello Giraud); M. Savelli (Mimi); Maria Martelli (Mus); G. Polese (Mar); G. Di Grazia; Luis Muñoz Degrain (Schaun); A. Rossi (buffo); L. Fiesoli (comp. ten); Emanuele Candella (comp. bs.); C. Campanini cdr. (Mar 8 De Lucia *festa*, opera given with *Iris*: Serenade; 'A suon di baci' (A. Baldelli); *Rigoletto*: 'La donna è mobile'.)
	Mefistofele	Feb 28*	[Faust]; C. Bonaplata-Bau (Marg/Elena); L. Berlendi (Marta/Pantalis); G. Di Grazia (Mef); C. Ragni (Wagner?); C. Campanini cdr. (* Prologue & Act II.)
	Concert	Mar 17,18	Benefit Missoes Ultramarinas: *Mefistofele*: Epilogue; *Rigoletto*: 'La donna è mobile'; 'Ideale' (Tosti); 'A suon di baci' (Baldelli); & an unidentified Neapolitan song.
	Concert	Mar 20	
London: Covent Garden	*Pagliacci*	May 9,17, Jul 8	[Canio]; Thevenet/Suzanne Adams/Febea Strakosch/McDonald (Ned); M. Ancona (Ton); Maurice Cazeneuve (Bep); J. Bars (Sil); L. Mancinelli cdr.

16 Often Pietro.

Venue	Work	Date(s)	Cast / Notes
	Rigoletto	Jun 12, Jul 22	[Duke]; N. Melba/S. Adams (Gil); Louise Homer/G. Ravogli (Madd); M. Bauermeister (Giov); Maud Roudez (Countess); A. Scotti/M. Ancona (Rig); Marcel Journet (Spar); C. Gilibert (Mont); Thomas Meux (Mar); Roberto or Carlo Vanni (Borsa); Cernusco (Cep); L. Mancinelli cdr.
	La Bohème	Jul 1,7,12,20	[Rodolfo]; N. Melba (Mimì); Z. de Lussan (Mus); M. Ancona (Mar); C. Gilibert (Schaun); M. Journet (Coll); E. Dufriche (Ben. & Alcin.); M. Cazeneuve (Ton); M. Cazeneuve (Parp) L. Mancinelli cdr.
Windsor Castle	*Pagliacci*	Jul 4	[Canio]; S. Adams (Ned); M. Ancona (Ton); M. Cazeneuve (Bep); J. Bars (Sil); L. Mancinelli cdr. (w. *Le Chalet* (Adam))
Buckingham Palace Residence of George Ogilvie Haig, 65, Brook St.	Concert	Jun 30 Jul 19	State Concert: *Il Barbiere di Siviglia*: 'Ecco ridente'. 'Ancora' (Tosti); *Romeo e Giulietta*: Duet (w. E. Nevada); *Mignon*: 'Addio, Mignon';
Cava de' Tirreni: S. Maria dell'Olmo		Jul 28	F.A. Sewell, pf. Programme unknown.
Cava de' Tirreni: Cathedral		Sept 11	'Pietà, Signore' (Niedermeyer).

1899-1900

Venue	Work	Date(s)	Cast / Notes
Rome: T. Costanzi	*Werther*	Dec 30, Jan 1, 4,6,12	[Werther]; M. Savelli (Carl); Clara Rommel (Sof); C. Verdi (Prüfmann); Tina Cozzolino (Käthchen); Enrico Moreo (Alb); Ettore Borelli (Pod); Ettore Trucchi-Dorini (Schmidt); Giuseppe Gironi (Johann); L. Mugnone cdr.

1900

Venue	Work	Date(s)	Cast / Notes
Lisbon: T. Sao Carlos	*Rigoletto*	Feb 8,10,23	[Duke]/Fiorenzo Constantini;17 Amalia De Roma (Gil); Luiza Longhi (Madd); M. Sammarco (Rig); Oreste Carozzi (Spar); Oswaldo de Gennaro (comp. ten); N. Cervi (comp. bs.); E. Candella (comp. bs); Lorenzana; Emanuele Isquierdo; Annita.
	Fedora	Feb 13,15,17,19	[Loris]/Edoardo Garbin; G. Bellincioni/A. Stehle (Fed); M. Martelli (Olga); E. Isquierdo (groom); Giuseppe De Luca (De Siriex); A. Rossi (Cirillo); O. Carozzi; Andrea Perellò De Segurola; Oswaldo de Gennaro (Desiré & Rouvel); N. Cervi; L. Fiesoli; E. Candella; Lorenzana; A. Conti/Romualdo Moro cdr.
	La Traviata	Mar 1	[Alfredo]; G. Bellincioni (Viol); M. Sammarco (Ger); L. Longhi; Oswaldo de Gennaro; N. Cervi; E. Candella; Lorenzana.
	La Bohème	Mar 4	[Rod] (after A. Bonci); C. Ferrani (Mimì); M. Martelli (Mus); G. De Luca (Mar); N. Cervi (comp. bs); O. Carozzi; A. Rossi (buffo); L. Fiesoli (comp. ten); E. Candella (comp. bs).
	Pagliacci	Mar 6	[Canio] (after A. Garulli); Lina Cavalieri (Ned); M. Sammarco/G. De Luca (Ton); L.Fiesoli; E. Candella.

17 Probably Florencio Constantino.

Salao Sassetti Rome: T. Costanzi	*La Bohème*	Mar 20,22,24, 25, Apr 3,8	[Rodolfo]/Luigi Innocenti; Giorgina Caprile (Mimi); C. Rommel (Mus); Vincenzo Ardito (Mar); R. Galli (Coll);19 E. Moreo (Schaun); E. Borelli (Ben. & Alcin.); L. Mugnone cdr.
Seville:20 T. San Fernando	*La Bohème*	Apr 16	[Rodolfo]; C. Ferrani (Mimi); M. Martelli (Mus); G. De Luca (Mar); A. De Segurola (Coll).
	Il Barbiere di Siviglia	Apr 18	[Almaviva], R. Pacini (Ros); Oliva (Berta); A. De Segurola (Bas); A. Rossi; N. Cervi; Oswaldo de Gennaro.
Vienna: Hofoper	*Fedora*	May 16,19,23	[Loris]; G. Bellincioni (Fed); Rina Giachetti (Olga); G. Polese (De Siriex); A. Silvestri (Grech); Gerhard Stehmann (Nicola); Arthur Preuss (Sergio); Agostino Nava (Cirillo); Adalgisa Minotti (Dmitri); G. Paroli (Désiré & Rouvel); Teodor Görner (Michele); Attilio Pulcini (Boroff & Lorek); Franz Schalk/Gustav Mahler cdr.
	La Traviata	May 21	[Alfredo]; G. Bellincioni (Viol); G. Polese (Ger).
	Pagliacci	Jun 14	[Canio] (after Thomas Salignac); Fritzi Scheff (Ned); A. Scotti (Ton); Francesco Daddi (Bep); Maurice Decléry (Sil); L. Mancinelli cdr. (with *Cavalleria Rusticana*.)
London: Covent Garden	*Don Giovanni*	Jun 20	[Ottavio/Andreas Dippel]; Susan Strong (Anna); M. Macintyre (Elv); F. Scheff (Zer); A. Scotti (Don); E. de Reszke (Lep); C. Gilibert (Mas); M. Journet (Comm); L. Mancinelli cdr.
	La Bohème	Jul 6	[Rodolfo] (after Giuseppe Anselmi/Alessandro Bonci; N. Melba (Mimi); F. Scheff (Mus); M. Bensaude (Mar); C. Gilibert (Schaun); M. Journet (Coll); E. Dufriche (Ben./Alcin.); M. Caisso (Parp); L. Mancinelli cdr.
	Tosca	Jul 12,16,20, 25	[Cavaradossi]; Milka Termina (Tosca); A. Scotti (Scarpia); E. Dufriche (Angelotti); C. Gilibert (Sacris); J. Bars (Spol); L. Viviani (Sciarrone); Cernusco (Gaoler); L. Mancinelli cdr.
	Il Barbiere di Siviglia	Jul 23	[Almaviva]; N. Melba (Ros); M. Bauermeister (Berta); M. Bensaude (Fig); A. Baldelli (Bart); E. de Reszke (Bas); L. Viviani (Fior); G. Maestri (Off); L. Mancinelli cdr.
Buckingham Palace		Jun 25	State Concert: *La Bohème*: 'Air' & Duet (w. S. Adams); *Rigoletto*: 'Un dì, se ben rammentomi'(Quartet)(w. S. Adams, L. Homer & P. Plançon.)
Windsor Castle	*Cavalleria Rusticana*	Jun 26	[Turiddu]; E. Calvé (Sant); Fanchon Thompson (Lola); M. Bauermeister (Lucia); A. Scotti (Alf); L. Mancinelli cdr. (with *Carmen*, Act I.)

---

18 Unconfirmed.
19 Frajese, op. cit., gives Enrico Galli.
20 De Lucia was evidently replaced by Colli in two performances of Eslava's *Miserere* at Seville Cathedral (see pp. 290-1).

1900-01

Naples: T. San Carlo	*Tosca*	Dec 20,23, Jan 1,8,10,13, 23,28,Feb 2,9, 16,26,Mar 7,16, 19,23,24,Apr 1	[Cavaradossi]; A. Pandolfini (Tosca); E. Camera (Scar); Costantino Thos (Angelotti); E. Borelli/Raffaele Gaetani (Sacr); R. De Rosa (Spoleta); G. Gironi (Sciarrone); Vincenzo Medina/Antonino Giovesi (shepherd); L. Mugnone cdr.
	La Bohème	Jan 31, Feb 5,12,23, Mar 2,5,9,12	[Rodolfo]/P. Schiavazzi/Elvino Ventura; A. Pandolfini/R. Giachetti (Mimì); R. Giachetti/F. Toresella (Mus); E. Camera/Tullio Quercia (Mar); G. Gironi (Schaun); C. Thos (Coll); Carlo or Ettore Borelli (Ben. & Alcin.);[21] R. De Rosa (Parp); L. Mugnone cdr.
	Fedora	Apr 8,11, 13,15	[Loris]; A. Pandolfini (Fed); R. Giachetti (Olga); E. Camera (De Siriex); R. De Rosa (Désiré); C. Thos (Grech); E. Borelli (Cir/Boroff); V. Medina (Dmitri & Savoyard); Nicola Scotti; Ugo Jabbò; Alfredo Palumbò; Michele Bove; Luigi Finizio; L. Mugnone cdr.
T. San Carlo	Concert	Feb 27	Verdi Commemoration: *La Traviata* IV w. A. Pandolfini; E. Camera; L. Mugnone cdr.
T. San Carlo	Concert	Apr 12	Benefit of the Orphans of Civil Servants: Two unidentified Tosti romanzas; 'Giacchè' (Costa). Encores were 'Invano' & 'Ancora' (both Tosti); 'Napulitanata' (Costa).

1902

Budapest: Lipót Városi Casino	Concert	Jan 19	*Tosca*: 'Romanza'; 'Serenata' & 'Ideale' (both Tosti).
Budapest: Vigadó	Concert	Jan 23	*Werther*: 'Romanza'; *Tosca*: 'Romanza'; *Cavalleria Rusticana*: 'Siciliana'; 'Ideale' (Tosti); 'A suon di baci' (Baldelli); unspecified works by Bizet.
Warsaw: Filarmonica	Concert	Before Mar 15	Programme unknown.
Naples: T. San Carlo	*Il Barbiere di Siviglia*	Feb 27, Mar 2,6	[Almaviva] (after Pietro Lara); Regina Pinkert (Ros); L. Garavaglia (Berta); M. Ancona (Fig); E. Borelli (Bart); G. Scarneo (Bas); E. Mascheroni cdr.
	Carmen	Mar 12,17, 22,24	[José]/E. Colli; Amedea Santarelli/Edwige Ghibaudo (Car); Valentina Leopardi/Gilda Galassi (Mic); Rosa Garavaglia (Merc.); Lina Garavaglia (Fras.); Emanuele Bucalo/Ernesto Caronna (Esc); Virgilio Mentasti; M.? Olivieri; E. Mascheroni cdr.
	Fedora	Mar 29,Apr 1, 3,6,8,10	[Loris]; G. Bellincioni (Fed); L. Garavaglia (Olga); E. Bucalo (De Siriex); V. Mentasti (Cir. & Boroff); M.? Olivieri; O. Carozzi; Oscar Anselmi cdr.

Venue	Opera	Dates	Cast
T. Massimo		22,25,29	G. Tisci-Rubini (Cir); Guglielmo Niola (Boroff); Silvio Becucci (Grech); Ferdinando Gianoli-Galletti; Enrico Giordani (Rouvel); la Mancuso (Dmitri & Savoyar); R. De Rosa (Désiré); L. Mugnone/V. Lombardi cdr.
Naples: T. San Carlo	Manon	May 15,17	[Des Grieux] (after Enrico Caruso/Franco Mannucci); R. Giachetti (Man); E. Bucalo (Brétigny); C. Thos (Count); Savoia; E. Mascheroni cdr.

1903

Venue	Opera	Dates	Cast
Genova: T. Politeama Genovese	Fedora	Jan 20,22,24	[Loris] (after Gino Martinez-Patti); Enrica Canovas/G. Bellincioni (Fed); Amelia Campagnoli-Cremona (Olga); Carlo Silvestri (De Siriex); Filippo Aldobrandi; Edoardo Boccolari cdr.
Catania: T. Bellini	Fedora	Feb 7	[Loris] (after Remo Andreini/Salvo Panbianchi; Eugenia Burzio-Ravizza (Fed); Noëmi Casini (Olga); F. Fratoddi (De Siriex); Algos Gastone; Michele Fiore; Manlio Bavagnoli/O. Anselmi cdr.
	Tosca	Feb 21	[Cav]; E. Burzio-Ravizza (Tosca); Silla Carobbi (Scarpia); O. Anselmi cdr.
	La Traviata	Feb 28 (up to 12 perf) (4 perf)	[Alfredo]; Linda Brambilla (Violetta); Pasquale Amato (Germont); A. Gastone; Di Bianco; Doncich cdr.
Palermo: T. Massimo	La Bohème	Mar 14,17,19,22,25	[Rodolfo]/Francesco? Bravi; Giuseppina Uffredduzzi (Mimi); Amelia Campagnoli-Cremona (Mus); C. Buti (Mar); Vittorio Ferraguti (Schaun); G. Tisci-Rubini (Coll); G. Cremona (Ben. & Alcin.); Emilio Venturini (Parp); E. Mascheroni cdr.
Messina:	Concert		Tosca: 'Romanza'.
Rome: T. Argentino	Stabat Mater (Rossini)	Apr 8	w. Mary D'Arneiro; I. Di Spagny; F. Navarrini; Alessandro? Bustini cdr.
Milan: T. Lirico	Fedora	Nov 21,24,29, Dec 3,5,7	[Loris]; Marie Lafargue (Fed); Rapalli (Olga); G. Tisci-Rubini (Grech); Francesco Maria Bonini (De Siriex); Virginia Rigotini; Venturina Muggia; G. Paroli; C. Thos; il Rosci; il Gabutti; Giuseppe Sturani cdr.

1903-04

Venue	Opera	Dates	Cast
Lisbon: T. Sao Carlos	Fedora	Dec 13	[Loris]; M. Lafargue (Fed); Bice Silvestri (Olga); C. Buti (De Siriex); V. Lombardi cdr. (Gala perf. in honour of H.M. The King of Spain.)
	Carmen	Jan 15	[José]; M. Lafargue; B. Silvestri; C. Buti (Esc); G. Sturani cdr.
Oporto: T. Sao Joao	Fedora	Dec 22,26, Jan 1	[Loris]; M. D'Arneiro (Fed); Olga Sabbadino (Olga); Luigi Nicoletti-Korman; Rodolfo Angelini-Fornari (De Siriex); A. Conti cdr.
	Tosca	Dec 28,30	[Cavaradossi]; M. D'Arneiro (Tosca); E. Bucalo (Scar); L. Nicoletti-Korman (Angelotti); Luigi Tavecchia (Sacr. & Gaoler); R. Sillingardi (Spol); A. Pulcini (Sciarrone); Cesarine (Shepherd); A. Conti cdr.

1904

Place	Opera	Dates	Cast
Florence: T. Pergola	Werther	Feb 18,20	[Werther]; Romilda Nelli (Sof); M. Savelli (Carlotta); Mario Hediger (Alb); Giovanni Bellucci (Pod); Francesco? Baldini (Schmidt); Banti (Johann); Gialdino Gialdini cdr.
Naples: T. San Carlo	Fedora	Feb 27, Mar 1,3,6	[Loris] (after G. Martinez-Patti)/G. Anselmi; L. Pasini-Vitale (Fed); Amelia Fusco (Olga); F. Maria Bonini (De Siriex); Oreste Luppi (Cir); E. Vitale cdr.
Bari: T. Petruzzelli	Fedora	Mar 22,24,27,29	[Loris]/Frosini; Marta Currelich/L. Berlendi (Fed); Demarther (Olga); E. Sottolana (De Siriex); Umberto Macnez; M. Fiore (Grech); Carlo Farinetti (Cir); Egisto Tango cdr.

1905

Place	Opera	Dates	Cast
Naples: T. San Carlo	Vita Brettona (Mugnone)	Mar 14,16,19, 23?	[Yann]; G. Bellincioni (Gaud); Nini Frascani (Ivona); M. Sammarco (Gaos); F. Maria Bonini (Silvestro); Margot Kaftal (Marta); Mario Massa; G. Berenzone; Paolo? Poggi (Guermeur); L. Mugnone cdr.
Milan: T. alla Scala	Il Barbiere di Siviglia	Apr 5,8,10, 12,15,17	[Almaviva]; Maria Barrientos (Ros); Elvira Lucca (Bert); G. De Luca (Fig); Gaudio Mansueto (Bas); A. Pini-Corsi (Bart); C. Campanini cdr.
Paris: T. Sarah Bernhardt	L'Amico Fritz	May 9	[Fritz]; L. Berlendi (Suz); G. Kaschmann (David); Fede Fassini; R. Ferrari cdr.
London: Waldorf Theatre	Pagliacci	May 22,26, Jun 10,12,17, 24,28,Jul 1,8, 11,15	[Canio]; Irene De Bohuss/Aurelie Révy (Ned); M. Ancona/R. Angelini-Fornari (Ton); M. Massa (Beppe); R. Angelini-Fornari/Constantino (Silvio);[22] A. Conti cdr.
	L'Amico Fritz	May 30,Jun 7, 14,Jul 10	[Fritz]; Alice Nielsen (Suz); Eleonora De Cisneros (Beppe); E.? Lucca (Cat); M. Ancona (David); F. Foglia (Han); Riccardo? Sillingardi (Fed); A. Conti cdr.
	Il Barbiere di Siviglia	Jun 9,13,21, 30	[Almaviva]; A. Nielsen (Ros); E.? Lucca (Berta); M. Ancona (Fig); A. Pini-Corsi (Bart); F. Foglia (Fior); V. Arimondi (Bas); R? Sillingardi (Officer); A. Conti cdr.
	Cavalleria Rusticana	Jun 2	[Turiddu]; Inês Maria Ferraris (Sant); E.? Lucca (Lola); Marchetti (Lucia); A. Pini-Corsi/R. Angelini-Fornari (Alfio).[23]

1905-06

Place	Opera	Dates	Cast
Naples: T. San Carlo	Tosca	Dec 20,24,26,31, Jan 3, Feb 7,15,18,26	[Cavaradossi/Amedeo Bassi/Francesco Fazzini; Maria Farneti/Elena Bianchini-Cappelli (Tosca); Angelo Scandiani (Scar); M. Wigley; Ettore Panizza cdr.
	Il Barbiere di Siviglia	Dec 29, Jan 7,21,28	[Almaviva/Pietro Lombardi; R. Pacini (Ros); Emma Zaccaria (Berta); M. Battistini/M. Ancona (Fig); M. Wigley (Bart); C. Walter (Bas); P. Mascagni cdr.

22 Angelini-Fornari sang Silvio on at least June 12.

	Fedora	Feb 2,10 Feb 21,23 Mar 1,4,25,28	(Lot); G. Niola (Laer); E. Zaccaria (Fed); G. Berenzone; E. Panizza/Gaetano Zinetti cdr. [Loris]/F. Fazzini; E. Bianchini-Cappelli/M. Lafargue (Fed); E. Trentini (Olga); E. Zaccaria (Dmitri); A. Scandiani (De Siriex); C. Walter (Cirillo); P. Wulman (Grech); G. Zinetti/U. Giordano cdr.
	Pagliacci	Mar 11,19	[Canio] (after E. De Marchi & F. Fazzini); Isabella Orbellini (Nedda); M. Sammarco (Ton); Alfredo Costa (Silvio); Angelo Bada (Beppe); G. Zinetti cdr.
1907			
Naples: T. San Carlo	*L'Amico Fritz*	Jan 6,8,10,13, 15,20,27, Apr 22*	[Fritz]; M. Farneti/G. Caprile (Suz); Giuseppina Zoffoli (Bep); E. Moreo/Virgilio Bellatti (Dav); G. Berenzone (Han); R. De Rosa (Fed); J. Mannarino (Cat); Giovanni Calveri (violin); L. Mugnone/G. Scognamiglio cdr. (* Gala in honour of H.M. King Edward VII & Queen Alexandra.)
Monte Carlo: Casino	*Il Barbiere di Siviglia*	Mar 14,17,23	[Almaviva]; Rosina Storchio (Ros); Mary Girerd (Ber); Titta Ruffo (Fig); A. Pini-Corsi (Bart); Feodor Chaliapin (Bas); Paolo Ananian (Fior); Proferisce (Off); A. Pomé cdr.
Berlin: Königliches Opernhaus	*Il Barbiere di Siviglia*	Apr 13	[Almaviva]; R. Storchio (Ros); T. Ruffo (Fig); A. Pini-Corsi (Bart); F. Chaliapin (Bas); A. Pomé cdr. (Act II only, w. *Samson et Dalila* II & *Herodiade* III.)
Milan: T. Lirico	*Marcella*	Nov 9,11,14, 16,17,20,24, 28, Dec 4	[Giorgio]; G. Bellincioni (Marcella); Nunzio Rapisardi (Drasko); Leo Eral (Vernier); Cristina Pittarollo (or Pittirolla) (Raimonda); Maria Roberto (Eliana); Amelia Chiostri (Lea); V. Muggia (Clara); Aurelio Sabbi (Barthélemy); Romeo Boscacci (Flament); Ettore Perosio cdr.
1908			
Venice: T. la Fenice	*Marcella*	Jan 19,21	[Giorgio]; Lucia Crestani (Mar); Maria Avezza (Lea & Clara); Sandri (Eliana); V. Muggia (Raimonda); Gregorio Maccaroff (Vern); Renzo Minolfi (Dras); Zoni (Flament); Primo Maini (Bart); Giuseppe Baroni cdr.
Rome: T. Costanzi	*Il Barbiere di Siviglia*	Feb 15,18,22, 23,27 Mar 1,4,8,	[Almaviva/Fernando Carpi; Mignon Nevada (Ros); Ada Bellini (Bert); G. De Luca (Fig; Adamo Didur (Bas); R. De Rosa (Fior); Federico Carbonetti (Bart); G. Gironi (Official); L. Mugnone cdr.
Rome: T. Adriano	*Marcella*	Nov 12,14,17	[Giorgio]/E. Perea; Adelie D'Albert (Mar); R. Minolfi (Dras); L. Eral (Vern); Icilio Nini-Bellucci cdr.
1909			
Rome: Corea	Concert	Jan 15	Associazione della Stampa/R. Academia di S. Cecilia: Benefit of earthquake victims of Sicily & Calabria: *Tosca*: 'Recondita armonia'; *Manon*: 'Romanza'; Alessandro Bustini pf.

1910

Rome: Corea	Concert	Feb 18	Concert S. Cecilia: Benefit of French flood victims: *Werther*: 'Romanza'; unspecified Tosti romanza, Alessandro Bustini, pf.
Paris: Opéra	*Fedora* (Act II only)	Oct 20	[Loris]; L. Cavalieri (Fed); Rose Heilbronner (Olga); Louis Vaurs (De Siriex); Robert Pasquier (Cir); Raymond Gilles (Désiré); Paul Payan (Grech); U. Giordano cdr.

1914

Naples: T. San Carlo	*Fedora*	Jan 24,27,29, Feb 1,5,7, 12,15	[Loris]/Tito Schipa; Carmen Melis/Giulia Tess (Fed); Maria Donatello (Olga); E.? Venturini; la Padovano; Riccardo Tegani/E. Caronna (De Siriex); Gino De Vecchi (Cir); R. De Rosa (Désiré); L. Mugnone cdr.
Naples: T. San Carlo	Concert	c. Feb 20	Journalists' Concert: 'Marechiare' (Tosti), F. Paolo Tosti, pf, 'Napulitanata' (Costa), P. Mario Costa, pf, 'Durmenno' (De Leva).

1916

Milan: T. alla Scala	*La Bohème*	Feb 5,8	[Rodolfo] (after A. Bonci); Adelina Agostinelli (Mimi); Elisa Marchini (Mus); Armand Crabbé (Mar); Amedeo Bettazzoni (Schaun); Teofilo Dentale (Coll); G. De Vecchi (Ben); Vittorio Serra (Alc); Francesco Merli (Parp); Gino Marinuzzi cdr.
Rome: T. Adriano	*Fedora*	May 30, Jun 1,4,10	[Loris]; Olga Paradisi (Fed); Ida De Filippis (Olga); Leone Paci (De Siriex); Enrico Romano cdr.

1917

Naples: T. San Carlo	*L'Amico Fritz*	Feb 22,24,27, Mar 1,4,10,15, 25,Apr 9	[Fritz]; Nera Marmora (Suz); Celeste Vornos (Bep); Enrico Nani (Dav); R. Ferrari/Gino Colisciano cdr.
Naples: Sala Maddaloni	Concert	Mar 5	Tosti Commemoration: 'Ideale'; 'Aprile'; 'Marechiare' (w. chorus of Tina di Angelo, Graziella Pareto & M. Sammarco); Umberto Mazzone, pf. (All the songs are by Tosti)

1921

Naples: T. Politeama	Concert	Early Feb	Programme unknown.
Naples: Circolo Artistico	Concert	Feb 3	*Mattinata Il Giorno*: *Fedora*: 'Amor ti vieta'

S. Francesco di Paola

1922

Marechiaro:		Sept 9	Unveiling of commemorative plaque: 'Marechiare' (Tosti); Raffaele Calace cdr.

1924

Naples:		Mar 1	
Naples: S. Ferdinando	Stabat Mater (Pergolesi)	Apr 1825	Inauguration of Casa Musicale Editrice Marechiaro: Programme unknown.
Naples: 224, Via Roma		c. May 29	Unidentified romanza (Nadir De Lucia); Fedora: 'Amor ti vieta'

24 The Times, Aug. 4 1921 and Il Mattino, Aug. 3/4, state that the funeral would be held on Thursday [Aug. 4], a day confirmed, many years later, by the tenor's elder son, Rodolfo (Andrew Farkas, private communication). The Neapolitan papers Il Mattino, Il Giorno, and Il Mezzogiorno all report the ceremony in their editions of Aug. 5/6 but, since they do not specify the day or date, their reports, though not inconsistent with a date of Aug. 5, do not establish that date beyond doubt. The Times, Aug. 8, gives its own correspondent's brief report of the funeral, datelined 'Rome, Aug. 5th.' Salvucci, op. cit., p. 95, who was present at the ceremony, gives Aug. 5. Daspuro, Enrico Caruso, pp. 72-5, specifies that Caruso's body was immediately embalmed and, the same evening [as the day of his death, Aug. 2], was exposed to lie in state on the ground floor of the Hôtel du Vésuve, in Via Partenope. Daspuro then notes that 'the sad spectacle was prolonged for a further two days [Aug. 3 and 4] because the permission of the Royal House was required [to hold the funeral] at San Francesco di Paola. The greatly desired licence having at last arrived, the imposing funeral took place on August 5th'. However, The New York Times, Aug. 5 1921 quotes an Associated Press report of the event: 'Naples, Italy, August 4: The funeral of Enrico Caruso took place here today.' Although misprints in newspapers are not uncommon, and although the six hour time difference could well have permitted a late New York edition of August 5 to report an event taking place at noon in Naples that same day, this report would appear conclusive, and August 4th must therefore be preferred to Daspuro's entirely reasonable account and a date of August 5th.

25 Unconfirmed.

Chronology Index

Pozzi, Vincenzo, 409
Prampolini, Clotilde, 406
Preuss, Arthur, 423
Preziosi, Sig.a M., 406
Proferisce. Sig., 427
Puccini, Giacomo, 418
Pulcini, Attilio, 423, 425
Quadri, Sig., 420
Quaranta, Salvatore or Francesco, 404
Quarenghi, Osanna, 417
Quercia, Tullio, 424
Radicchi, Sig.a, 411
Ragni, Carlo, 416, 421
Randegger, Alberto, 407
Rapalli, Sig.a, 425
Rapisardi, Nunzio, 427
Rapp, Giuseppe, 404
Rappini, Federico, 405
Ravogli, Giulia, 411, 413, 415, 417, 422
Ravogli, Sofia, 413
Reggiani, Samuele, 408
Reid, Margaret, 419
Révy, Aurelie, 426
Ricci, Matilda, 405
Rigotini, Virginia, 425
Rinaldini, Antonio, 409, 413, 414, 415, 419
Risley, Grete, 414
Roberto, Maria, 427
Rolla, Kate, 414
Romano, Enrico, 428
Rommel, Clara, 422, 423
Rosci, Sig., 425
Rossi, Arcangelo, 419, 420, 421, 422, 423
Rossi, Emilia, 412
Rossi, Giulio, 408, 409, 410, 418, 419, 420
Rossini, Michelangelo, 420, 421
Rotoli, Donato, 409
Roudez, Maud, 422
Roussel, Mario, 420
Roveri, Sig. G., 418
Ruffo, Titta, 427
Ruta, Anna, 403
Sabbadino, Olga, 425
Sabbi, Aurelio, 427
Sabellico, Antonio, 412
Salassa, Gaudenzio, 405, 410
Salignac, Thomas, 423
Sammarco, G. Mario, 416, 419, 420, 422, 426, 427, 428
Sandri, Sig.a, 427
Santarelli, Amedea, 424
Sapio, Romualdo, 408
Savelli, Maria Stuarda, 412, 421, 422, 426

Savoia, 425
Savoldi, Bice, 405
Scalchi, Sofia, 414, 415, 416
Scandiani, Angelo, 426, 427
Scaramella, Massimo, 417, 418
Scarneo, Giovanni, 416, 424
Schalk, Franz, 423
Scheff, Fritzi, 423
Schiavazzi, Pietro (or Piero), 421, 424
Schipa, Tito, 428
Scognamiglio, Gaetano, 420, 4°·
Scotti, Antonio, 411, 422, 423
Scotti, Nicola, 424
Sembrich, Marcella, 417, 418, 419
Seppilli, Armando, 416, 419
Serra, Narciso, 418, 419, 420
Serra, Vittorio, 428
Sewell, F.A., 422
Siani, Angelo, 403
Signoretti, Leopoldo, 407
Sillingardi, Riccardo, 421, 425, ?426
Silvestri, Alessandro, 407, 408, 418, 419, 423
Silvestri, Bice, 425
Silvestri, Carlo, 425
Siragusa, Antonio, 409
Sivori, Ernesto, 405, 406
Smeroschi, Carolina, 405
Smitti, Maria, 404
Soarez, Ester, 411
Sottolana, Edoardo, 405, 412, 420, 426
Spangher, Francesco, 417
Sparapani, Senatore, 405, 411
Spreafico, Sig., 405
Sprugnolli, Cristina, 406
Stahl, Amelia, 409, 410, 418
Stehle, Adelina, 416, 422
Stehmann, Gerhard, 423
Storchio, Rosina, 427
Strakosch, Febea, 421
Strong, Susan, 423
Sturani, Giuseppe, 425
Synnerberg, Ortensia, 411
Tabayo, Ignazio, 411
Tagliacozzo, Margherita, 404
Talamo, Eduardo, 404
Tamburlini, Angelo, 417
Tanci, Camillo, 420
Tango, Egisto, 426
Tanzini, Giovanni, 408
Tavary, Marie, 414, 415
Tavecchia, Luigi, 425
Tegani, Riccardo, 428
Teodorini, Elena, 408, 412, 413
Ternina, Milka, 423
Terzi, Scipione, 408, 409, 410

Discography

Fernando De Lucia recorded for the Gramophone and Typewriter Company Limited (G&T) (later The Gramophone Company), the Società Italiana di Fonotipia, and Phonotype Record. For them he made 402 known records. Two further G&T titles are surmisable. Rumoured recordings for Zonophone and Edison cannot be substantiated.

The discography is adapted from that published in *The Record Collector*, which listed the records under Discography Numbers 1-401.[1] It maintains the same numerical order, adds two Fonotipias and one G&T (all three formerly unknown), and presents data for direct pressings manufactured by the original recording companies and their associates for regular or for subscription sale. For reasons of space it does not reproduce the detailed notes or the microgroove reissue data given in the earlier publication.

Discography numbers

Each selection is listed across the page against an assigned Discography Number. To avoid confusion, these numbers are identical to those previously published.

Matrix and catalogue numbers

G&T/Gramophone Company sessions appear chronologically; except for re-takes, titles within them are listed by matrix number. Victor catalogue numbers reflect the order of issue; double-faced numbers, given in italics, follow the single-faced numbers in the Victor column. As in the *Record Collector* discography, which was prepared when matrix data for them were incomplete, De Lucia's Fonotipias are listed by catalogue number. Three recently discovered titles are assigned Discography Numbers 22a, 100a, and 100b. Phonotype records are listed in the order set out in the registers, and are believed to reflect the actual order of recording.

Composers and poets

Operatic composers are given only on the first appearance of each opera. Full names of poets and composers of songs are given only for De Lucia's first recording of the song.

Language

Unless better known in translation, opera titles appear in the original language. The title of the selection is given in the language used by De Lucia, followed (in parenthesis) by its title in the original language. All are sung in Italian unless noted as:

Fr = French   L = Latin   N = Neapolitan dialect.

---

[1] Michael E. Henstock, 'Fernando De Lucia: Discography', *Record Collector*, Vol. 30, Nos. 5-9, June-Aug., 1985, pp. 100-39 and 148-213; *corrigenda* and *addenda*, ibid, Vol.33, Nos. 8-10, Aug. 1988, pp. 231-6.

Phonotypes which have not been heard by the writer have been assigned the language suggested by the entry in the recording register.

Phonotype recordings

Diameters

Documentation of the Phonotype recordings is drawn from available pressings and from the original recording registers. In the Phonotype Celebrity Series - for which only De Lucia, Pasquale Amato, Benvenuto Franci, and Angeles Ottein recorded as solo singers - two sizes of disc were offered. The prefix C in the registers generally represented a 27 cm recording, and M a 30 cm. Though there are a few known inconsistencies (such as an occasional 25 cm disc, a non-celebrity record with a celebrity prefix, or a celebrity record which lacks one) the registers are usually reliable on this point. Therefore, even in cases where copies are still unknown (and where a dash appears in the 'diameter' column of this listing), their *probable* diameter may be deduced from the registers. Some diameters have been determined from surviving matrices.

Matrix and serial numbers

The matrix number of each Phonotype recording is also its catalogue number; each side of a double-faced disc is labelled independently with the title and catalogue number of that recording. Thus, a double-faced Phonotype carries two independent catalogue numbers; there is no double-faced number which uniquely identifies the coupling.[2]

Speeds and transpositions

The speed and pitch relationships in De Lucia's Gramophone & Typewriter (G&T) recordings were analysed in the notes to the complete reissue of those records.[3] It showed the flaw in the natural presumption that the operatic items had, for the most part, been sung at score pitch. It also showed that previous impressions of De Lucia's voice were incorrect. At speeds reflecting not the score pitch but, instead, downward transposition by a semitone or, sometimes, by a tone - the most that then seemed possible given prevailing perceptions of the voice - the arias and songs revealed a new picture of the singer. That new concept serves as a starting point for the reconsideration which, a decade later, is required in the light of the information which has since become available on his vocal condition and stage practice at the time of his first records.

It is a strange commentary on the early recording industry that a company which employed men with the acumen and insight of Fred Gaisberg seemed so unconcerned over the possible effects on musical verisimilitude, and consequently on its sales, of variations in the recording (and playing) speed of its products, and made only half-hearted attempts to alert the public to such possibilities: the Foreword to certain Gramophone & Typewriter catalogues is said to have warned that the records should not be played faster than 72 rpm, but offered no other guidance.[4] Before speed standardisation, many so-called 78 rpm recordings were actually made at speeds varying from as low as 60 to as high as 90 rpm. Pitch and speed are related: at or about 78 rpm a speed increase or decrease of about 4 rpm will raise or lower the pitch by a semitone, with consequent - and noticeable - changes in vocal timbre and coloration. We

2 For details of the Phonotype numbering system see Henstock (1985), pp. 106-11.

3 Michael E. Henstock, Vivian A. Liff and Desmond Shawe-Taylor, 'Speeds and pitches for the Gramophone Company records of Fernando De Lucia', Notes to Rubini 305: *The G&T/Gramophone Company Recordings, 1902-1909* (released 1980).

4 Hurst, *The Golden Age Recorded* (1963), p. 39. The note cannot, however, be traced in any available copy of early G&T catalogues.

cannot overstate the importance of ensuring that a record plays at a turntable speed as close as possible to that used when the record was made. Failure to do so may give a quite inaccurate reproduction of a voice *over the entire vocal range recorded*; in this it differs from the obvious difficulties encountered only on the highest or lowest notes, or on those located around the so-called 'break', when an artist attempts something in an unsuitable key.

The problems of determining the playing speeds for the records of a singer such as De Lucia, for whom transposition in the studio seems to have been the rule rather than the exception, are inherently complex and troublesome. In general, records made at score pitch and reproduced at the wrong speed are readily detected by the observant because the selections emerge in the wrong keys. The detection of transposition is more difficult. If the record is of music which the singer would normally be expected to perform at score pitch we may have no reason to suspect a transposition. This is commonly the case with De Lucia. In fact, as will be shown later, his records frequently exhibit extensive downward transposition. Since this was often not realised they were, as a matter of course, played (and reissued on lp) at score pitch, i.e. at too fast a speed, whereupon vowels were distorted and so was the timbre of the voice. However, because the keys were correct, the errors went unnoticed by those who knew the voice only from records, and for successive generations the resulting thin, white, tremulous sound has been accepted as the legacy of Fernando De Lucia. Notes which he had actually sung (in, for instance, pieces transposed by a tone) as high A flats became - when played at speeds which produced score pitch - forced-up, artificial, and ugly B flats. And there are worse cases: when his 1902 G&T record of the 'Flower Song' from *Carmen* was reissued in the HMV 'Archive' series its label carried the legend: 'Speed 78'. In reality, this well-known record plays a tone below score pitch (at around 64 rpm) and to play it at 78 rpm is to hear it in a key almost two full tones higher than that in which it was recorded. The damage to the vocal quality, and to the tenor's reputation, may be imagined. Ironically, transpositions made for his own vocal comfort in the studio may well have caused De Lucia to be more seriously misrepresented than any other singer whom we can call to mind.

Before assessing the extent of De Lucia's transpositions we should first examine the possible influence of fluctuations in Standard Pitch, a matter much discussed in the context of Caruso's records.[5] The question arises because pitch standards have varied over the past two centuries; examples are known of A = 393.2 (1713) and A = 457.5 (1897). In 1859, a commission appointed by the French government fixed pitch (French pitch) as A = 435.45 at 15º Celsius (59º Fahrenheit). In England, the French *diapason normal* of A = 439 at 68º Fahrenheit (20º Celsius), which is actually the same as A 435 at 59º F, was adopted in 1896, and was called Philharmonic Pitch.[6] This, in turn, is substantially the same as the A = 440 at about 70º F (21º C) which became standard in the United States and which reflects the somewhat higher temperatures prevailing in concert halls there.[7] A range from 415 to 429 corresponds to about one quarter of a

---

[5] Aida Favia-Artsay, *Caruso on Records*, pp. 19-23.

[6] Sometimes 'new Philharmonic Pitch' to distinguish it from other pitches to which the name 'Philharmonic' had previously been applied. When, in 1846, Sir Michael Costa became conductor of the Philharmonic Society (replacing Sir George Smart, whose 'Philharmonic Pitch' had been A = 433.2), he adopted A = 452.5 (so-called 'high pitch') which, except for relatively few exceptions which involved even higher pitches, then prevailed as 'Philharmonic Pitch' in England until 1896. In 1878, for instance, the Royal Italian Opera at Covent Garden used a pitch of approximately A = 450.

[7] In 1989, there are reports that some orchestras are tuning to a pitch decidedly higher than A = 440 at about 70º F (21º C). For a discussion of the subject of standard pitch, as it relates generally to singers, see John Stratton, 'Some Matters of Pitch', *The Opera Quarterly*, Vol. 6, No. 4, Summer 1989, pp. 49-60. However, Stratton makes some debatable assumptions: it has always been accepted that the French commission on pitch erred in setting the relevant temperature (15ºC/59ºF) unrealistically low and, in stating (p. 55) that 'Tamagno [at Monte Carlo] would not have had to sing any higher than French pitch', Stratton appears to overlook that pitch - even if starting at A = 435 - would certainly, at theatre temperatures, have risen to A = 440, or something close to it, during the course of the evening. Similarly, no objective evidence is cited for the statement (p. 55) that: 'In Milan, at the Gramophone Company studios, the pitch seems actually to have been

tone, and the range 435 to 440 proportionately less, perhaps one twelfth of a tone.[8] This is consistent with the calculation that an uncertainty of 5 Hz in either direction in the pitch standard used prevents us from determining the speed at which a record was made (to place it in a given key) more closely than 0.8 rpm at 70 rpm or about 0.9 rpm at 80, i.e. about one fifth of a semitone.[9] We can, by changing the turntable speed, accurately match it to a pitch standard of A = 435, 440, or any other value at a given temperature, but we cannot usually be certain of which, if any, of them was actually used in the recording 'laboratory' in question. It should, in any case, be noted that a variation of 5 Hz in the pitch standard is at the very threshold of discrimination of many trained musicians, and is probably quite imperceptible to most non-musicians. In 1902, one authority ended his article on musical pitch with a list of the orchestral pitches which he had measured in New York and in various European cities in 1899; at 68⁰ F (20⁰ C) they varied from A = 435 (Leipzig) to A = 442.4 (Paris). They were, he concluded, '. . . measurements [which] prove how chimerical it is to hope for greater accuracy than is found between 435 and 440 vibrations per second . . . inasmuch as temperature must always be reckoned with.'[10]

Such uncertainties are, moreover, matched by those of some of the musical instruments themselves. Depending on the quality of the instrument, a piano - which may in any case flatten by one quarter tone between tunings - will flatten as the temperature rises or will sharpen as relative humidity increases. A temperature rise of 5⁰ Celsius may sharpen wind instruments by 4 Hz. Though errors of opposite sense may cancel one another out, errors are additive: the *maximum* possible error is the sum of the individuals. An uncertainty of at least 5 Hz because we do not know which standard pitch was *nominally* employed eighty years ago by the Gramophone Company in Milan (most likely A = 435) must be added to one of similar magnitude arising from the unknown state of tune of the piano used: 'studios' were not permanent (hotel rooms were often pressed into service), and pianos which - probably after having been moved from room to room - had to be lifted on to platforms (often improvised from packing cases) to bring their level nearer to that of the horn doubtless experienced handling which affected their state of tune. We must also consider pitch variations resulting from changes in humidity and temperature between cool morning (when tuning might last have taken place) and the noonday heat of a room sealed against external noise. The total possible uncertainty may, therefore, be plus or minus at least 10 Hz, a spread of between one quarter and one half of a tone which, at or around 78 rpm, corresponds to as much as plus or minus almost 2 rpm. This takes no account of instabilities in primitive recording turntables, which sometimes appear to have slowed down by about 2 rpm during the recording; on playback at constant speed the pitch of records made under such conditions rises and their tempo increases throughout the side.

Thus, although a keen ear, supplemented by a modern electronic reference source of A = 440, may be able to decide that a record should play precisely at 70 (actually 69.77 for a 50 Hz stroboscope) instead of at 69 rpm (actually 68.97), such determinations could easily be 2 rpm slow or fast of the speed actually used early in the century and under unknown conditions, with a consequent error of plus or minus a quarter tone.

Bearing in mind these uncertainties, we cannot, then, read too much into apparent discrepancies of one or two revolutions per minute, or be too dogmatic about them, since they lie within the margin of inevitable uncertainty discussed above. The speeds *suggested* here for the G&T records were determined using an A = 440 pitchpipe and a piano nominally tuned to A = 440. Speeds for the Fonotipias and for most of the

---

A = 435; and now [1906] Patti's piano seems to have risen [relative to the A = 428-433 which Stratton *presumes* to have been used for her first group of recordings, in 1905] to about the same.' It is, of course, perfectly possible that the very reason that Marconi, Patti, and Tamagno all insisted, at some stage, on recording in their own homes was that their own pianos were tuned to some pitch that the singers - all of them over fifty - found congenial.

8 *Grove's Dictionary of Music and Musicians*, 2nd edition, Vol.III, pp. 756-8.

9 Paul Lewis, *The Record Collector*, Vol.34, No. 1-2, Jan. 1989, p. 46.

10 A.J. Hipkins, *Encyclopædia Britannica*, tenth edition, Vol. 31, 1902, p. 782.

Phonotypes were determined using an electronic reference source of A = 440.

Setting aside the imponderable, a basic principle is that the speed chosen must be one which, at the pitch standard decided upon, produces a specific key for the piece rather than one which is between keys. Of the several possible keys the choice is limited to those in which the singer's voice sounds realistic - in so far as we may be able to judge a singer whom we have never heard in the flesh - and in which both the key and any transposition are likely ones for the piece and for its accompaniment. Another principle is that there is a strong (and logical) tendency for the speed of records made at a single session, i.e. those with consecutive or very close matrix numbers, to remain more or less constant. Sometimes a session may include records by several artists, perhaps of different voice types, whose records may provide a useful cross-check. When a speed change occurs it may usually be attributed to some adjustment (possibly unintentional) of the recording apparatus; the next few matrix numbers will again remain constant at the new speed. This useful feature is, however, only a rule of thumb and cannot be applied indiscriminately or extended indefinitely. Changes are known to occur within sessions; waxes may not have been numbered systematically as and when they were cut, and matrix number sequences may therefore not reflect the order of recording. We cannot, in many cases, even be sure of the precise date of a G&T session and, therefore, of the matrix numbers with which it began and ended. Since, for most acoustic records, few - if any - listeners can have any real idea of how the voice sounded in the period when they were made the speeds must perforce be determined by successive approximation. The present analysis of De Lucia's records strongly suggests that he transposed not just a few but most of his operatic selections, and that he did so to a greater extent than the semitone (occasionally a whole tone) that was formerly thought to be the heaviest conceivable transposition in all but exceptional cases, such as those of the pieces from *I Puritani*. The problems of determining their correct speeds are, in some measure, those of overcoming preconceptions produced by years of listening to his records played at score pitch and, therefore, with an unwittingly falsified timbre, and of accepting the possibility, however unlikely it may appear, that he regularly recorded familiar arias with transpositions of a tone or a minor third. Since score pitch is almost an irrelevance in his recordings the score not only offers little help but may actually delude the listener into mistaken prejudgement of the keys used. Arguably, it has been the sheer improbability of such heavy transposition that has caused us, in De Lucia's case, to disregard the evidence of our ears and to ignore, for instance, distorted vowels. It must be accepted that, while logical deduction serves up to a point, the choice between two speeds and their respective keys ultimately demands subjective judgements. These may require us, for instance, to evaluate the relative credibility of the pinched high notes and exaggerated vowels of a selection reproduced at score pitch as against the baritonal quality of many of the notes heard with a downward transposition. In his day, De Lucia was known as a tenor of many different timbres and, as an Argentine critic wrote in 1895, '... not all of them equally pleasant' (see p. 216). However, since there is usually nothing artificial or unpleasant about this baritonal quality itself - unaccustomed though we may now be to hearing it from him - and since every stage (even the earliest) of De Lucia's career yields reviews which describe his vocal quality as baritonal, the lower speed often seems the more likely. Downward transposition to limit his top notes to A or A flat, with - given that we cannot always be certain of the precise transposition - *possibly* an occasional B flat on good days, is entirely consistent with the evidence of Fred Gaisberg, who made many of De Lucia's G&T records and who described him as having a top note of barely an A natural, and with contemporary references (some actually using the word 'baritone') to transpositions made in the theatre in the years following 1900. It is also consistent with the observations made in 1898 by Mascagni (see p. 259), and with De Lucia's need for the transpositions which Giordano was making for him that same year (see p. 277). Early studio conditions would have offered still greater freedom: it can hardly be doubted that obliging accompanists would agree to any transposition that De Lucia - arguably the most distinguished and influential Italian tenor of the day and one whom the Gramophone Company, at least, was demonstrably eager to retain on its roster - might request and, from the results, we may sometimes suspect that the transposition in question was not one for which the pianist was prepared. There are consequent penalties to be paid at the lower end of the range of these transposed pieces, and the obvious difficulty that De Lucia sometimes has in that region is also consistent with Gaisberg's description of his voice as a 'short' one.[11] The analysis which follows has frequently required subjective judgements, and in most cases the decisive factor has been the sound of the vowels. Considering De Lucia's records as, first and foremost, those of a native Italian speaker rather than those of an operatic tenor, it appears to the writer that, for most of De Lucia's G&T recordings, the balance of probability is in favour of a further semitone transposition relative to previous opinion.

The records of De Lucia's first session, matrix numbers 2861-2870, when played at 77.92 rpm (the nearest band to 78 rpm for a 50 Hz stroboscope), emerge with the *Manon* aria a whole tone and three other arias a semitone above score pitch.[12] Whilst downward transposition is not uncommon (the records of Caruso, McCormack, and Schipa, to name but three famous tenors, include many examples), upward transposition by tenors is rare. Hence, as a first step, the speed of the first group may be reduced to bring the *Manon* aria into score pitch, at about 70 rpm: at this apparently reasonable speed all the other arias of the session are transposed downwards, by a semitone or a tone, from score pitch. It is, however, De Lucia's vowels which suggest a further semitone transposition, and that the speed of this session was not 70 (69.77) but 66 (65.93): at 70 rpm one hears white, slightly pinched tones as he descends from his top A in 'Ideale'; at the words '... *che fido v'adoro*' in 'Se il mio nome'; at many points of 'Marechiare' and 'Napulitanata'; and at '*ritrar costei*' and other passages of 'Recondita armonia'. Even if, as reviews suggest, the voice was by then in decline, what we hear at 70 rpm seems implausible in a singer whose tonal beauty was so often commended during a long and distinguished operatic career which had, at that time, still some years to run. At 66 rpm most - though not all - of the apparent tonal defects disappear; what remains is a voice which appears more credible, natural, and attractive.[13]

The recordings of Session II pose, as will be seen, complications such that they are best discussed in conjunction with Session VI.

In Session III a uniform speed of 77 (76.92) brings the *Adriana Lecouvreur*, *Faust*, and *La Traviata* items into score pitch, and it is therefore the *highest* speed likely to have been used for this session. At this speed, when we hear a tone transposition in the (almost always transposed) 'Una vergine', each of the two *Fedora* items, in G flat major and F sharp minor respectively, emerges a semitone below score pitch. Again, it is the vowels, especially in the *Fedora* arias, which suggest that they were recorded a semitone lower still, at a speed of about 73 rpm (73.17). Since they lie no higher than does the other *Fedora* item, 'Amor ti vieta', these transpositions are consistent with that of the latter in Session I (from C to B flat). In the *Faust* duet it is Boninsegna's quality as much as De Lucia's which benefits from a semitone transposition, at 73 rpm. At this speed the *La Traviata* item 'Un dì felice' [No. 19] is convincing with a semitone transposition and, in phrases such as '*che mi ferì*', even the famous 'Ecco ridente' [No. 25] sounds better with a tone rather than a semitone transposition.

At 77 (76.92 rpm) several records of Session IV display unpleasant vowels; too pronounced an 'eee' on the Italian vowel 'i' in the words '*periglio*' [No. 27], '*sospir*' [No. 28], and '*Dio*' [No. 30] are notable examples. The first four are more natural at 73 (73.17 rpm), with the 'Addio, Mignon' perhaps a revolution slower. Similar points may be made regarding Session V: in [No. 31], Pini-Corsi sounds too light at 77 (76.92 rpm), and his evident difficulty in reaching the lowest notes of 'All'idea' [No. 35] suggests downward transposition; De Lucia experiences similar discomfort in the lower reaches

11 F.W. Gaisberg, 'Enrico Caruso', *Gramophone*, Jan. 1944, pp. 117-8.

12 The reasons for giving stroboscope speeds to two decimal places are discussed on pp. 446.

13 Favia-Artsay, op. cit., pp. 51-8 assigns a speed of 68 (68.18 rpm) to the contiguous Caruso matrices (starting at 2871). This conclusion should, however, be viewed in the light of the several attendant uncertainties discussed above.

of 'Salve! Dimora' [No. 33], suggesting that the aria is more heavily transposed than the semitone previously supposed; the 'vivere' of 'De' miei bollenti' [No. 38] becomes totally credible with a tone rather than a semitone transposition, and so on. For this session, a speed of 73 (73.17 rpm) is strongly indicated.

In Session VI there are some slight speed fluctuations, which are unimportant except as mechanical frailties. It is, though, significant that at the speed which renders the *Manon* aria and the *Faust* duet in the same keys in which De Lucia apparently recorded them in Session I and Session III respectively, the Flower Song appears with a tone transposition, i.e. in B. Ample evidence for such a transposition is internal to Session VI: vowel sounds in *Lohengrin* 'Mio salvatore ... Mai devi domandarmi' [No. 46] are especially unnatural at score pitch (c. 76 rpm), and both Ernesto Badini's timbre in the *L'Elisir d'Amore* duet [No. 42] and Josefina Huguet's unaccustomed shrillness in several of the duets suggest that the 77 rpm previously suggested is incorrect. There are, however, implications for Session II, whose matrix numbers are sufficiently close to those of Session I for the two occasions to have been separated only by days. Played with a very small speed increase (c. 67.5 rpm) over that of the first batch, two of the operatic items of Session II emerge with a semitone transposition, the *Cavalleria Rusticana* 'Siciliana' in E minor and the Flower Song in C. It seemed natural, therefore, to assume that all four were recorded at about 67.5 rpm, which gives 'A suon di baci' in the score pitch of E flat and 'Sei morta ne la vita mia' in B flat. That assumption, though, reckoned without the evidence of the 1907 30 cm recording of the Flower Song (matrix 1175c, 052185). To pitch the latter in C assumes that at the very end of De Lucia's series of recordings (in which [No. 42] and [No. 46] clearly appear to have been transposed, at a speed of c. 73 rpm) the speed of the recording turntable was either inadvertently or intentionally increased by 4 rpm. By far the most probable explanation, reinforced by subjective evidence of timbre, is that the Flower Song was recorded at the same speed as were the other records of Session VI, i.e. at 72-73 (72.29-73.17 rpm), when it emerges in B. It is possible, of course, that De Lucia was obliged - either through advancing age, or perhaps because he was not in his best vocal form on the day of the recordings in 1907 - to make a heavier transposition than he had needed in 1902, and that the earlier version was sung i. C. But to play the two versions of the Flower Song side by side, first in C, and then in B, is to feel convinced that in both cases B is correct, for reproduction in C gives that familiar over-white and unnaturally pinched quality to many words and, specifically, to many vowels in *both* versions. If, therefore, we accept a tone transposition in the 25 cm Flower Song and assume a speed of about 64 (63.82 rpm) for the second batch (2897-2900), we find the 'Siciliana' a tone down, in E flat minor (where, it must be said, it sounds splendid), and 'A suon di baci' in D, (where *'Perchè april non è aprile'* sounds much less constricted), and 'Sei morta' in A.

There follows a small gap of four recordings by other singers (matrices 2901-2904), after which we reach the isolated *Lohengrin* disc ('Mercè, mercè, cigno gentil', matrix 2905) [No. 15]. This is a most curious case. In so short a passage, never rising above F sharp, transposition would appear intrinsically unlikely. Nevertheless, the 30 cm version (matrix 1174c, 052184) [No. 49] exhibits a semitone transposition if played at the speed shown, in the previous paragraph, to be required by its predecessors in Session VI. To bring the 1902 *Lohengrin* into score pitch requires an increase of more than 10 rpm compared with the other records of this session, i.e. to about 74 rpm; furthermore the voice again sounds much more comfortable and natural, particularly in the vowels, with a tone transposition to G at a speed of about 66 (65.93) rpm. The slight speeding up of the turntable, from 64 (63.82) to 66 (65.93) rpm between 2900 and 2905, could easily be accounted for by so routine a matter as the the oiling of the mechanism.

The discrepancy with the 30 cm version may seem surprising, but it is not inexplicable. Whereas it would have been a simple matter to ask a pianist to play the passage in almost any desired key, in the later version, with a 'chorus' and 'orchestra' on hand (even on the modest scale then provided) - and performing on their own for the bulk of the record - more extensive transposition might well have seemed not worth while or perhaps even slightly embarrassing for the tenor.

Session VII has a few speed variations. After [Nos. 51-52], where the choice seems to be between 76 (75.94) or 72 (72.29), there is some slowing down for [Nos. 53-56], where the choice is between 74 (74.07) or 70 (69.77). The 30 cm records [Nos. 57-60], formerly thought to play at 75 rpm, may be reassessed at 71 rpm. At the slower speeds, 'Ecco ridente' in B flat and 'Se il mio nome' in F sharp minor show the same transpositions as exhibited in, respectively, Sessions III and I. It is not impossible that the tenor would choose, in 1907, a smaller transposition of a piano-accompanied solo piece than that needed in 1902; indeed, some of the much later Phonotype recordings may actually exhibit smaller transpositions than those used in the equivalent G&T titles which were made at a period when, as we have seen, he may have been in poor health. However, this decision may be justified, for 'Se il mio nome', on internal evidence: at 74 rpm, for example, we again hear *'aneema'* instead of *'anima'*. There is some slight speed fluctuation throughout the session, but pitching of 'Se il mio nome' (matrix 11167b) [No. 54] in G minor at 74 rpm requires a speed that, assuming that the matrices were recorded in numerical order, implies either that 'Ah! qual colpo' (11168b) [No. 55] was sung at score pitch (unlikely, when we consider than he evidently recorded the same piece earlier [No. 39] with a tone transposition), or else requires a sudden increase of as much as 4 rpm in the speed of the recording turntable for 'Se il mio nome', *followed by a 4 rpm decrease*. Detailed examination of phrases such as *'Sorgi alfin'* in the *Romeo* piece [No. 51], *'man sentia'* in the *Luisa Miller* aria [No. 60], and *'infedel'* in the *La Sonnambula* solo [No. 56] emphatically suggests that all three were sung a semitone lower than previously thought. Less obvious are the cases for transposing 'Il mio tesoro', though the vibrato on the long *'cercate'* is less noticeable at 70 than at 74, or 'Dalla sua pace', where only *'s'ella non ho'* causes disquiet at 76 compared with the marginally-preferable 72. The two *La Sonnambula* duets seem acceptable at either 75 or 71, but the evidence of the adjacent *Luisa Miller* aria makes 71 decidedly the preferred speed for all three, with a tone transposition in each case.

The items in *La Sonnambula* need a word of explanation. As is well known, the abnormally high keys in which these selections were written did not long survive the period of Rubini, for whom they were composed. Thus, although some scores give 'Ah! perchè non posso' in the original key of D, the Ricordi score gives B flat, a difference of two whole tones; a transposition of one tone is shown between the earlier and later scores for the two duets, 'Prendi, l'anel ti dono' (B flat/A flat) and 'Son geloso' (G/F). De Lucia, therefore, sang all three pieces with a tone transposition from the keys *normally* used for these pieces and not, as has been suggested, a major third for 'Ah! perchè'.

Session VIII contains a group of songs with no 'score pitch' as such. Hence, subjective judgements are necessary. Previous analysis had suggested that the choice lay between 70 and 74 rpm; while several songs sounded acceptable (though different in timbre) at either speed others, such as 'Sulla bocca amorosa' and 'Era de maggio', produced an over-white sound on the high notes at 74 rpm. It was concluded then that there had been a speed change within the session, and that conclusion is unaltered.

To come to these songs with the accumulated experience of so many operatic selections which, with very few exceptions, seem to sound so much more natural a semitone lower than previously accepted is to be persuaded that many, or even most, of them are more convincing at a slower speed. It is difficult to reach definite conclusions for the very rapid and rhythmic 'Oilì, oilà' [No. 65], and no unequivocal decision in favour of 70 rpm (which seems generally more satisfactory than 74 rpm) is possible even for ' '0 sole mio' [No. 66]. But [Nos. 61-64] at 70 rpm show a quite different timbre from that of the operatic items at the speeds now thought likely for the latter, and a semitone transposition to 66 rpm seems very likely. At 70 rpm, [Nos. 67, 68, and 70] regain the velvety vocal texture exhibited in, for example, the *La Sonnambula* duets. And in ' 'A Surrentina' [No. 69], played at 74 rpm, the phrase *'Vurria passar la vita'* is, for the writer, definitive in setting the speed as no higher than 70 rpm.

Corroboration of a highest key of C (and, therefore, a highest speed of 70) for 'Triste ritorno' is given by the sheet music of the song. It dates from 1899, is in C major and, unusually for a song of that date, appears to have been issued by the publishers in no other key. The lowest vocal note is the low C and the highest only high G. Since the song is dedicated to De Lucia (not, as sometimes stated, to Caruso) and was, presumably, written to suit his voice as it was in 1899, we may well believe Gaisberg's description of his range, since it is unlikely that anyone dedicating a song to a singer with effective high notes would fail to provide an opportunity to display them. Similarly, 'Voce 'e notte!' (1904), another song dedicated to De Lucia, rises only to G.

The example of the 'Flower Song' illustrates the necessity, when pitching the records of singers who recorded over several years, of assessing all available evidence. In this analysis the whole corpus of De Lucia's G&T and HMV records has been considered, and it is felt that the speeds determined are *internally* consistent. Only in the case of Session II are there some residual problems. It may be that some of these records sound strange because the enunciation is not good; in fact, certain words lying on the highest notes still sound curious when the records are revolving so slowly that the lowest notes are grotesquely distorted. 'Sei morta ne la vita mia' seems to have slowed down during recording, so that at constant playback speed the pitch progressively rises. We conclude that there is no one speed at which it may be made to sound beautiful or comfortable.

The Fonotipias (made in 1911) present a simpler challenge, since they are a more or less homogeneous group of songs. To compare the timbre that they display with that of the G&T records of 1909 is to believe that they were recorded at a speed of about 75 rpm, when they emerge approximately a semitone lower than previously thought. Although the keys of songs are often altered, to suit singer and accompaniment, at this lower speed the Fonotipia 'A suon di baci' emerges at the score pitch of E flat.[14]

There are no accessible copies of some Phonotypes, and pitching must be done piecemeal.[15] From available data, however, we may fix provisional speeds for most De Lucia sessions; those *suggested* (which are only opinions and must be treated as such) have been derived for the direct pressings available to the writer, or have been reported by eminent collectors worldwide. It is clear that De Lucia did not necessarily transpose more heavily as he grew older. It also emerges that, at the slower speeds now adopted - reflecting contemporary descriptions of his voice and range - some of his partners on the records sound decidedly more credible than hitherto, providing additional supporting evidence. In particular, Angela De Angelis (1888-1939), with whom De Lucia recorded many duets, may have been as ill-served as has he by playing their records at score pitch. Though transposition obliges her, no less than De Lucia, to sing uncomfortably low notes, De Angelis - who in 1917 was not yet 30 - begins, at the suggested speeds, to resemble a plausible singer (albeit an indifferent one) rather than the caricature heard at faster speeds, and in pitching such records particular note has been taken of her vocal quality.[16] We must, however, conclude that, on certain Phonotypes, both De Lucia's highest and lowest notes sound equally uncomfortable *at the same speed*, evidence of the shortness of his voice at that time; in the final phrases of 'O paradiso!' [No. 152] he changes the music to avoid low notes, and in extracts from *I Pescatori* [No. 115] and *I Puritani* [No. 183] he sings low-lying phrases an octave higher than written.

Not only are these problems complex, but it has gradually emerged, after much detailed work, that long experience of De Lucia's records played at too high a speed and pitch (on the once natural assumption that most of them had been recorded in the score key) has given a generally false notion of his characteristic timbre and vocal colour. To cite a well-known and often reissued 1906 recording, 'De' miei bollenti spiriti' (Matrix 622c, 052129) [No. 38]: until lately we had assumed (probably like most listeners) that it was sung with a semitone transposition, in D, and accepted the pinched sounds

---

14 All of the published Fonotipias have been reissued, with some of De Lucia's G&T and Phonotype recordings of songs, on Opal CDS 9845.

15 See, for example, Paul Steinson, 'Repressed De Lucia Phonotypes - Keys and Speeds', *Record Collector*, Vol.32, Nos. 1-2, Jan. 1987, pp. 19-24, and related comments, ibid., p. 25.

16 De Mura, *Enciclopedia della Canzone Napoletana*, Vol. I, p. 104, states that De Angelis, who recorded for G&T in 1905-06, sang in many Italian theatres in operas such as *Aida*, *Andrea Chénier*, *Un Ballo in Maschera*, *Cavalleria Rusticana*, *La Gioconda*, *La Forza del Destino*, and *Il Trovatore*. The rôles are not specified.

towards the end as slight flaws in a delightful performance; in what now seems to be the more likely key of D flat the record appears more natural and tonally attractive.[17]

The suggested speeds represent the writer's considered views, based on a study both of the records and of the available *contemporary* evidence concerning De Lucia's voice and his transpositions on stage. They produce a darker vocal timbre than that to which we have become accustomed, and one which will probably cause surprise. In what amounts to a balance of probabilities - and the writer is fully aware that we can, with sufficient exposure, become accustomed to almost any timbre - the speeds may always be controversial. Some respected opinions are, it must be said, in disagreement - generally to the extent of a semitone - over transpositions in the G&T records.[18] Communicated speeds, or those thought the most likely on the basis of communicated speed and pitch relationships, are given in square brackets. Those drawn from the sleeve-notes of reissues appear in parentheses.

Keys

Downward transposition is represented by one asterisk for each semitone. No upward transpositions of operatic pieces have been found. The key given is that in which De Lucia is *thought* to have sung the piece and, unless otherwise stated, is the major. Many pieces modulate from one key to another; wherever possible the main key is the one given. However, some pieces modulate so frequently that it is difficult to assign a single key to them, and this consideration applies still more markedly to the recitatives. In such cases, the keys at the beginning and end are given.

Stroboscopes

Speeds are reported to two decimal places. This is not to claim such precision but to reflect the fact that the speeds given correspond to those on stroboscopes constructed for a 50 Hz light source. A stroboscope with 84 divisions appears stationary not at 71 but at 71.43 rpm, and one with 85 divisions at 70.59 rpm. Rounding to the nearest whole number can be misleading, since the 71 rpm band (the worst example) of a 50 Hz stroboscope can actually correspond to a speed of *either* 71.43 (84 divisions) or 70.59 rpm (85 divisions), a difference (0.84 rpm) which is sometimes detectable. Similarly, the 67 rpm band is almost midway between 66.67 (90 divisions) and 67.42 rpm (89 divisions). Rounding introduces the risk that they might be thought identical. In the range 64-83 rpm, only 75 rpm (80 divisions) and 80 rpm (75 divisions) are definable as integers, although most of the deviations from whole numbers are small.[19] A speed quoted to two decimal places corresponds, then, to the band so named on a stroboscope designed for a 50 Hz lamp or, for speeds which fall between bands, to an arithmetical average of the speeds of two named bands which appear to be revolving at the same rate but in opposite directions. For completeness, the actual speeds which correspond most closely to the rounded numbers of a 50 Hz stroboscope are:

64 63.83	69 68.97	74 74.07	79 78.95
65 65.22	70 69.77	75 75.00	80 80.00
66 65.93	71 70.59 (71.43)	76 75.95	81 81.08
67 66.67	72 72.29	77 76.92	82 82.19
68 68.18	73 73.17	78 77.92	83 83.33

17 The reissue of the complete G&T recordings of De Lucia (Rubini 305) will reproduce uniformly in what are now thought to be the correct keys if a single downward adjustment of a semitone be made.

18 Fagan and Moran, *The Encyclopedic Discography of Victor Recordings*, Vol. III, base their conclusions on speeds derived for records with adjacent matrix numbers to those of De Lucia.

19 There is a corresponding set of values for a 60 Hz stroboscope; here also, in the range 68-88 rpm, only 75 and 80 rpm are definable as integers.

Gramophone & Typewriter/Gramophone Company Recordings

Orchestral accompaniment except where noted.
Matrix suffix 'c' signifies a 30 cm recording; all others are 25 cm.[1]

Matrix no.	HMV sf	HMV df	Victor sf/*df*	Other reissue	Speed	Key used	Trans- position

Milan, c. November 30th 1902 (Session I)[2]

1 Ideale (Carmelo Errico - F. Paolo Tosti)(Pf)

| 2861R | 52410 | - | 5027 91022 | IRCC 5003 | 65.93 | A flat | |

2 *Werther:* Ah! non mi ridestar (Pourquoi me réveiller) (Massenet)(Pf Cottone)

| 2862R | 52435 | - | - | - | 65.93 | E flat min | *** |

3 *Rigoletto:* La donna è mobile (Verdi)(Pf)

| 2863R | 52411 | - | 5026 91021 | HRS 2001 | 65.93 | A | ** |

4 *Il Barbiere di Siviglia:* Se il mio nome (Rossini)(Pf)

| 2864W2 | 52427 | - | 5049 91038 | - | 65.93 | F sharp min | *** |

5 *Fedora*: Amor ti vieta (Giordano)(Pf Cottone)

| 2865W2 | 52436 | - | - | - | 65.93 | B flat | ** |

6 Marechiare (Salvatore Di Giacomo - F.P. Tosti)(N)(Pf)

| 2866R | 52412 | - | - | - | 65.93 | C sharp min | |

7 Napulitanata (S. Di Giacomo - Pasquale Mario Costa)(N)(Pf)

| 2867W2 | 52413 | - | - | - | 65.93 | B min | |

8 *Tosca:* Recondita armonia (Puccini)(Pf)

| 2868R | 52414 | - | 5028 91023 | HRS 2001 | 65.93 | E flat | ** |

9 Fenesta che lucive (Giulio Genoino & Mariano Paolella - Guglielmo Cottrau)(N)(Pf)

| 2869R | 52415 | - | - | - | 65.93 | E min | |

10 *Manon:* Chiudo gli occhi (En fermant les yeux)(Il sogno) (Massenet)(Pf)

| 2870W2 | 52416 | - | 5025 91020 | - | 65.93 | D flat | * |

Milan, c. December 3rd 1902 (Session II)

11 *Cavalleria Rusticana:* O Lola ch'ai di latti (Siciliana) (Mascagni)(Pf)

| 2897b | 52652 | - | - | - | 63.82 | E flat min | ** |

12 A suon di baci (- Antonio Baldelli)(Pf)

| 2898W2 | 52651 | - | - | - | 63.82 | D | |

13 *Carmen:* Il fior che avevi a me tu dato (La fleur) (Bizet)(Pf)

| 2899R | 52437 | - | - | HRS 1025 VA 13 | 63.82 | B | ** |

14 Sei morta ne la vita mia (G. Capitelli - P.M. Costa)(Pf)

| 2900R | 52438 | - | - | - | 63.82 | A | |

15 *Lohengrin:* Mercè, mercè, cigno gentil (Nun sei bedankt) (Wagner)(Pf)

| 2905W2 | 52650 | - | - | HRS 1025 VA 13 | 65.93 | G | ** |

---

1 With one exception [No. 11], these recordings carry matrix numbers with handwritten suffixes, 'R' and 'W2', which denote the recordist. These suffixes were later deleted and replaced by 'b', the standard letter for this 25 cm (10") series.

2 Some (but not all) labels of records from this session bear the name of Salvatore Cottone, whom Kelly, op. cit., gives as the accompanist for all De Lucia's 1902 records.

Milan, c. October 6th 1904 (Session III)

16 *Fedora:* Mia madre, la mia vecchia madre (Pf Sabajno)
2153L   52077   -   -   -   73.17   F   **
17 *Fedora:* Vedi, io piango (Pf Sabajno)
2154L   52078   -   -   -   73.17   F min   **
18 Occhi di fata (Tremacoldo - Luigi Denza)(Pf Sabajno)
2155L   52079   -   -   -   73.17   G flat
19 *La Traviata:* Ah sì, da un anno ... Un dì felice, eterea (Verdi)(Pf Sabajno)
2156L   52080   -   -   VA 15   73.17   E   *
20 *La Favorite:* Una vergine, un angel di Dio (Donizetti)(Pf Sabajno)
2157L   52081   -   -   -   73.17   F sharp   ***
21 La Serenata (G.A. Cesareo - F.P. Tosti)(Pf Sabajno)
2158L   52082   -   -   -   73.17   E
22 Lontananza (Francesco Cilea)(Pf Francesco Cilea)
2159L   52084   -   -   -   73.17   C sharp min
23 *Adriana Lecouvreur:* L'anima ho stanca (Cilea)(Pf Cilea)
2160L   52083   -   -   -   73.17   A min   **
24 *Faust:* Tardi si fa (Il se fait tard) (Gounod)(Pf Sabajno)(w. Celestina Boninsegna)
213m   054043   -   -   IRCC 15   73.17   E   *
25 *Il Barbiere di Siviglia:* Ecco ridente in cielo (Pf Sabajno)
214m   052078   -   92029   HRS 1053   73.17   B flat   **
                   76000
                   88602
                   6399

Milan, September-October 1905 (Session IV)

26 *Lohengrin:* Di, non t'incanta (Atmest du nicht)(Pf Sabajno)
7339b   2-52472   -   -   -   73.17   B   *
27 *Lohengrin:* S'ei torna alfin (Kommt er dann heim) (Pf Sabajno)
7340b   2-52473   -   -   -   73.17   F sharp   *
28 *Les Pêcheurs de Perles:* Della mia vita (De mon amie) (Bizet)(Pf Sabajno)
7341b   2-52474   -   -   -   73.17   C min   **
29 *Mignon:* La tua bell'alma (Ah! que ton âme enfin)(Thomas)(Pf Sabajno)
7342b   2-52475   -   -   -   73.17   E flat   *
30 *Mignon:* Addio, Mignon! (Adieu, Mignon!)(Pf Sabajno)
549c   052111   -   -   15-1024   72.29   F sharp   *
                   IRCC[3]

Milan, c. May 1st 1906 (Session V)

22a Lontananza (Francesco Cilea)[4]
31 *Il Barbiere di Siviglia:* Numero quindici (Pf Sabajno)(w. Antonio Pini-Corsi)
8053b   54293   -   -   -   73.17   F sharp   *
32 *Mignon:* Ah! non credevi tu (Elle ne croyait pas) (Pf Sabajno)
8054b   2-52518   DA 124   -   -   73.17   B   *
33 *Faust:* Salve! Dimora (Salut! Demeure) (Pf Sabajno)
8058b   2-52519   -   -   -   73.17   F sharp   **
34 *Les Pêcheurs de Perles:* Mi par d'udir ancora (Je crois entendre) (Pf Sabajno)
8059b   2-52520   -   -   -   73.17   F sharp min   ***
35 *Il Barbiere di Siviglia:* All'idea di quel metallo (Or. cond. Sabajno)(w. A. Pini-Corsi)
619c   054080   DB 388   -   -   73.17   F   **

---

3 The IRCC issue was not assigned a number.
4 The background to this recording (whose matrix number is unknown) is discussed on pp. 322 and 327.

36 *La Traviata:* Parigi, o cara (Or. cond. Sabajno)(w. Josefina Huguet)
620c   054081   DB 368   88361   ABHB 6   73.17   G flat   **

37 *Les Pêcheurs de Perles:* Non hai compreso (Ton coeur n'a pas compris)(Or. cond. Sabajno)(w. J. Huguet)
621c   054082   DB 570   92054   IRCC 64   73.17   A min   *
                                89147   VB 34
                                8058

38 *La Traviata:* De' miei bollenti spiriti (Pf Sabajno)
622c   052129   -   -   15-1024   73.17   D flat   **
                                IRCC 24

39 *Il Barbiere di Siviglia:* Ah! qual colpo (Pf Sabajno)(w. J. Huguet & A. Pini-Corsi)
630c   054083   DB 388   -   VB 1   73.17   E flat   **

40 *Rigoletto:* E il sol dell'anima (Pf Sabajno)(w. J. Huguet)
638c   054084   DB 368   92056   ABHB 6   73.17   A flat   **
                                89142

Milan, July-September 1907 (Session VI)

41 Pietà, Signore (Aria di Chiesa)(L.A. Niedermeyer)(Pf Sabajno)
10512b   2-52608   -   -   73.17   B min   *

42 *L'Elisir d'Amore:* Ecco il magico liquore...Obbligato, obbligato (Donizetti)(Pf Sabajno)(w. Ernesto Badini)
10513b   54357   -   91079   AGSA 25   73.17   F sharp   *
                                87562

43 10514b is unidentified, possibly an unpublished De Lucia recording.[5]

44 *Manon:* Chiudo gli occhi (En fermant les yeux)(Il sogno)(Pf Sabajno)
10515b   2-52607   -   87049   IRCC 57   73.17   D flat   *
                                66001   AGSA 25

45 *Lohengrin:* Cessaro i canti alfin! (Das süsse Lied)(Or. cond. Sabajno)(w. J. Huguet)
1170½c   054171   DB 237   92055   -   72.29   E flat   *
                                89141
                                8056

46 *Lohengrin:* Mio salvatore...Mai devi domandarmi (Mein Held, mein Retter...Nie sollst du mich befragen)(Or. cond. Sabajno)(w. J. Huguet)
1171c   054175   DB 237   -   IRCC 104   72.29   A flat,   *
                                          then G

47 *Carmen:* La tua madre...Mia madre io vedo ancor (Votre mère avec moi sortait de la chapelle...Ma mère je la vois!)(Or. cond. Sabajno)(w. J. Huguet)
1172c   054172   DB 359   92052   VB 34   72.29   A then   *
                                89140   F sharp

48 *Faust:* Tardi si fa (Il se fait tard) (Pf Sabajno)(w. J. Huguet)
1173c   054173   DB 570   92053   -   73.17   E   *

49 *Lohengrin:* Mercè, mercè, cigno gentil (Nun sei bedankt)(Or. cond. Sabajno) (w. La Scala chorus, chorus master Giuseppe Cairati)
1174c   052184   DB 605   92033   -   73.17   A flat   *
                                76002
                                88603
                                6399

50 *Carmen:* Il fior che avevi a me tu dato (La fleur)(Or. cond. Sabajno)
1175c   052185   DB 359   92028   -   73.17   B   **
                                76001

---

5 G&T recording contracts for this period were usually (but not invariably) for five or ten titles. Hence, the session of May 1906, from which ten records were issued, may be regarded as complete. This single gap in a session which produced nine published records suggests that 10514b might be an unpublished De Lucia title. The documentation at EMI shows a gap between 10513 and 10515b.

Milan, c. May 1908 (Session VII)

51 *Don Giovanni:* Dalla sua pace (Mozart)(Pf)
11164b   2-52666   -   -   72.29   F   **
52 *Romeo et Juliette:* Deh, sorgi il luce in ciel (Ah! lève-toi soleil)(Gounod)(Pf)
11165b   2-52660   -   -   72.29   A flat   **
53 *Don Giovanni:* Il mio tesoro (Pf)
11166b   2-52661   DA 124   -   VA 65   69.77   A   *
54 *Il Barbiere di Siviglia:* Se il mio nome (Pf)[6]
11167b   2-52667   -   66000   -   69.77   F sharp min ***
55 *Il Barbiere di Siviglia:* Ah! qual colpo (Pf)(w. Galvany)
11168b   54384   -   -   69.77   E   *
56 *La Sonnambula:* Ah! perchè non posso odiarti (Bellini)(Pf)[7]
11169b   2-52676   -   -   69.77   A flat   **
57 *Il Barbiere di Siviglia:* Ecco ridente in cielo (Pf)[8]
1442c   052250   -   -   71.43   B flat   **
58 *La Sonnambula:* Prendi, l'anel ti dono (Pf)(w. Galvany)
1443c   054217   -   89045   IRCC 64 71.43   G flat   **
                               8057
59 *La Sonnambula:* Son geloso (Pf)(w. Galvany)
1444c   054215   -   -   IRCC 104 71.43   E flat   **
60 *Luisa Miller:* Quando le sere al placido (Verdi)(Pf)
1445c   052239   -   -   71.43   G flat   **

Naples, May 21st 1909 (Session VIII)

61 Sulla bocca amorosa (- Riccardo Barthélemy)
13331b   2-52698   -   87048   IRCC 5001 65.93   A
                               66002
62 Era de maggio (S. Di Giacomo - P.M. Costa)(N)
13332b   2-52699   -   66003   IRCC 5003 65.93   B min/maj
63 Triste ritorno (L. Forzati - R. Barthélemy)
13333b   2-52700   -   -   65.93   B
64 Serenamente (Silvio Marvasi - R. Barthélemy)
13334b   2-52772   -   -   IRCC 5001 65.93   E
                                       HMA 2
65 Oilì, oilà (S. Di Giacomo - P.M. Costa)(N)(Violin, Pf)(w. chorus)
13335b   2-52722   DA 333   -   65.93   E
66 'O sole mio (Giovanni Capurro - Eduardo Di Capua)(N) (Violin, mandolin, pf)
13336b   2-52701   DA 335   87047   -   69.77   G flat
                               66004
67 Carmela (Words and music by G. De Curtis)(N)(w. chorus)
13337b   2-52773   -   66006   IRCC 57 69.77   G flat
68 Nun me guardate 'cchiù (Ferdinando Russo - Salvatore Gambardella)(N)(Violin, pf)
13338b   2-52723   DA 333   -   69.77   F sharp min/maj
69 'A surrentina (G. De Curtis - Ernesto De Curtis)(N)(Violin, pf)
13339b   2-52774   -   -   HMA 2   69.77   G sharp min
70 Luna, lù! (Teodoro Rovito - Vincenzo Ricciardi)(N)(Violin, mandolin, pf)(w. chorus)
13340b   2-52724   DA 335   -   69.77   E flat min/maj

---

6 [No. 54] gives both verses, whereas [No. 4], which is also piano accompanied, gives only one verse.

7 The marked keys for the *La Sonnambula* titles [Nos. 56, 58, & 59] relate to the modern Ricordi score and not to that used by Rubini, the first interpreter.

8 Compared with the 1904 recording [No. 25], this version is distinguishable by its more flamboyant piano introduction and by the fact that, five bars into the aria, De Lucia sings '. . . *sorgi mia dolce speme*' instead of the written '. . . *e tu non sorgi ancora*'.

Fonotipia Recordings

All orchestrally accompanied, all 27 cm
Speed 75.00 rpm

Recorded in Milan

Jan. 10th 1911 XPh 4461-65
Jan. 11th 1911 XPh 4466-73
Jan. 12th 1911 XPh 4474-82
Jan. 13th 1911 XPh 4483-90
Jan. 14th 1911 XPh 4491-92

	Matrix no.	Catalogue no.	Key
71 Mattinata (Ruggero Leoncavallo)			
	XPh 4491	92695	D
72 A suon di baci (A. Baldelli)			
	XPh 4492	92696	E flat
73 Matenata (Ernesto Murolo - Evemero Nardella)(N)			
	XPh 4469	92697	G sharp min/maj
74 Serenata scumbinata (Libero Bovio - Vincenzo Valente)(N)			
	XPh 4466	92698	C sharp min
75 Marechiare (S. Di Giacomo - F.P. Tosti)(N)			
	XPh 4467	92699	C sharp min
76 Lu cardillo (Ernesto Del Preite - Pietro Labriola)(N)			
	XPh 4468	92700	E flat min
77 'O sole mio (G. Capurro - E. Di Capua)(N)			
	XPh 4488	92701	G flat
78 Luna nova (S. Di Giacomo - P.M. Costa)(N)			
	XPh 4465	92702	A
79 Durmenno (Roberto Bracco - Enrico De Leva)(N)			
	XPh 4473	92703	E
80 Vo' turnà (Edoardo Nicolardi - E. De Curtis)(N)			
	XPh 4489	92704	F sharp min/maj
81 Torna a Surriento (G. De Curtis - E. De Curtis)(N)			
	XPh 4484	92705	E flat min
82 'O marenariello (Gennaro Ottaviano - S. Gambardella)(N)			
	XPh 4474	92706	F sharp min/maj
83 Dimme (E. Murolo - S. Gambardella)(N)			
	XPh 4485	92707	E
84 Carmela (Words and music by G. De Curtis)(N)			
	XPh 4481	92708	F sharp
85 Serenata a Surriento (Aniello Califano - S. Gambardella)(N)			
	XPh 4490	92709	E
86 Voce 'e notte (E. Nicolardi - E. De Curtis)(N)			
	XPh 4480	92710	F sharp min/maj
87 Comm 'o zuccaro (Raffaele Ferraro-Correra - Pasquale Fonzo)(N)			
	XPh 4470	92711	A flat
88 Era de maggio (S. Di Giacomo - P.M. Costa)(N)			
	XPh 4483	92712	B min/maj
89 Scetate (F. Russo - P.M. Costa)(N)			
	XPh 4461	92713	F sharp min
90 Napulitanata (S. Di Giacomo - P.M. Costa)(N)			
	XPh 4486	92714	B min

91 Fenesta che lucive (G. Genoino & M. Paolella - G. Cottrau)(N)
　　　　　　　　　　　　　XPh 4462　　92715　　F min
92 Canta pe' me! (L. Bovio - E. De Curtis)(N)
　　　　　　　　　　　　　XPh 4482　　92716　　E flat min
93 Serenata napulitana (S. Di Giacomo - P.M. Costa)(N)
　　　　　　　　　　　　　XPh 4479　　92717　　E flat
94 Chi sa? (F. Russo - F.P. Tosti)(N)
　　　　　　　　　　　　　XPh 4463　　92718　　F sharp min/maj
95 Palomma 'e notte (S. Di Giacomo - Francesco Buongiovanni)(N)
　　　　　　　　　　　　　XPh 4472　　92719　　E
96 Luna, lù! (T. Rovito - V. Ricciardi)(N)
　　　　　　　　　　　　　XPh 4487　　92720　　E flat min/maj
97 Tu sola! (F. Russo - S. Gambardella)(N)
　　　　　　　　　　　　　XPh 4478　　92721　　F sharp min/maj
98 Si chiagnere me siente (L. Bovio & E. Murolo - S. Gambardella)(N)
　　　　　　　　　　　　　XPh 4477　　92722　　G sharp min
99 Mamma mia che vo' sapè?! (F. Russo - Emanuele Nutile)(N)
　　　　　　　　　　　　　XPh 4476　　92723　　F sharp min/maj
100 Ammore che gira (G. Capurro - F. Buongiovanni)(N)
　　　　　　　　　　　　　XPh 4471　　92724　　E
100a Serenata a Maria (A. Califano - S. Gambardella)
　　　　　　　　　　　　　XPh 4464　　Unpublished
100b Comme a na fronna (Vittorio F. Guarino - S. Gambardella)
　　　　　　　　　　　　　XPh 4475　　Unpublished

Phonotype Recordings

All recorded in Naples

Accompaniment by 'Orchestra [Salvatore] Sassano' except where noted.
An 'M' prefix signifies a 30 cm and a 'C' a 27 cm recording.

Pref.	Matrix no.	Dia. (cm)	Speed (rpm)	Key	Transposition

May 24th 1917

101 *Il Barbiere di Siviglia:* Ecco ridente in cielo[9]

| M | 1744 | 30 | 83.33 | B | * |

102 *La Favorite:* Una vergine (Un ange, une femme inconnue)

| C | 1745 | 27 | 83.33 | G | ** |

103 A suon di baci (A. Baldelli)

| M | 1746 | 30 | (83) | | |

104 *Carmen:* Il fior (La fleur)[10]

| M | 1747 | 30 | 83.33 | C | * |

105 *Il Barbiere di Siviglia:* Se il mio nome

| M | 1748 | 30 | 83.33 | G min | ** |

106 *Rigoletto:* La donna è mobile

| M | 1749 | 30 | 83.33 | [B flat] | * |

---

9 In a narrow band of grooves which, in the Symposium Records pressing, precedes the aria, De Lucia may be heard trying out his voice.

10 Both [No. 104] and [No. 261] were maintained in the catalogue: 261 is distinguished by a heavy opening orchestral chord which has no counterpart in 104.

107 *Mefistofele:* Dai campi, dai prati (Boito)
   M   1750   30   83.33   E   *
108 *Mefistofele:* (Epilogue) Giunto sul passo estremo
   M   1751   30

May 31st 1917

109 *Manon:* O dolce incanto...Chiudo gli occhi (Il sogno)(Instant charmant... En fermant les yeux)
   M   1752   30   [84.51]   [D flat]   [*]
110 *Mignon:* Addio, Mignon! (Adieu, Mignon!)
   M   1753   30   84.51   F sharp   *
111 *L'Elisir d'Amore:* Una furtiva lagrima
   M   1754   -
112 *Werther:* Ah! non mi ridestar (Pourquoi me réveiller)
   M   1755   30   84.51   E min   **
113 *La Gioconda:* Cielo e mar (Ponchielli)
   M   1756   30   84.51   D   *
114 *Mignon:* Ah! non credevi tu! (Elle ne croyait pas)[11]
   M   1757   30   84.51   B   *
115 *Les Pêcheurs de Perles:* Mi par d'udir (Je crois entendre)
   M   1758   30   (88.24)   (F sharp min)   (***)
116 *La Favorite:* Spirto gentil (Ange si pur)
   M   1759   -

June 3rd 1917

117 *Mefistofele:* (Epilogue) Giunto sul passo estremo[12]
   M   1751/2   30   68.97   A flat   -
118 *Tosca:* E lucevan le stelle[13]
   M   1760   30   [68.97]   [B flat min]   [*]
119 *Rigoletto:* Questa o quella[14]
   C   1761   27   68.97   G   *
120 *La Traviata:* Lunge da Lei...De' miei bollenti spiriti
   M   1762   30   68.97   D   *
121 *Aida:* Celeste Aida (Verdi)
   M   1763   30   [68.97]   [A]   [*]

---

11 A footnote in the Italian vocal score (Casa Editrice Madella) remarks: 'This air may be transposed to Bb, as sung at the Opéra Comique.'

12 All known 30 cm pressings of *Mefistofele*: 'Giunto sul passo' are from a matrix which lacks the designation /2. Nevertheless, they play at score pitch at 68.97 and so clearly fit well into this session rather than that of May 24, where 83.33 was the prevailing speed. Hence, the second matrix, from which the /2 was inadvertently omitted, was clearly the one used. As one of relatively few of De Lucia's operatic records to emerge at score pitch it has particular significance in the determination of the session speed and, indeed, in the pitching of his records in general. Since *upward* transposition would seem most unlikely, this record indicates a *maximum* session speed of 68.97, which might otherwise be thought very slow for as late as 1917.

13 Copies of M 1760 are known from both matrices, 118 and 182.

14 A Phonotype 25 cm. dubbing of this title, also numbered C 1761, plays in G, with a semitone transposition, at 68.97.

June 17th 1917

122 *I Puritani:* A te, o cara (Bellini)
   M   1764   30   72.29   B flat   ****
123 *Cavalleria Rusticana:* O Lola, ch'ai di latti (Siciliana)
   M   1765   30   72.29   E flat min   **
124 *L'Africaine:* O paradiso! (O paradis!)(Meyerbeer)
   M   1766   -
125 *La Bohème:* Che gelida manina (Puccini)15
   C   1767   27   72.29   B   **
126 *La Bohème:* In poverta mia lieta
   C   1768   -
127 Fenesta che lucive (G. Genoino & M. Paolella - G. Cottrau)(N)
   M   1769   30   [72.29]

June 24th 1917

128 *La Traviata:* Un dì felice, eterea (w. Angela De Angelis)
   M   1770   30   74.07   E   *
129 *La Traviata:* Parigi, o cara (w. De Angelis)
   M   1771   30   74.07   G   *
130 *Aida:* La fatal pietra (w. De Angelis)
   M   1772   30   [74.07]   [D min/G flat/B]   [**]
131 *Aida:* O terra addio (w. De Angelis)
   M   1773   30   [74.07]   [E]   [**]
132 *L'Elisir d'Amore:* Una furtiva lagrima
   M   1754/2   30   74.07   A min   *

July 1st 1917

133 *Cavalleria Rusticana:* Mamma, quel vino è generoso (Addio alla madre)
   (w. unidentified soprano, presumably De Angelis)
   M   1774   30   73.17   G flat   **
134 *Faust:* Tardi si fa (Il se fait tard)(w. De Angelis)
   C   1775   27   [73.17]   [E flat]   [**]
135 *Faust:* Sempre amar (Eternelle)(w. De Angelis)
   C   1776   27   [73.17]   [B]   [**]
136 *Rigoletto:* Ah, inseparabile...E il sol dell'anima (w. De Angelis)
   M   1777   30   [73.17]   [A flat]   [**]
137 *L'Africaine:* O Selika, io t'adoro (O ma Sélika, vous régnez sur mon âme)
   (w. De Angelis)
   C   1778   27   73.17   D flat   **
138 *Cavalleria Rusticana:* Tu qui, Santuzza? (w. De Angelis)
   M   1779   30   [73.17]   [G min]   [**]
139 *Cavalleria Rusticana:* Ah! lo vedi che hai tu detto? (w. De Angelis)
   M   1780   30   [73.17]   [G flat]   [**]
                             (at 'No, No, Turiddu')

---

15 Instead of remaining on the opening note on the words *'Che gelida manina'*, De Lucia sings the rising orchestral phrase. In [No. 314], except for a transposition, he sings the phrase as written.

July 15th 1917

140 *Il Barbiere di Siviglia:* All'idea di quel metallo (w. Giorgio Schottler)
   M   1781   30   74.07   F   **
141 *Il Barbiere di Siviglia:* Numero quindici (w. Schottler)
   M   1782   30   74.07   F   **
142 *La Forza del Destino:* Solenne in quest'ora (Verdi)(w. Antonio Armentano)
   M   1783   30   (74)   (B min)   (*)
143 *La Forza del Destino:* Le minaccie (w. Armentano)
        1784   27   [74.07]   [F sharp min]   [**]
144 *La Forza del Destino:* Non si placa il mio furore (w. Armentano)
   C   1785   27
145 *Ruy Blas:* Ah, tu mi fuggivi...O dolce voluttà (Marchetti)(w. De Angelis)16
   M 1786   30   74.07   D/E flat   **

July 29th 1917

146 *Tosca:* Recondita armonia
   M   1787   30   [74.07]   [E]   [*]
147 *Fedora:* Amor ti vieta
   C   1788   27   74.07   B flat   **
148 *Il Guarany:* Pery! Che brami?...Sento una forza (Gomez)(w. De Angelis)
   C   1789   27   74.07   E   ***
149 *Il Guarany:* Ah! Lo sguardo tuo...Ma deh! che a me (w. De Angelis)17
   C   1790   27   74.07   E
150 *Il Trovatore:* Ah! sì, ben mio coll'essere (Verdi)
   M   1791   30   74.07   E flat min   **
151 *Luisa Miller:* Quando le sere al placido
   M   1792   30   74.07   G flat   **
152 *L'Africaine:* Mi batte il cor...O paradiso! (Pays merveilleux...O paradis!)
   M   1766/2 30   74.07   E   **

August 5th 1917

153 *Manon Lescaut:* Donna non vidi mai (Puccini)
   M   1793   30   75.00   A flat   **
154 *Manon:* Io son solo...Ah! dispar vision (Je suis seul!...Ah! fuyez, douce image)
   M   1794   30   75.00   D flat   **
155 *Rigoletto:* Ella mi fu rapita
   C   1795   -
155 *Rigoletto:* Parmi veder le lagrime
   C   1796   27   75.00   E   **
157 *La Forza del Destino:* La vita è inferno
   M   1797   30   75.00   E flat   **
158 *La Forza del Destino:* O tu che in seno
   M   1798   30   75.00   G flat maj/min   **
159 *La Favorite:* Spirto gentil (Ange si pur)
   M   1759/2 30   75.00   B flat   **

---

16 The Symposium Records pressing is from matrix 1786/2, which is not documented in the recording register. The suffix may be a recordist's error. In the absence of other evidence it is attributed to this session.

17 No score is to hand of this section of the *Il Guarany* duet.

160 *La Bohème:* In poverta mia lieta[18]
M   1768/3   -

August 19th 1917

161 *La Gioconda:* Enzo Grimaldo! (w. Armentano)
M   1800   -
162 *La Gioconda:* O grido di quest'anima (w. Armentano)
M   1801   -
163 *Lohengrin:* Da voi lontan (In fernem Land)
M   1802   30   74.07   G   **
164 *Pagliacci:* No! Pagliaccio non son; (Leoncavallo)
M   1803   30   74.07   D flat min/maj   **
165 *Faust:* Qual turbamento...Salve! dimora (Quel trouble...Salut! demeure)
M   1804   30   74.07   G flat   **
166 *Faust:* O bei lochi (O nature)
M   1805   30   74.07   G flat   **
167 *Andrea Chénier:* Colpito qui m'avete (Improvviso, Pt. I)(Giordano)
M   1806   -
168 *Andrea Chénier:* E volli pien d'amore pregar (Improvviso, Pt. II)
M   1807   -

September 2nd 1917

169 *Le Roi de Lahore:* Sia benedetto il dolore (Oui, je bénis la souffrance)
     (Massenet)   (w. De Angelis)[19]
M   1808   30   74.07   D   *
170 *I Puritani:* Nel mirarti (w. De Angelis)[20]
C   1809   30   74.07   A flat   ****
171 *I Puritani:* Vieni, vieni fra queste braccia (w. De Angelis)
M   1810   -
172 *Ernani:* Mercè, diletti amici...Come rugiada al cespite (Verdi)
M   1811   30   74.07   B flat   **
173 *Les Huguenots:* O qual soave vision...Bianca al par (Ah! quel spectacle...Plus
     blanche)(Meyerbeer)[21]
M   1812   30   74.07   A flat   **
174 *Lucia di Lammermoor:* Tombe degli avi miei (Donizetti)
M   1813   30   74.07   D flat   **
175 *Lucia di Lammermoor:* Fra poco a me ricovero
M   1814   30   74.07   C   **

---

18 There is no 1768/2 in the recording register.
19 De Angelis is very out of tune in her final note, making [No. 169] easily distinguishable from [No. 181].
20 The C prefix in the register is an error since the disc, though having a wide blank rim, is clearly intended to be 30cm. As may be heard from the Symposium Records repressing in 30 cm format, this 27 cm master was cut on a 30 cm blank left over from an earlier session and already partly used by De Lucia in an attempt to record the *Chénier* 'Improvviso', presumably [No. 167].
21 Score pitch is here taken as the B flat of the Ricordi score rather than the A of other scores, for which the transposition would be only a semitone.

September 16th 1917

176 *La Traviata:* Invitato a qui seguirmi...Mi chiamate? (Scena della borsa)
(w. De Angelis & chorus)
  M   1815   30   74.07   B/B flat   **

177 *Les Huguenots:* Stringe il periglio (Le danger presse)(w. De Angelis)
  M   1816   30   74.07   E flat min/maj/E   **

178 *Carmen:* Io ti vengo a cercar...Mia tu sei (Moi je viens te chercher...Ah! Je te tiens,
fille damnée)(w. De Angelis)22
  M   1817   30   [74.07]   [A flat/F]   [**]

179 *Rigoletto:* Ella mi fu rapita23
  C   1795/3 27   74.07   C sharp min   *

180 *La Bohème:* In poverta mia lieta
  C   1768/4 27   74.07   F maj   ***

September 30th 1917

181 *Le Roi de Lahore:* A te...Sia benedetto il dolore (Oui, je bénis la souffrance)
(w. De Angelis)
  M   1808/2 30   74.07   D   *

182 *Tosca:* E lucevan le stelle
  M   1760/2 30

183 *I Puritani:* Dunque m'ami, mio Arturo...Vieni, vieni fra queste braccia
(w. De Angelis)24
  M   1810/2 30   74.07   G   *****

184 *Lucia di Lammermoor:* M'odi e trema...Sulla tomba (w. De Angelis)
  M   1818   30   74.07   F min/maj   **

185 *Lucia di Lammermoor:* Ah talor del tuo pensiero...Verranno a te sull'aure
(w. De Angelis)
  M   1819   30   74.07   A flat   **

186 *Les Pêcheurs de Perles:* Non hai compreso (Ton coeur n'a pas compris)
(w. De Angelis)25
  M   1820   30   74.07   A flat min   **

November 11th 1917

187 *Pagliacci:* Bada, Pagliaccio...Un tal gioco (w. unidentified tenor as the villager in
the opening phrases)
  M   1843   30   74.07   E   *

188 *L'Amico Fritz:* Ed anche Beppo amò...O amore, o bella luce (Mascagni)
  M   1844   30   74.07   E   **

189 *Les Pêcheurs de Perles:* Del tempio al limitar (Au fond du temple saint)
(w. Schottler)
  M   1845   -

190 *Fedora:* Mia madre, la mia vecchia madre
  C   1846   27   74.07   G

---

22 The words sung by De Angelis are indistinct. 'Io ti vengo' is the translation commonly given in Italian libretti.

23 There is no 1795/2 in the register.

24 Transposition to avoid the high D obliges De Lucia to sing some low-lying phrases an octave higher.

25 A distinguishing feature of [No. 186] is that someone, presumably De Lucia, makes an indistinct aside just before the final phrase of the duet. This aside is absent from [No. 293].

November 18th 1917

191 *Lohengrin:* Cigno fedel! (Mein lieber Schwan)
  C   1857   27   [74.07]   [A flat]   [*]
192 *Lohengrin:* S'ei torna alfin (Kommt er dann heim)
  C   1858   27   [74.07]   [F sharp]   [*]
193 *Lohengrin:* Di non t'incanta (Atmest du nicht)
  C   1859   27   [74.07]   [B]   [*]
194 Rimpianto (Come un sogno d'or)(Alfredo Silvestri - Enrico Toselli)
  M   1860   30   74.07   D

December 30th 1917

195 Autunno (L. Bovio - E. De Curtis)(N)
  C   1867   -
196 Scetate (F. Russo - P.M. Costa)(N)
  M   1868   -
197 'O munasterio (S. Di Giacomo - P.M. Costa)(N)
  C   1869   27
198 'O marenariello (G. Ottaviano - S. Gambardella)(N)
  M   1870   -
199 'O sole mio (G. Capurro - E. Di Capua)(N)[26]
  M   1871   30
200 Catarì (S. Di Giacomo - P.M. Costa)(N)
  M   1872   30

January 20th 1918

201 Pietà, Signore (Aria di chiesa)(Niedermeyer)
  M   1879   30   74.07   C min
202 Ave Maria (J.S. Bach, arr. Gounod)(L)
  M   1880   30   74.07   F
203 Sérénade (Quand tu chantes)(Victor Hugo - Gounod)(Fr)[27]
  C   1881   27   74.07   F sharp
204 Serenata (Sérénade)(Quando canti)(- Gounod)
  C   1882   27

January 27th 1918

205 *Rigoletto:* Alla chiesa...Ah! veglia o donna (w. De Angelis, Armentano & an unidentified singer as Giovanna)[28]
  C   1886   25

February 3rd 1918

206 *Stabat Mater:* Vidit suum, Pt. I (G.B. Pergolesi)(L)
  C   1895   27

---

26 This version has an orchestral false start.

27 The Symposium records 30 cm pressing reveals that this 27 cm master employed a 30 cm blank previously used for a few bars of *Rigoletto*, 'Cortigiani', probably a trial for the Armentano version (M 1876), which was made on the same day.

28 De Lucia sings only '*Sua figlia*'. He is not mentioned in the register.

207 *Stabat Mater:* Vidit suum, Pt. II (G.B. Pergolesi)(L)
    C   1896   27
208 *Les Pêcheurs de Perles:* Della mia vita (De mon amie fleur endormie)
    C   1897   27   74.07   C min   **
209 Leggenda Valacca (Marcello - Gaetano Braga)
    M   1898   30   74.07   G
210 Autunno (L. Bovio - E. De Curtis)(N)[29]
    -    1867/2   30

April 3rd 1918

211 *Rigoletto:* Partite? Crudele! (w. Vida Ferluga, Armentano, chorus & unidentified singer as Borsa)
    C   1910   27
212 *Rigoletto:* M'odi! ritorna a casa (w. De Angelis, Ferluga, Armentano, Luis Muñoz & chorus)
    -    1911   27   [71.43]   [C]   [*]
213 *Rigoletto:* Povero giovin! (w. De Angelis, Ferluga, Muñoz & chorus)
    C   1912   27   [71.43]   [G flat]   [*]

April 6th 1918

214 *Rigoletto:* La donna è mobile...E là il vostr'uomo (w. Armentano & Muñoz)[30]
    C   1915   27   74.07   B flat   *
215 *Rigoletto:* E l'ami? (w. De Angelis, Armentano & Muñoz)
    -    1916   27
216 *Rigoletto:* Un dì, se ben rammentomi (w. De Angelis, Ferluga & Armentano)
    C   1918   27   74.07   E flat   *
217 *Rigoletto:* Bella figlia dell'amore (w. De Angelis, Ferluga & Armentano)
    M   1919   30   74.07   C   *

April 8th 1918

218 *Rigoletto:* Della mia bella incognita...Questa o quella (w. unidentified singer as Borsa)[31]
    C   1920   27
219 *Rigoletto:* Egli è là...morto! (w. Armentano)
    C   1921   27
220 *Rigoletto:* Ch'io gli parli (w. Armentano, Muñoz & chorus)
    M   1922   30
221 *Rigoletto:* Gran nuova! gran nuova! (w. Armentano, Muñoz, two unidentified singers (Borsa & Count Ceprano), & chorus)
    C   1923   27   [74.07]   [G]   [*]

April 11th 1918

222 *Rigoletto:* Giovanna, ho dei rimorsi... (w. De Angelis & unidentified singer as Giovanna)
    C   1930   27   [74.07]   [D flat]   [**]

---

29 The register gives only one duplicate take, which it erroneously lists as 1795/3.
30 The Phonotype 25 cm dubbing, numbered C 1915, also plays in B flat at 74.07.
31 The register lists De Lucia only.

223 *Rigoletto:* Che m'ami, deh! ripetimi...Addio, addio (w. De Angelis & two
unidentified singers, as Giovanna & Count Ceprano)
-     1931   27   [74.07]   [B] ('Addio, addio')   [**]

April 13th 1918

224 *Rigoletto:* Duca, duca!...Scorrendo uniti (w. Muñoz, two unidentified singers (Borsa
& Count Ceprano) & chorus.)32
-     1934   25

June 2nd 1918

225 *Il Barbiere di Siviglia:* Ecco ridente in cielo
C   1943   27   72.29   B flat   **
226 *Il Barbiere di Siviglia:* Oh sorte! già veggo
-     1944   27   72.29   B flat   **
227 *Il Barbiere di Siviglia:* Se il mio nome (w. Maria Resemba)
C   1945   27   72.29   G min   **

June 6th 1918

228 *Il Barbiere di Siviglia:* Oh cielo! Nella stanza...All'idea di quel metallo
(w. Francesco Novelli)
-     1948   -
229 *Il Barbiere di Siviglia:* Voi dovreste travestirvi (w. Novelli)
C   1949   -
230 *Il Barbiere di Siviglia:* Dunque? All'opra...Numero quindici
(w. Novelli)
C   1950   -

June 9th 1918

231 *Il Barbiere di Siviglia:* Alfine, eccoci qua...Ah qual colpo (w. Resemba & Novelli)
M   1964   30   72.29   E   **
232 *Il Barbiere di Siviglia:* Mio Signor!..ma..voi..Zitti, zitti, piano piano (w. Resemba &
Novelli)33
C   1965   27   [72.29]   [E flat]   [**]
233 *Il Barbiere di Siviglia:* Ma vedi il mio destino!...Pace e goia (w. Schottler)
C   1966   27   A flat   **
234 *Il Barbiere di Siviglia:* Insomma, mio Signore, che è lei? (w. Resemba & Schottler)
C   1967   27   C   -
235 *Il Barbiere di Siviglia:* Bella voce! bravissima!...Quando mi sei vicina (w. Resemba,
Novelli & Schottler)
C   1968   27   Recit.   *
                      Arietta in G flat   *

---

32 De Lucia is not listed in the register, which lists only '*coro*'; Muñoz is the *probable* Marullo. The disc,
which does not seem to be a dubbing, is 25 cm with no visible matrix number.

33 The keys given are those determined for a reissue (Rubini SJG 121) of Almaviva's music from *Il
Barbiere*. Since this was done not directly from originals but from tapes (whose speed was then adjusted as
necessary) of originals in the possession of several collectors it was unnecessary to determine the actual
speeds of the originals.

July 14th 1918

236 'A canaria (L. Bovio - Gaetano Lama)(N)
  C   1978   -
237 Nuttata napulitana (E. Murolo - Nicola Valente)(N)
  C   1979   -
238 La mia canzone (- G. Lama)
  -    1980   27
239 Torna al paesello (- Amerigo Giuliani)
  C   1981   -
240 Scetate (F. Russo - P.M. Costa)(N)
  C   1982   -

July 21st 1918

241 *Il Barbiere di Siviglia:* Finora in questa camera...Ehi di casa...buona gente
   (w. Resemba, Schottler, & Nina Sabatano)
  M   1984   30   [72]   [B flat]   [**]
242 *Il Barbiere di Siviglia*: E Rosina: or son contento (w. Resemba, Sabatano,
   Schottler, & Stefano Valentino)
  M   1985   30   [72]   [B flat]   [**]
243 *Il Barbiere di Siviglia*: E quel briccon che al conte (w. Resemba, Novelli, Schottler,
   & Valentino)
  C   1986   27   D   *
244 *Il Barbiere di Siviglia*: Colla febbre, Don Basilio...Buona sera (w. Resemba,
   Novelli, Schottler, & Valentino)
  M   1987   30   D/G flat   *
245 *Il Barbiere di Siviglia*: Buona sera...Stringi! (w. Resemba, Novelli, Schottler, &
   Valentino)
  M   1988   30   G flat/A/D   *

July 27th 1918

246 *Il Barbiere di Siviglia*: Piano, pianissimo (w. Angelo di Tommaso & chorus)
  -    1989   27   G flat   *
247 *Il Barbiere di Siviglia*: Ehi, Fiorello? (w. Di Tommaso, Novelli & chorus)
  M   1990   30   [72]   Recit   [**]
                            [then G flat]   [*]
248 *Il Barbiere di Siviglia*: Ecco qua! sempre un'istoria (w. Resemba, Novelli, Schottler,
   Valentino, Sabatano, & chorus)
  C 1991   27   [72]   [E flat]

August 11th 1918

249 *Il Barbiere di Siviglia*: Ah! Ah! che bella vita (w. Novelli & Schottler)
  M   1996   30   [72]   [**]
250 *Il Barbiere di Siviglia*: Fermi tutti. Nessun si muova (w. Resemba, Sabatano,
   Novelli, Schottler, Valentino, chorus, & an unidentified singer as The Official)
  M   1997   30   A flat   -

251 *Il Barbiere di Siviglia*: Ma signor....Zitto tu! Mi par d'esser colla testa (w. Resemba, Sabatano, Novelli, Schottler, Valentino, & chorus)
  -    1998   27   C   -
252 *Il Barbiere di Siviglia:* Ah disgraziati noi! (w. Resemba, Novelli, Schottler, Valentino, & chorus)
  M   1999   30   G   -

August 19th 1918

253 Torna al paesello (- A. Giuliani)
  C   1981/2   27
254 'A canaria (L. Bovio - G. Lama)(N)
  C   1978/2   27
255 Nuttata napulitana (E. Murolo - Nicola Valente)(N)
  C   1979/2   27
256 La mia canzone (- G. Lama)
  C   1980/2   27
257 *Il Barbiere di Siviglia*: Oh cielo! Nella stanza..All'idea (w. Novelli)
  -    1948/2   27   F   **
258 *Il Barbiere di Siviglia*: Voi dovreste travestirvi (w. Novelli)
  C   1949/2   27   F   **
259 *Il Barbiere di Siviglia*: Dunque? All'opra...Numero quindici (w. Novelli)
  C   1950/2   27   F   **

September 1st 1918

260 *Les Pêcheurs de Perles:* Mi par d'udir (Je crois entendre)
  M   2012   -
261 *Carmen:* Il fior (La fleur que tu m'avais jetée)
  M   1747/2   30   (78)   (D flat)
262 *Lohengrin*: Cessaro i canti alfin (Das süsse Lied verhallt)(w. De Angelis)
  M   2013   30   [72.29]   [E]
263 *La Traviata:* Dammi tu forza, o cielo...Amami, Alfredo (w. De Angelis)
  C   2014   27   (72.29)   (F sharp min/E)   (*)

September 11th 1918

264 Salve Maria (Pt.I)(Mercadante)
  C   2018   27   72.29   F
265 Salve Maria (Pt.II)
  C   2019   27   72.29   F
266 *La Sonnambula:* Perdona, o mia diletta...Prendi, l'anel ti dono (w. Olga Perugino)[34]
  M   2020   30   72.29   G   *
267 *La Sonnambula:* Sposi or siamo (w. Perugino)
  C   2021   27   72.29   G   *

---

34 See *notes* above regarding keys in *La Sonnambula*. The semitone transposition relates to the later score. The matrix number of the Symposium Records pressing appears on the record as 2020/2, but no second take appears in the register. Original pressings, from a matrix which lacks the /2 suffix, measure differently across the grooves and play for 4 min 48 sec, compared with 4 min 32 sec for 2020/2 at the same speed and with the same semitone transposition as 2020/2.

September 15th 1918

268 *La Gioconda:* Cielo e mar
    C   2035   27   [72.29]   [D]   *
269 *Manon:* O dolce incanto...Chiudo gli occhi (Il sogno)(Instant charmant...En fermant les yeux)35
    C   2036   27   [72.29]   [D flat]   *
270 *Mefistofele:* Dai campi, dai prati
    C   2037   27   72.29   E   *

May 24th 1919

271 Bambola infranta (Enrico Frati - J.W. Tate)
    C   2098   27
272 Perchè mi baci (- Ernesto Tagliaferri)
    C   2099   27
273 'Ncopp' 'a ll'onna (L. Bovio - Vincenzo Fassone)(N)
    C   2100   27   77.92   B min
274 Quanno canta Pusilleco (E. Murolo - E. Tagliaferri)(N)
    C   2101   27
275 Sta luna 'o vvo' (E. Murolo - N. Valente)(N)
    C   2102   27
276 Voce 'e notte (E. Nicolardi - E. De Curtis)(N)
    M   2103   30
277 Torna a Surriento (G. De Curtis - E. De Curtis)(N)
    M   2104   30

July 6th 1919

278 Mandulinata (L. Bovio - E. De Curtis)(N)
    C   2111   27   75.95   G sharp min
279 *Adriana Lecouvreur:* L'anima ho stanca (Cilea)
    C   2112   27   75.95   A min   **
280 *Adriana Lecouvreur:* Mi basta il tuo perdono...No, più nobile
    C   2113   27   [75.95]   [E flat]   [**]
281 Serenata medioevale (Nell'alta notte)(- Giuseppe Silvestri)
    M   2114   30   75.95   C min
282 *La Sonnambula:* Prendi, l'anel ti dono
    C   2115   27   [75.95]   [G flat]   [**]
283 Scetate (F. Russo - P.M. Costa)(N)
    C   1982/2   27

July 27th 1919

284 *La Forza del Destino:* La vita è inferno all'infelice
    C   2116   27   [75.95]   [G flat](aria)   [**]
285 *Otello:* Niun mi tema (Verdi)
    M   2117   30   75.95   G flat/E flat   *
286 *Lohengrin:* Mercè, mercè, cigno gentil (Nun sei bedankt, mein lieber Schwan)
    C   2118   27   [75.95]   [G]   [**]

---

35 Unlike [No. 109], this version has an unwritten high note just before the final 'Ah! Manon'.

287 *Pagliacci:* Vesti la giubba
   C   2119   -
288 *Lucia di Lammermoor:* Tu che a Dio
   C   2120   27   75.95   B   ***
289 A suon di baci (- A. Baldelli)
   C   2121   27   75.95   E flat

September 7th 1919

290 *La Bohème:* O soave fanciulla (w. De Angelis)36
   M   2134   30   80.00   A flat/B   *
291 *Carmen:* Ah! mi parla di lei (Parle-moi de ma mère)(w. De Angelis)
   C   2135   27   [80.00]   [A]   [*]
292 *Carmen:* Ti baciava mia madre...Mia madre io vedo ancor (Un baiser de ma mère...Ma mère, je la vois) (w. De Angelis)
   C   2136   27   [80.00]   [A/G flat]   [*]
293 *Les Pêcheurs de Perles:* Non hai compreso (Ton coeur n'a pas compris) (w. De Angelis)
   M   1820/2   30   [80.00]   [A flat min]   [**]
294 *La Bohème:* Sono andati? (w. De Angelis)
   M   2137   30   [80.00]   [B min]   [*]
295 *La Bohème:* Sono andati? (w. De Angelis)
   C   2138   27   [80.00]   [B min]   [*]
296 *La Bohème:* Tornò al nido (w. De Angelis)
   C   2139   27   [80.00]   [G]   [*]

October 5th 1919

297 *L'Amico Fritz:* Suzel, buon dì (w. De Angelis)
   M   2153   30   80.00   G/F sharp min
298 *L'Amico Fritz:* Tutto tace (w. De Angelis)
   M   2154   30   80.00   A flat min/maj   *
299 *La Traviata:* Ah non più (w. De Angelis)37
   M   2155
300 *La Traviata:* Ah non più...Ah! gran Dio! morir si giovine (w. De Angelis)
   C   2156   27   [80]   C ('Gran Dio!')
301 *Tosca:* Recondita armonia
   C   2157   27   80.00   E flat   **
302 *Fedora:* Ma chi m'accusa...Vedi, io piango (w. De Angelis)
   C   2158   27   [80.00]   [F sharp min]   [*]
303 *Fedora:* Addio!...Addio! a domani (w. De Angelis)
   C   2159   27   [80.00]   [E flat]   [*]

---

36 This title was later re-made [No. 307], probably to eliminate the heavily over-recorded passage early in the side rather than the (presumably simulated) kiss which, in a test pressing, is distinctly audible at the words 'No, per pietà!'

37 [No. 299], which has not been heard, is given here as listed in the register, which shows [No. 300] as 'Gran Dio! morir si giovine'. This phrase actually occurs near the end of [No. 300], which starts at: 'Ah!, non più'. [No. 299] is presumably a longer extract than is [No. 300].

November 23rd 1919

304 *Tosca:* Tu?...di tua man l'uccidesti...O dolci mani (w. unident. soprano, presumably De Angelis)

| C | 2220 | 27 | 77.92 | E | | * |

305 *Tosca:* Amaro sol per te (w. De Angelis)

| C | 2221 | 27 | [77.92] | [F] | | [*] |

306 *Tosca:* E non giungono...Trionfal di nuova speme (w. De Angelis)

| C | 2222 | 27 | [77.92] | [D flat/E flat] | | [*] |

307 *La Bohème:* O soave fanciulla (w. De Angelis)

| M | 2134/2 | 30 | (80) | (A flat/B) | | (*) |

308 *L'Elisir d'Amore:* Una parola, o Adina (w. De Angelis)

| M | 2223 | 30 | 77.92 | D flat | | ** |

309 *L'Elisir d'Amore:* Chiedi al rio (w. De Angelis)

| M | 2224 | 30 | 77.92 | D flat | | ** |

January 18th 1920

310 *Mefistofele:* Giunto sul passo estremo (Epilogue)[38]

| C | 2230/2 | 27 | [81.08] | [G] | | [*] |

311 *Mignon:* Ah! non credevi tu (Elle ne croyait pas)

| C | 2231 | - |

312 *Mignon:* La tua bell'alma (Ah! que ton âme enfin)

| C | 2232 | 27 | 81.08 | E flat | | * |

313 *Tosca:* E lucevan le stelle

| C | 2233 | 27 | 81.08 | B flat min | | * |

314 *La Bohème:* Che gelida manina[39]

| M | 2234 | 30 | 81.08 | B | | ** |

March 30th 1920

315 *La Traviata:* Concluding phrases in the recording of 'Sempre libera' by Angeles Ottein.[40]

| C | 2304 | 27 | [73.17] | [G] | | * |

April 11th 1920

316 *La Gioconda:* Enzo Grimaldo! (w. Benvenuto Franci)[41]

| C | 2340 | 27 | 76.92 | F | | ** |

317 *La Gioconda:* O grido di quest'anima (w. Franci)

| C | 2341 | 27 | 76.92 | B flat | | ** |

318 *Les Pêcheurs de Perles:* Del tempio al limitar (Au fond du temple saint)(w. Franci)

| M | 2342 | - |

---

38 The matrix number clearly appears as 2230/2 on the records, but no second take is listed in the register.

39 See note to [No. 125]. De Lucia avoids the low D flat (E flat at score pitch) on the word *'belli'*.

40 De Lucia is not mentioned in the register but his name appears, with Ottein's other records and also in the *La Traviata* section, in certain editions of the Phonotype catalogue.

41 M 2338, a Franci solo which was made at this session, plays in score pitch at 76.92 rpm.

April 18th 1920

319 *Mefistofele:* Forma ideal purissima
   C   2343   27   78.95   A   *
320 *Mefistofele:* Ascolta...Colma il tuo cor
   C   2344   27   78.95   B flat   **
321 Napule! (E. Murolo - E. Tagliaferri)(N)
   C   2345   27
322 'O mare canta (L. Bovio - G. Lama)(N)
   C   2346   27
323 *L'Elisir d'Amore:* Una furtiva lagrima
   C   2347   27
324 *L'Elisir d'Amore:* Un solo istante i palpiti
   C   2348   27
325 *La Bohème:* Che gelida manina
   M   2234/2 -

May 16th 1920

326 *L'Elisir d'Amore:* Quanto è bella
   C   2367   27
327 *L'Elisir d'Amore:* Adina! quest'oggi, no ... Adina, credimi
   C   2368   27
328 *Don Pasquale:* Sogno soave e casto (Donizetti)
   C   2369   27   [78.95]   [G]   [*]
329 *Don Pasquale:* Com' è gentil
   C   2370   27
330 *Don Pasquale:* Cercherò lontana terra
   C   2371   27

August 15th 1920

331 *Andrea Chénier:* Come un bel dì di maggio
   C   2392   27   75.00   F min   *
332 *Cavalleria Rusticana:* O Lola ch'ai di latti (Siciliana)[42]
   C   2393   27   75.00   E flat min   **
333 *Les Pêcheurs de Perles:* Mi par d'udir ancora (Je crois entendre encore)
   C   2394   27   [75.00]   [F sharp min]   [***]
334 *Carmen:* Il fior che avevi a me tu dato (La fleur que tu m'avais jetée)
   C   2395   27   [75.00]   [B]   [**]
335 *La Bohème:* Quest'è Mimì
   C   2396   27   75.00   D min/maj   **

September 12th 1920

336 Sogno (Lorenzo Stecchetti - F.P. Tosti)(Pf)
   C   2403   27
337 Dopo! (Ferdinando Martini - F.P. Tosti)(Pf)
   C   2404   27   75.00   D flat

---

42 Faint studio conversation at the end of [No. 332] distinguishes it from De Lucia's other orchestrally-accompanied version, [No. 123].

338 Ideale (C. Errico - F.P. Tosti)(Pf)[43]
    C   2405   27   75.00   A flat
339 Occhi di fata (Tremacoldo - L. Denza)(Pf)
    C   2406   27   75.00   A flat
340 Malia (Rocco E. Pagliara - F.P. Tosti)(Pf)
    C   2407   27   75.00   E
341 Se... (E. Mancini - L. Denza)(Pf)
    C   2408   27
342 La mia bandiera (prob. traditional - Augusto Rotoli)(Pf)
    C   2409   27   75.00   B flat min/maj
343 Ave Maria (C. Errico - F.P. Tosti)(Pf)
    C   2410   27
344 Torna (R.E. Pagliara (From English of A. Chapman) - L. Denza (Pf. & violin)
    C   2411   27

October 24th 1920

345 Tristezza (R. Mazzola - F.P. Tosti)(Pf)
    C   2430   27   75.00   E min
346 Musica proibita (N. Mapaldi - Salvatore Gastaldon)(Pf)
    C   2431   -
347 Quando tu sarai vecchia (L. Stecchetti - F.P. Tosti)(Pf)
    C   2432   27   75.00   A
348 Amour! Amour! (Victor Hugo - F.P. Tosti)(Fr)(Pf)
    C   2433   27   75.00   E
349 La serenata (G.A. Cesareo - F.P. Tosti)(Pf)
    C   2434   27   75.00   E
350 Aprile (R.E. Pagliara - F.P. Tosti)(Pf)
    C   2435   27   75.00   B
351 Segreto (L. Stecchetti - F.P. Tosti)(Pf)
    C   2436   27
352 La gondola nera (Raffaele Salustri - Augusto Rotoli)(Pf)
    C   2437   27   75.00   A flat

November 7th 1920

353 L'avessi tu compreso (- L. Denza)(Violin)
    C   2450   27
354 Ave Maria (Gounod)(L)(Violin)
    C   2451   27
355 *Iris:* Apri la tua finestra (Serenata)(Mascagni)(Pf)   ***
    C   2452   27   75.00   D
356 La mia canzone (Francesco Cimmino - F.P. Tosti)(Pf)
    C   2453   -
357 Povera mamma! (P. Ferrari - F.P. Tosti)(Pf)
    C   2454   -
358 Mattinata (Words & music by R. Leoncavallo)(Pf)
    C   2455   27

---

[43] De Lucia avoids the low note on the first syllable of *'splendori'*. He sings both verses, making the record easily distinguishable from [No. 1], which gives only one verse. [No. 400] has not been heard.

359 Amor fa morire! (S. Nurisio - A. Rotoli)(Pf)
  C 2456 -
360 L'alba (R. Salustri - A. Rotoli)(Pf)
  C 2457 27 75.00   C sharp min
361 Inverno triste (F. Cimmino - F.P. Tosti)(Pf)
  C 2458 27
362 Ninon (A. De Musset - F.P. Tosti)(Fr)(Pf)
  C 2459 27 75.00   F sharp min/maj
363 In mare (L. Stecchetti - F.P. Tosti)(Pf)
  C 2460 -

January 23rd 1921

364 L'ultima canzone (F. Cimmino - F.P. Tosti)(Pf)
  C 2506 -
365 Vorrei (M. De Fiori - F.P. Tosti)(Pf)
  C 2507 27 75.00   A min/maj
366 Caro mio ben (- Tommaso Giordani)(Pf)[44]
  C 2508 27 75.00   E
367 Se tu m'ami (Paoli Rolli - attrib. G.B. Pergolesi)(Pf)
  C 2509 27
368 Apri (L. Stecchetti - F.P. Tosti)(Pf)
  C 2510 -
369 Oblio! (V. Campanini - F.P. Tosti)(Pf)
  C 2511 27 75.00   A flat
370 Mattinata (Enrico Panzacchi - F.P. Tosti)(Pf)
  C 2512 27
371 Musica proibita (N. Mapaldi - Gastaldon)(Pf)
  C 2431/2 27 75.00   G flat
372 Amor fa morire! (S. Nurisio - A. Rotoli)(Pf)
  C 2456/2   75.00   F sharp min

February 6th 1921

373 *Werther:* Ah! non mi ridestar (Pourquoi me réveiller)
  C 2527 27
374 *I Puritani:* A te, o cara[45]
  C 2528 27
375 *La Favorite:* Spirto gentil (Ange si pur)
  C 2529 27
376 *Luisa Miller:* Quando le sere al placido
  C 2530 27
377 *Andrea Chénier:* Colpito qui m'avete (Improvviso, Pt.I)
  C 2531 27 75.00   A   ***
378 *Andrea Chénier:* E volli pien d'amore pregar (Improvviso, Pt.II)[46]
  C 2532 27 75.00   A   ***

---

44 Variously attributed either to Giuseppe or Tommaso Giordani.

45 De Lucia comes in a bar late while the orchestra plays seven triplets instead of four. In [No. 122] he enters correctly.

46 The lively studio chatter at the end of this recording is tantalisingly close to being intelligible.

April 17th 1921

379 *Manon Lescaut:* Donna non vidi mai
    C   2558   27   77.92   A flat   **
380 *Manon Lescaut:* Tra voi belle
    C   2559   27   77.92   E flat   *
381 *Pagliacci:* Recitar!...Vesti la giubba
    C   2560   27   77.92   E flat min   *
382 *Pagliacci:* No! Pagliaccio non son;
    C   2561   27   77.92   D flat min/maj   **
383 *Pagliacci:* O Colombina (Serenata)
    C   2562   27   77.92   G min   **

May 1st 1921

384 'O marenariello (G. Ottaviano - S. Gambardella)(N)
    C   2569   27   72.29   F sharp min/maj
385 Voce 'e notte (E. Nicolardi - E. De Curtis)(N)
    C   2570   27   72.29   F min/maj
386 Marechiare (S. Di Giacomo - F.P. Tosti)(N)
    C   2571   27
387 Salomé (Sotto la volta del cielo)(Riccardo Rossi - Robert Stolz, Op.355)(German verses by Artur Rebner)[47]
    C   2572   27   72.29   E min/maj
388 'O sole mio (G. Capurro - E. Di Capua)(N)
    C   2573   27   [72.29]   [G flat]
389 Fenesta che lucive (G. Genoino & M. Paolella - G. Cottrau)(N)
    C   2574   27   [72.29]   [F sharp min]
390 Napulitanata (Uocchie de suonno)(S. Di Giacomo - P.M. Costa)(N)
    C   2575   27

September 11th 1921
(With mandolins and guitars)[48]

391 Oilì, oilà (S. Di Giacomo - P.M. Costa)(N)
    C   2724   27
392 Funiculì, funiculà (Giuseppe Turco - L. Denza)(N)(w. chorus)
    C   2725   27   75.95   E flat
393 Palummella zompa e vola (Words & music by Teodoro Cottrau)(N)
    C   2726   27   75.95   A min
394 Nu mazzo 'e sciure (- Vincenzo De Meglio)(N)
    C   2727   27   75.95   A min
395 Mariannì (T. Cottrau - V. De Meglio)(N)
    C   2728   27   [75.95]   [E]
396 Lu cardillo (E. Del Preite - P. Labriola)(N)
    C   2729   27   75.95   E flat

---

[47] A voice, apparently De Lucia's, may be heard counting time between the verses.

[48] The register gives the accompaniment as mandolins and guitars but its actual composition is debatable.

November 20th 1921

397 Elégie (Louis Gallet - Massenet)(Fr)('Cello Sergio Viterbini)
    C   2761   -
398 Ave Maria (Gounod)(L)('Cello S. Viterbini)
    C   2762   27
399 Torna (R.E. Pagliara (from English of A. Chapman) - L. Denza) ('Cello S. Viterbini)
    C   2763   27
400 Ideale (C. Errico - F.P. Tosti)(Pf)
    C   2764   27

September 24th 1922

401 Marechiare (S. Di Giacomo - F.P. Tosti)(N)(Mandolins & guitars, cond. Raffaele Calace)(w. chorus)
    C   3148   27   73.17   C sharp min

The Complete Operas[49]

Rigoletto

Duke of Mantua	Fernando De Lucia	(tenor)	a
Rigoletto	Antonio Armentano Anticorona	(baritone)	b
Gilda	Angela De Angelis	(soprano)	c
Sparafucile	Luis Muñoz	(bass)	d
Count Monterone	Luis Muñoz	(bass)	e
Marullo	Luis Muñoz	(bass)	f
Maddalena	Vida Ferluga	(mezzo-soprano)	g
Countess Ceprano	Vida Ferluga	(mezzo-soprano)	h
Borsa	Unidentified	(tenor)	i
Count Ceprano	Unidentified	(bass)	j
Giovanna	Unidentified	(mezzo-soprano)	k
A Page	Unidentified	(mezzo-soprano)	l
An Usher	Unidentified	(bass)	m

Some sets are known to contain records made by:

Gilda	Angeles Ottein	(Side 14)	(soprano)	n

Chorus, o, and orchestra, p, of the Teatro San Carlo, Naples

Conductor: Salvatore Sassano

---

[49] The two complete operas recorded by Phonotype, *Rigoletto* and *Il Barbiere di Siviglia*, included some existing recordings of individual items from the operas, made by De Lucia and other singers. The remaining *Rigoletto* pieces were recorded in the spring of 1918, and the bulk of the *Barbiere* music in the summer of that year. Since, however, the orchestral items from the latter were not made until several months later, *Il Barbiere* was presumably not available until early 1919.

Recording sessions

I	July 1	1915	1566 - 1567
II	July 14	1915	1592
III	July 1	1917	1777
IV	Aug. 5	1917	1795 - 1796
V	Aug. 19	1917	1799
VI	Sept.16	1917	1795/3
VII	Jan. 13	1918	1875
VIII	Jan. 27	1918	1883 - 1887
IX	Apr. 3	1918	1910 - 1913
X	Apr. 6	1918	1914 - 1919
XI	Apr. 8	1918	1920 - 1923
XII	Apr. 11	1918	1929 - 1931
XIII	Apr. 13	1918	1932 - 1936
XIV	Apr. 17	1918	1939
XV	Mar. 29	1920	2299

Unissued Takes

C 1795	Ella mi fu rapita		a,p	Session IV

Act One, Scene One

1 Prelude and Introduction[50],[51]

-	C	1883	p				VIII

2 Della mia bella incognita...Questa o quella

218	C	1920	a,i,p				XI

3 Partite? Crudele!

211	C	1910	a,b,h,i,o,p				IX

4 Gran nuova! gran nuova!

221	C	1923	a,b,f,i,j,o,p	[74.07]	[G]	[*]	XI

5 Ch'io gli parli

220	M	1922	a,b,e,f,i,j,o,p				XI

Act One, Scene Two

6 Quel vecchio maledivami

	M	1914	b,d,p	X

7 Pari siamo

-	M	1799	b,p	V

8 Figlia! Mio padre!...Ah! Deh non parlare al misero

-	M	1884	b,c,p	VIII

9 Il nome vostro ditemi...Già da tre lune

-	C	1885	b,c,k,p	VIII

10 Alla chiesa...Ah! veglia o donna

205	C	1886	a,b,c,k,p	VIII

---

50 With few (accidental) exceptions prefixes were assigned only to recordings featuring one or more of Phonotypes four celebrity singers, Amato, De Lucia, Franci, and Ottein. The prefix listed corresponds to the diameter of known pressings. Otherwise, it is that listed in the register.

51 The participants listed are those required by the score.

11 Giovanna, ho dei rimorsi
    222   C   1930   a,c,k,p   [74.07]   [D flat]   [**]   XII

12 Ah, inseparabile d'amore...E il sol dell'anima
    136   M   1777   a,c,p   [73.17]   [A flat]   [**]   III

13 Che m'ami, deh! ripetimi...Addio, addio
    223   1931   a,c,i,j,k,p   [74.07]   [B]   [**]   XII

14 Gualtier Maldè...Caro nome
    -    M   1939   c,p   XIV

14 Gualtier Maldè...Caro nome
    -    M   2299   n,p   XV

15 Gualtier Maldè...(Riedo!...perchè?)
    -    C   1932   b,c,f,i,j,o,p   XIII

16 Zitti, zitti moviamo a vendetta
    -    C   1933   b,c,f,i,j,o,p   XIII

Act Two

17 Ella mi fu rapita[52]
    179   C   1795/3   a,p   74.07   C sharp min   *   VI

18 Parmi veder le lagrime
    156   C   1796   a,p   75.00   E   **   IV

19 Duca, duca!...Scorrendo uniti
    224   -   1934   a,f,i,j,o,p   XIII

20 Povero Rigoletto[53]
    -    -   1592   b,f,i,j,l,o,p   II

21 Cortigiani, vil razza dannata
    -    -   1566   b,p   I

22 Miei signori
    -    -   1567   b,p   I

23 Mio padre! Dio! mia Gilda!
    -    -   1935   b,c,f,i,j,o,p   XIII

24 Tutte le feste
    -    M   1936   c,p   XIII

25 (Solo per me l'infamia...)...Piangi, piangi fanciulla
    -    M   1887   b,c,p   VIII

26 Compiuto pur quanto a fare mi resta...Si, vendetta
    -    C   1929   b,c,e,m,p   XII

Act Three

27 E l'ami?
    215   -   1916   a,b,c,d,p   X

28 La donna è mobile...E là il vostr'uomo[54]
    214   C   1915   a,b,d,p   [74.07]   [B flat]   [*]   X

29 Un dì, se ben rammentomi
    216   C   1918   a,b,c,g,p   74.07   E flat   *   X

---

52 There was no 1795/2. C 1795 [No. 155], which was not recorded as part of the set, was made on August 5th 1917.

53 Not made for the set.

54 See note to [No. 214]. The register gives only De Lucia. The Rigoletto and Sparafucile heard on the record were presumably Armentano and Muñoz, who were present that day.

30 Bella figlia dell'amore								
	217	M	1919	a,b,c,g,p	74.07	C	*	X
31 M'odi! ritorna a casa								
	212	-	1911	a,b,c,d,g,o,p	[71.43]	C	[*]	IX
32 Povero giovin!55								
	213	C	1912	a,c,d,g,o,p	[71.43]	[G flat]	[*]	IX
33 Eppure il danaro								
	-	M	1913	c,d,g,o,p				IX
34 Della vendetta alfin giunge l'istante								
	-	-	1917	b,d,p				X
35 Egli è là! morto!								
	219	C	1921	a,b,p				XI
36 Oh, mia Gilda...Lassù in cielo								
	-	M	1875	b,c,p				VII

Il Barbiere di Siviglia

Count Almaviva	Fernando De Lucia	(tenor)	a
Figaro	Francesco Novelli	(baritone)	b
Rosina	Maria Resemba	(soprano)	c
Doctor Bartolo	Giorgio Schottler	(bass)	d
Don Basilio	Stefano Valentino	(bass)	e
Fiorello	Angelo di Tommaso	(bass)	f
Berta	Nina Sabatano56	(soprano)	g
Ambrogio	Unidentified	(bass)	h
An Official	Unidentified	(bass)	i

Some sets contain records by:

Figaro	Benvenuto Franci	(Side 7)	(baritone)	j
Rosina	Angeles Ottein	(Sides 13/14)	(soprano)	k
Don Basilio	Luis Muñoz	(Side 16)	(bass)	l

Chorus, m, and orchestra, n, of the Teatro San Carlo, Naples

Conductor: Salvatore Sassano

---

55 The register also gives Armentano who is, however, not required in his passage.

56 Catalogues attribute the part of Berta to Maria Giuliano instead of to Nina Sabatano, the singer given in the register. Both register and catalogues ignore the parts of Ambrogio and The Official, and the singers performing them.

Recording Sessions

I	Apr. 8	1918	1924
II	June 2	1918	1942 - 1947
III	June 6	1918	1948 - 1950
IV	June 9	1918	1962 - 1970
V	July 14	1918	1983
VI	July 21	1918	1984 - 1988
VII	July 27	1918	1989 - 1991
VIII	Aug. 11	1918	1996 - 1999
IX	Aug. 19	1918	1948/2 - 1950/2
X	Aug. 20	1918	2000 - 2002, 1942/2, 1946/2, 1947/2
XI	Sept. 1	1918	2015
XII	Jan. 3	1919	2067 - 2069
XIII	Mar. 29	1920	2297 - 2298
XIV	Apr. 11	1920	2337

Unissued Takes

M	1942	Largo al factotum	b,n	II
C	1946	Una voce poco fa	c,n	II
C	1947	Io sono docile	c,n	II
-	1948	Oh cielo! Nella stanza...All'idea	a,b,n	III
C	1949	Voi dovreste travestirvi	a,b,n	III
C	1950	Dunque? All'opra...Numero quindici	a,b,n	III

Act One, Scene One

1 Overture, Pt.I
-	C	2068	n			XII

2 Overture, Pt.II
-	C	2069	n			XII

3 Piano, pianissimo
246	-	1989	a,f,m,n		G flat	*	VII

4 Ecco ridente in cielo
225	C	1943	a,n	72.29	B flat	**	II

5 Oh sorte! già veggo
226	-	1944	a,n	72.29	B flat	**	II

6 Ehi, Fiorello?....Signor Conte
247	M	1990	a,b,f,m,n	[72]	[Recit then G flat]	[**] [*]	VII

7 Largo al factotum
-	M	1942/2	b,n		X

7 Largo al factotum
-	M	2337	j,n		XIV

8 Ah! Ah! che bella vita[57]
249	M	1996	a,b,c,d,n	C	VIII

---

[57] A cut removes Rosina's phrases.

9 Se il mio nome[58]
227	C	1945	a,b,c,n	72.29	G min	**	II

10 Oh cielo! Nella stanza...All'idea di quel metallo
257	-	1948/2	a,b,n		F	**	IX

11 Voi dovreste travestirvi
258	C	1949/2	a,b,n		F	**	IX

12 Dunque? All'opra...Numero quindici
259	C	1950/2	a,b,n		F	**	IX

Act One, Scene Two

13 Una voce poco fa
-	-	1946/2	c,n	X

13 Una voce poco fa
-	C	2297	k,n	XIII

14 Io sono docile
-	-	1947/2	c,n	X

14 Io sono docile
-	C	2298	k,n	XIII

15 Si, si, la vincerò[59]
-	M	2000	b,c,d,e,g,h,n	X

16 La calunnia[60]
-	C	2001	e,n	X

16 La calunnia[61]
-	M	1924	l,n	I

17 Ah! che ne dite?
-	-	2002	b,c,d,e,n	X

18 Dunque io son
-	-	1969	b,c,n	IV

19 Che ne dite? Non vorrei...
-	-	1970	b,c,n	IV

20 Ora mi sento meglio
-	-	1962	c,d,n	IV

21 Manca un foglio
-	C	1963	d,n	IV

22 Finora in questa camera...Ehi di casa...buona gente
241	M	1984	a,c,d,g,n	[72]	[B flat]	[**]	VI

23 E Rosina: or son contento
242	M	1985	a,c,d,e,g,n	[72]	[B flat]	[**]	VI

24 Ecco qua! sempre un'istoria
248	C	1991	a,b,c,d,e,g,m,n	[72]	[E flat]	VII

25 Fermi tutti. Nessun si muova...Fredda ed immobile
250	M	1997	a,b,c,d,e,g,i,m,n	A flat	VIII

26 Ma signor...Zitto tu!...Mi par d'esser colla testa
251	-	1998	a,b,c,d,e,g,m,n	VIII

---

58 A cut removes Figaro's phrases. Resemba, the presumed Rosina, is not mentioned in the register.

59 Cuts remove the phrases of Berta and Ambrogio.

60 Although no celebrity artist is involved the register gives C; the record is, in fact, reported to be 30 cm.

61 No pressings of M 1924 were accessible; the prefix is that given in the register.

Act Two

27 Ma vedi il mio destino!...Pace e gioia sia con voi

    233 C   1966   a,d,n   A flat   **   IV

28 Insomma, mio Signore, chi è lei, si può sapere?

    234 C   1967   a,c,d,n   C   IV

29 Lesson Scene: Variations (H. Proch)

    -   C   2015   c,n   XI

30 Bella voce! bravissima!...Quando mi sei vicina (Don Bartolo's arietta)

    235 C   1968   a,b,c,d,n   Recit.   *   IV

                                                        Arietta in G flat

31 E quel briccon che al Conte...Don Basilio! Cosa veggo!

    243 C   1986   a,b,c,d,e,n   D   *   VI

32 Colla febbre, Don Basilio...Buona sera, mio signore

    244 M   1987   a,b,c,d,e,n   D/G flat   *   VI

33 Buona sera...Stringi...Bravissimo...Bricconi! birbanti!

    245 C   1988   a,b,c,d,e,n   G flat/A/D   *   VI

34 Che vecchio sospettoso[62]

    -   -   1983   c,d,e,g,h,n   V

35 Temporale

    -   -   2067   n   XII

36 Alfine, eccoci qua...Ah qual colpo

    231 M   1964   a,b,c,n   74.07   E   *   IV

37 Mio signor!...ma...voi...Zitti, zitti, piano piano

    232 C   1965   a,b,c,n   [72]   [E flat]   [**]   IV

38 Ah disgraziati noi!...Di sì felice innesto [63]

    252 M   1999   a,b,c,d,e,g,i,m,n   G   VIII

---

[62] Bartolo and Ambrogio should share a brief scene before Berta's aria, which is in turn followed by two scenes for Bartolo, the first with Rosina and the second with Basilio. The record has not been heard and it is not known how much of the music is actually included. The register gives Sabatano only.

[63] The register makes no mention of Sabatano, who should be present in this ensemble.

Discography Index

The index serves to identify, by discography number, all recordings of a given selection, listed by the opening words of the principal musical item, or of that by which the extract is usually known in the language used. Introductory recitatives are generally not included; full details of these, where available, are to be found in the main listing. Operatic items are listed in the order in which they occur in the work, with Roman numerals dividing the selections by act. Composers are given only where several well-known versions exist under a single title, eg.'Ave Maria'.

Bibliography

The bibliography includes books, unpublished monographs, and chapters in multi-author works. It also includes magazine and journal articles and other printed sources, such as record documentation, which are cited several times; those quoted only occasionally are, together with newspaper references, documented in footnotes.

Abbiati, Franco. *Giuseppe Verdi*, Milano, Ricordi, 1959.

Adami, Giuseppe. *Letters of Giacomo Puccini*, translated by Ena Makin, London, Harrap, 1931.

Alcari, C. *Il Teatro Regio di Parma nella sua storia dal 1883 al 1929*, Parma, Officina Grafica Fresching, 1929.

Anon. *Cento Anni di Vita del Teatro San Carlo, 1848-1948*, Napoli, Ente Autonomo del Teatro di San Carlo, 1948.

---- *Cook's Tourist's Handbook for Southern Italy, Rome and Sicily*, London, Thomas Cook, 1899.

---- *Fernando De Lucia: Madrid, Gennaio e Febbraio 1895 - Milano, Marzo e Aprile 1895*, Introduction by C.D'Or. [Carlo D'Ormeville], no publication details available, (probably Milan, 1895), (SPM).

---- *Guide through Naples and its Neighbourhood*, Naples, Libreria Detken and Rocholl, 1914.

---- *Il Teatro di S. Carlo*, Naples, Ente Autonomo del Teatro di San Carlo, 1951.

Apicella, Domenico. *Sommario Storico-Illustrativo della Città della Cava*, Cava de' Tirreni, Edizioni Il Castello, 1964.

Ardoin, John. 'Horn of Plenty', *The Opera Quarterly*, Vol. 4, No. 1, Spring 1986, pp. 50-1.

Artieri, Giovanni. *Napoli Nobilissima*, second edition, Milano, Longanesi, 1959.

Baedeker, Karl. *Italy: Handbook for Travellers. First Part: Northern Italy*, Leipzig, Baedeker, twelfth edition, 1903.

---- *Southern Italy and Sicily: Handbook for Travellers*, Leipzig, Baedeker, tenth edition, 1890, and fifteenth edition, 1908

Barblan, Guglielmo & Eugenio Gara. *Toscanini e la Scala*, Milano, Edizioni alla Scala, 1972.

Bastianelli, Giannotto. *Pietro Mascagni*, Napoli, Riccardo Ricciardi Editore, 1910.

Bates Batcheller, Tryphosa. *Glimpses of Italian Court Life*, New York, Doubleday Page, 1907.

Bellincioni, Gemma. *Io e il Palcoscenico*, Milano, Soc. An. Editoriale Dott. R. Quintieri, 1920.

Berlioz, Hector. *Evenings in the Orchestra* (translated from *Les Soirées de l'Orchestre* by Charles E. Roche), Introduction by Ernest Newman, New York, Knopf, 1929.

Bernardini Marzolla, Ugo. 'Spunti di Storia delle Opere di Pietro Mascagni da un Carteggio Perduto', in: Various authors, *Pietro Mascagni. Contributi alla Conoscenza della sua Opera nel 1o Centenario della Nascita,* pp. 59-189 (q.v.).

Biblioteca di Storia Moderna e Contemporanea, *Memoria fotografica (1908-1923) Dall'album romano di Alfredo De Giorgio*, Roma, Ministero per i Beni Culturali e Ambientali, 1985.

Bispham, David. *A Quaker Singer's Recollections*, New York, Macmillan, 1920.

Blyth, Alan (ed.). *Opera on Record*, London, Hutchinson, 1979.

---- *Opera on Record* 2, London, Hutchinson, 1983.
---- *Opera on Record* 3, London, Hutchinson, 1984.
Borgatti, Giuseppe. *La Mia Vita d'Artista*, Bologna, L. Cappelli, 1927.
Borelli, Giovanni. 'Il necrologio', in *Angelo Masini: Il tenore angelico*, p. 56 (q.v.).
Borovsky, Victor. *Chaliapin*, London, Hamish Hamilton, 1988.
Boutet, Edoardo. *Sua Eccellenza San Carlino. Macchiette e Scenette*, Roma, Soc. Editrice Nazionale, 1901.
Briggs, John. *Requiem for a Yellow Brick Brewery*, Boston and Toronto, Little, Brown and Company, 1969.
Burney, Charles. *The Present State of Music in France and Italy*, London, T. Becker and Co., J. Robson and G. Robinson, 1771.
Caamaño, Roberto. *La historia del Teatro Colón 1908-1968*, Buenos Aires, Editorial Cinetea, 1969.
Calvé, Emma. *My Life*, translated by Rosamond Gilder, New York, Appleton, 1922.
---- *Sous tous les ciels j'ai chanté*, Paris, Librarie Plon, 1940.
Canonico, Valerio. *Noterelle Cavesi*, Cava de' Tirreni, Arti Grafiche Ditta E. Di Mauro, Vol. I, 1967, Vol. II, 1970, and Vol. III, 1972.
Carelli, Augusto. *Emma Carelli. Trent'anni di vita lirica*, Roma, Casa Libraria Maglione, 1932.
Carner, Mosco. *Puccini. A Critical Biography*, London, Duckworth, 1958.
Catalani, Luigi. *I Palazzi di Napoli*, Napoli, Colonnese Editore, 1979 (originally published 1845).
Celletti, Rodolfo (ed.). *Le Grandi Voci*, Roma, Istituto per la Collaborazione Culturale, 1964.
---- 'Gli interpreti giordaniani', in: Morini: *Umberto Giordano*, 1968, pp. 193-222 (q.v.).
---- 'La voce di Angelo Masini', in: Various authors, *Atti del Convegno su Angelo Masini*, 1977, pp. 45-52 (q.v.).
Chaliapin, Feodor. *Man and Mask*, London, Gollancz, 1932.
Chorley, Henry F. *Thirty Years' Musical Recollections*, London, Hurst and Blackett, 1862.
Collison-Morley, Lacy. *Naples through the Centuries*, London, Methuen, 1925.
Coote, Colin R. *Italian Town and Country Life*, London, Methuen, 1925.
Crutchfield, Will. 'Vocal Ornamentation in Verdi: The Recorded Evidence', *19th Century Music*, Vol. 7, No. 1, Summer 1983, pp. 3-54.
---- 'Twin Glories I', *Opera News*, Dec. 19 1987, pp. 10-13.
---- 'Twin Glories II', ibid., Feb. 27 1988, pp. 10-14.
Da Fonseca Benvenides, Francisco. *O Real Theatro de S.Carlos de Lisboa, Memorias 1883-1902*, Lisboa, Typographia e Lithographia de Ricardo de Souza & Salles, 1902.
Danzuso, Domenico & Giovanni Idonea. *Musica, Musicisti e Teatri a Catania*, Palermo, Publiscula Editore, 1984.
Daspuro, Nicola. *Enrico Caruso*, Milano, Sonzogno, 1938.
---- 'Memorie Postume' (unpublished MS), 1936 (BLP).
Davis, Ronald. *Opera in Chicago*, New York, Appleton-Century, 1966.
De Carlo, Salvatore (ed.). *Mascagni Parla*, Milano-Roma, De Carlo Editore, 1945.
De Filippis, F. *Napoli Teatrale dal Teatro Romano al San Carlo: Aneddoti e Figure*, Milano, Edizioni Curci, 1962.
De Giorgio, Achemenide & Carlo D'Ormeville. *Fernando De Lucia*, Milano, Tipografia Capriolo e Massimino, 1897.
De Giorgio, Alfredo. *Chicchere e Chiacchiere*, Roma, Giuseppe Marino Editore, 1926.
De Giorgio, Vincenzo. *Canto e Cantanti*, Napoli, Tipo Ruggiani, 1891.
De Gregori, Luigi. *El Tenor Francesc Viñas*, Barcelona, Tipografia Emporium, 1935.
De Lara, Isidore. *Many Tales of Many Cities*, London, Hutchinson, 1928.
Della Porta, A. *Il Santuario di S. Maria dell'Olmo*, Cava de' Tirreni, Scuola Tipografia 'Ragazzi di S. Filippo', 1966.
---- *Da Corpo di Cava a Dupino*, Cava de' Tirreni, Di Mauro, 1974.
---- *Incontri*, Cava de' Tirreni, Palumbo e Esposito, 1976.

Dell'Arco, Mario. *Café-Chantant di Roma*, Milano, Aldo Martelli Editore, 1970.

Dell'Erba, Francesco. 'Il debutto di un divo', chapter in: *Napoli. Un Quarto di Secolo*, Napoli, Edizione S.E.G. 'Il Pungolo', 1963, pp. 169-75.

De Mura, Ettore. *Poeti Napoletani dal '600 ad oggi*, Napoli, Conte-Editore, 1950.

---- *Enciclopedia della Canzone Napoletana*, Napoli, Casa Editrice Il Torchio, 1969.

Depanis, Giuseppe. *I concerti popolari ed il Teatro Regio di Torino*, Torino, S.T.E.N., 1914.

De Roberto, Domenico, Domenico Scardaccione & Domenico Majolo, *La Signora Itala De Giorgio contro Il Sig. Fernando De Lucia, Memoria a Stampa*, Tribunale Civile di Napoli, 1a Sezione, 1895, included in: 'Procedimento penale, Tribunale Penale di Pretura, No. 591,' Napoli, May 27 1909.

De Schauensee, Max. 'Passionate Believer', *Opera News*, Mar. 19 1960, pp. 10-12.

De Segurola, Andres Perello. 'Through My Monocle', 1949, (unpublished MS), (LCML).

De Vries, Leonard. *Victorian Inventions*, London, John Murray, 1973.

Dickens, Charles. *Pictures from Italy*, Introduction & notes by David Paroissien, London, André Deutsch, 1973.

Di Massa, Sebastiano. *Il Café-Chantant e la Canzone a Napoli*, Napoli, Fausto Fiorentino Editore, 1969.

---- *Storia della Canzone Napoletana*, Napoli, Fausto Fiorentino Editrice, 1982.

Duval, J.H. *Svengali's Secrets and Memoirs of the Golden Age*, New York, Robert Speller, 1958.

Eaton, Quaintance. *Opera Caravan*, London, John Calder, 1957.

---- *The Miracle of the Met*, New York, Meredith, 1968.

Encyclopædia Britannica, ninth edition, Edinburgh, Adam and Charles Black, 1875; tenth edition, London, Adam and Charles Black and *The Times*, 1902.

Erskine, Mrs. Steuart. *The Bay of Naples* (illustrations by Major Benton Fletcher), London, A. and C. Black, 1926.

Erskine Clement, Clara. *Naples: The City of Parthenope and its Environs*, Boston, Estes and Lauriat, 1894.

Fagan, Ted & William R. Moran. *The Encyclopedic Discography of Victor Recordings, Matrix Series: 1 through 4999*, Westport, Greenwood Press, 1986.

Favia-Artsay, Aida. *Caruso on Records*, Valhalla, New York, The Historic Record, 1965.

Fitzgerald, Augustine & Sybil Fitzgerald. *Naples*, London, A. and C. Black, 1904.

Fraccaroli, Arnaldo. *La Vita di Giacomo Puccini*, Milano, Ricordi, 1925.

Frajese, Vittorio. *Dal Costanzi all'Opera*, Roma, Edizioni Capitolium, 1978.

Frassoni, Edilio. *Due Secoli di Lirica a Genova*, Genova, Cassa di Risparmio di Genova e Imperia, 1980.

Fuller Maitland, J.A. (ed.). *Grove's Dictionary of Music and Musicians*, second edition, London, Macmillan, 1904-10.

Gaisberg, F.W. *Music on Record*, London, Robert Hale, 1947. [*The Music Goes Round*, New York, Macmillan, 1942.]

Gallus, A. [pseudonym for Arthur Wisner]. *Emma Calvé*, New York, R.H. Russell, 1902.

Gara, Eugenio. *Caruso. Storia di un emigrante*, Milano, Rizzoli, 1947.

---- Mario Morini, & Raffaele Vegeto (a cura di). *Carteggi Pucciniani*, Milano, Ricordi, 1958.

---- 'Cantanti mascagnani tra pregiudizio e verità', in: Morini, *Pietro Mascagni*, Vol. I, pp. 201-49, 1964 (q.v.).

---- *Cantarono alla Scala*, Milano, Teatro alla Scala/Electa Editrice, 1975.

Garcia, Manuel. *Hints on Singing*, London, Ascherberg, Hopwood and Crew, 1894.

Gargano, Pietro & Gianni Cesarini. *La Canzone Napoletana*, Milano, Rizzoli Editore, 1984.

Gatti, Carlo. *Il Teatro alla Scala*, Milan, Ricordi, 1964.

Gatti-Casazza, Giulio. *Memories of the Opera*, London, John Calder, 1977.

Gavazzeni, Gianandrea, 'La Musica di Mascagni, Oggi', in Morini, *Pietro Mascagni*, Vol. I, pp. 11-43.

Girard, Georges. *Emma Calvé: la cantatrice sous tous les ciels*, Veyreau, Editions Grands Causses, 1983.

Girbal, F. Hernández. *Julián Gayarre*, Madrid, Ediciones Lira, 1970.

Glackens, Ira. *Yankee Diva*, New York, Coleridge Press, 1963.

Glover, James M. *Jimmy Glover His Book*, third edition, London, Methuen, 1911.

Gorky, Maxim. *Chaliapin: An Autobiography as told to Maxim Gorky,* translated by Nina Froud and James Hanley, London, Macdonald, 1968.

Greenfield, Howard. *Puccini*, London, Robert Hale, 1981.

Gualerzi, Giorgio. 'Cavalcata canora di mezzo secolo' in: Various authors, *Pietro Mascagni. Contributi alla Conoscenza della sua Opera nel 1º Centenario della Nascita*, 1963, pp. 343-66 (q.v.).

---- 'Appunti per la Carriera di Angelo Masini', in: Various authors, *Atti del Convegno su Angelo Masini*, 1977, pp. 29-43 (q.v.).

Gunn, Peter. *Naples: A Palimpsest*, London, Chapman and Hall, 1961.

Haggin, B.H. *Conversations with Toscanini*, New York, Dolphin, 1959.

Hain, Edward. 'Commentary [on the records of De Lucia]', *Record Collector*, Vol. XI, No. 6, June 1957, pp. 129-33.

Hanslick, Eduard. *Fünf Jahre Musik* [1891-1895] (Der 'Modernen Oper' VII. Teil), Berlin, Allgemeiner Berein für Deutsche Literatur, 1896.

Hauk, Minnie. *Memories of a Singer*, London, A.M. Philpot, 1925.

Henstock, Michael E. 'The London Career of Fernando De Lucia', *Record Collector*, Vol. XVII, No. 7, Aug. 1967, pp. 160-7.

---- 'Some notes on Angelica Pandolfini', *Recorded Sound*, No. 38, April 1970, pp. 622-5.

---- 'Fernando De Lucia: Discography', *Record Collector*, Vol. XXX, Nos. 5-9, June/Aug. 1985, pp. 100-213, addenda and corrigenda, ibid., Vol. XXXIII, Nos. 8-10, Aug. 1988, pp. 231-6.

Homer, Anne. *Louise Homer and the Golden Age of Opera*, New York, William Morrow, 1974.

Homer, Sidney. *My Wife and I*, New York, Macmillan, 1939.

Hurst, P.G. *The Age of Jean de Reszke*, London, Christopher Johnson, 1958.

---- *The Golden Age Recorded*, Henfield, Hurst, 1946; second (revised) edition, Lingfield, The Oakwood Press, 1963.

Kellogg, Clara Louise. *Memoirs of an American Prima Donna*, New York and London, G.P. Putnam's Sons, 1913.

Kelly, Alan. *His Master's Voice / La Voce del Padrone*, New York, Westport and London, Greenwood Press, 1988.

Kesting, Jürgen, *Die Grossen Sänger*, Düsseldorf, Claasen, 1986.

Key, Pierre V.R. & Bruno Zirato. *Enrico Caruso*, London, Hurst and Blackett, 1923.

Key, Pierre V.R. (transcriber) & John Scarry (ed.). *John McCormack. His own life story*, New York, Vienna House, 1973. (Originally published Small, Maynard and Co., 1918.)

Klein, Hermann. *Thirty Years of Musical Life in London, 1870-1900*, New York, The Century Co., 1903.

---- *The Golden Age of Opera*, London, George Routledge, 1933.

---- *Great Women Singers of My Time*, London, George Routledge, 1931.

---- *The Reign of Patti*, London, T. Fisher Unwin, 1920.

Kolodin, Irving. *The Story of the Metropolitan Opera 1883-1950*, New York, Knopf, 1953.

Krehbiel, Henry Edward. *Chapters of Opera*, New York, Henry Holt, 1908.

---- *A Second Book of Operas*, New York, Garden City Publishing, 1917.

Kutsch, K.J. & Leo Riemens. *Unvergängliche Stimmen*, Bern, A. Francke, 1975.

Lancellotti, Arturo. *Le Voci d'Oro*, Roma, Fratelli Palombi Editori, 1953.

Leiser, Clara. *Jean de Reszke and the Great Days of Opera*, London, Gerald Howe, 1933.

Lewis, Norman. *Naples '44*, London, Eland Books, 1978.

Limoncelli, Mattia. *La Musica nei Salotti Napoletani tra l'800 e il 900*, Napoli, Il Fuidoro, 1956.

Lombardo, G.A. *Annuario dell'Arte Lirica e Coreografica Italiana*, Milano, G.A. Lombardo, 1899.

McQueen Pope, W.J. *Theatre Royal Drury Lane*, London, W.H. Allen, 1945.

Mackinnon, Albert G. *Things Seen in the Bay of Naples*, London, Seeley, Service and Co. (undated).

Mancini, Roland. *Georges Thill*, Paris, Société de Diffusion d'Art Lyrique, 1966.

Mapleson, J.H. *The Mapleson Memoirs 1848-1888*, London, Remington, 1888.

Marchesi, Blanche. *Singer's Pilgrimage*, London, Grant Richards, 1923.

Marchesi, Mathilde. *Marchesi and Music*, London and New York, Harper and Brothers, 1897.

Marek, George. *Puccini*, London, Cassell, 1952.

Marinelli Roscioni, Carlo. (a cura di) 'La Cronologia 1737-1987', in: Various authors, *Il Teatro di San Carlo*, Napoli, Guida, 1987 (q.v.).

Marotta, Giuseppe. *The Gold of Naples*, translated by Frances Frenaye, London, Harborough Publishing, 1960.

Massie, Robert K. *Nicholas and Alexandra*, London, Gollancz, 1968.

Monaldi, Gino. *Cantanti Celebri*, Roma, Edizioni Tiber, 1929.

Moore, Jerrold Northrop. *A Voice in Time: The Gramophone of Fred Gaisberg 1873-1951*, London, Hamish Hamilton, 1976.

Moran, William R. *Nellie Melba. A Contemporary Review*, West Port and London, Greenwood, 1985.

---- 'Mario Ancona (1860-1931)', *Record Collector*, Vol. XVI, Nos. 5-6, April 1965, pp. 100-39.

Moreau, Màrio. *Cantores de Opera Portugueses,* Vol. I, Lisboa, Livraria Bertrand, 1981.

Morini, Mario. 'Iris e i Progetti Non Realizzati', in: Various authors, *Pietro Mascagni. Contributi alla Conoscenza della sua Opera nel 1º Centenario della Nascita*, 1963, pp. 191-285 (q.v.).

---- (a cura di) *Pietro Mascagni*, Milano, Casa Musicale Sonzogno di Piero Ostali, 1964.

---- 'Per la storia delle opere: Carteggi, documenti, cronache', in: Morini, *Pietro Mascagni*, Vol. I, pp. 251-426, 1964 (q.v.).

---- (a cura di). *Umberto Giordano*, Milano, Casa Musicale Sonzogno di Piero Ostali, 1968.

Mormone, Salvatore. 'Cimbellino', *Roma*, Feb. 20 1891.

Munthe, Axel. *Letters from a Mourning City* (Naples. Autumn, 1884), translated by Maude Valérie White, London, John Murray, 1887.

---- *The Story of San Michele*, New York, E.P. Dutton, 1929.

Neville-Rolfe, Eustace & Holcombe Ingleby. *Naples in the Eighties* (reprint of *Naples in 1888*), Naples, Emil Prass, 1899.

Neville-Rolfe, E. *Naples in the Nineties*, London, A. and C. Black, 1897.

Norway, Arthur H. *Naples. Past and Present*, second edition, London, Methuen, 1905.

Odell, George C.D. *Annals of the New York Stage*, New York, Columbia University Press, 1949.

Osborne, Conrad L. 'The Evolution of the Tenor Voice from Handel to the Present', *Musical Newsletter*, Vol. III, July 1973, pp. 3-8, 17-20.

Osborne, Richard. 'Il barbiere di Siviglia', in *Opera on Record* (1979), pp. 142-53 (q.v.).

Palermo, Santo. *Saverio Mercadante*, Fasano di Puglia, Schena Editore, 1985.

Paliotti, Vittorio. *Storia della Canzone Napoletana*, Milano, Piccola Biblioteca Ricordi, 1958.

---- *La Canzone Napoletana. Ieri e Oggi*. Milano, Ricordi, 1962.

---- *Il Salone Margherita e la Belle Epoque*, Roma, Edizioni di Gabriele e Mariateresa Benincasa s.r.l., 1975.

---- *Napoletani si nasceva*, Napoli, Editrice Fiorentino, 1980.

---- 'C'è un Esposito nella Storia del Disco', *Mattino Illustrato*, Anno 4, No. 5, Feb. 2 1980, p. 14ff.

Pannain, Guido. *Il R. Conservatorio di Musica 'San Pietro a Maiella' di Napoli*, Firenze, Felice Le Monnier, 1942.

Piccini, G. [Jarro]. *Attori, Cantanti, Concertisti, Acrobati*, second edition, Firenze, R. Bemporad e Figlio, 1897.

Pompei, Edoardo. *Pietro Mascagni nella vita e nell'arte*, Roma, Tipografia Editrice Nazionale, 1912.

Porcaro, Giuseppe. *Piedigrotta*, Napoli, Fausto Fiorentino, 1958.

Priestley, Harold. *The What it Cost the Day before Yesterday Book*, Havant, Kenneth Mason, 1979.

Rasponi, Lanfranco. *The Last Prima Donnas*, New York, Alfred A. Knopf, 1982.

Ricci, Luigi. *34 Anni con Pietro Mascagni*, Milano, Edizioni Curci, 1976.

Robinson, Michael F. *Naples and Neapolitan Opera*, Oxford, Clarendon Press, 1972.

Roncaglia, Gino. 'Pietro Mascagni: L'Operista', in: Various authors, *Pietro Mascagni nel 1º Centenario della Nascita*, pp. 19-57 (q.v.).

Rosenthal, Harold. *Two Centuries of Opera at Covent Garden*, London, Putnam, 1958.

Rosselli, John. *The Opera Industry in Italy from Cimarosa to Verdi*, Cambridge, Cambridge University Press, 1984.

Rubboli, Daniele. *Ridi Pagliaccio*, Lucca, Maria Pacini Fazzi Editore, 1985.

Sackville West, E. & D. Shawe-Taylor, *The Record Year*, London, Collins, 1952.

Sadie, Stanley (ed.). *The New Grove Dictionary of Music and Musicians*, London, Macmillan, 1980.

Salvucci, Antonio. *Confidenze e Anedotti di Cantanti Celebri e Maestri Compositori*, Roma, Arti Grafische Demer, 1964.

Sartori, Claudio (a cura di). *Casa Ricordi, 1808-1958*, Milano, Ricordi, 1958.

Scalera, Erminio. *I Caffè Napoletani*, Napoli, Arturo Berisio Editore, 1967.

Schlitzer, Franco. *Salvatore Di Giacomo. Ricerche e Note Biografiche*, Edizione postuma a cura di Gino Doria e Cecilia Ricottini, Firenze, Sansoni, 1966.

Schmidl, Carlo. *Dizionario Universale dei Musicisti*, Milano, Sonzogno, 1926.

Scholes, Percy A. *The Oxford Companion to Music*, London, OUP, 1938.

Scott, Michael. *The Record of Singing: To 1914*, London, Duckworth, 1977.

---- *The Great Caruso*, London, Hamish Hamilton, 1988.

Segond, André. *Georges Thill ou l'âge d'or de l'Opéra*, Lyon, Editions Jacques-Marie Lafont, 1980.

Seligman, Vincent. *Puccini Among Friends*, London, Macmillan, 1938.

Seltsam, William H. *Metropolitan Opera Annals*, New York, H.W. Wilson, 1947.

Serao, Matilde. *Il ventre di Napoli*, first edition, Milano, Treves, 1884, and second edition, Napoli, Perrella, 1906.

---- *Il paese di cuccagna*, Milano, Treves, 1891.

Shaw, Bernard. *London Music in 1888-89 as heard by Corno Di Bassetto*, London, Constable, 1937.

---- *Music in London 1890-94*, London, Constable, 1932.

---- (Dan H. Laurence, ed.) *The Bodley Head Bernard Shaw*, London, The Bodley Head, 1981.

Shawe-Taylor, Desmond. 'A Gallery of Great Singers: 5 - Fernando De Lucia (1860-1925)', *Opera*, Vol. 6, No. 7, July 1955, pp. 433-8.

Slonimsky, Nicolas (reviser). *Baker's Biographical Dictionary of Musicians*, seventh edition, New York, Schirmer, 1984.

Specht, Richard. *Giacomo Puccini. The Man - His Life - His Work*, translated by Catherine Alison Phillips from the German edition, 1932, London and Toronto, Dent, 1933.

Stagno-Bellincioni, Bianca. *Roberto Stagno e Gemma Bellincioni Intimi*, Firenze, Casa Editrice Monsalvato, 1943.

Steane, J.B. *The Grand Tradition*, London, Duckworth, 1974.

Stivender, David, *Mascagni*, White Plains, New York, Pro/Am Music Resources, 1988.

Stratton, John. 'Some Matters of Pitch', *The Opera Quarterly*, Vol. 6, No. 4, Summer 1989, pp. 49-60.

Strong, L.A.G. *John McCormack. The Story of a Singer*, London, Methuen, 1941.
Subira, José. *Historia y Anecdotario del Teatro Real*, Madrid, Editorial Plus-Ultra, 1948
Sutherland Edwards, H. *The Lyrical Drama*, London, W.H. Allen, 1881.
---- *The Prima Donna. Her History and Surroundings from the Seventeenth to the Nineteenth Century*, London, Remington, 1888.
Thompson, Oscar. *The International Cyclopedia of Music and Musicians*, Philadelphia, Blakiston, 1944.
Trezzini, Lamberto (a cura di). *Due secoli di vita musicale, Storia del Teatro Comunale di Bologna*, Bologna, Edizioni Alfa, 1966.
Tribble, Edwin. 'The Prima Donna as Goddess: A Life of Adelina Patti', 1972, revised 1976 (unpublished MS) (LCML).
Turati, V. *Pietro Mascagni: Cavalleria Rusticana*, Milano, Sonzogno, 1891.
Uda, Michele. *Arte e Artisti* (Mary Scott-Uda, ed.), Napoli, Stab. Tip. Pierro e Veraldi nell'Istituto Casanova, 1900.
Various authors. *Enciclopedia dello Spettacolo*, Roma, Le Maschere, 1954-62.
---- *Pietro Mascagni: Contributi alla Conoscenza della sua opera nel 1o Centenario della Nascita*, Livorno, Comitato Onoranze nel 1o Centenario della Nascita, Livorno, 1963.
---- *Angelo Masini: Il tenore angelico*, Forlì, Comitato Cittadino per le Onoranze ad Angelo Masini nel Quarantesimo della Morte, 1966.
---- *Atti del Convegno su Angelo Masini*, Forlì, Comune di Forlì, 1977.
---- *Il Teatro di San Carlo*, Napoli, Guida Editori, 1987.
Vaughan, Herbert M. *The Naples Riviera*, fourth edition, London, Methuen, 1925.
Walsh, T.J. *Monte Carlo Opera 1879-1909*, Dublin, Gill and Macmillan, 1975.
Weinstock, Herbert. *Donizetti*, London, Methuen, 1964.
---- *Vincenzo Bellini*, London, Weidenfeld and Nicolson, 1972.
Whitaker's Almanack, London, Joseph Whitaker, 1885-1890 editions.
Wier, Albert E. (compiler and ed.) *The Macmillan Encyclopedia of Music and Musicians*, New York, Macmillan, 1938.
Ybarra, T.R. *Caruso*, London, The Cresset Press, 1954.

General Index

D. = Fernando De Lucia

221; opinion of Toscanini, 221-2,
222n; opinion of *Iris*, 270; considers
setting *Tosca*, 285; casting of *Tosca*,
240; wishes D. to create
Cavaradossi, 240; première of *Tosca*,
287; on *La Bohème*, London, 1900,
295; on *Tosca*, London, 1900, 296
Ragusa, Giuseppe, 365, 367
Rainieri, 74
Randegger, Giuseppe, 280
Rapp, Giuseppe, 35
Rappini, Ida, 233
Ravazzolo, Alessandro, 304
Ravogli, Giulia, 165; 191
Ravogli, Sofia, 165
Renaud, Maurice, 354
Rendle, Frank, 279
Resemba, Maria, 335, 460-2, 473, 475n
Ricci, Ugo ('Mascarillo'), 304, 311, 348
Ricciardi, Riccardo, 162n
Ricco, Giovanni, 300
Ricco-De Giorgio, Pia: see De Giorgio,
Pia
Ricordi, Casa, 18, 37, 98, 121, 257, 323;
negotiations to give *Cimbellino* at
Naples, 1891, 112-13, 115, 117, 120
Ricordi, Giulio, 18, 37n, 41, 196, 201,
221, 222, 222n, 223n, 224n, 240n,
242, 269n, 271, 271n, 273n, 281;
pseudonym 'J. Burgmein', 112; on D.
in *Silvano*, 200; casting of *La
Bohème*, 222-5; corresponds with
Verdi on conductors, 257; genesis of
Iris, 257-8; R. and *Iris*, Rome, 1898,
259-60; remonstrates with D. over
Iris, 268-9; Milan première of *Iris*,
1899, 265-73; seeks to mollify
Mascagni over *Iris*, 267; persuades
Franchetti to relinquish libretto of
Tosca, 285; comments on D. as
Cavaradossi, 296
Ricordi, Tito, 223, 233, 235, 242, 261,
271, 287, 323n; preparations for
première of *Iris*, 1898, 260
Robin, Mado, 388n
Roche, Agostino, 312n, 380, 383
Rolla, Kate, 174
Rosa (maid to Itala De Giorgio), 128
Rosa, Carl Opera Company, 58
Rossi, Arcangelo, 213, 243
Rossi, Enrico, 70
Rossi, Ernesto, 93n, 143
Rossi, Giulio, 77, 243, 250
Rossi, Lauro, 5, 68
Rossini, Gioachino, 283n
Rossi-Trauner, Carolina, 111

Rotoli, Augusto, 10n, 12, 181
Roussel, Mario, 251
Rousselière, Charles, 372
Rubini, Giovanni Battista, 29, 30, 31,
32, 46, 75, 450n
Rubini-Scalisi, Fanny, 10
Ruffo, Titta, 10n, 33, 354, 360, 394
Ruggieri, Ruggiero, 380
Russ, Giannina, 323
Russell, Henry, 354, 356
Russia, Imperial Theatres, 226-7; on
rail travel, 225-6; lyric artists, 226-7;
Russitano, Giuseppe, 317, 318
Russo, Ferdinando, 20, 69, 70, 72
Russo, Giuseppe, 373
Russo, Luigi, 334
Ruta, Anna, 11
Ruta, Michele, 11
Sabajno, Carlo, 230, 328, 328n, 448-9
Sabatano, Nina, 378, 378n, 383n, 398,
461-3, 473n, 476n
Saléza, Albert, 295
Salignac, Thomas, 294
Salsomaggiore, 127
Salvi Bros (outfitters), 298, 302, 309,
311
Salvini, Tommaso, 93n, 143, 319
Salvucci, Antonio, 393, 394
Sammarco, G. Mario, 243, 245, 323,
351, 384, 384n
San Vitaliano (Vitagliano), 4
Sani, Giovanni, 28, 106, 155
Sanmartino, José, 291
Santley, Charles, 61
Santos, General (President of
Uruguay), 49, 82
Sassano, Salvatore, 452, 470, 473
Savelli, Barone, 24
Scalchi, Sofia, 59, 171, 178, 191
Scalisi, Carlo, 10, 12, 22, 23, 25, 26, 102
Scaramella, Sig., 378
Scarpetta, Edoardo, 316
Schaumberg-Lippe, Princess Victoria,
105
Scheff, Fritzi, 295
Schiavazzi, Piero (Pietro), 308, 323
Schipa, Tito, 148, 379, 379n, 380, 442
Schottler, Giorgio, (posteggiatore), 329
Schottler, Giorgio, (operatic baritone),
329, 335, 399, 455, 457, 460-2, 473
Scoppetta, Enrico, 70
Scott, Michael, 339-41
Scotti, Antonio, 243, 279, 280, 296;
Klein on S. as Scarpia, 296
Sembrich, Marcella, 204, 229, 229n,
230, 237, 239, 336n